UNDERSTANDING AND EXPLAINING ADJUDICATION

Understanding and Explaining Adjudication

WILLIAM LUCY

OXFORD
UNIVERSITY PRESS

OXFORD
UNIVERSITY PRESS

Great Clarendon Street, Oxford OX2 6DP

Oxford University Press is a department of the University of Oxford.
It furthers the University's objective of excellence in research, scholarship,
and education by publishing worldwide in

Oxford New York

Athens Auckland Bangkok Bogotá Buenos Aires Calcutta
Cape Town Chennai Dar es Salaam Delhi Florence Hong Kong Istanbul
Karachi Kuala Lumpur Madrid Melbourne Mexico City Mumbai
Nairobi Paris São Paulo Singapore Taipei Tokyo Toronto Warsaw

with associated companies in Berlin Ibadan

Oxford is a registered trade mark of Oxford University Press
in the UK and in certain other countries

Published in the United States
by Oxford University Press Inc., New York

First published 1999

British Library Cataloguing in Publication Data
Data available

Library of Congress Cataloging in Publication Data
Lucy, William.
Understanding and explaining adjudication / william Lucy.
p. cm.
Includes index.
1. Law—Methodology. 2. Jurisprudence. 3. Law—Philosophy.
I. Title.
K212.L77 1999
340'.1—dc21 99-34492
ISBN 0-19-826025-3

1 3 5 7 9 10 8 6 4 2

Typeset in Times
by Best-set Typesetter Ltd., Hong Kong
Printed in Great Britain
on acid-free paper by
Biddles Ltd., Guildford and King's Lynn

To Joyce and Stuart
one couldn't hope for better

Acknowledgements

It is a pleasure and a duty to say thanks in one's acknowledgements; one is also duty-bound to avoid a kind of maudlin effusion that makes the process unseemly. Here goes. A number of colleagues, friends and institutions helped a great deal with the writing of this book. The following read portions of the text at one time or another and I am very grateful for their comments and thoughts: John Bell, Patrick Birkinshaw, Alan Brudner, Bruce Chapman, Neil Duxbury, John Finnis, John Gardner, Allan Hutchinson, Matthew Kramer, Neil MacCormick, Chris Riley and Stuart Toddington. I owe special thanks to Gerry Johnstone who has read more of this book than he will care to remember. No one will be happier than he that it is finished at last. I am also grateful to Dino Kritsiotis, Ian Ward and Matthew Festenstein for invitations to present portions of the book at seminars and to the participants for their comments and forbearance. In addition, there are two people whose example exerted a great deal of influence upon me: Nigel Simmonds and Hillel Steiner. Simmonds got me going, if indeed this counts as 'going', and was a great teacher; his teaching and writing, like Steiner's, set standards that one should always aspire to achieve.

Whether or not the academic world will think this book worthy or distinctive, I do not know. Of one thing, however, I am reasonably sure. It has one distinction few jurisprudential works can claim, having been completed in a dental surgery. Thankfully, this had nothing to do with my teeth but everything to do with the fact that, during the first half of 1998, I found myself homeless and without a study. In addition to his other responsibilities, David Hillary, family friend and dentist, was generous enough to offer refuge in his own well-appointed study. I owe him a great deal for that and only hope that the ethos of the surgery—drills, pills and fills—is not reflected in the prose. Colleagues and friends in my department helped in a number of ways with logistical support and I must in this context thank both Catherine Mitchell and Diamond Ashiagbor. Patrick Birkinshaw, Cosmo Graham and, before him, David Freestone, respectively Dean and Research Director of the department, also provided a good deal of support and I thank them for that. Ann Ashbridge and Sue MacDonald smoothed my path in a huge number of ways. By contrast, Wendy Sunderland didn't help at all, but I am nonetheless grateful. Some work on the book was done in the convivial surroundings of the University of Toronto, Faculty of Law, and I owe thanks to that institution for putting up with me. Also, thanks are owed to my editors at OUP for their colossal patience.

Finally, versions of some of the chapters have been published in journals and I thank the publishers and editors for permission to reprint. They are:

Chapter 2. A shorter version was published under the title 'Criticizing and Constructing Accounts of Legal Reasoning' in (1994) 14 *Oxford Journal of Legal Studies* 303–333. A much shorter version was presented as a paper at the 16th World Congress of the IVR, Reykjavik, May 1993 and published in A. Soeteman and M. Karlsson (eds.), Law, Justice and the State III, *ARSP-Beiheft 60* (Stuttgart, Franz Steiner Verlag 1995), 70–87.

Chapter 4. A version was published in (1996) 16 *Oxford Journal of Legal Studies* 369–405 under the same title.

Chapter 7 was published in (1998) 48 *University of Toronto Law Journal* 61–123 and is only slightly changed here.

Contents

1 Introduction 1

PART I

2 Criticising and Constructing the Orthodoxy 45
3 The Sovereign Individual 93
4 Adjudication for Pluralists 135

PART II

5 Constructing the Heresy 187
6 The Sovereign Structure 249
7 Adjudication for Visionaries 295

8 Conclusion 351

Index 387

1
Introduction

Yet another book about adjudication requires justification. This chapter takes some steps along that path by sketching the area of discourse with which the book is concerned and identifying the specific problems addressed. The chapter also provides some hints as to the nature of the arguments needed to resolve those problems and indicates what is distinctive about them; it concludes by making some preliminary gestures toward terminological tidiness.

I ORTHODOXY AND HERESY

Contemporary accounts of adjudication can be divided, albeit rather crudely and notwithstanding the many differences of detail and emphasis among them, into those that are 'orthodox' and those that are 'heretical'. Composite pictures of these two types of account can be constructed, first, by delineating the constitutive claims of each and, secondly, by determining the scope or range of each. Clarifying what each account maintains and which issues they usually avoid enables us to appreciate the similarities and differences between them. Hopefully, this advantage outweighs the usual disadvantage of composite pictures, namely, their tendency toward caricature. Moreover, although the list of works from which these composite pictures are compiled is not exhaustive, I hope it is credible, because the list of heretics and orthodox includes authors who can be considered exemplars. No one familiar with the field would, I hope, object to authors on each list although it is likely that some will find the lists rather short and somewhat restrictive.

By 'orthodox' accounts of adjudication I refer to those that, on the whole, fall within the positivist tradition in Anglo-American legal theory and affirm four core claims. Exemplars of this tradition include Neil MacCormick, Joseph Raz and, despite his many differences with the aforementioned, Ronald Dworkin.[1] This is indeed a limited list of authors and it

[1] The main sources of these writers' views are: N. MacCormick, *Legal Reasoning and Legal Theory* (Oxford, Clarendon 1978; revised ed., 1993) hereinafter referred to as '*LRLT*'; J. Raz, *Practical Reason and Norms* (London, Hutchinson 1975; New Jersey, Princeton U. P. 1991) and *The Authority of Law* (Oxford, Clarendon 1979), hereinafter '*AL*'; R. Dworkin, *Taking Rights Seriously* (London, Duckworths 1978) hereinafter '*TRS*', *A Matter of Principle* (Oxford, Clarendon 1985), referred to as '*MP*' and *Law's Empire* (London, Fontana 1986) referred to as '*LE*'. In one way or another, all these works take as their starting point the arguments in H. Hart, *The Concept of Law* (Oxford, Clarendon, 2nd ed. 1994).

is justifiable, if at all, on two grounds: there is neither time nor space to consider all orthodox works and these writers have had considerable influence both within the common law world and beyond. The list is not exclusive in the sense that many other legal scholars' work will be touched upon, particularly those North American writers, such as Steven Burton, Joel Levin and Cass Sunstein, who echo, extend and question key orthodox claims.[2] But, these writers' work will be examined as supplements to that of MacCormick, Raz and Dworkin; the work of the latter group will always be our first port of call and is accepted as setting the agenda in this area. Only when other non-heretical work supplements, extends or improves upon this notional 'first wave' of orthodox scholarship, will it be discussed. A group of authors is notably absent from this list and the omission requires explanation. The group is that body of European legal scholars whose work embodies many if not all of the core orthodox claims.[3] Their work does not feature here simply because consideration of it would expand an already long volume and would raise issues that go beyond the scope of this work. It is undoubtedly true that some European contributions to the orthodox corpus are far more ambitious, being developments of general theories of ethics, politics, rationality and discourse, than their Anglo-American equivalents. Thus, I have chosen a relatively small number of Anglo-American orthodox works for consideration in the hope that a restricted focus will allow a more sustained and detailed analysis.

Although it is undoubtedly true that there are many, many differences between the works of the writers on this list, it is also true that they share the following four claims. That is, orthodox accounts of adjudication characteristically contend, first, that adjudicators' claims that they decide cases *relatively* constrained by standards *relatively* determinate of the dispute before them must be taken seriously. Adjudicators are 'relatively' constrained because even the orthodox on these matters do not hold that adjudicators have no choices open to them when making decisions. Rather, the orthodox hold, albeit in different ways and for different reasons, that these choices are *justifiable* in principle and often in practice.[4] That is the second

[2] See S. Burton, *Judging in Good Faith* (Cambridge, C. U. P. 1992); J. Levin, *How Judges Reason* (New York, Peter Lang 1992) and C. Sunstein, *Legal Reasoning and Political Conflict* (New York, Oxford U. P. 1996).

[3] Many of the best works in this rich tradition of orthodox scholarship are now also available in English. The translation of R. Alexy's *A Theory of Legal Argumentation* (Oxford, Clarendon 1989), published originally in German in 1978, and the publication of, *inter alios*, A. Aarnio's *The Rational as Reasonable* (Dordrecht, D. Reidel 1987), K. Gunther's *The Sense of Appropriateness* (Albany, SUNY Press 1993) and J. Habermas's *Between Facts and Norms* (Cambridge, Polity Press 1996), make possible an assessment of the similarities—of which there are many—and differences—of which there are relatively few—between orthodox Anglo-American and European approaches to legal reasoning.

[4] That the justifiability of judicial decisions is *the* crucial concern of the orthodox is obvious: see the remarks of MacCormick, *LRLT*, pp. 14–18, chs. 2 and 5; Dworkin, *TRS*, ch. 4, particularly pp. 106–107, p. 112, p. 115, pp. 117–118; *LE*, ch. 7, particularly pp. 227–228, p. 239 and p. 245; Raz, *AL*, p. 184 and pp. 186–187.

claim constitutive of the orthodoxy and it feeds directly into the third, which affirms that the strategies of justification adjudicators use when making these choices form a limited and recognisable class of arguments. These arguments are constrained by, *inter alia*: (i) requirements of 'fit' with the extant legal materials and the values that are assumed to underlie and give point to them;[5] or (ii) by requirements of consistency and coherence with extant legal materials and a consequentialist evaluation of the effects of a decision one way or another upon the world.[6] The fourth orthodox claim is the culmination of the first three: it holds that the law has some degree of predictability and certainty, that adjudication takes place, again to some degree, within the law. Given adequate knowledge and understanding of the law, the orthodox hold that academics, practitioners and observers can form fairly stable expectations about the outcomes of the vast majority of cases. As we will see, this claim is also made by heretics, but the crucial difference in each case is its alleged basis. For the orthodox, outcomes in the vast majority of cases are reasonably predictable and certain because the choices judges make are in principle justifiable, drawing upon a limited range of arguments.

Translated into the field of doctrinal legal scholarship, the orthodoxy becomes 'rational reconstruction'.[7] That is, orthodox doctrinal scholars take their task to be a good faith rebuilding of the law from the sometimes imperfectly expressed statements of it contained in judicial decisions and statutes. Law makers and law appliers are sometimes blind, by virtue of their role and its constitutive pressures (they must, for example, decide case Y and decide it within period x, or enact statute Z in period q and in the face of objections a, b and c), as to the consequences of their actions, or take action without being fully informed, or are unable to articulate and justify their actions fully. The job of the doctrinal scholar is to fill these gaps whenever they appear, but to do so with an eye to both generic rule of law values such as consistency, intelligibility and fairness, and to the practicability of any legal change or intervention in any aspect of social life. This job means that the orthodox doctrinal scholar is neither fawningly quiescent nor sceptically dismissive toward existing legal doctrine. The law reviews of the Anglo-American legal world abound with criticism of existing judicial decisions and statutes, but, in orthodox hands, criticism is tempered by a shared faith: that the law is basically intelligible, that it, either across the system as a whole or within particular doctrines, imperfectly embodies a rational and valuable scheme for human interaction. Orthodox doctrinal scholars aim to ensure

[5] Dworkin, *LE*, pp. 254–258.

[6] MacCormick, *LRLT*, chs. 5, 6, 7 and 8.

[7] Some standard orthodox treatments of this issue are N. MacCormick and R. Summers (eds.), *Interpreting Statutes: A Comparative Study* (Aldershot, Dartmouth 1991), pp. 16–24; A. Aarnio, 'Is Legal Science a Social Science?' and N. MacCormick, 'Four Quadrants of Jurisprudence', especially pp. 55–58, both of which appear in W. Krawictz, N. MacCormick and G. v. Wright (eds.), *Prescriptive Formality and Normative Rationality in Modern Legal Systems* (Berlin, Dunker and Humblot 1994).

that the law remains on this track, that it develops in such a way as to embody the values of intelligibility, consistency, fairness and practicality in fuller measure. Their creed is but the doctrinal analogue of the jurisprudential position constituted by the four claims just noted. If anything, this creed is more deeply and unreflectively embedded than its jurisprudential partner, for at the jurisprudential level, at least, the position is contested. At the doctrinal level, the orthodox approach is still regarded by many as unquestionably correct, there being no alternative.

In addition to the four constitutive claims, orthodox accounts of adjudication can be identified by the fact that they share four restrictions upon their scope. First, these accounts are almost exclusively concerned with the decision-making process in the appellate courts. This restricted focus is not beyond criticism since, although it is undeniable that these courts oversee the decision-making of all other legal decision-making bodies, it might be a mistake to concentrate exclusively upon them. For, until it is established that the patterns of reasoning prevalent in the appellate courts are replicated throughout the legal system, we should be cautious about regarding decision-making in these courts as representative of what goes on in the system as a whole. The second restriction follows directly from the first. The orthodox confine themselves to saying relatively little about 'easy' cases, probably because it is assumed that the arrival of a case in the appellate courts is linked to its degree of difficulty. Easy cases allegedly exist when the facts of a dispute are uncontested and there is no doubt about either the applicable proposition of law or its interpretation. For MacCormick, judicial decisions in these cases can in principle be justified deductively;[8] judges are therefore rationally compelled to reach the decisions they do and have few choices, if any, open to them. Moreover, decisions such as these are rationally unimpeachable—they have the most powerful justification possible. Although it is true that few among the orthodox explicitly address MacCormick's account of easy cases, it seems safe to say that there is little in it with which they could legitimately disagree.[9] So, for example, although Dworkin does not share MacCormick's account of the nature of hard case legal reasoning, he nevertheless accepts that there are in principle easy cases and the examples he uses suggest that the decisions in them could be deductively justified.[10]

The third way in which the scope of orthodox accounts is limited follows

[8] *LRLT*, ch. 2.

[9] Most of the orthodox criticisms of MacCormick's account of easy cases have called into question his use of propositional logic: see A. Wilson, 'The Nature of Legal Reasoning: a commentary with special reference to Professor MacCormick's theory' (1982) 2 *Legal Studies* 269–285 and MacCormick's reply at 286–290; P. White, book review (1979–80) 78 *Michigan L. R.* 737–742.

[10] *LE*, pp. 353–354 and note 14 at p. 449 ('"It goes without saying" that the speed limit in Connecticut is 55 . . .').

from the second. To anyone familiar with disputes in appellate courts, 'easy' cases seem rare indeed. According to the orthodox, the disputes that preoccupy appellate courts predominantly raise legal issues (to say nothing of factual disputes) of the following three kinds. First, there is doubt about whether or not there is indeed a proposition of law applicable to the case; secondly, the dispute is about the correct interpretation, out of a range of two or more, of the agreed applicable proposition of law; and, thirdly, there is doubt about which out of two or more incompatible propositions of law should be applied in the case. These 'hard cases', where 'no settled rule dictates a decision either way', 'in which reasonable lawyers will disagree . . . and neither will have available any argument that must necessarily convince the other',[11] provide the fulcrum of orthodox accounts of adjudication: they aim to articulate how hard cases are and should be decided.

Furthermore, the issue of how hard cases are and should be decided is one about which the orthodox disagree. Take just one example. MacCormick argues that the reasons judges do and should use to justify their choices in hard cases can be divided into three: arguments from coherence, consistency and consequences.[12] He thinks arguments of the last type crucial because in many hard cases arguments from consistency and coherence do not determine the decision.[13] Consequentialist arguments are concerned with whether or not a decision one way or another in a hard case 'makes sense in the world'.[14] The criterion of sense is yielded by evaluating the consequences in the world of the competing possible decisions: 'choosing between rival possible rulings in a case involves choosing between what are to be conceived as rival models for, rival patterns of, human conduct in . . . society'.[15] At least part of these evaluations consist of a rule–utilitarian calculation of the effects of a decision one way or another upon the welfare or preference satisfaction of the whole community, or a substantial segment thereof.[16] By contrast, Dworkin's view is that in hard cases '[j]udges must make their . . . decisions on grounds of principle, not policy'.[17] Arguments of principle have the following structure: they 'justify a political decision by showing that the decision respects or secures some individual or group right'.[18] These arguments are derived from an interpretation 'which shows the community's structure of institutions and decisions—its public standards as a whole [including, of course, its law]—in a better light from the

[11] *TRS*, at p. 83 and p. xiv respectively. [12] *LRLT*, chs. 5–8.

[13] See his discussion of *Donoghue* v *Stevenson* in *LRLT*, p. 110.

[14] *Ibid*, p. 103. [15] *Ibid*, p. 104.

[16] MacCormick is not entirely comfortable with utilitarianism, of whatever type, but he nevertheless invokes it: *ibid*, pp. 115–116 and p. 105, fn.1.

[17] *LE*, p. 244.

[18] *TRS*, p. 82. See also p. 90. Note that Dworkin is unclear about the relevance of rights based arguments to hard cases in the criminal law: *ibid*, p. 94, fn 1. See also *MP*, ch. 3.

standpoint of political morality'[19] than any other. Opposed to arguments of principle are arguments of policy, which Dworkin thinks are not and should not be the basis of judicial decision-making. Policy arguments 'justify a political decision by showing that the decision advances or protects some collective goal of the community as a whole'.[20] Understood thus, Dworkinian policy arguments are structurally very similar to the consequentialist arguments that MacCormick thinks are the justificatory core of legal reasoning.[21] Hence, for the orthodox there is disagreement in the midst of agreement. For, despite the fact that Dworkin and MacCormick agree that hard cases are decided via relatively determinate processes and yield relatively determinate outcomes, they nevertheless disagree over the nature of the arguments judges do and should use to decide such cases.

The final limitation on the scope of orthodox accounts of adjudication is that they have little to say about the institutional constraints within which judges make their decisions, the most obvious being the rules of precedent, statutory interpretation, evidence and procedure. These are matters which judges cannot ignore but which rarely completely determine the decisions they have to make and justify in hard cases. This is so because the institutional constraints are themselves often so vague as to create room for a judicial choice exactly similar to that which must be made in a hard case about some substantive legal issue. So, for example, while it is true that most legal systems have a number of canons of interpretation detailing the way in which judges should interpret statutory or judicial legal materials, it is also true that those legal systems rarely have priority rules assigning greater and lesser weight to each of these canons.[22] In the absence of such priority rules judges have an important choice open to them. Even where some priority rules exist, there is no guarantee that their application will not raise difficulties of the kind judges face in 'standard' hard cases (for example, should an unambiguous priority rule that holds that 'in circumstances Z apply canon of interpretation P', be applied where to do so would allow a party to benefit from his own wrong?). For reasons such as these the orthodox would concur with Robert Alexy's judgment that '[t]he weakness of the canons of interpretation . . . does not mean that they should be dismissed out of hand. But it does exclude the possibility of considering them as

[19] *LE*, p. 256. [20] *TRS*, p. 82.

[21] However, the difference between consequentialist arguments and arguments of principle and policy is not, for Dworkin, a simple one: see *TRS*, pp. 294–327. MacCormick seems to be of the view that there is almost an exact match between his consequentialist arguments and Dworkinian policy arguments: see MacCormick, 'On Legal Decisions and Their Consequences: From Dewey to Dworkin' (1983) 58 *New York University L. R.* 239–258, pp. 244–245.

[22] For the plethora of canons of statutory interpretation in England see, for example, J. Bell and G. Engel, *Cross: Statutory Interpretation* (London, Butterworths, 2nd ed. 1987) and F. Bennion, *Statutory Interpretation* (London, Butterworths, 2nd ed. 1991). On the rules for interpreting judicial decisions see R. Cross and J. W. Harris, *Precedent in English Law* (Oxford, Clarendon, 4th ed. 1991).

sufficient in themselves as rules for constructing justifications of legal decisions'.[23]

American scholars are by far the most influential proponents of heretical accounts of law and legal reasoning, although it is a mistake to think either that there is no European heretical work or that it is unworthy of attention.[24] However, the reasons that restrict the range of orthodox works considered in this volume hold good in relation to heretical work, with the added caveat that there may indeed be important differences between geographical instances of the heresy.[25] Thus we will be concerned in the main only with the writings of Roberto Unger, Duncan Kennedy, Mark Kelman, Joseph Singer, Clare Dalton, Drucilla Cornell and Pierre Schlag.[26] Their works have directly and indirectly influenced many and appear to have set

[23] Alexy, *supra,* note 3, p. 4.

[24] Much of the literature is Francophone and as yet unavailable in English. For an introduction, now somewhat dated, see I. Stewart, 'Critical Legal Studies in France' (1981) 9 *International Journal of the Sociology of Law* 225–231. Some important works are P. Legendre, *Law and the Unconscious: A Legendre Reader* (trans. by P. Goodrich and A. Pottage, London, MacMillan 1997); M. van der Kerchove and F. Ost, *Legal System Between Order and Disorder* (Oxford, Clarendon 1994) and their *Jalons pour une théorie critique du droit* (Brussels, Facultés Universitaires Saint-Louis 1987). For an introduction to the sometimes quite different contours of German critical legal thought see C. Joerges and D. Trubek (eds.), *Critical Legal Thought: An American-German Debate* (Baden-Baden, Nomos 1989).

[25] P. Goodrich has argued along these lines. His agenda for a distinctively 'British' or 'English' critical legal theory is suggested in 'Critical Legal Studies in England: Prospective Histories' (1992) 12 *Oxford Journal of Legal Studies* 195–236, especially pp. 195–203 and pp. 232–236. See also his 'Sleeping with the Enemy: An Essay on Critical Legal Studies in America' (1993) 68 *New York University L. R.* 389–425. For some examples of British critical legal scholarship see C. Douzinas, R. Warrington with S. McVeigh, *Postmodern Jurisprudence* (London, Routledge 1991); C. Douzinas and R. Warrington, *Justice Miscarried* (London, Harvester Wheatsheaf 1994) and P. Goodrich, *Oedipus Lex: Psychoanalysis, History, Law* (Berkeley, University of California Press 1995). Unlike their American counterparts, however, British critical scholars are not self-consciously part of a 'movement' with a manifesto, have as yet lacked the influence to recreate large bodies of legal scholarship in their own image and, fortunately, have avoided the battles—curricular and political—that have engulfed American heretics.

[26] The main works are: R. Unger, *Knowledge and Politics* (New York, The Free Press 1975), hereinafter '*KP*'; *The Critical Legal Studies Movement* (Cambridge, Mass., Harvard U. P. 1986), henceforth referred to as '*CLSM*'; *Politics, A Work in Constructive Social Theory*, three volumes (Cambridge, C. U. P. 1987); *What Should Legal Analysis Become?* (London, Verso, 1996); D. Kennedy, 'The Structure of Blackstone's *Commentaries*' (1979) 28 *Buffalo L. R.* 205–382 (henceforth referred to as '*BC*'); 'Form and Substance in Private Law Adjudication' (1976) 89 *Harvard L. R.* 1685–1778 (referred to as '*FS*'); *Sexy Dressing Etc.* (Cambridge, Mass., Harvard U. P. 1993); *A Critique of Adjudication* (Cambridge, Mass., Harvard U. P. 1997), hereinafter '*CA*'; M. Kelman, *A Guide to Critical Legal Studies* (Cambridge, Mass., Harvard U. P. 1987), henceforth referred to as '*GCLS*'; J. Singer, 'The Player and the Cards: Nihilism and Legal Theory' (1984) 94 *Yale L. J.* 1–70; C. Dalton, 'An Essay in the Deconstruction of Contract Law Doctrine' (1985) 94 *Yale L. J.* 997–1114; D. Cornell, *The Philosophy of the Limit* (London, Routledge and Chapman Hall 1992); and P. Schlag, ' "Le Hors de Texte, C'est Moi"—The Politics of Form and the Domestication of Deconstruction' (1990) 11 *Cardozo L. R.* 1631–1674 and 'The Problem of the Subject' (1991) 61 *Texas L. R.* 1627–1743. The work of S. Fish can be located at the margin of this group: see his *Doing What Comes Naturally* (New York, Oxford U. P. 1989) chs. 4–7 and chs. 16–19.

the agenda for much legal scholarship of the last two decades. It would be tempting, on seeing this list of scholars, to regard what is hereinafter called the heresy as but an eccentric composite made up of the works of some leading lights from the field of 'critical legal studies'. Yet this would be a mistake.

First, because the 'critical legal studies' label often obscures as much as it illuminates. It is sometimes used, for example, as a means of lumping together the work of some of the North American legal scholars referred to hereinafter as heretics with the work of North American proponents of Derridean deconstruction, critical race theory and feminism.[27] There is little justification for doing this, given the great differences in method, aims and strategy between these diverse bodies of thought. Furthermore, taking the label 'heresy' to be but a synonym for critical legal studies suggests that being a heretic, like being a critical legal scholar, is predominantly a matter of self-definition. This impression arises from the fact that critical legal studies became, and perhaps still is, a 'movement', in the sense of being an organisation designed to achieve specific goals for its membership and, apparently contingently, the disadvantaged in society at large. The label 'heretic' carries no such impression. It is intended to capture nothing other than a number of claims, an intellectual position, which may or may not be a 'movement' and which those labelled by it might or might not *explicitly* share and profess. Certainly, there are serious disagreements among those labelled heretics in this book, disagreements which suggest that if there is indeed a 'movement' here, it is pluralistic and fractious. Self-definition is not therefore a good guide to membership.

The heretics on our list certainly do not speak with one voice. They argue with one another and sometimes draw upon quite different sources for inspiration and argument. Moreover, those in the vanguard have subsequently marched under slightly different banners, albeit banners informed and inspired by the initial aims of the heresy.[28] However, despite this apparent diversity, the suggestion has been made that heretics pursue a single

[27] This is a very limited list of examples of each approach. On deconstruction, see M. Kramer, *Legal Theory, Political Theory, and Deconstruction* (Bloomington, Indiana U. P. 1991); J. Balkin, 'Deconstructive Practice and Legal Theory' (1987) 96 *Yale L. J.* 743–786 and his 'Transcendental Deconstruction, Transcendent Justice' (1994) 92 *Michigan L. R.* 1131–1186. Some early examples of critical race scholarship are included in 'Symposium: Minority Critiques of the Critical Legal Studies Movement' (1987) 22 *Harvard C. R.—C. L. Law Review* 297–449; K. Crenshaw, 'Race, Reform and Retrenchment: Transformation and Legitimation in Antidiscrimination Law' (1988) 101 *Harvard L. R.* 1331–1387; and A. Cook, 'Beyond Critical Legal Studies: The Reconstructive Theology of Dr. Martin Luther King, Jr.' (1990) 103 *Harvard L. R.* 985–1044. Feminist legal scholars include C. Mackinnon, *Feminism Unmodified* (Cambridge, Mass., Harvard U. P. 1987) and *Toward a Feminist Theory of the State* (Cambridge, Mass., Harvard U. P. 1989); D. Cornell, *Beyond Accommodation* (London, Routledge 1991) and M. J. Frug, *Postmodern Legal Feminism* (London, Routledge 1992).

[28] Kennedy, *Sexy Dressing*, *supra*, note 26, ch. 2 and G. Peller, 'Race Consciousness' (1990) *Duke L. J.* 758–847.

left/modern/post-modern project. The politically left-wing dimension of this project is its goal 'to change the existing system of social hierarchy, including its class, racial, and gender dimensions, in the direction of greater equality and greater participation in public and private government'.[29] The modern/post-modern dimension revels in 'the ethos of post-ness, doubleness, yearning, irony and the aesthetic, the element of self-conscious formal manipulation in the name of unknowable primal underforces and dangerous supplements, cut by the critiques of the subject and representation'.[30] One obvious problem with understanding the heresy in this way is the tension that arises between its left-wing political programme—'the struggle for a more egalitarian and communitarian society'—and its alleged intellectual underpinnings, which are 'supposed to put in question . . . claims of rightness'.[31] For it seems clear that the intellectual foundations of the heresy undermine its political aims: if the struggle for a more communitarian and egalitarian society is not, either implicitly or explicitly, ultimately a claim of rightness, then what can it be?

More problematic, perhaps, is the elision of modern and post-modern intellectual influences. Lumping them both together, Kennedy turns them into a single refrain, namely, a chorus of rupture. Kennedy takes the transgressive artefact as the motif of this position and his lumping together of 'post-modern' or deconstructive thought with the modernist moment in literary and artistic thought is superficially quite plausible. For, just as post-modern philosophers supposedly preach the end of certainty and the collapse of meta-narratives, modernist writers such as Pound and Joyce challenged and sought to topple the dominant forms of literary style and content.[32] The works of both groups can be seen as an attempt to attack, to rupture, pre-existing styles and stabilised patterns of thought. However, two things are lost in this picture. First, the modernist literary and artistic programmes are overlooked—that is, the ideas, goals and aims that animated efforts at rupture—and, second, modernist social theory is entirely invisible. These oversights are significant because they succeed in making modernist thought far too post-modern, if a hallmark of the latter is indeed an absence of guiding blue-prints, plans and meta-narratives. So, when Kennedy claims that the modern/post-modern project 'is a critique of the characteristic forms of rightness of . . . [our] culture and aims at liberation from inner and outer experiences of constraint by reason, in the name, *not of justice and a new system*, but of a dialectic of system and anti-system', he over-inflates and thus traduces modernism.[33] For, since modernism existed only at the

[29] Kennedy, *CA*, p. 6. [30] *CA*, p. 339. [31] Both statements are from *CA*, p. 341.

[32] For useful introductory discussions of the modernist 'style' in literature see P. Faulkner, *Modernism* (London, Methuen 1977) and M. Bradbury and J. McFarlane (eds.), *Modernism 1890–1930* (Brighton, Harvester Press 1978).

[33] *CA*, p. 340.

literary–artistic and architectural levels, having discernible analogues neither in human sciences such as sociology, anthropology, political and moral philosophy nor in practical politics, it hardly explicitly eschewed 'liberation in the name of justice and a new system'. Since it was in no sense (other than the most banal and trivial) 'political' (the sense in which 'everything is political'), modernism cannot be tarred with this brush.[34] This is not to say that there is no self-proclaimed 'modernist' heretical work. Roberto Unger's work is proudly modernist but, of course, he offers a new *system*, unfurls a banner inscribed with ideas like participation, equality, autonomy and solidarity under which we are to re-make and re-imagine society. Aspects of that programme are analysed in chapter 7, as is some avowely post-modern or, more accurately, deconstructive heretical work which, in its search for the ethics of deconstruction, invokes notions of justice and otherness.

For these reasons, Kennedy's rather grandiose statement of what unites our sample heretics is best ignored. It raises many more difficult questions than it answers; pursuing it further would enmire us in nice questions of intellectual genealogy and influence that we do not have time to examine. For our purposes, what unites heretics is far more mundane. For, although their influences are often quite different, and although they often vigorously disagree with one another, they nevertheless share the following claims. They accept the third and fourth orthodox claims. They accept that there is some degree of predictability and certainty in the law and that adjudicators generally adopt only a limited number of justificatory strategies when deciding cases. However, in opposition to the orthodox, heretics deny that this is the result of adjudicators applying relatively determinate standards and invoking determinate justificatory strategies to achieve closure of a choice open to them. For heretics, these choices are not in principle capable of justification. Adjudicators may believe their choices are justifiable and thus decide cases predictably, on the basis of this belief combined with a range of values and assumptions which as a group they share.[35] Yet this belief, inculcated through socialisation perhaps prior to, but certainly during, professional and academic training, is a mistake: there are at least

[34] See the sources in *supra*, note 32, for modernism's non-existent 'politics' and its lack of resonance in many of the human sciences. R. Unger sings from the same vague hymn sheet as Kennedy in his discussions of 'modernism': see *Passion* (New York, The Free Press 1984), pp. 1–89. Unger's only suggested analogues to literary modernism in the human sciences are 'the writings of such philosophers as Heidegger and Sartre': *Politics*, Vol. 1, *supra*, note 26, p. 222. G. Hawthorn notes the potential (I would say actual) political emptiness of Unger's modernism in 'Practical Reason and Social Democracy: Reflections on Unger's *Passion* and *Politics*' (1987) 81 *Northwestern University L. R.* 766–790, p. 771.

[35] For heretical statements that legal reasoning is relatively determinate and predictable for 'sociological' or 'ideological' reasons see: D. Kairys (ed.), *The Politics of Law: A Progressive Critique* (New York, Pantheon 1982), p. 15; Singer, *supra*, note 26, pp. 19–25; Kelman, *GCLS*, p. 4 and pp. 46–47.

three reasons why the choices open to adjudicators cannot be justified. They are: the truth of language and value indeterminacy, and the truth of the ideology critique. A brief sketch of each is necessary here.

Simply put, both types of indeterminacy entail that neither legal standards, nor the values nor purposes they serve, determine any legal decision. This is because, first, heretics such as Singer and Peller assume that language yields meaning only conventionally. That one word means or refers to X rather than Y is a purely contingent matter. The word could have had another, radically different meaning or referred to any number of other things.[36] It just so happens that it means X. The meaning and reference of words is therefore analogous to stipulative definitions of the form: henceforth I use the word 'fish' to mean 'a hairy quadruped at least two metres high with a bushy tail'. Such definitions have no rational power and are not compelling—we can accept or reject them as we wish.[37] Thus in relation to any interpretation or definition of the word, sentence or proposition X, there is always another, equally 'valid' or 'compelling' interpretation available. As this is true of language in general it is held by heretics to be true, *a fortiori*, of legal language. The implication heretics draw is that, despite appearances, legal doctrines are severely indeterminate: in particular cases, 'opposing arguments can be made with *equal* force'; in general, there is always 'a wide variety of precedents and a still wider variety of interpretations and distinctions . . . from which to *pick and choose*'.[38]

Secondly, heretics assume either that values are beyond the bounds of rationality *tout court* or that the orthodox are explicitly or implicitly committed to this view. This uncomfortable conjunction is necessary because when heretics speak of values it is far from clear whether they are simply attacking what they take to be the orthodox position or invoking a general truth about values. For Unger and Kelman the orthodox, insofar as they are 'liberals', are committed to the subjectivity (or indeterminacy) of values. That commitment entails 'that values—beliefs about what is worth pursuing—are seen as nothing more than tastes, the purely arbitrary assertions of individuals'.[39] By contrast, heretics such as they favour an account in

[36] For a good statement see G. Peller, 'The Metaphysics of American Law' (1985) 73 *California L. R.* 1152–1290, pp. 1160–1170 and S. Fish, *supra*, note 26, ch. 1. One heretic who seems ambivalent about language indeterminacy is Kelman: *GCLS*, p. 13, note 21 and pp. 45–48.

[37] For useful discussion see R. Robinson, *Definition* (Oxford, Clarendon 1954). G. Williams in 'The Controversy about the Word "Law" ', *Philosophy, Politics and Society* (First Series) P. Laslett (ed.) (Oxford, Basil Blackwell 1956), seems quite happy to 'resolve' the dispute about the nature of law by reference to stipulative definitions. Humpty Dumpty was also much impressed by stipulative definitions: 'When I use a word . . . it means exactly what I want it to mean—neither more nor less': L. Carroll, *The Annotated Lewis Caroll*, M. Gardiner (ed.) (London, Penguin 1975), p. 269.

[38] The quotations are from, respectively, Dalton, *supra*, note 26, p. 1007 and Kairys, *supra*, note 35, p. 14; (emphasis supplied). See also J. Frug, 'Argument as Character' (1988) 40 *Stanford L. R.* 869–927, p. 871.

[39] Kelman, *GCLS*, p. 64. See also Unger, *KP*, pp. 76–100.

which values and the good are more than just a function 'of the satisfaction of individual desires'.[40] Values have an objective existence over and beyond individual desires, part of that objective existence deriving from the fact that values and the good are embedded in communities and groups.[41] Hence it is unlikely that for Unger and Kelman the subjectivity of values is a general truth—it is true only of orthodox or liberal accounts of value. However, other heretics seem to accept that the subjectivity of values is a general truth. For example, when Kennedy notes that private law doctrine is informed by both individualistic and altruistic values, he seemingly assumes this observation can, without more, conclusively establish that this conflict of values cannot be resolved. This claim is acceptable only if there is some independent reason to support it (invoking the existence of different values does not show that they must conflict).

Such a reason could be provided by the subjectivity of values claim: if it is the case that values are agent-specific, arbitrary assertions, then it is difficult to see how different assertions could be compatible (in the same way that it is difficult to see how your view that coffee tastes better with sugar could be made compatible with my view that it is better without). What is there in Kennedy's argument to suggest that when he invokes the subjectivity of values he is doing more than reconstructing the orthodox or liberal position? What grounds do we have for thinking that Kennedy takes the subjectivity of values as a general truth? Simply this: his many *general* statements—statements about the human situation *simpliciter*, not the human situation within supposedly liberal societies—that conflicts between values are an inescapable feature of our lives, be those conflicts a function of a deeper 'fundamental contradiction' or just a consequence of the fact that there is more than one value or list of values open to us.[42] However, Kennedy makes statements such as these while simultaneously ascribing the subjectivity of values claim to the 'individualist' and, since he is out of sympathy with individualism, the implication is that the subjectivity of values is the last claim he would want to accept.[43]

[40] Unger, *KP*, p. 240.

[41] For a tentative statement by Kelman along these lines see *GCLS*, p. 82; for his reservations about Unger's account of the community 'embeddedness' of values (found in *KP*, pp. 243–247) see p. 84. See also Kennedy, *FS*, pp. 1771–1774.

[42] On the fundamental contradiction between self and other see Kennedy, *BC*, pp. 211–218. On the analogous conflict between the values constitutive of altruism and individualism see Kennedy, *FS*, p. 1712 (there is an 'unresolvable conflict' between the values we accept); p. 1762 (there can be no justifiable choice between values constitutive of individualism and altruism); pp. 1766–1767 (the contradiction is unavoidable); pp. 1774–1776 (ditto, plus the claim that the choice between altruism and individualism is not reasoned but 'existential', a pure matter of commitment). Both versions of the contradiction crop up in Kennedy's later work (see *Sexy Dressing*, *supra*, note 26, pp. viii and 70 and *CA*, pp. 54, 83, 95, 151–2 and 207) despite his effort to retract it. The bogus retraction is discussed in chapter 6.

[43] *FS* at p. 1765 and p. 1769. Kennedy's 'individualist' seems to have a deal in common with the orthodox or 'liberal'.

We need not attempt to resolve this ambiguity here. It will suffice to note that the indeterminacy or subjectivity of values claim amounts to this: we cannot—generally, or insofar as we are liberals—be *rationally* compelled to accept that any values are 'correct' or 'true' and hence cannot be *rationally* persuaded that one value or set of values is better than any other. When combined with the observation that members of modern societies manifest a vast range of incompatible values, this view allows reason little scope in evaluative matters. If it is further accepted that (i) for interpretation of legal standards (by which I mean to refer to legal rules, principles and policies) to be possible, recourse must be had to the values or purposes they track; and (ii) value indeterminacy is true, then it seems plausible to deny that any adjudicator's choice, being based upon the interpretation of legal standards in light of their value or point, can be justified. A choice one way, it seems, is only as good as a choice the other way. Remember, also, that for heretics this argument is offered in addition to the argument about the indeterminacy of language. That argument holds that legal language, like language in general, yields meaning only conventionally and therefore there is always another alternative to any judicial interpretative choice. Taken separately or together, these two indeterminacy arguments are regarded by many heretics as sufficiently powerful either to induce scepticism about, or to lead to the outright rejection of, the first two orthodox assumptions.

The truth of the ideology critique can make judicial decisions impossible to justify in a number of ways: a great deal turns upon what is meant by 'ideology'.[44] In one sense, ideology signifies propositions, attitudes and beliefs that are systematically misleading, that prevent us from seeing things—the world or perhaps even our selves—as they really are. In some accounts of ideology the obfuscatory nature of these propositions, attitudes and beliefs serves a particular purpose or set of interests whereas, on other accounts, this 'false consciousness' is entirely neutral between such purposes or interests. Now, if it could be shown that legal reasoning peddles in obfuscation—that judicial decisions embody systematically misleading beliefs, etc.—then the task of attempting to justify that process and its constitutive decisions seems foredoomed to failure. A rational justification for what is systematically misleading is not impossible—the notion of the noble lie, is after all, not unknown to us—but it is certainly an unpromising foundation for a system of law and adjudication.

In another sense, ideology refers to a body of ideas, beliefs and interests held by a particular group. The group can be large or small and the ideas

[44] This question is addressed in more depth in ch. 7, below. Useful treatments of the issues are J. Larrain, *The Concept of Ideology* (London, Hutchinson 1979); J. Thompson, *Ideology and Modern Culture* (Cambridge, Polity Press 1990) and M. Rosen, *On Voluntary Servitude* (Cambridge, Polity Press 1996).

and beliefs can be conventional or eccentric—those of the campaign for the protection of rural England or those of the flat earth society. The interests in question are usually the reason why the group exists—its actions are geared toward protecting or furthering those interests. Such interests can be political, moral, prudential, cultural or aesthetic. When the notion of ideology is employed in this sense, showing adjudication to be ideological, and thus a series of unjustifiable choices, must entail a demonstration that the ideas, beliefs and interests embodied in judicial decisions are in some sense illegitimate. Hence, if it can be shown that judicial choices always favour the interests of a particular group in society, then those choices are *prima facie* very difficult to justify. For, if claims about equality before the law are taken seriously, it is hard to justify judicial choices that always favour a particular group. Moreover, the problem might not be the fact that the outcomes of judicial decisions always favour particular interests; rather, the problem might instead be the intrusion of certain types of interests, beliefs or ideas into the process of adjudication. For example, it might be maintained that 'political' factors unavoidably enter into adjudication despite the fact that many judges and orthodox legal scholars insist upon a strict separation between politics and law. If the ideology critique highlights the existence of such illegitimate factors in adjudication, then it does indeed suggest that judicial choices are impossible to justify.

There are two points to note about the range of heretical accounts of adjudication. First, their range can appear simultaneously wider and narrower than orthodox accounts. They appear wider and more ambitious than orthodox accounts because, when tackling adjudication, a standard heretical strategy is to move from what they take to be general truths or assumptions, like those about the indeterminacy of language and values, to the implications these truths must have for law and adjudication in general. This concern with large philosophical issues of language and value is far less explicit in the work of the orthodox; certainly the latter generally deal with these issues as and when they arise at a lower level of abstraction. The orthodox, unlike heretics, rarely offer 'total critiques' of broad traditions of thought and articulate the consequences of such critiques for adjudication.[45] Although heretics sometimes do this, they also often concentrate upon particular instances of legal reasoning and doctrine. However, there is an important difference between their approach and that of the orthodox which suggests a more restricted focus. For, at the level of doctrinal analysis, heretics eschew the orthodox task of rational reconstruction and their

[45] A total critique of liberal thought is, of course, Unger's enterprise: *KP*, ch. 1. Heretical works which one might think, from their titles, would focus on some specific examples of legal reasoning do not: see P. Gabel, 'Reification in Legal Reasoning' (1980) 3 *Research in Law and Sociology* 25–51 and D. Kennedy, 'Freedom and Constraint in Adjudication: A Critical Phenomenology' (1986) 36 *Journal of Legal Education* 518–562.

analyses of specific cases therefore manifest a relatively lax attitude to the 'surface' of the legal text.[46] The text is not taken too seriously because any and all judgments or statutes embody the rational and evaluative defects that arise from the general issues of language and value indeterminacy. Furthermore, because legal texts purport to be determinative but are not, they make good candidates for rhetorical, ideological, psychological and sociological analysis. In general terms, analyses such as these purport to explain how what in reality is contingent, arbitrary and without justification, comes to be regarded as natural, legitimate and correct. Therefore, these modes of analysis seem obvious sources upon which to draw so as to explain why an indeterminate process—adjudication—is regarded as determinate.

The second point to note about the range of heretical accounts is this. They have a wider range than orthodox accounts because, in opposition to the latter, some heretics do not confine their accounts of adjudication to hard cases. They reject the hard case/easy case dichotomy. For these heretics '[t]here are . . . no easy cases, though there may be ones whose outcomes are perfectly predictable'.[47] It is obvious why heretics should come to this conclusion. If value and language indeterminacy are indeed true—and the first and second orthodox assumptions are rejected—then it seems obvious that the law lacks the determinacy necessary for there to be such things as easy cases. Hence the easy case/hard case distinction is one of the crucial sites for the dispute between heretics and orthodox. That is not to say that the orthodox are blind to the problems that arise for their attempts to draw the distinction.[48] Thus, while heretics draw upon wider philosophical and historical perspectives than the orthodox (explicitly) do, and therefore their accounts seem to have a greater range, their accounts also seem narrower than some orthodox accounts in so far as the latter concern themselves with the details of adjudicative practices that some heretics ignore. However, it is also true that orthodox accounts concentrate on a very limited class of hard cases and that heretics regard the hard case/easy case classification as mistaken.

Orthodox and heretical accounts of adjudication constitute the realm of thought and dispute with which this book is concerned. The nature of that concern must, however, be briefly delineated so as to avoid an obvious misunderstanding. The misunderstanding is this: it may be assumed that what follows will take issue, in a detailed, blow-by-blow way, with the claims

[46] The difference between orthodox and heretical emphases is well put by G. Frug, 'A Critical Theory of Law' (1989) 1 *Legal Education Review* 43–57, p. 55.

[47] Kelman, *GCLS*, p. 4. But see Kennedy, *CA*, p. 60.

[48] For orthodox discussions of the problem of easy cases see: MacCormick, *LRLT*, ch. 8; A. Marmor, *Interpretation and Legal Theory* (Oxford, Clarendon 1993), ch. 7; and F. Schauer, 'Easy Cases' (1985) 58 *Southern California L. R.* 399–440.

heretics and orthodox make about the scope and nature of accounts of adjudication. That is not the case. I do not, as is common in discussions of accounts of adjudication, seek to reject one or other of these accounts by examining particular cases that purport to be counterexamples to them. (Some reasons for not doing this are offered in chapter 2.) Nor do I concern myself entirely with the task of determining the internal coherence of these accounts. Rather the book examines assumptions about the nature of explanation and understanding made by heretical and orthodox scholars who turn minds and pens to the practice of adjudication. In a sense, therefore, the book is a second-order enquiry—an enquiry about how to conduct a particular kind of enquiry. By contrast, the majority of works examined here could be called first-order, since they often grapple head-on with the phenomenon to be explained. They wrestle with particular judicial decisions, the details of the arguments therein and attempt to determine the way in which those arguments are best interpreted and categorised. However, the first order/second order dichotomy is potentially misleading. It implies that those engaged in first-order enquiry can in an unproblematic sense just do it—that they can just apprehend the phenomenon to be understood or explained without considering what a good explanation or understanding might look like. That is nonsense. As will become plain in what follows, heretics and orthodox have fairly clear ideas, although often implausible and incompletely formulated, on these issues that inform their work.

There is much, although I do not document it in any detail here, in both orthodox and heretical accounts with which I agree. There is also much in each of these supposedly contradictory accounts that is compatible, though some will find this claim controversial. I take some trouble to try to highlight these similarities for it is important as a means of puncturing the inflated rhetoric that surrounds this 'debate'. It is portrayed by some participants as a crusade, a war of opposing sects, a fight for hearts and minds. It is thus surprising and useful to find that these alleged enemies do not disagree as radically and deeply as they say they do, that their positions on a number of matters are quite close, if not actually indistinguishable. This task of charting the real differences and similarities between orthodox and heretical accounts of adjudication is pursued in the book through the consideration of three problems. For, another claim I make and seek to substantiate against both heretics and orthodox is this. Orthodox and heretical accounts of adjudication must respond to the three problems outlined below and they often either fail adequately to respond to each of the problems or fail to appreciate the problematic implications of some of their responses. Of course, I do not argue that each and every heretical and orthodox position in response to these problems is wrong, only that they sometimes overstate their arguments, thus exaggerating their differences, and are sometimes completely blind to the similarities in their positions. Furthermore, the commendable and plausible aspects of both types of accounts are often quite compatible. Let us, however, turn to the three problems: what are they and why should they concern us?

II PROBLEMS AND SOLUTIONS

The three problems will be tiresomely familiar to anyone schooled in the philosophical and methodological controversies of the human sciences.[49] Since the first two problems are usually only briefly and cryptically alluded to in the Anglo-American jurisprudential literature, both heretical and orthodox, I make no apology for the pedestrian and utterly predictable account that follows. I assume that an explicit but pedestrian statement of the problems is far better than either no, or only a cryptic, statement. Moreover, all three problems deserve explicit and sustained attention because both orthodoxy and heresy must, and implicitly do, take up a position, often unsatisfactory, in response to them.

(a) The problem of method

The first problem orthodox and heretical accounts of adjudication must address is that of method. It has at least two dimensions. The first consists of a response to the 'What question': what should be examined in order to explain and understand social action (of which the practice of adjudication is but part) and its constitutive rules, roles and institutions? Within the history of the human sciences two answers have been offered to this question although there are in fact three available. Each answer has a strong and a moderate version. Although the answers have sometimes been thought incompatible one with another and sometimes regarded as consistent, it is the case that only the strong versions of each answer are incompatible. Since the two moderate versions are compatible then, taken together, they constitute a third answer to the question.

The moderate version of the first answer holds that explanations and understandings of social action can be generated by reference to information about the individuals whose behaviour constitutes the action in which we are interested. (The distinction between 'behaviour' and 'action' here, and in what follows, is that the former is merely a range of bodily movements whereas the latter includes such movements but situates them within

[49] General accounts of these controversies are found in collections such as A. Ryan (ed.), *The Philosophy of Social Explanation* (Oxford, Clarendon 1973) and R. Beehler and A. R. Drengson (eds.), *The Philosophy of Society* (London, Methuen 1978).

a web of goals, rules and meanings.[50] The dubious supposition upon which the distinction rests—namely, that behaviour can be identified and described independently of webs of goals etc.,—will not be questioned here.) The strong version of the first answer must hold, further, that (i) explanations and understandings of social action are generated *solely* by reference to information about individuals; and (ii) the individual behaviour constitutive of social action is also *completely* constitutive of social rules, roles and institutions. This stronger claim, that 'facts' or information about individuals can tell us all we need to know about social life, including its rules, roles and institutions, is the hallmark of the methodological individualist. Methodological individualists hold that 'social processes and events should be explained by being deduced from (a) principles governing the behaviour of participating individuals and (b) descriptions of their situations'.[51]

A second answer to the 'What question' holds that explanations and understandings of social action must be constructed by reference to social or 'societal' facts, that is, information about the rules, roles and institutions within which individual action takes place. This answer is incompatible with the strong version of the first answer. It would only be incompatible with the moderate version of the first answer if it were extended to hold, additionally, that (i) no adequate explanation and understanding of social action could escape reference to 'societal' facts; and (ii) societal facts are not reducible to information about individuals.[52] This strong version of the second answer has been labelled, not too discriminatingly, 'methodological holism'.[53]

Thus there are at least three answers to the question of what should be examined in order to explain and understand social action. First, that our accounts of social action must begin and end with either information about individuals or, secondly, with supra-individual societal facts or, thirdly, with both. A shorthand way of putting these options is this: when we are to explain and understand social action are we to begin with agents, structures or both? The second dimension of the method problem consists of answers to what we can call the 'How question': given our starting point—agents, structures or both—how are we to go about explaining and understanding these features of the world? Again, within the history of the human sciences, at least two answers have been offered to this question; again, the

[50] In the human sciences and philosophy generally this point is often put in terms of the possibility or otherwise of explaining and understanding others without reference to 'intentionality'. For some traditional objections to accommodating this notion in the human sciences, and a rebuttal of them, see C. Taylor, *The Explanation of Behaviour* (London, Routledge and Kegan Paul 1964), ch. IV.

[51] J. W. N. Watkins, 'Ideal Types and Historical Explanation' in Ryan, *supra*, note 49, p. 88.

[52] For discussion see M. Mandelbaum, 'Societal Facts' in Ryan, *supra*, note 49, ch. VI.

[53] By, for example, Watkins, *supra*, note 51.

answers have been thought by some to contradict one another and by others to be consistent; again, we can distinguish moderate and strong versions of each answer and note that only the strong versions of each are incompatible.

The first answer is that one can only begin to explain and understand social action when one can predict it, if it has not already occurred, or deduce it, if it has already occurred, from a set of initial conditions and a corpus of general or probabilistic laws.[54] Because of the importance of general and probabilistic laws and the notions of deduction and induction, this answer is properly named the deductive-nomological or inductive-probabilistic method (hereinafter the 'D-N method'). Proponents of this answer regard it as applicable to the subject matter of both the human and natural sciences, although many have doubted that it does indeed provide a good account of natural scientific practice.[55] In the human sciences the strong version of this answer holds that the D-N method is the *only* way in which one can hope to explain and understand social action, the moderate version that the method is an important component of any adequate explanation and understanding of social action. Both versions agree on what an explanation and understanding of social action looks like. Suppose we want to explain and understand social action E. On the D-N approach this reduces to two questions: either 'why did E occur?' or 'do we have grounds to believe that E will occur?'. 'In order to answer the [first] question, we point to certain other events or states of affairs $E_1, \ldots, E_m$ and to one or several general propositions or laws $L_1, \ldots, L_n$ such that the occurrence of E (on the occasion in question) follows logically from those laws and the fact that those other events (states) have occurred (obtain)'.[56] Suppose further that action E is X's behaviour of stopping her vehicle at traffic lights. If we have a list of initial conditions and previous events such that we know X knows (i) that most other agents do this; (ii) that the consequences of refraining from stopping at traffic lights are 'unpleasant'; (iii) that the probability of some or all of those unpleasant consequences occurring as a result of a single omission to stop is thus and so; and we also know (iv) that there is a well established 'general' law to the effect that human beings structure their behaviour in such a way as to avoid 'unpleasant' consequences, then

[54] Exemplars of this method are C. G. Hempel, 'The Function of General Laws in History' and 'Aspects of Scientific Explanation' in his *Aspects of Scientific Explanation* (New York, The Free Press 1965) and E. Nagel, *The Structure of Science* (London, Routledge and Kegan Paul 1961) chs. 3–4 and 13–15.

[55] See, for example, the diverse and often incompatible accounts offered by K. Popper, *The Logic of Scientific Discovery* (London, Hutchinson 1968), chs III–VI; T. S. Kuhn, *The Structure of Scientific Revolutions* (Chicago, University of Chicago Press 2nd ed. 1970), chs. III–IX; and M. Hesse, *The Structure of Scientific Inference* (Berkeley, University of California Press 1974), chs. 1–3 and 7–9.

[56] This accurate and non-controversial statement is taken from G. H. Von Wright, *Explanation and Understanding* (London, Routledge and Kegan Paul 1971), p. 11.

we can explain and understand E by deducing it from these initial conditions and this general law. With knowledge of this general law and the initial conditions we could predict that in the future X would engage in action similar to, or of the same general type as, E.

The second answer to the 'How question' makes two initial claims. First, that social action has a dimension of sense, meaning or value for its authors and, secondly, that an adequate explanation and understanding of social action must capture this dimension. The strong version of this answer holds that the D-N method of explanation and understanding must but cannot accommodate the meaning dimension of social action which, of course, is not to say that the D-N method is completely redundant. That would only follow were it true that social action has nothing but a meaning dimension. Yet it is neither *a priori* implausible nor inconsistent with the strong version of this answer to suggest that social action, just like events in the natural world, has a causal dimension that the D-N method may be employed to explain. To say this is to limit the range of the D-N method but not to reject it completely;[57] that would require further argument. Were such argument forthcoming, it would be necessary to distinguish an ultra-strong version of the second answer from the strong and moderate versions. The latter version holds that most accounts of the D-N method already do, or can in principle be amended so as to, accommodate the meaning dimension of social action.

Both versions of the second answer hold that to capture the meaning dimension of social action one must take a particular approach that has been labelled interpretative, hermeneutic or *Verstehen* (from this point on I adopt the latter label). The *Verstehen* approach holds, *inter alia*, that the language, values and discriminations of the authors of social action must be grasped if we are to be able fully to understand and explain social action.[58] Why? Because the meaning dimension of action is only available to us through the language, values and discriminations of its authors. Without access to the meaning dimension of action we will mistakenly believe that

[57] This is Weber's position: see *Economy and Society* (New York, Bedminster Press 1968), G. Roth and C. Wittich (eds.), pp. 4–22.

[58] A. Giddens rightly notes that this approach has developed in the history of the human sciences from what can be called a 'subjectivist' version—first associated with W. Dilthey and in the later parts of this century with the work of A. Schutz—in which the emphasis is upon the meaning action has for its particular author (hence Dilthey's notion of 'reliving' or 're-experiencing'), to an 'ontological' version—associated with, *inter alios*, H-G. Gadamer, P. Winch and post-Wittgensteinian analytical philosophy—in which the meaning of action is determined by language and language is regarded as our only means of relating to the world and each other (hence Gadamer's claim that language constitutes our world). See A. Giddens, *Studies in Social and Political Theory* (London, Hutchinson 1977) pp. 170–175. It seems Giddens errs when he ascribes the subjectivist position to Weber for, as G. Oakes notes, the subjectivist reading of Weber fits uneasily with the 'objectivist' implications of his ideal types: see his *Weber and Rickert* (Cambridge, Mass., The MIT Press 1988), pp. 29–32.

ostensibly the same behaviour must have the same meaning. To see this, think, for example, of someone raising their arm. Suppose we have some way of determining that a good deal of this behaviour takes place in a community. It would be a mistake to assume that, because in various instances the behaviour is similar, its meaning is exactly the same on each occasion it is observed. For we know, because we share a language, rules and institutions, as well as some discriminations and some values, that in our community this 'unitary' behaviour could be, *inter alia*, a manifestation of St. Vitus's dance, an attempt to gain or to distract the attention of another, a method of directing traffic, a vote (for or against), the award of a free kick in association football or an indication that competitors (swimmers, jockeys, runners, cyclists, etc.) are under starter's orders. What, then, is to stop similar instances of behaviour having a different range of meanings in another community? Absolutely nothing. In order to establish whether or not this behaviour has a range of different meanings from, or similar meanings to, the 'same' behaviour in our own community, and what meaning some specific instance of this behaviour actually does have, we need to learn the language, values and discriminations of its authors.

There are two further points to note about the method problem before turning to the remaining problems. The first is that the responses to the 'What' and 'How' questions outlined above are little more than sketches. They do not purport to be exhaustive nor to address all the questions that arise for each response (such as, for example, how do we gain knowledge of general laws? What, exactly does the *Verstehen* approach entail over and beyond learning the language, values and discriminations of others? Is *Verstehen* truly incompatible with the D-N method?). These questions will be addressed as and when necessary in the substantive chapters of the book. Secondly, a potential confusion must be dispelled. It arises from the assumption that either a response to the 'What question' must determine a response to the 'How question' or vice versa. This assumption is mistaken. Hence it is possible to give a methodological individualist answer to the 'What question' and either the D-N or *Verstehen* answer to the 'How question'. We may think that methodological individualism, with its emphasis upon agents, has an obvious *compatibility* with the *Verstehen* approach to explanation and understanding. This would be correct. However, we would fall into error were we to turn this compatibility into a necessary relationship holding that, if one is a methodological individualist, then one can only take up *Verstehen*. For it is undoubtedly the case that methodological individualism is compatible with the D-N method. Nor is it the case that the methodological holist is necessarily committed to either *Verstehen* or the D-N method. Explaining and understanding social action in terms of societal facts may be thought incompatible with *Verstehen* but is not. It is simply not a contradiction to affirm both methodological holism and the claim that knowledge of societal facts is only available to us through the language, values and discriminations of individuals. Equally, it is no contradiction to affirm both methodological holism and the D-N method.

(b) The causality problem

The second snag on which orthodox and heretical accounts of adjudication must stake out a position is the causality problem. The problem consists of at least three issues. Two of these issues (one of which is terminological) will be particularly important in the remainder of the book while one will be touched on *en passant*. The most important substantive issue for present purposes is that of determining the relationship between giving a causal account of social action and giving a non-causal account, of determining when the former or the latter is the most 'fruitful' or 'appropriate' means of explaining or understanding social action, or whether there is indeed an important difference between them. This issue is approached in the philosophical literature as one concerning the compatibility or otherwise of reason-based and cause-based explanations of social action and has sometimes appeared, albeit rather obliquely, in jurisprudential discussions as a contrast between 'external' and 'internal' accounts of a practice.[59] Moreover, it could quite legitimately be regarded as simply another dimension of the method problem (although I treat it separately on 'presentational' grounds). That is because, in the history of the human sciences, causal explanations and understandings of social action have been regarded as the exclusive domain of the D-N method, whereas non-causal or reason-based explanations have been assumed to be the fulcrum of the *Verstehen* approach. In so far as those engaged in the human sciences have propounded strong versions of either approach, then this characterisation is correct. It does not, however, hold good for proponents of the moderate versions of each answer to the 'How question'.

This historical association raises the second issue constitutive of the causality problem. It is terminological. During the historical association between, on the one hand, the D-N method and causal explanations and understandings and, on the other, the *Verstehen* approach and reason-based or non-causal explanations and understandings, it has become common to use the word 'explanation' to refer to the former conjunction and 'understanding' to refer to the latter.[60] That being so, it may be thought unwise to

[59] Within philosophy the argument involves, *inter alios*, G. E. M. Anscombe, D. Davidson, A. I. Melden and C. Taylor. Papers by the first three charting their preliminary positions (though a good deal of ink has been spilled on this issue since) are available in A. White (ed.), *The Philosophy of Action* (Oxford, Clarendon 1968). For Taylor's preliminary position see *supra*, note 50. For internal (supposedly non-causal) and external (supposedly causal) accounts of legal practice see Dworkin, *LE*, pp. 11–15.

[60] Examples are von Wright, *supra*, note 56 and K-O Apel, *Understanding and Explanation* (Cambridge, Mass., The MIT Press 1984), Introduction and part I.

lump explanation and understanding together in the undiscriminating way characteristic of this introduction. However, this is not a conclusive reason for adopting the traditional usage. That usage assumes a rather greater divergence between explanation and understanding than there may be in fact. If the D-N method is appropriate anywhere, its proponents have argued, it is within the realm of natural science, a realm supposedly dominated by causal explanation and prediction. This, in conjunction with the claim that the human sciences have a problematic meaning dimension, is the basis for holding that the natural sciences are concerned with causal explanation whereas the human sciences are interested in rule-based, meaning-based understanding. But this divergence has been questioned by many who have offered accounts of the history of natural scientific practice. The claim these studies have generated is that the practice of natural science has an important meaning dimension, that it is, in ways not fully appreciated by proponents of the D-N method, interpretative.[61] If this is so, we ought to be circumspect about a rather casual association of natural science, the D-N method, causality and explanation, on the one hand, and the human sciences, *Verstehen*, meaning and understanding, on the other. This is part of the justification for what many would regard as a failure to distinguish between explanation and understanding. In this book, the distinction is not taken to be of great importance, although there are *some* reasons and *some* circumstances that demand it be drawn. Hopefully, this claim will be substantiated to the satisfaction of supporters of the distinction by the arguments in chapter 3.

The third issue that the causality problem raises is the most obvious and the most difficult. Obvious because it asks: in what does causality consist? Since the other two issues constitutive of the causality problem invoke this notion, it is not unreasonable to expect it to be analysed. The difficulty is that there at least three such analyses available. They are the logical entailment analysis, in which causality is held to consist in a relationship of entailment between preceding and subsequent events; the constant conjunction analysis, wherein the relationship between X (cause) and Y (effect) consists of nothing more than the fact that in our experience X has always or usually preceded, or occurred simultaneously with, Y; and the ordinary language analysis, the exemplar of which holds that 'there is not a single concept of causation but a group or family of concepts . . . united not by a set of common features but by points of resemblance, some of them tenuous'.[62] While it is obvious that any attempt to explain and understand social

[61] See Kuhn and Hesse, *supra*, note 55.

[62] H. L. A. Hart and T. Honore, *Causation in the Law* (Oxford, Clarendon 2nd ed. 1985), p. 28. This is the classic ordinary language account of causation. The constant conjunction account of causation we owe to D. Hume, *A Treatise of Human Nature* (Oxford, Clarendon 2nd ed. 1978), part III, sections I-V, XIV and XV; the logical entailment account predates but is well expressed by A. C. Ewing, *Idealism: A Critical Survey* (London, Methuen 3rd ed. 1961), pp.

action—of which, obviously, adjudication is but a subset—must take up a position on the issue of the appropriateness of causal accounts of that action, and is hence committed to some analysis of causality, it is equally obvious that no thorough evaluation of analyses of causality can be undertaken here. That is a book length project in itself and one which I am even less well equipped to tackle than the present project.

(c) The problem of values

The third problem is the value problem. It concerns not only the role and status of values within any *account of social action* which, of course, will include the action or practice of adjudication. It also concerns the way in which values are conceived by both participants *within the action or practice which is the object of our account* and those who construct such accounts. There is now almost consensus within the human sciences that values—which we can regard for present purposes as generating moral, political or aesthetic reasons for some action, refraining, institution or practice—have a role within accounts of social action in so far as they have a role within that action itself. So, for example, if it is accepted that some social actions, rules and institutions are purposive, that is, they are thought of as means to particular ends, and some of those ends are values, then our attempts to understand and explain these actions, rules and institutions must register this, at least at the outset. Thereafter, the role of values—particularly moral values—in accounts of social action depends upon the way they are conceived by actors and those seeking to understand and explain their action and its constitutive rules, roles and institutions. Roughly, there seem to be two possibilities here, both of which accept that values can be, in some sense and in some degree, the springs of action and thus important in explaining and understanding action.

The first possibility holds that values, once we have registered their role in social action, must be ignored. They are not really a suitable subject for the human sciences and can pose a serious threat to them. This is because on this view 'statements of value cannot be refuted: they can be condemned but not shown to be untrue'; 'the testability of propositions . . . depends upon their non-valuative or non-hortatory content which alone can be publicly verified . . . since the feelings of the speaker are not open to public inspection'.[63] Within moral philosophy, this conception of values is

151–187 (although by the time of the third edition Ewing had amended his account slightly so as to hold that causality consisted in entailment or something 'closely analogous to' it: *ibid*, p. 440).

[63] Statements such as these, drawn from S. Andreski's crude and polemical *Max Weber's Insights and Errors* (London, Routledge and Kegan Paul 1984) p. 21 and pp. 25–26, are by no means uncommon within the relatively recent history of the human sciences. For example,

described as emotivist or non-cognitivist and has been characterised quite accurately, if the previous statements are representative, and elegantly by Alaistair MacIntyre as

> the doctrine that all evaluative judgments and more specifically all moral judgments are *nothing but* expressions of preference, expressions of attitude or feeling . . . Particular judgments may of course unite moral and factual elements. 'Arson, being destructive of property, is wrong' unites the factual judgment that arson destroys property with the moral judgment that arson is wrong. But the moral element in such a judgment is always to be sharply distinguished from the factual. Factual judgments are true or false; and in the realm of fact there are rational criteria by means of which we may secure agreement as to what is true and what is false. But moral judgments, being expressions of attitude or feeling, are neither true nor false; and agreement in moral judgment is not to be secured by any rational method, for there are none. It is to be secured, if at all, by producing non-rational effects on the emotions and attitudes of those who disagree with one.[64]

Thus values lack the properties needed to be the subject matter of a science and, while they must be taken account of, they need to be treated with care. Of course, we can attempt to find out whether specific actions were premised upon one or other value by means of questionnaires and surveys, but there is no way of verifying the results because all we have to go on in the attempt to explain and understand social action is outward, publicly available behaviour. More often than not, that is a highly ambiguous manifestation of an agent's value commitments. Since there is no way of checking the latter we must regard our survey results as incorrigible brute data or facts. Converting values into facts is thus one way of ensuring that they do not seriously undermine attempts at explanation and understanding.[65] Furthermore, values can be a suitable subject of the human sciences if our aim is to offer a causal account of their genesis which would probably be constructed in accordance with the D-N method. It is also accepted on this view that values can influence the work of the social scientist, conferring significance on certain events and thus making them 'worthy' objects of explanation and understanding.[66] Again, this is not thought to imperil the human sciences.

throughout the 1950s and 1960s this was the dominant position within Anglo-American political science: see D. Easton, *The Political System: An Inquiry into the State of Political Science* (New York, A. Knopf 1953), p. 221.

[64] A. MacIntyre, *After Virtue* (London, Duckworths 1981; 2nd ed. 1985), p. 12.

[65] A good account of this process as it occurs in political science is provided in C. Taylor, 'Interpretation and Sciences of Man' in R. Beehler and A. R. Drengson, *supra*, note 49, ch. 6 at pp. 169–179; for an account of the equivalent process in moral philosophy see C. Taylor, *Sources of the Self* (Cambridge, C. U. P. 1989), ch. 3.

[66] This is part of what M. Weber means by value relevance in the human sciences. Only 'part' because this formulation does not take account of Weber's views about the constitution of the subject matter of the human sciences, that is, what is and can become a cultural phenomenon worthy of attention (such phenomena are in no sense simply the 'brute facts' of social life).

The second possibility here is to conceive of moral values in either a rationalist or realist way (the two are not coextensive, but I treat them together because they share an opposition to emotivism). By moral rationalism a claim like the following is intended: some moral beliefs or principles can be rationally established in a compelling way such that, given certain truths or presuppositions about ourselves and our position in the world, they are binding upon us.[67] By moral realism I have in mind something like the claim that '[t]here are facts which make some moral judgments . . . true and others false, facts which are independent of anyone's beliefs about the matters in question'[68] (though this rather loose 'fact-talk' must be treated extremely cautiously). On either of these views, values—particularly moral values—are not as problematic for the human sciences as they are when conceived in emotivist terms. So, for example, on either rationalist or realist view the refutation of statements of value is in principle possible notwithstanding their hortatory content (although that, for realists and rationalists, is not their only content). Both rationalists and realists hold that value-statements can be publicly verified by reference to either the canons of standard logic (for the rationalist) or areas of allegedly non-problematic knowledge such as our knowledge of secondary properties (for the realist).[69] Therefore, neither view provides reasons to think values lack the properties necessary to be an object suitable for the human sciences.

It needs to be noted that the two incompatible ways of conceiving values—emotivism, on the one hand, and moral rationalism/realism, on the other—do not have a simple relationship to either the responses to the 'What' and 'How' questions or the responses to the causality problem. It is not the case that a response one way or the other to the 'What question' dictates the way in which one must conceive values. Equally, neither the D-N method nor the *Verstehen* approach compels one or other approach to values, though it is probably correct to say that historically proponents of the former have tended towards emotivism. We cannot, however, assume from this that proponents of *Verstehen* incline towards a moral realist or

Weber's thoughts on these matters are found in his methodological essays, particularly '"Objectivity" in Social Science and Social Policy' in his *The Methodology of the Social Sciences*, translated and edited by E. A. Shils and H. A. Finch (New York, The Free Press 1949), at pp. 76–84. A useful guide to Weber's dense and often disparate arguments in the methodological essays is provided by Oakes, *supra*, note 58, ch. 1.

67 An example is A. Gewirth, *Reason and Morality* (Chicago, University of Chicago Press 1978).

68 J. Waldron, 'The Irrelevance of Moral Objectivity' in R. George (ed.), *Natural Law Theory* (Oxford, Clarendon 1992), p. 158.

69 See Gewirth, *supra*, note 67, ch. 1 (the rationalist position) and J. McDowell, 'Values and Secondary Qualities', ch. 8 of G. Sayre-McCord (ed.), *Essays on Moral Realism* (Ithaca, Cornell U. P. 1988) (realist). Waldron, 'The Irrelevance of Moral Objectivity', *supra*, note 68, at pp. 172–175, expresses doubts about the realists' ability to come up with means of publicly verifying value statements.

moral rationalist position—certainly, Max Weber did not.[70] Thus the relationships here are just ones of tendency, nothing more. There is no logical or conceptual block to combining particular responses to the 'What' and 'How' questions with particular conceptions of the nature of values.

(d) Solutions

Why is what follows worthy of attention? Ought one to put both money and time at risk in considering the arguments developed here? There are three reasons why what is said here may be worthy of attention, all of which highlight the alleged distinctiveness of the solutions developed to cope with the three problems. The first reason is this: in highlighting the three problems and attempting to respond to them, the arguments of the book expose the limits of both orthodox and heretical accounts of adjudication and attempt to transcend those limits. Doing that entails a longer journey into the philosophy and methodology of the human sciences than either the orthodox or heretics have been willing to pursue. However, the journey is inescapable if we are to be able to establish the existence of criteria for the success and failure of accounts of adjudication.

The second reason why what follows may be worthy of attention consists of the direction that journey takes. The starting point is the following assumption. The task faced by those who offer accounts of adjudication is, despite the obvious superficial differences, the same as the task of those who attempt to explain and understand any aspect of social action, be it the practices of gift-giving, voting or religious observance in particular communities. Saying this does not, of course, commit one to denying that episodes of social action take place within a variety of institutional contexts and their constitutive rule structures. Rather, it commits one to holding that once the different institutional contexts and the constitutive rules in which social action takes place are identified, the same issues about the nature of understanding and explanation arise. So, despite the fact that the institutions and rules differ, the task of explaining and understanding what judges are doing when deciding cases is the same as the task of understanding and explaining, for example, what priests are doing in taking confession. Furthermore, the first step towards discharging the task of explaining and understanding any aspect of social action is surely to determine what a good explanation or understanding would look like. It needs be determined what, if any, criteria of success and failure are applicable to such explanations and understandings.

This starting point has an important consequence. In so far as the problem of method, that is, the general problem of explaining and under-

70 Weber, *supra*, note 66, pp. 83–84.

standing social action, ensnares accounts of adjudication, then disciplines other than legal theory and legal philosophy should preoccupy us. This is so for at least two reasons. First, legal theorists have rarely been attentive to the discussions of method in the human sciences, despite their apparent relevance.[71] Those involved in legal study of a non-philosophical kind—involving the chronicling of certain aspects of the law with an eye (sometimes wide open, sometimes almost completely shut) on both the underlying purpose, goal or value of that branch of law and the generic rule of law values that underlie it—have, perhaps with better reason, thought the methodological problems of the human sciences irrelevant. Secondly, if it is right to characterise the task of giving an account of adjudication as the task of attempting to understand and explain a segment of social action, then an interdisciplinary approach is unavoidable because social action is not a discipline-specific category. That is, the disciplines of legal theory and legal study can help us learn the language and rules, and understand the institutions, in which a specific segment of social action takes place, but those disciplines do not necessarily tell us anything about the best way in which to go about understanding and explaining that segment of social action. Thus, even though the accounts of methodology that influence the arguments which follow were not developed by legal theorists, nor were they developed with a view to understanding social action in legal contexts, I still hold that they are directly and obviously applicable here.

Thankfully, it is not necessary to begin considering anew the full range of disputes about method in the whole of the human sciences in order to determine what a good explanation and understanding of the social practice of adjudication would look like. This is so because those few contemporary legal theorists who have diverted their minds to this matter have moved or gestured in the right direction (or so I shall intermittently argue in the remainder of the book). They have taken up, albeit rather hesitantly and without full appreciation of the consequences of so doing, the method of *Verstehen* to understand and explain social action. Orthodox theorists have been the first to employ this method within jurisprudence and their treatments are examined in chapter 2. As will be seen from the arguments of that chapter, the orthodox are often blind to the implications of this method. Nevertheless, they are in a better position than those legal theorists, both heretical and orthodox, who have either ignored discussions of method altogether or have rejected this particular account of method.

[71] A flavour of the generally superficial orthodox and heretical discussions is provided by MacCormick's remarks, *en passant*, in *H. L. A. Hart* (London, Edward Arnold 1981) pp. 29–30 and Kennedy's equally brief comments in *BC*, pp. 211–223. Unger is an exception among heretics: see *KP*, pp. 1–28 and *Law in Modern Society* (New York, The Free Press 1976), chs. 1 and 4. An interesting non-orthodox, non-heretical exception is J. Finnis, *Natural Law and Natural Rights* (Oxford, Clarendon 1980), ch. 1.

Chapter 5 examines some heretical strategies designed to weaken the power of the *Verstehen* method and concludes that some of them are powerful and fruitful. Yet they do not, contrary to the heretical view, discredit that method altogether but are better regarded as a supplement to it. Some of these strategies, in particular the ideology critique, serve as a warning against exaggerating the power of the *Verstehen* method. That, though, is not to say that the ideology critique is incompatible with *Verstehen*. Thus the approach taken in this book to the problem of method is distinctive because it expands an approach that some accounts seek to embrace; it illustrates that these accounts are often blind to the problems that approach creates for them; and defends the approach from some exaggerated criticisms. The overarching argument is that the *Verstehen* approach *must* be taken up by heretics and orthodox alike, at least as a starting point.

There is more to the argument than this. For the method outlined and defended here not only seeks to make good the shortcomings of some of the arguments employed by heretics and orthodox, it goes beyond them. True, it is argued that the orthodox are right to begin with *Verstehen* but it is also argued that it is a mistake to rest there. Among the problems that exist with the orthodox method, the greatest is the failure to appreciate the limits of *Verstehen* or to exaggerate its power. In this regard, it is mistake to think, as chapter 3 shows, either that *Verstehen* rules out a cause-based account of social action or that it entails strong methodological individualism. Rather, it is quite compatible with a cause-based account and moderate methodological individualism—that is one reason why the method outlined and defended in chapters 3 and 6 is labelled 'compatibilism'. As against some heretics, chapters 3 and 6 show that the meaning dimension of action cannot be ignored. Attempts to ignore it, like those allegedly characteristic of structuralist thought of the type discussed early in chapter 6, are mistaken. While compatibilism entails a concern with both reason-based and cause-based explanations and understandings (it is, however, loath to draw a bright-line distinction here), it does not countenance a kind of methodological eclecticism embraced by some heretics. That, too, is discussed in chapter 6.

Since the book commends methodological arguments formulated in subdisciplines of the human sciences other than law, and seeks to apply those arguments to the enterprise of explaining and understanding adjudication, it can be called an interdisciplinary study. That can be both a benefit and a serious disadvantage. The benefit is the obvious one that arguments developed in other disciplines might solve the snags that beset our own discipline, thus helping to forward the discussion or to clarify the nature of the issues involved. The disadvantage is that the book may lapse into a type of infatuation that besets other efforts at interdisciplinary legal scholarship. This takes the form of an unquestioning acceptance of the assumptions, methods and 'truths' of the discipline which is used as a vehicle to understand law or some aspect of it. Since the claims of any discipline should never be taken for granted in this way, this infatuation is a dangerous one. It is also self-defeating since interdisciplinary legal scholarship which is so afflicted serves merely to reproduce the difficulties of its 'adopted' discipline. There are many examples of this phenomenon, more or less extreme.

A less extreme example is provided by Herbert Hart's reliance upon the ordinary language or 'analytical' philosophy of his day which, while it aimed to sharpen our understanding of phenomena by sharpening our understanding of words,[72] could not help us understand phenomena susceptible to different normative explanations.[73] Why would we accept such a philosophy, which can tell us so little about 'many of the central problems of legal philosophy',[74] were it not for the fact of some degree of infatuation? It is surely the case that many of the central concepts of legal philosophy—law, authority, legitimacy and rights—are indeed susceptible to different normative explanations. While the analytical tasks of sorting and tidying, of differentiating and contrasting, characteristic of ordinary language philosophy are crucial steps prior to normative argument, they surely do not exhaust the field of legal philosophy. However, it cannot be said that Hart propounded ordinary language philosophy in such a way as to exclude many areas of discussion traditionally open to legal philosophy. His infatuation was more muted than that. Nevertheless, his first public statement showing a self-conscious awareness of the limitations of the ordinary language approach came rather late in his academic life, after legal philosophy—in the UK, at least—had reinvented itself in ordinary language form. That style of philosophy now appears more of a stultifying straitjacket than a set of great liberating ideas.[75]

Disciplinary infatuation of an extreme form occurs in the Economic Analysis of Law (EAL) literature. Here we find EAL scholars applying neo-classical economics and its assumptions—moral, metaphysical and methodological—to particular areas of law and to the enterprise of understanding and explaining it in general terms.[76] What is surprising is that this

[72] H. Hart, *supra*, note 1, p.v.

[73] H. Hart, *Essays in Jurisprudence and Philosophy* (Oxford, Clarendon 1983), p. 6.

[74] H. Hart, *ibid*.

[75] The language belongs to I. Berlin, 'Does Political Theory Still Exist?' in P. Laslett and W. G. Runciman (eds.), *Philosophy, Politics and Society* (Second Series) (Oxford, Basil Blackwell 1962), p. 19.

[76] R. Posner aims to do for almost all aspects of the law what he claims he does for the common law: '[t]he common law is to most lawyers a collection of disparate fields, each with its own history, vocabulary, and bewildering profusion of rules and doctrines . . . Yet we have seen that the law of property, of contracts and commercial law, of restitution and unjust enrichment . . . can all be cast in an economic form that explains the principal doctrines . . .': *Economic Analysis of Law* (Boston, Little Brown 4th. ed 1992), p. 251. Parts III–VII of the book show the range of EAL in Posner's hands.

is done without any apparent awareness of the fact that these assumptions stand in need of defence and clarification. So, for example, the notion of efficiency employed in EAL is richly ambiguous, sliding between Pareto-optimal, Pareto-superior, Kaldor-Hicks and wealth-maximisation definitions, not all of which, when applied to similar cases, will generate the same results.[77] Moreover, it seems impossible for EAL to avoid the larger epistemological and methodological problems of neo-classical economics of which it is but a part.[78] Avoiding these larger questions while continuing to apply the methods of economic analysis to the law to yield putative 'insights' is a severe case of disciplinary infatuation.

The third reason why the arguments that follow may be worthy of attention is that they take a distinctive (some might say implausible) approach to what we have previously called the problems of causality and value. My hope is that the treatment of the causality problem is distinctive in the following ways. First, unlike many heretical and orthodox discussions, what follows is a sustained treatment of the problem rather than the more usual practice of tipping one's cap in its direction. Secondly, that treatment recognises but marginalises the differences between reason- (or purpose, or meaning, or value) based explanations and understandings of social action and causal explanations and understandings. In so doing, it must negotiate some snags in both the philosophy of the human sciences and the philosophy of action. These are old problems, but that does not mean that they need not be addressed. Longevity is no good reason for disdain. Thirdly, the solution to these problems—and hence the solution to the causality problem in general—is such as to yield protocols for the appropriate and inappropriateness of causal and non-causal explanations and understandings of social action. That is, I hope to offer reasons to show when each form of explanation and understanding should make its entrance upon and exit from the stage of the human sciences. The fact that many practitioners of those sciences have written scripts with roles for only one or the other approach ought not to be taken as conclusive proof that the two cannot be appropriately placed, albeit at different places, in the same drama. The reasons for believing in the possibility of peaceful coexistence between the two approaches are articulated in chapters 3 and 6 and parallel a number of other arguments offered by philosophers to the same end. For example, the interrelationship between cause-based and reason-based explanations of human action has been put in a

[77] For informed criticism on this point see J. Coleman, 'Efficiency, Exchange, and Auction: Philosophic Aspects of the Economic Approach to Law' (1980) 68 *California Law Review* 221–249 and his 'Efficiency, Utility, and Wealth Maximization' (1980) 8 *Hofstra Law Review* 509–551. Both are also available in J. Coleman, *Markets, Morals and the Law* (Cambridge, C. U. P. 1988), the former with a slight change of title.

[78] A useful account of these, though often tough on the non-specialist, exists in M. Hollis and E. Nell, *Rational Economic Man* (Cambridge, C. U. P. 1975).

marvellous, characteristically trenchant way (although perhaps too trenchant for our purposes) by Martin Hollis: it is 'that rational action is its own explanation and that departures from it have a causal explanation'.[79] While our argument does not take this exact form, it is hopefully not inconsistent with it.

The response offered in the book to the value problem holds that values (note that I concentrate almost entirely upon moral values) are inescapable features of social action and, further, inescapable when constructing understandings and explanations of social action. That is not news. However, it is argued in chapters 4 and 7 that some heretical and orthodox arguments about either the nature of values *tout court* or the nature of value conflict, are dubious and self-defeating. That is not to say that these arguments are in any way uncommon, either within the academy or the world at large. Far from it. The argument about the nature of (moral) value conflict discussed in chapter 4 invokes the very fashionable but not well understood notion of incommensurability, while some of the arguments analysed in chapter 7 embody an account of the nature of moral values which I have labelled emotivist or non-cognitivist. Such an account has dominated much social, political, legal and moral thought for a long time. It will become necessary during our discussion in chapters 4 and 7 to refine what incommensurability looks like, to elucidate what emotivism and non-cognitivism entail, and to refine the nature of the alternatives to them. Two alternatives, both of which initially appear in chapters 2 and 4, will be elucidated—moral realism and moral rationalism. Two arguments in their favour are considered. The first, developed in chapter 2, holds that either moral realism or moral rationalism is necessary if some of the difficulties generated by the problem of method are to be solved. Standing alone, that argument may appear weak. It can gain some strength from the second argument, offered in chapter 7, which holds that moral realism and rationalism are better able to support heretics' visionary accounts of the role of values in adjudication than any other meta-ethical theory. If either moral realism or rationalism is true, and it is true that moral values impinge upon the process of judicial decision-making, then it *might* also be true that an explanation and understanding of the practice of adjudication premised upon the former is significantly different from one based upon non-cognitivism/emotivism. Whether or not that is the case is another of the issues addressed in chapters 4 and 7. Of course, these arguments supporting moral realism/rationalism arise within the concerns of legal philosophy and they cannot stand in lieu of properly abstract, context-independent 'proofs' of the truth or falsity of these doctrines.

[79] M. Hollis, *Models of Man* (Cambridge, C. U. P. 1977), p. 130.

(e) Three general points

Before turning to terminological matters, three points must be made. The first is that the heretical and orthodox responses to the three problems, particularly those of method and causality, constitute an important tranche of criteria for assessing the success and failure of accounts of adjudication. This is because responses to the 'What' and 'How' questions tell us what the accounts purport to be and how they purport to achieve their aims. If we do not have this information—and it is rarely explicitly provided—it is difficult (if not impossible) to assess whether accounts of adjudication succeed or fail. How can one hope to evaluate something if one has no idea what it purports to be?

The second point is noteworthy because it highlights yet another limitation upon the range of the arguments of the book. The point, which for pragmatic reasons will not be further considered, is that within the history of the human sciences each response to the three problems only makes sense in light of a wider account of what can and cannot be knowledge and of what can and cannot constitute the world. However, to say this is not to say that there are only necessary connections here. There may be some such connections between specific epistemologies and ontologies, on the one hand, and particular responses to the problems of method, causality and values, on the other, but it is doubtful that they are the only kind of connections. Rather, many of the links are altogether looser. Hence, it is not solely the fact that there exist *some* logical connections between what can be called an empiricist epistemology, on the one hand, and an emphasis upon facts and laws, deduction and prediction, as well as a suspicion of values, on the other hand, that leads them to be run together.[80] All we can say of some aspects of such an epistemology and such an approach to social action is that they are not incompatible: they 'fit' together but one is not entailed by the other. So, the fact that some empiricist epistemologies hold that knowledge is constituted by a sphere of facts directly apprehended by the senses and a sphere of logical 'truths' or 'conventions' true by definition, makes sense of the view that in the human sciences the value dimension of social action is problematic. For, if values cannot be converted into, or regarded as if, facts or logical truths, then they seem not to qualify as being the objects of knowledge.

[80] A classic statement of the empiricist theory of knowledge is found in Hume, *supra*, note 62, Book I, parts I, II and III and the first enquiry of his *Enquiries Concerning Human Understanding and Concerning the Principles of Morals* (Oxford, Clarendon 3rd ed. 1975). An account of the methodology of the human sciences entirely compatible with Hume's epistemology is found in Book V of J. S. Mill, *A System of Logic* (Toronto, University of Toronto Press 1973). The work of Hempel and Nagel, *supra*, note 54, can be placed in the same tradition.

Alternatively, a rationalist epistemology seems to imply that direct apprehension by the senses of any categorisable, 'meaningful' information is impossible. On views such as these the world must first be categorised *a priori* before it can be understood, before it can be divided into realms of fact and value, meaning and meaninglessness, the empirical and non-empirical.[81] The realm of knowledge is a more expansive one here, constituted by a number of types with different methods of access and evaluation. Propositions regarded as suspicious or even excluded from the category of knowledge on the first view need not be so regarded on this view. Hence, both the meaning and value dimensions of social action, and approaches to social action that aim to explain and understand them (like the varieties of *Verstehen*) would be viewed more charitably on an epistemology such as this. However, it would again be folly to see nothing but relationships of entailment here; more likely, there is simply no incompatibility between aspects of such an epistemology and such an approach to understanding and explaining social action.

The relationship between the various approaches to explaining and understanding social action and accounts of the constituents of the world must be understood in the same way, with the following proviso. It is that epistemological and ontological claims are frequently run together. Take, for example, John Mackie's argument that 'if there were objective values, then they would be entities or qualities or relations of a very strange sort, *utterly different from anything else in the universe*. Correspondingly, if we were aware of them, it would have to be by some special faculty of moral perception or intuition, *utterly different from our ordinary ways of knowing everything else*'.[82] The epistemological and the ontological (Mackie calls the latter 'metaphysical') components of this argument are not freestanding: there is, as is usual, a strong relationship of dependence between the two. Assessing one component thus involves assessing the other. This adds an additional layer of complexity to the task of untangling the various epistemological and ontological commitments of the various approaches to understanding and explaining social action

The arguments considered and developed in the book—the various more or less implicit responses heretics and orthodox offer to the three problems and the criticisms directed at those responses—are undeniably implicated

[81] Within the realm of epistemology this position is associated with I. Kant: see *The Critique of Pure Reason* (trans. N. Kemp-Smith, London, Macmillan 1929), Introduction and pp. 92–175. This position does not translate in any straightforward way into accounts of the methodology of the human sciences. For discussion of important areas of overlap see W. Outhwaite, *Concept Formation in Social Science* (London, Routledge and Kegan Paul 1983), ch. 3. Giddens, *supra*, note 58, pp. 80–89 outlines accounts of methodology incompatible with empiricism that are not obviously indebted to Kant.

[82] J. L. Mackie, *Ethics: Inventing Right and Wrong* (Harmondsworth, Penguin 1977), p. 38 (emphasis supplied).

within a web of ontological and epistemological claims. Hence to offer an account of adjudication is not only to assume or explicitly take up some range of responses to the three problems but, in so doing, to incur various epistemological and ontological commitments. These commitments are, of course, eminently contestable and in need of justification. However, it is only the first step of this process with which we are concerned, for the following reason. The arguments involved in that step will no doubt be considered by lawyers, academic and otherwise, to be more than sufficiently 'abstract' and 'theoretical'. It would therefore be unwise to push both one's luck and the patience of part of one's audience too far by trying to swim, and perhaps beginning to sink, in the philosophically deep waters of epistemology and ontology (or metaphysics). Moreover, so much of our time will be devoted to showing that heretics and orthodox must and do take up positions in relation to the already 'abstract' and 'theoretical' three problems, that little time will be available to engage in epistemological and ontological chitchat.

The final point of this section is a note about the structure of the book. It has, remember, two aims. First, to determine what, if any, are the true differences between orthodox and heretical accounts of adjudication and, secondly, to explore this theme in relation to the problems of method, causality and values. The overarching argumentative refrains are that the differences between orthodoxy and heresy have been greatly exaggerated and that both orthodox and heretics offer fairly implausible responses to the three problems. Some considerable effort is devoted to showing what better responses to these problems would look like and entail. Part I of the book highlights the similarities between the various orthodox responses to the three problems. The orthodox are in rough agreement on the method used to yield plausible accounts of social action in general and of adjudication in particular. They are in broad agreement about the role and power of reason and value in both the process of adjudication and in the construction of accounts aimed at explaining and understanding that process. Having established this, it is argued that the positions adopted by these authors are severely problematic. Part I constructs an alternative approach to the explanation and understanding of social action which includes an improved account of the nature of *Verstehen* (chapter 2) as well as an argument as to when causal explanations and understandings are and are not appropriate (chapter 3). In addition, chapter 4 contains a critical analysis of the role of values in orthodox accounts of adjudication. Were these alternative arguments about method, causality and values incorporated in orthodox accounts of adjudication, then many snags would be avoided. This capacity to resolve the shortcomings of orthodox accounts I take to be a precondition for any other account to be regarded as better than they; if such an account can also maintain the undoubted insights of orthodox accounts, then it might legitimately be judged an improvement upon them.

Avoiding the problems that beset orthodox accounts of adjudication in the ways suggested in part I may, however, come with a very high price attached. The tariff could be, as many contemporary philosophers have thought, the invocation of some dubiously 'rationalist' or 'metaphysical' or 'foundationalist' approach to understanding social action and institutions. We are often told that such an approach is part of the now failed 'enlightenment project' and who, we are asked, wants to be part of such an obvious failure?[83] Part II of the book examines some of the arguments that underlie this line of thought and the way they have been incorporated into heretical accounts of adjudication. The background philosophical presuppositions and beliefs—in so far as they are univocal—that inform heretical accounts of adjudication often *appear* to contradict the background presuppositions upon which orthodox accounts depend. It is therefore reasonable to expect that the accounts of adjudication informed by incompatible background beliefs will contradict one another. Yet the matter is not that simple. For, while the book argues that the responses of both orthodox and heretics to the three problems are inadequate, the argument is not that the inadequacy lies in the privileging of one side or the other of a list of opposites. So, for example, the argument is not that some heretics are right to privilege causal accounts of social action over non-causal accounts and the orthodox wrong to privilege the latter. Rather, the argument is that in most instances the inadequacies of both accounts are different although they can be remedied in the same way. Whereas part I constructs an approach to the explanation and understanding of social action avoiding the weaknesses of orthodox accounts of adjudication, part II defends that approach against some arguments underlying heretical accounts, and extends and improves it in light of other heretical arguments. Part II suggest that many heretical accounts are committed to methodological tenets (chapters 5 and 6) and normative claims (chapter 7) which their polemical arguments rule out. Recommending the approach initially outlined in part I as but a component of the heresy might be too much for some heretics but it is, as I hope parts I and II show, a move they must make.

[83] Four philosophers notable for their influence upon this debate are A. MacIntyre, *supra*, note 64; *Whose Justice? Which Rationality?* (London, Duckworths 1988); *Three Rival Traditions of Moral Inquiry* (London, Duckworths 1990); R. Rorty, *Philosophy and the Mirror of Nature* (Oxford, Basil Blackwell 1980); *The Consequences of Pragmatism* (Minneapolis, University of Minnesota Press 1982); *Contingency, Irony and Solidarity* (Cambridge, C. U. P. 1989); J. Derrida, *Of Grammatology* (Baltimore, Johns Hopkins U. P. 1974); *Writing and Difference* (London, Routledge and Kegan Paul 1978); *The Margins of Philosophy* (Brighton, Harvester Press 1982); and M. Foucault, *The Order of Things: An Archaeology of the Human Sciences* (London, Routledge and Kegan Paul 1974); *The Archaeology of Knowledge* (London, Tavistock 1972).

While emphasising a few real differences between orthodox and heretical accounts, the book also argues that some supposed differences are merely apparent. This is the result of some rather slipshod scholarship that culminates in both sides to the debate operating with drastically caricatured versions of the others' arguments. Hence, it is not surprising to find proponents of orthodox accounts being portrayed as believers in a rigid 'rule formalism', holding that not only easy-case adjudication but also hard-case decision-making is a purely deductive or mechanical process.[84] It is equally unsurprising to find heretics dubbed as dangerous nihilists deserving no place in the Law School.[85] This kind of hyperbole makes it difficult to see the wood from the trees in this dispute and has led to a near complete failure to join issue on what exactly divides the putative disputants. I suggest that they are divided on fewer issues than either they or some observers are initially inclined to think. The risk in this argumentative strategy is akin to that of clambering into the no-man's-land between warring factions, counselling peace and goodwill: one may well be cut down by fire from both sides.

Nevertheless, it is argued that, despite appearances, some heretical and some orthodox responses to the problem of the role and status of values in social action and practices and in *accounts* of such action and practices are not incompatible. Nor is there a clear divergence between orthodox and heretical responses to the causality problem, although there is sometimes a difference of emphasis. In terms of the debate about adjudication, this difference is manifest in the supposed conflict between accounts constructed so as to capture 'the logic of decision' and those designed to elucidate 'the process of decision'.[86] Emphasis on the latter entails determining which causal factors influence adjudicators' choices, a process leading to the development of historical, sociological and psychological explanations of legal reasoning. An examination of the logic of justification is assumed to be a far more restricted, non-causal enterprise, concerned solely with the elucidation of the patterns and types of reason and argument used by adjudicators to justify decisions. It is often assumed that orthodox accounts concentrate upon the logic of decision while completely ignoring—on very weak grounds—the process of decision, whereas heretics are said to make

[84] For useful discussions of this old saw, which has many echoes throughout the history of Anglo-American legal thought, see J. Dewey, 'Logical Method and the Law' (1924) 10 *Cornell L. Q.* 17–27; D. Kennedy, 'Legal Formality' (1973) 2 *Journal of Legal Studies* 351–398; T. Grey, 'Langdell's Orthodoxy' (1983) 45 *University of Pittsburgh L. R.* 1–53; F. Schauer, 'Formalism' (1988) 97 *Yale L. J.* 509–548.

[85] See Dean Paul Carrington's thoughts on the American CLS movement in 'Of Law and the River' (1984) 34 *Journal of Legal Education* 222–228.

[86] The distinction is drawn by *inter alios* W. Twining, *Karl Llewellyn and the Realist Movement* (London, Weidenfeld and Nicolson 1985), pp. 229–231 and Z. Bankowski et al., 'On Method and Methodology', ch. 2 of D. N. MacCormick and R. S. Summers, *supra*, note 7, pp. 16–18.

the opposite mistake.[87] A better response to the problems of causality and method—an approach called compatibilism—is suggested by arguments in both parts of the book. Compatibilism accommodates both the logic and process of decision. Furthermore, it is a method that both orthodox and heretics avouch, usually implicitly yet sometimes explicitly. Chapters 3 and 6 aim to show this, in addition to highlighting compatibilism's many virtues.

III TERMINOLOGY AND STYLE

Many think that matters of intellectual or philosophical or writing style should not be raised in polite company. The usual reason for this attitude is entirely laudable, for this is a matter of tolerance: each to his or her own. I have no quarrel with this, but one feature of what follows should be highlighted. It might be thought that an inordinate amount of time is spent upon matters of 'target identification', involving extensive quotation from the sources under discussion and much effort at clarification of ambiguities, exaggerations and mistakes. Surely, readers of the book might complain, we all know what heretical and orthodox scholars say and hence we can be spared the boring work of explicating what they say. I am generally sympathetic to this kind of view: the more that is taken for granted, the less needs to be said, and hence the likelihood of what is said being clear, succinct and, hopefully, illuminating, is increased. But within the present context—the debate between orthodoxy and heresy—this approach has caused problems and mystification rather than illumination. Many of the parties to the dispute seem loath to accord their opponents the respect of reading their work closely and carefully and have instead been content to peddle in misrepresentation, stereotype and hyperbole. Perhaps this is inevitable when a set of arguments is portrayed as a crusade, perhaps not. Whatever the reasons for it, this tendency is resisted here. I attempt to get clear what the participants to the debate say by, wherever possible, using their own words and extrapolating from them. This is a rather time consuming and sometimes dull job, but in this context there is no alternative. As a general approach it is commendable—it cannot, after all, be wrong to get clear the exact nature of the views one is discussing. R. G. Collingwood

[87] For orthodox examples see: Dworkin, *LE*, pp. 11–15; MacCormick and Summers, *supra*, note 7, pp. 16–24. In *The Transformation of American Law 1780–1860* (Cambridge, Mass., Harvard U. P. 1977), M. Horwitz gives an account of American law that often appears to emphasise the process of decision to the exclusion of its logic. However, Horwitz gives little attention to the nature of such 'explanations', their conditions of success and failure etc., in that volume. We had to wait until *The Transformation of American Law 1870–1960* (New York, Oxford U. P. 1992), pp. vii-ix, for that and the discussion is, at best, cursory.

set down the approach which I aspire to follow with his usual erudition. Speaking of his teaching, Collingwood said

> I . . . taught my pupils, more by example than precept, that they must never accept any criticism of anybody's philosophy which they might hear or read without first satisfying themselves that this was a philosophy he actually expounded; that they must always defer any criticism of their own until they were absolutely sure they understood the text they were criticising; and that if the postponement was sine die it did not greatly matter.[88]

This is a difficult standard to achieve and I am sure that what follows often falls short. Nevertheless, the aspiration to this standard explains the style of the discussion. The starting point is that the views of both orthodox and heretics must, initially at least, be taken seriously. So doing requires scrupulous attention to what they say; I therefore resist the trite and not uncommon view among (orthodox) legal *philosophers* that much of what heretics say is just not worth reading, as if we can know *a priori* whether or not this is true.[89]

Next, terminology. So far I have spoken what for some will be a mysterious language. I have referred without discrimination to 'explaining' and 'understanding' accounts of adjudication. Yet those worried that no unambiguous distinction between explanation and understanding has been drawn should not despair, since a calming notice was issued on this point in section II (b) above. It is extended in chapter 3. Despite the lax attitude taken herein to that distinction, it is, however, occasionally appropriate in order to highlight a wrong-headed debate in the philosophy of social science about two supposedly different and incompatible approaches to making sense of the social world. In one sense this distinction maps onto the division between orthodoxy and heresy yet, in another, it is manifest within both orthodoxy and heresy. For the time being, though, it is not worth worrying about. In addition to clouding this distinction, it might be said that I neglect the obvious in favour of the oblique by the conceit that has me refer to 'accounts' of adjudication when it is clear that such accounts are either 'theories' or 'descriptions' or 'models'. The reason for the conceit is simple. It is far from clear, in the discussions of legal theorists at least, what 'theories' are supposed to be and do, what their criteria of success and failure are, and how they differ, if at all, from descriptions and models. Legal theorists rarely address the questions: 'what is it to construct a theory?', 'what is it to offer a description?', 'what is it to develop a model?'. That being the case, it would be unwise to rely, prior to critical reflection, upon common-sense hunches about what 'accounts' of adjudication are

[88] *An Autobiography* (Oxford, The University Press 1939), p. 27.

[89] This, of course, is rarely said in print. B. Leiter, 'Is There An "American" Jurisprudence?' (1997) 17 *Oxford Journal of Legal Studies* 367–387, pp. 385–386, comes close.

'obviously' or 'naturally' supposed to be. That must suffice, for the present, as a justification for this ostensibly curious usage; the issue of what theories, descriptions and models are supposed to be and how they differ arises in the arguments of chapter 2.

Speaking of accounts of *adjudication* may be thought odd, given the issues tackled in the book, because the more accurate label is surely *legal reasoning*. The reason for what may be thought of as an eccentric and unusual label has already been touched upon. Orthodox and heretical accounts of 'legal' reasoning are accounts of decision-making in the appellate courts. Clearly, these bodies have a supervisory function overseeing the decision-making of all other legal decision-making bodies. Yet the cases that arrive in the appellate courts, and the patterns of reasoning prevalent therein, need not be representative of the cases and methods of reasoning adopted in the plethora of legal decision-making bodies discharging quasi-administrative, quasi-judicial functions in the contemporary extended state. Therefore, there is no warrant for referring to what goes on in this segment of the system as *legal* reasoning, with the implication that this is the exemplar that all other decision-making bodies mimic. Furthermore, the label 'legal' reasoning carries with it the suggestion that the ways in which judges decide this numerically insignificant body of cases somehow embodies the essence of 'the legal'. It may well be true that in some sense the essence of the nature of law is indeed found in the processes by which judges decide appellate court cases. This should not be simply assumed; it requires argument. Hence, the preference for 'adjudication'.

However, had I the courage of my convictions, the book should properly be entitled 'understanding and explaining *judicial reasoning*' rather than '*adjudication*' or, even more accurately, 'understanding and explaining the patterns of justificatory reasoning used by judges in deciding the numerically few cases that arrive in the appellate courts'. While accurate, this is somewhat jarring on the ear, as is talk of judicial reasoning *simpliciter*. Aesthetic reasons therefore mandate the convention of speaking most often of 'adjudication', and only occasionally of 'legal reasoning'. This brings us, finally, to the title. Any self-obsessed author will lament that titles are a difficult business. I searched long and hard for a snappy, dynamic title that adequately characterised the central themes of this book and, as can be seen, failed miserably. 'Understanding and explaining adjudication' fits the book's contours well even though it lacks grace. Further, reversing Samuel Johnson, it can be said that although the title is not particularly concise, it has the virtue of being reasonably accurate.

While these gestures toward terminological tidiness will certainly leave the extremely pedantic reader entirely dissatisfied, I hope that moderate pedants (and those intrigued by both half-baked definitions and hints) will find enough in the gestures to encourage an examination of what follows. 'Beyond intrigue' could well be the subtitle of the remainder of the book, though I hope that one state beyond intrigue—complete confusion—is avoided and another—a degree of clarity—is achieved. Time and reviewers will tell.

I
Orthodoxy

2
Criticising and Constructing the Orthodoxy

> Critics' moments of greatest blindness with regard to their own assumptions are also moments at which they achieve their greatest insight.
> P. de Man, *Blindness and Insight* (1983), p. 109.

This chapter is a partial proof of Paul de Man's observation. He would, of course, object to that idea and, quite probably, to the use of his claim in a context far removed from that in which it was originally stated. Nevertheless it is true that some critics of orthodox accounts of adjudication, in being blind as to the nature of their assumptions and, we might add, the assumptions made by the orthodox themselves, prompt insight. For, in attempting to correct critics' blindness and mistakes, we see more clearly the problems the orthodox face, problems that prove very difficult to resolve. This is the insight within the illusion. Unlike de Man and the wave of deconstructive or post-structuralist literary scholars that have followed him, however, we accept that the problems highlighted by the illusion might be capable of resolution. Yet before these problems are examined we need turn to a set of questions the answers to which, although contested, are known and discussed by critics of just about everything, from literary works, to sculpture, poetry and drama. The questions concern the nature and point of that which is criticised and evaluated. Although there is a good degree of dispute, it is true that literary critics and writers have accounts of the nature and point of literature and the same is true of almost any other brand of critic. It is a surprising contrast, then, that thought about and criticism of adjudication often proceeds without ever directly facing such questions. These questions—what are accounts of adjudication supposed to be? how are we to determine whether or not they are successful?—are hardly ever explicitly raised nor directly answered in jurisprudential debate. Thus, unsurprisingly, both proponents and critics of accounts of adjudication indiscriminately and simultaneously describe them as either 'theories' or 'models' or 'descriptions' of judicial practice with no attempt to determine whether these words are indeed synonyms, as this usage would suggest, or whether they mark out significantly different enterprises.

This chapter fills that gap, seeking to answer these questions by considering (i) a prevalent strategy of criticism of orthodox accounts of adjudication and (ii) the orthodox understanding of the nature of the enterprise of constructing such accounts. The number of writers from which examples of the former strategy are drawn is a large one, although when speaking specifically there are only two targets at which their criticism is aimed, namely, the accounts of adjudication offered by Neil MacCormick and Ronald Dworkin. It is therefore pleasingly symmetrical that both authors' descriptions of the nature of the enterprise of constructing accounts of adjudication, in conjunction with the views of Joseph Raz, are the basis of most of what follows.

Remember that, being jurisprudentially orthodox, these writers take seriously adjudicators' claims that they decide cases *relatively* constrained by standards *relatively* determinative of the dispute before them. 'Relatively' because the orthodox do not believe that adjudicators have no choices open to them when making decisions but rather that, albeit in different ways and for different reasons, adjudicative choices are justifiable in principle and often in practice. The orthodox accept that the strategies of justification adjudicators use when making these choices form a limited and recognisable class of arguments. These arguments are constrained, *inter alia*, by either (i) requirements of 'fit' with the extant legal materials and the values that are assumed to underlie and give point to them;[1] or (ii) by requirements of consistency and coherence with extant legal materials and a consequentialist evaluation of the effects of a decision one way or another upon the world;[2] or (iii) by a combination of doctrinal, systemic reasons and moral considerations.[3] Thus, for the orthodox, law has some degree of predictability and certainty. Adjudication takes place, again to some degree, within the law; it is not a radically indeterminate process.[4] These features of orthodox accounts of adjudication are accepted by the proponents of the critical strategy considered in the first part of this chapter. These critics are not representatives of any branch of the heresy, and are best regarded as a mildly disaffected or misguided group within the orthodoxy.

It is also worth recalling, so as to be clear exactly what separates the orthodox from their non-heretical critics, two important respects in which their accounts of adjudication are restricted. First, orthodox accounts are

[1] R. Dworkin, *Law's Empire* (London, Fontana 1986), pp. 254–258. Hereinafter referred to in both text and notes as '*LE*' with page numbers.

[2] D. N. MacCormick, *Legal Reasoning and Legal Theory* (Oxford, Clarendon, revised ed. 1993), chs 5, 6, 7 and 8. Hereinafter referred to in the text and notes as '*LRLT*' with page numbers.

[3] J. Raz, *Ethics in the Public Domain* (Oxford, Clarendon 1994), pp. 323–324. Referred to in text and notes as '*EPD*'.

[4] Heretics, remember, argue that adjudication is radically indeterminate because, *inter alia*, both language and values, at least as the orthodox understand them, are indeterminate. For an example of a strong version of the indeterminacy of language argument see G. Peller, 'The Metaphysics of American Law' (1985) 73 *California L. R.* 1151–1290, pp. 1160–1175. The indeterminacy of values argument consists of the attempt to ascribe to the orthodox belief in the subjectivity of values: examples include R. M. Unger, *Knowledge and Politics* (New York, The Free Press 1975), pp. 76–81 and M. Kelman, *A Guide to Critical Legal Studies* (Cambridge, Mass., Harvard U. P. 1987), ch. 2.

not concerned with the causal genesis and determination of the justificatory strategies adjudicators use—they are not histories attempting to relate changes in adjudicators' patterns of reasoning to wider social and economic forces.[5] Nor do they explain on sociological or psychological grounds why adjudicators find some strategies and their constitutive values more appealing than others.[6] Whether or not the orthodox are right to be so cavalier about such matters is discussed in chapter 3. What they focus upon, by contrast, is the nature of the 'formal' reasons adjudicators offer for deciding a case one way rather than another, usually excluding consideration of the causes of, or motives for, accepting those reasons rather than others which would determine a decision the other way. This is not something with which orthodox critics disagree. Secondly, orthodox accounts are primarily interested in patterns of adjudication in hard cases. These are cases that raise legal issues, to say nothing of 'factual' questions, such as: (i) is there a proposition of law applicable to the issue in this case? (ii) which is the correct interpretation, out of a range of two or more, of the agreed applicable proposition of law? (iii) which proposition of law out of a range of two or more competing propositions should be applied to this case? Such cases, where 'no settled rule dictates a decision either way', 'in which reasonable lawyers will disagree . . . and neither will have available any argument that must necessarily convince the other',[7] are the fulcrum of orthodox accounts of judicial reasoning. Again, this restricted focus is accepted by non-heretical critics of the orthodoxy.

The argument of this chapter is that questions about the nature of accounts of adjudication—what are such accounts supposed to be? are they theories, models or descriptions? how do we determine whether or not they succeed?—cannot be convincingly answered by our sample critics and proponents of accounts of adjudication. Critics are blind as to the problems inherent in their approach, for their critical strategy apparently commits them to a defective programme for the explanation and understanding of social action of which, obviously, judges resolving disputes are but a part (this is their 'illusion'). These problems can be avoided if another approach to explanation and understanding social action is adopted, an approach which, as we will see, is partially accepted by proponents of orthodox

[5] An example of such a history lauded by American heretics is M. Horwitz, *The Transformation of American Law 1780–1860* (Cambridge, Mass., Harvard U. P. 1977). The second volume of this work (*The Transformation of American Law 1870–1960* (New York, Oxford U. P. 1992)) is strangely reticent about such matters. For a fine non-heretical study see L. Freidman, *A History of American Law* (New York, Simon and Shuster 1973).

[6] A crude attempt at this is J. A. G. Griffiths, *The Politics of the Judiciary* (London, Fontana 4th ed. 1991). It seems that Griffiths's argument is that judges in the appellate courts routinely decide cases in favour of the 'establishment' because the majority of them are educated in similar environments and hail from a similar class background.

[7] R. Dworkin, *Taking Rights Seriously* (London, Duckworth 1978) at pp. 83 and xiv respectively.

accounts of adjudication (this is the occasion of the critics' insight). Consequently, they face fewer methodological problems than our sample critics; the problems the orthodox face arise almost entirely from their failure to appreciate and thus to pursue the implications of this alternative approach to explanation and understanding. It is an approach, moreover, which in our contemporary intellectual culture may appear counter-intuitive because it both harks back to the promise of classical social theory and hints at what, for many, is an uncongenial account of moral values.[8] It is, nevertheless, an approach that both critics and proponents must take up if they are to avoid a number of snags.

I CRITICISING THE ORTHODOXY

A first step towards answering these questions about the nature of accounts of adjudication outlines an often made criticism of the orthodoxy. When we know what is wrong with this criticism we will understand better what orthodox accounts of adjudication purport to be. On the assumption that the criticism is offered in good faith, then its proponents must believe that they know what the objects of their criticism are about or for, and hence they must assume that these objects—orthodox accounts of adjudication—have criteria of success and failure. The substance of the criticism can be briefly stated: orthodox accounts of adjudication do not 'fit the facts'. Henceforth, it is labelled the 'fit criticism'. Many have thought this a worthwhile, even powerful criticism. Here are a number of examples, some of which are general statements about accounts of judicial reasoning, others being directed at specific accounts. The examples, although diverse, are not exhaustive, yet there are enough of them to rebut the claim that what follows attacks a straw man.

[8] By classical social theory I have in mind not only the work of Durkheim, Marx and, particularly, Weber but also some members of what has been called the 'orthodox consensus' in post-war sociology. It is often alleged by 'postmodernist' social theorists that classical social theory (i) has been outdated by events in the contemporary world and (ii) makes a number of methodological and epistemic mistakes (e.g., in accepting that an all-embracing social theory is possible; that such a theory can be respectably grounded as 'knowledge'). For useful introductions to this line of critique see: Z. Bauman, *Intimations of Postmodernity* (London, Routledge 1992), chs. 2–5; B. Smart, *Postmodernity* (London, Routledge 1993), chs. 2 and 3. The account of moral values hinted at in section IV will be uncongenial to many because it is non-emotivist. Taken widely, emotivism is a hallmark of our culture: see A. MacIntyre, *After Virtue* (London, Duckworth 1982), chs. 1–3. Non-MacIntyrean alternatives can be labelled thus: moral rationalism, by which I mean claims to be able to show that some ends of human action, including some moral goals or values, rationally must be pursued; and moral realism, proponents of which hold that by virtue of certain facts or other properties, moral claims and values can be true or false. Examples are A. Gewirth, 'Can Any Final Ends be Rational?' (1991) 102 *Ethics* 66–95 and the essays in G. Sayre-McCord (ed.), *Moral Realism* (Ithaca, Cornell U. P. 1988).

(a) The general statements

'[I]t is an endemic weakness of the theoretical literature on judicial reasoning that it regularly presents an *oversimplified picture* of what is an extremely intricate process. *A few important steps tend to be selected and presented as the whole.*'[9] '[I]t is in the analysis of *real cases* that we can see the benefits, if any, of theories of adjudication.'[10] The cardinal sin of such theories is 'to show an ignorance of *reality*', 'to provide little *real* guidance to *real* judges in *real* cases'.[11] John Bell is deeply impressed by such arguments from legal reality. One of the main critical strategies of his study of three models of judicial reasoning and the judicial role is 'to consider the validity of these models in the light of judicial *practice*'.[12] The 'test' Bell uses to determine the success of the models is 'to examine judicial decisions for evidence'[13] that they are used; when assessed in this way two of the three do badly. He says that the 'consensus model of the judicial function, *even if not a fully adequate description of what judges do in England*, does point out important factors which limit the role the judiciary plays in government.'[14] It is, however, an inadequate description of actual judicial practice since it, like the rights model, provides only a partial picture of reality. The rights model, even if it 'is descriptively accurate *of the United States . . . does not work for countries like Britain*'.[15] By contrast, the interstitial legislator model 'offers *the best description of* the judicial function in England'.[16]

Other commentators share the assumption that there is something which accounts (or 'models' or 'theories') of judicial reasoning must 'fit' and of which they should offer accurate descriptions. For example, Max Weaver thinks because 'none of the models provides *a perfect fit*' with the reality of judicial practice, then the attempt to offer a general theory of adjudication is pointless: 'the realisation that each of the models *fits some of the facts* some of the time suggests that the jurisprudent's quest for a general theory is a vain one'.[17] For Weaver it seems that theories do well when they 'provide [an] *accurate description* or the most useful models' or are '*drawn directly from life*'[18] (where 'life' means legal practice or reality). Similarly, David Meirs holds that an important test of the quality of such theories is whether or not they are 'descriptively accurate'.[19]

[9] W. Twining and D. Miers, *How To Do Things With Rules* (London, Weidenfeld and Nicolson 3rd ed. 1991), p. 271. Unless stated otherwise in the text, emphasis in quotations is supplied.

[10] S. Lee, 'Law's British Empire?' (1988) 8 *Oxford Journal of Legal Studies* 278–292, p. 287.

[11] *Op. cit*, at p. 278 and 287 respectively.

[12] J. Bell, *Policy Arguments in Judicial Decisions* (Oxford, Clarendon 1983), p. v.

[13] *Op. cit*, p. 14. [14] *Op. cit*, p. 202. [15] *Op. cit*, p. 224. [16] *Op. cit*, p. 244.

[17] M. Weaver, 'Is A General Theory of Adjudication Possible? The Example of the Principle/Policy Distinction' (1985) 48 *Modern L. R.* 613–643, p. 643.

[18] *Op. cit.*, p. 625 and p. 628 respectively.

[19] Book Review (1992) 51 *Cambridge L. J.* 538–541, p. 540.

(b) The specific statements

These are directed at the accounts of adjudication offered by Dworkin and MacCormick. Alan Paterson criticises Dworkin on the basis of a questionnaire and interview survey of judges which ostensibly establishes how they decide cases. 'If it is simply a question of whose account *fits the available facts* better, on the crucial aspect of what the Law Lords themselves think, the answer is clear cut. Law Lords do exercise choices. Many cases do not have right answers which the Law Lords could divine if only they were sufficiently discerning'.[20] Exactly how this refutes Dworkin's account of adjudication is oblique; so far as I am aware, Dworkin denies only that judges have strong discretion and not that they must make and justify choices within the realm of weak discretion.[21] The argument is not one about the existence of choice but about the nature of that choice. How the agents doing the choosing understand that process, and its significance for theoretical explanation and understanding, is an issue to which we return.

Many others have offered a qualitatively identical criticism of Dworkin based upon judicial pronouncements in cases rather than responses to questionnaires. Kent Greenawalt argues that his examination of a number of cases shows that Dworkin's principle/policy distinction has no secure foundation. This is an especially acute problem, Greenawalt thinks, since the cases are such that, if the distinction is to be found at all, it should be apparent in them.[22] That it is not bodes ill for the descriptive accuracy of Dworkin's theory.

Exactly the same kind of critical argument has been directed at MacCormick's account of judicial reasoning. For example, Bernard Rudden gently chides MacCormick because his account of consequentialist arguments in adjudication does not completely fit judicial practice. This is because, says Rudden, there are at least two kinds of consequentialist argument used by judges which MacCormick overlooks. These are arguments based on behavioural consequences, instances of which exist in Admiralty cases, and arguments from 'inbuilt consequences'.[23] Joel Levin also points to standard cases that MacCormick's account of adjudication does not fit: this lack of fit 'leaves a gap in his [MacCormick's] description'.[24] By contrast, some think that the virtue of MacCormick's account is that it is

[20] A. Paterson, *The Law Lords* (London, Macmillan 1982), pp. 194–195.

[21] R. Dworkin, *supra*, note 7, pp. 31–39.

[22] K. Greenawalt, 'Policy, Rights and Judicial Discretion' in M. Cohen (ed.), *Ronald Dworkin and Contemporary Jurisprudence* (London, Duckworth 1984), pp. 93–94.

[23] B. Rudden, 'Consequences' (1980) *Juridical Review* 193–201, pp. 194–201.

[24] J. Levin, *How Judges Reason: The Logic of Adjudication* (New York, Peter Lang 1992), p. 194.

'descriptively accurate';[25] unlike most who offer accounts of judicial reasoning, 'MacCormick knows his law'.[26]

(c) How wrong can things be?

Two interrelated arguments are offered in the remainder of the chapter. First, it is argued in part (d) of this section that both the general and specific versions of the fit criticism are beset by three difficulties. Proponents of the fit criticism, because they do not address these three difficulties, mistake the nature of the enterprise of constructing an account of adjudication. Their criticism is either obviously confused about the nature of 'facts' and 'description' in the human sciences or compatible with untenable views about such matters. The argument proceeds by sketching two accounts of the nature of facts, description and theory which are embodied in two supposedly competing philosophies of the human and natural sciences. These accounts are ranked in order of plausibility, the first being the least, the second being the most, plausible. However, the second argument is that even if the fit criticism is reformulated so as to incorporate the most plausible account of the nature of facts and description (examined in part (e) of this section), that reformulation creates two additional problems. The first is the incorrigibility problem and the second is the plurality problem. Both problems also beset the accounts of adjudication offered by MacCormick, Dworkin and Raz: they arise from the method these scholars employ in order to explain and understand the social world. The problem of incorrigibility is examined in section III and the plurality problem, which will take more of our time and attention, is analysed in section IV. Three responses to the plurality problem are also considered in section IV although only one is a success. In the course of that discussion some doubt is raised as to the possibility of reformulating the fit criticism, so as to avoid the implausible account of facts, description and the incorrigibility and plurality problems, in a way consistent with the statements of it outlined above.

(d) Badly wrong: version one of the fit criticism

Hopefully, proponents of the fit criticism do not make the first mistake with which their statements are compatible. Those statements unambiguously hold that accounts of adjudication must in some way reflect 'reality' or 'judicial practice'; they must provide 'a fully adequate description of what judges do'; successful accounts 'fit the available facts better'; they are 'descriptively

[25] J. W. Harris, *Legal Philosophies* (London, Butterworths 1980), p. 205.
[26] P. S. Atiyah, Book Review (1979) 42 *Modern L. R.* 471–472, p. 471.

accurate'. These thoughts are certainly compatible with, and suggestive of, a particular conception of the way in which 'theories' in the human and natural sciences should be tested. On this view, theories must be 'tested' against a bedrock of facts or observations: a good theory can accommodate the facts, a bad theory cannot. Moreover, a good theory is one from which empirical regularities can be deduced and predicted. Within this approach to theory testing there is a conception of description at work. It is a conception which seems irrefutable and common-sensical: descriptions are supposedly neutral, bare reports corresponding to specific factual situations which theories have to fit and explain.

In so far as models are distinct from descriptions and theories, their difference might be thought to lie in the fact that they occupy an intermediate position between the former and the latter: they are neither supposedly simple descriptive reports nor restatements of theoretical propositions. However, some proponents of the fit criticism hold that models must fit or be tested against the facts and thus apparently regard them as akin to simple descriptions. We have already seen that Bell explicitly and unambiguously propounds the latter view: models must, remember, be tested in light of judicial practice. Yet others do not regard models in this way, although their understanding of what they may be is somewhat oblique. Weaver thinks models 'are neither accurate descriptions nor normative ideals but analytical or heuristic devices'.[27] It is therefore no surprise that models are never a 'perfect fit' with the domain they purport to capture or, more accurately, abstract from; this is true by virtue of Weaver's definition. Hence, Weaver concludes of models of adjudication, 'that each of the models fits some of the facts some of the time'.[28] Then to argue, as Weaver does, that 'general theories of adjudication' are impossible because they do not fit the facts, one reason for this being their employment of models, is disingenuous. If there is nothing wrong with the employment of models in 'general theories' (Weaver fails to show that there is), and if 'general theories' can succeed even when they do not replicate every detail of the domain they purport to illuminate and describe (Weaver has no argument to show they must fail in this case), then this criticism is clearly misplaced. Furthermore, Weaver leaves the most interesting questions unanswered. For, if he is right that models are indeed heuristic tools, he ought to provide some indication as to the ends to which they are used, how they are constructed and wherein lies their heuristic pay-off. Unfortunately, he provides no answers to these questions. What, then, are models? Hereinafter they are regarded as a type of simplified or abstract description, rooted in the domain they describe but not such as to replicate its every detail. Although the conceptions of models, description and theory sketched here compliment one another, they are

[27] Weaver, *supra*, note 17, pp. 613–614. [28] *Ibid.*, p. 643.

unacceptable because they generate at least three difficulties, the first and third being insuperable. Therefore, it is ultimately uncharitable, despite compatibility and suggestiveness, to ascribe such conceptions to proponents of the fit criticism.

The first difficulty can be called the 'clingfilm' problem. The problem arises from the view that facts and our observations of them are in some sense qualitatively distinct from theories, yet related to them, in the same way that clingfilm relates to that which it seals or covers. To keep a bowl of cream fresh one might seal it with clingfilm. To work, the film must fit the contours of the bowl exactly, allowing no gaps between the surface area of the bowl and the film, and seal in the cream. Now some crude 'empiricist' methodologies of the human and natural sciences appear to relate theories and facts in the same way. Theories must fit the facts in the same way that clingfilm must fit the bowl of cream and facts are as distinct from theories as bowl and cream are from clingfilm.[29] A problem arises for this view if it is true that the qualitative distinction between facts and theories cannot be maintained in an epistemologically respectable way. The argument that they cannot involves at least two closely connected moves: the denial of brute facts or data available to the senses independent of theories or conceptual schemes; and a demonstration of the impossibility of theory independent experiment or research, including the search for, and discussion of what is to be regarded as, data.[30] This argument has been powerfully deployed in relation to the natural sciences and those concerned with the human sciences have been quick to extend it, with good reason. For, if a strict qualitative distinction between facts and theories cannot be maintained within the natural sciences, it is doubly unlikely to be defensible within the human sciences. Not only can the points about the fallibility of the distinction be generalised to the human sciences, those sciences also have a dimension that undermines it: the 'facts' of these sciences are self-describing and interpreting and can quite easily appropriate 'theoretical' terms in their descriptions and interpretations. In addition, many methodologists of the human

[29] A few examples are: in the philosophy of natural sciences (with particular reference to physics), E. Mach, *The Analysis of Sensations* (London, Open Court 1914), chs. I and XIV; in the philosophy of the human sciences, J. S. Mill, *A System of Logic* (Toronto, University of Toronto Press 1973), Book V; in sociology, the preface to W. L. Wallace, *Sociological Theory: An Introduction* (London, Heinemann 1969). For an account of both 'crude' and 'sophisticated' empiricism in economics see B. Caldwell, *Beyond Positivism* (London, George Allen and Unwin 1982), parts one and two.

[30] I here crudely simplify a number of arguments offered by, *inter alios*, K. Popper, *Objective Knowledge* (Oxford, Clarendon 1981), Appendix 1 and his *The Logic of Scientific Discovery* (London, Hutchinson 1968), ch. 5; T. Kuhn, *The Structure of Scientific Revolutions* (Chicago, University of Chicago Press, revised second edition 1970), ch. 10; P. K. Feyerabend, *Against Method* (London, Verso, revised edition 1988), ch. 6; N. R. Hanson, *Patterns of Discovery* (Cambridge, C. U. P. 1958), chs. 1, 2 and 4; and M. Hesse, *Revolutions and Reconstructions in the Philosophy of Science* (Brighton, Harvester Press 1980), ch. 3.

and natural sciences have thought that arguments such as Willard Quine's denial of a strict distinction between analytic and synthetic statements make the fact/theory distinction untenable.[31]

The second difficulty, closely related to the first, concerns the nature of theory. If the fit criticism is interpreted in the way the clingfilm problem suggests, then it must hold that accounts of adjudication are theories in the relevant sense. The relevant sense—let us call it *theory in the tertiary sense*—is shared by crude and sophisticated empiricist methodologies of the human and natural sciences, as well as by a number of non-empiricist methodologies. It holds that

> 'theory' means in all empirical sciences the explicit formulation of determinate relations between a set of variables in terms of which a fairly extensive class of empirically ascertainable regularities can be explained. Furthermore, . . . neither the fact that these regularities have in the social sciences a rather narrowly restricted universality, nor the fact that they permit prediction only to a rather limited extent, constitutes a basic difference between the social and natural sciences, since many branches of the latter show the same features.[32]

It is, however, difficult to interpret orthodox accounts of adjudication in this way because they yield few explicit formulations and explanations of the relations between a set of variables. In jurisprudence, as in all the human sciences, such law-like propositions are few and far between. This being the case, we ought to be circumspect before ascribing this conception of theory to proponents of accounts of adjudication. It is not the case that proponents of the fit criticism explicitly accept this conception of theory. Rather, their apparent acceptance of the relationship between theories (or accounts) of adjudication and the facts of the matter, which culminates in the clingfilm problem, suggests that they are implicitly committed to this conception. It is a conception that may set standards of 'theoreticity' which proponents of accounts of adjudication, as well as accounts of many other aspects of social action, find difficult to satisfy.

Nevertheless, were accounts of adjudication understood as theories in this sense, then the fit criticism would appear quite plausible. For, if theories are to provide a corpus of statements from which empirical events are to be predicted and explained, then the dredging up of empirical events (particular judicial statements, specific cases, etc.) might be understood as attempts to confront such theories with facts they can neither explain nor

[31] W. Quine, 'Two Dogmas of Empiricism', ch. II of *From a Logical Point of View* (Cambridge, Mass., Harvard U. P. 2nd ed. 1961).

[32] A. Schutz, 'Concept and Theory Formation in the Social Sciences' in his *Collected Papers* Volume 1 (The Hague, Martinus Nijhoff 1971), pp. 51–52. Schutz certainly cannot be regarded as an empiricist in these matters but his conception of theory is shared by one of the most sophisticated empiricists: see E. Nagel, *The Structure of Science* (London, Routledge and Kegan Paul 1961), chs. 13–15.

predict. If only things, more particularly 'facts', were that simple. This line of argument could only lend plausibility to the fit criticism if the clingfilm problem did not exist. Proponents of the fit criticism need some response to it if their argument is to be interpreted in this way (for my part I can think of no defensible reply to it that would also fail to imperil the criticism).

The third snag raises the problem of access. It asks: 'how are we to get knowledge of the data or facts of social action?'. If such facts are not simply presented to our senses the way we assume, prior to reflection, visual and tactile sensations are presented to us, then the way we can come to know them is indeed a puzzle. Part of an answer (a compelling reply cannot be developed here) begins by noting some of the preconditions of obtaining any knowledge of social action. Such knowledge can only be obtained through language, for we are linguistically constituted beings,[33] and, in so far as that knowledge relates to social action, it must be assumed that such action is purposive. If these two preconditions are indeed unavoidable, two points seem to follow. First, in so far as social action is purposive, and in so far as purposive social action is (not necessarily completely) constitutive of social practices and institutions, then those institutions and practices must be regarded as purposive also. Secondly, initial access to purposive social action is perhaps best achieved through the accounts of the nature of that action provided by those whose behaviour constitutes that action. This knowledge is available to us through the languages of self-description, explanation and justification of those acting in accordance with the practices and involved in the institutional structures of a community. Moreover, there is a sense in which these languages are theories or conceptual schemes: they provide agents with maps of the rules, practices and institutions in which they operate, showing them how to manoeuvre in social space. Such conceptual schemes—or *theories in the primary or practical sense*—consist of a range of evaluations and distinctions conferring significance and meaning upon an agent's webs of interaction with others and his or her participation in practices and institutions. Hence, in so far as such conceptual schemes or theories in the primary sense constitute the 'facts' of social action, then those facts are clearly already 'theorised'. Drawing a distinction between facts, taken to be a theory independent realm, and 'theory' thus makes no sense here, whereas some distinctions between 'levels' of theory are invaluable.

The argument generated from the two preconditions of knowledge of social action is often thought sufficient to demonstrate that attempts to explain and understand social action must necessarily take up what has

[33] 'Language is not just one of man's possessions in the world, but on it depends the fact that man has a world at all': H-G. Gadamer, *Truth and Method* (London, Sheed and Ward 1975) p. 401.

variously been called an interpretative, hermeneutic or *Verstehen* approach (hereinafter I regard these terms as synonyms).[34] At the least, such an approach insists upon the points just made: that social action is purposive or meaningful and that our initial understanding of it must be gained through the self-understandings of those whose behaviour constitutes the action. However, it is important to note what is sometimes thought to follow from this approach. For example, it is often assumed that the self-understanding of those whose behaviour constitutes social action sets the limits of social scientific explanation and understanding. On this view, any account of social action is unsatisfactory if it does not correspond exactly to the views (about the meaning and purpose of the action) of those whose behaviour constitutes that action. Participants' views are thus rendered incorrigible. This, as the arguments in section III suggest, does not necessarily follow from the *Verstehen* approach. Furthermore, regarding participants' views as incorrigible makes a common kind of social scientific 'theory'—*theory in the secondary sense*—pointless. This kind of work is rooted in the languages of description and evaluation of the participants in some institution and practice (theory in the primary or practical sense). It attempts to retrieve and elucidate those languages in order to understand and explain them. Yet the latter task is often envisaged as going beyond those languages and involving something like theory in the tertiary sense; certainly, the possibility is accepted that an adequate explanation or understanding of some aspect of social life can go beyond, perhaps even ultimately reject, the self-understanding and evaluations of participants.

It is often also assumed that any move to embrace the *Verstehen* approach to understanding and explaining social action of necessity entails the rejection of causal 'explanations' of such action and, hence, the rejection of all or most of the strategies and methods of natural science. This argument is considered in some depth in chapter 3, yet it should be noted that the claims made here about the importance of *Verstehen* are far from having any direct relevance to the 'unity of science' thesis. One cannot derive from the two preconditions alone an argument to establish an impermeable, qualitative difference between the *methods* of the human sciences, on the one hand, and those of the natural sciences, on the other. Those preconditions tell us only that the *subject matter* of the human sciences is qualitatively different—because self-understanding and self-interpreting—from the subject matter of the natural sciences.

Within Anglo-American jurisprudence, discussion of the necessity of *Ver-*

[34] Max Weber is the most important exponent of *Verstehen*. See *Economy and Society* (New York, Bedminster Press 1968), G. Roth and C. Wittich (eds.), Volume I, ch. I. For comment see S. Toddington, *Rationality, Social Action and Moral Judgement* (Edinburgh, Edinburgh U. P. 1993), chs. 2 and 3. On hermeneutic or interpretative social science a useful introduction is Z. Bauman, *Hermeneutics and Social Science* (London, Hutchinson 1978).

stehen is phrased almost entirely in terms of the 'internal' and 'external' points of view.[35] The former phrase has a number of senses, two of which must be distinguished. First, the phrase highlights an approach to understanding and explaining social action. We can call this use of the phrase the methodological use or sense. According to it, the internal point of view accepts the two preconditions identified above, whereas the external point of view does not. A standard example will illustrate the supposed difference. In order to understand and explain what is happening when vehicles stop at red lights it is not sufficient, according to those who take up the internal point of view (and who are thus apparently committed to *Verstehen*), merely to detail a vast number of instances in which, when the lights are red, vehicles stop. One of the problems with such an 'explanation' or 'understanding' is that it leaves out of the picture the meaning or point or purpose of the behaviour as understood by participants. If the two preconditions for obtaining knowledge of social action are unavoidable, then the internal point of view seems to be the most obvious methodological injunction to follow. By contrast, the external point of view appears amusing: understanding chess is a matter of correlating the vast series of 'moves' one may witness (though that description will supposedly be unavailable to one who does not attempt to understand the language of participants) with one or more out of a perhaps infinite range of external variables (room temperature, body weight, number of observers etc.). Such external accounts of behaviour miss the fact that much behaviour is rule-governed.[36]

The second sense of the phrase 'internal point of view' is closely but not necessarily related to the first. In this second sense the phrase is not used so as to contrast and belittle an alternative approach to understanding and explanation. Rather, it is used as a label to elucidate what it is to follow a rule or practice. To do this, those whose behaviour constitutes the rule or practice must accept that practice. Acceptance must consist of a certain limited range of reasons for acting in the way specified by the rule or practice—not any old reason will do. This sense of the phrase we can call the participants' sense, for the internal point of view here signifies participants' reasons for acting as they do. This sense is related to the first in that the question the participants' sense raises—why does X act in accordance with this rule or practice?—is only intelligible if the first sense is accepted. But it does not follow from the first sense that the question must be put in this way. For the methodological sense holds, *inter alia*, that social action, prac-

[35] The terminology belongs to H. L. A. Hart, *The Concept of Law* (Oxford, Clarendon 2nd ed. 1994), pp. 54–56, 96–114, 197, 242 and 244. For further development of Hart's arguments see N. MacCormick, *H. L. A. Hart* (London, Edward Arnold 1981), ch. 3 (referred to hereinafter in both text and notes as '*HLAH*' with accompanying page numbers).

[36] This, of course, is Hart's criticism of Austin: *The Concept of Law*, *supra*, note 35, chs. 2–5. For a delightful illustration see MacCormick on Gulliver's watch: *LRLT*, appendix.

tices and institutions are in some degree purposive. It does not follow from this that the only way to try to elucidate, explain and understand those purposes is through the reasons agents have for accepting rules, institutions and practices.

If the arguments raised in this section are ultimately capable of being defended, then the conclusion must be that the fit criticism, despite the language of its proponents, ought not to be interpreted in such a way as to incorporate a dubious account of the nature of facts and description. Interpretative charity demands that we reconstruct or re-read the fit criticism (by adding to what is already there), so as to avoid such absurd results.

(e) An improvement: version two of the fit criticism

If the data with which we are concerned when attempting to understand and explain social action are already theorised—by those whose behaviour, beliefs and values constitute that action—and if those data are only accessible through the internal point of view, then simplistic recourse to the 'facts' of social action cannot amount to a compelling criticism of any explanation and understanding of a particular segment of social action. This is because there may be more than one practical or primary 'theory'—and hence more than one internal point of view in the participant's sense—providing access to, and thus generating different accounts of, the 'facts'. In so far as the fit criticism appeals to an unproblematic, univocal bedrock of fact against which accounts of social action are tested, it falls victim to a number of snags. In order to avoid them the criticism must be modified in such a way as to appeal to the facts as they appear from the internal point of view, in the languages of self-description, explanation and justification of those whose behaviour constitutes those 'facts'. The fit criticism then amounts to an argument that proponents of orthodox accounts of adjudication have failed to capture what they hoped to, namely, the way participants in that practice understand it. Hence, the orthodox misdescribe the internal point of view; their accounts 'do not fit the facts'. This appears an admirably simple and tidy way to resurrect the fit criticism. It might be thought silly to imagine its proponents invoke some crudely mistaken view as to the nature of facts and description in the human sciences; the criticism is made with a full appreciation of the nature and necessity of *Verstehen*. Thus chastised, we ought to give up our resistance to the fit criticism.

Clearly, if the fit criticism is reformulated in this way its proponents must amend their understanding of facts and description. The first version of the criticism embraced an implausible but apparently commonsensical understanding in which descriptions are simply neutral, bare reports corresponding to specific factual situations. But in the second version of the criticism it is accepted that the 'facts' of social action are not knowable in a non-theorised, non-evaluative way. We come to know and understand the 'facts' of social action only through the languages of self-description, explanation and justification of those whose behaviour is constitutive of those facts. Those 'facts' exist and have significance within conceptual schemes or theories in the primary sense. The method of *Verstehen* thus entails describing social action and practices from the viewpoint of those who perform the action and practices, incorporating their evaluations and distinctions. So, to describe is to give an account of some action or practice from a point of view—that of those whose behaviour constitutes the action or practice—maintaining the evaluations and distinctions contained in that point of view. To theorise social life is, then, to do either or both of the following: (i) to attempt to articulate the conceptual scheme of those whose action or practices one describes from the internal point of view (theory in the secondary sense); or (ii) to attempt to explain those practices, actions and conceptual schemes by reference to some corpus of supposedly law-like generalisations (theory in the tertiary sense).

Surely the fit criticism, reformulated so as to incorporate *Verstehen* and plausible conceptions of facts and description, escapes the difficulties outlined in part (d) above? The answer must be yes, with the following caveats. The first raises the incorrigibility problem. Reformulated so as to take seriously participants' viewpoints, the fit criticism is apparently committed to giving an account of an action, practice or institution solely in terms used by participants. The problem here is the 'solely': it suggests that an account of an action, practice or institution cannot go beyond what the participants think and, hence, that what they think—their accounts of the point, purpose or value of the practice or whatever—determines the meaning and nature of that which they think about. Many would balk at this, for they hold the perfectly intelligible view that social theoretic accounts of actions, institutions and practices ought not to be so closely tied to participants' views. They do not object to such accounts of a practice closely resembling the participants' views of the practice, but hold that they should not merely replicate or amplify participants' accounts. This is entirely understandable if it is accepted that it is possible for participants to be mistaken about the point, purpose or value of some action, institution or practice, that ideology affects the social world. Whether or not this problem is a genuine one, and the ways in which it might be avoided, are considered in section III.

The second caveat raises the plurality problem. For, reformulated so as to take up the participants' point of view, the fit criticism faces the following difficulty. Suppose that, among the participants in a practice or institution, there is a plurality of accounts as to the point, purpose or value of the practice or institution. If there is such a plurality, how are the fit criticism and orthodox accounts of adjudication to accommodate it and what problems, if any, does it cause? Section IV aims to answer this question by showing, *inter alia*, that the plurality problem does indeed affect the orthodoxy and, *a fortiori*, the reformulated fit criticism. It is argued that the consequences of adequately responding to the problem are significant. One consequence is such that it raises doubt as to whether or not the fit criticism can be amended so as to take account of the plurality problem; another is that orthodox accounts of adjudication must be amended in ways unforeseen by their authors. Nevertheless, these consequences must be accepted if the plurality problem is to be avoided. The following section briefly sketches the way in which the orthodox go about constructing accounts of legal reasoning so as to illustrate how the incorrigibility and plurality problems ensnare them.

II CONSTRUCTING THE ORTHODOXY

When constructing their accounts of adjudication, do MacCormick, Dworkin and Raz hold a methodological position similar to that which proponents of the second version of the fit criticism espouse? If so, they must construct those accounts from the internal point of view, and they would thus share an apparently plausible conception of the nature of facts and description. Or, are this trio instead committed to the untenable conception of facts and description embraced by those who expound the first version of the fit criticism? Despite some *apparently* troubling statements suggesting a commitment to the latter view, it is the case that these orthodox scholars take up the internal point of view and the conception of facts, description and theory upon which it depends. Before establishing that, the troublesome hints to the contrary must be discounted. Even when they are, all is not plain sailing for the orthodox. For, although they espouse the internal point of view and its plausible conception of facts, description and theory, they thereby court other difficulties. It is upon this common ground that the incorrigibility and plurality problems arise.

The apparently troublesome remarks are these. MacCormick, for instance, says that theories and hypotheses must be tested against or compared with some thing or bit of the world (*LRLT*, pp. 8 and 13). Dworkin espouses a similar view, albeit in the language of practices and interpretation. He holds that the former are 'brute facts' (*LE*, p. 255) of the social world which competing interpretations of their point or moral value must 'fit'; practices are the 'raw data' of interpretation (*LE*, p. 67). With these comments in mind, it might be said that MacCormick and Dworkin are committed to the untenable view of facts and description characteristic of the first version of the fit criticism. That view, remember, was one in which a sharp distinction was drawn between a supposedly non-problematically accessible realm of brute facts, on the one hand, and a realm of description and 'theory', on the other. Certainly, this dichotomy is echoed in MacCormick's and Dworkin's remarks but the dichotomy they draw is clearly not the same as that underpinning the untenable version of the fit criticism.

The reason for this is that neither MacCormick nor Dworkin accept that the domain with which interpretations or theories must be compared—the brute facts of legal history, for example—is a non-linguistic, non-theorised realm which can be simply discerned by the senses. Rather, that realm is already theorised and linguistically constructed by those whose behaviour constitutes it and, while it is to some degree distinct from theory and interpretation, the latter are undoubtedly vital in order to appropriate that realm. Participants whose language, actions and beliefs constitute that which is to be interpreted and theorised can themselves offer their own interpretations and theories and appropriate those offered by theorists. Hence, while MacCormick and Dworkin speak, for example, of comparing *interpretations* with *raw data*, they do not accept that these are *qualitatively* different; rather, they are different points on the same spectrum. Nor do they hold that the raw data, or the facts which our hypotheses must fit, are unproblematically knowable: they can be accessed only through the language of those whose actions, beliefs, institutions and practices we are attempting to understand and explain. Their emphasis upon the importance of the latter refutes any claim that either MacCormick or Dworkin espouses the view of facts and description underpinning the first version of the fit criticism.

The orthodox commitment to taking up the internal point view is unambiguous and it betokens a conception of facts and description identical to that which underlies the second version of the fit criticism. For Dworkin 'the historian [and any other exponent of the human sciences] cannot understand law as an argumentative social practice, even enough to reject it as deceptive, *until he has a participant's understanding*, until he has his own sense of what counts as a good or bad argument within that practice' (*LE*, p. 14; emphasis supplied). Dworkin therefore '*takes up the internal, participants' point of view*; it tries to grasp the argumentative character of our legal practice by joining that practice and struggling with the issues of soundness and truth participants face' (*LE*, *ibid*; emphasis supplied). There is not much in these remarks with which MacCormick would disagree. He holds that '[a]ny account of rules, norms and standards of conduct must be in terms of th[e] 'internal point of view'. That is to say, it must take account of the consciousness of those who use and operate with whatever standards of conduct may be in question' (*LRLT*, p. 284). MacCormick believes this approach is necessary because, *inter alia*, 'human beings act for reasons when they act at all, and no 'explanation' of human behaviour which omits reference to the subjective reasons for which it is performed can be a full or adequate one' (*LRLT*, p. 6). Raz rarely makes general methodological statements, but he does say that '[i]t is a major task of legal theory to advance our understanding of society by helping to understand how people understand themselves' (*EPD*, p. 221). This aim surely could not be achieved without taking up the participants' point of view; how else could Raz hope to understand how people understand themselves? Furthermore, Raz's development of the internal point of view, by means of the notions of detached legal statements and statements from a point of view, clearly underpins a commitment to *Verstehen*.[37]

Now, it would be a mistake to minimise the many differences between orthodox accounts of adjudication. Substantively, the political and moral implications of Dworkin's account of law as integrity appear very different from the implications of MacCormick's moderate consequentialist account. Raz's account of adjudication is far less systematic and consequently less ambitious than either. These differences, as well as other differences of emphasis and language—for Dworkin, to give an account of judicial reasoning is to offer a constructive interpretation of that practice (*LE*, p. 52), whereas for MacCormick it is a process of offering 'eminently falsifiable hypotheses' which are descriptively accurate and normatively acceptable (*LRLT*, p. 13), while Raz is really only concerned with answering the question '[i]s legal reasoning *sui generis*?' (*EPD*, p. 310)—flow from a shared assumption that the internal point of view represents the starting point of any serious attempt to provide an account of any social practice or segment of rule-governed behaviour. This assumption is a hallmark of the jurisprudentially orthodox and, if the arguments against the first version of the fit criticism are correct, it is an assumption they are right to make.[38] Yet the invocation of the internal point of view as a methodological starting point is not unproblematic. For MacCormick, Dworkin and Raz, as well as for proponents of the second version of the fit criticism, the most immediate difficulties are the incorrigibility and plurality problems.

[37] Raz's discussion of detached legal statements and statements from a point of view occurs in, *inter alia*, *Practical Reason and Norms* (New Jersey, Princeton U. P. 1990), pp. 170–177 and *The Authority of Law* (Oxford, Clarendon 1979), pp. 142–143 and 153–157.

[38] Some orthodox statements of method over and beyond those of MacCormick, Dworkin and Raz are: S. Perry's discussion of H. L. A. Hart in 'Interpretation and Methodology in Legal Theory', ch. 3 of A. Marmor (ed.), *Interpretation and Legal Theory* (Oxford, Clarendon 1995); S. Burton, *Judging in Good Faith* (Cambridge, C. U. P. 1992), pp. xv–xvi; O. Fiss, 'Objectivity and Interpretation' (1982) 34 *Stanford L. R.* 739–763, pp. 748–750 and his 'The Death of Law?' (1986) 76 *Cornell L. R.* 1–16, pp. 7–8. Two good illustrations of the orthodox method at work within private law scholarship are E. Weinrib, *The Idea of Private Law* (Cambridge, Mass., Harvard U. P. 1995) and A. Brudner, *The Unity of the Common Law* (Berkeley, University of California Press 1995).

III THE INCORRIGIBILITY PROBLEM

Taking up the internal point of view, in the way the orthodox and proponents of the reformulated fit criticism do, might be thought to entail that the views of the participants in practices and institutions as to the point, purpose or value of those practices and institutions are incorrigible. This is the incorrigibility thesis and, if it is true, it has the following rather startling consequences. First, it entails that the social theorist can get no better account of an action, practice or institution than that offered by the participant; participants' views on these matters cannot be improved and hence cannot be wrong. While many have thought it important to take up the internal point of view when attempting to understand and explain social life, few would agree that the social theorist cannot go beyond participants' views or that those views cannot be wrong.[39] If the orthodox method leads to this result, then we have good reason to look for a better method. Secondly, the truth of the incorrigibility thesis falsifies an important account of ideology. That account is the critical conception of ideology which holds, *inter alia*, that it is possible, under certain circumstances, for agents to be systematically misguided about some aspect of social reality.[40] If agents' views as to the nature of social reality are incorrigible, then this cannot be true. Again, if the orthodox method leads to this result we have cause to question it, or, at the very least, we must see the argument that has this dramatic effect unpacked. Finally, the truth of the incorrigibility thesis apparently entails the truth of methodological individualism, thereby making pointless a discussion that has persisted for at least one hundred and fifty years.[41]

On what grounds can it be argued that the orthodox and proponents of the reformulated fit criticism are committed to the incorrigibility thesis? They neither explicitly espouse the thesis nor do they explicitly reject it; hence the argument that they are so committed must proceed indirectly. One such indirect path, that may be thought promising, begins by asserting that the best available accounts of meaning analyse the concept in terms of a speaker's or writer's intentions. For example, to understand properly a speaker's utterance that 'the ice over there is very thin', we need not only grasp the relevant rules of grammar and reference, but also what the

[39] P. Winch is often associated with this view but the evidence is equivocal: see *The Idea of a Social Science and Its Relation to Philosophy* (London, Routledge and Kegan Paul 1958), pp. 86–91 and 116–120.

[40] Critical and non-critical accounts of ideology are discussed in chapter 5, section III. An excellent overview is provided by J. Thompson, *Ideology and Modern Culture* (Cambridge, Polity Press 1990), chs. 1 and 2.

[41] That discussion and the general nature of methodological individualism and its supposed opposite are tackled in the following chapter.

speaker intended by the utterance.[42] The rules of grammar and reference say that the utterance means there is, or the speaker thinks there is, ice over there, and that it is, or she thinks it is, very thin. But there might be much more to the meaning of this utterance that will be missed if the speaker's intentions are ignored. For, this utterance could be a recommendation to divers or fishermen on a frozen pond, a warning to ice-skaters, a line from a play, or the punchline of a joke. It is not obviously wrong to speak of these matters as displaying the 'meaning' of the utterance, a meaning that the rules of grammar and reference clearly do not disclose, but which reference to the speaker's intentions will. Let us assume that there is a general truth here, namely, that meaning is indeed determined by intention. What relevance is this to the incorrigibility thesis?

It would become relevant were the following substitutions made: the replacement, in 'intention determines meaning' of 'intention' by 'point, purpose or value' and the replacement of 'meaning' by 'nature of action, institution or practice'. Hence where we faced the claim that agents' intentions determine the meaning of their utterances we now have 'agents' accounts of the point, purpose or value of an action, institution or practice determine the nature of that action, institution or practice'. Obviously, the logical structure of these claims is not equivalent, but it is not surprising that the latter draws plausibility from the former. It is not, after all, a huge extrapolation from the claim about meaning and intention, although it does involve moving from statements about singular events and agents (what Y means by utterance q) to statements about a plurality of agents (what the participants in a practice take its point to be), and moving from talk of intentions to talk of point, purpose or value. Assuming that no major difficulties arise from these moves, and assuming that it is indeed right to hold that agents' intentions determine the meaning of their utterances, it does not seem completely implausible to maintain that participants' accounts of the value of a practice determine the nature of the practice. If the extrapolation is accepted, we are thereby apparently committed to the incorrigibility thesis. However, there are two powerful reasons why the incorrigibility thesis cannot be accepted. The first is simple: there is no account of the relation between intention and meaning such that it can support the incorrigibility thesis; the second holds that, even if there were such an account, it could not be accepted because it embraces an unacceptable social ontology. These reasons must be unpacked.

Paul Grice has insisted upon the importance of the connection between meaning and intention and his account has the look of a general semantic theory. By virtue of its generality it might be thought a valuable prop for

[42] The example is from Q. Skinner, ' "Social Meaning" and the Explanation of Social Action', ch. 4 of J. Tully (ed.), *Meaning and Context* (Cambridge, Polity Press 1988), p. 83; it originally belonged to P. Strawson.

the incorrigibility thesis. Grice's account of non-natural ($_{NN}$) meaning holds that '. . . "A meant $_{NN}$ something by *x*" 'is (roughly) equivalent to "A intended the utterance of *x* to produce some effect in an audience by means of the recognition of this intention"; and we may add that to ask what A meant is to ask for a specification of the intended effect'.[43] This looks promising for the incorrigibility thesis because, from Grice's emphasis upon the vital importance of speakers' intentions in determining the meaning of an utterance, it appears but a small step to maintaining that the utterer's intentions are incorrigible. Furthermore, there does not seem to be room for anything else to have a role in determining the meaning of an utterance given that Grice 'do[es] not think that meaning is essentially connected with convention'.[44] Also, if Grice's efforts to minimise the gap between non-natural and natural meaning are successful, then one inference that could be drawn is that the role of intention in determining meaning becomes even greater. (The inference does not necessarily follow since the opposite inference could also be drawn: eliding the difference between natural and non-natural meaning could, if intention has no role in determining the former, minimise rather than expand the role of intention.[45])

Despite appearances, Grice's account of meaning does not support the incorrigibility thesis. This is because he allows that there can be doubt as to a speaker's intentions and that those intentions are reflexive. In allowing that there can be doubt as to a speaker's intentions Grice is hardly making a bizarre point. Further, he says that in the presence of doubt the context does some work in allowing an assessment of what, after all, the speaker's intentions might be.[46] The significant point for present purposes is that there can be *doubt*—the speaker's intentions are thus not an incorrigible guide to the determination of meaning. Hence, this account of meaning cannot simply be extended so as to support the claim that participants' views of the point, purpose or value of a practice are conclusive. Moreover, the fact that speakers' intentions are reflexive also ensures that they are not incorrigible. Being reflexive, speakers' intentions are designed to produce a particular effect on the audience through their recognition of those intentions. The reflexivity of speakers' intentions entails that '. . . for *x* to have meaning $_{NN}$, the intended effect must be something which in some sense *is within the control of the audience*, or that in some sense of "reason" the recognition of the intention behind *x* is for the audience a reason and not merely a cause'.[47] Therefore, it is a speaker's intentions, taken in combination with the audience's understanding of those intentions, that determines the meaning of a sentence. The speaker's intentions are not incorrigible: they

[43] H. P. Grice, *Studies in the Ways of Words* (Cambridge, Mass., Harvard U. P. 1989), p. 220.
[44] *Ibid*., p. 298.
[45] This is a rare lapse for Grice who is otherwise so acute: *ibid*., pp. 290–297.
[46] *Ibid*., p. 222. [47] *Ibid*., p. 221 (emphasis supplied).

must be filtered through, and hence to some extent determined by, the understanding and expectations of listeners.

Quentin Skinner has provided another contribution to the discussion about the relation between meaning and intention. Unlike Grice, Skinner does not aim to offer a general semantic theory, but rather deploys an account of the relation between meaning and intention in his pathbreaking contribution to the history and analysis of political ideas. In the effort to analyse political texts in context, Skinner draws upon J. L. Austin's account of speech acts. Yet, although Skinner insists that intention determines meaning in some circumstances, his account of that relationship is not such as to support the incorrigibility thesis. The utterance already noted, that 'the ice over there is very thin' is one of Skinner's favourite examples. He uses it to show that the meaning of utterances must in *some* circumstances be discerned by reference to the intentions of the speaker. Those circumstances exist when the conventions which give utterances unambiguous meaning are lost, so that we are now unsure exactly what it is supposed to mean over and beyond the standard rules of reference and grammar, and when utterances are ironic or illocutionary acts (Skinner regards these as one and the same).[48] The essence of the latter is 'that any agent, in issuing any serious utterance, will be doing something as well as merely saying something, and will be doing something *in* saying what he says, and not merely as a consequence of what is said. . . . [T]o issue any serious utterance is always to speak not only with a certain meaning but with a certain intended force'.[49] The utterance about ice is naturally regarded as an illocutionary act because it not only means that the ice over there is very thin, but it is usually, depending on the context, intended to do something, to have a certain intended force: it is a warning. Whether or not the utterance actually is an illocutionary *act* is, in the main, dependent upon the speaker's intention, whereas whether or not a particular utterance has illocutionary *force* is determined by the context in which it is made. An utterance can have illocutionary force but not be an illocutionary act.[50]

Now there is some doubt as to how far Austin, at least, thought intention crucial to determining illocutionary meaning and Skinner candidly notes the equivocation.[51] In some work Austin clearly thought that the context surrounding an utterance conferred upon the utterance its illocutionary force, whereas at other points he plainly regarded speakers' intentions as crucial. Skinner accepts that both have a role in determining illocutionary

[48] J. Tully (ed.), *Meaning and Context*, *supra*, note 42, chs. 3, 4 and 14, especially pp. 270–271. Skinner's methodological writings must be supplemented with his work in the history of political thought, some of the most important and ambitious being his *Foundations of Modern Political Thought*, vols. I and II (Cambridge, C. U. P. 1978) and *Reason and Rhetoric in the Philosophy of Hobbes* (Cambridge, C. U. P. 1996).

[49] J. Tully (ed.), *Meaning and Context*, *supra*, note 42, p. 83.

[50] *Ibid.*, pp. 260–267. [51] *Ibid.*, p. 262.

meaning and hence rejects the view that intention and only intention determines (illocutionary) meaning. His account of meaning is therefore not an obvious prop with which to support the incorrigibility thesis. Since the connection between intention and meaning is important for Skinner (and Austin) only in relation to illocutionary meaning, there is some doubt as to the propriety of extending this analysis to the present question. That, remember, is this: does taking up the internal point of view commit the orthodox to regarding participants' views as incorrigible? This account of the relation between meaning and intention holds that the latter determines the former in the case of illocutionary acts. If this account is to support the incorrigibility thesis, it needs to be established that participants' views as to the point, purpose or value of an action, institution or practice are illocutionary acts. This seems implausible even though Skinner, in particular, thinks there are a great number of illocutionary acts in everyday language and is keen to extend the analysis as far as possible. What act or additional force would a participant in a practice want to attach to their account of its point? There is no answer to this question save to say that this does not seem like a forum for an illocutionary act, even though there is no guarantee that participants cannot or will not perform illocutionary acts when giving an account of the point of an action, practice or institution. For, illocutionary meaning is a facility of our language that can be drawn upon at any time and in an infinite variety of ways. Hence there is no limit upon when and how illocutionary acts can be performed or attempted. Nevertheless, it seems that there are some situations in which they are more and some in which they are less appropriate, and participants giving an account of the point, purpose or value of some practice is, I think, one of the latter. Finally, even were it accepted that illocutionary acts are (almost) everywhere, and that participants' accounts of the point, purpose and value of a practice or institution are examples of such acts, this would not support the incorrigibility thesis. Why? Because, as Skinner notes, this analysis does not entail that participants' views are incorrigible. There is

> no difficulty in principle . . . about reconciling the claim that we need to be able to characterise a writer's [or participant's] intentions in order to interpret the meanings of his works with the claim that it may sometimes be appropriate to discount his own statements about them . . . [This is] only to make the . . . charge that the writer [or participant] himself may have been self-deceiving about recognising his intentions, or incompetent in stating them. And this seems perennially possible in the case of any complex human action.[52]

If neither Skinner's nor Grice's account of the relationship between meaning and intention is capable of supporting the incorrigibility thesis, is there any other account that can? I do not think so. Moreover, accounts of

[52] J. Tully, (ed.), *Meaning and Context*, *supra*, note 42, p. 77.

meaning that emphasise the role of intention, such as Grice's, do not currently enjoy much philosophical popularity. Such accounts of meaning are not even on the agenda of one of the most important contemporary philosophers, Donald Davidson. He has made contributions to the analysis of action, events, causality, reasons, truth and meaning. The job of a theory of meaning for Davidson is to apply the Tarskian account of truth to natural languages and there is clearly no room for agents' intentions in such an account.[53]

However, those familiar with Davidson's account of agency might, mistakenly, assume that some support could be wrung from it for the incorrigibility thesis. For example, Davidson holds that in order to distinguish a class of events called actions from other events in the world, it is necessary to have reference to agents' intentions. Thus, '[i]f an event is an action, then under some description(s) it is primitive, and under some description(s) it is intentional'; '[a]ction . . . require[s] that what the agent does is intentional under some description, and this in turn requires . . . that what the agent does is known to him under some description'.[54] This is clearly not the same as insisting that intention determines meaning; rather, Davidson says intention determines whether or not some event is rightly regarded as an action. It might be said that this is indeed one way in which intention determines meaning and it is therefore a more than adequate peg from which to hang the incorrigibility thesis. Davidson's question is: 'is this event an action?'. The answer, generated by reference to the intentions of the agent, is either yes (if the event is intentional) or no (if it is not). If reference to the agent's intentions is necessary to determine whether or not event Y is an action, then does not intention determine meaning in this very narrow sense? This could be conceded, but it must be noted that Davidson's account of meaning is utterly unlike this one, so different, in fact, as to make it erroneous to ascribe any such claim to him. Moreover, any strong claim that intention determines meaning faces the additional difficulty of positing a *prima facie* dubious social ontology.[55]

The dubious social ontology takes this form: the social world is entirely a product of our thoughts, ideas and beliefs which, when changed, necessarily change that world and its constitutive institutions, structures and practices. This view holds that the rules and conventions constitutive of language (undeniably part of the social world) have no constraining force over us.

[53] D. Davidson, *Inquiries into Truth and Interpretation* (Oxford, Clarendon 1984), essays 1, 2 and 10.

[54] These statements are from D. Davidson, *Essays on Actions and Events* (Oxford, Clarendon 1980), p. 61 and p. 50 respectively.

[55] This point is taken from A. Altman, *Critical Legal Studies: A Liberal Critique* (Princeton, Princeton U. P. 1990), p. 169, but, as will be seen from the discussion in chapter 5, section I (b) (iii), I think he is mistaken in ascribing this view to heretics. To my knowledge, the person who comes closest to espousing this dubious view is P. Winch, *supra*, note 39, p. 133.

Just as intention determines meaning so, then, does it determine the content and structure of language as a whole. The consequence of this view when applied to other aspects of the social world is just the same: that aspect we label law is just as much a product of our thoughts, ideas and beliefs as meaning is a product of intention. The dubious social ontology is but a slight extension of the claim that intention and only intention determines meaning; this claim attributes to intention all the causal and rational power in this relationship; meaning is merely its by-product. That surely denies the conventions and rules of language any power in and of themselves and this, of course, looks very similar to the dubious social ontology. Why is it dubious? No alternative ontology can be developed here nor is that necessary to answer this question. What makes this social ontology dubious is that it is strongly counter-intuitive. Although it is easy to accept that our intentions, thoughts, ideas and beliefs certainly have some effect upon the social world beyond them, it is very difficult indeed to accept that there is no social world beyond and separate from them, that our thoughts and ideas constitute that world entirely, it being but a mirror of our minds. We ordinarily posit a social world beyond our intentions, thoughts, ideas and beliefs that operates upon them, that constrains not only our ideas and intentions but also our bodies. Our intuitive social ontology emphasises a world beyond our ideas and beliefs that we can to some degree change, but which also to some degree constrains us. We are both passive objects of the social world and active creators of it; parts of that world such as, for example, language, empower and constrain.

These reasons, then, require the rejection of the incorrigibility thesis; the supposed incorrigibility 'problem' is a red herring. The problem ensnares the orthodox and proponents of the reformulated fit criticism neither directly, by virtue of what they say, nor indirectly, as a consequence of some of their beliefs or arguments. The orthodox, however, should not be too quick to celebrate this escape. For, opening a gap between intention and meaning allows the possibility that participants' views are corrigible, that some can be mistaken or misguided about the point, purpose or value of some action, institution or practice while some are not. In this gap two other difficulties can arise. The first is that of deciding which participants' views as to the point of a practice are correct and which are not; this is exactly the kind of question posed by the plurality problem and it is tackled in the following section. The second raises the spectre of ideology. If agents can be mistaken about the nature of social reality, then the critical conception of ideology is on hand to explain why that may be so. Yet if we allow that there is ideology in the world, we run the risk, in taking up the internal point of view as our method of understanding and explaining the social world, of replicating in our social theories the ideological misconceptions of those whose behaviour constitutes that world. However, there is no insurance against this risk; it cannot be avoided. If there is ideology in the world, then we must accept that. The problem it presents is not unique to the orthodox method for it affects all who attempt to construct an account of some aspect of social reality whatever their method. All must have strategies to cope with ideology and, if there is a problem unique to the orthodox here, it is that they have relatively few such strategies. Ideology is a matter which the orthodox hardly trouble to address.[56] Hence, as things stand, the orthodox are open to the objection that their accounts of adjudication—or of any other aspect of social reality, for that matter—replicate ideology. This ideology critique cannot be dismissed *a priori* nor can it be ignored. Its power is examined in chapter 5. For the present, we must turn to the plurality problem.

IV THE PLURALITY PROBLEM

The plurality problem arises in the following way. If social action is purposive and rule-governed, then it can only be fully understood in light of the purposes or goals or values it supposedly serves. Access to those purposes, goals and values is best provided by determining what those whose behaviour constitutes the action think are its purposes, goals and values. In descriptive accounts of the nature of law, this issue is approached via consideration of the reasons participants in the practice 'law' have for accepting that practice and its rules. It is assumed in these accounts that participants' reasons for accepting the practice determine their understanding of the point, purpose or goal of the practice. It is far from clear that this *must* be so. It is surely in principle possible that participants could have very different reasons for accepting the practice yet agree as to its point, purpose or goal. Thus descriptive theorists who argue in this way are committed to establishing a link between reasons for acceptance and point or purpose, but that link cannot be a necessary one. They must therefore hold that, in many but not all instances, reasons for accepting a practice determine judgments about its point, purpose or goal.

When discussion of the internal point of view is framed in terms of the reasons participants have for accepting a practice and its rules, the argument to demonstrate a plurality of internal points of view easily follows. For it seems perfectly natural to observe that the participants in a practice will have a number of significantly different reasons for acceptance. For

[56] So far as I can see, the notion does not figure at all—even obliquely—in Raz's discussion of adjudication. It does appear obliquely in *LRLT*, pp. 15–17 and is briefly but explicitly discussed by MacCormick and colleagues in D. N. MacCormick and R. S. Summers (eds.), *Interpreting Statutes: A Comparative Study* (Aldershot, Dartmouth 1991), pp. 16–18. For Dworkin's brief remarks see *LE*, pp. 12–14 and 272–274.

example, among those whose behaviour constitutes the action or practice of stopping at traffic lights, some may do so for the reason that the practice represents adherence to a morally binding norm; some may conform with the practice because they think it the prudentially right thing to do (if they did not stop at the lights they or their cars might be damaged); or some may accept the practice either from fear of sanctions (legal or non-legal) or because they had never thought about following or rejecting the practice—they simply do as (almost) everyone else does. MacCormick, Dworkin and Raz recognise this. For example, MacCormick notes that '"[f]rom the internal point of view" acceptance of rules is not unreasoned, *though indeed different people may reason differently for acceptance of the same rule*' (*LRLT*, p. 64; emphasis supplied). Dworkin makes the same point but in the language of interpretation. He notes that one seeking to give an account of a social practice 'can, if he wishes, undertake only to report the *various opinions* different individuals in the community have about what the practice demands' (*LE*, p. 64; emphasis supplied). If MacCormick is right then there certainly will be a large number of different opinions to be reported. However, the student of social practices can go beyond this and offer an interpretation of the practice provided he realises that this 'different project . . . use[s] the methods his subjects use in forming their own opinions about what [the practice] really requires. He must, that is, join the practice he proposes to understand; his conclusions are then not neutral reports about what citizens . . . think but claims about [the practice] *competitive with* theirs' (*LE*, p. 64; emphasis supplied). Raz highlights this competitive dimension well when he observes 'that the law . . . is the product of the activities of human institutions intended to affect the law . . . [and] it is only natural that it reflects the *multiplicity of aims and beliefs* held by various people manning those institutions . . . It is natural to find reflected in the law conflicting values, goals and aims' (*EPD*, pp. 314–315; emphasis supplied). The only thing to add here is that what Raz takes to be true of agents in institutions affecting the law is, *a fortiori*, true of the law and its participants.

MacCormick, Dworkin and Raz accept that there is a large number of possible accounts, all constructed in accordance with the methodological sense of the internal point of view, about the point, purpose and value of any practice, rule or institution. The problem, however, is what to do in the face of this diversity. If we are to find the point or purpose or goal of a practice we must determine what those who accept that practice take to be its point, purpose or goal. Yet if they have diverse reasons for accepting the practice, and those different reasons generate different accounts of the point, purpose or goal of the practice, then this manoeuvre brings no benefit. It tells us only that there are conceivably a great number of internal points of view. The plurality problem is the problem of responding to this situation, of being able to take up, or differentiate between, one or another version of the internal point of view non-arbitrarily. That this is a problem requiring a response can be established, *prima facie*, by the following argument.

Were the plurality problem ignored, then both the fit criticism and orthodox accounts of adjudication would be trivial. This is because there is neither a singular, univocal internal point of view nor a privileged point of view within the multiplicity of views of the point, purpose or value of the practice. The orthodox and proponents of the fit criticism must construct their arguments by taking up the internal point of view. Since the many participants in the practice have different accounts of the point, purpose or value of the practice, it is impossible for these accounts and the fit criticism to conflict with one another genuinely. By 'genuine conflict' is meant a situation in which there are incompatible accounts of some univocal action, practice or institution. But competing accounts of adjudication, and the fit criticism often aimed at them, instead offer different views of the practice 'adjudication' that themselves are latent within the practice. The practice is thus not described in a univocal way and these different accounts of it are all apparently equally tenable. In MacCormick's and Dworkin's words, 'different people may reason differently for acceptance of the same rule'; the social scientist's account of a community's practices is 'competitive with' the many accounts the community may already have. Hence, orthodox accounts of adjudication and the reformulated fit criticism may rest upon different foundations, reflecting the different reasons participants in the practice have for accepting 'a' practice and, therefore, the different accounts of the point, purpose or goal of the practice those reasons generate. If this is the situation of accounts of adjudication and their orthodox critics, and of jurisprudence and the social sciences in general, then it is indeed a mistake for these disciplines 'to aspire to be more than a conjunction of lexicography with local history, or even than a juxtaposition of all lexicographies conjoined with all local histories'.[57] Assuming this to be a sorrowful situation, can it be avoided? In what follows three responses to the problem are considered. It is argued that the third is by far the most plausible. In addition, the implications of this response for the fit criticism and orthodox accounts of adjudication, as well as two objections to it, are discussed.

(a) Three responses

The first response to the plurality problem is found in MacCormick's work. It is unsatisfactory because partial. As already noted, MacCormick is unambiguous in his endorsement of the internal point of view as a methodol-

[57] J. Finnis, *Natural Law and Natural Rights* (Oxford, Clarendon 1980), p. 4. Hereinafter referred to in both text and notes as '*NLNR*' with page numbers.

ogical starting point. However, he says little about its implications. He notes, for example, that acceptance of rules or practices from the internal point of view embraces moral, non-moral and perhaps even self-interested reasons for acceptance, but does not try to distinguish between them. He simply says that the latter are parasitic upon the former and argues that the theorist need not take up the viewpoint of one who morally accepts the rule or practice in question (*LRLT*, Appendix; *HLAH*, ch. 3). This argument is one we shall return to in part (b) of this section. It is a partial response to the plurality problem because it prevents the descriptive theorist taking up only one version of the internal point of view. So, although the viewpoint of one who morally accepts the practice or rule in question is not, for MacCormick, one the theorist has to take up, there remain a number of other versions of the internal point of view open to her. Thus, the plurality problem is not avoided by MacCormick. In absence of arguments to show that it is a mistake to be concerned with the problem (arguments which MacCormick has not provided), it must be concluded that his response is not compelling.

A second response is found in some of Dworkin's remarks in *LE* (although he does not explicitly address the plurality problem). Our previous statement that Dworkin invokes the internal point of view as a methodological starting point is correct, but tells only half the story since it says nothing about the nature of interpretation. And for Dworkin, of course, theoretical disputes about the nature of law, as well as disputes about the law to be applied in particular cases, are interpretative. They involve disputes between competing constructive interpretations of the law, that is, interpretations 'aiming to make the best of what is interpreted' (*LE*, p. 61; also, p. 52). Judges and theorists 'should decide hard cases by trying to find, in some coherent set of principles about people's rights and duties, the best constructive interpretation of the political structure and legal doctrine of their community' (*LE*, p. 255). Constructive interpretations of the law have at least two independent dimensions (*LE*, p. 68). First, to interpret the law so as to make it the best it can be entails establishing that one's interpretation satisfies a requirement of fit with 'the brute facts of legal history' (*LE*, p. 255). Secondly, by contrast with other interpretations, one's interpretation must 'show . . . the community's structure of institutions and decisions—its public standards as a whole—in a better light *from the standpoint of political morality*' (*LE*, p. 256; emphasis supplied). So, for Dworkin, to give an account of a practice entails taking up the internal point of view. Doing that, he thinks, involves joining the practice and offering an account of its purpose, value or goal in the same form as participants' accounts. The form of those accounts, holds Dworkin, is that they are constructive interpretations and must satisfy requirements of fit and moral soundness.

It may be thought that Dworkin's account of constructive interpretation, when conjoined with the internal point of view, provides a response to the plurality problem. It is plain that in giving an account of a practice one should not, on Dworkin's view, construct that account on the basis of any old internal point of view, that is, on the basis of any old reasons for accepting the practice. For, as has been noted, those who accept the practice may do so for no good reason, or for self-interested, prudential or moral reasons. Their diverse reasons for acceptance may well condition their account of the point, purpose or value of the practice. The viewpoint one must take up, according to Dworkin, is that of one who tries to make the practice the best it can be, where 'best' means an account that is both a good fit with the brute facts of the practice and makes the practice compelling on grounds of political morality. That, of course, filters out some accounts of the point, purpose or value of the practice since we are to ignore participants' accounts if they are not constructive interpretations. Is this not a compelling response to the plurality problem? Does not this manoeuvre show how the theorist can non-arbitrarily distinguish between the various internal points of view?

There are at least three reasons that throw doubt upon the adequacy of this response. All three question Dworkin's account of constructive interpretation. If that account is questionable, then the response to the plurality problem is imperilled. That is because the response reduces the plurality of internal points of view that could be taken up in giving an account of a practice through the requirement that only accounts which are also constructive interpretations pass muster. Such interpretations, remember, must portray the practice in the best possible light and, when the practice in question is law, 'best' means, *inter alia*, '*best possible moral and political light*'. The first reason to doubt this account of interpretation raises this question: how does Dworkin legitimately restrict the range of 'best' interpretations so as to include only those that offer an account of a practice in the best possible *moral and political light*? Interpretations could attempt to make the best of a practice—whatever it may be—in light of other, non-political, non-moral values. Until Dworkin fills this argumentative gap neither the account of constructive interpretation nor the response to the plurality problem is compelling. This is not to say that the gap could not possibly be filled, but rather that Dworkin has yet to fill it.[58]

Were this the only difficulty with Dworkin's response to the plurality problem, he would have little to worry about. However, the second and third reasons to doubt the adequacy of his response are weightier. The second reason draws attention to the following contingent feature of our

[58] This argumentative gap is outlined by A. Marmor, *Interpretation and Legal Theory* (Oxford, Clarendon 1992), pp. 56–57. I noted a problem with Marmor's treatment of it in my review of his book: (1993) 56 *Modern L. R.* 269–272, p. 271.

world: there is a great deal of controversy about moral and political right and wrong. Because Dworkin's account of constructive interpretation is 'protestant', leaving the construction of interpretations almost entirely in the hands of individuals' perceptions of the moral and political value of a practice (there being no consensus on moral and political matters), then it should be no surprise to find that '[i]n Dworkin's interpretative approach . . . there will be as many different "descriptions" of a given legal system as there are persons thinking seriously about that system'.[59] This much seems to be implied by a number of Dworkin's remarks. For example, he tells us that the social scientist's interpretation of a practice is '*competitive with*' participants' interpretations; and that '*each* of the participants in a social practice must . . . try[. . .] to decide, *for himself*, what it really requires' (*LE*, p. 64; emphasis supplied). Hence it is not a massive exaggeration to say that there can be a vast number of competing constructive interpretations of a practice. If this is the consequence of Dworkin's response to the plurality problem, then it is indeed a poor response—it counsels an escape from plurality into plurality. Furthermore, this surely casts doubt upon Dworkin's right answer thesis. Add to this the third reason to doubt Dworkin's account of interpretation—that it lapses either into infinite regress or arbitrariness[60]—and it becomes difficult to accept his response to the plurality problem.

The third attempt to demonstrate that the theorist can non-arbitrarily distinguish between the many versions of the internal point of view is offered by John Finnis (*NLNR*, p. 13). It is found in the second and third steps of the four which constitute his methodological agenda for descriptive social and legal theory.[61] It will be worthwhile to sketch all the steps of Finnis's argument in order to, first, recap the discussion in parts (d) and (e) of section I (Finnis's first step relies heavily upon some of the arguments therein) and, second, to facilitate the discussion that follows in part

[59] B. Bix, *Law, Language and Legal Determinacy* (Oxford, Clarendon 1993), p. 108. The 'protestant' nature of Dworkin's account of interpretation and its consequences are thoroughly explored by G. Postema, '"Protestant" Interpretation and Social Practices' (1987) 6 *Law and Philosophy* 283–319, especially pp. 300–319.

[60] The argument is put by N. E. Simmonds, 'Imperial Visions and Mundane Practices' (1987) 46 *Cambridge L. J.* 465–488; A. Marmor, *supra*, note 58, at pp. 81–84, has tried to defend Dworkin against this critique by claiming that his account of interpretation is not, contrary to Simmond's view, hierarchical. Rather, it is non-viciously circular, related by means of reflective equilibrium or coherence. The textual evidence is, however, on Simmond's side: see *LE* pp. 424–425.

[61] Curiously, this ambitious methodological argument has been completely ignored by many commentators: see, for example, N. MacCormick, 'Natural Law Reconsidered' (1981) 1 *Oxford Journal of Legal Studies* 99–109; J. Harris, 'Can You Believe in Natural Law?' (1981) 44 *Modern L. R.* 729–735. An exception is S. Toddington, *supra*, note 34, ch. 4. Support for the second step in Finnis's argument is provided by: R. A. Duff, 'Legal Obligation and the Moral Nature of Law' (1980) *Juridical Review* 61–87, pp. 68–73; N. E. Simmonds, 'The Nature of Propositions of Law' (1984) *Rechtstheorie* 96–108, pp. 97–100.

(b) of this section. As a preliminary, it needs be noted that the first three steps of Finnis's argument purport to follow one from another whereas the fourth merely elucidates the relationship between the second and third steps. Thus the fourth step will be stated only in passing and will not occupy us again.

The first step holds that to give an account or description of social action and practices involves, *inter alia*, understanding the point, purpose or goal of that action or those practices. One way of finding out the point, purpose or goal of action or practices is through the language of those whose behaviour constitutes the action or practices: their languages of evaluation and self-description. This is part of what it means *for the theorist to take up the internal point of view*. This accords exactly with the methodological injunction upon which the internal point of view rests: in attempting to understand social action we must first determine the meaning or value that action has for those whose behaviour constitutes the action. However, as the plurality problem tells us, of any action or practice it is conceivable that those whose behaviour constitutes it will offer, in their languages of evaluation and self-description, a number of different accounts of its point, purpose or goal.

The second step responds to this plurality. It holds that, although participants in a practice may have a variety of reasons for accepting it, they *all* agree that one particular mode of acceptance of the practice—the mode of acceptance which consists in the moral acceptance of it—represents the essential or central case of the internal point of view. Of the variety of reasons participants in the practice 'law' might have for accepting the practice and its rules, 'any actor in the field' (*NLNR*, p. 13) would hold that reasons for acceptance other than moral approval are 'manifestly deviant, diluted or watered-down instances of the practical viewpoint that brings law into being as a significantly differentiated type of social order' (*NLNR*, p. 14). Hence, if

> there is a point of view in which legal obligation is treated as at least presumptively a moral obligation . . . , a viewpoint in which the establishment and maintenance of legal as distinct from discretionary or statically customary order is regarded as a moral ideal if not a compelling demand of justice, then such a viewpoint will constitute the central case of the legal viewpoint (*NLNR*, pp. 14–15).

This viewpoint represents part of what it means *for agents to manifest the internal point of view*. For agents such as these, the point, purpose or goal of a practice is conceived in moral terms via the notion of practical reasonableness (*NLNR*, p. 15 and ch. 5).

Accepting the practice 'law' from the central case of the internal point of view entails a concern with the existence of that practice: to 'bring it into being' or 'establish' the practice if it does not exist, to 'maintain' and uphold its 'distinctiveness' when it does exist. On the basis of these statements, it is safe to conclude that for Finnis those who morally accept a practice think the practice really matters; they will act so as to uphold or bring about the practice even when that conflicts with their self-interest. For those who do not morally accept it, the practice will not matter in quite the same way—they will perhaps be less willing to act so as to maintain it or to bring it about. If we want to understand the point, purpose or goal of some practices, then we must take up the viewpoint of those for whom those practices really—morally—matter.[62] Furthermore, all the participants in such practices accept that the central case of the internal point of view is the view of those who morally accept the practices: these participants supposedly have the best reasons for accepting the practice. Finally, note that this argument is purely contingent. It just happens to be the case that participants in particular practices regard the central case of acceptance (or the internal point of view) as consisting in moral approval of the practices. Things could well be otherwise in different communities.

Just as the second step is a response to plurality so, too, is the third. For, although Finnis has so far restricted the range of accounts of the point, purpose or goal of a particular practice to those accounts which conceive of their point, purpose or goal in moral terms, there can conceivably be a plurality of moral positions in relation to one and the same practice. (This, of course, was one of the snags that beset Dworkin's response to the plurality problem.) Think, for example, of the moral point of a practice like promising or contracting. Surely no single moral value obviously and preeminently gives point or purpose to this practice but, rather, a number of different and competing moral values could play such a role. Moreover, it could well be the case that what are thought to be moral values underpinning these practices turn out not to be such. What, then, is the descriptive theorist to do in the face of this second level of plurality?

The initial solution to the plurality problem, represented by the second step of the argument, does not work as a response to this question. This is because that solution rests entirely upon the contingency that a number (a majority? A 'significant' number? An informed minority?) of the participants in a practice happen to think that moral acceptance of a practice is the essence or central case of the internal point of view. Of course, that says nothing about the different and perhaps incompatible types of moral reason, including reasons mistakenly thought to be moral, for accepting the practice. What Finnis does say about plurality is, however, intriguing. For he thinks that a further distinction can be made by the theorist within the realm of the central case of the internal point of view. He claims that the theorist can distinguish

[62] This, of course, is not to say that all practices can and must morally matter: some may be morally neutral or insignificant.

> [a]mong those who, from a practical point of view [which entails or is closely related to the moral point of view], treat law as an aspect of practical reasonableness, [for] there will be some whose views about what practical reasonableness actually requires in this domain are, in detail, *more reasonable than others*. Thus the central case viewpoint itself is the viewpoint of those who do not only appeal to practical reasonableness but *also are practically reasonable* (*NLNR*, p. 15, emphasis supplied).

The intriguing aspect of this response to moral plurality is the promise it holds out—the promise of a union between two enterprises assumed to be very different, namely, that of giving an account of some aspect of social action and that of determining which, if any, are the moral prescriptions we must live by. This union is the consequence of the fact that, for Finnis, the theorist must discriminate between instances of accepting a practice for good moral reasons—regarding it as genuinely morally significant—and instances of accepting a practice for bad or putative moral reasons. To do that, of course, requires that the theorist know the difference between good and bad moral reasons. Being able both to know the difference and to justify that belief is close to being able to say that there exists a compelling moral viewpoint which agents and theorists alike must, either rationally or by virtue of some other condition, take up. And that takes us some way towards to embracing a form of moral realism or rationalism. For Finnis, then, there is clearly a 'dependence of even purely descriptive social theory on an implicit or explicit ethics and political theory'.[63] If this step in Finnis's argument is to avoid the plurality problem, then ethics and political theory must be taken to yield determinate answers to questions about how we ought to live and be.

The nature of the dependence between ethics or political theory, on the one hand, and descriptive social theory, on the other, is explicated by the fourth step in the argument. At least two types of dependence could be distinguished. They could range from a pure one-way process of determination and reliance, in which descriptive theory would depend, in order to be possible, upon the articulation of an ethics (or vice versa), to a two-way process of interaction and inter-dependence in which descriptive theory is made possible by, but also influences the nature of, an ethics (or vice versa). The textual evidence suggests that Finnis's view is a version of the latter. For example, Finnis speaks of the relationship between the theorists' ethical theory and his description of a practice or action from the internal point of view as being one of 'reflective equilibrium' (*NLNR*, p. 17): '[t]here is . . . a movement to and fro between, on the one hand, assessments of the human good and of its practical requirements, and on the other hand, explanatory

[63] J. Finnis, 'The Authority of Law in the Predicament of Contemporary Social Theory' (1984) 1 *Notre Dame Journal of Law, Ethics and Public Policy* 115–137, p. 115, fn. 1.

descriptions . . . of the human context in which human well-being is variously realised and variously ruined' (*NLNR*, p. 17). The relationship between political theory and descriptive social theory is, on this view, a matter of two-way interdependence, each side mutually supporting and influencing the other.

Before turning to the implications of Finnis's argument, as well as two objections that could be made to it, note two points. First, the argument purports to be an account of what is required if general descriptive theory is to be possible in the human sciences. If it is impossible then lexicography and local knowledge will be the fruit of these disciplines (and it is by no means obvious that we should be disappointed with such a crop).[64] General descriptive theory of the kind Finnis aspires to can, but need not, be closely related to theory in the tertiary sense; it must be a preliminary to Schutz's 'explicit formulation of determinate relations between a set of variables' which explain empirical regularities. It need not, however, collapse into that enterprise which many would regard as either impossible or objectionable. Descriptive theory, for Finnis, is thus theory in the secondary sense. Secondly, the descriptions constitutive of descriptive theory are doubly evaluative: they are rooted in the evaluations and distinctions of the conceptual scheme of those who morally accept the rule or practice in question; and those evaluations, distinctions and reasons for moral acceptance are themselves differentiated and evaluated by the theorist in the course of describing.

(b) Implications and objections

Finnis's response to the plurality problem avoids the snags that beset Dworkin's response. Is it therefore the case that the orthodox and proponents of the fit criticism should embrace it?

The key points in Finnis's response to the plurality problem are the second and third steps (the orthodox and proponents of the reformulated fit criticism clearly accept the first step). Moreover, of these two steps the third is most likely to be regarded as problematic. For, it is clear that if the orthodox and proponents of the reformulated fit criticism take the first step, then they cannot consistently refuse to take the second. This is because the second step is merely a restatement of the preconditions underpinning the first. The preconditions are, remember, that (i) social action is purposive and (ii) that knowledge of the purposes it tracks is initially only available

[64] Indeed, some philosophers and social and legal theorists are not. Two diverse examples, both based upon the same attempted rejection of the 'totalising' nature of classical social theory, are M. Jay, *Marxism and Totality* (Cambridge, Polity Press 1984), ch. 15 and Epilogue; J. Boyle, 'The Politics of Reason: Critical Legal Theory and Local Social Thought' (1985) 133 *University of Pennsylvania L. R.* 685–780, pp. 766–780.

to us through agents' languages of self-description, explanation and justification. If those preconditions upon knowledge of social action hold, then attention must be paid to the distinctions drawn in those languages. If it is indeed the case that all agents in the field think that the central or core case of accepting a rule or practice from the internal point of view means morally accepting that rule or practice, then there is no good reason for proponents of the fit criticism and accounts of adjudication to reject that. Of course, that is the argument Finnis makes against the undifferentiated internal point of view invoked by, *inter alios*, Hart and Raz. Of their account Finnis concludes, as already noted, that it is 'unstable and unsatisfactory because it involves a refusal to attribute significance to differences that any actor in the field . . . would count as practically significant'. If Dworkin, Raz, MacCormick and proponents of the fit criticism take the internal point of view seriously as a methodological injunction, then they, too, ought *not* to refrain from such attributions of significance.

Finnis's third step is likely to meet resistance for at least three related reasons. First, it hints at an uncongenial account of moral knowledge; secondly, it apparently collapses the conventional distinction between the descriptive human sciences and moral and political philosophy which entails, thirdly, serious amendments to the already reformulated fit criticism and orthodox accounts of adjudication. On the latter point, note that were proponents of the fit criticism to take Finnis's third step they would have to claim not only that orthodox accounts of adjudication misdescribe the practice because they fail to draw a distinction—between moral acceptance of the practice, which is the central case of the internal point of view, and non-moral acceptance, a diluted or deviant instance of the internal point of view—which those involved in the practice draw and regard as important. Rather, proponents would also have to claim that orthodox accounts mistake the nature of moral acceptance. That is, those accounts take as moral reasons for accepting the practice reasons which, on reflection, are either not moral reasons at all or are very weak moral reasons. This is the level at which the fit criticism must bite, if its proponents take the third step. Furthermore, were those who offer accounts of adjudication also to take the third step then they, too, must purport to have determined what are, and what are not, good moral reasons for accepting the practice. It is against such accounts of the nature of good moral reasons for accepting the practice that other accounts of the practice—offered by both theorists and participants—are to be judged. However, being able to take the third step, and thus being able to avoid the plurality problem, assumes answers are available to often asked and very difficult questions, namely, what is the nature and basis of morality? Can moral positions be rationally or objectively right or wrong, better or worse?

Before becoming involved in answering such questions, it is not unreasonable to imagine proponents of the fit criticism and orthodox accounts of adjudication raising another question: how, exactly, did we get here? At this point the first objection to the third step arises. The objection attempts to deny the necessity of taking this step even if the first two are accepted. Since it seeks to stop Finnis's argument somewhere between the second and third steps, it is labelled the half-way house objection; it has been powerfully put by, *inter alios*, MacCormick and Raz. It holds that, although an *agent* who accepts a rule or practice from the central case of the internal point of view must morally accept it, and that non-moral acceptance is 'parasitic' (*LRLT*, p. 287) upon moral acceptance, the *theorist* can nevertheless offer accounts of rule governed action and practices without morally accepting them.[65] The theorist need only accurately represent an agent's internal attitude to rules or practices without sharing it. Hence the natural language of the theorist is that of one 'who, without accepting [a rule or practice] . . . states the fact that others accept it';[66] 'what the legal theorist . . . must do is take as his standpoint that of a person who understands and seeks to describe legal rules as they are held from the internal point of view regardless of any commitment he himself has for or against these rules' (*HLAH*, p. 37). While cognitively aware of the fact that agents internally accept a rule or practice, the theorist may lack the volitional commitment to the rule or practice which is a condition of an agent actually manifesting the internal point of view (*HLAH*, p. 38). This ability to describe without moral commitment, to state rules and practices that others accept without accepting them personally, is manifest in what Raz has called 'detached statements'.[67] Such statements are relatively commonplace, consisting of a claim by X that, according to some rule or practice Y accepts but X does not, Y ought to do or refrain from some action. Thus meat eaters can say to vegetarian friends 'you ought not to eat this dish'; Catholics knowledgeable about Rabbinical law can tell ill-informed Jews what they ought to do; and MacCormick, a non-practising Christian, can, given sufficient time and exposure, provide an account of the rules and practices of a particular Christian sect without morally accepting those rules and practices.[68] The theorist's viewpoint, understood as (i) the ability to describe the way in which rules and practices are morally accepted by those whose behaviour constitutes them without (ii) thereby being morally committed to those rules and practices, is labelled by MacCormick the 'hermeneutic' or 'non-extreme

[65] For the same sentiments see J. Raz, *Practical Reason and Norms*, *supra*, note 37, p. 172; *NLNR*, pp. 233–237.

[66] H. L. A. Hart, *supra*, note 35, p. 99.

[67] J. Raz, *Practical Reason*, *supra*, note 37, pp. 170–179 and *Authority*, *supra*, note 37, pp.153–157.

[68] The examples are from J. Raz, *Authority*, *supra*, note 37, p. 156 and N. MacCormick, *HLAH*, p. 38.

external' point of view (*HLAH*, pp. 37–38). If this viewpoint is coherent and defensible, then it causes difficulty for Finnis's argument because it undermines the necessity of the move from step two to step three. Thus the dependency Finnis seeks to establish between descriptive and ethical theory is threatened.

How powerful is this objection? The examples used to illustrate it—of detached statements, of being able to understand a practice without being morally committed to it—are plausible, charting a position which seems intuitively right for the descriptive theorist. To hold that we have to be committed chess players or Catholics in order to understand the rules or practices of that game and that religion seems crazy. How could Finnis argue for such a position, a position which is surely the consequence of taking the third step in ignorance of the half-way house objection? There are two arguments in response, both seeking to demonstrate that the half-way house objection does not, despite appearances, provide an insurmountable block between steps two and three. Only the second argument is a success, however. To succeed this second argument must do more than simply show that the move from step two to three is not illegitimate. Noting that the move is not illegitimate does not show why it must—only that it can—be taken. It is fortunate indeed that the second argument also discharges this task.

The first argument to show that the half-way house objection does not block the move from step two to step three in Finnis's argument was suggested by Roger Shiner.[69] It holds that the examples which support the objection—of detached statements and, of what appears to be the same thing, one's ability to be cognitively aware of rules or practices and of the fact that others accept them from the internal point of view, without oneself being volitionally committed to those rules and practices—are not compelling. This is because they depend upon suspect supporting arguments drawn from Austinian ordinary language philosophy and the philosophy of mind and belief. From this step Shiner's argument appears to (i) rule out the legitimacy of detached statements altogether and (ii) provide the basis for an argument that the move from the second step to the third must be taken. The former is problematic for Finnis in light of a number of statements in which he embraces detached statements (*NLNR*, pp. 16, 21 and pp. 234–237). The latter is problematic for Shiner because he appears to reject the possibility of detached statements while denying that the consequence of this is that 'in order for the theorist . . . to "understand" a [practice] . . . , he or she must make a full moral commitment to . . . [the practice]'.[70] But rejecting the possibility of detached statements leaves

[69] See his *Norm and Nature* (Oxford, Clarendon 1992), pp. 54–65 and ch. 5.
[70] *Ibid*., p. 157.

Shiner with a choice between either external statements or statements of moral commitment (which are entailed by Finnis's third step). And, despite Shiner's assumption to the contrary, there does not appear to be a *via media* here.[71]

The second argument to refute the half-way house objection is more powerful. Moreover, one need look no further than Finnis's text in order to find it. At first glance it may appear contradictory that Finnis's argument as outlined so far, which accepts the possibility and hints at the necessity of moving from the second to the third step, stands alongside other statements in *NLNR* which suggest that this move need not, after all, be made. The recalcitrant textual evidence consists of: (i) his remarks about the independence of descriptive social theory from a 'concern about what ought to be done' (*NLNR*, p. 16) and about 'the different uses to which the more or less common stock of theoretical concepts will be put by . . . normative and . . . descriptive (historical) theorists' (*NLNR*, p. 21); (ii) his acceptance of the legitimacy of detached statements (*NLNR*, pp. 234–237). Can both sets of statements be consistently made in conjunction with an argument demonstrating the importance of taking the third step? That they can is clear, for the following reason. Finnis's initial remarks, which suggest that for the purposes of some kinds of descriptive theory the third step can be avoided, do not show it is a mistake to take the third step. However, if Finnis's conclusion is that the descriptive theorist can simply ignore the third step, then he is indeed in danger of undermining whatever positive argument he has for taking that step. By contrast, if his argument is that in *some* circumstances the descriptive theorist can *postpone* that step, can be *temporarily* less concerned about what ought to be done, then there is no such risk. An argument to that effect is found in *NLNR*.

The argument, which is conditional, has already been noted in passing. It holds that, if descriptive theory is to be more than 'a conjunction of lexicography with local history, or even . . . a juxtaposition of all lexicographies conjoined with all local histories' (*NLNR*, p. 4), then descriptive theorists must at some point take the third step. Otherwise the risk is that such theories collapse into 'a vast rubbish heap of miscellaneous facts described in a multitude of incommensurable terminologies' (*NLNR*, p. 17). These are strong claims and must be closely examined. To that end, consider the role of the descriptive theorist as sketched so far. To gain knowledge of social action she must presuppose that such action is engaged in by linguistically constituted, purposive beings. To have language is to have rules of language. Understanding those rules, and whatever other rules and practices a community may have, entails understanding that community's languages of self-description, explanation and justification. If the members of that

[71] *Ibid.*, pp. 157–158.

community are purposive beings, then their languages of self-description, justification and evaluation should disclose a range of accounts of the point, purpose or goal of particular practices and rules. Retrieving and understanding these accounts is part of what it means to take up the *Verstehen* approach to understanding social life. To understand social life, on such a view, is, at the very least, to make sense of it from the viewpoint and in terms of the language, with all its discriminations and evaluations, of those whose behaviour constitutes it. This much is the result of accepting the first step in Finnis's argument: the thrust of the first section of the essay was to show that this step must be taken. The alternative is to embrace an epistemologically dubious account of facts and description.

Now some rules and practices track moral purposes or goals. If that is the case, the descriptive theorists' account of those rules and practices must register this. This is the second step in Finnis's argument and it is one which few, if any, orthodox legal theorists have good reason to resist. (They agree, that is, that the central case of accepting some practices or rules from the internal point of view is to morally accept them, to be fully volitionally committed to them, and that other forms of non-moral acceptance are parasitic upon, or diluted versions of, the central case.) If our descriptive theorist takes the first two steps he or she will provide an account of a rule-governed practice, which, let us suppose, turns out to bear some relation to our own practice of gift-giving, in terms of the language of those whose behaviour constitutes the practice. Moreover, suppose it turns out that the practice is conceived by that community in moral terms as tracking, for example, the value of respect for persons. Furthermore, suppose also that it is accepted in the community that those who engage in this practice, having morally accepted it and thus conceived its point or purpose in moral terms, manifest the central case of the internal point of view. Surely the descriptive theorist can be content to leave matters here?

Only if two conditions are satisfied. First, moral acceptance of the practice must be clearly demarcated within the community's languages of self-description, justification and evaluation; secondly, those languages must speak with one voice about the nature of moral acceptance, about what good, bad and putative moral reasons for accepting the practice look like. If either of these conditions does not obtain, then descriptive theory appears to collapse into lexicography. That collapse can be avoided if the third step is taken. How?

Consider the absence of each condition in turn. Absence of the first condition entails that the theorist has to decide what, from the range of possibilities embodied in the languages, practices and rules of the community, constitutes moral acceptance. There are at least two ways of doing this. First, the theorist could attempt to find out more about what the community regards as moral acceptance by, for example, studying their culture more deeply or by having the community respond to questionnaires. As a result, the theorist will learn that the community has either a shared, implicit conception, or a range of competing conceptions, of what moral acceptance looks like. In each case, what constitutes moral acceptance is, eventually, seen by the theorist to be clearly demarcated by the community. In the first instance, the theorist would only need to take the third step so as to avoid lexicography if she aspired to comparative study of the practices and rules of various communities. However, if the theorist refrained from the third step and the communities under study differed in their accounts of moral acceptance, then the fruits of her labour would be a conjunction of lexicographies with local histories, a vast heap of miscellaneous facts described in incommensurable terminologies. She would be able to give an account of the practices and rules of various communities, attempting to show their similarities and differences in his or her own language (not the language of the communities under study). He or she could also note that they have various different accounts of the point of their respective practices (and thus, perhaps, incomparable practices) because they have different conceptions of what it is to morally accept those practices. This situation is an inter-community manifestation of the situation that would arise were the second condition not to obtain.

The second way in which the theorist can respond to the absence of the first condition is by discriminating between various accounts of moral acceptance by reference to her account of what good moral reasons for accepting a practice or rule look like. This process would allow room for the critical assessment of rules and practices because it leaves open the possibility that they do not have any genuine moral point or purpose. Moreover, this response must also be made to the failure of the second condition if lexicography is to be avoided. If the second condition does not hold then the community will disagree *inter se* about what moral acceptance looks like, having a range of competing candidates for the title 'good moral reasons for accepting rule or practice RP'. In light of this, the theorist can do one of two things. Either report this fact and thus provide a collection of local histories and lexicographies (a possibility which *ex hypothesi* should be avoided). Or attempt to discriminate between putative and genuine forms of moral acceptance within that community. The latter, a process in which descriptive theory depends upon an explicit ethics or political theory, entails taking the third step.

Thus the argument for taking the third step, which also shows when the descriptive theorist can and cannot avoid it, goes in this way: if lexicography is to be avoided in the face of the failure of the two conditions, then the descriptive theorist must invoke an ethical or political theory. At this point the second objection to taking the third step becomes pertinent. It is the potentially devastating argument that, whatever positive reasons there are for taking that step, they are a waste of time because moral and political arguments are beset, as Finnis himself sometimes seems to suggest, by incommensurability.[72] That is, the values in those arguments sometimes display a lack of transitivity which means we can neither rank them higher and lower than one another, nor establish that they are of equal value. Therefore, we cannot rationally choose between them, in the sense of having *compelling* reasons to choose one way or another, although such a choice is based on reasons and hence not arbitrary.[73] That being true, it follows that a number of moral and political positions cannot be compellingly justified. If the political or moral theories, or even segments thereof, upon which our descriptions of social action depend are unjustifiable, then the plurality problem reiterates once the third step is taken. (We will face a position rather like that faced by Dworkin's response to the plurality problem: there might be as many accounts of a practice as there are people who hold incommensurable value positions.) So why bother to take the third step if it no longer functions as a response to the plurality problem? In the face of widespread incommensurability there is no longer an advantage—the advantage of avoiding lexicography in descriptive social science—in ensuring that descriptive theory depends upon an explicit ethics or political theory.

There are three ways in which the power of this objection can be reduced.[74] First, proponents must offer compelling examples of incommensurable moral and political values and this they rarely do. That is not to say that the burden of proof falls entirely upon proponents of incommensurability; a similar burden must also be borne by proponents of commensurability. Neither burden looks easy to discharge in light of our third point. The second, however, is that over and beyond adducing plausible examples, proponents of incommensurability must show that it is widespread in our moral and political thought. For, if it is not, it is indeed unlikely to cause a problem for those faced with the plurality problem in the effort to explain and understand some aspect of social life. Showing incommensurability to be widespread, to be the rule rather than the exception, is quite a different task from that involved in making conceptual sense of the notion and every bit as difficult. Most recent work takes up the conceptual task, which is entire-

[72] A recent statement by Finnis is 'Natural Law and Legal Reasoning', ch. 6 of R. P. George (ed.), *Natural Law Theory: Contemporary Essays* (Oxford, Clarendon 1992), particularly pp. 136–148. The statement about incommensurability in the text owes a good deal to the excellent discussion in J. Raz, *The Morality of Freedom* (Oxford, Clarendon 1986), ch. 13 and J. Griffin, *Well-Being* (Oxford, Clarendon 1986), ch. 5.

[73] Raz, *The Morality of Freedom*, *supra*, note 72, p. 338–339.

[74] I explored two of these possibilities in a little more depth in 'Rights, Values and Controversy' (1992) 5 *Canadian Journal of Law and Jurisprudence* 195–213, p. 208 and 'Natural Law Now' (1993) 56 *Modern L. R.* 745–760, pp. 757–758 (on Finnis on incommensurability). We learn from B. Bix, *supra*, note 59, p. 97 that Dworkin has taken up a similar position—though he thinks moral experience far less equivocal than I do—in lectures.

ly commendable, but this has had the unwelcome consequence of encouraging the facile invocation of the notion.[75] Many mistakenly assume that the fact that incommensurability makes conceptual sense shows that it exists everywhere in our lives. The third way of deflating the objection consists of a question: how do we proceed with the argument if both proponents of incommensurability and commensurability produce plausible examples? In other words, what do we do if neither our intuitions nor our moral experience are univocal on this issue? Until these three issues are addressed the incommensurability objection cannot be compelling.

Suppose that there are sound reasons to take Finnis's third step, reasons that show his response to the plurality problem is compelling. What implications does this have for orthodox accounts of adjudication and the second version of the fit criticism? The consequences for the latter are severe. This is because it seems unlikely that the fit criticism can be twice reformulated and remain consistent with the statements of it outlined above. The first reformulation, remember, served to free the fit criticism from a dubious account of the nature of facts and description. That reformulation could be justified on the grounds of interpretative charity. Thus the second version of the criticism took on board the *Verstehen* approach and the methodological injunction to take up the internal point of view. The problem with reformulating the criticism in accordance with the third step of Finnis's argument is simple. From the sample statements of it, above, it is plain that proponents do not set up the criticism in that way. In fact, there is precious little to suggest that the vast majority of pedlars of the criticism are even aware of the problems with the internal point of view, not to mention the steps necessary to differentiate it and so avoid lexicography. Nor do they appear aware of the complexity of the apparently simple task of offering a description of any segment of social action. The reason for saying this is simple: if proponents of the criticism were indeed aware of the issues involved here, then they could not frame the criticism in the way they do. The criticism is invoked in such a way as to mask its complexity—with no appreciation that any argument appealing to 'social reality' or the 'facts' is, without more, dubious (how do we come to know what the facts of the matter are?). Appreciation of what is involved when invoking the criticism would, however, mitigate against flippant use. Until the criticism is recast it must be read as if its proponents had addressed these complexities—only then could it have any weight. However, charity—particularly in matters of interpretation—is not always a virtue. To expend it upon existing proponents of the fit criticism may be to encourage future laxity in the face of complexity and to obscure both the preconditions and duties of criticism.

[75] A useful collection of such recent work, some of it published elsewhere, is R. Chang (ed.), *Incommensurability, Incomparability, and Practical Reason* (Cambridge, Mass., Harvard U. P. 1997).

The dilemma for proponents of the criticism is this. Either stick with the criticism as outlined in section I (d) and so rely upon, or at least make statements consistent with, a dubious account of the nature of facts and description. Or, reformulate the criticism so as to avoid that dubious account. That, however, is something of an Odyssean journey, requiring not only the rejection of the original version of the criticism, but also the acceptance of an account of the relationship between descriptive theory and ethics or political theory, as well as an account of the nature of ethical and moral values, that they may find uncongenial.

A slightly different but equally grand either/or also ensnares orthodox accounts of adjudication. If proponents of those accounts seriously think that *Verstehen*, incorporating the methodological sense of the internal point of view, is the method by which to obtain knowledge of social action, then they must address the implications of that belief. One implication is the plurality problem and the either/or it poses is this: either accounts of the point, purpose or goal of social practices are constructed on the basis of a multiplicity of (perhaps incommensurable) points of view; or one such point of view can non-arbitrarily be chosen. Our discussion has suggested that a plurality of points of view about a practice—adjudication—are found in the range of different reasons participants might have for accepting the practice. If there is indeed a variety of kinds of acceptance, each representing a viewpoint which the descriptive theorist of a practice can take up, then descriptive social theory appears to be little more than a form of lexicography, confined to reporting a multiplicity of accounts of the nature of 'a' practice. (Although the very fact of such a plurality of views about the nature of the practice casts doubt upon the assumption that there is only one practice.) However, the only plausible argument offered to discriminate legitimately between competing internal points of view held that the viewpoint of one who has good moral reasons for accepting the practice can be privileged. For many, not the least problematic aspect of this argument is the claim that good moral reasons are knowable and that a claim to know them can be rationally defended. Claims such as these seem illiberal and dissonant with the moral temper of our culture. They are certainly incompatible with MacCormick's Humean account of moral values and practical reason, although he has recently come to doubt this account (*LRLT*, ch. 10 and foreword, p. *xvi*), and probably incompatible with Dworkin's coherentist moral epistemology. ('Probably' because it is by no means clear that a coherence account of practical deliberation such as Dworkin endorses—an account which holds that in particular problematic instances we ought to do what the account that makes our other intuitions, beliefs and values 'most' coherent tells us to do—is incompatible with either moral rationalist claims that some ends of human action, including some moral goals, rationally must be pursued or moral realist accounts of what makes statements such as these true.)[76] Nevertheless, it is claims such as these that proponents of accounts of adjudication must make if the plurality problem is as pressing as has been suggested. It was argued that a journey towards some account of substantive rationality—a rationality of ends among which we can include some moral and political ends—must be the orthodox response to the grand either/or they face. They may regard that response with suspicion, but it is one made necessary by the conjunction of the invocation of the internal point of view with a desire to avoid the plurality problem.

V CONCLUSION

A brief summary of the arguments in this chapter is necessary. It was argued, first, that the initial version of the fit criticism is compatible with an untenable account of the nature of facts and description and invokes a conception of theory (theory in the tertiary sense) that might be unsuitable to this domain. Second, that in order to avoid the problems which arise from the untenable account, the criticism must be reformulated so as to incorporate the *Verstehen* approach to explaining and understanding social action. Third, that approach—an approach also favoured by the orthodox—leads to the incorrigibility and plurality problems. We argued that the former is something of a red herring whereas the latter is an altogether more difficult snag. The fourth step was to argue that, of the responses to the plurality problem which were considered, the best was offered by Finnis. However, that Finnis's response was the only one the orthodox could take up in order to avoid the plurality problem has one unwelcome implication, namely, it apparently incorporates a discomfiting and unfashionable view of moral and political values. Yet the effects of this response to the plurality problem upon the orthodox are nowhere near as drastic as its consequences for the fit criticism, since it was argued that the criticism could not be amended so as to incorporate it. The inference to be drawn is unambiguous: so much the worse for existing versions of the fit criticism.

In the course of these arguments answers to the three questions with which we began were offered. Accounts of adjudication are descriptive theories. As such, they must begin by offering accounts of that practice from

[76] S. Hurley, 'Coherence, Hypothetical Cases, and Precedent' (1990) 10 *Oxford Journal of Legal Studies* 221–251, gives an account and defence of Dworkin's coherence account of legal deliberation. In her book *Natural Reasons* (New York, Oxford U. P. 1989), she defends a coherentist account of practical deliberation in general terms and argues in chs. 9 and 14 that such an account is consistent with ethical cognitivism (under which banner we might subsume moral realism and moral rationalism). For Dworkin's own remarks see *Taking Rights Seriously* (London, Duckworth 1978), p. 162 and p. 278 of 'A Reply by Ronald Dworkin' in M. Cohen (ed.), *supra,* note 22, 247–300.

the viewpoint of those whose behaviour constitutes the practice. The accounts offered must reflect the distinctions and evaluations made in the participants' languages of self-description, justification and explanation. To give an account of those languages is to give an account of a conceptual scheme or to indulge in what we have called theory in the secondary sense. How well or badly particular accounts fare in representing the languages and conceptual schemes of participants in a practice is a criterion of their success or failure. Moreover, another indicator of their success may well be the steps such accounts take beyond theory in the secondary sense. Note that while our discussion of orthodox accounts of adjudication shows that they are not best regarded as theories in the tertiary sense, and the conceptions of 'theory' and 'description' in play should be understood accordingly, no compelling arguments against the possibility of theory in the tertiary sense were offered here. Nor has any insurmountable incompatibility between tertiary and secondary theory been identified. Rather, the latter can be regarded as entirely compatible with the former, as the next chapter endeavours to show. The chapter takes issue with those discussions of method in jurisprudence and the human sciences which assume that the effort to understand and explain social life cannot go beyond secondary theory. The arguments to that end are disfigured by either exaggeration or *non sequitur*.

How well or badly do accounts of social action or practices accommodate or respond to the plurality of accounts of the point, purpose or value of the action, rule or practice in question and, hence, in some circumstances, a plurality of accounts of the moral value of that action, rule or practice? The answer to this rather verbose question is another indicator of the success or failure of accounts of adjudication. A response to the plurality problem that insists upon a dependence between descriptive theory, on the one hand, and ethical or political theory, on the other, was suggested here. In so far as that response is compelling, the degree to which it can be incorporated into orthodox accounts of adjudication and the fit criticism, is another way in which to assess their success or failure. Of course, it might be thought that this response has no advantage because it invokes a dubious account of normative (essentially moral) values. And, while it is indeed true that the supposed conflict between moral realist and rationalist accounts of the nature of values, on the one hand, and those non-realist, non-rationalist accounts, on the other, has implications for the particular argument suggested in this chapter, a broader point within the argument remains unscathed. It is a point about the obvious and unavoidable overlap between supposedly 'descriptive' and 'normative' theory, a point often and conclusively made with the human sciences and philosophy of the last fifty years but, judging from the remarks of critics of the orthodoxy noted at the beginning of this chapter, equally often forgotten within jurisprudence.

The point remains even if moral rationalism and realism are false, although how that might be established is difficult to imagine. Arguments by reference to moral experience or moral language will not carry much weight if it is true that such experience and language are not univocal. If we sometimes speak as moral realists, and sometimes as non-realists, what weight can this have? A better approach invokes the 'no-difference thesis' to show the redundancy of moral realism.[77] The argument is that, even if realism (or rationalism) be true, it makes no difference to our reasons, actions and significant non-meta-ethical beliefs. It would therefore make no difference to any solution to the plurality problem. This part of our business must for the moment remain unfinished, although it, like some other loose ends, will be tackled in the concluding chapter. Our immediate priority is an examination of the implications of the orthodox method as we have so far unpacked it.

[77] A fine discussion is J. Waldron, 'The Irrelevance of Moral Objectivity', ch. 7 of *Natural Law Theory, supra*, note 72.

3
The Sovereign Individual

> [T]he interpretation of action . . . [is] a . . . process in which the subject is not naively enthroned, but rather systematically and critically unveiled. J. Thompson, *Critical Hermeneutics* (1981), p. 143.

A common view of ourselves, found in much moral and political philosophy, in metaphysics and literature, and many of the supposedly separate human sciences such as economics and, perhaps less so, sociology, holds that 'we'—individual agents—are the source of all value in the world. Morally and ethically, 'we' matter most in the world both as a species and as creators of what is valuable. Yet it is not, on this view, as a collectivity or group that 'we' create this moral and ethical significance, but as individual agents. As individual agents we are capable of transcending the collective into which we are born and in which we initially flourish. Furthermore, the collective, with its institutions, practices and structures, only exists and has significance as a result of the actions of individual agents. If individual agents choose to do things differently then, in time, the nature of the collectivity will change. On this view, the individual is sovereign in a double sense: first, morally and ethically, because individuals are sole creators of moral and ethical significance in the world and, second, in explanatory terms, since the actions and beliefs of individuals determine the nature of social structures, institutions and practices. Both senses are often associated with the vague, loosely specified notion of individualism. The methodological sense in which the individual is sovereign appears in the approach to explanation and understanding in the human sciences that philosophers call methodological individualism; the moral and ethical sense arises as but an echo of many versions of political liberalism, on the one hand, and moral and ethical egoism, on the other.[1]

This chapter looks again at the orthodox method. The previous chapter clarified what this method amounts to and highlighted two difficulties. Both difficulties—that of resolving the plurality problem and that of accommodating ideology—are general in the sense that they affect this method wherever deployed, be it in the jurisprudential or any other context. However,

[1] A good introductory treatment of these matters is S. Lukes, *Individualism* (Oxford, Blackwell 1973), chs. 15, 16, 17 and part three. Good contemporary treatments of methodological individualism and its competitors are P. Birnbaum and J. Leca, *Individualism* (Oxford, Clarendon 1990) chs. 1–4, R. Bhargava, *Individualism in the Social Sciences* (Oxford, Clarendon 1992) and P. Pettit, *The Common Mind* (New York, Oxford U. P. 1996), part II.

when encountered in the former context the plurality problem raises an additional snag, namely, that a plausible solution to it suggests reliance upon what many will regard as an unacceptable account of moral values. The problem of ideology is not, of course, particularly acute for the orthodox nor is it unique to them. It arises because the orthodox must sever any necessary link between meaning and intention and, in so doing, ensure that the views of participants as to the point, purpose and value of the practices and institutions in which they act are corrigible. Severing the link between meaning and intention is, as was argued, the correct thing to do; that this creates conceptual space for the ideology critique does not in any way disgrace the orthodox. The only complaint appropriately laid at their door is that they do little to respond to the ideology critique. Whether or not that critique, as developed by heretics, is ultimately plausible, is explored in chapter 5. The task of the current chapter is to examine the degree to which the orthodox method subscribes to the picture just sketched of the sovereign individual. More precisely, we examine the degree to which the orthodox method takes the individual to be sovereign in the methodological rather than the moral and political sense. At least two connected arguments might be made to show that the orthodox method embraces the sovereign individual.

First, it might be argued that the internal point of view privileges a reason-based explanation and understanding of actions, institutions and practices over a cause-based explanation. Indeed, it might be thought that the internal point of view assumes that reason-based and cause-based explanations are actually incompatible. The truth of either of these accusations would seem to commit the orthodox to holding that the individual is the primary unit upon which attempts at understanding and explaining social actions, practices and institutions must be based. At least, this would seem to follow if it is assumed that reasons are a property ascribable only to agents and their actions and that causes are either not ascribable to agents and their actions; or, if they are, they are not the primary source of plausible explanations or understandings of agents and their actions. Secondly, it might be argued that either the internal point of view privileges a methodological individualist over a methodological holist explanation and understanding of action, institutions and practices, or that it takes the two different types of explanation to be entirely incompatible. The truth of either claim seemingly commits the orthodox to the explanatory primacy of the individual agent in an obvious way: it is the actions of individuals that drive and determine social institutions, practices and structures. The latter are but the side-effects—intended or unintended—of individuals acting in certain ways. On this view, a football club is but a collection of individuals held together by a common purpose; there is nothing to the institution other than these individuals—players, coaches, physiotherapists and investors—and their actions. There is no supra-individual 'thing' or social fact by reference to which the institution must be explained and understood.

Two points must be noted about these arguments. First, they gain support from an obvious feature of orthodox legal scholarship, namely, its almost exclusive fascination with the activities of judges when deciding (mainly hard) cases. Many of the orthodox devote themselves to a close textual analysis of particular judicial decisions and a slightly more generalised analysis of the ways in which such decisions change, affirm or conflict with pre-existing decisions. The dominant voice in their doctrinal scholarship is that of the independent counsel to judges, advising not just on a particular case, but on the general pattern of development in the area of law in which the case arises, and with an eye to generic rule of law values such as consistency and coherence. The compliment of this judge-centric approach is sometimes repaid by the judges themselves when they adopt or commend orthodox scholars' analyses of particular cases or of a particular branch of the law. Clearly, the near-exclusive concentration upon judicial decision-making betokens the view that this is indeed where the explanatory action is—the implication being that to understand the law one must understand the actions of these individuals. These individuals and the decisions they make are apparently the central point of the legal system, supposedly determining the nature and operation of that set of actions, institutions and practices. Thus the orthodoxy apparently embraces the sovereign individual and the sovereign individual is, unsurprisingly, a judge.

Second, the arguments as stated say nothing about the nature of explanation and understanding and how, if at all, they differ. In chapter 1 we were loath to draw any real distinction between these two notions and that position is ultimately defended here. However, the reasons for thinking the two are not worth distinguishing are not articulated until section III. It will therefore be useful to repeat the difference between explanation and understanding as traditionally understood. Briefly and simply put, it is that the former is regarded as the realm of causality, whereas the latter is the realm of meaning.[2] Attempts to *explain* social action, institutions and practices have traditionally been regarded as a matter of unearthing some causal law of which the phenomenon in question, in combination with some set of background conditions, is an instance. The human sciences aim, on this view, at the development and illustration of a corpus of causal laws, as is the

[2] Much more discriminating and informed accounts of the supposed differences between understanding and explanation are found in, *inter alia*, J. Habermas, *On the Logic of the Social Sciences* (Cambridge, Polity Press 1988); K-O Apel, *Understanding and Explanation* (Cambridge, Mass., The MIT Press 1984); G. von Wright, *Explanation and Understanding* (London, Routledge and Kegan Paul 1971); and P. Ricoeur, *Hermeneutics and the Human Sciences* (Cambridge, C. U. P. 1981).

alleged practice within the natural sciences. By contrast, *understanding* action, institutions and practices is said to be little more than a matter of recovering their meaning for the participants. Understanding is therefore unavoidably a matter of interpretation, of sympathetic reconstruction of the significance the action, institution or practice has for those engaged in it. This is sometimes characterised as a redescription of the action, institution and practice and said to generate genuine but non-causal understanding. Described thus, there is an obvious incompatibility between the process of explaining and that of understanding. In what follows it should be obvious from the context when I intend to invoke this traditional distinction between understanding and explanation and when I invoke the better usage, the usage which refrains from making a distinction between the two. Finally, note that the explanation/understanding cleavage spawns a whole family of related terms and a multiplicity of synonyms. So, the divide is often stated as a conflict between causality and meaning, or causes and reasons, and occasionally as a divide between interpretativism and something else, be it behaviourism, empiricism, positivism or the deductive-nomological method. Within legal philosophy the distinction has been drawn as a tension between the internal and external points of view. Some attempt is made here to contain the number of terms used to characterise the supposed conflict: the preferred argot is explanation versus understanding. However, it might be wise to highlight other ways in which the distinction will occasionally be drawn here by listing some opposites. The first list of terms that follows are synonyms for explanation and the second are synonyms for understanding: (i) causes (or cause-based), causality, external, empiricist; (ii) reasons (or reason-based), meaning, internal and interpretive.

The claim urged in this chapter is that the orthodox do not and should not embrace the sovereign individual. Section I uses an apparently simple example to show the range and complexity of the questions asked in an effort to explain and understand human action, institutions and practices. When we look instead at any reasonably complex segment of social life such as, for example, law, the questions remain the same but the level of complexity increases astronomically. It is banal but true that social life—with its range of constitutive actions, practices and institutions—is indeed complex. Section II examines the orthodox position towards the sovereign individual and shows, contrary to first impressions, that it is not a view they embrace. Section III offers an argument, albeit hesitant and incomplete, as to why it is right to reject the sovereign individual. The argument is developed via an analysis of a methodological position labelled compatibilism.[3] It is suggested that compatibilism is a compelling method for the human

[3] The reasons for using this term will become apparent in due course. For now, though, note that its use has nothing to do with the 'compatibilist' position in philosophical disputes about the nature of free will and determinism.

sciences and, hence, appropriate for those seeking to explain and understand law and adjudication. If there are good reasons to be a methodological compatibilist, then there are good reasons to reject the sovereign individual. That, at least, is what section III attempts to show.

I SAY IT WITH FLOWERS

The simple example is stolen from Martin Hollis and, like all of his work, illustrates the crucial issues in a marvellously succinct way. The example illustrates the range of questions which must be asked in order to explain and understand human action, practices and institutions. Furthermore, these questions can easily be overlooked when considering complex examples drawn from actual experience. Hence two other examples, drawn from actual, legal experience, are used to illustrate the level of complexity that can arise. They are the House of Lords decision in *R* v. *Caldwell* and the Court of Appeal judgment in *Re Selectmove*.[4] Hollis's example is this:

> Let us suppose that, soon after the balcony scene of some real-life Romeo and Juliet, Romeo sends Juliet a bunch of red orchids with a card inscribed, 'A beauteous flower for when next we meet.' This episode is the text and I shall use 'text' to refer not just to speech but to any act whose author intends others to understand something by it. What is its interpretation? The question is ambiguous between meaning and explanation and I introduce the elements of our discussion by splitting it into four. First, there is the overt meaning—in the case of speech [or any other 'text'], 'What did he succeed in saying?' Second, there is the covert meaning—'What did he intend to say and intend in saying it?' Third, there is the overt explanation—'Why was the utterance apt?' Fourth, there is the covert explanation—'What was his motive in uttering the text?'[5]

This example is a heuristic tool and does not beg any questions about the method appropriate to explaining and understanding social life. Anyone familiar with the range of methods expounded within the philosophy of the human sciences over the last century and a half will be able to recognise and label the possibilities it suggests. Suffice it to say that Romeo's 'text' is prima facie susceptible to analysis in terms of both meaning and causality and doing both requires not only an inquiry into the reason and motives he may have, but also an account of the context—the conventions, practices and institutions—'framing' the action. The fulcrum, for Hollis, of covert meaning and explanation is the range of possible intentions, reasons and motives Romeo could have had and did actually have. Since the range is vast, our way of determining them relies partially upon charting the inter-

[4] *R* v. *Caldwell* [1981] 1 All ER 961; *Re Selectmove* [1995] 2 All ER 531.

[5] M. Hollis, 'Say it with flowers', ch. 7 of J. Tully (ed.), *Meaning and Context* (Cambridge, Polity Press 1988), p. 136.

play between his act and its context (the latter being the domain of overt meaning and explanation). So, for example, the obvious meaning of the deed would be a declaration of courtship and Romeo's reason and motive in so acting would be to demonstrate his love for Juliet. There will, no doubt, be a limited number of moves that Romeo could make within this social context that could possibly be taken to be acts of courtship and, if giving flowers is one such move, then we are well on our way to determining its overt meaning and explanation. Romeo succeeded in declaring love for Juliet and, if he is indeed in love with her, that is why his deed is apt.

But there is no guarantee that Romeo succeeded in doing this, or even had reason and motive to do this, by sending red orchids. It could, for example, be the case that this particular flower, in this particular shade, is regarded as particularly base in this society. A social convention might well subvert what Romeo intends and has reason to say with flowers. Alternatively, once we learn of this convention our assessment of Romeo's reasons and motives might change. How could he be unaware of it? If we doubt that he could be so ignorant, we might instead think that his reasons and motives are altogether less elevated. What Romeo is saying with flowers might indeed be an insult. Whether insult or act of courtship is thus determined by a combination of the context and Romeo's reasons and motives and, when operating at the level of overt meaning and explanation, the former does most work. Although the overt meaning and explanation of the action seems quite easy to determine, being little more than a matter of understanding the context, charting the moves that could be made within it and fitting Romeo's move within them, its covert meaning and explanation is altogether more difficult to fathom. So difficult, indeed, that some historians and philosophers have eschewed it, except for one step: that of determining possible and plausible reasons the agent *could* have had for the action.

On this view, once the overt meaning of Romeo's deed is determined we need only find a range of plausible reasons he could have had for it. These scholars think it pointless to look much beyond the overt meaning of the action, beyond the list of plausible reasons Romeo *could* have had, since it is neither possible nor necessary to give a covert explanation of the action, to formulate Romeo's *actual* motive in acting this way, to determine which out of the range of reasons for the action was *really* his. As Hollis puts it, explanation and understanding on this account is a matter of gathering yarn (provided by one's understanding of context), knitting from it a cap for the actor to wear (a list of plausible reasons for the action), but refraining from questioning whether or not this cap was indeed the one he was wearing.[6] Hollis maintains that this extra step can be taken, but the job of determin-

[6] M. Hollis, p. 140.

ing whether Romeo was actually wearing the cap made for him demands an account of substantive rationality. The problems latent within that task cannot be explored here. Even if the fourth step of offering a covert explanation of action is eschewed, a great deal of work remains if we are to take steps one to three.

This apparently simple example raises a host of difficult questions. These questions remain the same, in qualitative terms, when we move from a supposedly simple hypothetical to an instance of actual social behaviour. However, they usually become even more difficult because of the richness and complexity of the action, or the practice or the institution of which it is part. This is especially so in relation to those practices and institutions that embody a reasonably high level of reflective concern among participants. That is, practices and institutions that attempt to monitor their own progress and development, and that make giving an account of this a significant part of the practice itself. Consider a trivial example. Part of the role of being a coach of any large, European football club is the duty, sometimes honoured, sometimes not, to account for the team's performance, to explain to the media and supporters how this game or series of games fits with the aspirations of the club. Particular players may be singled out for praise and blame, depending upon the team's progress and coaches are assessed not only by the team's progress but by virtue of their control over it. This practice and role is therefore one which insists on some degree of self-reflection and monitoring and encourages the effort to integrate present with past actions within the practice. It is not a practice in which there is a particularly high-level of such reflection and monitoring, but it undoubtedly exists. And, one might add, if it exists here, then it will exist almost everywhere.

It certainly exists within the contemporary practice and institution of adjudication. Indeed, it might be said that the very high degree of reflective concern and monitoring—embodied in, for example, the judicial convention or, in some jurisdictions, duty, to give reasons, usually in written form, for decisions—is one of the hallmarks of this practice. A good example is *R* v. *Caldwell.* One of the questions for the House of Lords in this case was about the contours of the *mens rea* concept of recklessness. The majority decided that recklessness included both knowingly running the risk of bringing about the *actus reus* of a crime and unwittingly running the risk of bringing about the *actus reus* of a crime, the risk in both instances being an unreasonable one to take. The minority dissenting judgment, delivered by Lord Edmund-Davies, held that recklessness included only knowingly running the risk of bringing about the *actus reus* of a crime, that risk being an unreasonable one to take. The decision was controversial, but for our purposes the crucial point is the steps the judges took in offering an account of the decision they came to, stating, *inter alia*, why they thought it was correct, how it was related to, perhaps even compelled by, pre-existing cases, and which from the range of potentially relevant pre-existing cases were 'good' authorities and which were not. In addition to this concern with the position of this particular decision within the range of other decisions and materials that constitute the relevant segment of the practice, the main judgments—that of Lord Diplock for the majority, and of Lord Edmund-Davies for the minority—were informed by general considerations about the way in which this area of the law was developing, how it ought to develop, how predictable and clear it was and how closely it tracked ordinary, non-legal understandings of recklessness, responsibility and blame. Hence, one of Lord Diplock's key arguments in favour of regarding unwittingly running a risk as being reckless was that there is no moral difference between knowingly and unknowingly running a risk. Since in our everyday ascriptions of blame there is no moral difference between the two, why then, thought Lord Diplock, should the law distinguish between them?[7] From the tenor of Lord Edmund-Davies's judgment, it is clear that he thought there was indeed a crucial moral difference here which had been and should continue to be marked within the law.[8] The decision in *Caldwell* is hardly remarkable for the degree of reflective concern and monitoring it manifests. Virtually all appellate court judgments go through the process of positioning the decision made in relation to other past decisions, of charting the progress of the relevant area of law and of highlighting the decision's virtues, both legal and extra-legal. In these respects, at least, *Caldwell* was tediously predictable.

In addition to high levels of self-reflection and monitoring, many practices have their own range of conventions, expectations and options for action within which any particular action must be integrated or which it must challenge. These conventions, expectations and options are (surmountable) constraints and it takes a great deal to be able to understand them. Those with no knowledge of contemporary European football would certainly not appreciate, for example, the significance of the current coach of F. C. Barcelona having his team play with nine strikers. This would be an innovation within the constraints of the current practice although not historically unknown (it was common, for example, in the early decades of this century for English football teams to play with a majority of strikers). To see this innovation requires a high degree of knowledge of the practice. The same is true of the constraints that affect judicial choices, be they explicit, such as the 'normal' institutional constraints of precedent and fidelity to the law, or implicit factors such as, for example, judicial temperament, professional goals, social background or whatever. To appreciate the innovative

[7] 'Neither state of mind seems to me to be less blameworthy than the other': [1981] 1 All ER 961 at 965.

[8] [1981] 1 All ER 961 at 969.

step open to Lord Justice Peter Gibson in *Re Selectmove* requires a good deal of knowledge not just of contract law doctrine, but also of the rules of precedent, the leeways of choice open to judges and their differing sense of the appropriateness of developing the law. That Lord Justice Peter Gibson declined to take the step of extending the rule in *Williams* v. *Roffey*[9] to partial payment of debt cases is entirely understandable *in the circumstances*, but, of course, those circumstances are rich and detailed, including not just the conventions and expectations of the practice, but Lord Justice Peter Gibson's attitude to and interpretation of them and the factors that influence both.

Furthermore, making sense—in both interpretative and causal terms—of Diplock's, Edmund-Davies's and Peter Gibson's actions requires even more work. For, not only must the action be situated within a complex practice and institution, and its *overt* meaning and explanation thereby discovered, but its *covert* meaning and explanation must also be unearthed. Determining the covert meaning is, perhaps, not too difficult since, under the conventions of the common law world, appellate court judges are required to articulate the reasons for their decisions. These reasons provide an entry point from which to consider the judge's intentions in deciding that way and what is intended thereby. Given that these reasons provide some degree of insight into what the judge intends, the quest for the covert explanation of the decision—the inquiry into the judge's *true* or *real* or *actual* reasons—might be thought pointless. Why go beyond the list of plausible reasons the judge may have had, and even says she had, and seek to determine which were really hers?

Since it was argued in the previous chapter that no strong connection can be affirmed between meaning and intention, the answer is obvious. Unless the views of actors as to the nature of their actions and the reasons they have for them are incorrigible, it must always be in principle possible for their views to come under scrutiny. This, of course, is not a recipe for discarding agents' views of their actions and reasons and the practices and institutions in which they occur; nor does it counsel that such views should always be regarded with suspicion. Rather, depending on the circumstances in which such views are articulated, they can be taken as fairly reliable although not incorrigible guides as to the *real* reasons agents have for their actions. Reliability comes into question only when there is reason for doubt and the sources of doubt are not unlimited. In relation to judicial decisions, the duty to articulate reasons surely raises a double presumption: that these decisions are indeed reasoned and that the reasons provided are the real reasons. Since these are only presumptions, they can be rebutted, and both heretical and orthodox legal scholars sometimes seek to rebut them. They

[9] [1990] 1 All ER 512.

argue, for example, that since the judicial decision in question was not, despite appearances, compelled by the reasons the judge articulated, then other, hidden reasons, must have held sway. Or, alternatively, that the judge did not in fact have good reasons for her decision even though she thought she did. That this scrutiny of an agent's reasons is a perfectly legitimate and common procedure shows how right Hollis is to insist upon the importance of the fourth step, of attempting to discover real, as opposed to merely listing possible, reasons for action.

A final point we must note about the complexity that besets the effort to ask Hollis's questions of the process of adjudication is this. Adjudication lies somewhere between individual actions, such as Romeo's, and collective action, where a group acts with a common purpose. Hollis rightly notes that, methodologically speaking at least, there is a fundamental difference between individuals and groups. He believes that collective action characterises the behaviour of the latter and that, for Hollis, is a joint venture:

> [w]hile Romeo and Juliet act singly, the likely response of each is an external factor in the planning of the other. When they join forces, they acquire a joint power to decide what both will do. Since what was external to each becomes internal to both collectively but not to either, the power of joint decision is an emergent property. Since it can include deciding the rules of their relationship, context is no longer the external fixed frame which it has been hitherto. . . . Rational manipulation of context emerges as a possibility and much of what was *explicans* becomes *explicandum*[10]

The action of judges deciding cases is in many ways like agents acting singly: the response of each is certainly a factor in the planning of another. This is certainly true contemporaneously, when a number of judges have to decide a case, and historically, in the double sense that a past judicial decision is a factor in a current judge's decision and that he knows his decision will be a factor in the decisions of future judges. Yet, judges share, as part of their role, a commitment to making the law intelligible and defensible, if not quite the morally best it can be and this wider, shared responsibility gives adjudication an air of collective action. However, it is just an air—the process and its judicial participants cannot really be regarded as part of a collective endeavour in Hollis's sense because they are free to contest the nature of that endeavour and often do so. They argue among themselves as to what they should be doing in some area of law or another and they are quite content, should the circumstances demand, to criticise one another's current and past decisions. Nevertheless, even though they occupy this hybrid position between acting singly and acting collectively in the form of a joint venture, Hollis's point is as true of judges as it is of genuine joint ventur-

[10] *Supra*, note 5, p. 143.

ers: that together they can decide how to act and thereby change the context in which they act.

The questions we can ask of judges deciding cases are exactly the same as those we ask when attempting to explain and understand any action, institution or practice. The questions turn out to be difficult to answer both in themselves and often because of the complexity of the action, institution or practice about which they are raised. They are, nevertheless, *the* crucial questions and their difficulty is no reason for ignoring them. In the next section we will consider whether or not the orthodox answer these questions in a particular way, namely, by invoking the sovereign individual.

II THE SUBJECT ENTHRONED

We know from the previous chapter that Neil MacCormick, Joseph Raz and Ronald Dworkin take up the method of *Verstehen*. Dworkin insists that in order to understand law, the theorist must have 'a participant's understanding' (*LE*, p. 14); he or she must 'take[...] up the internal, participants' point of view' (*ibid*).[11] Likewise, MacCormick holds that '[a]ny account of rules, norms and standards must be in terms of th[e] "internal point of view"' (*LRLT*, p. 284).[12] It was also noted in the previous chapter that general methodological statements are few and far between in Raz's work but, despite this, he clearly commits himself to the *Verstehen* method both through his analysis of detached legal statements or statements from a point of view, and through his account of the function of legal theory. The latter holds that '[i]t is a major task of legal theory to advance our understanding of society by helping to understand how people understand themselves' (*EPD*, p. 221).[13] How else could this be done if not by—initially, at least—taking up the internal point of view? The general import of statements such as these from MacCormick, Raz and Dworkin is repeated time and again by other members of the orthodoxy: it is their methodological mantra.[14] In this section we consider the degree to which this method commits the ortho-

[11] I use the same abbreviations in the text and notes of this chapter as in the last: *Law's Empire* (London, Fontana 1986) is referred to as '*LE*'.

[12] '*LRLT*' is *Legal Reasoning and Legal Theory* (Oxford, Clarendon, revised edition 1993).

[13] The abbreviated reference is to Raz's *Ethics in the Public Domain* (Oxford, Clarendon 1994). The abbreviation is used hereinafter in both text and notes. For a few of Raz's discussions of detached legal statements and statements from a point of view, see: *Practical Reason and Norms* (New Jersey, Princeton U. P. 1990), pp. 170–177; *The Authority of Law* (Oxford, Clarendon 1979), pp. 142–143 and 153–157.

[14] See S. Burton, *Judging in Good Faith* (Cambridge, C. U. P. 1992), pp. xv-xvi; J. Finnis, *Natural Law and Natural Rights* (Oxford, Clarendon 1980), ch. 1; O. Fiss, 'Objectivity and Interpretation' (1982) 34 *Stanford L. R.* 739–763, pp. 748–750 and his 'The Death of Law?' (1986) 76 *Cornell L. R.* 1–16, pp. 7–8. Two good illustrations of the orthodox method at work within private law scholarship are E. Weinrib, *The Idea of Private Law* (Cambridge, Mass.,

dox to the sovereign individual. This task can be broken down into two questions: does the orthodox invocation of the *Verstehen* method commit them to denying the relevance of causal explanations of actions, institutions and practices? Does their account of this method commit them to a strong version of methodological individualism? Sub-sections (a) and (b) examine the first question while (c) considers the second.

(a) Against causality?

Demonstrating that the orthodox reject causal explanations of actions, institutions and practices in favour of non-causal, interpretative approaches is extremely difficult. Indeed, the task seems almost impossible since many of the orthodox explicitly accept the value of causal explanations. Their methodological position is therefore well described as compatibilist, that is, as embracing both an interpretative approach in conjunction with efforts at causal explanation. MacCormick leaves us in little doubt on this matter:

> Human beings are not organisms set in motion by mere reaction to stimuli in the environment. Not merely can we give explanatory reasons to account for the actions of humans as for the ebb and flow of the tide; but it is also the case that human beings act *for reasons* when they act at all, and no 'explanation' or [of?] human behaviour which omits reference to the subjective reasons for which it is performed can be a full or adequate one. To any variety of behaviourism which expressly or impliedly denied that, there is a conclusive reply as devastating as it is simple; that it cannot be wrong to be anthropomorphic about people (*LRLT*, p. 6; emphasis in original).

There is a slight ambiguity here as to what explanatory reasons may be. MacCormick surely means explanatory *causes* when speaking of accounting for the ebb and flow of the tide and the reference to explanatory *reasons* is too anthropomorphic. Only agents have reasons for action, not natural phenomena, although both can undoubtedly be caused. Despite this, the overarching message is crystal clear: human action, institutions and practices can be explained and understood in both interpretative and causal terms, the only restriction being that efforts at understanding and explanation must register the meaning dimension of action, must begin with the reasons agents have for action and the meaning they attribute thereto. Note that MacCormick's compatibilism is no one-off; he has often affirmed this position.[15]

Harvard U. P. 1995) and A. Brudner, *The Unity of the Common Law* (Berkeley, University of California Press 1995). Although espousing the same method, Brudner and Weinrib offer very different accounts of the nature of contemporary private law.

[15] N. MacCormick and R. S. Summers (eds.), *Interpreting Statutes: A Comparative Study* (Aldershot, Dartmouth 1991), pp. 17–20; N. MacCormick and O. Weinberger, *An Institutional Theory of Law* (Dordrecht, D. Reidel 1986), pp. 82–91 and 102–107; N. MacCormick, 'Four

Dworkin, too, explicitly affirms compatibilism. He does so through the language of the internal and external points of view. The latter is the 'point of view of the sociologist or historian, who asks why certain patterns of legal argument develop in some periods or circumstances rather than others' (*LE*, p. 13) and raises questions such as: 'How far, and in what way, are judges influenced by class consciousness or economic circumstance? Did the judicial decisions of nineteenth century America play an important part in forming the distinctive version of American capitalism? Or were those decisions only mirrors reflecting change and conflict but neither promoting the one nor solving the other?' (*LE*, pp. 12–13). By contrast, the internal point of view is the viewpoint 'of those who make . . . [legal] claims. Their interest is not finally historical, though they may think history relevant; it is practical. . . . They do not want predictions of the legal claims they will make but arguments about which of these claims is sound and why; they want theories not about how history and economics have shaped their consciousness but about the place of these disciplines in argument about what the law requires them to do or have' (*LE*, p. 13). Lest it be thought that Dworkin is here ruling out one approach in favour of the other he says that

> both perspectives on law, the external and the internal, are essential, and each must embrace or take account of the other. The participant's point of view envelops the historian's when some claim of law depends on a matter of historical fact: when the question whether segregation is illegal, for example, turns on the motives either of the statesmen who wrote the Constitution or of those who segregated the schools [. . .]. The historian's perspective includes the participant's more pervasively, because the historian cannot understand law as an argumentative social practice, even enough to reject it as deceptive, until he has his own sense of what counts as a good or bad argument within that practice. We need a social theory of law, but it must be jurisprudential just for that reason. Theories that ignore the structure of legal argument for supposedly larger questions of history and society are therefore perverse. They ignore questions about the internal character of legal argument, so their explanations are impoverished and defective (*LE*, pp. 13–14).

Raz neither denies nor affirms this compatibilist consensus. His remarks relevant to methodological matters are inconclusive and pull in both directions. It could be argued that, since Raz often unambiguously endorses the *Verstehen* method, then he must be a compatibilist. While it is undoubtedly true that some of the most notable proponents of this method, such as Max Weber and Jürgen Habermas, have been compatibilists, compatibilism is not entailed by the *Verstehen* method. This much is clear from the fact that, despite its many problems, there is no contradiction in Peter Winch's methodological programme between his affirmation of *Verstehen* and his

Quadrants of Jurisprudence' in W. Krawietz, N. MacCormick and G. v. Wright (eds.), *Prescriptive Formality and Normative Rationality in Modern Legal Systems* (Berlin, Dunker and Humblot 1994), pp. 59–61.

affirmation of the redundancy of explanatory-cum-causal accounts of social action.[16] In fact, some of Raz's remarks suggest endorsement of just this kind of Winchian incompatibilism, a view holding that *only* non-causal interpretative methods can yield adequate explanations and understandings of social action. For example, he says that an analysis of law should not be judged by its 'theoretical sociological fruitfulness' (*EPD*, p. 221). Now it is not transparent what theoretical sociological fruitfulness entails, but Raz thinks assessing analyses of law in this way leads to a serious mistake: that of ignoring the meaning dimension of human action. It seems Raz is here assuming that 'theoretical sociological fruitfulness' is a matter of causal explanation and that such an explanation of law, as opposed to an 'understanding' or 'interpretation', obliterates its meaning dimension. Furthermore, the tenor of Raz's remarks suggest that he thinks causal explanation inappropriate even if care is taken to first capture the meaning dimension via the *Verstehen* method: it is just '*wrong* to conclude . . . that one judges the success of an analysis of the concept of law' (*EPD*, p. 221; emphasis supplied) in causal-cum-explanatory terms.

Lest the waters were in danger of clearing, we can muddy them further by noting Raz's caution 'that there is something inherently implausible in adopting the lawyer's stance as one's fundamental methodological stance' (*EPD*, p. 187). Were we, perhaps too hastily, to take 'the lawyer's stance' to be but an aspect of taking up the internal point of view, then the conclusion might follow that Raz is a compatibilist after all. For, despite appearances, this caution is not against using the *Verstehen* method; it is a caution against taking it to be the *only appropriate method*. In speaking of the importance of the legal profession and the judicial system he says that

> [i]t is . . . unreasonable to study such institutions *exclusively* from the lawyer's perspective. . . . The law is of interest to students of society generally, and legal philosophy, especially when it inquires into the nature of law, must stand back from the lawyer's perspective, *not in order to disregard it*, but in order to examine lawyers and courts in their location in the wider perspective of social organisation and political institutions generally (*EPD*, pp. 187–188; emphasis supplied).

So, if the lawyer's perspective is indeed the internal point of view, Raz does not intend to give it up as a methodological position. Rather, he acknowledges its limitations and teasingly hints that other methods might well be appropriate. If attempting to study law in the wider perspective of social organisations and society is akin to employing causal, explanatory methods

[16] See P. Winch, *The Idea of a Social Science and its Relation to Philosophy* (London, Routledge and Kegan Paul 1958), ch. 4, especially pp. 111–120. For the view that causal explanations are 'wholly irrelevant' to understanding action see A. I. Melden, *Free Action* (London, Routledge and Kegan Paul 1961), p. 184.

in addition to the *Verstehen* method, then Raz might indeed be a methodological compatibilist. In what follows this will be assumed, despite the doubts Raz's own remarks raise.

Since there is little doubt that MacCormick and Dworkin are compatibilists and we will assume Raz is, it seems pointless to maintain that they, and the orthodox in general, invoke the sovereign individual. Their compatibilism shows that they neither deny the importance of causal explanation in the human sciences nor do they regard causal explanation and interpretive understanding as contradictories. Nevertheless, some do attack the orthodoxy because of its alleged commitment to incompatibilism, in particular that version which insists upon explaining and understanding social reality solely in interpretive terms. From this a commitment to the sovereign individual quickly follows. How are we to make sense of this? An immediate and none too charitable response is to regard this criticism as plain wrong, made in ignorance of the various affirmations of compatibilism noted above. Roger Cotterrell appears guilty on this count. He says that

> Dworkin's method presupposes a participants' discourse of law. It sees the legal world *entirely* through the eyes of practical interpreters of legal doctrine and *refuses explicitly* to admit any other perspective on law into its field of concerns. In this way *it firmly excludes all external (sociological) perspectives*. As has been seen, the price paid for this is a theory of judicial interpretation which necessarily cannot rely at all on sociological information about the nature of judiciaries as interpretive communities. Thus, it cannot really recognise social constraints on judges arising from the institutional settings of judging.[17]

This was not written prior to the publication of *Law's Empire*, but it certainly seems to have been written in ignorance of some of its crucial arguments. How can it be said, in light of Dworkin's remarks about the compatibility of 'internal' and 'external' approaches to law, that he *refuses explicitly to admit* other, presumably 'external' or sociological, perspectives? How could a reader conscious of the passages already quoted from Dworkin possibly maintain that he, Dworkin, *firmly excludes* all external approaches? As if a reminder were needed, Dworkin actually says that '[b]oth perspectives on law, the internal and the external, are essential, and each must embrace or take account of the other' (*LE*, pp. 13–14). On the assumption that intersubjective meaning is possible, and by applying the 'normal' protocols for establishing such meaning, this clearly does not mean, nor could it possibly be taken to mean, that Dworkin rejects the external perspective. He does not; nor, as we have already seen, do Raz and MacCormick.

But there might be a kernel of truth, admittedly small, in Cotterrell's

[17] R. Cotterrell, *The Politics of Jurisprudence* (London, Butterworths 1989), pp. 232–233 (emphasis supplied).

point. For it might be said that Dworkin does, *in a way*, devalue external approaches and privilege internal approaches. He does so by his practice: 'although his method, in theory if not in practice, calls for reference to both external (sociological and historical) and internal (jurisprudential) points of view, the latter is given priority'.[18] Generalising the point: Dworkin, MacCormick and Raz affirm compatibilism, but their scholarship does not embody it; they say that both external and internal approaches are equally important, but then ignore their own advice. Their work exclusively takes up the internal perspective, aims solely at an interpretive understanding of the practices and institutions we know as law. Rarely, if ever, do the orthodox actually offer, for example, accounts of the law from an historical or economic perspective, accounts that seek to chart causal connections rather than explicate meaning. Is there anything wrong with this?

(b) Some problems

In a superficial sense, the answer to this question must be 'no'. For, having affirmed compatibilism, Dworkin, Raz and MacCormick are then surely free to take up whatever approach they want within that framework. If that happens to be an interpretive approach, then so be it: that is a legitimate choice. Subsequently asserting that they ignore a causal approach is to complain that they do not discharge a task they have not set themselves. However there are some deeper issues here that could incline us to think that there is indeed something wrong with the orthodoxy's exclusive concern with the *Verstehen* approach. It courts at least two, closely related problems.

First, taking up the internal point of view to the exclusion of the external point of view, concentrating upon meaning to the exclusion of causality, can have the baleful result that theorists might miss the overall effects of a range of individual actions. Certainly, it is possible that the particular authors of a number of specific actions (e.g., judges deciding cases) might not, at the time of those actions, appreciate their cumulative effect. Taking up the internal point of view ensures that theorists will replicate this limited perspective and will therefore miss something significant about the practice or institution. At this juncture internal and external accounts of law can work fruitfully together, yielding a more complete picture of the institution and practice. At least part of what Lawrence Friedman and Morton Horwitz claimed to capture in their accounts of the development of American law

[18] V. Kerruish, 'Coherence, Integrity and Equality in Law's Empire: A Dialectical Review of Ronald Dworkin' (1988) 16 *International Journal for the Sociology of Law*, 51–73, p. 54. Unfortunately, like many of the other judgments in her essay, Kerruish does not trouble to argue the point. The next three or so paragraphs in the text attempt to fill this argumentative gap.

is what the orthodox, focusing almost exclusively on particular decisions and the reasons judges offer for them, might be led to overlook: the cumulative, extra-legal effects of a whole body of judicial decisions.[19] We must be careful not to exaggerate the orthodox interest in the reasons for *particular* judicial decisions since this suggests they have no concern with the overall patterns of development in the law. And this, of course, is untrue. The concern with particular cases is just an aspect of orthodox efforts to disclose the unfolding pattern and coherence of the law: new cases must be integrated with old, their effects upon the pre-existing law analysed, and the hints they provide as to future developments considered.

The crucial point about the orthodox concern with the way in which the law is developing is that it is almost exclusively intra-systemic. It is almost solely a matter of charting the effects of decisions within the legal system and, of course, it can be no surprise that this is a major concern of some participants—mainly practitioners and judges—in the practice. Those participants are rarely concerned with the effects of a decision or a whole body of decisions outside the legal system, although it is undoubtedly true, as MacCormick has shown, that extra-systemic consequentialist arguments are used to justify decisions in particular cases (*LRLT*, ch. 6). Yet these extra-systemic considerations form a very limited class of arguments unlikely to be expanded—they concern matters such as the alleged unfairness, inconvenience or efficacy of a decision one way or another upon aspects of the wider society. Now, the actual assessment of these extra-systemic considerations—the charting, via survey, or cost-benefit analysis, or any other kind of 'empirical' research, of the consequences of a decision upon the wider community or aspects thereof—should be grist to the orthodox scholarly mill, but rarely is. Furthermore, there is no reason in principle why legal scholars cannot go beyond the consequentialist considerations articulated by judges and assess, for example, the ways in which bodies of decisions adversely affect particular groups in our culture or benefit others. Some, in fact, do this, but it is important to appreciate that this kind of work leaves the views of the participants in the practice some way behind. If the participants do not appreciate this particular consequence of their actions and practice, then their views are of little use in understanding and explaining it. Of course, we must know what participants think of the practice in order to orient ourselves, to be sure we are studying the right practice and appreciate its nuances.

[19] See, for example, their discussions of tort law: L. Freidman, *A History of American Law* (New York, Simon and Schuster 1973), part III, ch. VI and M. Horwitz, *The Transformation of American Law 1780–1860* (Cambridge, Mass., Harvard U. P. 1977), ch. III. The follow-up volume to the latter—*The Transformation of American Law 1870–1960* (New York, Oxford U. P. 1992)—is a very different kettle of fish, being far more concerned with thought about, rather than application of, the law

But, if the practice has consequences that participants do not or cannot see, then their views are, in this respect, useless.

The second problem is this. Just as concentration upon the participants' views can blind theorists to the wider consequences of actions, practices and institutions, so, too, can it obscure the effects upon participants and the actions, practices and institutions in which they are engaged, of other actions, institutions and practices. Taking up the internal point of view to the complete exclusion of any causal analysis gives credence to the view that all changes in the practice or institution with which we are concerned are solely the product of the actions and reasons of the participants. But changes in practice or institution Y could well be a causal consequence of changes in practice and institution Z and it is quite possible that participants in Y will be unaware of this. This is not to say that they do not have reasons for their actions, but that those reasons may well be either determined by events in another institution or practice or simply become salient because of those events. Our reasons for action are context dependent and when the context changes it is likely that our reasons also change. The point, then, is that participants in practice or institution Y will almost always have reasons for their actions, but that changes elsewhere might determine those reasons; furthermore, those changes need not be registered in those reasons. Hence, participant A, in practice Y, does * for reasons 1, 2 and 3. These reasons might now be salient for A because of developments in practice or institution Z of which A is unaware; hence those changes, although they *influence* A's reasons for action, do not have to figure *as* A's reasons for action.

Is this kind of analysis ignored by the orthodox? Not completely, although some of Dworkin's remarks appear to suggest that it should be. For, despite his general affirmation of compatibilism, and his particular commendation of 'external' legal histories—they 'are useful to Hercules . . . because . . . [they] remind[.] him that nothing in the way his law was produced guarantees his success in finding a coherent interpretation of it' (*LE*, p. 273)—he seemingly thinks Hercules immune to the causal forces that influence all other social actors. He accepts that law creators act in the thrall of ideology and interest and that the work of heretical and other legal historians illuminates this; they show that the law was not created in accord with any overarching rational or moral plan. Hercules, though, is supposedly immune to the forces of ideology and interest when applying the law: '[h]e tries to impose order over doctrine, not to discover order in the forces that created it. He struggles toward a set of principles he can offer to integrity, a scheme for transforming the varied links in the chain of law into a vision of government now speaking with one voice, even if this is very different from the voices of the past' (*LE*, p. 273). Now, if the notions of ideology and interest are taken as exemplars of causal forces that operate upon social action, whether or not they also operate through the medium of reason, it might be inferred that Hercules is either immune to, or acting against, causal forces. This hasty inference conceals a snag.

In relation to social action, at least, it assumes that causes and reasons are incompatible. That is, an action can be explained and understood either in causal terms or by reference to reasons, not both. Hence, when Hercules attempts to decide cases independently of interest and ideology our objector apparently assumes that Hercules is acting contra-causally or is immune from causality, that the factors that lead him to decide a case one way or another are not themselves causes. These factors are, of course, part and parcel of Hercules's story of the law, a story that presents the law as coherent as it can be. This story is undoubtedly a reservoir of reasons for decision. Why think that reasons cannot be causes? If we do not think this way, then Hercules's action in deciding a case can be caused by reasons. Hence, when deciding cases he is neither immune from, nor acting against, either reasons or causes. Of course, more argument on this point is required and it will be provided in section III. For the moment, let us just problematise the assumption that reasons and causes are incompatible. Doing this casts considerable doubt over whether or not Dworkin denies the importance of causality in adjudication. (There are other objections our critic could make against this argument of Dworkin's—such as, for example, the difficulty of sustaining such a sharp distinction between law creation and application—but they are hardly relevant here.)

Analysis of the factors that causally determine the law figures in orthodox work and practice only in a piecemeal way. So, for example, in some exceptional instances judges justify changing the law by reference to wider, socio-cultural changes. These extra-legal developments are thought to require recognition and incorporation in the law.[20] It is rather more common for orthodox doctrinal scholars to appeal for reform of some area of the law on the ground that economic, or social, or cultural changes make legal change necessary. However, there is little effort towards an overarching and systematic account of the way in which non-legal aspects of our society impact upon the legal system, either at the level of the creation of new bodies of law or at the level of decision-making in particular cases. Hence, orthodox legal history is traditionally a matter of charting the changes *within* legal doctrine: there is little or no effort to sketch which extra-legal factors may have made these changes either possible, necessary or desirable.[21] While some of these histories of legal doctrine are undoubt-

[20] See, for example, the remarks of Lord Keith in *R* v. *R* (rape: marital exemption) [1991] 4 All ER 481 at 483–484.

[21] Two good examples are S. Milsom, *Historical Foundations of the Common Law* (London, Butterworths 2nd. ed. 1981) and J. Baker, *An Introduction to English Legal History* (London, Butterworths 3rd. ed. 1990). The narrow focus upon doctrine is peculiarly English and some-

edly fine scholarly achievements, their limited focus lends plausibility to the dubious view that changes in the law are best or only properly understood by reference to the activities of judges and legislators, that the law is sufficient explanation for its own development.[22] Again, this can be no surprise if the orthodox do little more than take up the internal, participants' point of view in their effort to understand law. For the perspective of many participants in the practice does not go beyond the demands of the practice: they are concerned to make correct or justifiable moves within the practice rather than to chart how the practice has come to take the form it has and to highlight the forces which have determined it. As Dworkin remarked, most participants 'want theories not about how history and economics have shaped their consciousness but about the place of these disciplines in argument about what the law requires them to do or have' (*LE*, p. 13). By contrast, a legal history that reaches beyond the participants' point of view can take 'law . . . not as a kingdom unto itself, not as a set of rules and concepts, not as the province of lawyers alone, but as a mirror of society[,] . . . as . . . moulded by economy and society'.[23]

What other objections might be made to the compatibilist position of Dworkin, Raz and MacCormick? The two problems just noted amount to a tendency argument, highlighting some bad consequences that flow from an exclusive concern with only one aspect of the compatibilist programme. General objections to the very idea of compatibilism will be considered in the following section. For now, are there any plausible objections to compatibilism as our sample of orthodox scholars understand it? Such objections are difficult indeed to find.

One red herring is this. It might be argued by some that Dworkin's position on the historian's practice is mistaken. That is, exception might be taken to his claims that the historian must enter a practice and understand it as the participants do in order to give an account of it. (This is a claim MacCormick and Raz are also committed to making.) It is unclear, however, what the objection can be: since the meaning dimension of social action is accepted by members of all methodological schools—although there are a few dissenters—it cannot be maintained that Dworkin's claim supports one methodological position against another. Furthermore, he

what eccentric when viewed from the perspective of North American orthodox legal history. See Horwitz and Friedman, *supra*, note 19 and the essays in D. Flaherty (ed.), *Essays in the History of Canadian Law II* (Toronto, The Osgoode Society 1983). For the first steps towards an English legal history of wider compass see G. Rubin and D. Sugarman (eds.), *Law, Economy and Society: Essays in the History of English Law, 1750–1914* (Abingdon, Professional Books 1984).

[22] This complaint is an echo of the young Edmund Burke's complaint about Matthew Hale's *History of the Common Law*. See J. G. A. Pocock, *Politics, Language and Time* (Chicago, University of Chicago Press 1989), pp. 222–225.

[23] Friedman, *supra*, note 19, p. 10.

explicitly states that methods which, for example, offer a causal, historical or cultural or economic account of the development of law, are quite legitimate, provided they begin with an insider's understanding of the practice. Yet it might be said that historians actually do and should give accounts of actions, practices and institutions without reference to participants' understandings. Again, this seems implausible. We are asked to imagine an historical account of some practice making no reference at all to the ways in which participants understood it. Is this not akin to the historian reading his primary material, a good deal of which—depending on the period—will consist of participants' thoughts and observations, and then proceeding to ignore it completely? Rather than being regarded as good history, this would surely be taken as eccentric and bad history. While there is no absolute unanimity among historians on methodological matters, very many agree with, and actually engage in, something like R. G. Collingwood's hermeneutic practice.[24] And that, of course, is in some respects both an exaggerated yet more sophisticated echo of Dworkin's method in particular, and the orthodox method in general.[25]

A second argumentative red herring is not all herring, for it contains some potentially important points. The argument is made by J. Balkin and holds that Raz's, MacCormick's and Dworkin's invocation of the internal point of view has two principal ideological effects. First, taking up the internal point of view 'makes the other purposes of legal understanding and the other social roles in which understanding occurs irrelevant, conflates them with rational reconstruction, or else relegates them to a peripheral and dependent status'. Secondly, 'this . . . makes invisible the subject's contribution to the particular form of understanding dubbed the "internal perspective"'.[26] Both effects may indeed be brought about by the orthodox method and Balkin is right to highlight them. The first effect in particular seems common and we have already addressed it—it has been shown that the orthodox are inchoate compatibilists. The second effect raises a large topic which reappears in chapters 5 and 6. No position is taken on that issue now, except to say that if the orthodox method does function thus, then some explanation is necessary. Balkin's argument goes awry because these important points are dressed up in a misconception about the nature of the internal point of view in orthodox hands. He thinks the orthodox 'believ[e]

[24] R. G. Collingwood, *The Idea of History* (Oxford, Clarendon, revised edition 1993), pp. 210–228 and his *An Autobiography* (Oxford, The University Press 1939), chs. 5 and 10. One of the most distinguished contemporary proponents of Collingwood's method is Quentin Skinner. See, *inter alia*, his 'A Reply to My Critics', ch. 14 of Tully, *supra*, note 5, pp. 234–235 and 274–275.

[25] The similarity exists only in *some* respects because, for example, Collingwood was no compatibilist. See, for example, *The Idea of History*, *supra*, note 24, p. 214.

[26] Both statements are from J. Balkin, 'Understanding Legal Understanding: The Legal Subject and the Problem of Legal Coherence' (1993) 103 *Yale L. J.* 105–176, p. 133.

in a single internal perspective' when there is indeed a 'plurality of forms of legal understanding'.[27] The error here is that there is not, as we saw in chapter 2, a single internal perspective for the orthodox. Of course, it was argued there that there should be, that the orthodox should make some effort to justify the response they make to the plurality problem, but it was also noted that some have very little to say in relation to it. In particular, MacCormick and Dworkin sometimes seem to embrace the plurality problem, the former occasionally remarking that some viewpoint must be taken up but offering no argument as to which, the latter apparently revelling in a protestant theory of interpretation. Thus, if part of the argument of chapter 2 is right, namely, that the orthodox are beset by the plurality problem and have no satisfactory response to it, then Balkin's claim must be wrong. If by criticising the belief in a single internal perspective Balkin means to criticise the displacement of causal or 'external' accounts of law, then the point is worthwhile but misleadingly put. His objection here is not to the belief in a single internal perspective, but to the belief that this is the *only* useful or appropriate method in understanding or explaining social life.

(c) Against holism?

Commitment to the *Verstehen* method, if not the sovereign individual, might be thought to imply both a commitment to strong methodological individualism and a denial of strong methodological holism. To understand how this may be so, our terms need to be defined. This is not easy, given the history of confused debate about these matters, but we can hazard the following. Strong methodological individualism holds that adequate explanations and understandings of social action must be either explicitly formulated solely in terms of truths about, or properties of, individual agents, or be ultimately reducible to such truths or properties. By contrast, strong methodological holism holds that adequate explanations and understandings of action must be explicitly and solely formulated in terms of truths about supra-individual social 'facts' or structures, or be capable of translation into such truths.[28] Defined in this way, there is no doubt that these two positions are incompatible and, although it is hard, in the history of the dispute, to find unequivocal proponents of either strong position, we will stick with these formulations.[29] For, our question is not 'who, in the history

[27] Both statements are from J. Balkin, p. 132 (the first statement) and p. 131 (the second).

[28] E. Durkheim comes close to espousing a view such as this: see *The Rules of Sociological Method* (New York, The Free Press 1965), chs. I, II and V.

[29] In addition to the sources referred to *supra*, note 1, good but dated discussions of methodological individualism and holism are found in A. Ryan (ed.), *The Philosophy of Social Explanation* (Oxford, Clarendon 1973), in particular the essays by G. Homans, J. W. N. Watkins, M. Mandelbaum and S. Lukes.

of this debate, espoused these views?', but 'do the orthodox espouse strong methodological individualism?'. If they do, we need also consider what, if anything, is wrong with that.

On what grounds could it be argued that the orthodox commitment to *Verstehen* entails a commitment to strong methodological individualism? Any such argument is intensely problematic. Taking up the viewpoint of agents involved in action, practices and institutions just does not commit the orthodox to holding that good explanations must begin and end with truths about, or properties of, individuals. Remember that, for the orthodox, *Verstehen* is but the starting point of their method and, of itself, appears neutral between methodological individualism and holism. True, taking up the internal point of view commits them to an explanation or understanding in terms of what the participants think or understand, but not exclusively so. For example, the explanation could quite easily be couched in terms of participants' views about supra-individual explanatory facts, like particular social structures, or the Hegelian notion of *Geist*, which influence their actions, or by situating their account of the action or practice in light of such facts (whatever their views about those facts). Nor is there anything here to commit the orthodox to holding that these supra-individual social facts must be reducible to statements about individuals.

These considerations mitigate against regarding Dworkin's 'protestant' theory of interpretation as an affirmation of strong methodological individualism and as a denial of strong methodological holism. Recall the consequences of Dworkin's account of interpretation, as illuminated by Gerald Postema: every participant in the practice can offer her own interpretation of the practice, these interpretations enjoy equal prima facie validity and compete with one another.[30] Postema highlights a number of problems with this account but they need not detain us here. Rather, note that Dworkin's interpretative protestantism seemingly ensures the task of understanding law begins and ends with the views of participants in the practice. And this, of course, looks a great deal like an affirmation of strong methodological individualism. To appreciate that this is deceptive we need not invoke Dworkin's brief and confusing rejection of methodological individualism (*LE*, p. 64). That is best ignored. Instead, a reconsideration of Dworkin's compatibilism shows that he cannot be taken to affirm strong methodological individualism. For example, when recognising the value of 'external' legal histories, Dworkin accepts that supra-individual facts have a role in explanation and understanding. The notions of ideology and interest are vital in understanding the way in which law is created (*LE*, p. 273). Further, these notions are not well understood if taken solely in methodological

[30] G. Postema, '"Protestant" Interpretation and Social Practices' (1987) 6 *Law and Philosophy* 283–319.

individualist terms, that is, as disclosing only truths about, or properties of, individuals. Both notions imply more than some truths about what a collection of individuals think or believe.

Taken in the critical sense, ideology implies a disjunction between some of the ideas, attitudes and beliefs of individuals, on the one hand, and an accurate picture of social reality, on the other.[31] This reality, while not completely independent of individuals' actions and beliefs, exercises some influence over them: it is not just a function of those actions and beliefs. Further, it can act upon individuals' ideas and beliefs so as to distort them, to induce mistakes the causes of which are not solely the ideas, attitudes and beliefs of other agents. The notion of interest, taken as but the expressed preferences of a group, might seem more appropriately understood in individualist terms than ideology. However, this is not so in relation to some senses of interest. For example, in some hands the notion of *real* or *class* interest is not reducible solely to the attitudes, ideas, beliefs and other properties of individuals.[32] It of course includes these factors but has often been taken to have an 'objective' dimension, be this a group's position in relation to the means of production or its location in some other structural hierarchy, not obviously explicable in methodological individualist terms. It is therefore not possible to derive an unequivocal commitment to strong methodological individualism from Dworkin's protestant account of interpretation. Hence, it seems true that, both in general, and in the particular case of Dworkin, a commitment to *Verstehen* does not imply strong methodological individualism.

The failure of this argument might generate another, slightly different point. It might be said that a commitment to *Verstehen* entails the denial of any role for causality in explanations and understandings of action. If the orthodox deny any significance to causality in explaining and understanding action, then, it could be further argued, they would obviously be committed to strong methodological individualism. Even supposing, contrary to the evidence, that the orthodox are Winchian incompatibilists will not help this argument. First, it is just not true that affirming *Verstehen* entails the rejection of causal explanation; for instance, Weber's combination of the two is certainly not contradictory.[33] Second, the denial of the importance of causality in efforts at understanding and explaining social action simply does not entail strong methodological individualism. For, any non-causal

[31] The critical conception of ideology is discussed in greater depth and defended in ch. 5, below.

[32] See G. A. Cohen, *Karl Marx's Theory of History: A Defence* (Oxford, Clarendon 1978), pp. 70–77. However, some analytical Marxists offer an account of class that appears more obviously in tune with methodological individualism: see, for example, J. Elster, *Making Sense of Marx* (Cambridge, C. U. P. 1985), ch. 6.

[33] M. Weber, *Economy and Society*, G. Roth and C. Wittich (eds.), (New York, Bedminster Press 1968), ch. 1.

explanation and understanding can in principle invoke supra-individual social facts. Pointing to the (non-causal) explanatory significance of these facts is not made impossible by a general denial of the importance of causal explanation. Nor does affirming strong methodological individualism entail the denial of the importance of causality in explanation and understanding. Many methodological individualists have indeed affirmed, without contradiction, the importance of causality in the explanation and understanding of action. Their methodological individualism is quite consistently subsumed under, for example, a commitment to the D-N method.[34] It cannot therefore be said that affirming the importance of causality in explanation is to embrace methodological holism, since the causal forces accepted as affecting an agent's actions might well be the actions of others and not supra-individual social facts or other 'holist' entities. Thus the status of causality in efforts at explanation and understanding is not relevant to resolving the dispute between methodological individualism and holism. Furthermore, the orthodox compatibilist method clearly does not commit proponents to a strong version of either methodological individualism or holism.

This is convenient for the orthodox since neither of these doctrines is particularly plausible. No compelling or even prima facie plausible argument has yet been formulated for the strong version of either and it is difficult to know what form such arguments could take.[35] While nothing the orthodox say commits them to the strong version of either doctrine, their comments suggest support for weak versions of each. Weak methodological individualism maintains that properties or truths about individuals must be at least part of a good explanation and understanding of some aspect of social life. By contrast, weak holism holds that truths about, or properties of, supra-individual facts must be part of an adequate explanation and understanding. These doctrines are quite compatible and it seems that the orthodox implicitly affirm both. Take, for example, their affirmations of compatibilism. MacCormick and Dworkin accept the legitimacy of both external and internal approaches to law and, in so doing, also concede that both 'facts' about individuals and 'facts' about supra-individual entities are relevant to each approach. Dworkin, as we have already noted, accepts that ideology and interest play a role in law creation and these notions, in some senses at least, are not well understood if taken in individualist terms. MacCormick, remember, accepts that individual action can be partially explained and understood by reference to 'explanatory reasons' (which we took to mean explanatory causes since it risks confusion to speak of the behaviour of the seas in terms of reasons), but a complete or adequate

[34] See Watkins, *supra*, note 29, pp. 93–104. For some scepticism about this combination see Bhargava, *supra*, note 1, ch. 3.

[35] This point is well made by Lukes, *supra*, note 29, pp. 124–129.

explanation must also refer to agents' 'subjective reasons'. Since the latter look like truths about or properties of individuals, and the former can clearly include supra-individual facts, it is not eccentric to take this as an affirmation of weak methodological individualism.

It seems, then, that the orthodox are neither strong methodological individualists nor strong methodological holists. A commitment to the sovereign individual might entail a commitment to strong methodological individualism, but the orthodox do not affirm the sovereign individual. Nor is it plausible to maintain that the *Verstehen* method entails strong methodological individualism. Moreover, orthodox statements on these matters, such as there are, suggest a commitment to weak methodological individualism and that is not a dangerous doctrine. Espousing it does, though, entail a denial of strong methodological holism but, since there is no question of the orthodox ever even hinting that they accept this doctrine, there is no problem with that.

The point we have arrived at is this: the orthodox are methodological compatibilists. They explicitly affirm this doctrine, but their practice favours only one aspect of it—the interpretative or meaning dimension. Moreover, although the orthodox affirm compatibilism they devote very little time to unpacking it. They seemingly pay lip service to this method but it does not impact upon their scholarly practice in any direct or pervasive way. This leads to the problems highlighted in section (b). Unpacking and understanding the implications of compatibilism would help circumvent these problems and the following section begins that task. It offers a picture of what compatibilism amounts to, seeks to show that it is the right method for the human sciences in general and jurisprudence in particular, and finally sketches, albeit briefly, the impact a sustained commitment to compatibilism would have upon legal scholarship.

III THE SUBJECT UNVEILED: COMPATIBILISM

Methodological compatibilism holds that efforts at understanding and explanation must be informed by the whole range of methods available within the human sciences and, therefore, that not all of these methods are incompatible. In particular, compatibilists contend that different methods, such as, for example, hermeneutic analysis of the meaning of an action or practice, on the one hand, and the causal account of the cultural and economic conditions in which an action or practice exists, on the other, are both appropriate in the attempt to understand and explain the action or practice. This tendency to argue that what were once regarded as entirely incompatible methods are indeed compatible, this spirit of methodological ecumenicalism, is found in much social scientific and philosophical work of the last two decades. It is a refrain found in the work of Habermas, Karl-Otto Apel, Quentin Skinner and Georg von Wright, that echoes in the writings of Anthony Giddens and which thunders to the fore in the methodological essays of Paul Ricoeur.[36] These scholars' works are diverse and difficult and they will not be examined in any depth, either singly or collectively, here. These works constitute a massive and ambitious corpus, some of which is still unfolding and undergoing development. Any adequate consideration of this corpus would place massive strain upon both the available space and competence. Hence, a short cut is surely permissible. It takes the following form: the work of only one compatibilist is examined in any depth. It is the work of John Thompson, selected for the reasons, *inter alia*, that it is admirably clear, thorough and synthetical. That is, Thompson is one of the few writers in this area who has attempted to draw connections between, for example, the work of Habermas and Ricoeur, to highlight similarities that are often lost, and to orchestrate these many different, though rarely completely dissentient voices into some degree of harmony.[37] So, while this short cut certainly reduces the number of works with which we have to grapple, there is no resultant reduction in quality: Thompson's project of synthesis is every bit as ambitious and as demanding as the work he discusses.

Thompson's methodological compatibilism has two hallmarks. The first is a claim that seems almost ontological, namely, that the most fundamental constituents of social reality are human action, social practices and institutions, and social structures. Furthermore, these diverse constituents are interconnected and influence one another, although it is unclear which, if any, is the more influential. The second, more obviously methodological claim is that, since the fundamental constituents of social life are diverse, and since they have a number of dimensions and interrelationships, it should not be thought that they can be understood and explained using a single method.

The first claim is unpacked thus by Thompson. He offers a fairly uncontroversial characterisation of human action. It is goal directed behaviour which agents could refrain from if they so wished, and hence not simply something that happens to them; yet the meaning of this goal directed

[36] See the works of Habermas, Apel, von Wright and Ricoeur cited in note 2, above. Some of Q. Skinner's important essays on method are gathered together in Tully, *supra*, note 5, chs. 2–6. There are at least two volumes of A. Giddens's methodological essays, both of which expound a version of compatibilism: *Studies in Social and Political Theory* (London, Hutchinson 1977) and *New Rules of Sociological Method* (London, Hutchinson 1976). Of course, contemporary compatibilism lives in the shadow of Weber, *supra*, note 33.

[37] See his *Critical Hermeneutics* (Cambridge, C. U. P. 1981); *Studies in the Theory of Ideology* (Cambridge, Polity Press 1984); and *Ideology and Modern Culture* (Cambridge, Polity Press 1990), pp. 20–23 and ch. 6; the first book is hereinafter referred to, in both text and notes, as '*CH*'.

behaviour is not determined solely by the intentions of the subject (*CH*, pp. 140–143). Thompson takes the latter point to be the most controversial aspect of his account of action since, in contending that the meaning of an action is specified by the manner in which it is described, and that the subject's description is not conclusive, he appears to run up against a number of powerful arguments. Both Donald Davidson and Quentin Skinner have argued, albeit in quite different ways, that action must be described by reference to an agent's intentions.[38] Davidson, remember, argues that for any event to be an action it must be intentional under some description, whereas Skinner maintains that reference to an agent's intentions is indispensable in order to understand the illocutionary meaning of any utterance. As we saw in chapter 2, neither of these positions entails that agents' views of their actions or utterances are incorrigible. Davidson's argument is only a means of distinguishing action-events from other events and it does not follow from his argument that no other descriptions of an action are either possible or plausible. Hence, Thompson's opposition to it is misplaced. Skinner's argument relates only to illocutionary meaning and, as we noted, even here he does not accept that agents' accounts of their intentions are conclusive—they can, in some circumstances, be departed from by the theorist. Again, Thompson's opposition is misplaced. With these caveats in mind, let us accept Thompson's statement that human action is 'the implementation of specific means for the attainment of particular ends, privately or publicly defined' (*CH*, p. 144).

The other two constituents of social reality are important because 'the performance of action must be situated within a wider context of social institutions and structural conditions' (*CH*, p. 143). The former are described as 'specific constellations of social relations, together with reservoirs of material resources which are associated with them' (*CH*, p. 144), whereas the latter—more often labelled as 'social structure'—is 'conceived as a series of elements and their interrelations, which conjointly define the conditions for the persistence of a social formation and the limits for the variation of its component institutions' (*CH*, p. 145). The most important difference between institutions and structures is that the latter set the conditions within which the former exist. The form of institutions—Thompson's two examples are the University of Cambridge and the Ford Motor Company—is dependent upon the social structure, which has two distinguishable elements. First, there are those elements of the structure that 'represent necessary conditions for the persistence of social life as such' (*CH*, p. 145) and which include, for example, arrangements for the production of the means of survival. Secondly, there are 'those elements which are

[38] See D. Davidson, *Essays on Actions and Events* (Oxford, Clarendon 1980), essays 3 and 6; Q. Skinner, '"Social meaning" and the explanation of social action', in J. Tully, *supra*, note 5.

necessary conditions, not for the persistence of social life as such, but rather for the continuation of a particular type of social formation' (*CH*, p. 145). Elements of the latter type directly influence the nature and type of social institutions. As Thompson notes, whereas production is a crucial part of any social structure, production by means of capital and wage labour is not—the latter is but a necessary element for a set of social institutions to be regarded as capitalistic.

The relationship between action, institutions and structure is 'multiple and complex' (*CH*, p. 145). However, Thompson contends that institutions determine actions via flexible institutional schemata, but that actions can transform those schemata, the institutions of which they are part and the social structure in which they exist. Institutional schemata, which agents acquire during socialisation into the institution, provide recipes as to how to act within particular institutional contexts. The schemata ensure that 'certain courses of action are open while others are relatively closed' (*ibid.*), but they certainly do not completely compel action.[39] For, 'action is an essentially creative and potentially transformative process' (*ibid.*) which can change schemata even when governed by them (and not all action is so governed). Action can slightly change such schemata or directly contradict them; in the latter case 'either the agent's career or the continuation of the institution' (*ibid.*) is put at risk. The limiting conditions of the institution are found in the social structure and, should action challenge the institutional schemata and hence the institution itself, we can expect transformations in the social structure. 'So long as the transformative capacity of action does not propel institutions beyond the limiting conditions, then action may be said to reproduce social structure . . . [;] [h]owever, one cannot preclude the possibility that these conditions may be exceeded by the cumulative consequences of collective action' (*ibid.*).

The picture that emerges from this limited sketch is one in which the constituents of the social world—action, institutions, practices and structures—are related through a series of interlocking causal webs. One aspect of the social world, X, can be influenced by another, Y, and yet itself influence Y; further, both can influence and be influenced by other aspects of social reality. While there are indeed causal influences and patterns here, this is not a billiard ball world in which there exist only one-way patterns of causal influence. No aspect of social reality is deemed completely causally determinative of another and, unlike an orrery, changes in one aspect will not lead automatically to changes in another. But this talk of interlocking causal webs, of multiple patterns of influence, might be prone to an obvious

[39] An almost exact parallel to this account of action and its context is found in G. Postema, *supra*, note 30, pp. 302–304. This is less surprising than might at first appear since both Postema and Thompson rely upon P. Bourdieu's account of action and practice: see his *Outline of a Theory of Practice* (Cambridge, C. U. P. 1977), pp. 6–22 and ch. 2.

objection. For, is it not the case that there are really no clearly delineated causal patterns in the compatibilist world because that world is but a causal mish-mash? In their efforts to avoid a one dimensional view of causation, have not compatibilists given an essentially non-causal view instead? On their picture of the social world, as so far developed, it is not possible to say exactly which aspect of social reality actually causes changes in another and with what degree of stringency. Yet this objection might be overstated. True, the compatibilist causal picture of the world is not a clear and simple one in which the initiation of change in one domain clearly entails change in another. Surely the compatibilist cannot be blamed for the world being more complicated than proponents of more reductive accounts of causality would have us believe. Compatibilists can and should be called to justify their picture of the world, but their task here—the epistemological and ontological one of attempting to show that their picture of the social world is plausible and justifiable—is no different from that which faces proponents of other views of the social world. Compatibilism's account of the causal patterns constitutive of social reality thus faces no especial or unique problems.

There might, however, be a more pressing snag in store for another part of compatibilism's first claim, namely, the idea that action takes place within a context of practices, institutions and structures. The difficulty is that this is surely accepted by almost all contestants in the methodological debate: it cannot therefore mark out a distinctive methodological position. What actually sets disputants apart is their competing accounts of how action and the context in which it takes place are to be explained and understood. There are many different accounts of the nature of the method that should be used here, but most of them have one thing in common: they take up a reductive position. That is to say, while almost all contestants in the debate accept the point about the context of human action, few also accept that, in order to understand and explain such action and its context, a range of methods is required. Rather, it is often held that the many facets of social action—its interrelationship with, and determination by and of, social institutions and structures—can be explained by invoking just one method or just one limited set of protocols. Participants in this debate dispute exactly which single method or set of protocols is best for this purpose. The compatibilists' problem, then, is that merely highlighting the context of action and the diverse range of institutions, practices and structures constitutive of that context, cannot, without more, show compatibilism to be the right and only methodological response.

Since the claim about the rich context of action neither sets compatibilists apart from proponents of other methods, nor does it show that compatibilism is the right path, there is a serious argumentative gap here. Moreover, a plausible argument showing that the fact that action takes place within a rich context demands compatibilism is unlikely to be forthcoming. How could such an argument work, since this 'fact' is, without more, neutral between contending methods? It neither rules out a purely causal nor purely interpretative explanation of the action in question nor does it commend compatibilism. Thus, compatibilists need an argument to show their method is the better response to the problem of understanding and explaining human action—this is the added extra, the 'more' that fills the gap between the claim about the context of action and compatibilism. What might such an argument look like? This takes us to the heart of the second compatibilist claim. Before examining the arguments that might be used to support it, two things must be done. First, the details of the second claim are unpacked; secondly, two difficulties it supposedly generates are considered. Finally, the arguments that might be invoked to support the second claim, arguments which recommend methodological compatibilism, are examined.

The core of the second claim is the *entente cordiale* proposed between methods of understanding and those of explanation. Thompson proposes 'a systematic interrelation between the understanding of human action and the explanation of its social genesis' (*CH*, p. 176). This interrelation is thought necessary, as we have already noted, because of the nature of action and its context. Two features of this context in particular require recourse to explanation: the first is the schematic generation of action, while the second is the dimension of social structure. Explanatory, causal methods are appropriate here in order to chart the nature and degree of influence between action and institutional schemata, on the one hand, and action, institutions and structure, on the other. Again, Thompson is keen to point out that the relationships here are not one way. Hence, 'not only is action circumscribed by structure through the medium of social institutions, but structure is reproduced by action through the process of schematic generation; and yet action may replace a particular structure, in which case the social structuration of institutions gives way to the active transformation of social structure' (*CH*, pp. 175–6). If it is accepted that explanation does have a role in the attempt to make sense of human action, because action is both influenced by and influences its context, then compatibilism seems plausible. For, if this explanatory dimension can be combined with a concern for the meaning of the action in question, compatibilism—or, as Thompson calls it, depth hermeneutics—surely follows.

Compatibilism is 'oriented towards a specification of the meaning of action' (*CH*, p. 176), yet takes this task to entail more than just the recapitulation of the meaning agents take the action to have. For, it also involves the elucidation of the effect upon the action of institutional schemata and social structure and its effect upon them. Hence, two steps are necessary when implementing the method. The first involves 'the reconstruction of institutional schemata . . . [which] may be elucidated through the process of comparison and abstraction, whereby one elicits a formula for the production of multifarious acts' (*CH*, p. 177). This formula 'may permit the action to be redescribed, and thereby reunderstood, in light of its schematic genesis' (*ibid.*). The second step is a matter of reconstructing the structural elements, that is, of specifying those conditions that determine the nature of the institution in question. 'Such a reconstruction enables one to grasp various aspects of institutions which would otherwise remain concealed, including the limits of the exercise of power and the efficacy of ideology, as well as the dynamics of institutional persistence and collapse' (*ibid.*). This reconstruction can situate agents and their actions within a context of institutional conditions of which they are 'ignorant or only dimly aware' (*ibid.*). Finally, note that both steps of the method are closely interrelated. 'For just as the understanding of action is enhanced by an account of its schematic generation, so too the comprehension of institutions is enriched by an analysis of their social structuration' (*CH*, p. 178).

There is a major difficulty with the second claim. It apparently entails that social action, and perhaps also institutions and structures, are prior to and determinative of the method used to explain and understand them. So, for example, Thompson maintains that 'the development of a more adequate methodology . . . is closely linked to the theory of action, for methodological issues *cannot be divorced* from the conceptualisation of an object domain' (*CH*, p. 173; emphasis supplied). Furthermore, since, as we have already noted, the object domain must be conceptualised in a particular way—namely, 'the performance of action *must* be situated within a wider context of social institutions and structural conditions' (*CH*, p. 143; emphasis supplied)—it seems certain that method is determined by ontology. How is this possible? How do we know what social action looks like prior to employing our method? Surely we need a method or 'theory' in the first instance, so as to perceive social action?

These questions raise, again, the relation between 'theory' and 'reality' or 'facts' and 'method'. In holding that action determines method, it might well be thought that Thompson is thereby committed to holding that there is a realm of 'facts' accessible prior to the deployment of any method or theory. And that, it might be argued, is a thoroughly discredited methodological and epistemological position.[40] However, the matter is not as cut and dried as this objection makes it appear. Thompson could surely accept that some theory or method is necessary in order to register social action, to be able to 'see' it in the first place, and that we do indeed have such a theory. We *have* one because such a theory is a necessary condition for understanding to be possible and, assuming understanding is an everyday occurrence

[40] See the discussion in chapter two, section I (d), for sources.

amongst agents, such a theory must exist. Indeed, it is a theory we have *already*—a practical, day-to-day set of hermeneutic and other protocols that allow us to communicate and understand, to some degree, one another—prior to the deployment of any more abstract, social-theoretic method. This 'practical' theory defines our practical, hermeneutic condition—we are interpreting beings.[41] If this is true, then action does at least determine method in one, preliminary sense: if we are interpreting beings, then some kind of interpretative method must always be our *starting point* in attempting to understand and explain social action.[42] An absurd, 'scientific' or empiricist method that proposed to ignore this feature of our condition entirely would thus be mistaken. Then, again, very few of the many methods in the human sciences have suggested that this dimension of our condition be completely ignored. Even the 'standard' empiricist response is to register this dimension, but then to suggest that it is only a minor aspect of the effort to understand and explain social action.[43] Just as the fact that social action takes place in a rich context does not entail compatibilism, neither does the fact of its meaning dimension entail that interpretativism is the only correct method with which to understand and explain such action.

So, the compatibilist can reply that 'theory' is indeed necessary in order to get access to the object domain—it tells us, *inter alia*, what is and is not social action. However, that theory is our everyday, practical theory—theory in the primary sense—which makes some degree of communication and understanding possible between us. We do not at this preliminary stage need the more abstract and quite possibly critical theories that our method might yield (theory in the secondary and tertiary senses).[44] True, these more

[41] See, for a vivid statement of the point, H-G. Gadamer, *Truth and Method* (London, Sheed and Ward 1975), p. 401.

[42] Some exaggerate this point, thinking that simply stating we are interpreting beings closes the debate about method, that this is somehow a knock-down argument against empiricist or causal methods. One example from the many available is W. Outhwaite, *Understanding Social Life: The Method Called 'Verstehen'* (London, Allen and Unwin 1975), pp. 16–17.

[43] Two examples are A. J. Ayer, 'Man as a subject for science', ch. 1 of P. Laslett and W. Runciman (eds.), *Philosophy, Politics and Society* series III (Oxford, Basil Blackwell 1967) and C. Hempel, 'Rational Action' in (1962) *Proceedings and Addresses of the American Philosophical Association* 5–24. One of the few philosophical examples of an empiricist denial of the significance of the meaning dimension of action is O. Neurath, *Empiricism and Sociology* (Dordrecht, D. Reidel 1973), ch. 10, especially pp. 353–358. Never afraid of overstatement, Neurath observes, at p. 357, that *Verstehen* is no more useful to the social theorist than 'a good cup of coffee'! The denial nowadays seems more common in the methodologically eccentric world of socio-legal studies: see B. Tamanaha, *Realistic Socio-Legal Theory* (Oxford, Clarendon 1997), pp. 61–65.

[44] As defined in chapter 2, section I (d): theory in the secondary sense entails excavating the languages of description and evaluation—the conceptual schemes—of the participants in the area of social life one is examining; theory in the tertiary sense is a matter of formulating determinate relations between a set of variables in terms of which an extensive class of empirically ascertainable regularities can be explained.

abstract 'social-theoretic' theories must begin from the practical theory that defines our condition, but they certainly need not be, *pace* Winch and A. R. Louch, just a reflection of the latter in more abstract language.[45] The problem that arises now is not one of circularity—our method being conditioned by the nature of action but that method must be employed in order to perceive action—but of the relationship between secondary and tertiary theory, on the one hand, and practical theory, on the other. How closely should or must social-theoretic descriptions and understandings be related to practical-theoretic descriptions and understandings? We have said already that they need not be just more or less abstract reflections of one another but, beyond that, what is their relationship?

The only rule here is that social-theoretic accounts of action, practices and institutions should always be related to practical-theoretic accounts. This is so because participants' views are either part of the explanation (*explanans*) of the actions, practices and institutions to which they relate, taken in conjunction with accounts of the causal power of institutional schemata and other elements of the social structure, or part of that which requires explanation (*explanandum*). Whether participants' views feature as *explanans* or *explanandum* depends upon the degree to which the theorist has reason to question their corrigibility. The more dubious particular participants' views as to the nature of the action, practice or institution in question seem, the more likely they are to be regarded as *explanandum*, whereas the more reliable they are, the more likely they are to be taken as *explanans*. Moreover, the reasons for casting doubt upon participants' views are not infinite. The grounds upon which they can be challenged are limited, including factors such as the distance between one participant's view of the action and that of the vast majority, or the distance between it and the views of those to whom the practice is morally important, and the degree to which the participant's view utilises the rules of standard logic and inference. Failure on any one of these dimensions will not automatically turn a participant's view from *explanans* to *explanandum*, but failure in more than one—such as the participant's view of the practice being completely out of sync with the views of the many other participants *and* being inconsistent—usually will.

When we say social-theoretic accounts must be *related* to practical-theoretic accounts we mean that the former must be based upon the latter. That is, the concepts and discriminations of participants must inform, but not completely compel the content of, social-theoretic accounts of a practice, institution or body of rules. Do not mistake this for a one-way

[45] Winch, *supra*, note 16, p. 89; Louch's notion of moral explanation ensures that efforts to explain and understand social action must be closely tied to participants' understandings: A. R. Louch, *Explanation and Human Action* (Berkeley, University of California Press 1966), chs. 2 and 8.

process of dependence, though, for it is perfectly possible for the concepts of social-theoretic accounts to be appropriated by participants; this is indeed a defining condition of the human sciences. Thus, although the distinction between different levels of theory can be easily and plausibly made in the abstract, the reflexivity characteristic of the social condition ensures that the levels can be thoroughly inter-mixed in practice.[46] Compared with some, this account affirms a relatively weak relationship between practical-theoretic and social-theoretic accounts. Alfred Schutz, for example, maintained that a condition of adequacy for social theories was that their concepts be in principle translatable into the everyday language of participants in the practice in question. That this is far too demanding a condition seems obvious; it would prevent the invocation in explanations and understandings of social life of any concept the participants do not expressly affirm, albeit by synonym, in their behaviour. So, for example, the economists' notion of liquidity preference, despite the fact that it relates to the behaviour of market actors in the sense we have specified—it takes their accounts of what they are doing as a starting point—must be rejected by Schutz unless there is an obvious equivalent in the language of participants.[47] Further, since the requirement is one of translatability, we may suppose that the criteria of equivalence are fairly demanding, so that a match like that between 'snow' and 'neige', 'pomodoro' and 'tomato' is necessary. On our account, some relationship between the two levels is still required, even though it is not as strong as that which Schutz affirms.

We turn now to a question left unanswered for too long. What arguments support compatibilism? The answer has two parts. The first considers arguments against compatibilism not already touched upon and shows that they fail. It therefore constitutes, at most, an indirect argument for compatibilism, showing that pursuing this method is not obviously pointless. The second part states, in positive spirit, the reasons why this method is attractive.

Three arguments against compatibilism come to mind, two of which have been lurking, not quite behind the scenes, in the previous discussion. The first seeks to convert an argument we have already made to a much more destructive purpose. The argument is a negative one: the denial, on our part, of the efficacy of an ontological argument for compatibilism. The ontological argument is the claim that some feature or features of social reality mandate a particular method for understanding and explaining action, institutions and practices. As we saw above, this kind of claim was made by Thompson and has also been made by

[46] This point has been made often and eloquently by A. Giddens. See, for example, his *Central Problems in Social Theory* (London, Macmillan 1979) pp. 245–248.

[47] The discussion and criticism of Schutz is taken from Giddens, *ibid.*, pp. 246–247.

others.[48] In the course of denying it, though, we rescued a kernel of truth: the ontological truth that we are linguistically constituted beings mandates that any method for understanding such beings register this fact. Yet we also noted that almost every method offered for understanding social life in some way takes account of, or certainly does not deny, its 'meaning dimension'. Objectors to compatibilism might be galvanised by this to maintain that, since the ontological argument does not support this method, then nothing can. There are two mistakes here. First, the failure of the ontological argument to support compatibilism is replicated in relation to any form of incompatibilism. That is, an argument from ontology cannot support *any* method—that, at least, is the position taken here. It is extremely difficult to see how any argument about what there is can be sufficiently fine grained and deep as to show conclusively that one particular method and its various injunctions and protocols must be employed to understand and explain social reality. Take, for example, a standard ontological argument to show that there are abstract particulars. However interesting and important such an argument might be in general philosophical terms, it beggars belief to imagine that it somehow demands a particular method be adopted to understand and explain social life. Secondly, the failure of the ontological argument does not show that there are no arguments in favour of compatibilism unless it is the only argument. As we will see, it is not.

The second and third objections to compatibilism are connected. The second makes what can be called the redundancy point. It says it is pointless to seek to understand and explain social life in both causal and interpretative terms since either one of these generates a sufficient account of any action, institution or practice. If there is, for example, a good causal explanation of my raising my arm, then there is no need to find out what I intended by this, or what the point of the action was (if indeed it was an action properly so called). Similarly, if it is known what I intended by raising my arm, then a causal account of that action is redundant. Now, there are many snags with this objection but only one will be examined. The objection assumes that reasons and causes are incompatible: action can be explained either by reference to causes or reasons but not both. This assumption underpins the redundancy point and, should it turn out to be wrong, that argument must fail. Furthermore, the denial that reasons can be causes also appears to entail the redundancy point since it is difficult to see how, in making the denial, one could avoid a commitment to either limb of that point.

The argument that reasons cannot be causes is the third objection to compatibilism. It traditionally rests upon a number of sub-arguments to the

[48] One example: 'the nature of explanation depends upon the kinds of things investigated': Louch, *supra*, note 45, p. 233.

effect that, for example, reason-based explanation and understanding is a matter of redescription and so cannot be causal; that the relation between reasons and actions is one of logical necessity but the relation between causes and effects cannot be of this order; and that to allow that reasons can be causes is to embrace determinism. This argument takes us to the heart of the positive case for compatibilism. For, one of the central arguments in its favour is that reasons can indeed be causes—it is therefore a direct denial of the third objection. Moreover, the argument that reasons can be causes is, at least in Donald Davidson's hands, as close to conclusive as possible within philosophy. Davidson's case consists of a refutation of the three objections noted above in conjunction with a simple question: in what, other than causation, can the relationship between reasons and actions consist?

The refutation of the first sub-argument is obvious: 'from the fact that giving reasons merely redescribes the action and that causes are separate from their effects', it does not follow that reasons are not causes. For, '[r]easons, being beliefs and attitudes, are certainly not identical with actions; but, more important, events [of which actions are a subset] are often redescribed in terms of their causes'.[49] Hence, redescription need not elide the distinction between cause and effect. The second sub-argument fails because it mistakes the logically necessary connection between two descriptions of a single action for the connection between cause and effect which, on David Hume's account at least, is only a matter of constant conjunction. Debate about this point has centred upon the example of a driver raising his arm. A. I. Melden insisted that from a driver's statement that he raised his arm in order to inform others of what he was about to do, it follows logically that he was signalling. This can be conceded, for it does not show a logical connection between cause and effect here unless we assume that the cause is the driver's intention to signal and the effect is his arm raising. This assumption is dubious for there are not two events here—an intention and an arm raising—but one: the act of signalling. This act has just been described in two different ways by Melden and, of course, each description is logically connected to the act described. As Simon Evnine puts it: '[w]hat Melden needs to show is that, from "he wanted to raise his arm in order to inform others of what he was about to do", it follows logically that he was signalling. This is obviously not true, since the agent could have the desire and yet not perform any relevant action at all'.[50] Finally, accepting that reasons can be causes is not, for Davidson, to embrace determinism in relation to human action because of the anomalism of the mental. By that he means at least that human actions and mental events can never be completely captured within 'the nomological net of physical theory', that it is

[49] Both statements are from essay 1, *supra*, note 38, p. 10.
[50] S. Evnine, *Donald Davidson* (Cambridge, Polity Press 1991), pp. 48–49.

not possible to develop a corpus of psycho-physical or psychological laws that can completely causally explain mental events and actions.[51]

If it is true that reasons are causes, then that is a feather in the compatibilist cap—compatibilism holds that an explanation or understanding of some act, practice or institution can be both cause- and reason-based. What other arguments support this method? There are at least two. One holds that an important advantage which compatibilism has is its open-mindedness toward issues of explanation and understanding. Unlike those incompatibilist positions that take for granted the explanatory power of one or other of the natural sciences, and then seek to construct a method for the remaining natural and human sciences in the image of the exemplar, compatibilism eschews the notion of a master discipline whose method all other disciplines should follow. This is just as well for, despite their amazingly immodest and self-assertive claims, no such reductive incompatibilist position has yet triumphed—proponents have still not succeeded in reducing the human and natural sciences to the method of either geometry or physics. Yet it might be said that what such reductive programmes have on their side is a commitment to methodological parsimony. They seek to show that there is only one way, whatever it may be, to generate adequate explanations and understandings of action, institutions and practices. Hence espousing one or other kind of incompatibilism—either that which claims that only cause-based approaches are adequate or that which pins all its hope on a reason-based method—is better than compatibilism. Unless it is established that there are good reasons to value parsimony in this context—and the trite invocation of Ockham's razor will not suffice—the point is entirely groundless.

Another argument in favour of compatibilism picks up and amplifies a refrain in the previous argument: incompatibilism has failed. Of course, this is hardly conclusive—it is not an argument to show that incompatibilism is impossible. Rather, it holds only that most versions of incompatibilism so far developed suffer from grievous infirmities. Just as those versions of incompatibilism obsessed with imposing upon all the natural and human sciences the method of one or other exemplary science have failed in their task, so those which have sought to apply only non-causal, interpretive methods have come undone. The overarching problem for incompatibilists of the latter stripe is that of getting beyond merely reporting what agents and participants in institutions and practices take themselves to be doing. While many accept that this should be the social scientist's starting point, many have thought that there is more to the task of understanding and explaining social life. The incompatibilists' refusal to take this extra step seemingly robs the human sciences of a role, leaves them with very little to

[51] See Davidson, *supra*, note 38, essay 11, p. 207.

explain and understand. Social life, on this view, is a great deal less complex and problematic than initially appears.

These reasons make compatibilism hard to resist. Further, its adoption of both causal and interpretive means of explanation easily accommodates the range of questions we ask in order to understand action, institutions and practices. Think back to Romeo's deed—compatibilism has us openly address each question. No question is ruled out in advance as being meaningless as some might according to incompatibilist approaches. Remember also that Hollis says the general question about the meaning of Romeo's deed is ambiguous between meaning and explanation and by this, no doubt, he has in mind the reasons/causes dichotomy. On a compatibilist view, however, this ambiguity is not a problem: compatibilism holds that causal and interpretative approaches are equally applicable in the attempt to answer any such question. The meaning of Romeo's deed is a function of both causes and reasons. Furthermore, since compatibilism asserts the appropriateness of both causes and reasons in the effort to understand and explain and, since reasons can be causes on this view, there is little point in drawing the traditional, strict distinction between understanding and explanation. The former can be used to refer to efforts to elicit the meaning dimension of action and the latter to the excavation of causal influences but, since both are united within the same method, there is little point in so doing. If reasons and causes are regarded as incompatible, if we can *either* explain *or* understand actions, practices and institutions, then the distinction has more force than it ever can under compatibilism. For compatibilists, there are reasons and there are causes, they are not always utterly qualitatively distinct, and reference to both is necessary in order to appreciate the nature of social life.

What, then, might compatibilism mean in legal scholarship? One answer would be: not much. Since the orthodox are compatibilists, it might be thought that the adoption of this doctrine would change nothing. Yet, as we noted, the orthodox espouse compatibilism in word but not in deed. Taking the doctrine seriously would open up a range of questions that have so far been regarded as marginal. Confining our remarks to accounts of adjudication only, compatibilism considers not just the distinctive modes of justification for decision, be they principled arguments of integrity or of coherence, consistency and consequences. It also insists upon an analysis of the factors that determine the salience of these kinds of argument, factors that operate within the legal system, from its own internal congeries of expectation, socialisation and prudence, and those which operate upon the legal system from outside. A. W. B. Simpson put factors of the first sort on the agenda of orthodox legal philosophy when he noted the inadequate account legal positivism gave of the common law. In arguing that the common law cannot be conceived as a system of rules, Simpson came to the unsurprising view that it is instead better understood as a customary system. That raises the following question: how is coherence possible in such a system? Simpson's answer highlights intra-systemic factors and mechanisms designed to uphold continuity and cohesion. He says there was a raft of such mechanisms within the common law of earlier centuries:

> The law was the particular possession of a small, tightly organised group comprising those who were concerned in the operation of the Royal courts, and within this group the serjeants and judges were dominant. . . . [I]deas were transmitted largely orally, and even the available literary sources were written in a private language . . . A wide variety of institutional arrangements tended to produce cohesion of thought. The organisation of the profession was gerontocractic, as indeed it still is, and promotion depended upon approval by senior members of the profession. The system of education and apprenticeship, the residential arrangements, the organisation of dispute and argument . . . all assisted in producing cohesion . . . and continuity.[52]

Factors such as these, generated from within the profession, are no less likely to operate now, but one could be forgiven for knowing nothing at all of their existence were one's reading solely confined to orthodox accounts of adjudication. The orthodox rarely register the wider conditions that make certain kinds of argument possible at a particular time, conditions that both constitute and determine institutional schemata. The latter, remember, are recipes as to how to act within particular institutional contexts, ensuring that certain courses of action are open while others are relatively closed. The kind of factors identified by Simpson constitute part of the institutional schemata of the ancient common law: they served to constrain what could and could not be thought, said and done. Of course, such schemata are not exclusively the product of the actions of those whose behaviour constitutes the institution or practice in question. They are also determined by developments in other institutions and practices and by structural changes at an even higher level of abstraction. For a complete account of the conditions of possibility of certain kinds of argument within the ancient common law, more is required than even Simpson's fine but partial analysis of institutional schemata. Some effort at providing an account of the extra-institutional or extra-systemic factors that mould the schemata is also required, although there is no guarantee that such an account will be found. In Simpson's case, it might involve, for example, a discussion of how the professional organisation of this institution was somehow determined by that of another, perhaps the clergy.

Work like this cannot be done on a wing and a prayer. In so far as the sketchy, half-baked analysis offered in the previous paragraph suggests it

[52] 'The Common Law and Legal Theory', ch. IV of A. W. B. Simpson (ed.), *Oxford Essays in Jurisprudence* (Second Series) (Oxford, Clarendon 1973), p. 95.

can, it is wrong. The aim, though, was not to engage in the kind of legal scholarship that compatibilism encourages but simply to note some of its contours. Once they are noted they seem to be embodied in a good deal of heretical scholarship. This brings us to what else compatibilism might mean in legal scholarship. By far the most important thing it means, for the purposes of this book, is a reconsideration of the supposed incompatibility between orthodoxy and heresy. Why? Well, not only because some heretical work does the jobs that properly compatibilist, orthodox work should do,[53] but also because heresy and orthodoxy share a commitment to methodological compatibilism. At least two notable heretics espouse compatibilism. First, Roberto Unger rejects either form of incompatibilism and thereby commits himself to compatibilism:

> If we disregard the meanings an act has for its author and for the other members of the society to which he belongs, we run the risk of losing sight of what is peculiarly social in the conduct we are trying to understand. If, however, we insist on sticking close to the reflective understanding of the agent or his fellows, we are deprived of a standard by which to distinguish insight from illusion or to rise above the self-images of different ages and societies. Thus, subjective and objective meaning must somehow both be taken into account.[54]

While this is undoubtedly an affirmation of compatibilism, the reasons Unger adduces for compatibilism are weak. For example, most incompatibilist positions which fall on the explanation side of the explanation/understanding divide accept that 'subjective and objective meaning must be combined'; they differ from a compatibilist position because they hold that both dimensions are subject to explanation by some version or other of the D-N method or some related, cause-based variant. Moreover, sticking close to agents' understandings of the action, practice or institution in question does not, as Unger thinks, make it impossible to distinguish insight from illusion. This becomes impossible only if, in addition to sticking close to agents' understandings, one also holds that there is a strong connection between meaning and intention such that agents' views as to the point, purpose or value of a practice are incorrigible. That connection can be severed without taking up an incompatibilist position.

Secondly, Duncan Kennedy has recently explicitly espoused compatibilism. During his analysis of adjudication he says his 'goal is to identify the aspects of legal discourse that suggest to *informed observers* of adjudica-

[53] Two examples: almost any of R. Gordon's historical work, a good starting point being 'Critical Legal Histories' (1984) 36 *Stanford L. R.* 57–125, and Horwitz, *supra*, note 19. This is not to suggest that there will be no areas of disagreement between heretics and orthodox. For example, the orthodox would reject Gordon's rather facile invocation of indeterminacy, 'Critical Legal Histories', pp. 114–116.

[54] R. Unger, *Law in Modern Society* (New York, The Free Press 1976), p. 15. See also his *Social Theory: Its Situation and Its Task* (Cambridge, C. U. P. 1987), p. 11.

tion that ideology is a major influence'. The viewpoint of informed observers is a matter of taking up the external point of view. He thus continues, immediately after the above, to refer to '[t]he external point of view of this chapter' and that clearly involves a departure from the views of the participants.[55] In addition, Kennedy 'attempt[s] to reconstruct the situation of the judge from the inside . . . asking how the judge experiences and responds to the body of legal materials when he has an ideological preference for a particular rule choice', thereby taking up the internal point of view.[56] He does not 'think there is anything inconsistent about adopting these different approaches one after the other' and, in so far as he is a methodological compatibilist, he is quite correct.[57] Whatever complaints might be made about Kennedy's methodological position (we will examine some in a later chapter), statements such as these show that he cannot be faulted as an incompatibilist of any type.

The orthodoxy and heresy cannot, then, be clearly distinguished on methodological grounds. This can only help to highlight the nature of the dispute between them. It must involve non-methodological matters, those concerning more obviously philosophical or epistemological or normative issues. They might, perhaps, be divided about the nature of values and their role in adjudication or the question of 'indeterminacy' might bring them into conflict. These matters are examined in subsequent chapters. Even then, less might divide orthodoxy and heresy than is initially assumed. Before turning to those other matters, though, the argument of this chapter should be summarised. First, the claim that the orthodox embrace the sovereign individual was rejected. It was shown that the orthodox neither deny a role to causality in the explanation and understanding of social life nor do they affirm strong methodological individualism. Secondly, the orthodox methodological position was characterised as compatibilist and, although some problems were noted in the orthodox employment of this method, they were not particularly serious. They were problems of emphasis rather than substance. Finally, some arguments in favour of compatibilism were offered and some effects of a full-blown commitment to this method upon legal scholarship were noted, albeit briefly. The orthodox are compatibilists but so, too, are some heretics. What, then, sets them apart? A step toward answering this question will be taken in the next chapter where the orthodox position on values in adjudication is discussed. It may well be that their position is different from that of heretics but, of course, that will only be certain when the heretical position on the same matter is analysed. That is the task of chapter 7.

[55] Both quotations are from D. Kennedy, *A Critique of Adjudication* (Cambridge, Mass., Harvard U. P. 1996), p. 134 (emphasis in original).

[56] *Ibid.*, p. 157.

[57] *Ibid.*, p. 135.

4
Adjudication for Pluralists

> The Supreme Court in *Bakke*, as on occasion in other cases, played the role of a peacemaking or truce-keeping body by negotiating its way through an impasse of conflict, not by invoking our shared moral first principles. For our society as a whole has none. A. MacIntyre, *After Virtue*, 1981 p. 236.

> Law is the dictate of reason determining every rational being to that which is congruous and convenient for the nature thereof. Viscount Stair, *Institutions of the Law of Scotland*, 1893 I. i.1.

Suppose value pluralism is true. So what? Will its truth have any effect whatsoever on the beliefs, self-understandings and practices of legal academics, practitioners and judges? I argue that almost all of the jurisprudentially orthodox think value pluralism is true. This is important because many of the orthodox who believe in value pluralism are blind to some significant consequences of this belief. In particular, they fail to appreciate that the invocation of value pluralism ensures that their accounts of adjudication become all but indistinguishable, in two important and soon to be specified respects, from heretical accounts. This argument, if successful, can be regarded in two very different ways: either as an attempt to steal the thunder of heretics within contemporary legal scholarship or as an illustration of the surprisingly radical nature of orthodox jurisprudence. From either perspective, the conflict between orthodoxy and heresy in contemporary legal thought is less dramatic than it initially appears. This reorientation will hopefully serve to reduce the heat generated by the conflict between orthodox and heretics and throw more light on the issues involved.[1] Of course, this brighter light may lead us to wonder what, exactly, is at issue in this dispute.

The chapter is divided into four sections. The first introduces the two conditions which, if affirmed by the orthodox, would in tandem constitute a crucial difference between their accounts of adjudication and those offered by heretics. The second establishes that many of the orthodox affirm value pluralism and that this serves to endanger one condition that might distinguish orthodoxy from heresy. Some orthodox responses to this argument are also considered but they are found wanting. Section three analyses the effect affirming value pluralism has upon the other condition that would serve to distinguish orthodoxy from heresy. The argument is that the affir-

[1] I am, of course, stealing and mangling H. Hart's delightful *bon mot* in his comments about L. Fuller: see *Essays in Jurisprudence and Philosophy* (Oxford, Clarendon 1983), p. 363.

mation of value pluralism is incompatible with the affirmation of this condition. The final section offers a brief summary and introduces some of the arguments developed in part II of the book.

I ORTHODOXY AND HERESY (AGAIN)

Before we can appreciate the way in which the orthodox invocation of value pluralism narrows the gap between their accounts and heretical accounts, three points must be made. First, the putative differences between orthodox and heretical accounts must be elucidated. This is done by recalling the two composite pictures of these accounts offered in chapter 1. Although they tend towards caricature, these pictures are informed by work that I think all would agree to be exemplars of these two apparently very different approaches to understanding and explaining adjudication. Secondly, the point of repeating these differences between orthodoxy and heresy is important. From these composites two distinctions—labelled the determinacy and legitimacy conditions—are constructed. It is argued that if the orthodox affirm value pluralism then they imperil their often voiced commitment to the determinacy condition. Further, the costs of giving up the determinacy condition cannot be mitigated by affirming the legitimacy condition since the orthodox struggle to show that judicial decisions which fail the determinacy condition can be legitimate. If the orthodox must—as a matter of consistency with, and in deference to, their other commitments—reject the determinacy condition, and cannot sustain the legitimacy condition in the face of indeterminacy, then two significant differences between their accounts of adjudication and those offered by heretics are lost. For heretics have often denied the truth and validity of both the determinacy and legitimacy conditions and affirm their contraries (labelled, hereinafter, as the *in*determinacy and *il*legitimacy conditions). Thirdly, it needs be shown that values are indeed implicated within the process of adjudication. If they are not, then affirming the truth of value pluralism will neither impact upon the beliefs, self-understandings and practices of legal academics, practitioners and judges nor imperil the determinacy and legitimacy conditions.

(i) The composite pictures

Orthodox and heretical accounts of adjudication have two features worth highlighting for present purposes (four were elucidated in chapter 1). While orthodox accounts are the fulcrum of this chapter, only the work of Neil MacCormick, Joseph Raz, Ronald Dworkin and a few others are tackled. There is neither time nor space to consider all orthodox works and these particular writers have had considerable influence both within the common law world and beyond.[2] Moreover, our focus is not exclusively upon the orthodoxy because, in order to appreciate the significance of the determinacy and legitimacy conditions, the heresy must also be considered. The role of the heresy in this chapter is, though, that of ghost at the feast, a disturbing background presence. Our picture of the heresy is based upon a limited number of exemplary works—by, *inter alios*, Roberto Unger, Duncan Kennedy and Mark Kelman—which have directly and indirectly influenced many legal scholars.[3] Thus, not all heretical work is examined. In particular, the diverse kinds of heretical work initially inspired by the likes of Kennedy and Unger, but now portrayed under banners as different as 'deconstruction', 'critical race theory' and 'critical legal feminism', are all but ignored here, although some is examined in subsequent chapters. Also ignored are the various and supposedly different geographical instances of 'critical legal' thought.[4] Since deconstructive, feminist, critical race and, perhaps, Anglo-European critical legal scholarship each raise substantive and methodological issues of their own,[5] they are not considered here.

The two features constitutive of orthodox and heretical accounts of adjudication stand in conflict with one another. The first feature of orthodox accounts narrows their focus. These accounts concentrate solely on appellate court cases that are 'hard', that is, cases where 'no settled rule dictates a decision either way' and 'in which reasonable lawyers will disagree . . .

[2] N. MacCormick, *Legal Reasoning and Legal Theory* (Oxford, Clarendon 1978; republished with a new foreword 1993) herein after referred to in text and notes as '*LRLT*'; J. Raz, *Practical Reason and Norms* (London, Hutchinson 1975 and New Jersey, Princeton University Press 1991) and *The Authority of Law* (Oxford, Clarendon 1979), referred to hereinafter as '*PRN*' and '*AL*' respectively; R. Dworkin, *Taking Rights Seriously* (London, Duckworth 1978) hereinafter '*TRS*'; *A Matter of Principle* (Oxford, Clarendon 1985), referred to as '*MP*'; and *Law's Empire* (London, Fontana 1986), referred to as '*LE*'.

[3] R. Unger, *Knowledge and Politics* (New York, The Free Press 1975); *The Critical Legal Studies Movement* (Cambridge, Mass., Harvard U. P. 1987), henceforth referred to as '*KP*' and '*CLSM*', respectively; and *What Should Legal Analysis Become?* (London, Verso 1996). D. Kennedy, 'The Structure of Blackstone's *Commentaries*' (1979) 28 *Buffalo L. R.* 205–382 and 'Form and Substance in Private Law Adjudication' (1976) 89 *Harvard L. R.* 1685–1778, hereinafter '*BC*' and '*FS*' respectively; also his *Sexy Dressing Etc.* (Cambridge, Mass., Harvard U. P. 1993) and *A Critique Of Adjudication* (Cambridge, Mass., Harvard U. P. 1997) hereinafter '*CA*'. M. Kelman, *A Guide to Critical Legal Studies* (Cambridge, Mass, Harvard University Press 1987), henceforth '*GCLS*'; J. Singer, 'The Player and the Cards: Nihilism and Legal Theory' (1984) 94 *Yale L. J.* 1–70; C. Dalton, 'An Essay on the Deconstruction of Contract Law Doctrine' (1985) 94 *Yale L. J.* 997–1114; G. Peller, 'The Metaphysics of American Law' (1985) 73 *California L. R.* 1152–1290; and the contributions in D. Kairys (ed.), *The Politics of Law: A Progressive Critique* (New York, Pantheon 1982), referred to as '*PL*'.

[4] See the sources referred to in chapter 1, above, at notes 25 and 27.

[5] Contrast, for example, Peller's deconstructive turn, *supra*, note 3 with D. Cornell, *The Philosophy of the Limit* (London, Routledge and Chapman Hall 1992) and M. Kramer, *Legal Theory, Political Theory, and Deconstruction* (Bloomington, Indiana U. P. 1991); and C. Mackinnon's feminism in, for example, her *Feminism Unmodified* (Cambridge, Mass., Harvard U. P. 1987) and *Toward a Feminist Theory of the State* (Cambridge, Mass., Harvard U. P. 1989) with D. Cornell's *Beyond Accommodation* (London, Routledge and Chapman Hall 1991) and M. J. Frug's *Postmodern Legal Feminism* (London, Routledge and Chapman Hall 1992).

and neither will have available any argument that must necessarily convince the other'.[6] In such cases the issues that arise are usually categorised thus by the orthodox. Hard cases (i) raise doubts about whether or not there is indeed a proposition of law applicable to the case; or (ii) generate disputes about the correct interpretation, out of a range of two or more, of the agreed applicable proposition of law; or (iii) raise doubts about which out of two or more valid and incompatible propositions of law should be applied to the case.[7] By implication, easy cases are those in which none of these issues arise and in which reasonable lawyers will agree as to the outcome: hence, the orthodox are usually uninterested in such cases. In stark contrast, the first feature of many heretical accounts is an unequivocal denial of the hard/easy case dichotomy. For heretics '[t]here are . . . no easy cases, though there may be many ones whose outcomes are perfectly predictable'.[8]

One, but probably not the only, reason for this divergence can be found in the second feature of each account. The second feature of orthodox accounts is that they take seriously adjudicators' claims that they decide hard cases *relatively* constrained by standards *relatively* determinate of the dispute before them. 'Relatively' because not even the orthodox on these matters believe that adjudicators have no choices open to them when making decisions. Rather, they hold, albeit in different ways and for different reasons, that these choices are justifiable in principle and often in practice.[9] Moreover, the strategies of justification which adjudicators use when making these choices form a limited and recognisable class of arguments. However, the exact nature of, and weight to be attached to, the various types of justificatory arguments is something about which the orthodox disagree: recall the dispute between Dworkin and MacCormick as to the nature and relevance of policy considerations in judicial decisions.[10]

The second feature of heretical accounts of adjudication stands in direct opposition to the second feature of orthodox accounts. Heretics deny that adjudicators apply relatively determinate standards and invoke relatively determinate justificatory strategies to achieve closure of a choice open to them. For heretics, these choices are not in principle capable of justification because of the truth of both language and value indeterminacy (only the latter type of indeterminacy figures in this chapter). These types of inde-

[6] Dworkin, *TRS*, p. 83 and p. xiv respectively.

[7] See MacCormick, *LRLT*, p. 100; Dworkin, *TRS*, p. 81; *LE*, pp. 3–6.

[8] Kelman, *GCLS*, p. 4. Kennedy has now apparently given up this article of faith: *CA* 3, p. 60.

[9] That the justifiability of judicial decisions is *the* crucial concern of the orthodox is obvious: see the remarks of MacCormick, *LRLT*, pp. 14–18, chs. 2 and 5; Dworkin, *TRS*, ch. 4, particularly pp. 106–107, 112, 115, 117–118; *LE*, ch. 7, particularly pp. 227–228, 239 and 245; Raz, *AL*, pp. 184 and 186–187.

[10] See chapter 1, section I.

terminacy allegedly entail that neither legal standards nor the values or purposes they serve compel any legal decision. This is because, first, heretics assume language yields meaning only conventionally. That one word means or refers to X rather than Y is a purely contingent matter. The word could have had another, radically different meaning or referred to any number of other things. Hence, the meaning and reference of words is analogous to stipulative definitions: they have no rational power and are not compelling.[11] Thus in relation to any interpretation or definition of the word, sentence or proposition X, there is always another, equally 'valid' or 'compelling' interpretation available. As this is true of language in general it is held by heretics to be true, *a fortiori*, of legal language. The implication heretics draw is that, despite appearances, legal doctrines are severely indeterminate. In particular cases, 'opposing arguments can be made with *equal force*'; in general, there is always 'a wide variety of precedents and a still wider variety of interpretations and distinctions from which to *pick and choose*'.[12]

Second, some heretics assume either that values are beyond the bounds of rationality *tout court* or that the orthodox are explicitly or implicitly committed to this view. This uncomfortable conjunction is made necessary because when heretics speak of values it is unclear whether they are simply attacking what they take to be the orthodox position or invoking a general truth about values. For Unger and Kelman the orthodox, in so far as they are 'liberals', are committed to the subjectivity (or indeterminacy) of values. That commitment entails 'that values—beliefs about what is worth pursuing—are seen as nothing more than tastes, the purely arbitrary assertions of individuals'.[13] By contrast, heretics such as they favour an account in which values and the good are more than just a function 'of the satisfaction of individual desires'.[14] Some heretics, however, appear to accept that the subjectivity of values is a general truth. For example, in his early work Kennedy noted that private law doctrine is informed by both individualistic and altruistic values. He assumed that this observation, without more, conclusively established that this conflict of values cannot be resolved, but this claim could only be accepted where there is some independent reason to support it. Merely invoking the existence of different values does not show that they must conflict. Such a reason could be provided by the subjectivity of values claim. If it is the case that values are arbitrary assertions of individuals, then it is indeed difficult to see how different value assertions could be compatible (in the same way that it is difficult to see how your view that coffee tastes better with sugar could be made compatible

[11] For useful discussion see R. Robinson, *Definition* (Oxford, Clarendon 1954), ch. 4.

[12] Dalton, *supra*, note 3, p. 1007; Kairys, *PL*, p. 14. For a similar refrain see also J. Frug, 'Argument as Character' (1988) 40 *Stanford L. R.* 869–927, pp. 869–874.

[13] Kelman, *GCLS*, p. 64. See also Unger, *KP*, pp. 76–100.

[14] Unger, *KP*, p. 240

with my view that it is better without). This, combined with Kennedy's many apparently general statements—statements about the human condition *simpliciter*, not the human situation within supposedly liberal societies—that conflicts between values are an inescapable feature of our lives, suggest that for him the subjectivity of values claim is a general truth.[15]

(ii) Two important distinctions

The task of highlighting two important distinctions between orthodox and heretical accounts can be discharged quite briefly since our composite pictures have served to introduce them. The determinacy and legitimacy conditions and their contraries arise from, respectively, either the affirmation or denial of the second feature of orthodox accounts. Affirming that feature does not immediately entail the determinacy condition; rather, that condition can be derived from it in a few steps. The condition maintains that the choices judges make in hard cases are justifiable in principle and often in practice. A corollary of this is that decisions in easy cases are, *a fortiori*, justifiable. Proponents of the determinacy condition therefore believe that judicial choices in both hard and easy cases often have the maximum justification quotient; this means at least that those choices are compelled by reasons (and, therefore, Reason). Hereinafter, when judicial decisions are spoken of as 'determinate', this is what is meant. Denying the determinacy condition commits one to holding that the choices judges make—certainly in hard cases but probably also in easy cases—are neither justifiable in principle nor practice. Those choices therefore suffer from a justification deficit; they are not compelled by reasons (yet they may still be rooted in Reason). Such a denial, which we can call the indeterminacy condition, can follow from the truth of either or both types of indeterminacy constitutive of the second feature of heretical accounts of adjudication (remember that only value indeterminacy will be of interest in what follows). That, of course, is not to say that language and value indeterminacy are the only possible foundations for the indeterminacy condition.

It is often thought that affirming the determinacy condition commits one to affirming the legitimacy condition.[16] The latter holds that judicial deci-

[15] Kennedy, *FS*, pp. 1712, 1762, 1766–1767, and 1774–1776. Kennedy attempts to retract the claim that there exists a fundamental contradiction between individualism and altruism and between self and other (Kennedy, *BC*, pp. 211–221) in 'Roll Over Beethoven' (1984) 36 *Stanford L. R.* 1–55, pp. 15–18. However, the notion of contradiction reappears in his later work: see *Sexy Dressing Etc.* (Cambridge, Mass., Harvard U. P. 1993), pp. viii and 70 and *A Critique of Adjudication* (Cambridge, Mass., Harvard U. P. 1997), pp. 151–152. The existence of apparently unavoidable value conflict does not inhibit Kennedy from making value judgements and moral arguments: *Sexy Dressing*, p. x.

[16] A notable example is J. Habermas who, in *Between Facts and Norms* (Cambridge, Polity Press 1996), often unwittingly elides the difference between the two conditions. See, for example, p. 198, where he observes that 'the claim to legitimacy [Habermas's equivalent to the

sions and other sources of propositions of law can in some circumstances be authoritative. That is, they can generate a legitimate obligation to obey and hence give good reasons for acting in accord with their content. Its contrary, the illegitimacy condition, simply denies that propositions of law—judicial or statutory—can be legitimately authoritative. Now the circumstances in which propositions of law can have legitimate authority will vary according to the account of political authority espoused and there are many such accounts available to us, being more or less plausible. However, given the close relationship between intellectual and practical authority (of which political authority is but a species), it seems plausible to hold that one condition for the latter is that the rule or direction offered up as authoritative is justifiable in principle and practice. In this way we may be led to think that affirming the determinacy condition entails the legitimacy condition. This would be a mistake. For the fulfilment of the determinacy condition is only one possible condition for a rule or directive to have legitimate authority and then, perhaps, not even a necessary condition. At least, this is the case if we accept that mistaken directives, rules or decisions can sometimes have legitimate authority and thus generate obligations to obey. Pending a more thorough discussion of this possibility, it appears sensible to draw a bright line between the determinacy and legitimacy conditions. We must avoid over-simplifying the relation between them.

This characterisation of the determinacy and legitimacy conditions and their contraries has a number of advantages. First, our statement of the determinacy and indeterminacy conditions minimises the potential that those words have to generate confusion in the discourse of both orthodox and heretics. This potential for confusion is not surprising given that the use of those words within the legal context could refer to any or all of the following. One could be speaking of the indeterminacy or determinacy of either legal *processes* or *outcomes*, and have in mind by those words the *predictability* of judicial decisions and/or law-making procedures, or the *legitimacy* of those decisions and/or procedures, or the *justifiability* of those decisions and/or procedures. The *inter se* links between these ideas and their links with notions like arbitrariness and impartiality are complex and would require a great deal of analysis. That task cannot be tackled here. However, there is one clear advantage in defining the notions of determinacy and indeterminacy, as they appear in the determinacy and indeterminacy conditions, narrowly, in terms of the *justifiability* of judicial decisions or *outcomes.* For that narrow definition fits better the language of both heretics and orthodox. It accommodates the fact that both orthodox and heretical accounts of adjudication are concerned exclusively with outcomes; and, that both types of account, when they speak the language of determinacy and

legitimacy conditions] requires decisions that are . . . rationally grounded [his equivalent to the determinacy condition] . . . so that all participants can accept them as rational decisions'.

indeterminacy, are in the main concerned with the justifiability of judicial choices.

Secondly, the characterisation of the determinacy and legitimacy conditions and their contraries offered here has the advantage of clearing up a number of puzzles that arise in some discussions of these matters. The first puzzle consists of the hasty inference from the supposed fact of the indeterminacy of judicial choices to the conclusion that such choices are illegitimate.[17] This inference is correct in so far as it must define indeterminacy narrowly, as relating to the absence of a justification for judicial choices, but problematic because it apparently assumes that justifiability is a necessary condition for legitimacy. If indeterminacy is given any other than the narrow meaning—if, for example, it is used to refer to the existence of a range of unpredictable judicial choices, then the inference is a *non sequitur*. For it is surely possible that in some areas of the law judges could be granted, by a presumably legitimate statute, a wide and unstructured domain within which they are free to choose any of a number of ways of resolving a case.[18] Such choices would be legitimate but indeterminate (in the sense that they lack predictability). However, the narrow definition of the indeterminacy condition taken in conjunction with an elucidation of the legitimacy condition highlights that there are indeed two distinct issues here and clearly counsels against linking the conditions in the way this inference does. For our previous analysis of these two conditions suggests that the relation between them is not a necessary one.

The second puzzle is cleared up by invoking the narrow definitions of determinacy and indeterminacy. Bearing them in mind, we can see why some discussions of these matters err. The mistake ascribes to heretics the view that adjudication generates unpredictable outcomes, a view taken to follow from the affirmation of widespread indeterminacy in the law.[19] But heretics do not hold that view; rather, they frequently affirm that adjudication does indeed generate predictable outcomes. The basis of the mistake is to equate indeterminacy with a lack of predictability. Yet, when indeterminacy is defined narrowly, as referring to a justification deficit, we can see that there is no contradiction between heretics' indeterminacy talk, on the one hand, and their affirmations of the predictability of adjudication, on the other. Defining indeterminacy as a lack of predictability just does not fit the claims heretics make. Hence, it is idle to point to easy—that is, completely predictable—hypothetical case outcomes (for example, that the

[17] One example of which is K. Kress, 'Legal Indeterminacy' (1989) 77 *California L. R.* 283–337, pp. 285–295.

[18] This example is a much exaggerated instance of what can be called a 'permissive gap' in the law: see J. Gardner, 'Concerning Permissive Sources and Gaps' (1988) 8 *Oxford Journal of Legal Studies* 457–461, p. 458.

[19] K. Kress, *supra,* note 17, pp. 296–297; L. Solum, 'On the Indeterminacy Crisis: Critiquing Legal Dogma' (1987) 54 *University of Chicago L. R.* 462–503 pp. 471–472.

first paragraph of this essay does not defame Gore Vidal) in an attempt to refute the heresy.[20] The obvious and charitable interpretation of indeterminacy regards it as raising only the issue of justifiability. Hence, both heretics and orthodox affirm that adjudication is a relatively predictable, certain process. Both camps agree that, given adequate knowledge and understanding of the law, academics, practitioners and observers can form fairly stable expectations about the outcomes of the vast majority of cases. Yet, while accepting that the outcomes of cases are quite predictable, the reasons orthodox and heretics offer in explanation differ radically. For the orthodox, one reason why adjudication is reasonably predictable and certain is because the choices judges make are in principle justifiable, drawing upon a limited range of arguments. Contrary to this view, heretics hold that although adjudicators may believe their choices are justifiable, this belief—inculcated through socialisation perhaps prior to, but certainly during, professional and academic training—is a mistake. The choices open to adjudicators cannot be justified because of the truth of language and value indeterminacy. The choices adjudicators make are nevertheless predictable because as a class they share a range of values and assumptions upon which they base their choices.[21] For heretics, these choices remain indeterminate even when informed by values, the reason being that values and choices between them are incapable of justification.

Finally, this interpretation avoids another puzzle that ensnares many discussions of determinacy and indeterminacy. It is the spectre of the 'objectivity' of legal doctrine and interpretation. This notion is problematic because, *inter alia*, it is far from clear what exactly it means to predicate it of legal doctrine or adjudication or of any practice, entity or institution. Within contemporary philosophy of language and epistemology the notion is as oblique and problematic as it appears within legal discourse. Therefore, a characterisation of determinacy and indeterminacy that avoids the notion surely has some advantages.[22]

(iii) Values and adjudication

Are values implicated within the practice of adjudication? That they are can be demonstrated by reference to some examples and by invoking an old but compelling jurisprudential lesson about the nature of rule applica-

[20] The example belongs to Solum, *ibid.*, p. 471.

[21] For heretics these values and assumptions are ideologies and hence socially determined; they are not rationally articulated and assented to nor could they be so, given the truth of value indeterminacy: see Kairys, *PL*, p. 15; Singer, *supra*, note 3, pp. 19–25; Kelman, *GCLS*, pp. 4 and 46–47.

[22] For a noble attempt to clarify the variety of issues for which objectivity talk in legal discourse may be a proxy, see J. Coleman and B. Leiter, 'Determinacy, Objectivity, and Authority' (1993) 142 *University of Pennsylvania L. R.* 549–637, pp. 594–635.

tion and interpretation. There are two kinds of examples that illustrate the point. The first consists of those propositions of law that invoke and require interpretation of moral concepts and their constitutive values. Propositions of law that include notions such as, *inter alia*, good faith, dishonesty, reasonableness and fairness are obvious instances. Secondly, even when dealing with propositions of law that do not explicitly incorporate any moral concepts or other kind of normative values, judges often interpret and apply those propositions in the light of generic rule of law values. These values take the form of, for example, rather abstract notions such as consistency (with other propositions of law and decisions, so that like cases be treated alike) or more specific principles such as that criminal law statutes are to be interpreted restrictively.

Now it might be the case that legal systems exist which do not incorporate values in either of the two ways—so familiar in our legal system—just noted. It could then be argued that the role values play within the process of adjudication is purely contingent. However, a compelling jurisprudential lesson suggests that, whether incorporated into propositions of law in the ways suggested by our two examples or not, values are apparently unavoidably implicated within the process of rule application and interpretation. The lesson begins with some over-simplified instances of rule application and interpretation. The examples used are rules like: 'no vehicles in the park' and 'no blood to be spilled in the streets'.[23] Setting aside issues about core and penumbral meanings, the interpretation and application of these rules in particular cases will, it is said, unavoidably implicate values of some kind. This is because being able to apply these rules in particular situations assumes some understanding of their point, purpose or value. It is only by reference to such understandings that we can decide whether or not the park warden's pick-up truck, war veterans' memorial jeep, a child's roller skates and the postman's bicycle are excluded from the park. The lesson, that even elementary instances of rule interpretation and application such as these depend upon an account of the point, purpose or value of the rule, seems undeniable. Furthermore, the lesson holds when applied to the much more complex and interrelated rules and standards we find in actually existing legal systems and holds, *a fortiori*, if the rules and standards in question raise any of the issues said by the orthodox to be the hallmarks of hard cases. Obviously, the lesson gives no guidance on either the number of cases that are hard or the number in which values play a role.

Having outlined, albeit briefly, the nature of orthodox and heretical accounts of adjudication, the determinacy and legitimacy conditions, and the way in which values are implicated in adjudication, the next steps in the

[23] These well-worn examples belong to L. Fuller, 'Positivism and Fidelity to Law—A Reply to Professor Hart' (1958) 71 *Harvard L. R.* 630–674, pp. 661–669; Hart, *supra*, note 1, pp. 62–72; Unger, *KP*, p. 92.

argument can be taken. There are two. The first consists of: (i) an attempt to unpack the notion of value pluralism; (ii) a demonstration of who, among the orthodox, accepts value pluralism; and (iii) a demonstration, premised upon the suppositions that values do have a role in adjudication and that value pluralism is true, of one *adverse* consequence value pluralism has for orthodox accounts of adjudication. The argument is simply that the orthodox affirmation of the existence of value pluralism in adjudication undermines the determinacy condition. Embracing value pluralism commits the orthodox to affirming some characteristically heretical claims. The second step of the argument considers an obvious way in which the orthodox could attempt to minimise the damage this point causes. They could maintain that, even though some judicial choices do not satisfy the determinacy condition, such choices are nevertheless legitimate and create compelling reasons to act in accordance with their content. This strategy depends for its success upon: (i) a plausible account of the conceptual and normative contours of the notion of legitimate authority; and (ii) the applicability of such an account to indeterminate judicial decisions. Our conclusion is that the arguments to support the strategy lack plausibility. Hence the orthodox are, by dint of their inability to support the legitimacy condition, uncomfortably close to accepting the truth of the *il*legitimacy condition. This is another instance in which they are apparently committed to a characteristically heretical claim.

II VALUE PLURALISM AND THE DETERMINACY CONDITION

This section addresses three connected questions.

(i) What is value pluralism?

The strongest and most interesting answer to this question consists of three claims labelled, respectively, the plurality, conflict and incomparability claims. A weaker, but not the weakest, answer comprises only the plurality and conflict claims. The very weakest answer makes just the plurality claim (it must do so in order to deserve the label 'pluralist').

Taken alone, the plurality claim is the least interesting of the three because, within the sphere of thought about moral, political and other values, it is one with which just about everyone could agree. It holds, obviously, that we believe the human world constituted by a multiplicity of values. Those—let us call them value monists and include among their ilk utilitarians—who hold that our moral and political thought embraces only one ultimate and fundamental value, could quite easily accept this claim with the following caveat. It is that the multiplicity of values evidenced in our thought and language are less fundamental, particular manifestations of some single fundamental value. Similarly, those who have reasons for rejecting single value views of the human world—we will label them value pluralists—accept the plurality claim. Generally speaking, however, neither value monists nor value pluralists accept the plurality claim on its own. Rather, what distinguishes these views as two separate classes and what also distinguishes between members of the same class is the nature of the wider claims with which the plurality claim is conjoined and to which it purports to provide support. For value monists, in particular utilitarians, one such wider claim consists of the alleged truth that there is indeed one ultimate, fundamental value—be it utility, welfare or preference satisfaction—that we do and should embrace. For strong value pluralists, by contrast, there are two such wider claims—the conflict and incomparability claims—that constitute a competing, putative truth about the nature of values. The conflict claim insists that some or all of our fundamental values conflict; the incomparability claim holds—unsurprisingly—that some or all of those conflicting values are in some sense beyond comparison. Answers to our question that have this structure are more interesting than those that affirm only the plurality claim because these other claims serve to draw a sharp distinction between value pluralists and value monists.

In the stronger answers to the first question, the conflict claim is admirably clear. It usually has two dimensions. The first consists of an observation about the human world. Its basis is that some value conflict is a consequence of the fact that the world does not bend itself to our purposes: '[i]t is beyond argument that the world as we know it gives us grounds for regret and conflict even if we do what is to be done . . . The present world, and those worlds we should think we could bring about, are worlds of conflict'.[24] If a world could be engineered in which conflict creating features were absent—a world, for example, in which it was logically impossible for our commitments to one another to conflict—then on this view much value conflict would not arise. Value conflict would not, however, be completely avoided for the reason stated in the second dimension of the conflict claim. It holds that we have good reason for accepting values that are substantively very different and which can quite plausibly conflict, in the sense of requiring incompatible courses of action in particular situations.

The incomparability claim is equally clear but it is difficult to assess or even think of ways in which it could be supported or denied. The standard argumentative strategy adopted by pluralists consists of the affirmation of incomparability (the language of incommensurability is often used) in con-

[24] M. Stocker, *Plural and Conflicting Values* (Oxford, Clarendon 1990), p. 125. For slightly different statements of the same point see: B. Williams, *Problems of the Self* (Cambridge, C. U. P. 1973), pp. 166, 170–171, 181 and his *Moral Luck* (Cambridge, C. U. P. 1981) pp. 74–75. Williams, however, seems to think this is the only interesting source of value conflict.

junction with both the conflict claim and some actual or hypothetical examples of the phenomenon. J. O. Urmson provides a clear and representative example of this. He says, first, that there is 'a plurality of first principles [and values] which may conflict to give contrary directives in particular types of cases: and second, . . . [that there is] no explicit method, no priority rules, for weighing these principles [and values] against one another'; he adds, third, a few examples that purport to illustrate the truth of the previous two claims.[25] Now the second part of Urmson's statement is the fulcrum of many contemporary discussions of incomparability, despite the fact that for Urmson it stands as part and parcel of a doctrine about the foundation and justification of moral values—moral intuitionism—that few other proponents of the incomparability claim accept.[26]

It is important to note one obvious implication that appears to follow from affirming all three claims that constitute the strongest answer to the first question. For, were the human world indeed constituted by a multiplicity of values and were it true that some or all of those values conflict, then there would be no obviously rational way—because of the absence of priority rules—of resolving the conflict. This becomes clear when Joseph Raz's account of the incomparability claim is considered. Raz is one of the few proponents of that claim who actually attempts to elucidate the nature of the relationship between incomparable values (he is not content just to affirm incomparability and point to some examples of it). He is concerned to do this because, quite rightly, he wants to determine whether or not there is conceptual room for talk of values being incomparable or incommensurable (like Raz, I regard these two words as synonyms). In order to do some distinctive conceptual work for us, the notion of value incommensurability must refer to something other than the difficulty we sometimes have in choosing between conflicting values, since that process does not need that label in order to become salient for us. Similarly, the notion of incommensurability will be redundant if it merely refers to the possibility that conflicting values can sometimes be of exactly equal weight. For how does the notion of incommensurability, used in this sense, convey more than talk of

[25] The quotation is from p. 111 of J. O. Urmson, 'A Defence of Intuitionism' *Aristotelian Society Proceedings* (1975) lxxv 111–119. The examples appear on pp. 118–119. That Urmson accepts both dimensions of the conflict claim is clear. Some of the examples of conflict he uses (see pp. 116–117) suggest that he agrees that conflict is a product of certain contingencies occurring in the world. Yet he also speaks as if conflict were simply a result of systematic tensions and inconsistencies *within* our moral thought ('I am inclined . . . to believe that there is a certain strain and disharmony within the moral requirements I must acknowledge and that there could be a decision-procedure only *within an harmonious set of moral beliefs*': p. 119, emphasis supplied). For an account of incomparability that tackles both dimensions see C. Sunstein, 'Incommensurability and Valuation in Law' (1994) 92 *Michigan L. R.* 779–861.

[26] Neither Stocker nor Williams, *supra*, note 24 accept it; nor do others who have made the incomparability claim, such as T. Nagel, *Mortal Questions* (Cambridge, C. U. P. 1979), ch. 9.

'conflict between values of equal weight'? However, the notion does useful work when interpreted thus: as highlighting the fact that the relationship between two or more values is not transitive.[27] A transitive relation between values holds when value X is more valuable than Y, and Y is more valuable than Z, then X is more valuable than Z. By contrast, were those values incommensurable there would be no warrant for making that claim. Hence, 'A and B are incommensurate if it is neither true that one is better than the other nor true that they are of equal value' (*MF*, p. 322). Obviously, a failure of transitivity between values entails the claim that there is no neutral metric with which to value them should one have to choose between them. Thus Raz's notion of a failure of transitivity is a detailed elucidation of the substance of the incomparability claim. Since there is no way in which incommensurable values can themselves be valued and a choice made between them on the basis of a higher level evaluation, it seems that the choice between them cannot be made by reference to compelling reasons. Raz is unambiguous on this point: '[w]here the considerations for and against two alternatives are incommensurate, reason is indeterminate. It provides no better case for one alternative than for the other. . . . Incommensurability speaks not of what does escape reason but of what must elude it' (*MF*, pp. 333–334). That, however, is not to say that the choice is completely uninformed by reason and hence arbitrary and random. Rather, it is to say that the reasons one has for a choice one way or another do not completely determine that choice: one has reasons for choosing both options.[28]

Having sketched what value pluralism is, it will be worthwhile in order to avoid any confusion to note what it is not. It is not—at least, not necessarily—a thesis about the foundation and justification of values. That is, it does not necessarily commit one to any position about how we can have knowledge and beliefs about moral, political and other values. Rather, in its strongest version it holds only that there is a plurality of values some of which can conflict, the conflict being in some sense insoluble. Nothing has to follow from this about the foundation and possibility of knowledge of values. So, for example, within the limited sphere of moral values, affirming value pluralism carries no meta-ethical commitments about how knowledge of those values can be established. One could just as easily affirm value pluralism in conjunction with a non-cognitivist position about the nature of moral values (which would make a claim along these lines: moral values cannot be rationally established, having their basis not in reason but in

[27] See J. Raz, *The Morality of Freedom* (Oxford, Clarendon 1986), pp. 324–328. Referred to hereinafter, in both text and notes, as '*MF*'.

[28] This explains away the apparent inconsistency between Raz's statements, *ibid*., and his remarks (at pp. 338, 339 and 352) that a choice between incommensurable options can be 'reasoned'.

either our desires or sentiments) as a moral realist position (holding that there are facts in the world that make certain statements about moral values either true or false). This is not to deny that some meta-ethical theories are more and some less sympathetic to value pluralism. One can say, on purely contingent grounds, that the more rationalist one's meta-ethics, the less room one has for insoluble conflicts between moral values.[29] This does not *have* to be the case: the link is merely contingent.

(ii) Who affirms value pluralism?

This second question must now be addressed. Given that the strongest version of value pluralism makes the three claims just sketched, who, among the orthodox, affirms that doctrine? In what follows, I show that MacCormick and Raz affirm it while Dworkin does not (he affirms a weaker version of value pluralism).

The textual evidence to show that MacCormick is a strong value pluralist is both plentiful and, with one exception, unambiguous. He is committed to the plurality and conflict claims by virtue of statements such as these:

> I go along with Hume in supposing that a determinant factor in our assent to some or another normative principle lies in our affective nature, in our sentiments, predispositions of will . . . That people have different affective natures, differences of sentiment, passion can then be adduced in explanation of fundamental moral disagreement (*LRLT*, p. 5).

Furthermore, '[h]onest and reasonable people can and do differ even upon ultimate matters of principle, each having reasons which seem to him or her good for the view to which he or she adheres' but 'the reasons which can be given are not in their nature conclusive' (*ibid.*). MacCormick is equally unambiguous in stating that the plurality and conflict claims are general truths manifest *within* the process of adjudication. Hence his value pluralism cannot be regarded as applicable to the general realm of value-talk but inapplicable to some specific instances, such as judicial value-talk. So, for example, MacCormick says that the consequentialist arguments judges invoke to decide hard cases are 'in part at least *subjective*' (*LRLT*, p. 105; emphasis in the original). Why? Because

> [j]udges evaluating consequences of rival possible rulings may give different weight to different criteria of evaluation, differ as to the degree of perceived injustice, or of predicted inconvenience which will arise from adoption or rejection of a given ruling. Not surprisingly, they differ, sometimes sharply and even passionately, in relation to their final judgment of the acceptability or unacceptability all things considered of a ruling under scrutiny. At this point we reach the bedrock of value preferences which inform our reasoning *but which are not demonstrable by it. At*

[29] B. Williams, *Problems of the Self*, *supra*, note 24, notes this contingent link: pp. 204–205.

this level there can simply be irresolvable differences of opinion between people of good will and reason (*LRLT*, pp. 105–6; emphasis supplied).

The only ambiguity about MacCormick's invocation of the plurality and conflict claims arises because of his recent renunciation of the Humean account of the foundation of moral and, presumably, other values (*LRLT*, p. xvi).[30] In so far as that account is *one* of the reasons underlying MacCormick's invocation of these claims, then its rejection partially imperils those claims. Moreover, the danger is partial in another sense. For MacCormick has as yet only stated his dissatisfaction with the Humean account; he has articulated no alternative to it. It is equally unclear how far, if at all, MacCormick's rejection of the Humean account impacts upon his commitment to the incomparability claim. He certainly appears committed to some version of that claim, as the following statements—again about judges' consequentialist arguments—make clear. Those arguments are, says MacCormick, 'intrinsically *evaluative*' (*LRLT*, p. 105). That is, they

> ask[..] about the acceptability or unacceptability of . . . consequences. *There is however no reason to assume that* . . . [they] *involve*[..] *evaluation in terms of a single scale*, such as the Benthamite scale of supposedly measurable aggregates of pleasures and pains. Judges characteristically refer to criteria such as 'justice', 'common sense', 'public policy', and 'convenience' or 'expediency' in weighing the case for and against given rules. *It should not be assumed without proof that these really all boil down to the same thing* (*LRLT*, *ibid.*; emphasis supplied).[31]

MacCormick is less equivocal in his discussion of whether or not there can be a single right answer to a hard case. He says that consequentialist 'evaluation *does not* use a single scale of measurable values . . . *It involves multiple criteria* . . .' (*LRLT*, pp. 252–253; emphasis supplied; see also pp. 114–115). Because this is so, then in hard cases 'we find ourselves faced with a disagreement which it is in principle impossible to send to any theoretical "Hercules" for objective resolution by delivery of the right answer' (p. 254). Presumably, the existence of multiple scales for the evaluation of the consequences of a decision means that there can be no single right decision, for what is right on one scale may well be wrong on another. To regard this talk of a plurality of scales of evaluation as expressing a commitment to the incomparability claim is surely neither unfair nor perverse. For if, as seems obvious from MacCormick's remarks, he is not making the simple

[30] This is contained in the new foreword to the 1993 reprinting of *LRLT*. That MacCormick travelled this road to Damascus recently is clear from the fact that in essays published several years after the first edition of *LRLT* he was still an unreconstructed Humean. See his 'Contemporary Legal Philosophy: the Rediscovery of Practical Reason' (1983) 10 *Journal of Law and Society* 1–18, pp. 13–14 and (with O. Weinberger) *An Institutional Theory of Law* (Dordrecht, D. Reidel 1986), pp. 193–196 and 204–205.

[31] For a similar statement embracing plurality and incomparability see MacCormick, *supra*, note 10, p. 255.

points that value judgements can sometimes be either very difficult or be 'tied', then what else—other than some version of the incomparability claim—could he have in mind?

On this evidence it seems safe to conclude both that MacCormick is a value pluralist in the strong sense and that he believes value pluralism arises within the adjudicative context. What evidence is there to suggest that Raz shares this view? The evidence is found in Raz's political philosophy and it establishes beyond doubt that he affirms the plurality, conflict and (as we already know) incomparability claims (*MF*, chs. 13 and 14; the plurality and conflict claims also appear in *PRN*, p. 159). The only doubt about Raz's value pluralism is this: does he accept that it arises within the adjudicative context? The question is not otiose because it is quite possible to affirm value pluralism and hold that some segments of value-talk (such as judicial value-talk) are beyond its range. There is no sustained response to this question in Raz's work but an unambiguous answer can be gleaned from a number of his disparate remarks about adjudication. Those remarks show he accepts that value pluralism arises within the adjudicative context.

The first step towards showing this consists of noting Raz's remarks that values and, in particular, moral judgements play a role within the process of adjudication. In speaking of unregulated disputes (which for present purposes we will regard as exactly akin to hard cases) Raz says 'judges do rely and should rely on their own moral judgement' (*AL*, p. 199); he holds that 'it is our normal view that judges use moral arguments . . . when developing the law' (*ibid.*, p. 49). Those arguments, when brought to bear on the question of whether or not an 'authority' should be overruled, consist of *inter alia* an assessment of the benefits and disadvantages of a new ruling (*ibid.*, p. 190 and p. 114).[32] It is therefore no surprise that for Raz '[l]egal reasoning is an instance of moral reasoning'.[33] The nature of the legal standards with which judges have to operate guarantees that values have a role in adjudication. This is because, as we have already noted, some legal standards embody moral and other values. Raz accepts this but with one caveat.[34] For, in order to maintain his version of legal positivism, which relies upon the 'strong social thesis' (*AL*, pp. 45–47), he has to insist that 'while the rule [or legal standard] referring to morality is indeed law . . . the morality to which it refers is not thereby incorporated into law' (*ibid.*, p. 46). This, of course, does not contradict the claim that adjudication is a value laden process. Secondly, it needs be noted that Raz says incomparability arises within the adjudicative context on at least two occasions. He says that in some instances the reasons judges have for deciding an unregulated dispute

[32] Raz is a little more specific on this issue in 'Facing Up: A Reply' (1989) 62 *Southern California L. R.* 1153–1235, pp. 1208–1209.

[33] J. Raz, *Ethics in the Public Domain* (Oxford, Clarendon 1994), p. 324.

[34] For an example of Raz accepting this, see *ibid.*, pp. 227–228.

one way rather than another 'are incommensurate as to strength . . . [;] [n]either is stronger nor are they equal in strength' (*ibid.*, p. 75). If those reasons are generated by incommensurable values then this is to be expected. And Raz does indeed suggest that judges can be faced with a choice between incommensurable values. [35]

Thus we can be certain that Raz is a strong value pluralist and that, on the basis of statements like those above, he thinks value pluralism arises within the adjudicative context. Just as we can be certain that Raz does affirm strong value pluralism, we can be equally certain that Dworkin does not. That is because, although Dworkin makes both the plurality and conflict claims, he denies—albeit sometimes with a hint of equivocation—the incomparability claim. The plurality and conflict claims appear many times in Dworkin's work. He holds that there are a plurality of moral positions—about issues such as homosexuality, pornography and abortion—that can conflict (*TRS*, pp. 248–249; *MP*, p. 203). He also thinks that conceptions of the good life, which are surely agglomerations of moral and other values, differ between members of the same political community, this truth being one reason why a version of liberalism grounded upon a right to equal concern and respect is preferable to any other (*MP*, pp. 191; 193–194). Furthermore, Dworkin's interpretative account of law contains many indications that it is 'Protestant'.[36] That means that accounts of law offered in the course of both adjudication and theorising depend upon the values of the adjudicator or theorist and that values differ significantly between members of the same community. Hence '[f]or every route Hercules took from . . . general conception to a particular verdict, another lawyer or judge who began in the same conception would find a different route and end in a different place' (*LE*, p. 412; see also pp. 411 and 413). A Protestant account of interpretation is therefore one that appears to endorse both the plurality and conflict claims. However, there is no such endorsement of the incomparability claim in Dworkin's work. There are instead some more or less qualified denials of that claim. This is not particularly surprising when it is noted that Dworkin's commitment to the 'right answers thesis' is conjoined with the affirmation that hard case adjudication is a value-laden process. For, were Dworkin to embrace incomparability then, obviously, it would be possible for the values in play within adjudication to be incomparable. That being so, it would be very difficult if not impossible to claim—on something like Raz's definition of incomparability—that there was a single right answer in those hard cases in which incomparable values were in play. No wonder, then, that in responding to John Mackie's criticisms Dworkin says that 'my thesis [about right answers and the assumption that ties will be

[35] For an example of Raz accepting this, see *ibid.*, pp. 322–323.

[36] The phrase belongs to G. Postema, '"Protestant" Interpretation and Social Practices' (1987) 6 *Law and Philosophy* 283–319, especially pp. 300–319.

rare in hard cases] . . . presupposes a conception of morality other than some conception according to which different moral theories are frequently incommensurate.'[37] Dworkin has gone further than this elsewhere, expressing the view that no argument has yet established widespread incommensurability within moral and political theory (*MP*, pp. 144–145). He has also cast doubts, albeit *en passant*, upon the relevance of incommensurability to adjudication.[38] Thus it is impossible to maintain that Dworkin is a strong value pluralist. The problems that flow from affirming that doctrine do not trouble him.

(iii) Why worry about value pluralism?

Does anything of significance follow from the fact that some of the orthodox (we are currently concerned with MacCormick and Raz) affirm value pluralism? The answer is 'yes'. In so far as values and value choices are unavoidably part of rule application and interpretation, and in so far as some or all of those values conflict and are incomparable, then some judicial choices cannot be rationally justified. What is meant by the latter is that a choice one way or the other cannot be based upon compelling reasons: in the face of incommensurability reasons are indeterminate. There is, in relation to these judicial choices, a rationality or justification deficit. Why should that be regarded as significant? Might not the orthodox suggest that this situation is of no interest at all since it merely tells us what follows from the truth of strong value pluralism? Under strong value pluralism some choices—by judges, practitioners and citizens—will be underdetermined by reasons because they will be choices between incommensurables. That is not to say that such choices will be either random or arbitrary. Choices based upon incommensurable reasons or between incommensurable values are still informed by, still based upon, Reason. However, in the face of incommensurability, no single choice is given pre-eminent salience by virtue of Reason—we are not rationally compelled to choose X rather than Y. Hence, choosing X rather than Y does not show that favouring Y would be a mistake. So, the orthodox could maintain, judicial choices between incommensurables are not compelled by reasons but are nevertheless unobjectionable provided that they are informed by Reason. That is the best we

[37] 'A Reply by Ronald Dworkin' in M. Cohen (ed.), *Ronald Dworkin and Contemporary Jurisprudence* (London, Duckworth 1983), p. 272. For more of the same see *MP*, pp. 143–145. Lest one be led to think that Dworkin's later work downplays the right answer thesis, see *LE*, pp. 412–413; also, he has often publicly defended the thesis since the publication of *LE* in lectures.

[38] In P. Amselek and N. MacCormick (eds.), *Controversies About Law's Ontology* (Edinburgh, E. U. P. 1991), pp. 88–90. See also B. Bix, *Law, Language and Legal Determinacy* (Oxford, Clarendon 1993), p. 97 where we learn that Dworkin has expressed numerous reservations about incommensurability in lectures.

can hope for if strong value pluralism is true. What more could be expected?

Many orthodox scholars have argued that nothing more can be expected, that it is a mistake to hope for any higher degree of rationality than this. Let us call this the modest response, for it counsels that we really ought not to expect too much from adjudication in particular, and, perhaps, from Reason in general. In some circumstances reasons simply run out and we must decide and act; one such circumstance is the existence of incommensurability; another might be the existence of factors other than incommensurability which ensure that completely determinate reasons are unavailable in a particular situation of choice. Consider just two instances of the modest response.[39] The first belongs to Steven Burton and, although he rarely invokes the notion of incommensurability, he sketches an account of adjudication such that the kind of rationality deficit characteristic of choices between incommensurables is, for him, a normal feature of judicial decisions. The second belongs to Joel Levin and he, too, holds that it is normal for judicial decisions to suffer from the kind of rationality deficit characteristic of a choice between incommensurables. Besides the particular problems unique to the arguments of Burton and Levin, both face a snag that ensnares any version of the modest response. The snag is that this response endangers the distinction between 'law' and 'politics'. Both anticipate this snag and offer brief replies, but neither is successful.

Burton is untroubled by the kind of rationality deficit characteristic of choices between incommensurables. Indeed he celebrates this deficit, regarding it as characteristic of all hard case adjudication. Further, this celebration is appropriate once it is realised that what Burton calls the determinacy condition is false. That condition entails 'that a judge can fulfil the judicial duty to uphold the law only if the law determines one correct result in each case and the judge reaches that result' (*B*, pp. 199 and 102).[40] Burton's version of the determinacy condition (hereinafter 'determinacy condition$_B$') is unlike the one adopted earlier in this chapter (henceforth 'the determinacy condition'), in the sense that his version incorporates Dworkin's one right answer thesis. The version of the determinacy condition used here—which holds that 'the choices judges make in hard cases are justifiable in principle and often in practice', having the maximum justification quotient and therefore being compelled by reasons—does not. It does not follow from this version that there must be a single right answer

[39] J. Levin, *How Judges Reason* (New York, Peter Lang 1992) and S. Burton, *Judging in Good Faith* (Cambridge, C. U. P. 1992). Other instances of the modest response are: J. Finnis, 'Natural Law and Legal Reasoning', ch. 6 of R. P. George (ed.), *Natural Law Theory: Contemporary Essays* (Oxford, Clarendon 1992); and, probably, C. Sunstein's idea of incompletely theorised agreements (*Legal Reasoning and Political Conflict* (New York, O. U. P. 1996), ch. 2). The latter might qualify as an instance of the modest response, but it is so oblique that I cannot be sure.

[40] 'B' is a reference to Burton, *supra*, note 39.

compelled by reasons; it is quite possible for there to be more than one answer that is so compelled, each having the maximum justification quotient. However, the point which determinacy condition$_B$ and the determinacy condition share is that reasons *completely* determine the choice made. It is that with which Burton disagrees. He thinks it neither plausible nor desirable to insist on this requirement being satisfied in judicial decisions. If he is right in this, then we are wrong to worry about the existence of incommensurability in adjudication.

What arguments does Burton offer against the expectation that reasons should compel judicial decisions? Some of his arguments are directed only at determinacy condition$_B$ and need not trouble us much, save to say that some of the positions he thinks might support that condition look most peculiar. For example, he suggests that the commitment to determinacy condition$_B$ is rooted in a discredited empiricist epistemology (*B*, ch. 4). This might be contingently true of the work of Oliver Wendell Holmes, which Burton mentions, but this is of little more than historical interest. For, a commitment to determinacy condition$_B$ is just as compatible with an epistemology antithetical to empiricism. This much is clear when Dworkin's work is considered—he is no empiricist yet he undoubtedly espouses determinacy condition$_B$. The implication is that matters of epistemology have very little, if any, impact upon whether or not one espouses a version of the determinacy condition. A more plausible point Burton makes against the determinacy condition is the argument in favour of his own position, which he labels 'the good faith thesis'. As the plausibility of that thesis is increased, so the plausibility of the belief that judicial decisions are and should be compelled by reasons is reduced. What does the good faith thesis look like and why should we accept it?

In the more banal formulations, the good faith thesis does not amount to very much. If it merely insists 'that the judicial duty to uphold the law requires judges to act on the reasons provided by the law and not on reasons excluded by judicial duty or the law's standards' (*B*, pp. 36–37; 92), then it is not very interesting. However, this idea becomes much more engaging when it is unpacked. Burton extends the claim in at least three directions. First, he says that all legal actors 'can agree on all the relevant legal reasons [in a case while] at the same time we disagree on the result due to disagreement on matters of weight' (*B*, p. 89). Hence, 'the law can constrain judges and other legal actors without determining a single result' (*B*, p. 17). Secondly, he holds that the relevant legal reasons are disclosed by the 'conventional law' and the facts of the case (*B*, pp. 54–59) and that these are knowable in a non-controversial way. Thirdly, he affirms that controversy begins in adjudication when judges have to weigh these reasons in order to decide a case. There is no agreed single scale that judges use to weigh the legal reasons relevant to a particular case. They can therefore assign different weight to the same legal reason and thus disagree either as to the outcome of the case before them or about the reasons supporting that outcome. Provided judges weigh only the relevant legal reasons, scrupulously ignoring *ad hominem* and other supposedly non-legal reasons (*B*, p. 156), and provided that process is carried out by reference to the facts of the case, they cannot be criticised. That, in taking these steps, judges come to different decisions in the same case, or reach the same decision but by weighing the relevant reasons very differently, is no cause for complaint. We should not assume, says Burton, that the law supplies judges and other actors only with compelling reasons for decision and action. Rather, he suggests that the normative force of the reasons the law offers is often inchoate, determined only after the process of weighing; hence they do not compel the decisions judges reach. This is as rational as the process of adjudication can be, given the nature of law and legal reasons.

Is this picture of adjudication sufficiently plausible to break our commitment to the determinacy condition? Three reasons dictate that the answer to this question must be 'no'. First, the notion of weight and the weighing of reasons is shrouded in mystery. Indeed, talk of 'weighing' in the absence of any agreed upon scale is, at best, misleading. Without a scale it is just false that '[i]t helps to conceive of weighing as a *gauging* of the relative normative force of the reasons that properly enter judicial deliberations' (*B*, pp. 50–51; emphasis supplied). For, if weighing without a scale is a matter of 'gauging', then how are we to gauge? The notion of 'gauging' surely implies a gauge, that is, a metric or tool that enables us to measure some property or dimension of some thing. Is that not just the same as a scale? If there is a gauge, is there then not, *a fortiori*, a scale? Similarly, if '[j]udges *balance* concrete reasons for action in cases' (*B*, p. 54; emphasis supplied), there must surely be a mechanism for balancing. But all this talk of weighing, balancing and gauging is metaphorical for Burton since the mechanism of these actions—scale, gauge or metric—does not exist. Or, more precisely, no single, agreed upon scale, gauge or metric exists. Things become no clearer when Burton shifts to apparently less metaphorical language. For example, he speaks of the 'grounds of weight' as if this provides some guidance as to the nature of the weighing process:

> [t]he grounds of weight are internal to each case in a way that can be modelled as follows[. . .]. Suppose a judge has an 'action threshold' consisting of the amount of normative force just sufficient to move him or her to act dutifully. . . .
>
> Accordingly, the weight of each legal reason would be a share in the total amount of normative force at the action threshold. In judicial deliberations, one might start by assigning each legal reason an equal share. Each legal reason has equal weight, upon its identification, due solely to its status qua legal. It would be silly, however, simply to count the reasons on each side and let the majority prevail. During the consideration of reasons, weight can vary from the starting point due to the play of

> background justification for the law . . . the weight of one reason ultimately depends on the justifications for the other reasons invoked by the circumstances.
>
> Giving one reason too little weight hence may be checked by the need to give another too much and vice versa. A judge in good faith seeks to give each and every relevant legal reason a proportional share within the frame fixed primarily by the judicial duty to uphold the law . . . The judge proceeds by gauging the weight of each legal reason in turn while standing on the ground provided by other relevant reasons, as one might rebuild a boat plank by plank while at sea . . . The grounds of weight are internal to the case because a congeries of reasons grounds the weight of each reason (*B*, pp. 56–58).

This explication of the weighing process adds little, except to cast doubt on our claim that Burton believes in weighting without a scale. For, it might be thought that the fact that judges initially allocate a fixed sum of weight to all the relevant reasons in a case, and that they subsequently redistribute some of that fixed sum of weight between reasons, shows that there is a single scale: how else can we make sense of these ideas? However, no such single scale is ever disclosed by Burton. Add to the absence of any agreed scale Burton's claim that the weight of one reason is determined by the weight of other reasons—'a congeries of reasons grounds the weight of each reason'—and one is faced with a mysterious process indeed.

The second reason why Burton's account of adjudication is not sufficiently powerful to loosen the grip of the determinacy condition consists of the claim that participants in the practice accept that condition. This much is obvious from *Patterson* v. *Mclean Credit Union*, an example Burton uses to highlight the supposed advantages of his good faith and permissible discretion theses. The minority and majority judgments Burton quotes evince a commitment to the determinacy condition and perhaps even determinacy condition$_B$ (*B*, pp. 73–78). His criticism of these judgments consists of simply affirming the good faith thesis and then proceeding to demonstrate its advantages. We are given no reason in advance to think that the judges in *Mclean* were wrong to accept the determinacy condition, other than Burton's worry that believing it leads to controversy and disagreement about the correct way to decide cases. Why worry about that? The participants in the enterprise do not, as evidenced by *McLean*; they take it to be part of the normal course of events. Nor will it do for Burton to ignore the participants' views, if his task is even partially descriptive, without good reason. Attempting to reduce, and being worried about, the level of controversy surrounding hard case adjudication is not in itself a good reason, especially when the participants are not so exercised. Finally, Burton does not and cannot succeed in discrediting the determinacy condition if one significant distinction between law and politics is to be maintained. That Burton's account of adjudication, when combined with the modest response, imperils this distinction, counts against him. We will see why this is so below, since Levin's account of adjudication and the modest response also imperils the same distinction.

Levin's account of adjudication simply concludes that compelling justificatory reasons are impossible in hard cases. These cases thus suffer from a rationality deficit but that, for Levin, is not worth worrying about; it is just the ways things are. Whether or not this conclusion is palatable depends upon the normative and descriptive power of his account of adjudication. It consists of 'a conventionalized, tertiary, internally consistent, truth functional, propositional schema . . . [t]he schema being determined by a conception of the judicial role' (*L*, pp. 95–96).[41] The three tiers of adjudication consist of 'initial or first order, judicial questions which require concomitant answers . . . [and] . . . the grounds or criteria for those answers [which] constitute the second level, and the grounds or justifications for the second level [which] constitute the third level' (*L*, pp. 95–97). Levin holds that the propositions of law and their grounds which occupy the first and second level are true or false by virtue of third level propositions. Third level propositions 'are drawn from the set of political, ethical, and prudential (and other) beliefs and attitudes' (*L*, p. 49) which justify lower level propositions. Third level propositions are the 'final level'(*L*, p. 42) in the model and, moreover, they 'are not able to be labelled as true or false' (*L*, p. 105). Hence, if this model is instantiated in practice, as Levin suggests it is, then there is a good deal of room for judges to disagree over the best way to justify an agreed result in a particular case and over the right result in any case. This is why Levin calls his account of adjudication 'pluralist': 'it suggests that there exists a number of co-equal third order views' (*L*, p. 65) or propositions. The third-order set of propositions which a judge accepts will, says Levin, be 'a function of an individual's understanding of what the judicial role involves' (*L*, p. 49). Since third-order choices are neither true nor false, neither right nor wrong, since they are all 'co-equal' in this regard, and are a function of an individual's 'home-made' private conventions and understandings, they are clearly not completely compelled by reasons. They therefore look very much like choices between incommensurables.

So far, this account is neither descriptively nor normatively objectionable. However, there are some problems lurking, by far the most interesting and pertinent for present purposes being those clustered around the idea of third-order propositions. Although such propositions lack truth value, Levin denies this entails that judicial choices are arbitrary—because unpredictable and indefensible—and relativistic—because what is right for one judge need not ever be right for another. His denial can rest on either of two grounds. First, that conceptions of the judicial role serve as a brake

[41] '*L*' in brackets and accompanied by a page number is, hereinafter, a reference to Levin, *supra*, note 39.

upon the number of available, plausible third-order propositions or, secondly, that such propositions are conventional, where that means something like 'widely accepted'. Neither ground is unproblematic. The first is unlikely to block the collapse into arbitrariness and relativism if it is true, as Levin seems to think, that conceptions of the judicial role are 'irreducibly individual' (*L*, p. 2), that is, they differ from judge to judge. Hence the argument that third-order propositions, even though they lack truth value, must be conventional and need not lead to arbitrariness and relativism, seems more promising. It is only promising, however, when 'conventional' is given a meaning along the lines just suggested. That meaning is rejected by Levin (*L*, pp. 64–82). He argues, implausibly, that 'convention is rooted in *individual* choice' (*L*, p. 65; emphasis supplied) and that 'a judicial convention can be unique to *a single* individual' (*L*, p. 75; emphasis supplied). This argument is weak because, first, it collapses by stipulation the distinction between personal precept and convention and, secondly, the idea of an individual inventing his or her own 'convention' is surely as flawed as the idea of inventing one's own private language. Both languages and conventions are irreducibly social and inter-subjective. Only if conventions are understood thus can Levin's argument succeed, for the public and intersubjective nature of conventions will then stop the slide into arbitrariness and relativism. If, however, there are as many conventions as there are persons, we are already deep within the realm of arbitrariness and relativism.

Yet even if there are problems in Levin's account of third-order propositions, it might be said that they are not such as to undermine his whole account and thus imperil his version of the modest response. The reply is to redeploy and unpack the third reason—stated but not elaborated—that undermined Burton's account of adjudication, namely, the blurring of the law/politics distinction. Levin, too, blurs that distinction and this counts powerfully against both his and Burton's arguments. Any version of the modest response will have this result. Before showing why that is so, our understanding of the distinction needs to be elucidated, for it might be thought folly even to speak of *the* law/politics distinction when a multiplicity of factors could be used to distinguish the two domains. The account of the law/politics distinction employed here is best stated by recalling some standard heretical claims about law and adjudication. For example, Singer informs us that the truth the heresy yields about adjudication is that 'no rational decision procedure . . . is possible'; this is because '[e]xisting legal doctrines are sufficiently ambiguous or internally contradictory to justify any result we can imagine'. Therefore, 'we [have] to give up the idea that the legal system has a foundation, a rational basis'.[42] If by phrases like

[42] The statements are from pp. 19–20, 46 and 66 of Singer, *supra*, note 3. For similar thoughts see Kelman, *GCLS*, chs 1–3 and p. 258.

'a rational basis' and 'rational decision procedure' we take Singer to mean 'no *completely determinate or completely compelling* rational basis or decision procedure', then his point is well made against orthodox value pluralists.

The orthodox might be tempted by the modest response, holding that to expect adjudication to satisfy such high standards of rationality is misguided, but this reply is extremely costly. If the orthodox want to maintain a significant distinction between legal and non-legal disputes, if—like Unger's formalists—they manifest 'a commitment to, and therefore a belief in the possibility of, a method of legal justification that contrasts with the open-ended disputes about the basic terms of social life, disputes that people call ideological, philosophical or visionary'[43], then the reply invites trouble. Disputes of the latter kind are surely based upon and informed by reasons in exactly the same way as are judges' choices between incommensurables, or in the same way as are any judicial choices in hard cases according to Burton and Levin. Clearly, ideological, philosophical and visionary disputes are not resolved by making choices and decisions that are given pre-eminent salience by reasons and neither, it seems, are disputes in hard cases. Hence, the inability of the orthodox to affirm the determinacy condition in the face of value pluralism leads to the conclusion that, if incommensurable judicial choices inform much legal doctrine, then doctrinal disputes are in principle apparently just as 'open-ended', as indeterminate and as incapable of compelling rational justification as philosophical or ideological disputes. In the face of incommensurability, the orthodox have great difficulty maintaining 'a contrast between *the more determinate rationality* of legal analysis and *the less determinate rationality* of ideological contests'.[44] And if they cannot maintain that significant distinction between law and politics, then it becomes very difficult to see in what else a significant distinction could consist. This is especially so once we rid our minds of the plethora of trivial and purely contingent ways in which legal disputes differ from other kinds. *A fortiori*, the orthodox also have great difficulty in showing that adjudication is compelled by reasons, driven by a 'rational decision procedure'. Bearing these difficulties in mind, the heretical conclusion that, within the realm of adjudication, '*settled* justificatory schemes are in fact unobtainable' is prima facie plausible.[45]

Distinguishing between law and politics in terms of the degree of rationality characteristic of disputes in each realm—the former being a domain in which disputes can be solved by compelling reasons whereas the latter is not—may be objectionable for some. For example, Levin takes the law/politics distinction to be between a normative and a non-normative

[43] Unger, *CLSM*, p. 1. [44] *Ibid.*, p. 2. See also pp. 9 and 11.
[45] Kelman, *GCLS*, p. 13 (emphasis supplied).

realm. The latter corresponds to law and the former to politics. Having drawn the distinction thus, he then proceeds to make mincemeat of it, concluding that '[n]o final distinction between law and politics is worth making' (*L*, p. 27). This is no doubt correct when, like Levin, one regards 'the issue of politics . . . [as] really an abbreviation for a myriad of other parallel issues [such as] [r]eligion, ethics, custom, social goals, convention, manners, economics, [and] even science' (*L*, p. 28), since everyone can accept that these factors can 'all bear on judicial reasoning' (*ibid.*). However, regarding politics as the domain of the normative, which Levin seems to do on the basis of this list (with the exception of 'science'), inflates unacceptably the realm of politics while misrepresenting the nature of law, for who would now deny that law is a normative system? Hence, although Levin's version of the law/politics distinction is not a dangerous one for the orthodox, it should nevertheless be rejected by them because trivial and misleading.

The latter vice is also displayed by Burton's effort to distinguish between law and politics. His usual move is to regard law as a realm where *ad hominem* reasons have no role whereas they 'animate ordinary and transformative political contests' (*B*, p. 156). Yet, once it is plain what Burton has in mind by '*ad hominem*' reasons, it is clear that he misrepresents politics in holding it to be characterised by such reasons. These reasons 'depend on advantage to *self*, friends or groups with which one identifies' (*B*, p. 46). Now, this seems to assume an interest-group conception of politics in which political actors act so as to maximise their own individual and group goods.[46] The only reasons for action are taken to be prudential and the rightness or wrongness of action is a function of some kind of cost-benefit or utility-maximising calculation. Political action is the means by which groups and individuals pursue and advance their interests. Setting aside the question as to how well this conception characterises contemporary polities, note that there is nothing distinctly 'communal' about the political on this account—it is just another realm in which self- or prudential- interests hold sway. Citizenship is an alien concept here, as is genuinely altruistic political action. The activities of those political actors, from Socrates to Nelson Mandela, whose lives are spent working for political, economic and social change, are inexplicable on this conception of politics, except as advancing their own interests or those of the interest group to which they belong. Presumably, those who act on behalf of humanity or future generations are either misguided or lying. We do not have to regard the realm of politics as exactly coextensive with that of friendship in order to make sense of altruistic political action. All that is needed is an appreciation of the category of other-regarding, non-self-interested reasons that can operate in a range of contexts, both political and

[46] See, for discussion, R. Dowse and J. Hughes, *Political Sociology*, 2nd ed. (Chichester, John Wiley 1986), chs. 2 and 13 and S. Hargreaves-Heap *et al.*, *The Theory of Choice* (Oxford, Blackwell 1992), part III.

non-political.[47] Furthermore, the law side of Burton's distinction requires more work since, although propositions of law and legal reasons for action are rarely if ever formally characterised in *ad hominem* terms (imagine a statute that at some point stated that 'this Act is for the benefit of group Y [let us say the judges' socio-economic 'class' or gentleman's club] and should be interpreted with this in mind'), there is nothing to prevent them being so interpreted and applied. In fact, it is a commonplace that particular pieces of legislation are often applied so as to impact differently upon different groups in the polity.[48]

Considerations such as these do not, of course, show that using the determinacy condition to construct a distinction between law and politics is the only sensible way in which that distinction can be drawn. They show, rather, that Levin's and Burton's efforts to construct such a distinction are severely flawed. On the supposition that our version of the law/politics distinction is not prima facie absurd, the conclusion here must be that, in the face of incommensurability or any other rationality deficit, the modest response is untenable. It endangers one significant version of the law/politics distinction and therefore plays into heretical hands. Returning to the question with which this subsection began, we can now restate our answer. What follows from the orthodox affirmation of strong value pluralism is that it becomes very difficult indeed to satisfy the determinacy condition. That is significant because the orthodox position on the determinacy condition becomes indistinguishable from the heretical position. For heretics, too, think the condition very difficult to satisfy. They have concluded, as the statements above make clear, that it cannot be satisfied and have affirmed the indeterminacy condition instead.

Heretical and orthodox attitudes to the determinacy condition differ only in that the latter begin from a position of faith. Initially at least, they appear committed to maintaining the condition. That they cannot ultimately do so is a consequence of affirming strong value pluralism. By contrast, many heretics thought the determinacy condition unsustainable from the outset. They never shared the initial commitment of the orthodox to it. Despite appearances and despite rhetoric, heretical and orthodox positions on this issue are, in substance, indistinguishable. Nor does it help to say that they arrive at substantively similar conclusions by different routes. That is true as between some members of the orthodoxy and some heretics, but it is also

[47] For excellent introductions to these matters see M. Hollis, 'Friends, Romans and Consumers' (1991) 102 *Ethics* 27–41 and his 'Reasons of Honour' (1986–87) *Proceedings of the Aristotelian Society* 1–19.

[48] A reliable starting point is W. Chambliss and R. Seidman, *Law, Order, and Power*, 2nd ed. (Reading, Mass., Addison-Wesley 1982), chs. 6, 8 and 10. For an argument that the form and content of certain procedural rules benefits particular social groups, see M. Galanter, 'Why the "Haves" Come Out Ahead: Speculations on the Limits of Legal Change' (1974) 9 *Law and Society Review* 95–160.

true within the orthodoxy and within the heresy. Furthermore, the difference between the routes taken by heretics and orthodox to the conclusion that the determinacy condition is difficult to sustain are not perhaps so very different. The source of trouble for the orthodox is strong value pluralism; for heretics it is value (and language) indeterminacy. Given that orthodox and heretical positions on the determinacy condition are all but indistinguishable, and assuming that the orthodox would wish to maintain some distance between their accounts of law and adjudication and those offered by heretics, the question arises: is there any way in the orthodox could distinguish their position from that of the heretics? In the next section one such orthodox argument is examined. Contrary to the heretical position, it consists of affirming the legitimacy condition in the face of the failure of the determinacy condition.

III VALUE PLURALISM AND THE LEGITIMACY CONDITION

The legitimacy condition holds that propositions of law can in some circumstances generate an authoritative obligation to obey and hence give good reasons for acting in accord with their content. (Note that in this formulation and in those that follow 'authority' and 'legitimacy' are used interchangeably; we are primarily concerned with legitimate not *de facto* authority, even though it is probably true that any person or group having the former must have the latter.) The question to be answered here appears disarmingly simple. Can the orthodox plausibly maintain that indeterminate judicial decisions—decisions resting upon a choice between incommensurable values—are nevertheless legitimate? No easy answer is available since this question brings in its wake at least two other questions separable only in a heuristic sense: conceptually, what does the notion of authority entail? Normatively, how, exactly, can authority be justified?[49] Only when answers are provided to these questions will we be able to decide whether the orthodox can affirm the legitimacy condition when the determinacy condition is not satisfied.

Answering these conceptual and normative questions will prove even more difficult if the orthodox, while in agreement in invoking the legitimacy condition, nevertheless disagree about the contours of the concept of, and the best justification for, legitimate authority. There are indeed many accounts of legitimacy compatible with, or actually components of, orthodox accounts of law and adjudication. Constraints of time and space dictate that each account cannot be considered. Moreover, other considerations also reduce the list of candidates for consideration. So, for example, some

[49] For Raz's treatment of the relationship between the two questions see *MF*, pp. 62–66.

accounts of legitimacy can be ruled out early on, as being either over-ambitious or incomplete. Into the former category falls the account of Jürgen Habermas.[50] In itself, of course, ambition is not a fault, but the range of Habermas's account of legitimacy, drawing as it does on the whole corpus of his work in social, political and moral philosophy, is such that it cannot be adequately dealt with here. Indeed, Habermas's discussion generates some difficult snags that are not central to our present concerns, such as the true degree of similarity between his and Dworkin's work, and the effort either to reconstruct or simply just find his reasons for refusing to distinguish between legitimacy and determinacy conditions.

The work of Burton and Philip Soper must be included among those accounts of legitimacy compatible with the orthodoxy but incomplete. These two accounts are incomplete in exactly the same respect, namely, neither offers a prima facie plausible account of the nature of the obligation to obey the law. This is not the complaint of the disappointed authoritarian, who hopes for an obligation to obey yet finds that the existence of such an obligation is doubtful, but of a disappointed sophist. The most difficult problem in Burton's contextual account of legitimacy is that the argument either yields an obligation to obey the edicts of those, including political and legal 'authorities', that do one no harm, or is unable to distinguish between laws and state directives, on the one hand, and the directives of campaigners for good, on the other. The first horn of this dilemma arises from Burton's view that '[c]rises of legitimacy probably can be avoided justifiably so long as the legal and political system as a whole respects the most basic rights and interests of all significant groups in the society and contains open avenues of legal change that . . . [allow] the law better to protect . . . basic rights and interests'.[51] Taken as an argument for an obligation to obey, this is woefully inadequate. It seemingly entails that, if one's neighbour refrains from harming one, then one has an obligation to obey her. That she does not threaten one's basic rights and liberties seems entirely irrelevant to the question of the legitimacy of her directives and this is so, *a fortiori*, in relation to state or legal directives. Burton seemingly bases the obligation to obey in our gratitude that the 'authority' has refrained from doing us harm and that is far from satisfactory. The other horn of the dilemma is a consequence of Burton's attempt to base an obligation to obey upon an instrumentalist calculation. He holds that if a legal and political system 'adequately contributes to a more orderly and just society', then there is an obligation to obey its directives.[52] This is more promising than the previous

[50] *Supra*, note 16, chs. 5 and 6.

[51] S. Burton, *An Introduction to Law and Legal Reasoning* (Boston, Little, Brown and Co. 1985) p. 203. The account of legitimacy developed at pp. 187–215 is incorporated by reference into Burton's more recent account of adjudication, *supra*, note 39.

[52] *Ibid*., p. 202.

move, but the instrumental dimension of the argument means a line cannot be drawn between legal and state directives, on the one hand, and those of, for example, campaigners for a more just society, on the other. In one sense, this might not be a problem, for it is undoubtedly the case that we have an obligation to ameliorate the position of those, such as the homeless and destitute, badly placed in our society. To see this obligation as akin to the obligation to obey the law is no bad thing. Yet, what is missing here is the uniqueness, if any, of the latter type of obligation and it is to accounts of political or legal obligation that the task of illuminating that uniqueness falls. Of course, there may be nothing unique about such an obligation—it may be all of a piece with other obligations—but an argument to that end is required. It cannot just be assumed that all obligations are indistinguishable from one another.

Soper holds 'the features that should be sufficient to establish political obligation . . . are (1) the fact that the enterprise of law in general —including the particular system, defective though it may be, that confronts an individual—is better than no law at all; and (2) a good faith effort by those in charge to govern in the interests of the entire community, including the dissenting individual'.[53] As to the second feature, '[i]t is the claim of justice, rather then [sic] justice in fact' that is significant.[54] Soper's problem is making the transition from either of these claims to the claim that there is indeed an obligation to obey. It seems that both claims can be accepted yet the question whether there is an obligation to obey not be answered affirmatively. Some think the most Soper establishes is that the existence of a legal directive is one factor, among others, impinging upon the process of practical reasoning. It can influence our decision whether or not to act in a particular way but does not give us a protected or exclusionary reason for action.[55] And, if legal directives do not generate a reason of the latter type, how, then, can they be said to generate an obligation? Beyond this difficulty, further analysis of Soper's position discloses that two arguments might generate the supposed obligation to obey. One is a duty deriving from the fact that a job needs to be done—the job of authoritative coordination—and, since the makers of legal directives are doing that job in good faith, we should obey them. The other is a duty not to frustrate and upset people who are doing their best. If the makers of legal directives are doing

[53] P. Soper, *A Theory of Law* (Cambridge, Mass., Harvard U. P. 1984), p. 80. Soper has developed his account and defended it against some critics in, *inter alia*, 'Legal Theory and the Claim of Authority' (1989) 18 *Philosophy and Public Affairs* 209–237 and 'The Moral Value of Law' (1986) 84 *Michigan L. R.* 63–86.

[54] P. Soper, *A Theory of Law*, *supra*, note 53, p. 55.

[55] The argument put here is developed by J. Raz, 'The Morality of Obedience' (1985) 83 *Michigan L. R.* 732–749 and S. Burton, 'Law, Obligation, and a Good Faith Claim of Justice' (1985) 73 *California L. R.* 1956–1983. The points made in the remainder of this paragraph are all derived from Raz's essay.

their best, in good faith, then we should obey them. Yet neither argument on its own looks compelling nor is it clear that they can be consistently combined. Finally, note that each argument supporting the obligation to obey only has weight, on Soper's account, if it is indeed true that the enterprise of law is in general better than no law. Soper assumes this, but he does not seem to appreciate the problematic nature of the assumption. It might look reasonable if the deck is stacked against a reasonable and pacifist anarchism by assuming, as Soper often does, that the options here are either law or the most solitary, most nasty, most brutish state of nature. This contrast is hardly tenable. As we know from legal anthropologists, the distinction is better put in terms of 'formal' legal regulation and protection as opposed to 'informal' social customs and norms. A choice between these two possibilities is unlikely to be obviously and always made in favour of the former.

What of the remaining 'orthodox' accounts of legitimacy? As between Raz and MacCormick there is not unanimity on every aspect of the nature of and justification for authority. In particular, MacCormick does not share Raz's account of the nature of the reasons for action that authorities generate, although the grounds of this disagreement have yet to be unpacked.[56] However, the accounts of authority they offer are similar in that both identify as crucial to the justification of authority an authority's capacity to solve coordination or cooperation problems. Note, though, that MacCormick's remarks on authority court a problem that Raz avoids. It is that the argument from capacity to solve coordination or cooperation problems—let us, following standard practice, call such accounts of the nature and justification of authority 'conventionalist'—invites a number of objections which MacCormick does nothing to quell.[57] By contrast, Raz's account of authority avoids the snags ensnaring standard conventionalist accounts by amending one of their crucial features. His account should therefore be labelled modified conventionalism. 'Conventionalism', because it shares two features with standard conventionalist accounts of authority, namely, an emphasis upon the role of practical authorities in solving coordination problems and the claim that the content of the solutions to such problems—their substantive rightness or wrongness—does not always determine their

[56] MacCormick's objection is reported in his review of *MF*: 'Access to the Goods', *Times Literary Supplement*, 5 June 1987, 599.

[57] Standard conventionalist accounts of the nature of and justification for authority invoke game-theoretical conceptions of coordination problems, the Prisoner's Dilemma and their solutions. They are expertly discussed and criticised by L. Green, 'Authority and Convention' (1985) 35 *Philosophical Quarterly* 329–346. Neither standard nor modified conventionalist accounts of authority should be confused with the interpretation of law Dworkin calls conventionalism: see *LE*, ch. 4. MacCormick's support for conventionalist accounts of authority is found in: *Legal Right and Social Democracy* (Oxford, Clarendon 1982), pp. 76–80; 'Contemporary Legal Philosophy', *supra*, note 39, p. 10; and 'Legal Reasoning and Practical Reason' (1982) VII *Midwest Studies in Philosophy* 271–286, pp. 281–282.

success qua solutions. 'Modified', because the notion of a coordination problem is here understood in a non-standard way. Raz's modified conventionalism is nuanced, thorough, compelling and, at first glance, appears admirably suited to the job of allowing the orthodox to affirm the legitimacy condition when the determinacy condition does not obtain. This account of authority I regard as *the* orthodox account, even though Raz is principally responsible for it, because it is a type of account that both fits MacCormick's remarks about conventionalism and rescues him from the snags that beset the standard forms of that doctrine. On these matters MacCormick must follow Raz's path. That path is certainly not taken by Dworkin, a recalcitrant member of the orthodoxy, since modified conventionalism is not the kind of account of authority he accepts.[58]

Modified conventionalism is an account of practical and not theoretical authority. That is, it concentrates upon the nature of and justification for authorities that purport to generate reasons for action and not, or not exclusively, those that generate reasons for beliefs. This is to deny neither that reasons for action and for belief can be closely related nor that there are degrees of overlap between theoretical and practical authority.[59] For example, the authoritative directive 'do X' is, of course, reason to believe that an authority has issued that directive and a meteorological expert's statement that it will rain is reason to take one's umbrella. But it is quite possible that some reasons for belief have no impact whatsoever on the reasons for action agents have. Reasons to believe that there is a ninth planet in the solar system will have little or no influence on the practical reasoning of agents who are not in the least interested in astronomy. According to Raz, practical authority impacts upon agents' practical reasoning in a dramatic way: for a person or group to have practical authority over another involves having 'a right to rule, where that is understood as correlated with an obligation to obey on the part of those subject to the authority' (*MF*, p. 23). This right to rule creates obligations to act independently of one's calculation of the merits or demerits of the action in question. Authoritative utterances are, for agents subject to them, exclusionary reasons: that is, 'reasons for not acting on the balance of reasons as they see it, even when they are right' (*PRN*, p. 64).[60] Of course, this does not rule out agents actually determining what they think is required on the balance of reasons. Rather, it rules out agents' compliance with authoritative directives being conditional upon their weighing of the reasons for and against.

[58] See *LE*, pp. 190–224.

[59] For Raz's thoughts on the relationship see pp. 2–3, 4–5 and 9–10 of the introduction to J. Raz (ed.), *Authority* (Oxford, Basil Blackwell 1990).

[60] Raz offers some further thoughts on exclusionary reasons in the postscript to the 1991 edition of *PRN*, pp. 178–199.

Moreover, the reasons that an authority acts upon are, in an important sense, reasons applicable to the agents subject to authority. So, although agents subject to authority ought to do as the authority says just because the authority says so, this directive is the result of the authority's weighing of reasons that are applicable to the agents themselves. When an authority says 'do X', that 'is not . . . just another reason to be added to the others when one reckons which way [doing X or not X] is better supported by reason. The . . . [authority's] decision is meant to be based on the other reasons, to sum them up and to reflect their outcome' (*MF*, p. 41). Hence, authoritative directives generate exclusionary reasons that are also 'dependent reasons' (*ibid.*), where what is meant is that those directives are based upon the authority's assessment of the reasons for and against the conduct, those reasons being applicable to agents and authority alike. In addition, authoritative decisions and directives are 'pre-emptive reasons' in the sense that they 'replace the reasons on which . . . [they] depend[. . . :] [t]he point is that reasons that could have been relied upon to justify action before . . . [the] decision cannot be relied upon once the decision is given' (*MF*, p. 42). Within an agent's practical reasoning the authority's decision takes the place of those reasons. It is therefore not merely one reason for an action to be taken in conjunction with the other reasons for that action.

The main way in which authority can be justified, according to Raz, is through 'the normal justification thesis'.[61] It holds that

> the normal way to establish that a person has authority over another person involves showing that the alleged subject is likely better to comply with reasons which apply to him (other than the alleged authoritative directives) if he accepts the directives of the alleged authority as authoritatively binding and tries to follow them, rather than by trying to follow the reasons that apply to him directly (*MF*, p. 53).

Clearly, this way of justifying authority is plausible only if it is true, first, that authorities invoke dependent reasons and, secondly, that authorities are indeed better placed than agents subject to them to recognise the reasons agents have for acting. It need not be the case that authorities, to be justified, must *always* be better able than agents to determine the reasons agents have. Rather

> [a]n authority is justified . . . if it is *more likely than its subjects* to act correctly for right reasons . . . If every time a directive is mistaken, i.e. every time it fails to reflect reason correctly, it were open to challenge as mistaken, the advantage gained by

[61] There are, according to Raz, other 'secondary' arguments that can in some circumstances be used in addition to, and, rarely, instead of, the normal justification thesis to justify authority: *MF*, pp. 80–99. These arguments—invoking, *inter alia*, the idea of consent—are not examined here because they have no obvious role in relation to indeterminate judicial decisions.

accepting the authority as a more reliable and successful guide to right reason would disappear (*MF*, p. 61; emphasis supplied).

Authorities do not have to be infallible in order to be legitimate.

In what circumstances will authorities be better placed than agents themselves to determine the reasons agents have for acting? The most obvious instance will be that in which the authority is not just a practical but also a theoretical authority. In this situation the authority's expertise will by definition ensure that it is in a better position than agents to determine which reasons are and are not applicable. Another, more complex, situation in which an authority may be better placed to determine the reasons applicable to agents than agents themselves is that in which coordination between agents is necessary to ensure that certain benefits are obtained.[62] In this situation the authority must be better than agents are at determining both when problems of coordination exist and how they can be solved. Coordination here is not to be thought of in technical, game-theoretical terms but as a common-sense idea understood thus.[63] Coordination 'means getting people to act in ways which are sensitive to the way others are guided, or are likely, to act, so that benefits can be expected which are less likely if they act without coordinating their efforts, i.e., without basing their own actions on a view as to how others should or are likely to act'.[64] Coordination in this sense can be desirable for at least two reasons. First, it can ensure that a good that would be lost were agents to try to bring it about without coordinating their efforts will be achieved. Secondly, although coordination may not make a difference to the achievement or not of a particular good (because, for example, a minority can bring it about), it is nevertheless desirable that all agents coordinate and contribute to bringing about the good for reasons of justice or morality (it is, for example, unfair for the minority to take up the burden of bringing about the good even though they can).

Note that in this second situation the claim that authorities may be better than agents at knowing when the need for coordination arises and how that need should be fulfilled is based upon both an authority's expertise (or theoretical authority) and the agent's weakness or lack of expertise. Raz imagines agents reasoning thus:

[62] These examples and much of the next two paragraphs are informed by Raz's discussion in 'Facing Up', *supra*, note 32, pp. 1179–1194.

[63] Game-theoretical conceptions of coordination problems and their solutions, which are the fulcrum of standard conventionalism, must be avoided by Raz and others, such as John Finnis, because the properties of such problems and their solutions are such as to make authority unnecessary. It has also been persuasively argued that justifications of authority premised upon game theoretical accounts of coordination problems cannot account for some features of most legal systems: see L. Green, *supra*, note 57 and his 'Law, Coordination and the Common Good' (1983) 3 *Oxford Journal of Legal Studies* 299–324. See also J. Finnis, 'Law as Coordination' (1989) 2 *Ratio Juris* 97–104, especially pp. 99–101.

[64] 'Facing Up', *supra*, note 32, p. 1189.

[k]nowing the limits of my knowledge and understanding, and being aware of the danger that my judgment will be affected by bias, and my performance by the weakness of my resolve, I am aware of the possibility that another person, or organisation, might be better able to judge when there are strong or sufficient reasons for social coordination in which I should participate.[65]

If that other person or organisation is free from bias and is of stronger will than the agent, then there is good reason to follow its directives:

[i]n such a case I should adopt a rule to follow the instructions of such a person or body, to regard them as authorities within certain specified bounds. The rule will be justified by the fact that following it will lead me to participate in justified coordinated social behaviour more reliably than if I should try to decide for myself when the conditions of a coordination problem exist, and when I should follow a certain course of conduct as a way of participating in a justified coordinative practice.[66]

Now if it is the case that many people are in the position of this particular agent, then they have a reason to adopt a general coordinative practice to accept the directives of a certain body within certain limits. For doing so allows all

to establish and preserve coordinative practices which would otherwise evade . . . [their] grasp. The reason is that by sharing the knowledge that . . . all [have] assigned to this body the power to decide . . . when coordination problems . . . exist and the responsibility to make generally known its proposed solutions, . . . [they] solve the problem of making sure [that coordination problems are recognised and resolved].[67]

Raz calls rules that set up a person or body as capable of authoritatively determining whether or not there is a coordination problem and, if there is, what should be done in response to it, 'second order coordinative practices'. Such 'rules justify the legitimacy of an authority . . . in accordance with the normal justification thesis. They enable all of us to solve coordination problems better than we might when we try to judge for ourselves whether there is a coordination problem and whether the . . . conditions for its solution are met.'[68]

Does modified conventionalism show that the state, its government and its legal system can be, and sometimes or perhaps always are, legitimate? In particular, can it serve to confer legitimacy on judicial decisions that fail to satisfy the determinacy condition? An affirmative answer to the first, general question would make providing an affirmative answer to the second, specific question a reasonably easy task. It would, however, be a mistake to think that an affirmative answer to the first question entails an affirmative answer to the second. That is so because it would be quite coherent to claim that the legal system of a particular state is, on the whole, legiti-

[65] 'Facing Up', *supra*, note 32, p. 1192. [66] *Ibid.* [67] *Ibid.* [68] *Ibid.*, p. 1193.

mate, except for those parts of it constituted by judge-made law. (The plausibility of this claim would, of course, depend upon the definition and amount of 'judge-made law' within the jurisdiction in question.) Nevertheless, if a general argument can be provided showing under what circumstances legal systems can be and sometimes are legitimate, then an important part of the task of attempting to show the legitimacy of indeterminate judicial decisions within particular legal systems has been accomplished.

Unfortunately for the orthodox, modified conventionalism does not appear to provide an affirmative answer to the general question. For, Raz's modified conventionalism 'denies the existence of a *general* obligation to obey the law even in a reasonably just society' (*MF*, p. 70; emphasis supplied). Prima facie, the law of such a society lacks legitimacy. This point should not be exaggerated. Modified conventionalism will indeed generate an obligation to obey the law in some circumstances even though it cannot generate a 'blanket' obligation. This is because the normal justification thesis is responsive to, first, the capacities of both subject and authority to uncover the reasons for action they have and, second, the circumstances in which these capacities are exercised. To determine whether or not the state, its legal system or any other institution or person legitimately has authority,

> [t]he test is . . . : does following the authority's instructions improve conformity with reason? For every person the question has to be asked afresh, and for every one it has to be asked in a manner which admits of various qualifications. An expert pharmacologist may not be subject to the authority of the government in matters of the safety of drugs, an inhabitant of a little village by a river may not be subject to its authority in matters of navigation and conservation of the river by the banks of which he has spent all his life (*MF*, p. 74).

So, although it is the case that there is no general obligation to obey the law, particular agents may have an obligation to obey particular laws in particular circumstances. Furthermore, if there is a particular kind of situation that affects many agents—for example, when collective action is subject to coordination problems—and in which (i) the state is better at recognising the reasons agents have for acting and (ii) is able, through a particular law or corpus of laws, both to tell agents that and to announce a solution to the problem, then in those circumstances the state and its law are legitimate.

Now, even if we take this as an albeit circumscribed affirmative answer to the general question, a number of other questions also have to be answered in the affirmative before the orthodox can plausibly maintain that indeterminate judicial decisions are legitimate. Those other questions are: do, or can, indeterminate judicial decisions generate exclusionary reasons for action? Are the reasons they generate, or can they be, dependent and pre-emptive? And, finally, do they, or can they, satisfy the normal justification thesis? In what follows, I concentrate upon the latter, normative question to the exclusion of the two conceptual questions. This is not because conceptual questions are unimportant. Rather, in tackling the normative question and the answer to it we can shed a good deal of light upon the conceptual questions because, as Raz notes, there is an overlap between both types of question. If, therefore, there is, as the argument that follows seeks to show, severe doubt as to whether a plausible affirmative answer to the normative question can be provided, then answers to the conceptual questions become redundant.

Our account of both the normal justification thesis and modified conventionalism's response to the general question suggest that the thesis might be fulfilled by indeterminate judicial decisions in three ways. The first two, which I label the direct and indirect arguments, are fairly obvious and are related while the third is independent and ambitious. Although the third argument is not a success, it requires rather more elucidation than the other two. I label it the fallibility argument. The direct argument would show that the general class or particular instances of indeterminate judicial decisions and the directives that issue from them (decision in favour of A for reasons e, f and g; therefore damages in the amount of £ to be paid by B to A) function so as to allow agents subject to them to comply with the reasons they have for acting more effectively than they would were they to try to determine those reasons for themselves. The indirect argument attempts to demonstrate that either a particular judicial decision and directive or a general class thereof serve to show that the parties and those affected by the dispute: (i) were in the grip of a coordination problem that they were unaware of; and (ii) that they had reason to cooperate which they were either unaware of or incapable of realising. If, furthermore, the decision and directive solved the coordination problem by ensuring actual cooperation between the parties to the dispute and those affected by it, then the normal justification thesis must have been satisfied. The fallibility argument holds that the reasons modified conventionalism uses to show that mistaken directives are authoritative can be used to show that indeterminate judicial decisions and the directives that flow from them are also authoritative. In order to do justice to these arguments they will be treated separately.

(i) The direct argument

This argument maintains that indeterminate judicial decisions can satisfy the legitimacy condition in an immediate way, by simply directing the parties in dispute to the reasons that are applicable to them but which they have, for one reason or another, failed to perceive. To be plausible this argument must assume that the parties either do not know they have reasons for action or are unaware that the reasons for action they have and the values that generate them are incommensurate. (Let us take it for granted—and this is surely acceptable to almost all who have offered an account of the nature and foundations of moral, political and other values—that values can be reasons for action.) If this assumption of ignorance is not made, then an indeterminate judicial decision cannot possibly satisfy the normal justification thesis. Remember that an indeterminate judicial decision, for the orthodox, is one that rests upon a choice between two or more incomparable values. When values are incomparable 'the considerations for and against [the] two alternatives are incommensurable' (*MF*, p. 333). If that is the case then it is true that when faced with a choice between incommensurables 'reason is indeterminate. It provides no better case for one alternative than for the other' (*ibid.*). Now if the parties in dispute know this, how can an indeterminate judicial decision enable them 'better to comply with the reasons which apply to . . . [them]' (*MF*, p. 53) than if they did not accept the decision?

The answer is that it cannot. It merely repeats what the parties already know, namely, that the reasons and values applicable to them are incommensurable. By contrast, where the parties are unaware either of the existence or of the nature of the reasons and values applicable to them, an indeterminate judicial decision that highlights one or other of these facts allows the parties better to comply with the reasons and values applicable to them. It may be thought, though, that where the decision merely highlights the nature of the reasons applicable to the parties by showing that they are incommensurable, the normal justification thesis will not be satisfied. For in this situation the decision cannot be said to make the parties better able *to comply* with reason because, in highlighting the incommensurability of reasons, the decision does not facilitate compliance with them. Rather, it only highlights their nature. However, this objection is misguided in so far as a proper understanding of the nature of the reasons applicable to one is a necessary prerequisite to acting upon, and hence complying with, those reasons.

The conclusion that, in order for indeterminate judicial decisions to satisfy the normal justification thesis, the parties to the dispute must be ignorant in the two senses noted, could be objected to on another, apparently more compelling, ground. It might be maintained, for example, that the discussion so far has concentrated upon the judicial *decision* to the exclusion of the *directive* that follows from it. And that, of course, is rarely ambiguous even though the decision from which it flows is indeterminate. It could be said, furthermore, that the directive can satisfy the normal justification thesis even though the decision does not and even though the parties know that their dispute is one based upon a conflict of incommensurable reasons or values. But how? There seem to be only two possibilities here. The first holds that the directive simply brings the dispute to an end and in so doing satisfies the normal justification thesis because there are good reasons, applicable to the parties, to resolve the dispute. The directive can do this even when the parties in dispute know that the reasons and values applicable to them are incommensurable and that they are beset by a coordination problem they have good reasons to avoid. For in this situation the parties could nevertheless be in dispute about the best way in which to solve the problem and it is that dispute which the directive curtails. However, there is a snag that besets this response. It can be briefly stated in the form of a question: if there are good reasons to bring the dispute to an end—and hence to make a choice and issue a directive one way rather than another—is the dispute really between incommensurables? Since this snag also besets all versions of the indirect argument it will be examined in the following subsection.

The second possibility modifies the first by insisting that the parties are *unwittingly* in the thrall of a coordination problem. It then holds that the directive which flows from the indeterminate judicial decision satisfies the normal justification thesis because it *solves* a coordination problem which the parties did not perceive or could not resolve and which they had good reasons to overcome (there being good reasons to cooperate). Since this response invokes the authority's greater ability at spotting and solving coordination disputes, it is in fact an indirect justificatory argument and best treated in the following subsection. As will be seen, it succumbs to the disabling problem that besets all versions of the indirect argument. Are there any other ways in which a directive that issues from an indeterminate judicial decision could satisfy the normal justification thesis? If we assume that the parties to the dispute know the nature of the reasons applicable to them and in play in the dispute, then it is indeed difficult to imagine an affirmative answer.

(ii) The indirect argument

This argument holds that indeterminate judicial decisions and the directives flowing from them satisfy the normal justification thesis by identifying and solving coordination problems. Such decisions and directives identify the reasons the parties in dispute have to act—the reasons, that is, they have for cooperating—and direct the parties how cooperation can be facilitated. For this argument to be plausible at least two hurdles must be cleared. I sketch the grounds for thinking these hurdles might be surmounted and conclude that, even if they are, this argument cannot demonstrate that indeterminate judicial decisions satisfy the normal justification thesis without denying the existence of incommensurability. The orthodox, in seeking to avail themselves of this indirect argument, therefore face an uncomfortable dilemma. Its horns are these: either apparently indeterminate judicial decisions satisfy the normal justification thesis by recognising and solving coordination problems, but in so doing serve to deny incommensurability; or they do not satisfy the normal justification thesis, in which case they lack legitimacy.

The first hurdle is that it must be appropriate to regard the parties' dispute—a dispute rooted in incommensurability of reasons and values—as a coordination problem. In the ordinary (not game-theoretical) sense that means the dispute, whether the parties know it or not, is about identifying the ways in which they should coordinate their action in order to obtain benefits that would not, in absence of cooperation, be forthcoming. It is not difficult to imagine how disputes rooted in incommensurability create coordination problems. Where the reasons and values applicable to the parties are incommensurable, then they do not have compelling reasons to prefer one reason or value to another; they therefore lack compelling reasons to act one way (so as to bring about cooperation, for example) or the other (so as to thwart cooperation). Now, it cannot be said in advance of an examination of the structure of particular disputes rooted in incommensurability that they will all satisfy this condition. But, given that the condition is not a demanding one, it is not reckless to assume that it will often be satisfied. When it is, the claim the orthodox make is that indeterminate judicial decisions rooted in incommensurability, or the directive flowing from them, solve the coordination problems to which incommensurability gives rise.

However, such decisions and directives must do a little more than that. They must surmount a second hurdle and actually fulfil the normal justification thesis. To do that the decisions and directives must dissipate the parties' ignorance of one or more of the following facts: (i) the fact that the reasons and values in play in their dispute are incommensurable; (ii) the fact that they are beset by a coordination problem; (iii) the fact that they have good reason to overcome that coordination problem. If the parties to the dispute are ignorant of one of these facts then it is more than likely that they will also be ignorant of one or more of the others. Similarly, if the parties are aware of one—for example, that their dispute rests upon incommensurability—then they will surely be aware of one or more of the others—in this example, that incommensurability is one important consideration preventing them from cooperating and hence bringing them into dispute. It just does not seem plausible that the parties could be aware of incommensurability but unaware of the fact that they are beset by a coordination problem or vice versa. Were it the case that the parties in dispute know some or all of these facts, an indeterminate judicial decision would merely reiterate that point. It tells the parties what they already know and is therefore incapable of satisfying the normal justification thesis. For how can an indeterminate judicial *decision*, one that rests upon incommensurability and the coordination problem it generates, both of which the parties already know about, allow the parties better to comply with reason?

An objection that does not reject the normal justification thesis could be made to the direction which the discussion of this second hurdle has taken. It was hinted at in the previous subsection and consists of an affirmative answer to the last, supposedly rhetorical question. The answer begins by noting that we have overlooked the *directive* that flows from the indeterminate judicial decision. It holds that this directive can satisfy the normal justification thesis even when the decision does not and even when the parties know the applicable reasons are incommensurable and that they are beset by a coordination problem. For the directive *solves* the problem: the directive forces the parties to cooperate because they have good reasons to do so. Since the directives that flow from judicial decisions rarely say 'do either X or Y or Z' but generally state unambiguously that one action must be taken or refrained from, they seem admirably suited to solving coordination problems. They unambiguously direct the parties how to act. If that way of acting solves the coordination problem and there are good reasons to want that—reasons found in the good of, or good that flows from, cooperation—then the normal justification thesis is undoubtedly satisfied.

This objection is instructive, but for what its proponents would surely regard as the wrong reasons. For it serves to show not that the indirect argument works but instead that, whether it relates to judicial decisions or directives, it must in this context fail. Why? Recall that the basis of the disputes in question is incommensurability of reasons and values. Further, that is why the parties in dispute face a coordination problem. Remember also that when the choice between reasons and values is incommensurable, then it is a choice not compelled by reason: 'incommensurability speaks not of what does escape reason but of what must elude it' (*MF*, p. 334). The indirect argument, however, surely denies this. For the indirect argument, to satisfy the normal justification thesis, must show that the parties in dispute have good reason to cooperate, that they have missed the fact that they are beset by a coordination problem and that there are good reasons to cooperate. Those reasons are found in the benefit or good that flows from cooperation or which is internal to it. Are these good reasons to cooperate also good reasons to choose one value or to act upon one reason, on one side of an incommensurable choice, rather than the value and reason on the other side? The situation we are imagining is one in which (i) the parties to a dispute are in dispute because the reasons and values applicable to them are incommensurable; and (ii) the parties are beset by a coordination problem by virtue of incommensurability. If there are good reasons for avoiding the coordination problem in (ii), reasons found in the good inherent in or flowing from cooperation and highlighted either by the judicial decision or directive, then there must be good reasons for exercising the choice in (i) one way— in favour of those reasons or values that promote cooperation and the values it generates—rather than another. That choice—the choice in (i)—is not therefore incommensurable. Despite appearances it is, after all, a choice compelled by reasons. The choice only temporarily eluded reason and then presumably as a result of oversight. This shows the way in which all versions of the indirect argument fail, in this context. For one crucial feature of the context is that it is one in which disputes and decisions are premised upon incommensurability. The indirect argument cannot work—nor can I imagine a form of it that would—because it must deny that feature of the context of dispute and decision. The argument can work only if incommensurability is false. And, as is obvious from section II of this essay, some orthodox value pluralists think incommensurability true. Moreover, the indirect argument fails for this reason whether its proponents have in mind indeterminate judicial decisions or the directives that flow from them. Given that the orthodox will probably not renounce their commitment to value pluralism and incommensurability, then their only remaining option is to reject the indirect argument.

(iii) The fallibility argument

This argument raises the following question in the hope that the answer to it is equally applicable to indeterminate judicial decisions and directives: why are mistaken directives authoritative? We have already noted that modified conventionalism makes conceptual room for mistaken but supposedly authoritative directives. We need examine how this is possible. If it is possible, and if the same reasons that make mistaken directives authoritative can also serve to make indeterminate judicial decisions and the directives that flow from them authoritative, then the orthodox can affirm both strong value pluralism and the legitimacy condition without difficulty.

The first task is to get clear about the ways in which supposedly authoritative directives can be mistaken. From Raz's discussion it seems that there are three ways in which directives can be mistaken. One such mistake ensures that the directive can have no authority at all: '[m]istakes which . . . [authorities] make about factors which determine the limits of their jurisdiction render their directives void. They are not binding as authoritative directives . . .' (*MF*, p. 62). Such mistakes can henceforth be ignored. The other two kinds of mistakes are not explicitly distinguished and labelled by Raz but his remarks are such as to show that he does implicitly draw a distinction and that he is (although he may not recognise it) committed to treating the two types of mistakes in very different ways. An objection to Raz's account of authority holds that a directive based upon a mistake about the reasons justifying the directive robs it of authority. Raz responds thus: '[r]easons which authoritative directives should, but fail to, reflect are none the less among the reasons which justify holding the directive binding' (*ibid*., p. 61). The type of mistake Raz has in mind here is what we can call an *Ealing* mistake: there is a good directive, in the sense that there are good reasons for it, based upon a mistaken assessment of its justifying reasons. That is, the authority issues a directive in the belief that it is justified by reasons Q when in fact only reasons U can justify the directive. Since, let us suppose, reasons U obtain, we are faced with a situation that can crudely be described as one in which we have the right directive justified by the wrong reasons, there being good reasons available. Raz thinks that in this situation the directive can be authoritative and, if it is, it must satisfy the normal justification thesis. The second kind of mistake we can call a *Wednesbury* mistake. Here an authority issues a directive that is mistaken in the sense that there are no good reasons for it at all: this situation can be characterised, albeit crudely, as consisting of the wrong directive and the wrong reasons.[69] Raz seems to have such a scenario in mind when he imagines a 'legitimate authority . . . [being] limited by the condition that its directives are not binding if *clearly wrong*' (*ibid*., p. 62; emphasis supplied). Somewhat strangely, Raz completes this remark with the caveat that 'I wish to express no opinion on whether it is so limited' (*ibid*.). He does not consider whether or not such directives could satisfy the normal justification thesis.

What reasons does Raz forward to support his claim that *Ealing* directives certainly satisfy the normal justification thesis? There are two, his argument beginning with a statement of the thesis and ending with a warning about losing its advantages:

> An authority is justified . . . if it is more likely than its subjects to act correctly for the right reasons. That is how the subjects' reasons figure in the justification, both when they are correctly reflected in a particular directive and when they are not. If every time a directive is mistaken, i.e. every time it fails to reflect reason correctly, it were open to challenge as mistaken, the advantage gained by accepting the authority as a more reliable and successful guide to right reason would disappear (*MF*, p. 61).

[69] My labels are drawn from two administrative law cases: *Associated Provincial Picture House Ltd* v. *Wednesbury Corporation* [1948] 1 KB 223 (under which a 'wrong' directive based upon the 'wrong' reasons would certainly come to grief) and *R* v. *Ealing LBC ex p. Times Newspapers Ltd.* (1986) 85 LGR 316 (in which an otherwise justifiable decision was made for the 'wrong' reasons). It would, however, be a mistake to think that there is any straightforward overlap between the types of mistakes identified in the text and those that will trigger judicial review of administrative action.

Now this restatement of the normal justification thesis seems intended to illustrate the point that an authority need not *always* be a better assessor of the right reasons applicable to agents than agents themselves are. Hence, in a number of cases the authority will be wrong. How does this establish that wrong directives are authoritative? The argument shows merely that, if we are satisfied that an authority tracks right reason in the majority of cases, then we ought to accept its authority in the majority of cases. The most it could establish beyond this is a fairly weak presumption in favour of all the authority's directives. The argument would take the following form: since in the majority of cases the authority tracks right reason and the majority of its directives are therefore authoritative, *all* its directives should be presumed to be authoritative. The reason why this can only be a weak presumption in favour of the authority is obvious—the fact that the authority has tracked right reason in a majority of cases in the past cannot guarantee that it will continue to do so either in the present or the future. So some *Ealing* directives might be taken to be authoritative on the basis of this presumption, but only some, and, one must assume, only for a limited time. If the authority is continuously mistaken its directives surely cannot satisfy the normal justification thesis. The fact that this argument falls far short of establishing that all *Ealing* directives are authoritative should not surprise us.[70] For this kind of limited claim fits snugly with Raz's view that there is no general obligation to obey the law. Rather, the existence of any obligation depends, *inter alia*, on the circumstances of both subject and authority (see *MF*, pp. 70 and 74).

Raz's second reason to show that *Ealing* directives are authoritative is also somewhat weak. It consists of the truism that when directives are mistaken we will lose the advantage of acting in accordance with an authority. However, it is equally true that once an authority issues directives that are *ultra vires* we will lose the advantage of authority. What this seems to amount to is that when authorities act contrary to the normal justification thesis their directives lack authority. In that case we will indeed lose the benefits of authority but avoiding that loss surely cannot justify, under the normal justification thesis, unconditional compliance with mistaken or *ultra vires* directives. So, the most that Raz establishes about *Ealing* directives is that some of them might be authoritative in that they might be covered by the weak presumption. That is hardly a sound basis for the claim that all such directives are authoritative.

Were we to consider what a particular *Ealing* directive that fell within

[70] For a similar argument that all mistaken directives cannot be taken to be authoritative see: S. Perry, 'Second-Order Reasons, Uncertainty and Legal Theory' (1989) 62 *Southern California L. R.* 913–994, pp. 933–936. D. Regan also raises the problematic status of mistaken directives at pp. 1030–1031 of his essay 'Authority and Value' in the same volume. Raz's reply (*supra*, note 32) hardly mentions mistaken directives at all.

the weak presumption must look like in order to satisfy the normal justification thesis convincingly, we would have to return to the two alternative conditions that indeterminate judicial decisions must satisfy. Since these are conditions that any directive must satisfy, one or other of them needs be satisfied by *Ealing* directives. The conditions are: either (i) the directive must function so as to allow agents subject to them to comply with the reasons they have for acting more effectively than they would were they to try to determine those reasons for themselves; or (ii) the directive must show that agents were in the grip of a coordination problem they were unaware of and that they had reason to cooperate which they were either unaware of or incapable of realising. Now, in so far as *Ealing* directives are based upon a mistaken account of the reasons justifying the directives they cannot satisfy the first condition: how can a directive that rests upon such a mistake allow the agents subject to it to comply with the reasons that apply to them more effectively than if they attempted to determine those reasons for themselves? Such a directive could only partially satisfy the second condition in that, though mistaken as to why coordination was worthwhile, it could nevertheless solve the coordination problem. (If the directive solved the problem and did so because it was based upon an accurate account of the reasons why coordination was worthwhile it would not, *ex hypothesi*, be mistaken.) Hence, Raz's confidence that *Ealing* directives are legitimate is misplaced since, even if they do fall within the weak presumption, they can only partially satisfy the normal justification thesis.

By contrast, it is unlikely that *Wednesbury* directives could satisfy the normal justification thesis at all. While there are some good reasons available to justify *Ealing* directives no such reasons support *Wednesbury* directives. So as to be sure that the latter type of mistaken directive does not satisfy the normal justification thesis, let us consider again the two alternative conditions which any directive must satisfy in order to be legitimate. The first condition need not delay us long: since *Ealing* directives cannot satisfy it there is no hope that *Wednesbury* directives can. If there are no good reasons for the directive, how can it help agents track right reason better than they otherwise would? And, whereas *Ealing* directives can partially satisfy the second condition—they solve the coordination problem and ensure cooperation even though they are based upon a misunderstanding of the reasons for cooperation—*Wednesbury* directives cannot. These directives, remember, are wrong both about the reasons for cooperation and the nature of the directive required to bring cooperation about. The seemingly insurmountable difficulties that ensnare any attempt to show that *Wednesbury* directives satisfy the normal justification thesis make Raz's caveat about 'clearly wrong' directives extremely puzzling. For, it seems that if they are clearly wrong in the *Wednesbury* sense, then they just cannot be legitimate. In this instance, Raz's caution is surely misplaced.

The argument to show that mistaken directives are legitimate is, then, rather limited. Using this argument to show that indeterminate directives are also legitimate is not therefore a promising strategy. Particular mistaken (*Ealing*) directives can only partially satisfy the normal justification thesis and then only if they fall within the realm of the weak presumption. So far, it might seem that although weak as a means of establishing the legitimacy of indeterminate judicial decisions and directives, this argument is no weaker than the direct argument. Therefore, it might be thought that the fallibility argument can be used to show that indeterminate judicial decisions and directives are legitimate. This would be a mistake, for the following reason. It consists of highlighting the way in which *Ealing* directives can partially satisfy the normal justification thesis. They do so by solving a coordination dispute albeit on the basis of a mistaken account of the reasons why the dispute should be solved (we are faced, remember, with the right directive but the wrong reasons). The crucial point here is that there are, even though the authority has got them wrong, *good reasons* to solve the dispute the one way or another. And, as we have noted in our discussion of the indirect argument, if there are good reasons to solve a dispute supposedly based upon incommensurability one way rather than another, that must call into question the fact that we are indeed dealing with a conflict between incommensurables. The difficulty that scuppered the indirect argument arises here also and serves to disable the fallibility argument.

The yield from the direct, indirect and fallibility arguments is indeed meagre. The direct argument can only show that indeterminate judicial decisions and their directives are legitimate when the parties in dispute are misguided about either the existence or nature of the reasons and values applicable to them. It is thus a very limited success, the authority of decisions and directives completely dependent, as is the normal justification thesis in general, upon the knowledge, abilities and context of the parties to whom they are applicable. By contrast, the indirect and fallibility arguments are not even partially successful: neither can show that indeterminate judicial decisions are legitimate without denying that those decisions are indeterminate. And, of course, that denial is not available to the orthodox by virtue of their commitment to value pluralism and incomparability. The obvious question that now presents itself is this: why should the orthodox, or anyone else for that matter, worry about this meagre yield? Those of us who take up the posture of world weary and cynical 'realists' will not regard the conclusion that indeterminate judicial decisions often lack legitimacy as news. Can the orthodox afford to take up the same pose of bored indifference? Not if they want to maintain some substantive distance between their position and that of the heretics on this issue.

For heretics, judicial decisions lack real legitimacy although mechanisms outwith and within the law serve to generate an appearance of legitimacy.[71] In this vein David Kairys observes that '[t]he judge makes a choice, and legal reasoning provides *a stylised rationalisation that legitimates* that choice within the legal and social order'; adjudication is one of the 'many areas of our lives . . . [in which] essentially social and political judgments gain legitimacy from notions of expertise and analysis that *falsely purport* to be objective, neutral, and quasi-scientific'.[72] Similarly, Unger holds that deceit is necessary if judicial decisions are to be regarded as authoritative: '[t]he concealment of . . . assumptions is vital to the *persuasive authority* of the dominant legal ideas; seemingly uncontroversial technical conceptions commonly depend upon highly controversial, nontechnical premises'. The legitimacy of these assumptions cannot stand the light of day: they are 'made controversial if not implausible in the very process of being exposed'.[73] Now, the orthodox can only maintain the legitimacy condition in very limited circumstances. First, if there are such things as easy cases (many heretics deny that there are), then the condition might be satisfied in them. Secondly, it can be satisfied in those hard or unregulated cases that manifest incommensurability if, as will rarely be the case, the parties are ignorant of either the existence or nature of the reasons and values applicable to them. The difference between heretical and orthodox positions on the legitimacy condition is therefore not great, particularly if heretics are right about hard cases. Perhaps, to echo the conclusion arrived at in the discussion of the determinacy condition, the only real difference between heretics and orthodox here is that the latter begin from a position of faith in the legitimacy condition, but subsequently find that faith very difficult to sustain, whereas the former are non-believers from the outset. This slight difference may lead one to wonder if it is indeed worthwhile to distinguish orthodoxy from heresy and to agree with the poet Michael Drayton that 'What late was truth, now turn'd to Heresie'.[74]

IV CONCLUSION

The argument is easily summarised. It was that many orthodox accounts of law and adjudication become indistinguishable from heretical accounts because they cannot maintain the determinacy and legitimacy conditions.

[71] See Kelman, *GCLS*, pp. 262–268 and ch. 9.

[72] These two statements (the emphasis is supplied) are from D. Kairys, 'Law and Politics' (1984) 52 *George Washington L. R.* 243–262, p. 246 and *PL*, p. 17.

[73] The two quotations are from Unger, *CLSM* pp. 88 and 89 respectively (the italics are supplied).

[74] M. Drayton, *The Legend of Matilda* (1596).

Both conditions are imperilled by the orthodox commitment to strong value pluralism: its presence within the realm of adjudication apparently ensures that neither condition can be plausibly affirmed. There is, however, an important orthodox exception that has not been considered. It was noted that Dworkin is not a strong value pluralist and he is therefore prima facie able to maintain the determinacy condition. Indeed, his right answer thesis is a good deal more demanding than that condition. Moreover, Dworkin also has an interesting account of authority which he unpacks through the notion of associative obligation.[75] Unlike many of the orthodox, he might be able to maintain both the determinacy condition *and* the legitimacy condition. Of course, we cannot rightly cast Dworkin in the role of saviour of the orthodoxy until his work is thoroughly examined and that task is not undertaken here.[76] Suffice it to say that many of the orthodox face what they will regard as an unpalatable choice: either maintain the orthodoxy by becoming Dworkinians or jump ship and become heretics.

If the orthodox decline this choice the consequence is that, despite appearances, their position on the justifiability and legitimacy of some judicial decisions is virtually the same as the heretical position. The moral of the story is this: either heretical accounts of adjudication are far less—or orthodox accounts far more—radical than might be assumed from the self-descriptions of each group of scholars. Armed with this insight we are, no doubt, better placed to determine what is at stake in the dispute between orthodox and heretics or whether there is indeed a genuine dispute at all. One thing is, however, abundantly clear. It is that heretics and orthodox must look beyond the determinacy and legitimacy conditions if, in an attempt to win minds and souls, they are to distinguish themselves as radically different sects. While the high temperature, conflictual rhetoric characteristic of their 'debate'—one in which, *inter alia*, 'toadying jurists' battle with dangerous 'nihilists'—is both amusing and arresting, it is neither a necessary nor sufficient condition for a genuine dispute to exist between them.

The three chapters in the second part of the book take a closer look at the heresy. The overarching question remains: what, besides different taste in rhetoric, distinguishes orthodoxy and heresy? We will examine the heretical method—in so far as heretics espouse a single method—and contrast it with that employed by the orthodox. This is done in two stages, beginning with heretical attempts to displace the orthodox method and then continuing with an analysis of the implications and difficulties of their own method. The heretical position on the role of values in adjudication is then

[75] See *LE*, pp. 195–216.

[76] I am not the first to cast Dworkin in this role: see Habermas, *supra*, note 16, p. 203. For a more amusing casting and a wonderful exaggeration of Dworkin's heroic status, see A. Hutchinson, 'Indiana Dworkin and the Temple of Doom' (1986) 96 *Yale L. J.* 637–665.

examined. This journey again exposes us to much amusing rhetoric and bombast. We will no doubt also be led to ponder the social and cultural conditions that gave rise to, and which currently nourish, the dispute between orthodoxy and heresy although that, as has been said many times, is not the object of our concern. Our interest is in substantive differences between orthodoxy and heresy, differences of method or of values, differences that might be called 'philosophical', were that a neutral and uncontentious label. Although we have not as yet compiled a very long list of such differences, we need not be discouraged. For, being able to come up with only a very short list, or even no list, would be an advance in our knowledge and a considerable improvement on the self-descriptions and rhetoric of the participants in this dispute. Even then we would be better able to distinguish wood from trees.

II
Heresy

5
Constructing the Heresy

The critic spits on what is done,
Gives it a wipe—and all is gone.
Thomas Hood, 'A Joke', 1897.

EXCURSUS

In 1982 a small storm broke in the world of art history and criticism. In his catalogue for the Tate Gallery exhibition of the works of Richard Wilson, David Solkin suggested that the paintings in question embodied a quietist, almost Burkean ideology of hierarchy, station and individual worth. Friction arose because Solkin attempted to understand and explain Wilson's work not just in terms of its technical quality, iconography and pattern of influences, but also in terms of its political cartography, its assumptions about, and representations of, the political society in which it was created. This approach was objectionable to some who thought it the *modus operandi* of Thomas Hood's critic, a scrupulous ignoring of the details and quality of the work in question, a displacement of the artist's aims and achievement, a metaphorical wiping clean of the slate upon which was written the vital concerns of traditional art history and criticism. For traditional art historians, Solkin either failed to engage sufficiently thoroughly and directly with the work, or failed to engage with it in the proper way. Furthermore, his puzzling concern with matters supposedly external to the work, such as the social and political context of its production, was regarded as an illegitimate departure that called into question the scholarly integrity of the art historian.[1]

This brief characterisation of the birth-pangs of the 'new' art history has an almost exact correspondence within contemporary legal philosophy. For the orthodox, many heretical attempts at understanding and explaining particular judicial decisions or bodies of law ape the structure of the explanatory accounts of the new art history. That is to say, heretics either fail to engage with the details of that which they hope to explain and understand in the way orthodox scholars think necessary; or, they take an apparently

[1] An informed account of the storm and its aftermath is M. Kitson's introduction to the fifth edition of E. Waterhouse, *Painting in Britain 1530–1790* (New Haven, Yale U. P. 1994). The cause of the storm was D. Solkin, *Richard Wilson: The Landscape of Reaction* (London, Tate Gallery 1982), some of the themes of which are developed in his *Painting for Money* (New Haven, Yale U. P. 1992).

dismissive view of some features of the phenomena in question and of the traditional attempts at understanding and explanation. They see judicial decisions and bodies of law not as specific attempts to resolve specific problems in a coherent, consistent and legitimate way, but rather as products of external factors such as the judge's values, ideology or preferences. Heretics are not particularly concerned with rational reconstruction of the judge's reasons for her decision, but rather with what may have given those reasons salience for her or for a whole class of judges. For many heretics, the rational reconstruction of judicial decisions is not an intellectually viable option, since they believe that adjudication cannot be rational in the first place.

There is a more radical heretical response to law and legal scholarship which is also echoed in the new art history. What is most disturbing, for some, about Solkin's claim that Wilson's paintings are vehicles of a specific set of political claims and assumptions, is the implication that this occurred regardless of Wilson's own aims and intentions. Traditional art history usually assumes that the painter is a fully autonomous human being, admittedly situated in a particular social and cultural context, but in some significant sense independent of it. So, although paintings are analysed by such historians for various patterns of influence—highlighting the artist's indebtedness to, and borrowing from teachers, for example—it is assumed that the artist can choose those influences, can accept or seek to liberate himself from them. Some heretics would maintain that, if we substitute judge for artist, this view comfortably fits the conception of the self that underpins orthodox legal scholarship. Moreover, this view of the self as rational and autonomous is general: it is an account of the nature of *any* self in our culture, be it artist, judge, critic, commentator or citizen. And, some heretics maintain, this picture of the self is completely and utterly misleading and mythical. If this is correct, we have here a particularly bold heretical critique that exceeds even Hood's critic. This is not just, as in the first heretical strategy, a wiping clean of the slate—or a reassessment of the nature of the 'product' in question, be it a painting or a judicial decision—but the erasure or calling into question of that which we assumed wrote upon and read from the slate. 'Producer' and 'consumer', artist and audience, judge and citizen, seem to disappear.

I THE DEATH OF INDETERMINACY

> [T]he radicalization of the indeterminacy thesis makes us realize that something has long since gone wrong in the terms of this discussion.
> R. M. Unger, *What Should Legal Analysis Become?* (1996), p. 121.

(a) Method and indeterminacy

Heretics are dismissive of orthodox doctrinal scholarship. The central task of the orthodox enterprise is the rational reconstruction of segments of law upon the basis of the judicial and statutory materials.[2] The orthodox usually regard such extant legal materials as but incomplete accounts of the true picture of the law. Put crudely, the law is regarded as hidden treasure buried beneath the sand of judgments and statutory provisions. Orthodox doctrinal scholars pore over the details of particular judgments and statutes in the belief that they contain hints as to the true picture of the law and the nature and whereabouts of the hidden treasure. Having gathered together such hints, the orthodox then highlight how the decisions and statutes in question do or might conflict with other areas of law and how they might thwart, or enhance, the law's future development. Overall, both orthodox doctrinal scholarship and legal philosophy unite behind the banner of sympathetic, rational reconstruction. It is a style of scholarship that is neither fawningly quiescent nor sceptically dismissive towards the existing legal system and its doctrines.

That many heretics are dismissive of this enterprise does not imply they are dismissive of the details of the phenomena—particular segments of law—the orthodox attempt to explain and understand. Many heretics spend a good deal of time examining particular cases or areas of law. Their analyses are, however, quite different from orthodox scholarship since heretics renounce the reconstructive, sympathetic task that animates the former. Gerald Frug, in concluding his discussion of a hypothetical consideration and modification case, captures the difference well:

> [m]any [orthodox] law professors would have adopted an alternative approach to the case, attempting instead to 'make sense' of it through an effort to rationalise all modification cases into one coherent legal framework. In fact, many law professors would say that this is obviously how a law professor should discuss a case . . . [But] [a]n attempt to rationalise cases is based on the controversial assumption that law is a consistent and a coherent whole rather than a forum for conflict over basic values. This assumption should not simply be an unstated premise of law teaching . . .[3]

This somewhat dismissive approach to rational reconstruction is not without justification. It is based upon a number of arguments designed to

[2] For discriminating statements of what the orthodox take rational reconstruction to involve see: N. MacCormick and R. S. Summers (eds.), *Interpreting Statutes: A Comparative Study* (Aldershot, Dartmouth 1991) pp. 18–24; A. Aarnio, 'Is Legal Science a Social Science?' and N. MacCormmick, 'Four Quadrants of Jurisprudence', pp. 55–58, both of which appear in W. Krawictz, N. MacCormick and G. v. Wright (eds.), *Prescriptive Formality and Normative Rationality in Modern Legal Systems* (Berlin, Dunker and Humblot 1994).

[3] G. Frug, 'A Critical Theory of Law' (1989) 1 *Legal Education Review* 43–57, p. 55.

redress the emphasis of legal scholarship. Whereas the jurisprudential and doctrinal orthodoxy explicitly invokes the internal point of view—from which is derived a commitment to consistency, coherence and rational reconstruction—the heresy explicitly or implicitly rejects that method. While the orthodox attempt to argue that participants—practitioners, clients, citizens and commentators—in the practice 'law' accept that consistency and coherence are but two of the values that inform the practice,[4] heretics seek to liberate legal scholarship from the shackles of the participants' point of view. At first glance, it seems an obvious error to construct an account of social action, practices and institutions upon the views of those whose behaviour constitutes the action, practices and institutions in question. For, if those participants live in a world riven with conflict, ideology, false-consciousness, bias and self-interest, then the theorists' account of the practice, built upon the participants' views of it, will be both founded upon and a perpetuation of bias, ideology, self-interest etc. This is the kind of claim which, if compelling, could discredit the orthodox method. It motivates most heretical thinking and is encapsulated in Jack Balkin's view that, in order to 'ground jurisprudence in a critical perspective, one that employs ideological critique to reflect on our internal experience of law[,] . . . [we must not] . . . tak[e] for granted the primacy of the internal point of view of participants in the legal system, [but] . . . ask how this internal experience comes about'.[5]

The initial step for the heretic is therefore to loosen the hold of the *Verstehen* method, and the commitment to consistency, coherence and rational reconstruction the orthodox think it yields, over legal thought. This section and the remaining two consider three arguments heretics use to this end. The first is in fact a very common family of arguments sharing the resemblance that all invoke some claim about 'indeterminacy'. This family of arguments is hereinafter labelled the indeterminacy theses, although it will be necessary to sort and label the arguments in a rather more refined way than this. The second argument is nowhere near as common as the first although its novelty is not solely a consequence of its rarity. The argument is strikingly ambitious and intended to call into question both orthodox and many heretical positions. It is nevertheless still discernibly an heretical position, albeit a dissentient voice within that broad church. It is the argument about the disappearance of the self. The third argument can flow from, or stand independently of, the indeterminacy theses. The argument will be labelled, for reasons that will become obvious, the ideology critique. It is

[4] The two most notable examples are N. MacCormick, *Legal Reasoning and Legal Theory* (Oxford, Clarendon 1978; revised ed., 1993), chs. V–VIII and R. Dworkin, *Law's Empire* (London, Fontana 1986), chs. 6 and 7.

[5] J. M. Balkin, 'Understanding Legal Understanding: The Legal Subject and the Problem of Legal Coherence' (1993) 103 *Yale L. J.* 105–176, pp. 110–111.

addressed in section III. It may seem odd to treat this argument last since, as a matter of chronology and association, it often appears in conjunction with one or other indeterminacy thesis. However, as noted, the ideology critique can stand independently of those arguments—it certainly is not entailed by, nor does it entail, them. The latter is clear from the argument considered in section II. The disappearance of self is an argument that makes no claim at all about any kind of indeterminacy yet it still invokes, at a vital stage, the ideology critique.

Of these three arguments, only the second and third operate as direct attempts to discredit the *Verstehen* method. The indeterminacy theses rarely have any explicitly methodological orientation. Nevertheless, the indeterminacy theses, if valid, would certainly serve to displace the orthodox method. The theses occupy us for some time because they have often been rather badly formulated by heretics and badly understood by both orthodox and non-aligned commentators. By contrast, the disappearance of the self is not such an intriguing mystery as to call for extensive consideration. The argument is somewhat underdeveloped but its most promising step is that which relies upon a version of the ideology critique. Hence, the ideology critique, though capable of standing independently, also functions to support either the indeterminacy theses or the argument about the disappearance of the self. The ideology critique is therefore an important and popular argument among heretics and its various strands and proponents will be noted. So, too, will some of the argument's problems.

More specifically, the discussion in this section attempts to substantiate two claims: (i) that only one indeterminacy thesis has any power; and (ii) that some of the putative rebuttals articulated by critics of the heresy do not endanger the indeterminacy theses at which they are directed. Section II argues that two of the three steps in the disappearance of the self argument are weak but one might succeed. Since that step of the argument invokes the ideology critique, its success depends upon the plausibility of that critique. An assessment of the power of the ideology critique is the fulcrum of section III. That section maintains that the ideology critique, taken independently of the indeterminacy theses and the disappearance of the self, is the heretic's most promising means of discrediting the orthodox method. The arguments offered here do *not* privilege the *verstehen* method in the sense of assuming it to be the 'right' or 'natural' or 'obvious' method for legal scholarship. True, that method is not critically analysed here, for our concern is with the arguments heretics use to loosen its grip upon us. But this should not be taken as an expression of support for that method which, as can be seen from the arguments of chapter 2, is problematic. Nor should the arguments here be regarded as in any way discrediting the method or range of methods that heretics invoke. Our concern is with prior matters—with heretics' arguments against the orthodox method rather than the details of the method heretics themselves adopt or espouse. The latter is the concern of chapter 6.

Before examining the indeterminacy theses, we must clarify exactly how these arguments are supposed to undermine the orthodox method. We have seen that, for the orthodox, a commitment to consistency, coherence and rational reconstruction flows from a commitment to *Verstehen* because participants in the practice espouse these notions. However, these notions are not directly refuted by any of the indeterminacy theses since they purport to show only the impossibility of justificatory determinacy within existing schemes of adjudication. That is, these theses supposedly undermine the orthodox claim that the choices judges make in hard and easy cases are justifiable (either in practice or principle). For heretics, all judicial decisions suffer from what we might call a justification deficit: the reasons judges offer for their decisions just do not rationally compel a decision one way or another. Such a deficit is supposedly guaranteed by the truth of the indeterminacy theses. If these arguments do indeed show that the choices made in adjudication are incapable of being justified, then the notions of consistency, coherence and rational reconstruction are imperilled as a (albeit fairly immediate) side-effect. Why is this so?

The answer depends upon what is meant by consistency and coherence. At one level, both notions can be regarded as merely surrogate terms for outcome predictability in the law. On this view, to maintain that the law is coherent and consistent is to say two things. First, that in the great mass of judicial decisions in some area of the law, the *outcomes* of later cases are compatible with the outcomes in earlier cases. Secondly, that given knowledge of those earlier outcomes, an informed commentator could predict with a reasonably high degree of accuracy the outcomes in later cases. Taken thus, the notions of consistency and coherence are untouched by heretical arguments to show the impossibility of justificatory determinacy. Since on this view these notions are simply concerned with predictability of legal outcomes and *nothing else*, they need make no claim about whether or not those outcomes are either justifiable or legitimate. Moreover, that the denial of justificatory determinacy in adjudication does not imperil any claim about the predictability of adjudicative outcomes is clear from heretics' own statements on these matters. They frequently propound one or other of the indeterminacy theses in conjunction with an acceptance of the fact that adjudicative outcomes are predictable.[6] Thus the indeterminacy theses cannot be intended to imperil the notions of consistency and coherence

[6] Two examples are: J. Singer, 'The Player and the Cards: Nihilism and Legal Theory' (1984) 94 *Yale L. J.* 1–70, pp. 19–25; and M. Kelman, *A Guide to Critical Legal Studies* (Cambridge, Harvard U. P. 1987), pp. 4 and 46–47.

understood as surrogates for outcome predictability. To think that they are so intended is to ignore what heretics themselves say.[7]

There is another view of what the notions of coherence and consistency entail, a view well represented among the orthodox. On this view, those notions incorporate a claim about predictability of outcomes in conjunction with a claim about justificatory consistency and coherence. Further, the best of the orthodox writers on these matters attempt to distinguish consistency and coherence, although for present purposes the distinction will be ignored. What the orthodox have in mind when they speak of coherence and consistency in justificatory terms is something like this: it is not enough if *only* the outcomes of judicial decisions fit with one another across time. Rather, in a good legal system the pattern of consistency and coherence must also be a matter of replicating in later cases the good reasons for the decisions in earlier cases. On this view, many but not necessarily all earlier cases are depositories of good, compelling reasons for decision and, in similar later cases, those good, compelling reasons should be followed. Of course, what 'good, compelling' reasons look like, and the criteria of 'relevant similarity', are topics for argument. This is not, however, relevant to the point in issue, namely, that for the orthodox the notions of coherence and consistency are understood not just as matters of predictability but also as matters of justification. When understood as involving a commitment to the possibility of good, compelling reasons for decision, these notions are very closely tied to the possibility of justificatory determinacy. Hence, when heretics attempt to discredit the latter they can thereby discredit the notions of consistency and coherence taken in justificatory terms. This, of course, need not necessarily be the case, since the orthodox could well amend their usage of those terms. Were they to employ consistency and coherence talk solely as a surrogate for outcome predictability, then—and supposing nothing else they say commits them to justificatory determinacy—they would be immune to the indeterminacy theses but not, as we will see in section III, the ideology critique.

One more point must be made. It concerns the ways in which indeterminacy theses could fail. From what we have just said, it will be obvious that one way in which these arguments could fail would be by failing to establishing the existence of justificatory indeterminacy. The indeterminacy theses would also fail were it established that their starting point was false, namely, that it is false that the orthodox espouse justificatory determinacy. And, the theses would fail were they internally inconsistent. The

[7] Three who make this mistake are: J. Stick, 'Can Nihilism be Pragmatic?' (1986) 100 *Harvard L. R.* 332–401, p. 353; L. Solum, 'On the Indeterminacy Crisis: Critiquing Legal Dogma' (1987) 54 *University of Chicago L. R.* 462–503, pp. 471–472; and K. Kress, 'Legal Indeterminacy' (1989) 77 *California L. R.* 283–337, pp. 285–295.

first and third types of failure will loom largest in what follows since, for the sake of argument, it will be taken for granted that the orthodox do indeed espouse justificatory determinacy. No position is actually taken up as to whether or not that is actually an accurate representation of the orthodox position nor are the problems with that position discussed. However, as is clear from the discussion in chapter 4, the orthodox position on these matters is often more complex than heretics think.

(b) The varieties of indeterminacy

Three indeterminacy arguments are examined. There are many more proponents of the three arguments than the following treatment suggests. The hope is that the sample is representative. Remember that, although quite distinct from one another and beset by different snags, the indeterminacy theses share the same burden: each aims to undermine the possibility of justificatory determinacy.

(i) Empirical indeterminacy

There are at least two versions of empirical indeterminacy in the heretical literature. One is true but banal, while the other is radical, challenging and quite implausible. They are examined here with three ends in mind. First, their internal coherence is assessed; second, some judgment is offered as to their effect upon either the orthodox method or substantive orthodox arguments about the nature of adjudication; third, they serve as an entrée to another type of heretical argument about indeterminacy.

The true but banal account of empirical indeterminacy is found in Duncan Kennedy's recent work. It 'does not assert that "law" "is" globally indeterminate' but only that in some situations the arguments judges use to support their decisions are not compelling.[8] Two such situations are identified by Kennedy. First, some judgments are not logically compelling even though the judges offering them think they are; secondly, some judgments 'are unconvincing because although of impeccable internal logic they don't confront obvious responses to their arguments' (*CA*, p. 89). Kennedy suggests that in these situations judicial decisions suffer from a rationality deficit which is filled by ideology since judges 'work in a medium saturated with ideology' (*CA*, p. 1). This account of indeterminacy deserves the label 'empirical' for the simple reason that it offers no general metaphysical, ontological or normative argument as to why indeterminacy exists. Indeterminacy does not affect the very nature of law on this view and hence determinacy is not impossible (*CA*, pp. 86, 92, 276–277). Simply put, the exis-

[8] D. Kennedy, *A Critique of Adjudication* (Cambridge, Mass., Harvard U. P. 1997), p. 279. Hereinafter referred to, in both text and notes, as '*CA*' with accompanying page numbers.

tence of determinacy and indeterminacy is for Kennedy a matter of 'look and see': the judgments in particular cases are placed before us and, by a close reading, we assess whether or not they are logically flawed or ignore obvious counter-arguments. It may well be true that many judgments are so flawed, yet it is difficult to envisage anyone, never mind orthodox scholars, objecting to this possibility. Any such objection must apparently be based on a prima facie odd belief about the infallibility of legal judgment which few have ever held. So, is anything at stake for the orthodox if they recognise the two kinds of indeterminacy identified by Kennedy? He would like us to think so, for his argument is that the notion of ideology does a lot of work when judges decide cases. For this to be more than a banal point that the orthodox can easily accept, however, the notion of ideology must amount to something more than a surrogate for value-talk. If it is not, then the argument is of no concern to the orthodox, since, as we saw in the previous chapter, they too affirm that adjudication is a value-laden process. Just what ideology looks like for Kennedy will be examined in the final section of this chapter. For now, simply note that the spectre of banality hovers over this account of empirical indeterminacy.

Joseph Singer's essay, 'The Player and the Cards: Nihilism and Legal Theory',[9] is a notorious, radical and challenging account of empirical indeterminacy. It contains a supposedly damning critique of orthodox legal theory and practice, an unequivocal endorsement of nihilism (a doctrine often assumed to be anathema to the intellectually serious), and, most importantly, it is an unqualified failure. Singer's account of nihilism and his arguments about the impossibility of objectivity in adjudication will not be considered here.[10] I will simply reaffirm the striking weaknesses in Singer's arguments about determinacy and indeterminacy.[11] Lest an examination, however brief, of this spectacular failure be thought useless, the points it serves should be stated. There are two. First, it is important to get clear why Singer's argument fails since at least one of his critics has perpetrated an insidious canard about the thrust of both Singer's indeterminacy thesis and, by implication, the other two indeterminacy theses. Secondly, this failure highlights the appeal of a different type of indeterminacy argument which promises an escape from the banality that threatens Kennedy and the problems that envelop Singer.

What, then, is empirical indeterminacy according to Singer? His argument that law is indeterminate is

> [f]irst, . . . an empirical claim about existing legal theories and arguments. It is not a claim that it is impossible to invent determinate theories. It is also not a claim

[9] *Supra*, note 6. Referred to hereinafter in text and notes as '*PC*'.

[10] *PC*, pp. 25–39; on objectivity, see also J. Coleman and B. Leiter, 'Determinacy, Objectivity and Authority' (1993) 142 *University of Pennsylvania L. R.* 549–637.

[11] A good analysis of Singer's essay is Stick, *supra*, note 7.

about the nature of reason or the human mind or anything like that . . . Second, it is an internal critique. This is a critique from within, a critique that uses premises of traditional legal theory against itself. Legal scholars and judges claim that the theories or arguments they develop necessarily lead to certain results, or at least define a narrow range of alternatives and thus severely constrain the possible outcomes . . . My contention that their theories do not determine the outcomes they propose falsifies a claim that they themselves have made (*PC*, p. 10).

However, the means Singer uses to show the orthodoxy's failure to comply with its own edicts actually falsifies those edicts. For, he holds that, regardless of what the orthodox say, a belief in determinacy entails a view of law in which the legal system must be: (i) comprehensive—that is, must cover all fact situations; (ii) consistent, in the sense that there is no possibility of contradictions within the system; (iii) directive—it must 'help us choose among alternative possible rules' (*PC*, p. 18); and (iv) self-revising. The last feature Singer characterises in a particularly informative way, casting light on what he takes to be the core of orthodox conception of law:

even if a legal theory or set of rules appears completely determinate—even if it appears comprehensive, consistent, and directive—*it may still allow choice* if it does not specify under what circumstances existing rules should be followed and when and how they should be changed . . . A fully determinate legal theory . . . must tell us when to follow precedent and when to reverse or overrule . . . precedent . . . If it does not do this, *we are free to choose* . . . (*PC*, pp. 18–19; emphasis supplied).

A belief in determinacy, then, apparently entails a belief in a legal system with these four features which supposedly make adjudicative choices impossible. But that is not what determinacy means for actually existing orthodox legal scholars nor is it what determinacy must mean on Singer's account. Contemporary orthodox jurists think that adjudication can be *relatively* determinate, that judges can decide hard cases by reference to *relatively* determinate standards and types of argument. What 'relatively determinate' means here is that judges have and make choices which they can attempt to justify in particular ways, namely by reference to arguments of consistency, coherence and consequences or by reference to arguments of principle and integrity.[12] Choice is not denied, but it is to some degree constrained because only a limited range of arguments can justify those choices. This is the orthodox position. No one among the orthodox nor, in adjudicative terms at least, their fellow travellers, subscribes to an account of adjudication which denies judges choice in hard cases.[13] That being so,

[12] These arguments are, of course, respectively formulated by MacCormick and Dworkin, *supra*, note 4. For orthodox variations on these two themes see S. Burton, *Judging in Good Faith* (Cambridge, C. U. P. 1992) and J. Levin, *How Judges Reason* (New York, Peter Lang 1992).

[13] By 'adjudicative fellow travellers' I have in mind those legal idealists who would disagree with Dworkin and MacCormick on the nature of law but who accept that adjudication is a matter of making and attempting, whenever possible, to justify choices: see J. Finnis, 'Natural

Singer's internal critique must fail if 'using the premises of traditional legal theory against itself' means using what the orthodox actually say about these matters against themselves. Nothing they say entails a commitment to the four features Singer describes. Of course, it could be replied that Singer's concern is not with what traditional or orthodox jurists say but with the implications of what they say. One of those implications could be a commitment to the four features and the possibility of adjudication without choice. That argument would be important but requires much to succeed. Singer does not establish it in this or in any subsequent essay.

Furthermore, Singer's attempt to foist upon the orthodox, via the notion of determinacy, a conception of law and adjudication which leaves no room at all for choice, conflicts with one of the two characterisations of determinacy he offers. The first holds that determinate judicial decision-making is a process in which 'theories or arguments . . . *necessarily* lead to certain results' (*PC*, p. 10). Taking 'necessarily' in its ordinary sense in this context, as denoting logical necessity, fits exactly with Singer's misguided assumption that, for the orthodox, adjudication excludes the possibility of choice. Logically necessary arguments in philosophy or mathematics do just this—they appear inexorable and unfold in one direction whether one likes it or not, provided one accepts the truth of the premises. If one is rational, there is simply no choice whether or not to accept the conclusion in the syllogism

I. All men are mortal
II. Socrates is a man
III. Therefore Socrates is mortal

provided the premises are true. This conception of determinacy undoubtedly 'presuppose[s] an axiomatic, deductive model of legal reasoning [and therefore] Singer appears to believe that legal reasoning, to be rational, must operate by means of deductive proof and agreed upon first principles, which function like axioms in Euclidean geometry'.[14] Yet proponents of the jurisprudential orthodoxy do not accept that hard case adjudication is anything like this.[15] Rather, the strongest claim the orthodox make about determinacy is something like Singer's second characterisation of determinacy. On this view, determinate adjudication entails that, when faced with *choices*, judges' arguments and theories 'define a narrow range of *alternatives* and thus severely *constrain* the possible outcomes' (*PC*, p. 10; emphasis sup-

Law and Legal Reasoning' in R. George (ed.), *Natural Law Theory* (Oxford, Clarendon 1992) and D. Beyleveld and R. Brownsword, *Law as a Moral Judgment* (London, Sweet and Maxwell 1986), ch. 9.

[14] Stick, *supra*, note 7, p. 346.

[15] The closest they get is in their account of easy case adjudication: see, for example, MacCormick, *supra*, note 4, chs. II and III.

plied). This, *ex hypothesi*, is not an axiomatic, logically necessary process excluding choice. It is a matter of reducing the options one faces, and attempting to justify the option taken, by reference to a fairly fixed menu of arguments (principle not policy, consistency and consequences etc.). Accepting this view of adjudication and determinacy commits one neither to the four features Singer outlines nor to a belief in the possibility of adjudication without choice.

In the course of attempting to show that the orthodoxy is committed to a conception of determinacy it cannot hope to satisfy, Singer also seeks to show that, despite the presence of widespread indeterminacy, adjudicative outcomes are nevertheless predictable (*PC*, pp. 19–25). This argument is important because it shows that Singer and, I would argue, just about every other heretic who invokes one or other of the indeterminacy theses, thinks indeterminacy undermines the justifiability, not the predictability, of judicial decisions. John Stick's otherwise acute evaluation of Singer's position is marred by his inability to understand how the indeterminacy and predictability arguments can be consistently conjoined. In fact, he conflates both ideas in a way that Singer clearly avoids: 'to show that the current practice of law is indeterminate, . . . [Singer] must show that legal decisions cannot be predicted by using the standards of the practicing lawyer'.[16] However, indeterminacy and predictability are separate issues for Singer. It is true that Singer argues that indeterminate judicial decisions lack rationality and legitimacy (*PC*, pp. 25–45); they suffer from what we earlier called a justification deficit. Yet he also maintains, perfectly coherently, that indeterminate decisions are nevertheless predictable because the factors that condition the ways in which judges decide such cases are well known. The crucial point is that such factors— 'legal culture, conventions, "common sense", and politics' (*PC*, p. 25)—are, for Singer, beyond the justificatory pale. Since '[c]ustom, rather than reason, narrows the choices and suggests the result' (*ibid.*), the result suffers from a justification deficit.[17] Hence, indeterminacy does not entail a lack of predictability and the distinction between the two is in principle unproblematic. Of course, there are many other points one could make about this aspect of Singer's argument and Stick does so, questioning, for example, Singer's view that custom and convention have neither rational power nor legitimacy. That does not imperil the indeterminacy/predictability distinction but instead questions Singer's

[16] Stick, *supra*, note 7, p. 353.

[17] This claim is the fulcrum of M. Tushnet's 'sociological' version of the indeterminacy thesis: see his 'Defending the Indeterminacy Thesis', ch. 11 of B. Bix (ed.), *Analysing Law* (Oxford, Clarendon 1998). In locating the determinacy of adjudication in the socialisation process lawyers undergo, Tushnet shows neither (i) that the process is the only explanation of determinacy (he merely assumes this) nor (ii) that, if it is, it is beyond the justificatory pale. That lawyers are socialised to think certain arguments are compelling does not show that those arguments are *not* indeed compelling.

placement of particular phenomena on one or the other side of the distinction which, of course, remains intact.

Singer's argument fails because he ascribes a standard of determinacy to the orthodox that they do not embrace. Showing the orthodox cannot achieve a standard they do not embrace, and affirming all-embracing indeterminacy in the face of (non-existent) orthodox declarations of complete determinacy, discomfits them not a jot. That the orthodox *do* tolerate some degree of justificatory indeterminacy seems obvious and the problems this generates were discussed in chapter 4 and will be revisited in chapter 8. Singer has nothing useful to say on this issue since he neither examines the problems within orthodox statements about these matters, nor shows that unexpectedly bad consequences follow from taking their statements seriously. His failure highlights two distinct ways of formulating indeterminacy theses, two ways which reflect, for want of a better word, the different 'levels' at which the theses could operate. One is the level Singer and Kennedy select, the level of empirical indeterminacy. Remember that for Kennedy this is a matter of examining the argumentative structure of actual judicial decisions. For Singer it is a matter of showing that the statements about a practice made by theorists and participants just do not match the actuality of the practice. The thrust of Singer's argument is that the orthodox say and think the practice of adjudication is much more determinate than it really is: his 'contention that their theories do not determine the outcomes they propose falsifies a claim that they themselves make' (*PC*, p. 10). Or so he says, in spite of the fact that his critique fails to satisfy the bare minimum requirement for an indeterminacy argument to work at this level, namely, that it embodies an accurate picture of what its objects actually say, or of what they are committed to by virtue of what they say. That does not mean this requirement can never be satisfied: the empirical indeterminacy option is still open to heretics even though it has not often been favoured.

Instead, some heretics have taken a 'metaphysical' path. Indeterminacy theses formulated at this level take a position on matters which Singer hoped to avoid. They make claims 'that it is impossible to invent determinate theories . . . [or] about the nature of reason or the human mind' (*ibid.*). In the days of a strident and self-confident logical positivism, many philosophers affirmed a rigorous distinction between metaphysical propositions, on the one hand, and empirical propositions and the truths of standard logic, on the other. It was thought that empirical and metaphysical propositions were easily distinguished since the former embodied clear, albeit sometimes complex, methods for determining their truth or falsity whereas there were no means at all by which to verify the truth or falsity of the latter. Few today hold the distinction to be as clear cut and impermeable as the logical positivists thought, but a qualified version can still be invoked.[18] It distinguishes between propositions that are more abstract and universal, and those that are less, between those that purport to be more 'foundational' within any particular set of propositions and beliefs and those that are less, between those with more uncertain or controversial methods of establishing their truth and those with less uncertain, less controversial methods.

This prolix way of putting the distinction at least has the virtues of, first, accepting that for many philosophers the distinction between metaphysics and other realms of knowledge is a matter of degree and, secondly, of recognising that there is no realm of empirical 'brute' facts available to the mind in an unmediated, unproblematic way. Accepting the distinction as formulated, we can see a difference between propositions like '[o]ur existence just involves the existence of our brains and bodies, and the doing of our deeds, and the thinking of our thoughts, and the occurrence of certain other physical and mental events' and '[b]etween the two dates the mean income rose by nearly 70 per cent, from about £1000 to nearly £1700'.[19] The first undoubtedly looks metaphysical: it purports to be an abstract, universal and foundational. It makes a claim arising above the realm of everyday particularity. It is unlike, for example, the claim that X is a fully integrated person. It applies cross-culturally and historically and is thus very different from the claim that 'people in Edinburgh are friendly'. Moreover, it supposedly either underpins or undermines many if not all of our other important beliefs and attitudes (unlike the belief that it is now raining). Metaphysical claims such as these are often combined with—as a cause, consequence or in some other relation—two other types of claims. One is epistemological, that is, a claim or set of claims about the means by which we can obtain, and the limits of, knowledge; the other is ontological, which is a claim or claims about the constituents of the world, about 'what there is'.

Clearly, developing an indeterminacy argument that functions at the metaphysical level is a daunting and complicated task, but that has not cowed many heretics. In fact, most heretical arguments about indeterminacy are constructed to operate at this level. Certainly, the two indeterminacy theses examined in the following two subsections appear to be metaphysical. The first apparently metaphysical indeterminacy thesis examined was originally developed by Kennedy and the second by Gary Peller. Each thesis will be examined with a view to establishing whether or not it imperils justificatory determinacy and thereby displaces the *Verstehen*

[18] One of the clearest statements of the undiluted doctrine is A. J. Ayer, *Language, Truth and Logic* (Harmondsworth, Penguin 1971), ch. 1. For what some would regard as a qualified version but others as a refutation, see W. Quine, *From a Logical Point of View* (Cambridge, Mass., Harvard U. P. 2nd. ed. 1961), ch. II.

[19] The first statement belongs to D. Parfit, *Reasons and Persons* (Oxford, Clarendon Press 1984), p. 216 and the second to H. Phelps Brown, *Egalitarianism and the Generation of Inequality* (Oxford, Clarendon Press 1988), p. 263.

method. The argument is that neither thesis succeeds, although each fails for very different reasons.

(ii) Contradiction and indeterminacy

Kennedy's early work was dominated by two arguments that purportedly move from the truth of one or other version of the fundamental contradiction to the truth of justificatory indeterminacy. The two arguments still occupy a role in his work, as we will see, and they may in fact be different sides of the same coin. Further, both arguments can be interpreted as either universal or parochial in range and, since Kennedy moves from one interpretation to the other without apparently noticing, he provides no grounds to prefer one to the other. It is worth briefly sketching the arguments before assessing their worth. (Since both arguments are examined again in the next chapter some economy of treatment is justifiable.)

The first version of the argument asserts a contradiction between self and other: '[o]thers . . . are necessary if we are to become persons at all—they provide us the stuff of ourselves and protect us in crucial ways against destruction . . . But at the same time . . . the universe of others . . . threatens us with annihilation and urges upon us forms of fusion that are quite plainly bad rather than good'.[20] The second version holds that 'we are divided, among ourselves and within ours[e]lves between irreconcilable visions of humanity and society, and between radically different aspirations about our common future'.[21] Whereas the first version operates at the level of a conflict between particularly abstract entities—'selves' and 'others'—the second represents a substantive conflict between different, slightly less abstract, moral and political positions labelled 'individualism' and 'altruism'.[22] While in this sense different, the arguments could plausibly be related since the more abstract formulation could be taken to imply the less, although Kennedy offers no such argument. In addition, Kennedy is inconsistent about the range of the arguments from the fundamental contradiction. Sometimes he seemingly regards both arguments as truths about the human condition *simpliciter*, as universal truths about our situation in this and all future societies. Yet on other occasions he hints that the contradictions can be transcended, that they are but truths about this particular society which can therefore be overcome.[23]

Fortunately, for present purposes, we need not tidy up the various loose ends and distinguish the many strands of argument in Kennedy's discussion

[20] 'The Structure of Blackstone's *Commentaries*' (1979) 28 *Buffalo L. R.* 205–382, pp. 211–212. Hereinafter '*BC*'.

[21] 'Form and Substance in Private Law Adjudication' (1976) 89 *Harvard L. R.* 1685–1778, p. 1685. Hereinafter referred to as '*FS*'.

[22] *FS*, pp. 1713–1717.

[23] For some hints—there are others—that the contradictions are universal, see *FS*, pp. 1685, 1767 and 1775; *BC*, pp. 210, 213 and 221.

of the fundamental contradictions. Nor need we discuss his somewhat bogus retraction of the contradictions.[24] For, whether the contradiction between self and others or between individualism and altruism is focused upon, and whether we take the contradiction as being universal or parochial, does not matter. Either version of the contradiction, interpreted in either way, is a metaphysical argument that aims to establish the existence of justificatory indeterminacy and thereby call into question the orthodox method. Both versions make, in Singer's words, a claim about the nature of reason or the human mind and the claim is neither more nor less metaphysical for being formulated in either parochial or universal terms. The claims made are certainly abstract and allegedly foundational since they underpin and condition those segments of our language and thought that are oriented to social life and the polity. It is also far from obvious how the truth of one or other of the fundamental contradictions could be established. They are not verifiable in any simple empirical sense, unlike Phelps Brown's claim about income levels or the claim that 'the Liverpool F. C. home-kit is red'. Neither does Kennedy show that they are a priori truths nor that they are 'transcendentally' true. Accepting, then, that the arguments from the fundamental contradiction are metaphysical, we must clarify how they purport to establish widespread justificatory indeterminacy.

The argument takes the following form. (i) There are contradictions between self and other, individualism and altruism; (ii) these contradictions cannot be transcended, either at all, or within our existing social world; (iii) these contradictions determine—that is, set limits upon—our language, thought and action, although it is quite possible to be blind to them, for them to be 'mediated';[25] (iv) one of the ways in which the contradictions determine our thought and action is that they make rationally defensible and legitimate choices between individualist and altruist values, or between protecting self and protecting others, impossible;[26] (v) one realm in which such choices arise is law. The conclusion drawn is that, despite appearances, judges' adjudicative choices cannot be rationally justified. If that does indeed follow from the previous steps in the argument, then the orthodox method of taking up the internal point of view—and hence participants' commitment to rational reconstruction—is called into question. What are we to make of this argument?

It is not a success and this can be shown without becoming too immersed in the deep waters of metaphysics. Three related reasons will suffice to cast

[24] D. Kennedy and P. Gabel, 'Roll Over Beethoven' (1984) 36 *Stanford L. R.* 1–55, p. 15. One or other version of the contradiction just will not go away: see D. Kennedy, *Sexy Dressing Etc.* (Cambridge, Mass, Harvard U. P. 1993), pp. viii and 70 and *CA*, *supra*, note 8, at, *inter alia*, pp. 83, 95, 151–152 and 207. My reasons for regarding the retraction as bogus are outlined in chapter 6.

[25] *BC*, pp. 214–216, 256–272 and 379–382.

[26] *FS*, p. 1775.

doubt upon the argument. The first maintains that the macro-level constructs Kennedy invokes—self and other, individualism and altruism—which supposedly ensure micro-level contradictions within legal doctrine, are not strictly speaking contradictions. The weakest formulation of this reason holds that neither Kennedy nor his imitators have done enough to show that, for example, altruism and individualism are logically incompatible;[27] the strong formulation asserts it is in principle impossible to show that either altruism or individualism or self and other are genuinely contradictory. Since there is a good deal of truth in the weak formulation—for Kennedy, and much more so for those that imitated him, the fundamental contradictions were little more than starting points for an analysis of other matters, such as the problem of form, the political economy of the *Commentaries* or some chunk of legal doctrine—the strong formulation need not occupy us further. Although caps were doffed vaguely in the direction of sources that supposedly generated the insight of the fundamental contradiction, no sustained analysis of why and how these notions contradict was ever offered. The starting point of the argument is therefore particularly shaky.

Whereas the first reason asserts that the macro-level contradictions have not been established, the second holds that the micro-level contradictions supposedly generated by macro-level contradictions have not been established. That is, it has not been shown that the micro-level 'contradictions' between, for example, different formulations of the liability rule for damages in tort, are indeed contradictions. Proponents of this objection make out their case by reconciling the supposed 'contradictions', showing that they are not ultimately in conflict and that the supposed tension between them can be understood and resolved without recourse to any argument from the fundamental contradiction. So, for example, Denise Meyerson shows with little difficulty that, despite some heretical statements to the contrary, the law of contract's underpinning principles are quite consistent; and Ronald Dworkin shows that the supposedly contradictory principles and doctrines within tort law can quite plausibly be regarded as merely 'competitors' and that the competition between them can be rationally resolved.[28] Since this objection often runs in conjunction with the first, proponents of an argument from one or other contradiction cannot have recourse to the 'truth' of a macro-level contradiction in order to support their claims about micro-level conflict. At least, this move cannot work until

[27] This argument, which underlies the other two reasons that discredit arguments from the fundamental contradiction, has not often been made explicit but see: D. Meyerson, 'Fundamental Contradictions in Critical Legal Studies' (1991) 11 *Oxford Journal of Legal Studies* 439–451, pp. 440–443 (directed at M. Kelman's version of the fundamental contradiction) and Dworkin, *supra*, note 4, pp. 271–275.

[28] See Dworkin, *supra*, note 4, pp. 269–271 and 443–444 and Meyerson, *supra*, note 27, pp. 442–443.

some effort is made to show that the macro-level tensions are indeed contradictions.

The third reason why the arguments from the fundamental contradiction fail shows that the macro-level 'contradictions' do not determine choices at the micro-level. Andrew Altman provides a compelling version of this objection.[29] His argument is made in relation to Kennedy's 'problem of form'. This consists of a choice lawyers have as to the structure of the specific law they can employ in an effort to resolve disputes and govern behaviour. Such a law can be more or less precise and more or less discretionary; the form it takes is not just a function of its purpose. Kennedy calls the most precise, least discretionary laws 'rules'—an example would be the age requirement law for the American president—and the least precise, most discretionary laws—such as the admittedly hypothetical requirement that the American president be 'mature' or 'wise'—'standards'. Both rules and standards have virtues and vices and it seems that, for Kennedy, the virtues of one are the vices of the other and vice versa.[30] Kennedy apparently holds that this doctrinal-cum-regulatory choice is determined by the values one espouses. And, since there is ultimately only one value choice open to us—the choice between altruism and individualism—our position here determines our position in relation to the problem of form. Kennedy suggests that individualists will prefer rules and altruists standards.[31] Others have traced the implications of the supposed contradiction between individualism and altruism into the details of particular legal doctrines and have claimed that, for example, the choice between a fault-based and natural consequences test for foreseeability of damage in negligence is ultimately one between individualism and altruism.[32] Of course, such a choice can be neither rationally justified nor legitimate.

Altman's point is twofold. He shows, first, in relation to the problem of form, that there is no contradiction between altruism and rules nor between individualism and standards. Kennedy himself seems occasionally to have accepted this and other heretics, most vividly Mark Kelman, have denied any entailment relationship here.[33] Secondly, Altman shows that what goes for the problem of form goes also for the choice of any particular rule of liability in tort, contract or any other area of law, namely, there is no contradiction between the preference for any particular liability rule and either

[29] A. Altman, *Critical Legal Studies: A Liberal Critique* (Princeton, Princeton U. P. 1990), pp. 111–130.

[30] *FS*, pp. 1710–1711.

[31] *FS*, pp. 1740–1766.

[32] A. Hutchinson, 'Of Kings and Dirty Rascals: The Struggle for Democracy' (1984) 9 *Queens L. J.* 273–292.

[33] See Kelman, *supra*, note 6, pp. 17 and 56–59; Altman, *supra*, note 29, pp. 111–117. Kelman's feeble reconstruction of the fundamental contradictions as merely matters of aesthetic connection (pp. 59–61) is powerfully criticised by Altman (pp. 113–114).

altruism or individualism. Particular rules of doctrine can just as easily be seen as a product of either altruism or individualism:

> [t]hus, the doctrines of fraud and unconscionability can be construed as conforming to the altruist demand that those who are cunning should not be allowed to take advantage of the uninformed, but it can also be construed as conforming to the individualist demand that bargains be enforced only when they are voluntary.[34]

Hence, macro-level contradictions do not generate micro-level contradictions. The best that can be said of the argument from one or other contradiction, according to Altman, is that one's choice at the macro-level generates defeasible reasons to resolve a micro-level doctrinal or regulatory choice one way rather than another. Defeasible reasons do not, however, give grounds to prefer one resolution of the problem of form or one formulation of a liability rule in *all* instances. If an altruist has defeasible reasons to prefer the standard rather than the rule form it does not follow that she can never accept the rule form.

> In certain cases, there may be rules that do a better job of implementing . . . altruist principles of sharing and sacrifice than the standards that could replace them . . . But conceding the existence and altruistic efficiency of such rules is not inconsistent with what I take to be Kennedy's claim: . . . that there are . . . modest logical links between rules and individualism, standards and altruism.[35]

These modest logical links make it impossible to argue that altruism entails a preference for standards while individualism entails a preference for rules.

Kennedy's arguments from one or other of the fundamental contradictions do not succeed because neither he nor his army of imitators establish that the alleged macro- and micro-level contradictions are indeed genuine contradictions; because a strong connection between the macro-level and micro-level 'contradictions' is not established; and because micro-level 'contradictions' are plausibly explained by factors other than macro-level contradictions. Since it is not established that legal doctrine is pervasively and unavoidably contradictory, the denial of justificatory determinacy cannot get off the ground (or must be founded upon reasons other than the existence of contradiction). That being so, the orthodox commitment to rational reconstruction and the *Verstehen* method is not called into question.

Even if these difficulties could be overcome, another lies in wait. Although it will be tackled in the discussion of linguistic indeterminacy, it is just as relevant here. The difficulty is highlighted by Stanley Fish. It denies any connection between metaphysical and 'theoretical' arguments, such as the argument from the fundamental contradictions, on the one hand, and arguments within a 'practice', such as those judges make in deciding a hard

[34] Altman, *supra*, note 29, p. 127. [35] *Ibid.*, p. 115.

case, on the other. This is part and parcel of Fish's challenging view that 'theory has no consequences'.[36] Before examining that claim, we must sketch another metaphysical indeterminacy thesis against which it can be invoked.[37]

(iii) The indeterminacy of language

Peller's 'The Metaphysics of American Law' has three principal aims. First, to show that legal discourse, like any other discourse, rests upon rationally and politically indefensible metaphysical categories. Secondly, to show how these categories operate ideologically, so as to make socially created institutions, practices and bodies of thought appear 'natural' and beyond our control; and finally, to demonstrate the first two claims by reference to the historical development of American legal thought and doctrine.[38] Only the first and second claims are examined here: the first, in this sub-section and the second, for obvious reasons, in the discussion of the ideology critique.

If Peller succeeds in his first aim the pay-off is substantial and would completely destabilise the orthodoxy. For,

> [t]he study of the underlying metaphysical assumptions of legal thought suggests that the purported distinction between rational legal argumentation and irrational emotional appeal is incoherent. Legal thought is merely one instance in a series of arational attempts to capture social experience in reproducible form. It is not qualitatively different from what it excludes as irrational.[39]

Since it is an attempt to represent social experience, legal thought, like any representational practice,

> relies on metaphors for perception and representation . . . [and this] inevitable reliance on socially created background categories of perception and communication inevitably filters the legal representation of social events through contingent metaphors. These assumptions [metaphors?] rest on particular substantive visions of the possibilities for social life and share a common inability to recognize various forms of social power (*MA*, pp. 1154–55).

Hence,

> representational practice . . . inevitably is ideological. There is no pure form of communication which merely represents rather than creates content; form and content are inseparable. As such, representational practice can never be neutral; represen-

[36] S. Fish, *Doing What Comes Naturally* (Oxford, Clarendon Press 1989), p. 26 (hereinafter '*Naturally*'). Just about every essay in the collection contains a version of Fish's argument to this end. For a slight variation on the refrain ('theory doesn't matter') that is directly relevant to Peller, see Fish, *There's No Such Thing as Free Speech* . . . (New York, Oxford U. P.), p. 191 (hereinafter, '*Speech*').

[37] For Fish's use of the argument against determinacy and indeterminacy theses see *Speech*, pp. 190–193.

[38] (1985) 73 *California L. R.* 1152–1290.

[39] *Ibid.*, p. 1155. Hereinafter referred to, in both text and notes, as '*MA*'.

tational activity, of which legal discourse is a part, *performs politically* (*MA*, pp. 1159–60; emphasis supplied).

Peller invokes two related arguments to show that legal discourse, like all representational practices, rests upon rationally and politically indefensible categories. The first is based upon a set of claims about the socially constructed nature of knowledge and the second denies the possibility of founding meaning upon some account of authorial intention or shared conventions. The first begins from the claim that language is not a neutral instrument through which meaning is expressed. Rather than merely representing the world, language to some extent creates it. By this Peller does not mean to deny that there is a world beyond language and consciousness (*MA*, p. 1170). That world, however, is accessible only through a medium that does much more than merely 'reflect' it. Peller attempts to support this claim by the following arguments. Words do not have meaning by virtue of the fact that they represent bits of the world because those bits can be conceived only through words. There is no pre-linguistic picture of the world available to us which we can then represent in language and which will guarantee that our language has meaning. (Its meaning would, presumably, be a function of, *inter alia*, how well it 'matched' the world.) Furthermore, it is extraordinarily difficult to conceive of any strong connection between language and the world, by which the former somehow necessarily hooks on to the latter, when it is realised that different languages use different words to refer to the same thing. This suggests that there is no necessary connection between any word and the bit of the world, if any, it represents: '[t]he bond between the signifier [the word] and the signified [the concept to which it relates] is arbitrary'.[40] But if words do not represent reality in this way, so that their meaning is not a function of how well they capture it, how is meaning possible?

The meaning generated by linguistic conventions is negative and differential rather than positive and fixed. The meaning of the word 'tree' is *artificial* in that it does not flow from anything in the nature of the word itself. Instead the meaning flows from the word's relationship to other words within the socially created representational practice. It acquires its meaning from not being another word, say, 'bush' or 'woods' (*MA*, p. 1164; emphasis in original).

From this account of the nature of meaning it follows, says Peller, that 'meaning is indeterminate . . . [because] the attempt to fix the meaning of an expression leads to an infinite regress. One must follow traces pointing

[40] *MA*, p. 1164. This is a quotation from F. De Saussure, *Course in General Linguistics*, although the most recent translation (by R. Harris (London, Duckworth 1983)) is slightly different from that used by Peller (see *ibid*., p. 67). There is a general problem in Peller's discussion of Saussure and Barthes which is his constant elision of the distinction between signified (the concept to which the word or signifier refers) and referent (that bit of the world, if any, to which the signifier refers).

away from expressions to other terms, which themselves contain traces leading to still other terms, and so on' (*MA*, pp. 1167–68). From the fact that 'there is no necessary connection between word and object' (*MA*, p. 1169), it follows that representational categories like the word 'tree' are merely 'metaphors [that] abstract particular features from the otherwise thick texture of the world. But there is no *necessary* reason to abstract some features rather than others' (*ibid.*; emphasis in original). That is, the features that we associate with tree-ness could easily be different; the word tree could quite possibly refer, to take an example from Jorge Luis Borges and quoted by Peller, to 'things that smile' (*MA*, p. 1167). And, what goes for this particular word goes, thinks Peller, for any word in our or any other language.

Peller's second argument to show that legal discourse depends upon politically and rationally indefensible categories adds little to the first. Rather, the argument uses the claims of the first to rebut a reply that might be made to the first. The reply invokes some account of either authorial intention or background context as the basis for an account of meaning. Although they accept that there is no necessary connection between words and the world, and accept that meaning is a matter of locating a word within a network of other words, proponents of this reply might nevertheless argue that determinate meaning is conferred upon words because the community of users accept, or the context of use implies, certain meanings, or because the author or speaker of words intends them to have a particular meaning. Peller shows, with little effort, how both possibilities are disabled by the reasons that underlie his first argument. That is, he shows that an author's or speaker's words have no stronger connection to the world than any other word and that the articulation of those intentions is not a matter of digging up some oddly private meaning, since intentions can only be formulated in a public language, that is, a representational practice. Further, he shows that the specification of context, or of the conventions of language users, is a process just as indeterminate, just as 'metaphorical', as that of specifying the meaning of any particular word.

Accept, for the moment, Peller's argument that legal discourse rests upon indefensible metaphysical categories. Accept also that this argument is undeniably a metaphysical argument according to the characterisation above. The argument supposedly imperils the orthodox method by making the task of rational reconstruction impossible. Since any representational practice rests upon unfounded assumptions and questionable categories—categories that are not rationally compelling—how can moves within such a practice be rationally justified? In so far as participants in the practice 'law' think the arguments and decisions made within the practice are rationally and normatively justifiable, then they are mistaken *because* the representational categories and metaphors that underpin those arguments and decisions are themselves without justification. Two questions designed to resist this conclusion immediately arise. The first asks how Peller's argument can be regarded as a critique since, if all representational practices rest upon unfounded, 'arational' assumptions and categories, why single out one such practice or set of practices for special critical treatment? If, as Peller suggests, all representational practices are equally arational—including the representational practice within which his own arguments are made—how can one be any more 'rational' than another? How can orthodox discourse about law and adjudication be less and heretical discourse more rational or determinate? Were Peller to take these questions seriously he would have to provide something like a metric by which such assessments could be made.

Such a metric might be found in Peller's observations about the way in which social practices and institutions can be founded upon representational practices and categories. For example, he uses the mind/body distinction as an illustration of the way in which a representational category can underpin a set of practices and institutions embodying a specific form of the division of labour (*MA*, p. 1176). Viewed in this light, representational categories clearly have consequences in the social world. Peller might argue that existing representational practices and categories have more bad consequences in the world than other such practices and categories. This argument looks unpromising because of the scale of the task it initially requires—an audit of the bad moral, political and other consequences of an existing representational category, practice or system and a comparison with the consequences of another, existing or imaginary category, practice or system. This seems a dizzyingly complicated task, but we should not assume it is impossible for that reason. However, we are entitled to look to the initiator of that task for guidance as to its discharge and, sadly, none is forthcoming. For, when Peller speaks about the consequences of representational practices or categories in the world, he either does so impressionistically, in the sense that he assumes bad consequences obviously follow, or makes a point about false consciousness, emphasising that we often take contingent representational categories to be natural and unchangeable. Neither point is helpful in relation to the audit before us although the latter surfaces again in the discussion of the ideology critique. Furthermore, there is an important gap in the argument that particular representational categories are the basis of certain social practices and institutions. Peller never articulates the exact nature of the connection here so it is uncertain whether representational categories in some sense 'cause' or necessarily lead to a particular, objectionable social practice or institution. An argument to show such a strong connection could in principle be made out but it must show that a particular representational practice or category—let us call it, unimaginatively, X—is the *only* basis for odious social practice or institution, Y. In the few examples he uses, Peller falls far short of discharging this burden.

Peller's remarks suggest another, perhaps more successful reply to the first question. He might maintain that the argument offered is critical in the sense that it aims to uproot the view that our discourse or representational practice is either rationally necessary—in the sense that the categories and language we use are somehow rationally tied to the world—or natural—in the sense that there is just no other way in which the world can be divided up and represented. In relation to legal discourse, the argument functions as an immanent critique demonstrating that the discourse cannot satisfy its professed standards of rationality and determinacy. In so far as legal discourse assumes the truth, necessity, rationality or naturalness of its categories, and assumes that it is therefore a rational or determinate discourse and set of practices, it is mistaken. The categories of legal discourse cannot, according to Peller, have the properties (necessity, rationality etc.) which it asserts they do, and the discourse cannot therefore satisfy its self-professed standards of determinacy and rationality. The crucial issue here is whether or not legal discourse does indeed assume the truth, rationality or necessity of its categories in such a way as to fall victim to Peller's indeterminacy argument. Even if it does, it can still be maintained that this is of no consequence because Peller's argument is itself redundant.

This objection can also take the form of a question: how can a 'theoretical' argument destabilise the operation of, or moves within, a practice? This objection is but part of a position about the irrelevance or inconsequentiality of 'theory' espoused by Fish which he thinks undermines both orthodoxy and heresy. The argument rests upon a distinction between theory, on the one hand, and practice and very general beliefs, on the other. '[T]heory, as I define it, is the name for a set of principles or rules and procedures that is attached to (in the sense of being derived from) no particular field of activity, but is of sufficient generality to be thought of as a constraint on (and explanation of) all fields of activity'.[41] Theory refers

> to an abstract or algorithmic formulation that guides or governs practice from a position outside any particular practice. A theory, in short, is something a practitioner consults when he wishes to perform correctly, with the term 'correctly' here understood as meaning independently of his preconceptions, biases or personal preferences.[42]

By contrast, '[t]o think within a practice is to have one's very perception and sense of possible and appropriate action issue "naturally"—without further reflection—from one's position as a deeply situated agent'. There-

[41] Fish, *Naturally*, p. 14. [42] *Ibid.*, p. 378.

fore, '[s]omeone who looks with practice-informed eyes sees a field already organised in terms of perspicuous obligations, self-evidently authorised procedures, and obviously relevant pieces of evidence'.[43] Fish argues that heretical and orthodox accounts of law and adjudication fail because, first, they are theoretical, and hence cannot do what they often purport to do, which is to offer guidance to participants in the practice law; or, secondly, because they are redundant, since they provide accounts of what participants in the practice already do and must do *qua* participants. The first limb of this argument is most relevant to Peller's position and for Fish's criticism to take hold two requirements must be met. First, Peller's indeterminacy thesis must be capable of being regarded as a theoretical position within Fish's typology and, second, that typology must be defensible.

There is little difficulty in satisfying the first requirement. Peller's indeterminacy thesis certainly appears to stand above all particular fields of activity and to operate as a constraint upon such fields. His claims about representational practices and language are abstract and purport to generate—from outside—implications for actions within practices. Hence, what we have called Peller's 'metaphysical' indeterminacy thesis is also, in Fish's terminology, a 'theoretical' position. What, then, of the second requirement? This is much more problematic. The foundation of the distinction is never explicitly formulated by Fish and there are doubts as to whether or not such a distinction could ever be defended in a non-circular way.[44] More pressing, however, is the difficulty that Fish's 'enriched notion of practice'[45] affords more than enough room for lashings of 'theory' because it allows that it is part and parcel of some practices to be theoretical, to be self-aware, to speculate about their own foundations and nature. This point has been made by Dworkin in one of his replies to Fish and, we may think, if Fish's notion of practice can incorporate enough theory to accommodate Dworkin's account of law as integrity, then can it not also incorporate Peller's 'theoretical' account of indeterminacy?[46] It is difficult for Fish to maintain that one of these positions is more theoretical than the other and therefore subject to his critique; moreover, both positions seem to share an 'obvious truism' that Fish would be unlikely to deny. It is that 'no institution or practice is what it is, or does what it does, independently of what anyone whatsoever thinks or feels about it. For institutions and practices are always, even if to differing degrees, constituted by what certain

[43] *Ibid.*, pp. 386–387.

[44] See P. Schlag, 'Fish v. Zapp: The Case of the Relatively Autonomous Self' (1987) 76 *Georgetown L. R.* 37–58, pp. 53–58.

[45] *Naturally*, *ibid.*; *Speech*, p. 224.

[46] The reply I have in mind is ch. 19 of M. Brint and W. Weaver (eds.), *Pragmatism in Law and Society* (Boulder, Westview Press 1991), at pp. 377–382. Fish discusses some of Dworkin's points in *Speech*, pp. 224–230 and 302–304.

people think and feel about them'.[47] That being so, if those people come to believe in widespread linguistic indeterminacy—or they accept law as integrity—then the practices and institutions in which they operate could well change. Theory might have consequences after all.

The two questions do not, it seems, denude Peller's indeterminacy thesis of all critical power. In relation to the first, Peller can quite easily affirm that his argument is an immanent critique and the second, although apparently powerful, is just too problematic to harm his case. Are there any other problems that his indeterminacy thesis faces? Altman thinks there are at least two, although, as we will see, he exaggerates the power of his objections.

The first objection is that Peller's argument makes meaning and communication impossible.[48] Altman goes about establishing this in two ways. He takes Peller's claim that 'meaning is indeterminate' to mean that meaning is impossible; and he holds that Peller's account of language is exactly analogous to that espoused by Willard Quine.[49] A consequence of the latter is that Peller supposedly cannot—because Quine cannot—explain how a language is learned and how communication is possible. If Peller does indeed claim that meaning is impossible, then Altman is right to say that Peller's 'argument means nothing and establishes nothing'.[50] Yet it is unlikely that Peller holds this view. He says that his arguments do not deny the possibility of meaning—and therefore of communication—and we should resist the conclusion that he so readily contradicts himself. The contradiction can quite easily be avoided once it is noted that the 'meaning is indeterminate' claim can be interpreted to mean something other than that meaning is impossible. On Peller's view of meaning and indeterminacy, language is not necessarily, rationally, locked on to the world. Meaning is not therefore a product of how well or badly language represents that world. Meaning is a process of contingent deferral and words could always have different meanings. Now this view does not reduce to the view that meaning is impossible. The fact that Peller is committed to the view that *meanings* could always be different suggests that meaning is possible, but that it is not always and ever the same. Peller's argument therefore refutes one account of meaning only to replace it with another, one which emphasises the indeterminacy—the in-principle changeability—of meaning without denying the possibility of meaning. Hence, 'I am not arguing that we never

[47] A. MacIntyre, *Against the Self-Images of the Age* (London, Duckworth 1971), p. 263. I am grateful to Matthew Festenstein for bringing this to my attention and indebted to him for a number of other points in my discussion of Fish.

[48] *Supra*, note 29, pp. 93–97.

[49] This, at least, is Quine's view: *supra*, note 18. For acute analysis of some of the changes in Quine's position see M. Dummett, *Frege, Philosophy of Language* (London, Duckworth 1973), pp. 611–627.

[50] *Supra*, note 29, p. 93.

communicate or understand each other when we speak or act. That would be absurd. Rather, there is no way to achieve *closure* with respect to the meaning of expressions or events' (*MA*, p. 1170; emphasis in original). Peller's view is that the meaning of some proposition cannot be guaranteed to remain the same always and ever.

Quine's account of language is unable to explain how language is learned and thus how communication is possible. This is because Quine is committed to the view that a single sentence can only have meaning in light of the whole body of sentences of which it is part. Micheal Dummett has plausibly argued that the consequence of this view is a sentence in a language cannot be understood unless the whole language is known and that, it seems, makes the normal way in which languages are learned impossible.[51] Word or sentence meaning is possible even though we do not know the whole of the language in which it is conveyed. Altman's claim that Peller's account of language is, broadly speaking, Quinean is hard to resist but it does not follow from this that Quine's problems must be Peller's problems. In particular, there is no great difficulty in Peller explaining the possibility of communication and language learning by invoking Donald Davidson's notion of prior and passing theories.[52] The former refers to everything an agent brings to the act of communication with another, including a range of conventions and assumptions about meaning, whereas the latter signifies the remnants and salient aspects of the former when put to work in an effort to understand a particular utterance here and now. The two are not co-extensive, simply because a particular utterance and the effort to understand it can shake or modify the assumptions and conventions constitutive of the prior theory, although the two obviously cannot be entirely discontinuous. The fact that there is overlap between prior and passing theories, and the fact that they can diverge and be amended, explains both the possibility of communication when the two theories match and when, by virtue of malapropisms and mistakes, they do not. We can communicate in the face of malapropisms and mistakes by virtue of a passing theory that temporarily amends our prior theory: what 'two people need, if they are to understand one another through speech, is the ability to converge on passing theories from utterance to utterance'.[53] Now, cannot the acquisition of a language take the form of an incomplete prior theory more regularly up for amendment and extension in light of an evolving passing theory or theories? And, if it can, this might provide some defence to the Peller/Dummett criticism. Davidson himself certainly entertains the thought that languages can be partly learned and, although he also suggests that the idea of a passing

[51] *Supra*, note 49, pp. 598–627.

[52] D. Davidson, 'A Nice Derangement of Epitaphs' in E. Lepore (ed.), *Truth and Interpretation: Perspectives on the Philosophy of Donald Davidson* (Oxford, Blackwell 1984), 433–446.

[53] *Ibid.*, p. 445.

theory might not capture how a language is learned, his treatment of this issue is far from complete. Moreover, if we take Davidson's advice and set aside the philosophers' conception of what a language must look like, there are few if any general objections to the suggestion that part learning occurs through an interplay between limited, revisable and tendentious prior and passing theories.

Altman's second objection to Peller's indeterminacy argument is that it incorporates a dubious social ontology. Peller's commitment to such an ontology is a consequence of the fact that his indeterminacy argument is premised upon an account of social reality which Altman dubs 'ultra-theory'. Peller is one among many heretical ultra-theorists who supposedly hold the view that 'there is no objective structure to the law or legal discourse because there is none to *any* element of social reality'.[54] Altman spends a good deal of time showing that this position is dubious. He argues, for example, that its proponents treat as equivalent the dissimilar claims that social structures can be manipulated and that they exercise no control over us at all. He also suggests that their views about the constraining power of human beings, on the one hand, and of social structures, rules and practices, on the other, are inconsistent. Thus, ultra-theory reduces to the implausible claim that social structures, rules and practices have no constraining power over us at all. Ultra-theorists' 'point is that it is human individuals, not the law or any other social structure, who exercise control. The very idea of a government of laws, rather than men, rests on the wrong-headed premise that social structures have an objective existence that enables them to exert power over individuals'.[55]

In attempting to ascribe this view to heretics, and to Peller in particular, Altman makes two blunders. First, he does not see that the heretical statements he relies upon—none of them, incidentally, made by Peller—are consistent with two versions of ultra-theory, extreme and modest. The extreme version is that characterised by Altman but the modest version—which is quite consistent with the heretical remarks Altman invokes—holds that social structures, rules and institutions do indeed constrain us, but not totally. That is, the power of such structures over us can be reduced and one set of constraints can eventually—by political action, changing our thought patterns and 'modes of consciousness' etc.,—be substituted with another. Hence, these constraints are both *binding* and doubly *contingent* (they can be changed and they lack rational power or necessity). It seems clear, despite Altman's view, that many heretics do indeed claim that social structures, rules and institutions are both constraining and contingent. What other view, after all, can make sense of heretics' many claims that conven-

[54] *Supra*, note 29, p. 169 (emphasis in original).
[55] *Ibid.*, p. 168.

tions, socio-economic background and socialisation ensure that judicial decision-making is predictable even in the face of justificatory indeterminacy? Altman's second blunder is that he does not see that this is indeed Peller's view. Peller says, often and unequivocally, that social structures, rules and institutions both constrain and are contingent, that they bind us but can also be changed. For example, when speaking of language (surely an undeniably obvious example of a social practice and set of rules), Peller says '[t]he assertion that communication is dependent upon existing linguistic conventions suggests that language speaks through us, rather than that we speak through language. But such an image of language overlooks that linguistic conventions are *social* creations' (*MA*, p. 1177; emphasis in original). If language speaks through us then it must constrain us. To be understood, we 'must articulate . . . [our] thought through the categories for communication in the linguistic community' (*MA*, p. 1161). We are therefore constrained. Yet the categories for communication can be changed, do not have to take the form they do. Hence 'it is difficult to articulate the simultaneous pregiven and external aspects of representational conventions with their socially contingent, political aspects' (*MA*, p. 1177). That difficult view—a combination of constraint and contingency—is clearly espoused by Peller. Equally clearly, that view is very different from the one Altman takes as constitutive of ultra-theory. The social ontology Peller expounds is not the dubious one Altman ascribes to him.

Peller's indeterminacy thesis is not as implausible as many would have us believe. The argument is neither redundant nor pointlessly metaphysical nor theoretical. It is not redundant because, interpreted as an immanent critique, it has positive critical power. Nor has the argument been shown to be pointlessly metaphysical or theoretical. Peller's indeterminacy thesis does not, contrary to Altman's view, either make meaning and communication impossible or incorporate a questionable social ontology. The problems that do beset the argument are neither particularly pressing nor unique to this particular position. One problem previously noted concerns the difficulty of showing that particular representational practices do indeed have bad moral, political or other consequences. This task is also effected by a version of the ideology critique and it will therefore be tackled in the discussion below. Another difficulty Peller faces is that of unpacking the simultaneously constraining and contingent nature of social practices, institutions and rules. Again, this problem is not unique to his argument, but is a central question for much sociology and philosophy of language.[56] The problems entangling Peller's position are in

[56] Peller's view that social structures, rules and institutions are both constraining and contingent is echoed by much work within sociology and the philosophy of language. See, for example, the discussion in A. Giddens, *Studies in Social and Political Theory* (London, Hutchinson 1977), ch. 4.

a sense generic and it would thus be unfair to criticise his failure to resolve them.

Before concluding that this indeterminacy thesis is the most plausible of the three considered—the weaknesses of the empirical indeterminacy thesis and the contradiction-based indeterminacy thesis appear so severe as to be insurmountable—one final, vexatious question must be asked. To what degree does Peller's indeterminacy thesis imperil the orthodox method? Remember that the argument operates as an immanent critique: it has critical power only in so far as participants in a particular representational practice overlook the contingency and wrongly affirm the necessity or naturalness of the foundational assumptions or categories of the practice. This certainly does not make the orthodox method and the enterprise of rational reconstruction impossible. Rather, this argument can quite consistently serve as a cautionary supplement to the orthodox method. The task of rational reconstruction can still be carried out even on the supposition, provided by Peller's indeterminacy thesis, that the foundational assumptions and categories of the practice are neither rationally necessary nor unchangeable.

This, of course, is not to reaffirm Fish's argument that theoretical or metaphysical positions such as Peller's lack consequences. The argument here does not, unlike Fish's argument, invoke a dubious distinction between theory-cum-metaphysics, on the one hand, and practice, on the other; nor does it hold that Peller's argument has no effect upon practice. The argument instead asserts that Peller's indeterminacy thesis, understood as an immanent critique, has effect only when participants in a particular representational practice mistakenly ascribe rational necessity and immutability to the foundational assumptions and categories of the practice. When they do not do this the argument has no effect. Further, one can quite easily take up the internal point of view as one's method for understanding and explaining any social action, institution or practice, and offer a rational reconstruction of it, with Peller's indeterminacy thesis in mind. The thesis serves not to make this task impossible but only to ensure that participants' views of the nature of the practice—in this case, the rationality or immutability of its basic assumptions—are not incorrigible. However, since the orthodox do not and, as we argued in chapter 2 should not, affirm that the views of participants in a practice are incorrigible, there is no conflict here. This indeterminacy thesis, then, seemingly buys plausibility and coherence at the cost of becoming compatible with the orthodox method. The thesis may yet destabilise that method in conjunction with the ideology critique but, in this situation, it is the latter argument that does all the critical work. It is therefore appropriate to turn our attention to that critique. Before doing so, however, we will examine another attempt to destabilise the orthodox method quite unlike the indeterminacy theses. As we will see, a number of the steps in this argument also fail. The most promising step invokes the ideology critique: just as that critique may be relied upon to shore up one or other indeterminacy thesis, it may also support the disappearance of the self.

II THE DISAPPEARANCE OF THE SELF

This is an apparently radical heretical challenge to both orthodox doctrine and philosophy, on the one hand, and much heretical scholarship, on the other. The challenge is labelled the disappearance of the self, although hereinafter I use 'self' and 'person' as synonyms. Further, by a 'conception' or 'picture' of the self or person, I mean some account of what we essentially are, involving not only an account of the constituents of our identity, such as has preoccupied philosophers and others for centuries. The main proponent of this challenge is Pierre Schlag, who attacks orthodox and heretical legal scholarship on a number of fronts. He argues, for example, that contemporary legal scholarship is blind to the 'politics of form'; that it is obsessively and disablingly 'normative'; and that it reinforces a dubious conception of the human agent or 'self'.[57] These three claims are ambitious and require a good deal of argument to be plausible, but only the last concerns us here. For, in challenging the conception of the self that allegedly underlies both heretical and orthodox legal scholarship, Schlag is indeed proposing a profound rotation in legal thought. He calls into question both the audience of legal thought—in the sense that what legal scholars and practitioners imagine their audience to be just does not exist (there is no such self)—and the perpetrator of legal thought—in the sense that what legal thinkers take themselves to be just does not exist (there is no such self). It just so happens, says Schlag, that perpetrator and victim, performer and audience, are envisaged in exactly the same dubious and misleading way.

Schlag's calling into question of legal thought's conception of the self destabilises the orthodox method by robbing it of audience and performer. He denies that the self orthodox legal thought takes to be its audience, and the self orthodox theorists take themselves to be, actually exist. At its strongest, the self the orthodox imagine taking up the internal point of view,

[57] See 'Fish v. Zapp', *supra*, note 44 (hereinafter '*FZ*'); '"Le Hors de Texte, C'est Moi"—The Politics of Form and the Domestication of Deconstruction' (1990) 11 *Cardozo L. R.* 1631–1674 (hereinafter '*Texte*'); 'Normative and Nowhere to Go' (1990) 43 *Stanford L. R.* 167–191 (hereinafter '*NN*'); 'Normativity and the Politics of Form' (1991) 139 *University of Pennsylvania L. R.* 801–932; and 'The Problem of the Subject' (1991) 61 *Texas L. R.* 1627–1743 (hereinafter '*PS*'). For related discussions of the conception of the self in legal scholarship see the essays by, *inter alios*, J. Boyle and C. Wicke in 'Postmodernism and Law: A Symposium' (1991) 62 *University of Colorado L. R.* 439.

and the self they take to be enmeshed in the actions, practices and institutions of the social world, is impossible and dangerous. The product of orthodox legal theory is thus not harmlessly otiose. True, it generates accounts of the nature of law and adjudication for beings who do not and perhaps cannot exist and is therefore legal philosophy for phantoms or Martians. But, because this picture of the self has a legitimation function, orthodox legal philosophy contributes to our subjugation by bolstering harmful institutions, practices and systems of thought.

The argument about the disappearance of the self consists of at least three steps. The first is that the self of contemporary legal thought is not us—it is a dubious and inaccurate picture of what we really are. The second step flows from and expands the first. It holds that the picture of the self embodied in contemporary legal thought has dangerous consequences. Chief among these is the legitimacy this picture confers upon existing bureaucratic-cum-economic power structures. The third step is directly connected to the first for, in holding that the self embodied in contemporary legal thought looks nothing like us, Schlag must at some point either commend a better, more accurate picture of what we truly are, or completely eschew that task. These three steps require further attention. The first and third steps will be examined together because they raise similar problems.

The first step answers the question 'what are we?' by default. Schlag is sure that there is one thing we are not, namely, the relatively autonomous or humanist self underpinning almost all contemporary legal thought.[58] The relatively autonomous self of legal discourse is '*a privileged individual subject . . . the author of his own thoughts, the captain of his own ship, the Hercules of his own empire*' (*Texte*, p. 1637; original emphasis). Hence

> [t]he legal thinker . . . *while he is speaking in role*—that is, while he is at the podium—. . . will *as a matter of form* present the self that is speaking—that is, his self—as an autonomous, coherent, integrated, originary self capable of rational argument and moral choice. Later on, out in the hall, in informal conversation, the legal thinker will, of course, readily admit that he is just as much a fit subject for sociological, economic, psychoanalytic explanations as the next guy. But when he is doing law, when he is in role, the rhetorical form of his statements will effectively deny all these twentieth-century knowledges in favour of eighteenth-century Lockean fantasies. What's more, the legal thinker will invite the authorized audience (i.e., the other members of the legal community) to participate in the same fantasies: the members of this authorized audience will be treated and thus constituted as autonomous, coherent, integrated, ordinary [*sic*; originary?] selves capable of rational argument and moral choice (*Texte*, pp. 1638–39; original emphasis).

[58] Schlag most often speaks of the relatively autonomous self as is clear from the passages cited in the text. Occasionally he labels the same conception of the self 'humanist': see *NN*, pp. 173–174.

This self 'is a fiction' (*FZ*, p. 51). Although this conception of the person is presupposed by many types of legal thought, one of which is dubbed the rule-of-law vision by Schlag and has many similarities with the orthodoxy, 'there is no longer a subject on the scene who is normatively and epistemologically competent to practice and realize th[is] [or any other legal philosophical] . . . vision' (*PS*, pp. 1726–1727). Of the various orthodox and heretical legal theories Schlag examines, he concludes that '[i]n each case the problem of the subject arises in the unwelcome recognition that the approach already presupposes the existence of a particular subject—and that this subject is nowhere to be found. This can, of course, be a disturbing recognition' (*ibid.*, p. 1729).

This first step contains a number of difficulties for Schlag. It shows that he is caught between affirming two rather different propositions and consequently lacks compelling arguments for either. The two propositions are: (i) that the orthodox avoid any account of the self or subject and (ii) that they have an account of the self and it is the relatively autonomous self. Taking what Schlag calls the rule-of-law approach to be his account of the orthodoxy, the first proposition is supposedly established in the central section of *PS* (pp. 1662–1679). Establishing this cannot, without committing a massive *ignoratio elenchi*, establish that the orthodox espouse any particular conception of the person. And, establishing the second proposition apparently refutes the first. Moreover, in this and other essays, Schlag neither labours hard to show that the orthodox do indeed espouse the relatively autonomous self nor establishes that the relatively autonomous self is objectionable. Again, establishing the first of these claims cannot establish the second, nor will demonstrating the second establish the first. As to the first, Schlag is content simply to assert that the orthodox are committed to the relatively autonomous self. The only instance in which he argues the point in any detail is in relation to the work of Stanley Fish, which is neither an instance of the orthodoxy nor the heresy. (Fish can seem simultaneously both more orthodox and more heretical than either.) As to the second, one promising way to show the objectionable nature of the relatively autonomous self would be to contrast it with a better picture.

Schlag's third step should, unless he eschews talk about the self altogether, offer a picture of a self better than that which underlies contemporary legal thought. That Schlag does not eschew talk of the self is clear: he offers no argument renouncing such talk nor does he refrain from such talk himself. However, he equivocates about whether he intends to offer an alternative to the relatively autonomous self or whether he merely aims to reduce its centrality in contemporary legal thought. Nevertheless, Schlag offers hints as to where we should look for a better conception of the person—either as an alternative to, or 'a decentring, not an annihilation of'

(*Texte*, p. 1671)—the relatively autonomous self. These hints obviously do not amount to a detailed picture of the person. The disciplines of history, sociology, economics and psychology are tipped by Schlag to provide a better, but probably more deterministic, picture of the self. Such disciplines, according to Schlag, treat the self of legal thought and practice as objects of study. Such disciplines are 'insulting' to legal thought, old and new:

> Given that law was an autonomous discipline, it was natural for the Langdellian thinkers to treat judges as conscious sovereign individual subjects—individuals beyond the reach of the insulting knowledges of social science, psychology, economics, and their (quasi-) deterministic structures. Indeed, little could be further from the Langdellian mind than to treat judges as an object of study—either generally or more particularly, as a class of bureaucratic decision makers whose rhetorical and cognitive patterns are prompted by the relatively intense socialization processes of law schools and law firms (*PS*, pp. 1734–5).[59]

These hints that some disciplines provide a more deterministic conception of the person is as far as Schlag goes on the journey of developing an alternative picture. Hence, not only does Schlag fail to sketch even the broadest contours of this conception of the person, he also falls victim to a remarkably naive understanding of the disciplines he invokes.

Schlag's failure to sketch, however vaguely, the contours of an alternative conception of the self is especially puzzling given the steps taken by others in this direction. The relatively autonomous self Schlag rejects bears more than a passing resemblance to the 'unencumbered' or 'punctual' self said to underpin much liberal moral and political philosophy.[60] This is a self free of any constitutive commitments and communities, capable of rational choice and with an identity independent of particular character traits or dispositions. The unencumbered self is unlike our empirical self because we define much of who and what we are by reference to the commitments we have (to place, family, group or nation), the roles we play (parent, citizen, activist, etc.,) and our and their history. Many who have rejected the unencumbered self have developed various 'narrative' conceptions of identity and selfhood.[61] It is odd that Schlag does not also follow this path, for it is such an obvious strategy. Having dismissed the relatively autonomous or unencumbered self, what is left but to develop an alternative? Of course, nothing Schlag says commits him to espousing a specifically narrative conception of the self, but this is undoubtedly an option. Further, Schlag's remarks about an alternative conception of the self are quite superficial. He invokes the human sciences to provide such a conception and thinks these

[59] For a similar refrain see *Texte*, pp. 1638–1639.

[60] By, *inter alios*, M. Sandel, *Liberalism and the Limits of Justice* (Cambridge, C. U. P. 1982), chs. 1 and 4; and C. Taylor, *Sources of the Self* (Cambridge, C. U. P. 1989), part I.

[61] See, for example, Taylor, *ibid.*; A. MacIntyre, *After Virtue* (London, Duckworth 2nd. ed. 1985), ch. 15.

disciplines speak with one voice on this matter and what they say must be accepted because they say it. Yet it is obvious that the human sciences do not speak univocally on this matter. And, it is equally obvious that an unquestioning invocation of the allegedly authoritative insights of any discipline breaches the protocols of critical thinking and is therefore somewhat dubious. Were these the only problems with Schlag's argument, things would not be too bad. After all, the third step is not crucial to his case against the conception of the self dominant in contemporary legal thought. Further, his unsatisfying hints about the nature of an alternative conception of the self could be taken as a promise of what may soon follow.[62] However, a closer look at the first and third steps of his argument shows that things are indeed much worse than this, that his conception of the self is still-born. Why is this so?

Consider what criticising or articulating a conception of the self might involve. One could be working metaphysically, that is, at the level of abstraction of traditional philosophical inquiries into the nature of the self and its identity. A dominant strand in this tradition sees its task as either unearthing or discrediting the non-empirical, non-analytical bases of our everyday, empirical conception of the self.[63] Alternatively, one could be concerned to articulate better the empirical self, the view or views individuals have in a culture as to the nature of selfhood. At this time in our culture we are most likely to turn to psychologists, anthropologists and sociologists for an insight into what we take the self to be, here and now.[64] A variation on this theme would be the cultural historian's genealogy of a particular conception of the self and the forces—intellectual and institutional—that have shaped its development. Then, again, in criticising or developing a conception of the self we might be operating normatively, that is, either criticising or commending a bundle of traits, beliefs and actions we take to be constitutive of a good person. Here an account of personhood or the self serves as an ideal and such ideal accounts have ranged from the Buddhist denial of a continuing self to the Nietzschean *übermensch*. They are invariably part of an account of the ethically and morally good life. These various levels of thought about the self can easily be related yet it would be a mistake to assume that there *must* be a strong connection between them. So, for example, an account of the empirical self need not have any implications for a metaphysical account of identity nor need it determine the contours of a normative account of the self. Furthermore, the methods of argument

[62] However, on the evidence of some of Schlag's recent work this promise is unlikely to be fulfilled. See his 'Law and Phrenology' (1997) 110 *Harvard L. R.* 877–921 and 'Law as the Continuation of God by Other Means' (1997) 85 *California L. R.* 427–440.

[63] See P. Strawson's distinction between revisionary and descriptive metaphysics in *Individuals* (London, Hutchinson 1959), introduction; and D. Parfit, *supra*, note 19.

[64] An excellent interdisciplinary collection is M. Carrithers et al., *The Category of the Person* (Cambridge, C. U. P. 1985).

and the standards of success and failure will differ according to the level at which one is operating. Clearly, it is no refutation of, for example, David Hume's metaphysical account of identity that few people in our culture take identity and selfhood to consist in nothing more than a bundle of perceptions and traits. This would indeed be a serious problem, were Hume's account of identity and the self taken (wrongly) to be a picture of the empirical self. [65]

The point of this brief excursus into the many discourses about the self is to illustrate how little Schlag has done to situate his criticism of, and alternative to, the conception of the self dominant in legal thought. Is his rejection of that conception based upon its lack of fit with what we actually, empirically, take ourselves to be and what the disciplines of history, sociology, etc. say we are? Or is he attacking, in the spirit of Karl Marx's reflections upon the inequality of standards of equality, the relatively autonomous self because it is something we can never be, and therefore embodies behavioural standards in the law beyond the reach of real persons? Perhaps his attack is upon a dubious metaphysical account of the self which he intends at some point to go beyond? These questions are unanswerable on the basis of Schlag's work. True, he criticises a supposedly dominant account of the self, but the basis of his criticism, over and beyond the unpalatable consequences of this account, is entirely oblique. He asserts time and again that this self is not us, but never articulates what he takes 'us' to be, other than quite implausibly hinting that the human sciences may contain a ready-made alternative. Now, Schlag's reticence about the alternative to the relatively autonomous self *could* be a consequence of the fact that his enterprise is neither metaphysical, normative nor straightforwardly empirical. He *could*, that is, be engaged in developing a genealogy of the self and that task certainly does not require one to develop an alternative conception of the self. Yet we need a clue in the texts which suggests that this is indeed Schlag's task and no such clue can be found. Even if it were, the genealogy in Schlag's work is sub-standard. It is 'historical' scholarship in a very restricted sense. It analyses only legal doctrine and thought; the cultural and institutional forces that might influence doctrine and its conception of the self are rarely examined; and the level of analysis is somewhat impressionistic.[66] It would therefore be unfair to think Schlag's work was directed to this task. The problem with this conclusion is that it leaves us no wiser as to the nature of the task Schlag is performing and its criteria of success and failure.

[65] For this account of identity see D. Hume, *A Treatise of Human Nature* (Oxford, Clarendon 2nd ed., 1978), Book I, part I, sections II and VI and the appendix.

[66] It therefore provides a stunning contrast to the excellent genealogical history of the self and subjectivity developed by N. Rose: see, for example, his *Governing the Soul* (London, Routledge 1989) and 'Authority and the Genealogy of Subjectivity' in P. Heelas et al. (eds.), *Detraditionalization* (Oxford, Blackwell 1996).

Schlag's second step holds that the conception of the person dominant in contemporary legal thought is pernicious. This conception portrays us as if we were relatively autonomous, capable of meaningful, free and rational choice when in fact we are not; in doing so, it distracts attention from the ways in which our behaviour is determined by existing bureaucratic power structures.

The political implications [of this false picture] are easy to describe. The constitution of legal thinkers and others as conscious sovereign individual subjects produces a politics that works perfectly—assuming that we do indeed have conscious sovereign individual subjects situated to control the levers of the social machinery.

. . . If the liberal subject disappears from the scene, a number of very troublesome questions immediately surface: who (or what) is controlling the levers running the social machinery? [. . .] And if there's no one operating the levers, then what has been the effect of all that good, admirable, serious, normative legal thought? [. . .]

As legal thinkers, we like to think that we are doing good, normative legal work—advancing noble causes and the like—but if the liberal subject is no longer operating the levers, our work product can take on a different character. We may simply be rehearsing and reproducing the instrumentalist logic of bureaucratic practices. [. . .] Indeed, the main significance of noble normative work is in the rehearsal of a false aesthetic of social life—one which falsely represents

instrumentalist strategies as within the control of individual subjects
the unfolding of bureaucratic logic as the choices of individuals
the discursive mechanism of coercion as normative dialogue.

. . . Viewed in this light, we can understand normative legal thought not as the attempt to criticize and reform the structures and practices of bureaucratic domination, but rather as a kind of discourse that has already been unconsciously captivated by those very same structures and practices. . . . Rather than contributing to our understanding or to the realisation of the good or the right, all this normative argument simply perpetuates a false aesthetic of social life—one that prevents 'us' [. . .] from even recognizing the sort of bureaucratic practices that constitute and channel our thought and action (*PS*, pp. 1738–40).

The talk of 'levers of power' and 'social machinery' is mysterious. Schlag provides no indication about the meaning of these phrases although they surely cannot be taken literally. Let us set them aside and interpret the second step as holding that the relatively autonomous self serves to obscure some important features of social reality. It is part and parcel of a view that 'falsely represents' the nature of that reality. No wonder, then, that Schlag believes '[t]he self becomes in effect one of the rhetorical spaces where ideology does its work' (*Texte*, p. 1670). Taking ideology to mean systematically misleading or obfuscatory beliefs or propositions, the self of contemporary legal thought becomes doubly ideological. First, because it is not us and, second, because it is complicit in legitimising existing power structures. Those structures are portrayed as a product of this self when in fact they produce it; moreover, this produced self is a seductive myth unrelated to how we really are. The effect of the myth is to legitimate power structures—their legitimacy derives from the fact that they are supposedly subject to the rationality and authority of the relatively autonomous self. Since that self is a myth, what then controls the operation of power? Whether or not Schlag is right as to what exactly the relatively autonomous self obscures, and the plausibility of his account of the mechanics of obfuscation, are issues that need not detain us. For the peg upon which the second step hangs is clearly some or other account of ideology and, from the tenor of Schlag's remarks, that account must be critical. That is, it must take the notion to refer to a baleful situation, must regard ideology as cognitively, or epistemologically, or otherwise objectionable. Often, critical accounts of ideology also indicate ways in which it can be avoided or overcome.

This, then, is the point at which the argument about the disappearance of the self invokes the ideology critique. It is unlikely, however, that the ideology critique can save this argument given the weakness of its other two steps. This is a pity because, as will be seen in the following section, the ideology critique is a promising argument. Since the other steps in the argument about the disappearance of the self are so weak, and cannot therefore increase the power of the ideology critique, the latter will, in what follows, be discussed independently of them.

III THE IDEOLOGY CRITIQUE

(a) Ideology: critical and non-critical accounts

The ideology critique can discredit the orthodox method either directly or indirectly. In the indirect use, the argument arises on the back of one or other indeterminacy thesis and purports to explicate how, in the face of justificatory indeterminacy, adjudicative outcomes are nevertheless predictable. In this form the argument does not itself show that the orthodox method is mistaken, but rather functions as a string in the bow of proponents of the indeterminacy theses. The latter theses supposedly show the impossibility of rational reconstruction; the ideology critique provides an explanation of how a widespread belief in rational reconstruction and justificatory determinacy can persist despite this 'truth'. The reservations expressed in section I about the indeterminacy theses dictate that we ought not to yoke the ideology critique to those rather dubious arguments. Therefore, only the direct use of the ideology critique will be considered.

The direct use can undermine the orthodox method in a simple way. It holds that taking up the internal point of view, and thus providing an account of a practice or institution in the language of its participants, is dangerous because participants may well have a mistaken understanding of the point, purpose or value of the institution or practice in question. Since direct and indirect uses of the ideology critique make the same core claim, namely, that *it is possible for agents to be systematically misguided* about either (i) aspects of social reality or (ii) the consequences of their beliefs, then agents' views about the nature of the institution or practice in which they participate constitute a dubious foundation for a social-theoretic description and explanation of that institution or practice. This emphasis upon the obfuscatory nature of certain beliefs and propositions ensures that the type of account of ideology we are dealing with here is critical.[67] That is, it holds, unlike non-critical accounts of ideology, that ideological beliefs and propositions are suspect, although it would be a mistake to assume that all critical accounts of ideology agree as to why such beliefs and propositions are suspect. There is disagreement as to what exactly ideology obfuscates: which aspects of social reality does it obscure—the real interests of a particular group, or the dominance of another group, or both? Alternatively, which consequences of which beliefs and practices does ideology blind us to: are we in the thrall of ideology when we cannot see the use of symbolic forms in upholding an asymmetrical distribution of power in society, or just when we mistake the socially created and contingent for the natural and immutable? Whatever it is that ideology obfuscates, such obfuscatory ideas and beliefs are, on critical accounts, clearly a bad thing; lives and polities would be better without them. That being so, critical accounts of ideology agree that ideology can be overcome and, further, that not all propositions and beliefs are ideological. Hence the malady is neither without remedy nor does it infect every part of the body politic, cultural, or social.

We must be careful here. For we have conjoined both direct and indirect uses of the ideology critique with a critical account of ideology. Indeed, a critical account is simply the foundation of the direct use; they are one and the same thing. While this conjunction generates an obvious means of attacking the orthodox method, it is clear that not all heretics take this path. In particular, some apparently reject the critical account of ideology that feeds into the ideology critique as we have so far formulated it, and invoke instead a non-critical account. Therefore, we need to distinguish the ideology critique when founded upon a critical account of ideology (which will

[67] I hope the bipartite formulation is broad enough to cover most of the major critical accounts of ideology. Important statements of such accounts are found in some of Marx's work, see *Capital I*, Vol. 35 of the *Marx-Engels Collected Works* (London, Lawrence and Wishart 1996), pp. 81–94; 185–186 and 537–542; *Capital II*, Vol. 36 of the *Collected Works* (London, Lawrence and Wishart 1997), p. 227; and *Capital III* (London, Lawrence and Wishart, 1974), p. 209, in D. Meyerson's *False Consciousness* (Oxford, Clarendon 1991) and in J. Thompson's *Ideology and Modern Culture* (Cambridge, Polity 1990), chs. 1 and 2. Both Thompson (*ibid.*, at pp. 31–33 and 55) and H. Williams, *Concepts of Ideology* (Brighton, Wheatsheaf Books 1988), p. xi, claim Napoleon was the first to state a (admittedly not very developed) critical account of ideology.

be labelled IC 1) from the ideology critique founded upon a non-critical account of ideology (hereinafter IC 2). IC 1 and IC 2 differ radically in terms of content and effect.

As to content, non-critical accounts of ideology deny that ideology is itself either objectionable or avoidable. Ideology can here refer to something as broad and abstract as a congeries of beliefs, attitudes and values constitutive of a 'world-view'; or to the political stance—party political or more general—of a group or class; or to the more mundane economic and social interests of a particular class or group. On this account almost all beliefs and propositions could be ideological, in so far as they embody and propound the beliefs, attitudes, values and interests of a particular group, and many ideologies can co-exist within a single community, state or group.[68] Furthermore, the effects of IC 2 are quite different from those of IC 1. Whereas the latter can function as a direct attack upon the orthodox method, the former cannot. To highlight the presence of ideology on IC 1 is to point to a baleful situation; to offer an account of an action, practice or institution that invokes participants' ideological views is to perpetrate obfuscation. IC 2 does not carry this obviously negative connotation, for ideology is not, on this account, automatically objectionable. Showing ideology is in play in any action, practice or institution is often simply an illustration of the inevitable, serving to remind those prone to overlook ideology that it cannot be forgotten.

This is not to say that IC 2 lacks critical power. In the context of adjudication IC 2 derives critical power not from the claim, made by IC 1, that judicial decisions peddle in myth and obfuscation, but rather that they rest upon considerations which orthodox legal thought regards as illegitimate. According to orthodox accounts of the rule of law and the law/politics distinction, some types of consideration ought never to inform judicial decisions. And it is just these considerations—considerations such as the class, party political, or interest group consequences of a decision—that heretical proponents of IC 2 maintain do indeed determine some judicial decisions. This, then, is not an attack upon the orthodox method but rather an immanent critique of a set of key orthodox claims about law, claims that loomed large in chapter 4. They are ignored in what follows in order to give close attention to the account of ideology which IC 2 invokes. The argument is

[68] Some claim Marx espoused such an account but he probably only did so, if at all, in segments of some early work: see the 1859 *Preface* to the *Critique of Political Economy* in *Early Writings* (Harmondsworth, Penguin 1975), p. 426 and *The German Ideology* (London, Lawrence and Wishart 1965), pp. 30–40; 60–64; and 90–95 (although there are many remarks in the latter suggesting Marx avouched a critical account). Many in the Marxist tradition have developed non-critical accounts: see V. I. Lenin, *What is to be Done*? in Vol. 5 of the *Collected Works* (Moscow, Foreign Languages Publishing House 1961); L. Althusser, *For Marx* (Harmondsworth, Penguin 1969), ch. 7 and 'Ideology and Ideological State Apparatuses' in his *Essays on Ideology* (London, Verso 1984).

that non-critical accounts of ideology are ultimately redundant, although this does not imply that the argument derived from such accounts—which problematises the law/politics distinction—is also redundant. Far from it, since this particular argument can be made out without reference to the dubious notion of ideology constitutive of non-critical accounts. Before examining the weaknesses of non-critical accounts of ideology another task must be discharged.

(b) Heretics and ideology

Since there are two accounts of ideology to choose from, we must clarify which account is espoused by whom; that is the task of this section. As already noted, most heretics invoke a critical account of ideology by affirming IC 1. One notable heretic, however, invokes a non-critical account of ideology, while others unwittingly attempt to combine critical and non-critical accounts. This section shows why the two types of accounts of ideology cannot be combined, that they are indeed inconsistent.

To clarify who, among the heretics, espouses IC 1, we must return to the core claim. It is important to distinguish its two limbs, even though they are not incompatible and are often run together. Each has quite different implications. The first has an epistemological dimension that the second does not, whereas the second has a consequentialist dimension which the first lacks. The first limb accepts the possibility of agents being systematically misguided about aspects of social reality and it must therefore entail a commitment to the existence or possibility of a better, more accurate account of that reality. It must accept that our understanding of the social can become less corrigible, that we can know it better and more accurately. Hence, this limb has an epistemological dimension: it suggests that our knowledge and beliefs about the social world can be improved and that some existing beliefs are suspect when judged against some standard of accuracy or truth. The second limb of the core claim need not carry this epistemological commitment. For its thrust need only be consequentialist, since it holds that some of our beliefs about the social world—regardless of their truth value—have bad consequences in the world. The idea is that some of our beliefs and patterns of thought inform our actions, practices and institutions and can thus cause harm to those who are affected by those actions, practices and institutions. This is quite different from, but not necessarily incompatible with, the epistemological thrust of the first limb. What both limbs share is the claim that agents can be systematically misguided about some of their beliefs.

Many heretics invoke IC 1 at some point in their work. While some affirm the epistemic limb of the core claim, others affirm the consequentialist; most, however, affirm both. The epistemological limb of the critique has long been propounded by Peter Gabel. According to Gabel and Jay Feinman, 'contract law today constitutes an elaborate attempt to conceal what is going on in the world'.[69] They maintain that in the aftermath of major economic and social changes, such as the transition to capitalism,

> the law of contracts . . . generated a new ideological imagery that sought to give legitimacy to the new order. To speak of ideological imagery is to imply that there is a reality behind the image that is concealed and even denied by the image. The reality was the new system of oppressive and alienating economic and social relations. Contract law denied the nature of the system by creating an imagery that made the oppression and alienation appear to be the consequences of what people themselves desired.[70]

Now there is undoubtedly a consequentialist dimension to this critique because contract law has a clear legitimating role. In portraying existing practices and institutions as fair and of universal benefit, it limits the likelihood of them being challenged and hence changed. The main thrust of the critique, however, is the falsity of the beliefs and propositions about the social world contained in the law of contract. Those beliefs and propositions *conceal* the real picture; they propagate an almost entirely false image of the social world. Hence, '[c]ontemporary capitalism bears no more relation to the imagery of contemporary contract law than did nineteenth-century capitalism to the imagery of classical contract law'.[71]

An early and typically lucid statement of both limbs of the critique was offered by Robert Gordon. He claimed that '[l]aw, like religion and television images, is one of [the] . . . clusters of belief . . . that convince people that all the many hierarchical relations in which they live and work are natural and necessary'. Such clusters of belief 'are profoundly paralysis-inducing because they make it so hard for people . . . even to *imagine* that life could be different and better'.[72] The epistemological dimension of Gordon's claim resides in the suggestion that it is a mistake to think existing social structures are indeed 'natural', 'objective' and hence beyond our control. The correct view, says Gordon in an oft-repeated heretical refrain, is that such structures are the work of our hands and we can therefore remake them. 'Though the structures are built, piece by interlocking piece, with human intentions, people come to "externalise" them, to attribute to them existence and control over and beyond human choice; and, moreover, to believe that these structures must be the way they are'.[73] The conse-

[69] 'Contract Law as Ideology' in D. Kairys (ed.), *The Politics of Law* (New York, Pantheon 1982), p. 183.

[70] *Ibid.*, p. 175. [71] *Ibid.*, p. 183.

[72] Both quotations are from his essay 'New Developments in Legal Theory', ch. 14 of Kairys (ed.), *supra*, note 69, p. 287 (emphasis in original). For an echo of these sentiments see also R. Gordon, 'Unfreezing Legal Reality: Critical Approaches to Law' (1987) 15 *Florida State University L. R.* 195–220 at pp. 198–201, 214–220.

[73] Kairys, *supra*, note 69, p. 288.

quentialist dimension occurs in the observation that thinking this way—mistaking the socially created and contingent for the necessary and unavoidable—blinds us to how things could be different. It limits our perception and reduces the vista of possible, alternative ways of organising our collective life: it is 'paralysis-inducing'.

A slightly more equivocal statement of both limbs of IC 1 is offered by Peller. The equivocation arises because he says a good deal about the first limb and relatively little about the second. Peller affirms the first limb by holding that legal discourse suppresses the socially created character of our roles and relations. In such discourse, 'the dependence of social hierarchies on a *contingent* articulation of the social space is replaced by a vision of social patterns as *having a life of their own, independent of the people who create and reproduce them*' (*MA*, pp. 1156–7; also p. 1285). This suppression Peller calls, echoing Marx, reification: 'the process by which social reality is experienced as fixed or objective. Social relations are reified when their socially created, contingent character is forgotten or suppressed' (*MA*, p. 1157). Hence the 'error of mainstream legal thought . . . [is] the mistaking of particular myths about the world for neutral and necessary truth' (*ibid.*). These statements unambiguously invoke the epistemological limb of the core claim since they posit a correct and proper picture of social reality—one in which that reality is an obvious human product and its practices, roles and institutions the contingent and therefore changeable work of our hands. The false picture is that in which social reality is regarded as immutable and natural.

Peller also occasionally invokes the consequentialist limb of the ideology critique. He maintains that harmful social institutions and structures arise upon specific representational metaphors. One such entirely contingent metaphor—the mind/body dichotomy—is not only assumed to represent some immutable and natural feature of the world but 'forms a metaphysical infrastructure legitimating contingent social practices such as the division of labor' (*MA*, p. 1176). For Peller, this metaphor and the social practices that arise upon it constrain how we act and think: they are exercises of power in the sense that they strike from the agenda of social life alternative ways of organisation and interaction (*MA*, pp. 1177–1181).

Kennedy's recent work embodies a non-critical account of ideology and IC 2. Hence, he holds, albeit obliquely, that there is a plurality of ideologies in the world—'there are several boats out in the ocean at the same time' (*CA*, p. 43)—and that ideologies are all pervasive. He poses the question '[i]s there a critical position "outside ideology"?' and abruptly answers '[o]f course not' (*CA*, p. 57; emphasis omitted). Just as judges cannot, despite their denials, decide cases without taking up ideological positions, neither can theorists offer accounts of that practice independent of ideology.

Kennedy approaches 'this study from my own left . . . ideological point of view, with the blinders that go with that position' (*ibid.*). Indeed, what else could he do, since there is no critical—or, it seems, any other—position outside ideology? Since on this account ideology is pervasive and inescapable, Kennedy cannot plausibly regard ideology as objectionable *per se*. The presence of ideology cannot, on this account, be a baleful situation. Lamenting its existence is therefore akin to lamenting the condition of man after original sin. Since the latter ensures that our condition in this world will always and ever be sinful, what point is there in complaining about this? Similarly, there is no point lamenting the existence of ideology if life without it is impossible.

Kennedy defines 'an ideology as a universalization project of an ideological intelligensia that sees itself as acting "for" a group with interests in conflict with those of other groups' and he specifies 'liberalism and conservatism as two primary examples of American ideology' (*CA*, p. 39; notes omitted). Note that liberalism and conservatism are just the *primary* examples of American ideology; there are other ideologies of which Kennedy's left-wing position is but one. Furthermore, it is probably the case that there are as many ideologies as there are groups with competing interests. This is because Kennedy defines interests as a group's orientation towards a particular resolution of a conflict (*CA*, p. 40) and then defines ideology as group interests portrayed as if they were the interests of all (this is what he means by an ideology being a 'universalisation project'). It should not be assumed that Kennedy objects to ideology because of the latter feature, namely, its apparently false portrayal of group interests *as if* they were universal interests, and is thereby committed to a critical account of ideology. For, to say ideology portrays group interests *as if* they were universal is not quite right: Kennedy concedes that an ideological conflict 'has to implicate the interests of *many people*' (*CA*, p. 41; emphasis supplied). So, while particular group interests may not be completely universal, they might nevertheless resonate with, and be an influence upon, many agents beyond the particular group. Also, to take the 'as if' dimension of ideology too seriously, to see it as implicating a critical rather than a non-critical account, is to ignore the fact that Kennedy's account of ideology 'reject[s] the idea of simple illusion or false consciousness'; his account is stripped 'of pretensions to truth' (*CA*, p. 19).

If there is nothing objectionable about ideology in itself on Kennedy's account, why does he think highlighting its presence in orthodox adjudication and theory is a worthwhile criticism? After all, is it in fact a criticism to show that judges and theorists do what they cannot avoid doing, namely, decide cases and offer accounts of law that are ideological? Kennedy's answer to the latter is affirmative and relies upon the following steps. First, he maintains, quite rightly, that the orthodox affirm a distinction between law and politics and that, however this is unpacked, one of its consequences is that factors on one side of the divide—the 'political'—are not a legitimate basis for adjudication. He also asserts that ideology as he understands it resides on the political side of this divide. His second step consists of the attempt to demonstrate the ideological stakes in judicial rule application and interpretation. That is, whenever judges apply and interpret rules in hard cases, that process 'dispose[s] significant ideological stakes either intrinsically or instrumentally' (*CA*, p. 64). When disposing ideological stakes intrinsically,

> the rules of law—the formal contents of the legal system—affect behaviour that is good or bad; right, wrong or indifferent; and fair or unfair, all according to one's ideological position . . . When the legal stakes in an appellate lawsuit include the choice between definitions of a rule of law, and the rule choice concerns behaviour about which there is ideological disagreement, then the legal stakes are also ideological stakes (*CA*, p. 58).

In addition,

> the rules of law affect behaviour in ways that in turn indirectly affect the distribution of the good things in life *other than compliance or noncompliance* with the rule in question, good things in life whose distribution is a matter of ideological dispute . . . The rules affect outcomes that ideological intelligensias care about by changing the balance of power between groups, their ability to get more for themselves in their relations of conflict and cooperation (*CA*, *ibid.*; emphasis in original).

When operating thus, rules of law and the process of their application and interpretation, are disposing ideological stakes instrumentally.

With his third step, Kennedy attempts to establish the following alternatives. First, that judges' arguments in hard cases do not determine their decisions; it is thus appropriate to find the factors that must or could have determined them. One plausible factor, he suggests, is ideology. In the face of indeterminate judicial reasoning, 'the only rational basis for making a decision seems to be to consider and evaluate [its] . . . effects on ideologized group conflict, and to choose between the arguments of the two ideological camps present' (*CA*, p. 85). Second, that judges' decisions in hard cases are determined, but only by invoking policy arguments. These are a '"Trojan Horse" for ideology' (*CA*, p. 97). The truth of either alternative, combined with the truth of the second step, guarantee that the distinction identified in the first is untenable. And this provides part of the force of Kennedy's critique. He argues that orthodox thought and practice cannot be true to its ideals, cannot uphold what it takes to be a vitally important distinction, namely, that between law and politics. Hence, the presence of 'ideology in adjudication . . . [ensures] the interpenetration of [the] . . . specific, technical rhetoric of legal justification and the general political rhetoric of the time' (*CA*, p. 1).

Kennedy's argument also derives some critical force from the notions of bad faith and denial. As we have seen, if his argument is successful it shows that ideology is indeed in play in adjudication. He correctly notes that orthodox judges and scholars deny that this is so—they seem unable to acknowledge or perhaps even to conceive that ideology is in play in adjudication. They are, says Kennedy, in a state of denial (*CA*, pp. 192–212). It is again important to appreciate that the notions of bad faith and denial do not commit Kennedy to a critical account of ideology. For, it is not ideology, on Kennedy's account, that is the cause or source of denial—ideology, for him, is not obfuscatory. Denial becomes necessary as a consequence of the presence of ideology in adjudication when combined with the belief, which is an important part of the orthodox conception of the judicial role, that ideology has no place in adjudication. This dissonance gives rise to denial. In many other contexts, where the role and beliefs in question are different, the presence of ideology does not require an account of denial or bad faith. For there is no necessary connection, on a non-critical account of ideology such as Kennedy's, between the two.

Of the heretics trapped in the uncomfortable position of apparently affirming both critical and non-critical accounts of ideology, the most notable are Peller and Kelman. It is clear from the statements above that Peller is committed to a critical account of ideology, but some of his remarks also evince support for a non-critical account. These occur in the argument about the indeterminacy of representational structures which, as will be recalled, begins from the claim that language cannot represent the world in a neutral or transparent way. Rather, language to some degree creates the world or, at least, abstracts from its 'thick texture' (*MA*, pp. 1177 and 1181). Brutally put, our language carves up the world in particular ways and there is, according to Peller, neither necessity nor rationality in this process. Everything could be represented differently. Speaking of the interpretation of texts, Peller says that '[e]ach interpretation rests on representational conventions which are ungrounded assumptions about the proper way to categorize the world. In this sense, *every* description or interpretation is prescriptive or *ideological*' (*MA*, p. 1181; emphasis supplied). And, lest there be any doubt: 'representational practice, *whatever its form*, inevitably is *ideological*' (*MA*, p. 1159; emphasis supplied).

Clearly, Peller cannot have in mind the critical account of ideology here because his comments commit him to the view that *all* representational practices—and hence probably *all* beliefs and propositions—are unavoidably ideological. They cannot be other than ideological because, on Peller's account of the relationship between language and the world, representational practices cannot avoid taking up rationally unfounded, non-necessary assumptions about the proper way to categorise the world. This, of course, is a very different view of what makes beliefs and propositions ideological from that embodied in critical accounts of ideology. In these accounts ideology can be avoided. Because it can be avoided it makes sense to regard ideology as something objectionable that should be transcended. Exactly how or why ideology is objectionable on a critical account depends upon which limb is affirmed or whether both are. By contrast, on a non-critical account such as that hinted at by Peller, ideology is inevitable and to regard it as objectionable is senseless. That both accounts of ideology are inconsistent is clear. Equally clear is the consequence of Peller's apparent affirmation of both: his argument is at best threatened, at worse actually overwhelmed, by contradiction.

Kelman, too, is haunted by the spectre of contradiction. Although he seems committed to a fairly standard, critical account of ideology by virtue of claims such as these—'[w]e treat the external world *as if* it determines our ideas, ascribing *false concreteness* to the categories we have in fact invented'[74]—he appears equally committed to a non-critical account. For example, in the sentence immediately prior to that just quoted, he says that reification is unavoidable. The concept, and the account of ideology of which it is part, is therefore non-critical. Since '[*a*]*ll* our thoughts *are, and seemingly must be*, language mediated, and as soon as we name, we invariably reify',[75] then reification cannot be avoided (unless language can in some way be avoided, a bizarre suggestion). It cannot therefore be a criticism of some language or body of thought that it reifies. Since all languages and bodies of thought cannot do other than this, how can this be a valid complaint against them? Kelman apparently mistakes a non-critical account of ideology for a critical account in just the same way as Peller does and with exactly the same consequence: it denudes his argument of any critical power. Pointing out the ways in which reification and other closely related mechanisms block counterhegemonic thought is almost entirely pointless if reification is an unavoidable feature of all languages and all bodies of thought. What little point such an observation could have may reside in an argument for a different reifying language, a different set of reifying concepts and ideas. As this argument could not claim that one reifying language was cognitively better than another, it must operate at a normative or pragmatic level. Suffice it to say that Kelman articulates no such normative or pragmatic basis for his arguments against orthodox legal thought except that, were we to liberate ourselves from it, counterhegemonic thinking would be easier. That, of course, does not show such thinking to be better. Nor is Kelman one of the heretics who has a moral and political vision for post-orthodox, post-liberal law to which this argument could be attached.

74 *Supra*, note 6, p. 270; emphasis supplied.
75 *Ibid.*, pp. 269–270; emphasis supplied.

(c) Against non-critical accounts

Critical and non-critical accounts of ideology cannot be consistently combined. Thus heretics must, when invoking the ideology critique, choose either the version founded upon a critical account of ideology (IC 1) or that based upon a non-critical account (IC 2). The argument here is that non-critical accounts of ideology are untenable; more precisely, that they are redundant. Redundancy sets in at a general level, when we consider the nature of the claims which non-critical accounts make about ideology, and at a specific level, when non-critical accounts are invoked to support a critique of orthodox legal theory and practice. However, the fact that non-critical accounts of ideology are redundant does not mean that the theories within which they are developed are useless. Rather, much of what they contain is important, but the force of the redundancy argument is that the notion of ideology does not make this so. The notion adds nothing of significance to the observations and arguments found in the theories in which it is articulated. This is especially so when IC 2 is in play, its critical thrust being wholly independent of a non-critical account of ideology. The argument heretics want to make can stand without recourse to the non-critical notion of ideology. So, a non-critical account of ideology adds nothing to what many of its proponents have to say at a general level about matters such as, for example, group interests and hegemony, and, in particular, adds nothing to the argument heretics invoke against orthodox theory and adjudication.

There are many quite different non-critical accounts of ideology, ranging from those developed in the Marxist tradition by, *inter alios*, V. I. Lenin, Antonio Gramsci and Louis Althusser, to the account offered by the conservative thinker Michael Oakeshott and his followers.[76] There is neither time nor space to consider in detail each non-critical account. Therefore the argument offered against these accounts is necessarily limited even though it claims to be general. It claims that the non-critical concept of ideology is redundant but does not show this in relation to every non-critical account. Rather, the argument shows why the redundancy claim has some plausibility by reference to a few non-critical accounts of ideology. It then, somewhat dubiously, infers from this that all existing non-critical accounts suffer from redundancy. Ultimately this inference is well founded, but that cannot be demonstrated here. Our question is thus: what lends even superficial plausibility to the suggestion that the non-critical conception of ideology is redundant?

[76] For the relevant works of Lenin and Althusser see note 68. Gramsci's elliptical remarks on ideology are found in *Selections from the Prison Notebooks*, edited by Q. Hoare and G. Nowell-Smith (London, Lawrence and Wishart 1971), part II; Oakeshott's account of ideology is contained in *Rationalism in Politics* (London, Methuen 1967) and developed by his followers in D. Manning (ed.), *The Form of Ideology* (London, Allen and Unwin 1980).

The response is that, in the hands of proponents of non-critical accounts, the concept 'ideology' picks out nothing we could not already talk and think about without that notion. Conceptually speaking, we already have a vocabulary for everything to which the non-critical notion refers; it confers salience on no 'thing' we would otherwise miss. This is surely the hallmark of conceptual redundancy. Pragmatically speaking, if the concept highlights nothing which is unfamiliar or new, nor does it provide greater insight than our existing language and its body of concepts, what is the point of invoking it? So, for example, many of those in the Marxist tradition who have developed non-critical accounts of ideology invoke the notion to refer to either group or class interests. Taking ideology as proxy for group or class interests explains the apparently bizarre claim made by some of these thinkers that ideology will persist even when class society has been transcended. For Marxists committed to a critical account of ideology, class domination is one reason why ideology (understood as false consciousness or fetishism or reification) exists; transcending class conflict means transcending ideology. For Althusser and others, however, ideology is neither a baleful situation nor is its existence purely a consequence of class conflict. Rather, ideology is simply taken to be the interests of any group or class in society. Even when class conflict has been transcended and we live in a classless or single class society, that class and segments of it will still have interests and aims. It will, therefore, still have an ideology in the non-critical sense.[77] The crucial question, though, is this: what does the notion of ideology actually add in this context? Since it seems to be but a synonym for class or group interests, the answer is 'nothing'. Althusser's point about the variety and persistence of group and class interests can stand without invoking the notion of ideology at all. The argument would lose nothing were every reference to 'ideology' replaced with 'class or group interest'. Of course, had this been done, the rhetorical impact of Althusser's work would have been seriously reduced.

Similarly, the non-critical concept of ideology could be dropped from Karl Mannheim's work and nothing would be lost. For, although Mannheim also invokes a critical concept of ideology, his non-critical concept is but a synonym for the social construction of knowledge.[78] In brutally simple terms, this captures two thoughts. The first, seemingly denied by some early empiricist philosophers, is that human beings lack any innate knowledge. Rather, our knowledge and concepts are learned through language and that, obviously, is an inter-subjective, socially-created medium. The second thought is that individuals share a pattern of beliefs and experiences in so

[77] See Althusser, *For Marx*, *supra*, note 68, pp. 234–236; Lenin, *supra*, note 68, at pp. 383–384.

[78] As anyone familiar with K. Mannheim, *Ideology and Utopia: An Introduction to the Sociology of Knowledge* (London, Routledge and Kegan Paul 1936) will know, a paragraph cannot do justice to the complexity of this work.

far as they are similarly placed in society and share similar experiences. It is their social conditions that determine their experience and, hence, their beliefs and attitudes. Now, much work has been done to illustrate the processes by which knowledge is socially created, how those processes are determined and what, if any, are the epistemological and other implications of this claim. And a good deal of this work takes Mannheim as a starting point. Yet the redundancy argument is as powerful here as it is in relation to Althusser's work. Nothing Mannheim says about the social construction of knowledge would be lost, or become oblique or silly, were the notion of ideology dropped. Indeed, it seems Mannheim himself was aware of this.[79] If it is true that there is a potentially debilitating confusion in Mannheim's work, brought about by his invocation of both a critical and a non-critical concept of ideology, then the latter must surely be dropped.[80] It adds nothing to the argument about the social construction of knowledge, as Mannheim hinted, and puts in peril his other, quite valuable claims, many of which depend for their power upon a critical account of ideology.

Kennedy's espousal of IC 2 and its underlying non-critical account of ideology courts redundancy in exactly the same way as those non-critical accounts developed beyond the context of adjudication. So, just as ideology operates in some of those accounts as an unnecessary synonym for other, perfectly intelligible and helpful notions like class interests, it functions in Kennedy's critique of adjudication as a pointless synonym for 'political factors'. The critical force of IC 2 is not, remember, derived simply from establishing the existence of ideology in adjudication, for on this account ideology is not in itself objectionable. Rather, as we have noted, there are three vital steps in Kennedy's version of IC 2. The first consists of a demonstration that the orthodox affirm the law/politics distinction, which entails that 'political factors' are never a legitimate basis for judicial decisions. The second is an argument showing that judicial rule choices dispose 'significant ideological [political] stakes' (*CA*, p. 64). And the third, an argument showing that hard case judicial decisions are indeterminate such that only policy, which is a trojan horse for ideology (political factors), or ideology plain and simple (political factors), can determine the decisions actually reached. The critical power of this argument is not increased by the non-critical notion of ideology since it is but a proxy for 'political factors'. After all, the main American 'ideologies' that Kennedy claims are in play when judges decide hard cases are liberalism and conservatism. What are these but more or less abstract political programmes? Is anything gained by calling them ideologies?

Perhaps we are being hasty. Redundancy might be denied by the sug-

[79] See his remarks about displacing the non-critical concept of ideology with the idea of 'perspective': *ibid.*, pp. 69 and 238–239.

[80] J. Larrain, *The Concept of Ideology* (London, Hutchinson 1979), pp. 117–118.

gestion that Kennedy's argument would, after all, be weakened were the non-critical concept of ideology dropped and the notion of 'political factors' put in its place. However, arguments to this end seem to lack plausibility. Could it be argued, for example, that the notion of ideology, given its connection in Kennedy's account to group or class interests and conflict, is a more refined and thus more useful concept than 'political factors'? It could, but the argument ignores the most obvious way in which to elucidate the nature of the 'political', namely, by reference to the relationship between the interests and wants of particular groups, on one hand, and the exercise of power, on the other. This account of the political can easily provide a list of 'political factors' which should not play a role in adjudication and it need not, in order to generate that list, invoke a non-critical account of ideology. What, then, of the close link between Kennedy's account of ideology and the idea of a 'project': does this ensure that the former is a valuable notion? Unfortunately not. 'Ideology is a project', Kennedy writes, because 'it is a mediation between interests and universal claims' (*CA*, p. 42). The process by which one group's interests come to serve the interests of other groups is not one, on a non-critical account, that entails any kind of misrepresentation or obfuscation. Like Gramsci, Kennedy seems to envisage a genuine unity of interest arising here which, in order to be possible, militates against the groups involved ruthlessly and single-mindedly pursuing their self-interest.[81] In order for there to be genuine mediation—that is, mediation in absence of misrepresentation or coercion—there must be some degree of compromise and cooperation. Now, there is no denying the value of the Gramscian account of this process of interest articulation and mediation, nor should the significance of his notion of hegemony, which describes aspects of this process, be understated. However, this account of mediation is quite transparent, and clearly a potential advance in our understanding of the social world, without any recourse to the notion of ideology. What power does this account of interest mediation and articulation gain from the notion of ideology? Does labelling this process as 'ideological' cast more light upon it than exists without that label? If the description of that process just given, which eschewed any reference to ideology, is both accurate and intelligible, then the answer must be 'no'.

Finally, it might be said that the value of Kennedy's non-critical account of ideology lies in the fact that it highlights a conflict we would otherwise miss. 'What gives ideology its particular character is the tension between group commitment . . . and [the] . . . requirements or directions or suggestions of the body of texts' (*CA*, p. 41). If ideology names this conflict then it does work that concepts such as class or group interests, mediation or political factors, do not already do. It apparently performs a

[81] Gramsci, *supra*, note 76, pp. 181–182.

useful role. Note what an odd usage, even when assessed from the perspective of non-critical accounts, this is. It confines the concept to an exceptionally narrow role having salience only when there is a very specific kind of conflict namely, between group interests, on the one hand, and a textual tradition, on the other. When group interests are either simply a product of, or deeply embedded in, that tradition—think, for example, of nationalist discourses and their perpetuation through an oral and written tradition of myth—ideology is impossible.

Furthermore, when Kennedy turns to examine the ideological stakes in judicial rule choices he plainly does not take ideology in this very narrow sense. Remember that when judicial decisions dispose ideological stakes either intrinsically or instrumentally they in fact benefit conservative or liberal political positions. In a different idiom, judicial rule choices have a displacement effect just like vessels floating on or moving through water. As the wake of a ship through a channel has certain consequences—such as the erosion of the shore on each side—so, too, do judicial decisions. Their effect, though, is upon one or other political programme and the logic of influence seems to be that one must be adversely, and the other beneficially, affected. One shore is eroded while the other is built up. When operating ideologically, then, judicial decisions do not elucidate a tension between a tradition, on the one hand, and group interests, on the other. Rather, the sense of ideology in play when Kennedy discusses adjudication is the sense in which ideology is but a proxy for political factors and, although redundant, this sense is most representative of Kennedy's thought. He seems driven to use ideology to highlight the tension between group interests and a tradition only in order to capture the thought that the two are to some degree independent of one another: for example, he says the tradition, the body of texts and ideas, 'has a "life of its own"' (*CA*, *ibid.*). However, something like Althusser's notion of relative autonomy, despite its problems, would surely serve Kennedy's purpose better.[82]

It seems that the non-critical notion of ideology adds nothing to Kennedy's argument. The removal of any reference to ideology will not reduce the argument's power. The thrust of IC 2—taken now to embody the contradiction between the orthodox affirmation that political factors play no role in adjudication, on the one hand, and the recognition that political factors must play a role in adjudication, on the other—is entirely unaffected by jettisoning the non-critical concept of ideology (except that the label IC 2 is no longer appropriate). The argument's crucial steps—first, showing that the orthodox do indeed espouse an appropriate version of the law/politics distinction which, secondly, cannot in fact be maintained—do not depend for their success upon an (apparently redundant) account of

[82] See *For Marx*, *supra*, note 68, pp. 111.

ideology. Whatever insight the argument contains, whatever challenges it poses for the orthodoxy, can and should be presented, so to speak, in the raw, free from obfuscatory or pointless encumbrances.

This point is, of course, the core of the redundancy problem: ideology, understood in the non-critical sense, adds nothing to those theories of which it is part. By contrast, if, in each of the theories noted above, a critical conception of ideology were deployed, then there would be no question of redundancy. Critical conceptions pick out some thing other than class or group interests, some thing other than the process by which these interests are mediated and something other than the abstract political programmes of certain groups. They promise to do useful work. They cannot be reduced to these other matters because they make a quite specific claim, namely, that it is possible for agents to be systematically misguided about either (i) aspects of social reality or (ii) the consequences of their beliefs. Such obfuscation could arise within the context of the articulation and mediation of group interests yet it need not do so. It could also arise within judicial decision-making, but its presence would not guarantee that judicial decisions influenced particular political programmes. In each case, the invocation of ideology triggers a distinctive claim; it adds something to the description, something—the existence of obfuscatory ideas or beliefs—we might otherwise miss. Conceptually speaking, the critical conception is therefore far from redundant. Yet nothing said here goes beyond conceptual cartography. The argument shows only that the non-critical conception of ideology occupies no distinctive conceptual space and hence does no useful work. There may well be other reasons—rhetorical or prudential—why it is still employed, but they are not addressed here.

(d) Ideology as critique: some problems

Non-critical accounts of ideology are redundant; heretics must therefore rely upon IC 1. This might be regarded as an undesirable position if the critical accounts of ideology underpinning IC 1 are infirm. This section argues that, while there are indeed problems associated with critical accounts of ideology, they are by no means insurmountable. Many of the problems are general ones within the human sciences and it would be unfair to expect heretical proponents of IC 1 to solve them. Of the remaining problems, they could well be solved if only heretics took time to do so. These problems are merely matters of unfinished business rather than insuperable obstacles.

One ostensibly important problem for critical accounts of ideology is ignored in what follows, partly because of pragmatic considerations of space and time, partly because of doubt—unpacked and unfounded—as to the seriousness of the difficulty. It concerns the relationship, if any, between the 'subjective' and 'objective' bases of ideology, that is, the degree to which it is a product of either individual consciousness or structural—cultural, social and economic—factors. So, it could be argued either that certain social or cultural factors bring into being and maintain ideology or that ideology originates entirely within the minds of those subject to it. Whether objective or subjective factors are dominant, or whether a combination of both call into being and sustain ideology, will not be discussed.[83] However, while this specific problem is overlooked, the more general difficulty of which it is part, namely, that of providing an account of the genesis and operation of ideology, is not.

Just four snags that ensnare proponents of IC 1 are examined. The first two parallel the two limbs of the critique. The first highlights the complexity of the issues involved in showing the corrigibility of some of our beliefs and propositions. The essence of the epistemological limb is that some of those beliefs and propositions misrepresent the world and this apparently implies a great deal. It seems to imply commitments to, *inter alia*, a theory of truth; an account of language such that it can in some way represent or mirror the world; an ontological claim about the constituents of the real world; and a methodological position designed to yield less corrigible beliefs about the world if not justified true beliefs (that is, knowledge). Each commitment requires a great deal of argumentation in order to be plausible. However, when Gabel and Feinman rightly say that 'to speak of ideological imagery is to imply a reality behind the image', they seem unaware of what must be done to unearth that reality. They accept the possibility of non-ideological knowledge of the world—that is, knowledge that represents the world as it really is—but are non-cognisant of, or least never feel it incumbent upon themselves to articulate, the complexities of a theory of truth.

Note that Gabel and Feinman are not committed to espousing any particular theory of truth, although it is sometimes wrongly assumed that proponents of a critical conception must endorse the correspondence theory of truth.[84] In the most abstract terms, such a theory holds that a proposition or sentence—about the social world, for example—is true if and only if it corresponds to the facts. This appears disarmingly simple but contains a nest of difficulties about issues such as access to the 'facts', the way in which a proposition or sentence 'corresponds' to them and the properties which sen-

[83] For a treatment of these issues see G. Lukacs, 'Reification and the Consciousness of the Proletariat' in his *History and Class Consciousness* (London, The Merlin Press 1971).

[84] Hans Barth comes close to making this assumption: see his *Truth and Ideology* (Berkeley, University of California Press 1976), p. 109. This assumption seems to inform Thompson's attempt to steer his critical account of ideology clear of 'the epistemological burden' with which it has traditionally been associated: Thompson, *supra*, note 67, p. 56. Some dislike critical accounts of ideology just because they connect with the notion of truth, however understood: see M. Foucault, *Power/Knowledge* (C. Gordon, ed; New York, Pantheon 1980), p. 118.

tences, propositions and beliefs must have in order for correspondence to be possible. The philosophical literature on the advantages and disadvantages of the correspondence theory of truth is vast and complicated and we cannot complain that proponents of IC 1 fail to resolve the problems in this theory.[85] That would clearly be unfair. Rather, the gripe is that they seem oblivious to the nature of the task they have set themselves and take up very difficult positions as if they were entirely unproblematic. This is not to imply that any other (non-correspondence) theory of truth would be any less difficult. It is merely to highlight that much work must be done if heretics are to support their position. The specific difficulties with the correspondence theory of truth cannot be avoided by severing the link between facts, on the one hand, and sentences, propositions and beliefs, on the other, and replacing it with one between human interests, on one side, and sentences, propositions and beliefs, on the other.[86] This just raises the equally difficult tasks of articulating an account of human interests—'real', expressed or otherwise—and of ensuring some link or even correspondence between them and knowledge.

The difficulties encountered but ducked by heretics in relation to the notion of truth are not unique. Nor are the other commitments supposedly incurred as a result of affirming the epistemological limb less difficult, demanding less effort to resolve or avoid. This is also true of the commitments incurred as a result of affirming the consequentialist limb of IC 1. The most obvious of these are the commitments to offer plausible accounts of both harm and causality. Neither notion is unproblematic and their difficulties have worried many. For example, the nature of harm to self and others—is it just a function of frustrating an agent's expressed preferences or is it rooted in some account of an agent's objective or real interests?—as well as questions of consent, are the fulcrum of traditional legal philosophical discussions about the limits of the law.[87] Equally, questions about harm and causality arise within analyses of the nature of actions and omissions and assume great importance in relation to the nature of violence.[88] The very notion of causality itself is immensely difficult: does the constant conjunction, or the ordinary language, or the necessary connection account

[85] For analysis see A. Tarski, 'The Semantic Conception of Truth' (1943) 4 *Philosophy and Phenomenological Research* 341–373; J. L. Austin, 'Truth' (1950) Supp. Vol. 24, *Proceedings of the Aristotelian Society* 111–128; J. Searle, *The Construction of Social Reality* (Harmondsworth, Penguin 1995), ch. 9; and P. Horwich, *Truth* (Oxford, Basil Blackwell 1990).

[86] This strategy would appeal to one writing under the influence of J. Habermas, *Knowledge and Human Interests* (London, Heinemann 1972), particularly the Appendix.

[87] The *locus classicus* is J. S. Mill, 'On Liberty' in *Utilitarianism, On Liberty and Considerations on Representative Government* (London, J. M. Dent 1972) which must now be supplemented with the first three volumes of J. Feinberg's *The Moral Limits of the Criminal Law* (New York, O. U. P. 1984, 1985 and 1986).

[88] An admirably clear but now somewhat dated contribution to this debate is J. Harris, *Violence and Responsibility* (London, Routledge and Kegan Paul 1980), ch. 2.

of causality underpin the consequentialist limb of IC 1?[89] Again, the gripe here is not that heretics have failed to solve the problems within these accounts of causation or harm, but rather that they take up problematic positions—positions at least in need of prima facie justification—as if they were completely unproblematic.

Since the nature of this criticism of IC 1 is so very limited—the argument amounts to little more than the somewhat patronising, but nevertheless true, school teacher's judgment of 'must try harder'—it cannot discredit the argument. Heretics have failed to make a compelling case for one or other or both limbs although they are not alone in this. Some of the originators of the ideology critique—among whom we must count some founders of the human sciences—also chose to ignore these difficulties. Of course, highlighting these difficulties does not imply that neither limb of the ideology critique can be plausibly unpacked. Each limb represents an as yet incomplete project for heretics and other philosophers and social critics who invoke them. Each limb ought to be, but a survey of recent work suggests they are not, part of the heretics' programme. However, there is a much more pressing difficulty for some heretical proponents of the ideology critique than the failure to develop it fully. This third snag may have troubled readers of the previous paragraphs where notions like truth and causality loomed large. For there is surely a tension between the ideology critique, on the one hand, and the claims of deconstruction—and the postmodern philosophy and social theory of which it is part—on the other. This conjunction only exists in the work of a few heretics, most notably that of Peller and Schlag. As we have seen, both affirm IC 1; furthermore, both invoke deconstruction and purport to write under the influence of Jacques Derrida. Although they would despise the phrase, it is no exaggeration to say that deconstruction is the 'foundation' of many of their arguments against the orthodoxy. They claim, quite explicitly, either to be 'doing' deconstruction (*Texte*, pp. 1631–1657) or, apparently the same thing, applying the insights of structuralist and post-structuralist thought (*MA*, pp. 1160–1170) within the legal academy.

What, then, is the tension? Look again at what the epistemological and consequentialist limbs require to be compelling. The former demands nothing less than an account of the true picture of social reality against which to judge our existing beliefs and propositions. Only if such a picture is available can we determine whether some beliefs are indeed mistaken or

[89] For statements of the different types of accounts of causality see D. Hume, *supra*, note 65, Book I, part III, sections I—V, XIV and XV; H. L. A. Hart and T. Honore, *Causation in the Law* (Oxford, Clarendon 2nd ed. 1985), preface and part I; J. L. Mackie, *The Cement of the Universe* (Oxford, Clarendon 1974) chs. 1–8; and the essays in M. Brand, *The Nature of Causation* (Urbana, University of Illinois Press 1976).

'false', be this a result of portraying the socially created and mutable as immutable or a consequence of giving a false impression of the nature of social reality. By contrast, the consequentialist limb requires a causal audit of the effects of some of our beliefs and propositions. The harmfulness of these beliefs and propositions must be established. That requires not just the implementation of an account of social causality, but also some articulation—moral, political or otherwise—of what counts as 'harm'. Now notions such as 'truth', 'representation', 'causality' and 'harm' are the fulcrum of what those supposedly writing under the influence of deconstruction and postmodernism maintain is 'the enlightenment project'. Let us forget the profoundly reductionist nature of this all too common claim—holding that there was and is some unitary 'enlightenment project' is every bit as dubious as affirming a unitary postmodern project—and forget also the variety of 'enlightenment' thought which prefigures many current deconstructive critiques. Concentrating instead on what are supposed to be the constitutive beliefs and aims of enlightenment thinkers—*inter alia*, '[d]emarcating truth from error and privileging science as knowledge'[90]—and the names bandied about in this context—in philosophy, David Hume, John Locke, Immanuel Kant and the Mills, in political and social theory, Emile Durkheim, Max Weber and Marx—it is clear that, superficially at least, all were directly concerned with issues of truth, representation, causality and harm. It is therefore not unreasonable to claim that the ideology critique is obviously part of this supposedly failed project. Certainly, the core concepts of the critique are central to the works of all the thinkers just noted.

The tension results from affirming the ideology critique—part and parcel of 'the enlightenment project'—whilst affirming deconstruction's denial of the sense of that project. Despite this formulation, it cannot be said that there is a contradiction here because the way in which the tension was established is just too abstract and lax. Much work would be required to unpack both potentially misleading, reductionist terms such as 'postmodernism', and the quite different arguments of the likes of Locke and Kant, Weber and Durkheim, so as to establish that there is indeed a contradiction here. Nevertheless, we can point to the brooding threat of such a contradiction and to the apparently quite different sources of the ideology critique, on the one hand, and deconstruction, on the other. Note also that neither Peller nor Schlag does anything to quell the threat of contradiction; both seem blissfully unaware of the tension between deconstruction and the ideology critique. They are therefore unable to take the obvious and,

[90] S. Seidman (ed.), *The Postmodern Turn* (Cambridge, C. U. P. 1994), p. 8. See also ch. 6 for Seidman's equally bland account of the supposed ailments of enlightenment sociological theory.

though it courts controversy to say so, *properly* deconstructive step of recognising and embracing the tension.[91] Doing that would, of course, raise a number of other issues that cannot be tackled here.

The final difficulty facing proponents of the ideology critique concerns the mechanism and genesis of ideology. The mechanism issue simply raises the 'how' question: how does ideology function so as systematically to misguide those in its thrall? The genesis issue poses the 'why' question: why is there ideology in the world? One of the few serious, critical accounts of ideology to offer answers to these questions is that derived from the work of Marx. In the hands of Gerry Cohen, one of the most acute Anglophone Marxist philosophers, Marx's answers are also admirably clear. A brief examination serves to clarify the nature of the task heretics must discharge when responding to these questions and provides a standard against which their efforts can be measured. (That, of course, does not imply that the Marxian answers to these questions, and the Marxian account of ideology in general, are beyond reproach. Whatever their faults, the Marxian answers are reasonably full and clear which, as we will see, puts them considerably ahead of the heretical answers.)

The 'how' question is answered thus by Marx. The social world of capitalist societies is bifurcated between appearance and reality. For example, the wage relation, viewed from the perspective of circulation, appears as a fair exchange between capitalist and labourer whereby the latter freely alienates labour in exchange for its true value or price. But this 'very Eden of the innate rights of man' is in reality—the reality yielded by viewing the wage relation from the perspective of accumulation—exploitative: it is robbery, theft, exploitation.[92] However, the dominant view of the wage relation, the one that both labourer and capitalist take up as most obvious and commonsensical, is that from the perspective of circulation. This view is false only in the limited sense that it does not go beyond the appearance of the relation and penetrate its underlying reality. It is true in the sense that the wage relation really does *appear* to be a fair and equal exchange in capitalist society. In capitalist societies there is, though, a world of appearances that does not necessarily correspond with the underlying reality: 'there is a gulf between appearance and reality when and only when the

[91] For an informed deconstructive analysis of ideology and reification see M. Kramer, *Legal Theory, Political Theory, and Deconstruction* (Bloomington, Indiana U. P. 1991), ch. 5. Kramer is aware of tension and, true to his deconstructive method, revels in it: see, in particular, pp. 238–269.

[92] The first statement is, of course, from Marx's *Capital I, supra*, note 67, p. 280; Marx's remarks about the wage relation being a form of theft, stealing or robbery are dotted about his works: see *Capital I*, pp. 728 and 761; *Grundrisse* (Harmondsworth, Penguin 1973), p. 705. Some of the clearest and most thorough treatments of Marx's views about the justice or injustice of the wage relation are two essays by N. Geras: 'The Controversy About Marx and Justice', ch. 1 of his *Literature of Revolution* (London, Verso 1986) and 'Bringing Marx to Justice: An Addendum and Rejoinder' (1992) 195 *New Left Review* 37–69.

explanation of a state of affairs falsifies the description it is natural to give if one lacks the explanation. Gulfs are due to the way reality itself appears'.[93] For Marx, ideology (or, perhaps more accurately, fetishism) is the name of the tendency, almost overwhelming, to regard appearance as reality, to elide the gap between the two. Those of our beliefs, propositions and ideas which elide the gap, which take appearance to be reality when it is not, are ideological. The Marxian response to the 'how' question, then, is that ideology misguides by having us mistake appearance for reality when there is indeed a gap between the two.

On hearing this, the immediate response is the 'why' question: why is it the case that some beliefs, propositions and ideas prevent us from perceiving the true nature of social reality? The Marxian reply, again admirably clear, gives two reasons. First, according to Cohen, there is a psychological thesis Marx never explicitly endorsed but which must be ascribed to him to make sense of much of what he says. It holds that

> [i]f the exploited were to see that they are exploited, they would resent their subjection and threaten social stability. And if the exploiters were to see that they exploit, the composure they need to rule confidently would be disturbed. Being social animals, exploiters have to feel that their social behaviour is justifiable. When the feeling is difficult to hide from the truth, the truth must be hidden from them as well as those they oppress.[94]

Secondly, '[i]llusion is . . . constitutive of class societies'; such societies have '"illusio-genic" properties'; they *create* distortions and errors of thought.[95] Further, because these illusions are part of social reality, bringing them to light will not dissipate them: that requires changing the social reality which gave them life. These two reasons might well be related: it could be argued, for example, that the first requires the second or they might be taken to be entirely independent of one another. The relationship of these reasons, their power and validity are not matters that need detain us here. For, taken in conjunction with the response to the 'how' question, these two reasons serve simply as a sample of what a reasonably clear—but not unimpeachable—treatment of the issues of genesis and mechanism should look like. The sample certainly highlights the kinds of considerations pertinent to the task.

Against this background, an examination of the heretical responses to the 'how' and 'why' questions produces disappointment. This arises, first, because very few heretics even make a start on these issues. Certainly, those—like Peller and Schlag—for whom a critical account of ideology does a great deal of work, do little to answer the 'how' and 'why' questions. Sec-

[93] G. A. Cohen, *Karl Marx's Theory of History: A Defence* (Oxford, Clarendon Press 1978), p. 329 (italics omitted).
[94] *Ibid.*, p. 330 (footnote omitted). [95] *Ibid.*, pp. 330 and 338.

ondly, disappointment arises because of the particularly limited and inadequate responses of those who make some effort to deal with these questions. Take just one example. Mark Kelman's answer to the 'how' question initially looks promising. He offers six examples of the ways in which, for those '"afflicted" by legal thinking . . . , counterhegemonic thoughts will simply make less sense, simply be harder to think'.[96] The six ways in which legal thought 'blocks critical stances'[97] are: reification; mistaking legal solubility with the existence of a problem (no legal solution, no problem); synthetic individualism; take and give; denial of contradictions within technical legal thought; and privileging.

This is an interesting and pertinent response to the 'how' question since the notion of 'blocking' looks like just the right kind of concept to explain how ideology misleads. There are some difficulties, however. For example, although each entry on this list shares a capacity to block counterhegemonic thought, we must question whether or not they are actually distinct from one another. Look at Kelman's notion of reification. It holds that

> [a]ll our thoughts are, and seemingly must be, language mediated, and as soon as we name, we invariably reify in the sense of ascribing identical traits to objects or situations we could otherwise imagine differentiating simply because we have given them the same name. We treat the external world as if it determines our ideas, ascribing false concreteness to the categories we have in fact invented.[98]

Understood as the process of labelling segments of the world, and coming to regard those labels as natural, objective or, what might amount to the same thing, as determined by the world, reification seems also to describe well what Kelman calls privileging, denial, and mistaking the legal solubility of a problem with the existence of a problem. If we cannot see a problem in the social world without it being conjoined with a legal solution, are we not thus 'ascribing false concreteness' to the contingent, legal categories we use to divide up the world? Similarly, if we deny the contradictions in our thought and practice by invoking non-contradictory legal categories, are we not engaged in exactly the same process?

This might not be a problem if the entries on this list are but slightly different specifications of the same thing, namely, reification. Yet, that being so, a more serious problem presents itself, a problem that also besets Kelman's response to the 'why' question. That response is nowhere near as developed as the response to the 'how' question but the bones of an argument can be cobbled together from Kelman's *obiter dicta*. It goes like this. There is ideology in the world because there is reification and there is reification because there is language. Language reifies. Yet since language is inescapable, reification (and hence ideology) is also inescapable. Kelman's

[96] *Supra*, note 6, p. 269. [97] *Ibid.* [98] *Ibid.*, pp. 269–270.

response to the 'how' question also apparently commits him to the latter claim. For, as we have seen, reification is a crucial source of 'blocking', a means—which seems quite obviously to overlap with and include many of the other instances of 'blocking'—of preventing counterhegemonic thinking. And, as we have already seen, reification is unavoidable in so far as representation is unavoidable. The difficulty with this conclusion is that it cannot possibly be a criticism of any representational system that it reifies because all language, all representation, as Kelman unambiguously says, reifies. Kelman is thus caught in the no-man's land between critical and non-critical accounts of ideology. The notion of blocking looks like a potentially useful explanation of how it is that some ideas, beliefs and propositions come to mislead or obfuscate. It suggests that Kelman is committed to a critical account of ideology. Yet all this promise is immediately wiped away when we consider his account of why ideology exists. Ideology and reification exist because language and representation exist. Since it is hard indeed to conceive of human life without language and representation of some kind, then life without ideology and reification seems impossible. Hence, this suggests that Kelman is in fact offering a non-critical account of ideology. We have already established that the two different types of accounts cannot consistently be affirmed. This, then, is the problem with Kelman's response to the 'how' and 'why' questions.

It is no exaggeration to say the Cohen-Marx response to the 'how' and 'why' questions is far superior to this. At the very least, it appears better simply because it generates clear and non-contradictory accounts of how and why ideology operates. That cannot be said for Kelman. Yet it must not be assumed that it would be impossible for heretics to provide better responses to the 'how' and 'why' questions than those Kelman gives. Indeed, some heretics—particularly Gabel—have provided a much more ambitious and detailed account of how ideology operates to mislead or obfuscate. However, the argument as to why ideology and reification exist becomes mired, in Gabel's case, in the difficulties of the donor work: his account of ideology is Sartrean and subject to many snags.[99] Nevertheless, it seems eminently possible for a critical account of ideology to be developed that plausibly responds to the 'how' and 'why' questions while escaping the snags of the best of the already existing, but somewhat problematic, critical accounts. If heretics were at some point able to outdo and improve upon either Marx or Sartre, then they would indeed have cause for celebration. For the moment, the task of developing a critical account of ideology and putting it to work within the legal and adjudicative context, is certainly a live one. The project should not be written off just because it is difficult. Heretics

[99] See, for example, 'Intention and Structure in Contractual Conditions: Outline of a Method for Critical Legal Theory' (1977) 61 *Minnesota L. R.* 601–643 and 'Reification in Legal Reasoning' in S. Spitzer (ed.), (1980) 3 *Research in Law and Sociology*, 25–51.

simply need high hopes: if ants can move rubber tree plants, then surely heretics can develop a defensible and critical account of ideology. Certainly, such an account would be the most direct and powerful means of calling into question the orthodox method.

CONCLUSIONS

The overarching question addressed here was: what arguments do heretics have to discredit the orthodox method? Three arguments to that end were discussed and three conclusions reached. First, it was argued that only one of the three indeterminacy theses is defensible, but only in such a way as to render it entirely compatible with the orthodoxy. In addition, it was argued that the attempt to destabilise the orthodox method—and much more besides—found in the argument about the disappearance of the self, is not a success. It fails not because it is compatible with the orthodoxy—far from it, since it is incompatible with much of what both heretics and orthodox believe. Rather, it fails because it has yet to be plausibly developed: despite its radical (and often amusing) claims, the argument is far from complete. This problem is compounded because it is impossible to be sure what, exactly, proponents of this kind of argument regard it as establishing. Both the argument about the disappearance of the self and that about linguistic indeterminacy sought support at crucial points from some or other claim about ideology. Two different types of argument about ideology were distinguished and it was argued, finally, that only one was both plausible and useful, namely, the type of argument which invoked a critical account of ideology. While it was accepted that critical accounts of ideology face some difficulties, the argument was that these are not overwhelming. Therefore, it seems that the ideology critique is the most powerful tool heretics have with which to discredit the orthodox method. The thrust of the critique, remember, is this: orthodox accounts of the practice and institutions of law peddle in myth and obfuscation in so far as the participants in that practice and those institutions are in the thrall of ideology. If true, that is a damning indictment.

6
The Sovereign Structure

It seems that in Paris, sometime during the late 1960s or early 1970s, the author first disappeared and was then found dead. Not long after, 'man' also perished. No particular author was declared dead, although doubtless some did die during this time in Paris and elsewhere. Rather, the idea of the author, the creator or initiator of a literary work or form of writing, was pronounced dead. The author was replaced with the 'text' which was not solely a product of the author, but of a system or structure of discourse and rules of literary production. These structures spoke through the author, who was, in one formulation, 'a kind of crossroads where things happen . . . purely passive' and, in another, an equally empty vessel: 'the *I* that writes the text is never, itself, anything more than a paper *I*'.[1] Coping with this loss was difficult enough, yet it was made even more appalling when 'man' died or, scarcely any better, was 'dissolved'.[2] Authors, a species of 'man' died first, but 'man', or in the usage of this chapter, 'agents'—the idea of autonomous human beings moving, manipulating and creating social rules, institutions and structures—quickly followed. When authors and agents perished, what was left?

There remained the family of labels like 'author', 'agent' and 'individual', yet these referred not to autonomous, creative forces in the social world—innovators of texts and creators of the social fabric—but to the products of texts and social structures. For Michel Foucault 'the author is an ideological product' since we present him 'as a genius, as a perpetual surging of invention' when, 'in reality, we make him function in exactly the opposite fashion'. In reality, the author does not precede and create literary works but is a 'functional principle by which . . . one limits, excludes, and chooses; in short, by which one impedes the free circulation, the free manipulation, the free composition, decomposition, and recomposition of fiction'.[3] Similarly,

> [t]he individual is not to be conceived as a sort of elementary nucleus, a primitive atom, a multiple and inert material on which power comes to fasten or against which

[1] The first statement belongs to C. Levi-Strauss, *Myth and Meaning* (London, Routledge and Kegan Paul 1978), p. 4; the second to R. Barthes, 'From Work to Text' in J. Harari, *Textual Strategies* (London, Methuen 1980) 73–81, p. 79. See also R. Barthes, 'The Death of the Author' in his *Image-Music-Text* (London, Fontana 1977) pp. 142–148. For a powerful argument that the author is never more alive than when declared dead, see S. Burke, *The Death and Return of the Author* (Edinburgh, Edinburgh University Press 1992).

[2] 'I believe the goal of the human sciences to be not to constitute, but to dissolve man': C. Levi-Strauss, *The Savage Mind* (London, Weidenfeld and Nicolson 1972), p. 247.

[3] M. Foucault, 'What is an Author?' in Harari, *supra*, note 1, 141–160, p. 159.

it happens to strike, and in so doing subdues or crushes individuals. In fact, it is already one of the prime effects of power that certain bodies, certain gestures, certain discourses, certain desires come to be identified and constituted as individuals.[4]

The announcement of this double death heralds a reversal of the traditional role assigned to author and agent. While they were once taken as the engines of social change and innovation, prior to and determinative of the rules, institutions and structures in which they operate, they are now merely the products of those rules, institutions and structures. The sovereign individual is apparently replaced by the sovereign structure.

The first section of this chapter uses this reversal, in conjunction with the strategies of unearthing binary oppositions and of highlighting the role of the unconscious in social life, as an introduction to the 'structuralist' thought which informs many heretical attacks upon the orthodoxy. Two of these strategies—that of reversal and the search for binary oppositions—were encountered in the previous chapter and the discussion will not be repeated in any depth here. The current approach is more general and, while particular instances in which heretics have invoked these strategies will be commented upon in passing, the strategies are examined as abstract types rather than specific tokens. This will hopefully elucidate both the promise and problems of a general structuralist approach to explaining and understanding social life and highlight the method—if there is a single method—which it embodies. The conclusion of section I is that heretics' deployment of particular structuralist strategies is rarely fatally flawed, although they do face some nagging problems. These difficulties are not such as to make the approach untenable. When sympathetically and non-dogmatically developed, structuralism at least highlights all the crucial questions that need be raised in the effort to understand and explain most aspects of social life. Furthermore, heretical laxity in evaluating the arguments against structuralism should not blind us to this.

For those who regard themselves as at the forefront of intellectual fashion, this concern with structuralism will seem *passé* and, in a sense, it is. Fashions have now moved on and some heretics have been keen to move with them. In this kind of world, the substance of the arguments against any particular position, structuralism included, are often given short shrift; in section III of this chapter those arguments are taken seriously. If doing that is *passé*, then we are guilty as charged. The closing part of section II notes, in passing, some arguments which those heretics initially enamoured of structuralism subsequently employed to refute it. The argument of section III is that heretics overestimate the power of these supposed objections.

[4] M. Foucault, 'Two Lectures' in C. Gordon (ed.), *Power/Knowledge: Selected Interviews and Other Writings 1972–1977* (Brighton, Harvester 1980), p. 98.

Like a jilted lover, structuralism finds itself discarded for apparently specious and half-articulated reasons. This simultaneously overhasty and overly dismissive approach to the problems of structuralism has the additional baleful consequence of tempting some heretics into an ill-judged theoretical and methodological agnosticism. The remainder of the section analyses that agnosticism and finds it wanting.

Section II is the filling in our structuralist sandwich. It begins with the discussion of yet another 'ism'—methodological eclecticism. Much heretical work flirts with this position but section II considers only Duncan Kennedy's contribution. The argument is that the reasons behind Kennedy's eclecticism actually support the methodological position outlined in chapter 3 and labelled compatibilism. The actual reasons Kennedy invokes to support eclecticism are, as will be seen, woefully weak. The section then actually takes Kennedy, along with Roberto Unger, as an exponent of compatibilism. It argues that, while they face some difficulties and risks, their conception of method for understanding and explaining social life is essentially sound. This, of course, raises again the question of what, if anything, distinguishes orthodoxy from heresy and it might be concluded that, methodologically at least, there is no great divide. This is only partially correct, though, since a group of heretics—the methodological agnostics discussed in section III—apparently regard 'method-talk' as unnecessary and irrelevant. Although this position does indeed promise a clear distinction between orthodoxy and heresy on matters of method, it is found wanting. More precisely, section III argues that this agnosticism issues from the chronic exaggeration of some tenets of post-structuralist thought.

I STRUCTURALISM

A complete answer to the question 'What is structuralism?' is not possible within the confines of this book, nor would a single volume devoted solely to this question do it justice.[5] For present purposes a more reductive, but hopefully not overly misleading approach is taken. The question can be answered by generalising some of the claims made in one author's work, that of the anthropologist Claude Levi-Strauss. This procedure is not based upon the contentious view that all aspects of Levi-Strauss's work represent

[5] Of the many general surveys of structuralist thought in the human sciences, some of the most useful are: P. Caws, *Structuralism: The Art of the Intelligible* (New Jersey, Humanities Press 1988); P. Pettit, *The Concept of Structuralism* (Dublin, Gill and Macmillan 1975); J. Sturrock, *Structuralism* (London, Fontana 2nd ed. 1993); J. Sturrock (ed.), *Structuralism and Since* (Oxford, Oxford University Press 1979); and A. Giddens, *Central Problems in Social Theory* (London, Macmillan 1979), chs. 1 and 2.

and exhaust the range of structuralist thought. Rather, it arises from the claim, unsupported herein, that three strategies constantly invoked by Levi-Strauss are the fulcrum of almost all subsequent structuralist thought, be it in the realm of literature, history, politics or sociology. Two of these three strategies are already familiar, since they concern the attempt to displace or de-centre the subject which is the thrust of much of Pierre Schlag's work and the search for binary oppositions characteristic of much of Kennedy's work. The third strategy consists of positing a large role for the unconscious in social reality, either as a general explanatory tool or as a means of impairing participants' understanding of social life and its constitutive practices, institutions and structures. This strategy usually figures only obliquely in heretical work, developed on the tails of the ideology critique. Hence, there are few general discussions of the nature and role of the unconscious in heretical thought but many assertions that judges and others are blind as to the nature or consequences of their position and actions. Although often closely connected, these three strategies will be examined separately and in the order just stated. Attention then turns to the advantages of structuralism as a method for understanding and explaining social life.

The deaths of both author and agent were presaged in Levi-Strauss's work by his entirely understandable preoccupation with the structures of myth, art and kinship in which those he studied lived.[6] Levi-Strauss was concerned to unearth the logical form of these structures and during this task he relied little on the views of those who lived within them. The emphasis is predictable, and not uniquely 'structuralist', because anthropology rarely concerns itself with individual agents.[7] Anthropologists purport to understand other societies, not just other agents, and regard the viewpoint of the individual as rarely appropriate. However, this should not be taken as a denial of the importance of the individual agent for, as Levi-Strauss said,

> [u]tterance is a function confined to subjects, and every myth, . . . must have its origin in an individual act of creation. This is no doubt very true, but in order to achieve the status of myth, the created work must cease precisely to remain individual and, in the process of generalization, must lose . . . those factors determined

[6] The notion of 'structure' is meant simply to refer to either explicit or implicit systematicity in the practice, institution or set of beliefs in question. This vague specification is a consequence of the fact that within structuralism the idea is rarely explicitly analysed and is employed in competing ways. For not completely successful efforts at clarification, see R. Boudon, *The Uses of Structuralism* (London, Heinemann 1971) and the response of C. Levi-Strauss to critics of his usage in *Structural Anthropology* (London, The Penguin Press 1968), chs. V and XV.

[7] The point is well noted by Sturrock, *Structuralism*, *supra*, note 5, p. 41, quoting A. R. Radcliffe-Brown, *Structure and Function in Primitive Society* (London, Cohen and West 1952), p. 190 (a distinctly 'structuralist' claim that anthropologists should concentrate upon structure and not individuals, made by a non-structuralist).

by probability ['chance' or 'contingency' might be a more appropriate translation] with which it was infused at the outset, and which could be attributed to the particular author's temperament, talent, imagination, and personal experiences.[8]

Hence we have a setting aside of the individual agent for the purposes of anthropological inquiry, although the individual is accepted as the origin of that which the anthropologist studies. Levi-Strauss's concern is principally with other societies' *systems* of art, kinship or myth and not with the meaning attributed to these systems by the participants. He charted the internal oppositions and similarities within and between these systems elucidating the moves and variations possible within them. True, individual agents act within and may even change those systems, and it is only through the actions and language of individuals that access to such systems of myth or kinship can be gained. But the systems themselves can subsequently be studied without any attention to participants' views.

In the hands of subsequent structuralist thinkers, Levi-Strauss's 'bracketing' of the individual is transformed. It changes from a methodological, discipline-specific setting aside, to a rumbling discontent with the underanalysed, taken-for-granted nature of our thought about the individual agent and consciousness. Structuralists after Levi-Strauss worried that standard philosophical and common-sense views regarded the agent as unproblematic, assumed consciousness was transparent to itself and took our knowledge of it to be virtually unimpeachable. By contrast,

[i]nstead of taking consciousness as a given, . . . [the structuralist approach] stresses the need for a genetic account of its production; consciousness is not regarded as a unitary or indivisible substance, but as a set of fractured and fragile processes; and the constitution of the 'I' is acknowledged to come about only through the 'discourse of the Other', that is, through signification.[9]

The approach questions our views about the agent and places our thought about our selves in a historical and cultural context rather than the philosopher's social vacuum. A history or genealogy of our thinking about the self, of ways in which it has changed and been determined, is an entirely laudable endeavour.

If orthodox legal thought is wedded to a conception of the self taken to be unproblematic and natural, then it is rightly open to the structuralist critique. This is the thrust of the work of Schlag and, before him, Thomas Heller. Remember that our criticism of Schlag was not aimed at his participation in this enterprise but at the manner of its execution. He is unclear about the nature of his task and, when taken as a genealogy of the autonomous legal self, his work is poor fare. This judgement holds, too, when

8 C. Levi-Strauss, *The Naked Man* (London, Cape 1981), p. 626.
9 Giddens, *supra*, note 5, p. 38.

Schlag's work is regarded either as an alternative to the autonomous legal self or as a moral and political critique thereof. Heller's account of the self is obviously and directly structuralist, giving an account of the agent 'as a product of culture, an identity created in language, a potentiality limited by the language that defined the conventions of a world'.[10] He attacks American law, in a refrain similar to many of Schlag's, because it embodies 'the existentially free subject . . . a being conscious of its autonomously selected normative principles and adept at the employ of instrumental reason in carrying out projects oriented to these norms'.[11] Structuralism, according to Heller, shows this account of the agent is false. Now, there is nothing wrong in principle with working towards a 'genetic account' of the production of consciousness, nor is it folly to excavate the assumptions and highlight the blindspots that surround any such existing account. In so far as this constitutes the structuralist account of the self, it is unobjectionable. The problems arise from a common two-fold exaggeration. First, the reversal is exaggerated, so that structuralism is deflected from developing a genetic account of the self and into empty sloganeering about the death of the author, agent or subject. Or, second, the determination of the self by social structures, institutions and practices is overstated, becoming the opposite of the alleged complete determination, beloved by non-structuralists, of structures, institutions and practices by autonomous agents.

Turning the de-centring of the subject into the death of the subject—maintaining, for example, as Schlag occasionally does, that the subject 'is a fiction'[12]—risks refuting structuralism itself. For, structures must have some 'thing' on which to operate, some 'thing' that they determine. If the self is dead, then it is an unlikely candidate even for the role of epiphenomenon of structures, unless conceived as the inanimate waste product of structures, churned out like smoke from chimneys. Moreover, such an inanimate side-effect can hardly function in the way selves are required to by structuralism, that is, as something more than the purely passive instantiations of structures. Think, for example, of the Saussurian account of language and its division between *langue* and *parole*.[13] The former is the language system, envisaged at a particular moment in time, with its range of grammatical and constitutive rules. The latter consists of the range of discrete everyday linguistic events, conducted by agents and made possible by, and in a sense taking place within, the language system. One or other point in this polarity cannot simply be abolished or declared dead without thereby robbing the other of meaning. They make sense only by reference to one another.

[10] T. Heller, 'Structuralism and Critique' (1984) 36 *Stanford L. R.* 127–198, p. 140.

[11] *Ibid.*, p. 175.

[12] P. Schlag, 'Fish v. Zapp: The Case of the Relatively Autonomous Self' (1987) 76 *Georgetown L. R.* 37–58, p. 51.

[13] F. de Saussure, *Course in General Linguistics* (London, Duckworth 1983), pp. 13–20.

Parole is an instantiation of *langue* and yet, without *parole*—without the possibility of discrete linguistic events—*langue* would be unintelligible: the idea of a language without speakers is senseless. The same is true of agents and structures. One cannot be abolished without making the other meaningless. Just as structures assume agents as the focus of their power, so, too, do agents assume structures. Agents are in fact the carriers of structures: without linguistic and other social structures agency would not be possible. If, as it seems, agency is indeed possible, then inter-subjective structures and conventions of some kind must exist. The notions of agent and structure, just like those of *langue* and *parole*, contain within themselves the kernel of their supposed opposites.[14]

This argument also shows why it is a mistake simply to substitute agent determination of structures with the structural determination of agency. If agency and structure, like *langue* and *parole*, require one another in order to make sense, then one cannot completely determine the other. Heller's otherwise excellent discussion is marred by occasional lapses suggesting that structuralism replaces a form of one-way determination with another. His (over)statement that '[t]he expressed behaviour of the subject, including his or her self-consciousness, is *determined* by the structural laws of, for example, semiotics, psychoanalysis, or historical materialism . . .' and that 'structuralist theory . . . assert[s] . . . the *primacy* of structural determination . . .' suggest this much.[15] In addition, this move suffers from one of the defects of the non-structuralist determination. For, if one of the problems with the latter was the very idea of *complete* determination of structures by agents, then the affirmation of the *complete* determination of agency by structure courts exactly the same snag. Of course, it is not clear beyond doubt that structuralists object to both complete determination and the direction of determination, or simply just the latter. Nevertheless, if hints and matters of 'tone' can stand in lieu of argument, it seems that the former is the better view.[16]

The elucidation of binary oppositions is an important feature of Levi-Strauss's work.[17] Having immersed himself, either directly or through the fieldwork of others, in the culture and beliefs of a diverse range of groups, he proceeds to unearth the oppositions underpinning their kinship, totemic

[14] The point 'is a crashing truism, but the fog emanating from Paris in recent decades makes it necessary to clutch it as a beacon in the darkness': C. Taylor, 'Foucault on Freedom and Truth' in D. Hoy (ed.), *Foucault: A Critical Reader* (Oxford, Basil Blackwell 1986), p. 90.

[15] *Supra*, note 10, p. 150; emphasis supplied. When writing as a 'post-structuralist', Heller is keen to avoid the death or complete determination of the agent: *ibid.*, p. 183.

[16] See the sources cited in notes 1 and 2, *supra*. Particularly noteworthy is Levi-Strauss's gloss on the 'dissolution of man' claim, pp. 247–248.

[17] See C. Levi-Strauss, *Tristes Tropiques* (London, Cape 1973), ch. 20; *The Savage Mind* (London, Weidenfeld and Nicolson 1972), chs 2, 3 and 4 (on which D. Kennedy often relies: 'A Semiotics of Legal Argument' (1991) 42 *Syracuse L. R.* 75–116, pp. 112–116); and *Structural Anthropology*, *supra*, note 6, ch. XI (hereinafter referred to as '*SA*' in both text and notes).

and other systems of categorisation. The idea of 'unearthing' is appropriate, for Levi-Strauss holds that these fundamental binaries usually lie beyond the consciousness of those whose beliefs and culture they support. The role of the unconscious in Levi-Strauss's work in particular, and in structuralism in general, will be discussed in due course. For now, note how distant the results of his excavations frequently are from the understandings of those whose cultures he studies. Although the starting point of his work is and must be an understanding, from the insider's point of view, of the language, culture and beliefs of a particular group, this is left a long way behind by Levi-Strauss's explanatory arguments. Indeed, the distance between the two is such as to lead to the well-founded criticism that he distorts the beliefs and practices he seeks to explain and understand, that his work is as a result altogether too reductive. The most succinct version of this objection belongs to Pierre Bourdieu, formulated in his discussion of Levi-Strauss's criticism of Marcel Mauss's work on the practice of gift-giving. Bourdieu shows that Levi-Strauss's effort to subject the practice to an explanatory system of mechanical laws of reciprocity, these laws being independent of the views of the participants within the practice, served to obscure the contingency of the practice, the tentative nature of the moves within it and the always present possibility of failure. According to Bourdieu, a consequence of this is that Levi-Strauss cannot distinguish between genuine instances of gift-giving and examples of swapping or loaning property.[18]

Now it is true that gift-giving is not an arena in which Levi-Strauss unearths many binary oppositions, but Bourdieu's point can be generalised. It highlights the almost ever present tension between respect for the participant's point of view, on the one hand, and the imperatives of one's explanatory theory, on the other. In Levi-Strauss's work this tension is almost always resolved, with no or little supporting argument, in favour of the latter, in favour of an explanatory scheme that gives pride of place to that which is beyond consciousness.[19] The fact that the binary oppositions unearthed, or the account of gift-giving he offers, are completely unrelated to the understandings of those whose societies are discussed, is therefore of little concern. By contrast, the methodological compatibilist sees a grave problem here, over and beyond the specific risk of distortion identified by Bourdieu. It is the failure to justify the move beyond the participant's point of view. Levi-Strauss does not think it necessary to show when and why this step is appropriate, yet the compatibilist insists upon exactly that. Compatibilists do not, remember, affirm that participants' views are incorrigible. Therefore, it is not the distance between Levi-Strauss's binaries and his

[18] P. Bourdieu, *Outline of a Theory of Practice* (Cambridge, C. U. P. 1977), pp. 4–7. See also Giddens, *supra*, note 5, pp. 25–26.

[19] See, for example, *SA*, pp. 281–282.

general accounts of kinship and totemism, on the one hand, and participants' understandings of these matters, on the other, that in and of itself troubles the compatibilist. Rather, it is the failure to address the gap, to explain why it is necessary to go beyond the internal point of view. Compatibilists, too, go beyond the internal point of view, but in holding that a justification for this step is necessary, they ensure a degree of integration between 'interpretative' and 'explanatory' aspects of their method and generate an account of when each is appropriate. The closest thing to an argument on this issue that could be found in Levi-Strauss's work would be the brooding presence of the unconscious: if it is half as important as he thinks, then it is perhaps understandable why he does not tarry long with participants' conscious views. To understand, of course, is not to excuse.

Some heretical exponents of 'the method of contradiction' might be open to the objection just levelled against Levi-Strauss, but Kennedy is not.[20] The reason is that much of Kennedy's unearthing of binaries, specifically those legal doctrinal oppositions or contradictions contained in 'argument bites' and 'nesting', is well-founded in the practice under discussion.[21] The practice is that of making and justifying legal doctrinal choices and, although participants rarely use Kennedy's language, the binaries he discovers arise from tensions in the practice of which participants are aware. Few if any participants in this practice, be they judges, practitioners, academics or students, would suggest that legal doctrinal choices are always completely compelled. Very many have an experience Kennedy and other heretics often ascribe to them, namely, of the law being fluid and malleable. Almost all will have had the experience of a legal position being arguable 'either way'. Legal doctrinal binaries are introduced by Kennedy as an attempt to make sense of this feature of the practice. They are deployed because participants and other theorists have as yet not adequately explained or understood it. Like Levi-Strauss, then, Kennedy's doctrinal binaries are based upon, but do not reproduce, the language, evaluations and understandings of participants in the practice. However, unlike Levi-Strauss, Kennedy offers some argument as to why participants' views cannot be conclusive. Furthermore, whereas for Levi-Strauss participants' views seem to be a formality that must be observed and then subsequently ignored or forgotten, rather in the way hungry atheists look upon grace before dinner, for Kennedy such views are both starting point and fulcrum. They set the contours of the enquiry, determining the need for and nature of explanation.

The problems Kennedy faces in the search for binaries arise almost

[20] The phrase is Kennedy's: 'Form and Substance in Private Law Adjudication' (1976) 89 *Harvard L. R.* 1685–1778, p. 1712.

[21] For sustained analysis of these notions see 'A Semiotics of Legal Argument' *supra*, note 17. Further discussion appears in *A Critique of Adjudication* (Cambridge, Mass., Harvard U. P. 1997), ch. 6.

entirely from, first, his claim to have unearthed one or other fundamental contradiction and, second, from the supposed link between fundamental contradictions, on the one hand, and doctrinal contradictions, on the other. These problems were tackled in the previous chapter and there is no need to repeat the argument here, save to note that Kennedy's difficulties would be reduced, although not entirely removed, were he to renounce the fundamental contradiction altogether. So doing would rid him of the apparently insurmountable problem of plausibly connecting fundamental and doctrinal contradictions. Convenient, then, that he has done just this. For, although a version of the fundamental contradiction informed almost all of Kennedy's early scholarship, he wrote, in 1984, that 'I renounce the fundamental contradiction . . . I recant it, and I also recant the whole idea of individualism and altruism'.[22] It would be hasty, however, to say this solves Kennedy's problems since a number of points suggest that bidding farewell to the fundamental contradiction is easier said than done. First, despite the language already quoted, Kennedy continues his 'retraction' by issuing both a warning against infatuations with slogans—'I really see the fundamental contradiction these days as a lifeless slogan that people can latch onto in completely good faith. No—in bad faith, but spontaneously trying to make things happen . . . and sort of think, well, the theory of Critical Legal Studies is somehow encapsulated in these phrases'—and an affirmation of the value of the idea: it is a 'substantive truth'.[23] That clearly does not bespeak an unqualified retraction.

Second, the retraction also looks dubious in light of Kennedy's inability to avoid the fundamental contradiction in subsequent work. It resurfaced, albeit obliquely, almost a decade after the retraction and then reappeared quite explicitly in 1997, looking as though it had never left the scene.[24] Third, even if this was an unambiguous retraction, it could not be taken to bind those writing under the influence of Kennedy's early work. Whatever Kennedy's status among heretics may be (one suspects the response to the retraction was similar to that of the masses when Brian claimed he was not the messiah: 'yes, messiah'[25]), he cannot speak for those who have thought the fundamental contradiction helpful. And it has indeed been thought so, having been used in accounts of tort, contract and the nature of public law and bureaucracy.[26] Finally, subsequent thinkers cannot, if they are to think

[22] D. Kennedy and P. Gabel, 'Roll Over Beethoven' (1984) 36 *Stanford L. R.* 1–55, p. 15.

[23] *Ibid.*, at pp. 16 and 17.

[24] See D. Kennedy, *Sexy Dressing Etc.* (Cambridge, Mass., Harvard U. P. 1993) at pp. viii and 70; *A Critique of Adjudication*, *supra*, note 21, at *inter alia* pp. 83, 95, 151–152 and 207.

[25] This, of course, is one of many brilliant moments in the film *Monty Python's Life of Brian* (1979).

[26] See C. Dalton, 'An Essay in the Deconstruction of Contract Doctrine' (1985) 94 *Yale L. J.* 997–1114; G. Frug, 'The Ideology of Bureaucracy in American Law' (1984) 84 *Harvard L. R.* 1276–1388 and A. Hutchinson, 'Of Kings and Dirty Rascals: The Struggle for Democracy' (1984) 9 *Queen's L. J.* 273–292.

freely, ascribe incorrigibility to the works of any previous scholar. So, just as those writing under the influence of Kennedy's early work ought not to take its arguments and ideas as beyond question—a tendency the tenor of Kennedy's retraction suggests he was worried about—so they ought not to regard his assessment of those ideas and arguments as incorrigible. For these reasons, then, 'the retraction' is a red herring. Provided one or other version of the fundamental contradiction, and a connection between it and doctrine, is still asserted by Kennedy, he faces a range of well-documented problems. And, while these problems are not the same as those that beset Levi-Strauss's search for binaries, they must be addressed.

What, then, of the unconscious? It is undeniably important in structuralist thought although there is doubt as to what exactly is meant by the notion. There are at least two, not necessarily connected senses in which the idea can be used. Both appear within structuralist thought, a likely explanation being that the use of either supposedly serves to distinguish structuralism from phenomenology, an intellectual predecessor and rival.[27] While there is some sense in the deployment of the two meanings of 'unconscious', the failure to distinguish them clearly is inexcusable. The first sense, in which the portentous locutions 'The Unconscious' and 'the unconscious mind' are appropriate, refers to a component of the mind, much discussed by Sigmund Freud but subsequently reformulated by him as a dimension of both id and ego. The second sense is simply a synonym for lack of awareness, highlighting a cognitive glitch or gap; the unconscious here is not a facet of mind but simply a statement about the existence or non-existence of particular beliefs. Freud called this unconsciousness in the descriptive sense.[28] While this second sense can often be a consequence of the first, this is not necessarily so; similarly, the second need not imply the first. Nor does the second sense carry the range of apparently unsustainable commitments the first has, although it is a mistake to assume that the second sense has no demanding epistemological and other commitments of its own. Although Freud invoked both senses of unconsciousness, the first is hereinafter dubbed the Freudian sense.

Levi-Strauss also invokes both senses. For example, when he says that '[k]inship systems . . . are built by the mind on the level of unconscious thought', he seems to be invoking the Freudian sense.[29] Moreover, Freud's work had a considerable influence on Levi-Strauss, appearing in his

[27] See Sturrock, *Structuralism*, *supra*, note 5, pp. 34–37 and Pettit, *supra*, note 5, pp. 68–69.

[28] For good introductions to Freud's discussion of the unconscious, in particular, and to the Freudian corpus in general (which is difficult to negotiate), see H. Ellenberger, *The Discovery of the Unconscious* (New York, Basic Books 1970), ch. 7; M. Macmillan, *Freud Evaluated* (Cambridge, Mass., M. I. T. Press 1997), ch. 13 and S. Gardner, 'The Unconscious' in J. Neu (ed.), *The Cambridge Companion to Freud* (Cambridge, C. U. P. 1991).

[29] *SA*, p. 34.

analyses of kinship, totemism and shamanism.[30] In discussion of the latter, the unconscious in something like the Freudian sense carries a great deal of explanatory weight, being 'reducible to . . . the symbolic function . . . which is carried out according to the same laws among all men, and actually corresponds to the aggregate of these laws'.[31] The unconscious serves to structure experience, 'imposing structural laws upon inarticulated elements which originate elsewhere—impulses, emotions, representations, and memories'; furthermore, these laws 'are the same for all individuals and in all instances where the unconscious pursues its activity'.[32] Yet, on many other occasions, the unconscious is simply a matter of unawareness, a cognitive problem. When Levi-Strauss notes that the anthropologist must often construct 'unconscious' models to understand a culture, that process is defined as building 'from phenomena the systematic character of which has evoked *no awareness* on the part of the culture'.[33] This is the unconscious as that of which one (or 'the culture') is unaware and is of a piece with Levi-Strauss's warning that '[t]he sociological representations of the natives are not merely a part or reflection of their social organisation. The natives may, just as in more advanced societies, be *unaware* of certain elements of it, or contradict it completely'.[34]

There are at least two difficulties with Levi-Strauss's particular invocation of the unconscious that are mirrored in structuralism as a whole. The first is that the Freudian sense of the notion is simply unreflectively and uncritically employed. While it is true that Freud's reputation may have been better in Levi-Strauss's day than it is now, having been tarnished by a number of revelations and critical analyses, that still cannot justify the uncritical deployment of parts of his work.[35] And, when critically considered, it seems that the notion of the unconscious and the explanatory role it is supposed to play is seriously flawed. That is not to say the notion cannot in principle be revived and its explanatory power harnessed; rather, the objection is that there is no general argument in Levi-Strauss to show that the notion has even prima facie plausibility. It is simply invoked to support some of his claims in the hope that this is a powerful and not merely *ad hoc* argumentative move. More pressing is the problem that Levi-Strauss and other structuralists obliterate a vital distinction when invoking both senses

[30] Moreover, chapter 6 of *Tristes Tropiques*, *supra*, note 17, sees Levi-Strauss explicitly acknowledging that Freud was one of his principal intellectual influences. For a somewhat laboured and not particularly persuasive argument demonstrating Freud's all-pervasive influence on Levi-Strauss, see T. Shalvey, *Claude Levi-Strauss, Social Psychotherapy and the Collective Unconscious* (Hassocks, The Harvester Press (no publication date stated)), chs 1–3.

[31] *SA*, p. 203. [32] *Ibid.*

[33] *SA*, pp. 281–282 (emphasis supplied).

[34] *Ibid.*, pp. 130–131 (emphasis supplied).

[35] For instances of the two sides in the contemporary debate about Freud's work see: R. Webster, *Why Freud Was Wrong* (London, Fontana 1996) and J. Forrester, *Dispatches from the Freud Wars* (Cambridge, Mass., Harvard U. P. 1997).

of the unconscious. Both senses, that is, seemingly assume that agents are either conscious of, for example, systems of kinship or myth, and therefore can articulate the rules of those systems, or they are not, in which case they cannot articulate the rules of the system. What is doubtful here, though, is the 'therefore', the claim that for X to be conscious of y, X must 'therefore' be able to articulate the nature of y or the rules for its use. If X cannot do this, she cannot, on Levi-Strauss's view, be conscious of y. Anthony Giddens is surely right, however, to note a *via media* here which makes it possible and plausible to say that X is conscious of y (for example, the grammar rules of a particular language), even though she cannot articulate the rules constitutive of y or that determine the use of y.[36] Yet it is likely that X uses those very rules each and every time that X uses language. Giddens labels the latter 'practical consciousness' and the former—the only kind of consciousness Levi-Strauss is conscious of—'discursive consciousness'. Now, Levi-Strauss's structuralism could be amended to accommodate practical consciousness, but so doing would require an altogether more refined account of the unconscious. As articulated by Levi-Strauss in particular, and by structuralists in general, the notion has a procrustean and reductive role.

In so far as heretics invoke the kind of account of the unconscious employed by Levi-Strauss, and do so without argument and without appreciation of its reductive nature, they are courting trouble. Fortunately, few do so. Most heretics avoid the Freudian sense altogether, invoking instead the second sense and appending it to some version or other of the ideology critique.[37] This is the usual way in which the notion is invoked by, for example, Heller and Peter Gabel. For Heller, structuralism entails the reinterpretation of self-consciousness, highlighting the determinants of behaviour of which agents are unaware. As a result, '[t]he subject is denaturalized because it recognizes its own mediation through structure. It rejects the sense that it has an ontologically given existence, perceiving itself instead as a social artefact'.[38] Hence, what agents were unaware of—their determination or mediation through culture—they now see clearly. Similarly, and despite a few hints that he is flirting with the Freudian unconscious, Gabel equates the unconscious with that of which agents are unaware. Agents are in the grip of false consciousness or ideology because, *inter alia*, they take the social to be natural; they are aided in this by current systems of thought,

[36] *Supra*, note 5, pp. 24–25.

[37] The Freudian account has recently been superseded or supplemented within the legal academy by scholars enamoured of the work of Jacques Lacan (see, for example, many of the essays in P. Goodrich and D. Carlson (eds.), *Law and the Postmodern Mind* (Ann Arbor, University of Michigan Press 1998)) and those at the margins of the heresy (see P. Goodrich, *Oedipus Lex: Psychoanalysis, History, Law* (Berkeley, University of California Press 1995)). The two groups are not, of course, mutually exclusive.

[38] *Supra*, note 10, p. 148.

including law, which constrain and distort their awareness of social reality. Hence, '[l]egal reasoning is an inherently repressive form of interpretative thought which *limits* our comprehension of the social world and its possibilities'.[39] Used in this sense, the notion of unconsciousness stands or falls with the account of ideology to which it is attached. And ideology, remember, is not a particularly problematic notion, except in the ways discussed in the previous chapter. Thus heretics' invocation of the unconscious is clearer and less problematic than that of Levi-Strauss and much of the other structuralist work they draw upon for inspiration.

Yet there is a noteworthy exception. Kennedy seemingly charts a position on the unconscious that goes beyond the straightforward illustration of blind-spots in our pictures of the social world and avoids the problematic Freudian sense of the unconscious. How? His account is based upon the notion of denial, understood as a situation in which two conditions are satisfied. First, an agent must misrepresent 'her own desire, emotion, opinion or intention or . . . important external facts about her situation, . . . in the special sense of a "refusal to acknowledge"' (*CA*, p. 193).[40] Secondly, the misrepresentation is neither conventional, 'as when you ask the terminally ill patient, "how are you?" and he responds, "I'm fine, how are you?"' (*ibid.*), nor 'a conscious, deliberate, strategic misrepresentation, . . . a lie designed to deceive its audience without the speaker having any belief at all in its truth' (*ibid.*), nor 'a cognitive glitch or random error'(*ibid.*). When these conditions are satisfied, Kennedy believes it is 'common practice to look for a "psychological" explanation, by which I mean an explanation that attributes the persistence of the misrepresentation to the needs or desires of the speaker' (*ibid.*). The need, in the case of judges, is to rid themselves of the anxiety caused by role conflict. The conflict results from the requirements that judges administer '"justice under law" . . . [on the one hand] and the categorical exclusion of the "personal", in the sense of the ideological, from the decision process [on the other]' (*CA*, p. 203). The argumentative burden of Kennedy's recent work is to show that judges cannot satisfy the first requirement without infringing the second prohibition. Whether or not this is indeed an accurate account of the judicial role is a moot point, but it need not be debated to understand Kennedy's account of denial. What judges deny, what they suppress, is that they

[39] P. Gabel, 'Reification in Legal Reasoning' (1980) 3 *Research in Law and Sociology* (S. Spitzer, ed.), 25–51, p. 25 (emphasis supplied). See also his 'Intention and Structure in Contractual Conditions: An Outline of a Method for Critical Legal Theory' (1977) 61 *Minnesota L. R.* 601–643. It is the latter that contains Gabel's flirtation with the Freudian sense of the unconscious: p. 606, fn. 4. However, while so flirting he simultaneously invokes the secondary sense of unconscious: see pp. 605, 606 (both fn. 4) and 615, fn. 23.

[40] This abbreviation, a reference to Kennedy's *A Critique of Adjudication*, *supra*, note 21, is used hereinafter in both text and notes.

routinely decide cases—indeed, on one version of Kennedy's argument, *must* decide cases—on the basis of ideology.

Denial is more than simple unawareness, on this account, since judges do indeed see the role conflict yet suppress it. Suppression is necessary because the systematic betrayal of a role requirement is extremely disturbing. Nor is it possible, says Kennedy, for judges simply to affirm the role conflict and decide cases candidly, since their denial is reinforced by the wider society (*CA*, pp. 205–212). Denial is not a product of the deeper forces of 'the unconscious' operating completely independently of the ideas and beliefs of judges. There is nothing, says Kennedy, 'particularly "Freudian" about' (*CA*, p. 201) his account of denial. Nor is it the same as the Freudian notion of repression, in which what is repressed is entirely obliterated from consciousness (*CA*, p. 199). Denial is not unconscious in that sense, for Kennedy maintains that judges must use a great deal of energy to suppress what they know, namely, that ideology plays a role in their decision-making. Hence denial is better understood as 'motivated error or wishful thinking, [in which] there is some part of the psyche that registers the possibility of the unpleasant truth and then mobilizes to keep from knowing it' (*ibid.*). In order to capture this, Kennedy sometimes speaks of denial being 'half-conscious' (*CA*, p. 191).

Is this *via media* a success? One immediate point in reply is to take issue with the claim that denial is half-conscious. This is an unhelpful description, for what, exactly, is it to be half-conscious? It sounds initially like some sleep-like state or a state of automatism and that is surely an unsatisfactory way of characterising the suppression of disturbing information. Far more enlightening is Kennedy's claim that denial is 'motivated error'. This hints at the role denial plays in practical deliberation, at the ways in which it can make sense. For, if the information provided is very disturbing, then there might be good reason for ignoring it, on exactly the same grounds employed in choosing to avoid particularly disturbing images or other things we find offensive. Another partial analogy with 'motivated error' is the deliberate suppression of information when its quantity, rather than quality, is disturbing in the sense of impeding decision and action. We all accept that at some point, in relation to some course of action or decision, deliberation has to stop and a decision made or action taken. To that end, we often have reason to ignore information, and do so, for example, by means of time limits upon deliberation or guillotines upon discussion. With these instances of rational suppression or avoidance of information in mind, the analysis of denial as motivated error (or, better, suppression), is very helpful. Nevertheless, it raises an obvious question: is the information suppressed by the judicial denial that cases are decided on ideological grounds so disturbing and harmful?

This question must be answered thus: it depends what is meant by 'ideology'. While Kennedy's account of denial is unlike many heretical invocations of the unconscious, in the sense that denial is more than simple unawareness, it is like them in that it rests upon a version of the ideology critique. Thus his notion of denial, just like their accounts of unconsciousness, stands or falls according to the strength of the account of ideology that supports it. The previous chapter argued that Kennedy's account of ideology was redundant, since it highlights nothing that does not already have salience, nothing that we could not already talk about with clarity. Indeed, it was concluded that ideology in Kennedy's non-critical sense referred to little more than value-systems, and that the claim that judges decide cases by reference to values is not one the orthodox would contest. Rather, it is a claim they have often made, as have many judges. Thus, the information that judges in denial supposedly ignore or suppress is hardly worth suppressing. It is information—that adjudication is an unavoidably value-laden process—that few would think could be denied. Many accept it as true beyond reasonable doubt and, moreover, are not troubled by this. This, then, is the crucial difficulty with Kennedy's account of denial. The notion itself is not incoherent and it successfully negotiates a path between unconsciousness as simple unawareness and unconsciousness in the Freudian sense. Yet what Kennedy claims is denied is just not worth denying. Indeed, what he says is denied has often been affirmed.

It is clear, then, that Kennedy's *via media* is not a complete success. The structure of the argument is unproblematic, but the content is dubious. Having outlined a plausible argumentative path between the two senses of unconsciousness, he spoils the argument by basing denial upon a redundant account of ideology. This qualified and somewhat bland judgement—there is both good and bad in Kennedy's work—represents the overall tenor of the discussion in this section. It has been shown that there are some problems with the three strategies characteristic of structuralist thought, both 'at large' and as embodied in heretical scholarship. The problems are not, however, overwhelming. For example, the task of de-centring the self is not in principle a worthless endeavour; far from it. Some of the difficulties that surround the task are simply the product of exaggeration, while others relate only to particular efforts at 'de-centring'. Similarly, the problems with the search for binaries do not make that search incoherent, but concern very specific argumentative gaps in the work of Levi-Strauss and Kennedy. Nor is the notion of the unconscious incoherent, although, as just noted, particular accounts of it are problematic. Thus, since structuralism is far from an intellectual write-off, it is appropriate to specify what it entails, methodologically speaking, and thereby outline its limits and advantages.

Commendably, structuralism places the agent within structures—literary, economic, linguistic, kinship, myth and others—as both product and producer. That is to say, the agent is created by and to some extent creates those structures. This might seem contradictory but it need not be. Recall the discussion in chapter 3 of institutional schemata and the ways in which they limit agents' actions: they set down specific recipes for action within particular institutions or practices. Simple examples would be the rules of games or the conventions for withdrawing money from banks. I cannot do the latter simply by shouting to the teller from the back of the queue nor by mailing a scribbled note to my branch. I must proceed in specific ways, fill out particular forms and repeat particular codes. But these requirements can be changed as a result of agents' actions. I can now, for example, conduct all my banking affairs on the telephone without ever going to a branch and standing in the customary queue. Institutional schemata can of course change to prohibit rather than allow particular actions: the tackle from behind, for example, is now regarded as always being an instance of foul play within the rules of association football. This is yet another instance of the many examples of the rules that 'govern' or 'determine' agents being changed or even rejected by them. Since in structuralist hands 'structure' is particularly vague, it is not obviously incorrect to draw an analogy between that concept, on the one hand, and the compatibilist's notions of institutional schemata and social structure, on the other. If the analogy is appropriate, then both structuralist and compatibilist accounts of the relationship between agent and structure are in broad terms indistinguishable. Since we accept the compatibilist account of the agent/structure relationship, we cannot criticise the substance of the structuralist account. What can and must be criticised is structuralist self-publicity.

Take, as an example, the dissolution or death of the agent. We have already argued that, were this taken seriously, it would subvert some of the central ideas of structuralist accounts of language and make the notion of structure unfathomable. The substance of the structuralist account of language and structure forces the conclusion that agents cannot be completely dissolved, yet structuralism's publicity suggests just the contrary. Therefore it must, like all advertising, be set aside or taken with a pinch of salt. So doing allows us to see that this talk of the death or dissolution of the subject is but a hyperbolic description of a particularly interesting set of tasks, including the de-centring the subject, the construction of a genealogy of the subject or even of 'subjectivity' itself. Part of the burden of these tasks is the explication of the ways in which our conception of ourselves, as 'persons', 'individuals' or 'agents' has changed and perhaps been influenced by other social, cultural and economic forces. There is nothing in principle objectionable or incoherent in this. Indeed, in so far as non-structuralist thought has been blind to the value of these tasks, structuralism deserves our commendation for bringing it to 'consciousness'.

The advantages of structuralism noted so far—its appreciation of the complexities of the agency/structure relationship and the advancement of the genealogy of the self—are not outweighed by the clouds of hyperbole surrounding it. Yet the latter also surround and cast gloom over another of the advantages which structuralism shares with compatibilism. Structuralism asks all the questions that should be asked in the effort to explain and understand social action, practices and institutions, even though some of these questions are often hidden from view. It hints at but is also sometimes blind to the interplay between reason- and agent-based explanations and understandings, on the one hand, and explanations independent of agents and their reasons, on the other. Think, for example, of Levi-Strauss's fieldwork, his vast knowledge of the conventions and mores of a range of different communities. This is obviously the product of taking up the internal point of view, of learning the language of those whose community he seeks to understand, and of appreciating the significance they attribute to various activities and institutions. He must therefore take agents and their reasons seriously in order for his work to begin.

Yet this is the bulk of the iceberg, hidden beneath the surface of Levi-Strauss's efforts to find a pattern within the beliefs, practices and institutions with which he is concerned. In his efforts to elucidate such patterns or systems, he has no hesitation in departing from participants' views. Predictably, the bulk of the iceberg is often forgotten or knowledge of it suppressed. Talk of the unreliable nature of participants' views, combined with news of the death of the agent and exaggerations about the all-pervasive power of 'structures', undoubtedly contributes to this. More measured claims are, however, available in the core of structuralist thought, claims which hold that agents' views, or 'conscious models' are sometimes just as important to the anthropologist as 'unconscious models'.[41] Agents and their reasons cannot therefore be always and completely ignored. This sounds suspiciously like the compatibilist credo, but that should not cause embarrassment. Our sketch of the similarities between structuralism and compatibilism, which doubles as an elucidation of the advantages of the former, hardly traduces structuralism. For, having set aside hyperbole and error, there is indeed overlap between the two. Of course, it might be said that what has been regarded as hyperbole here is in fact the fulcrum of structuralism, but this could only be established by playing scrupulous attention to that body of thought. Since that is what this section has endeavoured to do, its conclusions should not be flippantly dismissed. The conclusion our analysis yields is that structuralism's virtues derive almost entirely from its resemblance to compatibilism, while its vices are almost exclusively a result of hyperbole. While the tenor of structuralist discussions of method is quite different from compatibilism's inclusive emphasis, structuralism is almost

[41] *SA*, p. 282.

indistinguishable from compatibilism. Both employ the internal and external points of view, both accept that explanations and understandings of social life can be both cause-based and reason-based, although only compatibilism accepts that there is not a huge difference here since, in relation to human action, reasons can be causes. Some problems that supposedly undermine structuralism are discussed in section III but, for the moment, let us regard it as unproblematic and turn to two other heretical discussions of method.

II ECLECTICISM OR COMPATIBILISM?

The accounts of method analysed here are found in the work of Kennedy (again) and Roberto Unger. Both are compatibilists, the latter explicitly so, the former unwittingly. Indeed, some of Kennedy's remarks on method embody a position not far removed from compatibilism but pejoratively referred to as eclecticism hereinafter. This position is one that takes willy-nilly from other methods in the hope that a magpie-like collection of bits and pieces will add up to a single coherent method. A standard probability assessment would not show that this was impossible, but as an approach to methodological matters it seems altogether too contingent. Furthermore, were eclecticism advertised as being a matter of chance, it would be less objectionable. As things stand, though, this methodological position is often endorsed on the flimsiest grounds. That is the essential problem with eclecticism and Kennedy's work illustrates it vividly.

Kennedy's position is 'methodologically eclectic' because he has

> the conviction that each method . . . , and methodology in general, have been subjected to a critique that undermines any claim their practitioners might make to get at the truth of the objects they represent. So I don't believe that my object (adjudication) corresponds, in fact, only and truly, to a representation made in the 'correct' medium. It will transcend or surpass my representation, and indeed my understanding, no matter what method(s) I adopt . . . Nevertheless, I don't think the critique of methodology has come close to invalidating any of my own collection of methods in a way that would establish that what I do with them is necessarily a lie (*CA*, p. 15).

At first blush, this looks like a very bad argument to the effect that, since all methods have been discredited, the only option is to employ segments of each. Of course, even conceding the truth of the premise does not ensure that the conclusion follows. If all Xs (methods) are incorrect or false, then our conclusion must be, on the assumption that truth is a value worth tracking, that all Xs should be avoided. The opposite conclusion, namely, that all Xs—or segments thereof—must be pursued, could only be derived were a secondary premise added that was substantially more problematic than that which affirms truth to be a value. It is very difficult indeed to envisage a plausible suggestion to fill the gap between 'all Xs are false' and the conclusion 'pursue or invoke Xs', unless it were something like 'falsity is a value'. The problem here is that establishing this premise invokes some conception of truth, as well as a traditional set of philosophical paradoxes. Since there are independent arguments suggesting that truth is a value, or even a self-evident human good, the premise that truth is a value worth pursuing is better founded than that which would be required to support Kennedy's conclusion.[42]

If Kennedy is not making this bad argument, what is he affirming? He seems concerned with the notion of truth rather than method, his mistake being the assumption that attacks upon a particular account of truth discredit each and every method in the human sciences. Kennedy's remarks about 'getting at the truth' and about objects 'corresponding' with representations, suggest that the conception of truth he takes to be under attack is the correspondence theory. That theory holds, *inter alia*, that 'x' is true if and only if there is some fact to which it corresponds, and Kennedy is right that this theory has attracted some criticism. Yet the correspondence theory is not unique in having problems—so, too, do the other standard philosophical accounts of truth.[43] These problems are not such as to make particular methods *a priori* impossible. Whether or not some particular method is a failure would depend, in this argumentative matrix, upon the plausibility of the theory of truth it employs. Since particular methods can usually pick and choose between available theories of truth, and since there are as yet no compelling arguments to discredit whole classes of theory of truth, such that we could now say, for example, that there is no prospect of any defensible coherence theory of truth ever being developed, Kennedy's worry about truth is exaggerated. Of course, he is right in thinking that almost any method will at some point either make truth claims or provide protocols by which truth claims could be made. He is also right to be interested in what current theories of truth look like. Yet it is a mistake to think, prior to examining any particular method, that all methods are tied to one account of truth. If only things were that simple.

The source of this error might be Kennedy mistaking social theories—efforts at generalised explanations and understandings of aspects, or the whole range, of social life—for accounts of method. True, social theories of the kind mentioned by Kennedy—*inter alia*, 'neo-Marxism, Weberian

[42] An ambitious argument to show the value of truth is J. Finnis's 'Scepticism, Self-Refutation and the Good of Truth' in P. Hacker and J. Raz (eds.), *Law, Morality and Society* (Oxford, Clarendon 1977) and ch. III of his *Natural Law and Natural Rights* (Oxford, Clarendon 1980). For pragmatist doubts about the value of truth and its relationship to inquiry see R. Rorty, *Truth and Progress* (Cambridge, C. U. P. 1998), ch. 1.

[43] For good accounts see P. Horwich, *Truth* (Oxford, Basil Blackwell 1990) and J. Dancy, *Introduction to Contemporary Epistemology* (Oxford, Basil Blackwell 1985).

sociology, semiotics and structuralism, psychoanalysis, historicist narration' (*CA*, p. 15)—employ or develop a range of protocols specifying how theories should be constructed and what aspects of social life should be the focus of concern and why. Yet these distinctive theories do not, contrary to Kennedy's view, each employ a different method in order to generate their explanations and understandings. Rather, a number of them (neo-Marxism, structuralism and psychoanalysis) share a similar method, in the sense that they favour cause-based explanations over reasons-based understandings of social action, and endow 'structures'—economic, language, myth or whatever—with explanatory priority over 'agents'. Kennedy errs, then, in thinking that his account of adjudication is methodologically eclectic because it takes bits and pieces from these diverse social theories, since these do not themselves often employ different or incompatible methods. It would be more accurate to say that Kennedy's 'theory' was simply eclectic. His method, by contrast, is quite mundane, embodying many of the tenets of compatibilism.

Indeed, when the feeble reasons for Kennedy's eclecticism are set aside, it is easy to see that the appeal it has for him is but the appeal of compatibilism. That is, Kennedy sees that eclecticism allows the deployment of both reason-based, agent-relative and cause-based, structure-relative explanations and understandings, and these are not, as noted in chapter 3, ultimately incompatible. He deploys the internal point of view in the way compatibilism mandates, as the starting point for understanding the nature of rule-governed action, practices and institutions. So, for example, he takes up the internal point of view in order to understand what the participants in the practice 'adjudication' mean by 'policy'. It is, after all, the only way of understanding their language. For the purposes of this exercise, Kennedy becomes a 'participant observer' (*CA*, p. 97). In the effort to determine the role of ideology in adjudication, Kennedy 'attempt[s] to reconstruct the situation of the judge from the inside . . . asking how the judge experiences and responds to the body of legal materials when he has an ideological preference for a particular rule choice' (*CA*, p. 157). In addition, Kennedy takes up a view of adjudication independent of participants' views, a view he sometimes describes as 'structuralist' (*CA*, p. 133), sometimes as 'the external point of view' (*CA*, p. 134). However described, it is an approach to explaining and understanding actions, practices and institutions independent of the views of participants. Hence, it generates an account of 'ideological influence [upon judicial decisions] even in the absence of any showing of ideological preferences or intentions . . . in the person doing the argument' (*ibid.*). It is the viewpoint of '*informed observers*' (*ibid.*; emphasis in original) rather than *participant observers*.

Compatibilism provides no immutable rules as to when the internal and external points of view should be utilised by the theorist, save that the former is always necessary in order to understand the language of agents. Assuming it can never be wrong to understand the language of those whose actions, practices and institutions one seeks knowledge of, the internal point of view must be the theorist's starting point. The choice of particular protocols thereafter, and their role in the effort to explain and understand social life, is relatively unconstrained. However, one point at which resort to a causal or structural or external approach—one that is to some extent independent of the participants' viewpoint—becomes appropriate, is when doubts exist as to the accuracy of participants' accounts of their actions, practices or institutions. The reasons for doubt are not infinite. They involve considerations such as the degree of coherence or dissonance between participants' views, the internal coherence of those views, the level of self-consciousness about the action, practice or institution, and the degree of fit between participants' practical theories and the secondary and tertiary levels of social-theoretic theory. In the course of moving beyond participants' views, theorists must offer arguments that privilege the viewpoint they adopt and articulate why these views should be ignored. This cannot be avoided, nor should theorists be squeamish about the task. Whether or not particular theorists offer good reasons why participants' views should be rejected is a matter that can only be determined on a case by case basis.

Routine resort to 'a hermeneutics of suspicion' (*CA*, p. 55), in which participants' views are automatically ignored, is justifiable only in light of some compelling general argument showing why these views are always badly wrong. Kennedy's observation that the hermeneutics of suspicion, 'or a search for the hidden ideological motives in judicial opinions that present themselves as technical, deductive . . . or neutral, has been for a hundred years the most important characteristic of American debates about adjudication' may be true (*CA*, *ibid.*). If so, the observation is also an indictment, in so far as theorists involved in this search have failed to give a general and compelling account—beyond the claim that they really know better—as to why participants' views as to the nature of the practice should be rejected *carte blanche*. One objectionable legacy and misinterpretation of American legal realism is that no argument need be articulated to this end. The realists had somewhere and somehow established, in general terms, that participants' views (non-realist judges, practitioners and theorists) about the practice of adjudication cannot ever be trusted. This is both objectionable, because no such plausible general argument was ever offered, and inaccurate, misrepresenting many realists' actual practice of doctrinal analysis and critique.[44] They analysed particular cases, took seriously

[44] There is no such general argument if we rule out as implausible Jerome Frank's flirtation with psychology and psychoanalysis in *Law and the Modern Mind* (New York, Brentano's

participants' (mainly judges) views as to what they were doing, and only then—and not always—concluded that those views were inadequate.[45] At that point, participants' views were departed from and an explanation or understanding developed that was independent of them. In jurisprudential language, this marks the move from the internal to the external point of view.

This approach is adopted by Kennedy who is now keen, despite some of the claims in his early work, to distance himself from general arguments such as, for example, the proof of an all embracing 'indeterminacy', which purport to show *a priori* that participants' views cannot be trusted. Hence, Kennedy's current critique of adjudication 'does *not* assert that judicial opinions never convince us that the result was legally compelled, or that law "by its nature" can never determine an outcome . . . or anything of the sort' (*CA*, p. 86; emphasis in the original). Rather, the theorist must examine particular cases and might as a result find reason to doubt participants' views. Two grounds can give rise to such doubt. First, on examining a particular instance of the practice, the theorist finds that 'a judge's explanation of his or her choice of an answer to a question of law doesn't work, in the very specific sense of failing to establish that the rule interpretation was required by the materials, or was the interpretation that fit them best' (*CA*, pp. 84–85). Or, secondly, judicial opinions of 'impeccable internal logic . . . don't confront obvious responses to their arguments' (*CA*, p. 89). In each case, the theorist has good reason to depart from the participant's view of the action and to construct a better account, one that seeks to explain these obvious weaknesses or problems. We need not worry here about the substance of such a 'better', external account of particular instances of the practice. Our point is simply to note the circumstances in which Kennedy thinks it appropriate to depart from the participant's viewpoint and how well this fits with compatibilism.

The picture is not entirely rosy. In particular, Kennedy's compatibilism faces three problems. The first is that the fulcrum of Kennedy's particular effort at understanding and explaining adjudication—the notion of ideology—is developed in such a way as to be trivial. Consequently, even though his account of adjudication correctly embraces the compatibilist method, one of its central explanatory concepts is rather flimsy. Since we have already established that Kennedy's account of ideology is weak, this

1931). For a fine treatment of the range of realist themes, which also confirms the absence of any such argument, see N. Duxbury, *Patterns of American Jurisprudence* (Oxford, Clarendon 1995), ch. 2.

[45] Three oft-cited instances are: K. Llewellyn, 'What Price Contract?—An Essay in Perspective' (1931) 40 *Yale L. J.* 704–751; R. Hale, 'Coercion and Distribution in a Supposedly Non-Coercive State' (1923) 38 *Political Science Quarterly* 470–494 and his 'Bargaining, Duress and Economic Liberty' (1943) 43 *Columbia L. R.* 603–628.

problem is not pursued further. The second problem is not particularly acute in the sense that it does not threaten the core of the argument. It is more a matter of oversight. Kennedy thinks there are two good arguments for taking up the external point of view in addition to those already noted, but he misunderstands their power. He takes up

> [t]he external point of view . . . [because] the modernist/postmodernist theoretical current . . . emphasises two things about language. First, there is a discontinuity between speaker and speech, so that opportunistic or strategic use of language is always a possibility. Second, speech is never fully controlled by the speaker (the speaker is in some sense spoken by his or her language), so that speech 'exceeds' the speaker, propagating meanings independently of 'original intent' (CA, p. 134).

Assuming, although it is doubtful, that these two points are indeed distinct, neither provides a good argument to justify the move from the internal to the external point of view. That is because, conceding the truth of both points, they are not claims about specific instances of language but about language *simpliciter*. Jacques Derrida's point that 'iterability alters'—the possibility of being able to repeat words beyond the initial context of utterance ensures that their meaning can be changed[46]—which Kennedy echoes in the claim that meanings can exceed speakers, and the putatively different point that strategic use of language is always a possibility, hold across the board. They hold for theorists' language when they give accounts of actions, practices or institutions from the external point of view, just as much as they hold of participants' accounts of those actions, practices and institutions. That being so, neither point can justify rejecting or moving from one language, that of the participants, to another, namely, that of the 'external' theorist or vice versa. No single language is ensnared by the iterability and strategic use problems to any greater degree than any other. Hence, to use Kennedy's argot, neither point justifies the switch from the view of *participant* observer to that of *informed* observer.

The third problem goes to the core of Kennedy's argument. It holds that, as a method for understanding and explaining social life, Kennedy's compatibilism has a remarkably confused and self-defeating conception of what it is to explain or understand (hereinafter we will speak only of 'explanation'). This weakness is revealed in Kennedy's response to a hypothetical objection. His account of adjudication holds that judges decide some cases in accordance with ideological considerations. This occurs in cases in which the legal materials do not compel a particular decision either way: the logic of the judgment is so flawed as to make this obvious, or the judgment is constructed in such a way as to ignore all or most of the counter-arguments.

[46] See 'Signature Event Context' in his *Margins of Philosophy* (London, Harvester Wheatsheaf 1982).

If judges decide these cases by reference to ideological considerations then, Kennedy thinks, such considerations must be more determinate than legal-doctrinal considerations. He imagines the reply that ideological considerations are in every way just as indeterminate as legal-doctrinal considerations. Ideological considerations, like legal-doctrinal considerations, are 'just "texts" that each individual judge will have to interpret before he or she can decide what is "required"' (*CA*, p. 187). Kennedy accepts this. Hence, moving from the surface of the phenomenon—the judge's indeterminate, non-compelling legal-doctrinal reasons for the decision—to the true determining factors 'behind' or beneath them—ideological considerations—offers no enlightenment, since the latter are no more determinative of the decision than the former. Where else can Kennedy look for factors that truly determine judicial decisions?

> [W]e might follow Jerome Frank[...] and resort to explanation in terms of 'judicial temperament'. Then we could explain temperament in terms of childhood experience. But each level, from legality to ideology to temperament, requires 'the subject' to interpret and permits interpretative strategy based on the level behind . . . At each level, the attempt to persuade us that what happened was caused or required by the text will come up against the objection that the same text could have yielded the opposite outcome had the actor pursued a different interpretative strategy.
>
> It might at first appear that the infinite regress of interpretation simply invalidates each 'behind' in turn, so that 'explanation is impossible' (*CA*, p. 190).

Kennedy does not think that the last claim is right, but some of his reasons invoke the dubious account of explanation.

Some considerations which Kennedy advances to resist the infinite regress are weak in the sense that there is no reason to think they are not true of legal-doctrinal considerations as well as of ideological considerations. Hence, the observation that the meaning of ideological projects is stabilised by a number of factors (*CA*, *ibid.*) supposedly supports the claim that such projects are more determinative of judicial decisions than legal-doctrinal factors. Yet it cannot do so in the absence of an argument that such stabilising forces are unavailable in the legal-doctrinal realm. A. W. B. Simpson has identified a range of such forces in the common law and has argued that they are the essence of a customary law system.[47] If Simpson is even partially right about this, then Kennedy's observation is otiose, something he seemingly accepts when conceding that 'legal versions of ideological debate are sometimes stabilized in the same way' as ideological debate *simpliciter* (*CA*, *ibid.*). This particular effort to resist the infinite regress does not so much bespeak an inadequate conception of explanation as the

[47] 'The Common Law and Legal Theory', ch. IV of A. W. B. Simpson (ed.), *Oxford Essays in Jurisprudence*, Second Series (Oxford, Clarendon 1973).

absence of any such conception, for this move adds nothing at all to the case against the regress. Yet it is another of Kennedy's observations that embodies the dubious account of explanation; dubious because it relativises and pyschologises the criteria of explanatory adequacy.

The question troubling Kennedy is this: what does a good explanation of adjudication (or any aspect of social life) look like? He has so far answered, rightly, that an explanation mired in an infinite regress is unacceptable. His answer continues, though, in the following manner. A good explanation is one that induces *feelings of closure* in its audience and, presumably, in its creator:

> [f]or the observer, . . . what needs to be explained is the *event* (the judicial choice of a rule), and each level of textuality 'behind' the event is helpful. As critical observers, we sometimes feel we 'know what is going on', to the extent of explanatory closure, through the process of multiplying the levels available to make sense of the judge's action. As long as we don't expect more of the effort to explain than *these experiences of closure*, the infinite regress provides opportunities for richer description and more intelligent response, rather than a methodological disaster (*CA*, *ibid.*; emphasis supplied).

Kennedy glosses this statement in a note:

> [t]he point . . . is that we will sometimes reach explanatory closure, *in the sense that we feel constrained*, by our theory of why the case came out as it did, to respond in a particular way. If we feel constrained by the conclusion that the judge chose as she did because she felt constrained by her understanding of her liberalism [an ideological basis for decision], then it will make sense to offer her an alternative version of liberalism, to invest energy in internal critique (*CA*, p. 396; emphasis supplied).

There is little doubt or ambiguity in these statements as to Kennedy's answer to the question of explanation: a good explanation is one that feels right; it induces a feeling of closure; it makes us feel constrained. An acute problem is that no account of what might trigger these feelings, of their basis, is offered.

A traditional account of the feeling of constraint or closure would run along these lines. We feel constraint and closure when faced with a true and valid deduction because the premises cannot be accepted and the conclusion denied without contradiction. The notion of contradiction triggers 'feelings' of constraint and closure. An explanation of a particular judicial decision could take deductive form. Suppose Kennedy established that a particular decision was logically flawed; he could then, having established that the decision was not logically compelled by the legal materials, show that other factors, such as ideological considerations, could have determined it. He could reconstruct the judgment by adding-in these ideological considerations and then show that, with these in the picture, the decision is no longer logically flawed. When these hidden factors are made explicit and added into the reasoning in the case, the decision is logically compelling. This looks like a perfectly respectable explanation and a good basis for the feeling—and the actual existence of—explanatory closure. Unfortunately, this kind of explanation is not available to Kennedy because, as we have noted, he holds that ideology is no more determinate than legal doctrine. Since no potential explanatory factor—be it ideology, childhood experiences, judicial temperament or whatever—is any more 'fundamental' than any action or event it is adduced to 'explain', then it is impossible for Kennedy to derive one from the other in this way. Hence, Kennedy's notion of referring to different explanatory 'levels' to make sense of the judge's decision is misleading. In terms of explanatory power, all levels are the same, each being as indeterminate as the rest. Since no level is any more powerful than another, talk of 'levels' here is redundant in the same way as is talk of different 'levels' in a bungalow.

What, then, triggers the feeling of explanatory closure? If it is not the structure of the explanation tendered, is it something about the psychology or physiology of the audience and theorist? If so, what? One could imagine all kinds of silly things that might increase or decrease an audience's and theorist's susceptibility to a particular explanation, that might trigger or impede feelings of closure. Presumably those with trains to catch will be quicker to feel the sense of closure than those with time on their hands. Theorists taking Prozac could well find an explanation compelling sooner than those running on caffeine. This, of course, tells us nothing about the nature and quality of an explanation and much about the psychology and physiology of audience and theorist. Yet the one surely cannot be reduced to the other. Kennedy could not embrace such a reduction because it looks dangerously like explaining one thing, the nature of a good explanation, by reference to something more fundamental and determinate, namely individual psychology. Further, such a reduction is objectionable once it is accepted that good quality explanations can run counter to the feelings of those to whom they are offered and created by, and can actually take those very feelings as *explanans*.

The formal structure of a good explanation is not yielded solely, or perhaps even at all, by its capacity to induce the feeling of closure. Rather, in the human sciences factors such as logical form, range (does it explain much or little?), relationship with intuitions and practical theory (what was called 'theory in the primary sense' in chapter 3), truth-value and originality determine the quality of an explanation. These factors determine whether or not an explanation is good regardless of its effect on the psychology of its audience and creator. An explanation can be powerful on these criteria even if it has no impact at all on the psychology of the audience because, for example, it is unknown to them. It is true that the rhetorical style of a particular explanation can influence the degree to which it is taken up in a society, the extent to which it enters that society's practical-theory and its citizens' understandings of themselves and their social context, and it would be foolish to ignore this. Similarly, it would be silly to ignore the range of moral, political and religious factors that can impede the propagation of a particular good quality explanation or theory. (Think, for example, of Charles Darwin's secretive attitude, prior to 1859, to his theory of evolution, or Galileo Galilei's recantation, before the Church, of Copernicanism.[48]) But these factors certainly do not determine the validity of any particular explanation or tell us that an explanation is either good or bad.

So, while Kennedy's endorsement of methodological compatibilism deserves our praise, his squeamishness about offering an account of the nature of explanation, and failure to distinguish truly different explanatory levels, invites criticism. His deployment of compatibilism, his sensitivity to the advantages, and awareness of the compatibility, of both 'interpretative' and 'explanatory' methods, in conjunction with his appreciation of when to move between the two, is commendable. Although his account of adjudication does not explain that process by reference to factors beyond the law, for 'ideologies . . . are inside rather than outside legal discourse itself' (*CA*, p. 289), it deploys 'explanatory' methods to great advantage in highlighting what might be going on within the practice itself. Yet Kennedy's unwillingness to develop even a tentative account of the nature of explanation is a symptom of a greater difficulty. The difficulty is that of being in the constant grip of an exaggeration, of having a hyperbolic understanding of the effects of 'postmodern' or, perhaps more accurately, deconstructive philosophy. This apparently lies behind Kennedy's wildly exaggerated view that representation is impossible which, of course, is a feeble justification for his supposed methodological eclecticism. It looms over his misplaced suspicion about the notion of truth and is the cause of his squeamishness about the nature of explanation. Moreover, it is hardly likely that psychologising the criteria of explanatory adequacy avoids any of these exaggerated snags: is not a report that one has a feeling of explanatory closure a matter of representation? Is that not a proposition having a truth value? Is it not a sentence that can be altered by iterability? All Kennedy's worries are here, in the core of his own arguments. Of these worries, those that pose genuine problems do so in relation to all explanations and understandings. Moves within particular explanatory practices are not made impossible by 'truths' or arguments that attack the presuppositions of all practices. We return to this point in section III.

[48] On Darwin's doubts regarding publication of anything about evolution, see A. Desmond and J. Moore, *Darwin* (London, Penguin 1992), chs. 21–32. On Galileo's rather more serious problems see G. de Santillana, *The Crime of Galileo* (London, Heinemann 1958).

Kennedy's compatibilism is therefore a disappointment. Does Unger's compatibilist programme fair better? Before answering this question, let us briefly reassure ourselves that Unger is indeed properly regarded as a methodological compatibilist. An early statement to that effect was noted in chapter 3. They are echoed in the three volumes of Unger's social-theoretic *magnum opus*, *Politics*.[49] We must, he says, 'free ourselves from the hold of a single, exclusive model of explanation' (*P*, i, p. 187). Therefore, he aims to develop '[a]n antinecessitarian social theory [which] . . . reject[s] the choice between . . . scientistic social theory and a causally agnostic understanding' (*P*, i, p. 11). Unger equates the latter with strong interpretative methods that eschew all efforts to unearth causal forces at play in social action and which elide any difference between the approach of the social sciences and that of the humanities (although this distinction is somewhat dubious). Scientistic social theory is, for Unger, the quest to explain all aspects of social life by reference to a body of causal laws, regardless of the views of those whose conduct is thereby explained. With these definitions in mind, the aspiration to transcend the choice between the two options is clearly an affirmation of compatibilism. Unger hopes to accommodate and unify causal and interpretative approaches. He denies that his theory 'increases the tension between natural science and social understanding . . . [and] takes sides with the humanistic party, to relinquish rather than transform the practice of causal explanation' (*P*, i, p. 170). Rather, Unger's 'social theory can coexist with natural science without either imitating its methods or claiming an unjustified exemption from the responsibilities of causal analysis' (*ibid.*). Lest there be any doubt of Unger's compatibilist aspirations, consider his observation that 'intentional analysis: the comparison of social events and their consequences to the ideas and intentions of historical agents' (*P*, i, p. 191) is on its own an inadequate method to explain and understand social life.

> You cannot move from the ideas of and intentions of individuals to the large-scale structures of society unless you can find guidance in a more general conception of social reality and social opportunity. You cannot derive such a conception, in any simple or direct way, from the ideas and intentions of particular individuals and groups. Every approach to history has to account for a sense of constraints that hardly seem reducible to the intentions and ideas of particular individuals or (if you knew how to sum them up) of everyone's intentions put together. Every approach must allow for the possibility that the relation of actions to results over time may be shaped by forces the agents neither intend nor understand (*P*, i, pp. 191–192).

Many quibbles might be raised about these remarks and some will be aired shortly. Yet, whatever the force of these complaints, none could deny

[49] Cambridge, C. U. P. 1987. This is referred to hereinafter, in both text and notes, as '*P*', with accompanying volume and page number.

Unger's wish to develop a method that follows the compatibilist *via media*. While his method cannot be criticised for failing to be compatibilist, it is nevertheless open to objection as a dubious version of compatibilism. Why?

Two features undermine Unger's compatibilism. First, it appears inchoate. That is, despite his faith in a method that takes seriously both external and internal points of view, that marries both agent-based and structure-based explanations and understandings, the participant's viewpoint sometimes gets lost. This is the opposite mistake to that which the orthodox often make, namely, affirming compatibilism while ignoring 'external' accounts of actions, practices and institutions. Unger's error is not as gross as the orthodox mistake for, while it can plausibly be argued that they often ignore causal explanations, it cannot be said that Unger consistently ignores the viewpoint of the participants. Indeed, the explanatory part of Unger's work, in which the ideas of the plasticity and contingency of social structures, institutions and practices are developed and the dominant forms of social theory rejected, is informed by a participant's understanding of the economic and political institutions, practices and structures of a particular society, namely, Brazil (see, e.g., *P*, i, pp. 67–79). There is also a fairly obvious overlap between his notion of internal normative argument, on the one hand, and participants' understandings and evaluations of actions, practices and institutions, on the other. Internal normative argument is, for example, rooted in a shared tradition of moral and political ideals and schemes of human association (*P*, ii, p. 356); it 'benefits from the detailed texture of an assumed and accepted imaginative world' (*P*, ii, p. 360). It is founded upon the insider's perspective.

However, when the programmatic part of Unger's work is examined—the part that transforms the explanatory aspect into an alternative scheme of human association and suggests the means by which to achieve it—the views of participants disappear. Admittedly, such views must be hypothetical and it would be folly to spend much time speculating as to what agents might think in certain future circumstances. Yet it cannot be a mistake to inform our recipes for social change with some understanding of how participants in current institutions and practices understand and value them. This at least enables some slight degree of imaginative projection, however faulty and tentative, serving to illustrate what might and might not be possible and tolerable in the future. For each individual and group, taking steps toward widespread social change is, after all, a matter of having good reasons for action. One way of generating such reasons is to appeal to a better future, to sketch a goal—a better society—worth pursuing. That goal must make agents less adverse to the risks involved in attempting to bring about widespread social change. The problem with Unger's positive programme is that it embodies and apparently encourages risks that very few actually existing agents would countenance. Would many, for example, be as willing as Unger apparently is to unleash an equivalent to the cultural revolution of the Chinese Red Guard or encourage the messianic vigour and actions of a latter-day Napoleon I?[50] The difficulty here is not just of charting the relationship between means and ends, but of ensuring that the ends promised are indeed worthy of pursuit.[51] Unger's apparent distance from the views of what participants in existing practices, institutions and structures might find acceptable, never mind worthy, imperils this aspect of his work. Nor can Unger seek refuge here by saying he is operating on the normative level. For, normative arguments have to work for us, here and now, if they are to generate reasons for action; they cannot be formulated for Martians or for beings so unlike us that they make no sense. There is no reason in principle why normative arguments should not be rooted, just like social-theoretic explanations and understandings, in the views of participants and feed upon, and at some point be absorbed into, those views. Philosophical normative arguments should rest upon everyday normative arguments in just the same way as social-theoretic accounts of actions, practices or institutions (theory in the secondary or tertiary senses) rely upon practical-theoretic accounts (theory in the primary sense). In the normative realm, Unger ignores the implications of his sensible edict for the social-theoretic realm, namely, that '[e]verything people say and think about themselves and their life in common becomes the sketch of a picture that social theory can at best correct and complete' (*P*, i, p. 197).

The second snag echoes one that besets Kennedy, enveloping Unger's account of the nature of explanation. It has two dimensions. First, Unger apparently tries to show that explanation via the D-N model is impossible because the laws needed to make that method work do not exist. The qualifier 'apparently' is necessary because at some points Unger accepts his argument does not refute the existence of such laws, while at others he thinks it does (see, for example, *P*, ii, at pp. 252–253 and 276). The argument employed is of a familiar type, moving from an ontological claim about the constituents of social reality to a conception of explanation and method. Remember that some of the compatibilist work analysed in chapter 3 attempted to derive methodological arguments in the same way and that the ontological claims prayed in aid were unable to do the work needed. We noted that such ontological claims could be accepted by proponents of almost all methods; those claims cannot therefore succeed in commending

[50] W. Ewald is considerably vexed by Unger's use of these examples: 'Unger's Philosophy: A Critical Legal Study' (1988) 97 *Yale L. J.* 665–756, pp. 741–751.

[51] The issue has been raised many times, most notably in L. Trotsky, J. Dewey and G. Novack, *Their Morals and Ours* (New York, Pathfinder Press 1973). A fine discussion of the issue is also found in N. Geras, 'Our Morals: The Ethics of Revolution' in R. Miliband, L. Panitch and J. Saville (eds.), *The Socialist Register 1989* (London, The Merlin Press 1989), 185–211.

one method over another. Unger's problem is similar: he mistakenly ascribes methodological consequences to his ontological claim. The claim holds that the social world, one of three orders of reality Unger distinguishes, is simply too contingent, fluid or plastic to be explained by any corpus of causal laws. This

> third, distinctive type of order [is one in which] [p]eople act as if their thoughts and actions were governed by institutional and imaginative contexts with . . . self-reinforcing and self-regulating properties . . . and as if they could think and act, at a higher level, where they are ruled by no such frameworks or schemes. Sometimes one and sometimes the other aspect of their situation seems preeminent, but neither is ever entirely absent (*P*, i, 195).

Because the social world takes this infinitely revisable and contingent form, Unger thinks the D-N method is impossible: '[t]he facts about social reality and social change condemn this search [for the necessary and sufficient conditions of social change] to disappointment' (*P*, ii, p. 276). The difficulty is that this simply does not follow. The claim about the nature of the social world does not entail the claim about method. Conceding that the social world is indeed fluid, contingent and plastic, in which everything could have been otherwise, shows neither that the past events were uncaused nor that future events will lack causes. Nor can it show that a corpus of causal laws such as proponents of the D-N model espouse does not exist. The fact that reality is so plastic is not incompatible with the existence of such laws. For, rather than refuting the existence of general causal laws, social plasticity may be a result of either variability in the initial conditions of such laws or in the actual circumstances to which they are applied. That is, things could always have been otherwise, not because there are no general causal laws, but because the world to which they are applied is massively complex and varied.

Unger's illustrations of historical particularity, most of which are drawn from natural history, highlight this complexity and variety rather than deny the existence of general causal laws. One of his geological examples illustrates this perfectly. Unger suggests that the factors determining the properties of sedimentary rocks are far more diverse and complex than those determining the properties of either igneous or metamorphic rocks (*P*, i, pp. 187–188). Now, while the combinations of processes that create sedimentary rocks are far from simple, and lack close connections to 'general physical and chemical laws' (*ibid.*), this says nothing about the existence of such laws and everything about the complexity of the world to which they are applied. Indeed, Unger concedes as much when, in discussing an instance of animal evolution, he says that the vastly complex processes involved 'might be reducible to a single set of more basic regularities' (*P*, i, p. 189). He errs, though, in thinking that such a reduction is compromised by 'mediating links of explanation' (*P*, i, p. 190). If those mediating links reflect the complexity of the natural world they seek to explain, how can they be objectionable? How could they possibly refute the existence of a corpus of causal laws?

The first step of Unger's answer would likely invoke Willard Quine's attack upon the analytic/synthetic distinction, seeking to show that the conception of causal laws we have invoked assumes this unsustainable boundary (*P*, i, pp. 180–185 and 238). If causal laws are of exactly the same status as empirical 'facts', and can be in principle refuted or amended in light of such facts, then Unger's examples might have a point. Yet accepting the Quinean argument—and there are good reasons to reject at least parts of it—does not help Unger much.[52] For, as Quine noted, any old recalcitrant experience will not serve to destabilise embedded causal principles since we have a great deal of latitude in choosing which aspects, if any, of our belief system to amend.[53] Only exceptionally troublesome and copious empirical discoveries would have the desired effect and Unger's examples just do not fit the bill. The second step in Unger's reply might seek to foist some version of deep-structure social theory upon us by virtue of our affirmation of the existence—or, at least, of the possibility—of a body of causal laws. Belief in such laws clearly does not in any obvious way entail a particular method for explaining and understanding social life. That belief is compatible with both interpretative and causal methods and seems neutral between any particular type of social theory. It no more entails a commitment to Marxism than it does a commitment to 'positivist' political science. To show the contrary, Unger must offer much more by way of argument than he currently does.

The second dimension of Unger's problem with explanation concerns not his criticisms of other explanatory types but the nature of his own explanations. The problem is that it is difficult indeed to discern what Ungerian explanations of segments of the social world involve. Nor is it clear that the source of the problem is solely the sheer novelty and uniqueness of Unger's work. For, although he often promises a 'fundamental shift' or 'transformation' or, more modestly, 'a change' in or 'alternative' to, our understanding of the nature of explanation in the human sciences (*P*, ii, pp. 3, 7, 18 and 248), the substance of this startling development is elusive. True, his explanations eschew reference to the type of general laws which the D-N model invokes, but beyond that Ungerian explanations consist simply of charting the influence exerted by formative contexts and the ways in which it can be transcended (*P*, ii, pp. 246–277). Those seeking a quantification of this influence will be disappointed, as will those who want to know exactly

[52] For a beautifully succinct statement of some problems see M. Hollis, *Models of Man* (Cambridge, C. U. P. 1977), pp. 53–67.

[53] *From a Logical Point of View* (Cambridge, Mass., Harvard U. P. 1961), pp. 42–46.

how the task of charting influence escapes capture in the nomological net of the D-N model. (Unger cannot argue that the latter task is impossible because there are no general causal laws, since his arguments denying the existence or doubting the efficacy of such laws are inadequate.) At some points, Unger is bewitched by methodological eclecticism, holding that his theory 'generates a broad range of social and historical explanations: some comprehensive and abstract, others focused and concrete'(*P*, ii, p. 1), yet all of which are 'speculative'(*P*, ii, p. 7). In the absence of an abstract statement of the nature of Ungerian explanations, it seems the proof of the explanatory pudding is in the eating: '[t]he main test of such an explanatory argument is ultimately its ability to inspire detailed explanations more successful than the explanations made possible by current forms of social analysis' (*ibid.*). On this count, Unger's work is a success, for he does explain the cycle of retrenchment and reform more successfully than either deep-structure social theory or positivist social science. But note what an odd success this is. It is one in which Unger shows that some unquantified and supposedly unquantifiable influences have worked in a particular situation, contributing, in either a non-causal way, or in a way beyond the grasp of the D-N model, to a result that may have been otherwise. Furthermore, those influences are often characterised, and supposedly actually operate, independently of the understandings of the participants subject to them. This, then, is the picture, shorn of detail, which emerges from the second and third volumes of *Politics*. It is a picture of the nature of explanation more foggy than much that has gone before. It may be uncharitable to skip the detail that gives the picture depth and perspective, but detail cannot substitute for clarity of purpose. How can a wealth of detail make good the vagueness as to the nature or point of the picture?

Unger's compatibilism, like Kennedy's, faces problems. Clearly, these problems do not affect compatibilism *per se* but only these particular versions. The problems overlap to some extent but it would be a mistake to make too much of this. Although both Kennedy and Unger have difficulty with the notion of explanation, the specific root of the problem is quite different in each case. Both also have some problems with the deployment of the interpretative method yet their difficulties are quite distinct. Unger sometimes overlooks that method and the benefits it can bring, whereas Kennedy seems unsure why it should be adopted at all: his flirtation with methodological eclecticism makes the formulation of arguments to this end unnecessary. Nevertheless, both deserve commendation for their endorsement of compatibilism, whatever problems they face as a consequence. Of course, this raises an obvious question. If these heretics are compatibilists, and if structuralism, too, collapses into compatibilism, how do orthodoxy and heresy differ? The argument of this chapter, taken in conjunction with that developed in chapter 3, suggests a methodological *entente cordiale* between orthodoxy and heresy, and shows that there is no insuperable divide on these matters. Has the supposed conflict between them been a phoney war?

We are not yet able to say, in relation to non-methodological matters, since the heretical position on values in adjudication has not been considered. Confining ourselves to matters of method, the only restraint to giving a resounding affirmative answer to this question, is the following suspicion. It is that, in highlighting the different problems Kennedy and Unger face in their accounts of method, we have missed a unifying theme. For, while it is true that Kennedy's problems with explanation are quite different from Unger's problems with causal laws, their discomfort with both might have a common cause. That cause is not explicitly identified by these authors as the over-arching reason for their squeamishness about offering general accounts of the nature of explanation or invoking the D-N method. Yet it usually lurks in the background, occasionally in the foreground, of many of their discussions of method. It is the view that, in the most common shorthand phrases, there is some kind of 'crisis of representation', or there has been a 'collapse of meta-narratives' such that talk of method is as a result either impossible or inappropriate.[54] Moreover, these same ideas animate some heretical rejections of structuralism. Structuralism privileges its explanations of social life despite the fact 'that explanatory theory is but another practice, valid in itself, but no more privileged than other representations'; it is also committed to holding knowledge to be unmediated, certain and entailing 'positive truth'.[55] In a related refrain, David Kennedy regards this commitment as but a consequence of the idea that structuralism, like any general explanatory theory, endorses a 'stable origin, standpoint, agency or totalizer' as a foundation for its insights.[56] Supposedly, none of these moves is sustainable in light of the post-structuralist attack upon standard philosophical accounts of representation, epistemology and metaphysics. So, whereas the ideas of a crisis of representation and suspicion of metanarratives could well be the partially hidden roots of Kennedy's and Unger's discomfort with method, these ideas explicitly motivate those who maintain that a concern with method is pointless. This specific argument about method is rarely explicitly articulated by heretics, but the claims

[54] Kennedy, *CA*, pp. 186–190. For Unger, the Rortyean crisis of representation undermines some traditional methodologies and conditions his own: see *P*, i, pp. 166–169 and 237–238; *P*, ii, p. 604.

[55] Both statements are from Heller, *supra*, note 10, p. 183. See also p. 162 for Heller's invocation of R. Rorty's attack on representation and J. Derrida's rejection of the metaphysics of presence.

[56] D. Kennedy, 'Critical Theory, Structuralism and Contemporary Legal Scholarship' (1985–1986) 21 *New England L. R.* 209–289, p. 276. In fairness to Kennedy, it should be noted that his treatment of post-structuralist thought is unusual in being, on the whole, careful and considered.

that can support and nourish it, claims about the impossibility of ('privileged') representation or the absence of legitimating foundations for claims to knowledge, are often invoked. These claims therefore require our attention.

III AGNOSTICISM

What is a 'crisis of representation'? What does it mean to be suspicious of 'meta-narratives'? How, if at all, do these ideas impact upon discussions of method in the human sciences? The first problem in answering these questions concerns the fact that these phrases are but elliptical references to complex and ambitious arguments which are unpacked in a number of ways. In what follows just a few popular and plausible ways of supporting these claims, adopted by *inter alios* Jacques Derrida, Michel Foucault, Jean-Francois Lyotard and Richard Rorty, are examined.[57] Secondly, there is often a large gap between the specific arguments which proponents of 'the crisis' and 'the suspicion' use to support those claims and the way those arguments are invoked, either in legal scholarship in particular, or the human sciences at large. In the former, the arguments that supposedly impact upon method are invoked either far too hastily and used to prop up claims they cannot in fact support, or are taken, usually in footnotes and without analysis, to refute or make problematic whole styles, traditions and possibilities of argument. Joseph Singer provides an exemplary instance of the former strategy, whereas Unger, Kennedy and Heller occasionally illustrate the latter.[58] Within the human sciences in general, the specific arguments of Derrida, Foucault, Lyotard and Rorty that might influence discussions of method are again rarely unpacked and analysed. Rather, and in spite of the contrast with the often subtle and thorough way in which the normative dimensions of some of these writers' arguments have been analysed, their other arguments are simply taken to attack 'the foundations of Western thought' or, what is regarded as the same thing, 'the enlightenment project'.[59] The arguments generating these conclusions must be of exceptional power and range, being both abstract and universal, not to

[57] The starting points are J. Derrida, *Of Grammatology* (Baltimore, The Johns Hopkins U. P. 1974); M. Foucault, *The Order of Things: An Archaeology of the Human Sciences* (London, Routledge and Kegan Paul 1974); J-F Lyotard, *The Postmodern Condition* (Manchester, Manchester U. P. 1984); and R. Rorty, *Philosophy and the Mirror of Nature* (Oxford, Basil Blackwell 1980). Each author has, of course, written many subsequent works and I do not mean, in noting early works, to claim they are the most important elements of the corpus.

[58] For Kennedy and Unger see *supra*, note 54; Heller, *supra*, note 10, pp. 155–162. Singer's sometimes idiosyncratic invocation of Rorty was noted in chapter 5.

[59] A number of examples will be found in S. Seidman (ed.), *The Postmodern Turn* (Cambridge, C. U. P. 1994), beginning with pp. 8–13 of the introduction.

mention more than a little reductive (is 'the enlightenment project' such a simple and unitary package? Is not portraying it as such an instance of all the objectionable features of that project?).

Taken as an attack upon the foundations of Western thought, the arguments about a crisis of representation or the illegitimacy of meta-narratives appear to be instances of external scepticism and lack any critical power in relation to discussions within a practice.[60] It matters not whether the practice in question is that of considering the appropriate method to understand and explain social life or that of determining the best way to decide hard cases, for moves within practices are determined, in the main, by considerations internal to them and rarely by foundational factors. Hence, we do not need to know the general and special theories of relativity and time in order to catch a bus, nor is it likely that amendments to those theories will impact on this action. The possibility that changes in the foundations of some aspects of our knowledge and beliefs will influence practices cannot be ruled out, since the reflexivity of social life means participants' faith in the moves they make within practices could be shaken by factors and knowledge beyond them. Whether or not this has occurred could only be established on a case by case basis. Nor can a supposed proof that the practices of Western thought or the enlightenment project lack compelling foundations invalidate particular moves within those practices unless it is established that all practices are *not* in this respect the same. If they are, then showing that one (for example, the practice of tendering explanations of social life) lacks ultimate foundations is simply to repeat what is true of all.

The more sophisticated proponents of deconstruction recognise this and thus refrain from commending other practices because they are somehow foundationally 'better'. All are indeed in the same boat. Consider, for example, Derrida's demonstration that Levi-Strauss is in the grip of the metaphysics of presence. After attempting to show this, Derrida does not commend an approach that is better because free from such metaphysics since '[t]here is no sense in doing without the concepts of metaphysics in order to shake metaphysics. We have no language—no syntax and no lexicon—which is foreign to this history; we can pronounce not a single destructive proposition which has not already had to slip into the form, the logic, and the implicit postulations of precisely what it seeks to contest'.[61] Nor can we choose to interpret free from the metaphysics of presence, preferring a mode 'which is no longer turned towards the origin, affirms play

[60] The argument is derived from R. Dworkin, *Law's Empire* (London, Fontana 1986), pp. 76–86 and echoed, despite all his disagreements with the aforementioned, by S. Fish in, *inter alia*, *There's No Such Thing as Free Speech . . .* (New York, Oxford U. P. 1994), chs. 11 and 12.

[61] J. Derrida, *Writing and Difference* (London, Routledge and Kegan Paul 1978), pp. 280–281.

and tries to pass beyond man and humanism'.[62] For, although these two interpretations of interpretation are irreconcilable, we live by and with them in an uneasy, obscure 'economy'. Hence, the problems that supposedly gnaw at the foundations of Western thought are problems for the problems as well; they affect each and every practice within that tradition including the tradition of attacking the tradition.

Such consistent external scepticism is rare among heretical scholars. They are often unable to resist the temptation to invoke general, externally sceptical arguments to attack moves within particular practices. This temptation, as was noted in the previous chapter, threatens to undercut Peller's argument about the arbitrariness of legal systems of representation because he sometimes holds that *all* systems of representation are arbitrary. It also seems to underlie Kennedy's fear of insisting upon the explanatory priority of some factors rather than others, since he may think such a move entails a foundational claim that is ultimately ungroundable. And it animates both David Kennedy's view that structuralism is, balefully, committed to some such foundational claim, and Heller's observation that structuralism's explanations are but one set of representations among others. Yet, if it is true that *all* claims within *all* practices are ultimately ungroundable, because *all* practices lack rationally compelling and irrefutable foundations, how can this be regarded as a problem? The making of claims within a practice that, for example, X or Y is a better or worse explanation of p, seems untouched by such considerations, in the same way that my catching the bus is untouched by discussions of relativity and time. Of course, the claim about lack of foundations could be intended not as an attack upon a particular practice, but as a caution against unwittingly making claims that cannot be cashed. This cautionary use is unobjectionable but, again, does not invalidate wholesale the moves and claims within particular practices.

An argument that seems to straddle the boundary between internal and external scepticism, and which supports the delegitimation of metanarratives and the crisis of representation, has become popular among those writing under the influence of Foucault and Friedrich Nietzsche. The argument has two dimensions. The first is epistemological, holding that the notion of truth is best understood neither as a matter of the correspondence of our beliefs with the world, nor as the coherence of those beliefs as a 'web' or system, but as a reflection of our purposes and needs. This does not sound like a terribly dangerous claim and, as we will see in our discussion of Rorty, below, it need not be. In Nietzsche's hands, however, this account of truth is more challenging because it is a manifestation of both 'perspectivity' and the will to power. The former seemingly implies that knowledge—justified true belief—exists not as a single commodity with a life independent of

[62] J. Derrida, *Writing and Difference*, p. 292.

agents who discover it, but rather as a diverse range of commodities. Knowledge is created by a potentially vast range of producers and it has very many different and incompatible forms, some of which circulate in some areas and some in others, there being no universal currency. Hence, in some of his remarks at least, it seems that Nietzsche held that there are as many knowledges as there are people. 'In so far as the word "knowledge" has any meaning, the world is knowable: but it is *interpretable* otherwise, it has no meaning behind it, but countless meanings.—"Perspectivism"'.[63] Yet in conjunction with claims like these, Nietzsche also holds that interpretations and knowledges are a product of our needs and, if our needs are like Humean sentiments and thus fairly uniform, we are unlikely to be swamped by hundreds of 'truths', 'senses' or 'interpretations' of aspects of social life. If our needs are diverse then we might be so swamped.

It would be a mistake to think that the prospects for the idea of truth or knowledge could not, as a result of the first dimension of this argument, be worse. The second dimension places truth in an even more baleful light. It is a philosophical claim with immense practical implications, maintaining that the creation of truth is an instance of the will to dominate and control. '"Truth" is . . . not something there, that might be found and discovered—but something that must be created and that gives its name to a *process* . . . It is a word for the "will to power"'.[64] The argument holds that not only is there a plurality of truths, which in itself is a challenging enough argument for some traditional philosophical accounts of truth, but that the creation of truth is a method of domination. Truth is thus an objectionable and dubious concept, either internally, in its core, so to speak, since the very notion is inextricably violent, or because violence and domination are its constant side-effects. This relationship between truth, power and domination, particularly as it arises within the human sciences, was the fulcrum of Foucault's work. It in no way devalues that work to regard it as putting Nietzsche's insights to work in 'unmasking the human sciences'.[65] The true value and challenge of Foucault is his effort to replace the self-understanding of the human sciences as forums of reason and pathways to truth, with a demonstration of their complicity in, and legitimation of, the exercise and development of both 'formal' and 'informal' power.[66] (The latter was, of course, the primary focus of Foucault's attention.)

This shockingly superficial outline of the thought of Nietzsche and

[63] *The Will to Power* (New York, Vintage Books 1968), bk. III, sc. 481.
[64] *Ibid.*, sc. 552.
[65] This vivid characterisation of Foucault's enterprise belongs to J. Habermas, *The Philosophical Discourse of Modernity* (Cambridge, Polity Press 1987), p. 238.
[66] For Foucault's own account of the relationship between his work and Nietzsche's, see 'Nietzsche, Genealogy, History' in D. Bouchard (ed.), *Language, Counter-Memory, Practice* (Ithaca, Cornell U. P. 1977).

Foucault is justifiable, if at all, only on the ground that the exegetical and interpretative issues surrounding their work cannot even be adequately sketched here, never mind addressed. Also, our aim is only to reconstruct the bare bones of an ambitious argument so as to sketch the nature of one peg upon which methodological agnosticism could hang. Agnosticism might be assumed to follow from the two dimensions of this argument if they are taken to tar discussions of method with the same brush as that which discredited the notion of truth, in general, and its role within the human sciences, in particular. But we must be careful here, for the dimensions of this argument are open to interpretation and each interpretation has quite different consequences. Consider again the first. It reeks of external scepticism since it apparently holds that all knowledge is a product of our interests and needs. If all knowledge claims are in this respect the same, then this is a singularly pointless way of criticising particular knowledge claims, whether made within a discussion about method in the human sciences or a legal judgment. However, the criticism could take internal form, in the sense of being aimed at those moves within a practice which commit proponents to denying that truth is indeed a product of our needs and purposes, yet few truth claims within practices other than philosophy take such an abstract form. They entail some account of truth, but are often neutral between the contenders. Nor does conceiving knowledge in the way the first dimension demands support methodological agnosticism, unless it is true that humankind has a vast array of incompatible purposes and needs driving the creation of truth. If those purposes and needs are stable and limited, then justification of methodological protocols and knowledge claims relative to them has both sense and point. A raging sea of incompatible purposes and needs will not make justification by reference to some such needs and purposes senseless, but pointless. For what range could such a justification have, if each has her own incompatible and incommensurable needs and purposes?

The second dimension of the argument also equivocates between internal and external scepticism. It might be said, in a bout of external scepticism, that if truth is indeed a manifestation of the will to power, surely discussions of method are also. Such discussions are, after all, designed to provide tools for truth-seekers. Again, if all truth claims are in the same boat, then the point has critical power only as a caution against those who would overlook truth's situation and misrepresent it as something other than a manifestation of the will to power. Yet, if only some truth claims have this feature, then the argument takes on the mantle of internal scepticism. The crucial task then becomes the exposure of arguments, methodological and other, as well as assumptions and general patterns of thought or discourse, manifesting the will to power. In addition, some account must be provided of the property—presumably desirable—had by those truth claims which do not embody the will to power. The first part of this task is the fulcrum of Foucault's work, but it is unlikely that he willingly engaged in the second, although some have offered a 'moralised' or normative reading of his work. On that reading, the desirable property of truth claims free from the will to power is something like capacity for liberation or freedom or self-creation.[67] However, if liberation, freedom or self-enhancing knowledges and truths were indeed Foucault's goals (he would most likely have been appalled by the thought), he was exceptionally reticent about them. Thankfully, we need not become involved in this matter for, when taken as an instance of internal scepticism, Foucault's work provides very little support for methodological agnosticism. Why? First, the project of unearthing the human sciences' complicity with power is unlikely to show that the methodological segments of those disciplines have been and will continue to be the sole locus of that objectionable collusion. And, second, because it is unlikely that all the human sciences, as they have existed heretofore and as they will exist in future, invoke one and only one conception of truth, namely, that which is simultaneously blind to, but also a manifestation of, the will to power. It is surely possible that unobjectionable truth statements—those not tainted by the will to power—have already appeared in the human sciences and will appear again in the future. That being so, the task of determining the best means of generating such statements, often the primary concern in methodological discussions, cannot be regarded as obviously pointless.

In some other forms, claims about the crisis of representation and the collapse of meta-narratives are comfortably regarded solely as instances of internal scepticism. For, besides supposedly undermining the whole of Western thought, these claims are often taken to establish limited arguments about, for example, the problematic nature of some conceptions of truth or the abuse of reason.[68] In particular, the correspondence theory of truth is the main target of Rorty's arguments. What makes this an instance of internal rather than external scepticism is that the arguments are directed against a conception of truth dominant within a specific practice, namely 'Philosophy', albeit a practice that affects many others. The very idea of truth is not in question for Rorty (at least, this seems to be the view he repeats most often), but rather how it should be understood within a particular practice. So, in saying 'truth is not the sort of thing one should expect to have a philosophically interesting theory about', he is contesting not the very idea of truth but a particular, supposedly philosophical conception of

[67] On self-creation see C. Taylor, 'Foucault on Freedom and Truth' in D. Hoy (ed.), *supra*, note 14, pp. 98–99. A warning to those who would moralise Foucault is provided by I. Hacking's 'Self-Improvement', *ibid.*.

[68] For a stimulating and accurate analysis of the abuse of reason within American legal scholarship, see P. Schlag, *The Enchantment of Reason* (Durham, Duke U. P. 1998), chs 1–4.

it.[69] That conception holds the truth of any proposition to be a matter of determining how well it fits or corresponds with 'reality' and Rorty rejects it because, among other reasons, no satisfactory account of the correspondence relation exists. Rorty's alternative is a form of epistemological behaviourism, sometimes labelled pragmatism. It holds that 'justification [of our beliefs and knowledge claims] is a matter of social practice, and that everything which is not a matter of social practice is no help in understanding the *justification* of human knowledge, no matter how helpful it may be in understanding its *acquisition*'.[70] Pragmatists 'drop[. . .] the notion of truth as correspondence with reality altogether', maintaining that the notion is best understood as a reference to that which helps us cope better with world.[71]

Suppose everything so far reported from Rorty is correct (ignore the snag about just what 'correct' can mean here). Those heretics wishing to invoke this argument would have to take two steps. First, demonstrate that moves within the practice in question (either general practices such as law and adjudication or sub-practices such as discussions about the best ways to understand and explain those general practices) invoke the correspondence theory of truth. And, secondly, apply the arguments which purportedly show that this is indeed a dubious account of truth to the practice or practices. That neither step is often effectively taken in heretical scholarship need not prevent us from contemplating the consequences of so doing. At this point something very important is revealed. For, showing that the allegedly indefensible correspondence theory of truth is in play in legal methodological thought does not have the consequences some heretics imagine. Recall, for example, Kennedy's squeamishness about explanatory priority and representation. As to the latter, he hopes to avoid claiming that his explanation of adjudication represents or corresponds to that 'object' in a truthful way. As to the former, he is loath to explain judicial decisions by reference to ideological factors because to do so risks prioritising those factors and they, he says, are just as indeterminate as all other factors.

Now, although Rorty's work does not figure explicitly in Kennedy's critique of adjudication, it is not implausible to note the resonance between the former's attack upon the correspondence theory of truth and privileged representations, and some of Kennedy's worries. Yet this resonance is entirely superficial for, were Kennedy taken to be relying upon Rorty's arguments here, there would be a serious problem. It is that Rorty never claims that a pragmatist theory of truth, or epistemological behaviourism, makes the justification of choices—be they methodological, explanatory,

[69] R. Rorty, *The Consequences of Pragmatism* (Minneapolis, University of Minnesota Press, 1982), p. xiii.

[70] Rorty, *supra*, note 57, p. 186 (emphasis in original).

[71] *Supra*, note 69, p. xvii.

moral or otherwise—impossible. A Rortyean pragmatist need not be squeamish about prioritising certain claims rather than others in an explanatory matrix, nor need she worry about correctly representing any aspect of social life. What she must not do is hold that the explanatory priority of claim Y, or the accuracy of representation R, is a product of the fact that Y and R accurately reflect or mirror some world beyond language and representation. The denial of the possibility of correspondence of this type certainly does not make justification impossible; to think so is to be committed to this notion in the first place. There are still better and worse arguments in a world after the correspondence theory, just as representations and explanations will still be offered as more or less accurate, more or less justifiable. Epistemological behaviourism's 'essential point is that in characterizing an episode or state as that of knowing . . . we are placing it in the logical space of reasons, of *justifying* and being able to *justify* what one says'.[72] Hence, on Rorty's view, epistemological 'justification is not a matter of a special relation between ideas (or words) and objects, but of conversation, of social practice. Conversational justification, so to speak, is naturally holistic . . . The crucial premise of the argument is that we understand knowledge when we understand the social justification of belief, and thus have no need to view it as accuracy of representation'.[73]

If Rorty's epistemological behaviourism drives Kennedy's worries about explanation—and, remember, there is no textual evidence to suggest it does other than an overlap in vocabularies—then Kennedy is plainly in the grip of an exaggeration. Nothing Rorty says can ground Kennedy's worries, for the consequences of Rortyean pragmatism are nowhere near as radical and debilitating as Kennedy might think. Nor can the exaggeration be excused because encouraged by the originator of the argument for, when turning mind and pen to questions of method in the human and natural sciences, Rorty scrupulously avoids it. Yet it might be thought that we are about to traduce Rorty, for he concludes that the question 'What should be the method of the social sciences?' 'is badly posed'.[74] That does not encourage confidence in the argument that Rorty does *not* think methodological talk is redundant and is *not* a methodological agnostic. However, Rorty thinks the question badly posed for a very specific reason, namely, because it usually invokes 'traditional ideas of "an absolute ('objective') conception of reality" and of "scientific method"'.[75] Rorty takes these ideas to entail the correspondence theory of truth with all its associated snags and

[72] *Supra*, note 57, p. 185, fn 17 (emphasis supplied; original emphasis omitted; the quotation, cited with approval by Rorty, is from Wilfred Sellars). 'The realization that the world does not tell us what language games to play should not . . . lead us to say that a decision about which to play is arbitrary . . .': R. Rorty, *Contingency, Irony, and Solidarity* (Cambridge, C. U. P. 1989), p. 6.

[73] *Ibid.*, p. 170. [74] *Supra*, note 69, p. 195. [75] *Ibid.*

confusions. Once that theory is rejected and replaced with the pragmatic theory, methodological talk and protocols will continue to exist, will be meaningful and capable of justification. They will justified, though, not by reference to their accuracy in representing a reality beyond representation, but by virtue of the help they give us in coping with the world. Hence, '[t]o say that something is better "understood" in one vocabulary than another is always an ellipsis for the claim that a description in the preferred vocabulary is more useful for a certain purpose'; those that are not useful can be '"brushed aside" as either "nutty" or "primitive"'.[76] This is clearly not the refrain of a methodological agnostic. In fact, in many instances Rorty sounds like the archetypal methodological compatibilist, decrying the human sciences' misguided fixation with the explanation/understanding and fact/value cleavages, and their brooding, intermittent infatuation with the methods of the natural sciences.[77]

There are undoubtedly other arguments within deconstructive thought that might support methodological agnosticism but, as we have seen, those so far considered do not. In so far as heretics think they do, they are in the grip of an exaggeration or misunderstanding. The whirls of hyperbole that surround deconstructive or post-structuralist thought, just like those that surrounded structuralism, distract from the arguments themselves and can serve to deflect legal scholars from attending to their import. Hence exaggeration and misrepresentation gain a foothold in our thinking. It is important to try to uproot such worrisome problems and that is what this section tried to do. Nothing said here, nor anything said elsewhere in the book, can be taken to suggest that post-structuralist thought is unworthy of attention; nor have any arguments been produced herein that would seriously discredit that body of thought. It cannot be wrong for legal scholars to engage with it, but the manner of the engagement is crucial. An informed, sympathetic yet critically considered engagement, free from what we diagnosed in chapter 1 as disciplinary infatuation, would be commendable. Such infatuation is not an especial risk for heretics—it arises in equal if not greater magnitude in, for example, legal academy's engagement with neo-classical economics or systems theory. Finally, though, let us echo Unger and thereby highlight the possible roots of such infatuation. Although post-structuralist thought or 'ultra-theory' is undoubtedly a viable concern for legal scholars, Unger thinks its apparent antipathy to ambitious social theory—what he labels 'super-theory'—is objectionable. But, with admirable and entirely correct candour, he realises that there are no compelling (he says *a priori*) reasons determining the choice between the two (*P*, *i*, pp. 165–169). Since we do not yet know whether or not super-theory will succeed, nor do we

[76] *Supra.*, note 69, p. 197 (the first statement) and p. 200 (the remaining statements).
[77] *Ibid.*, pp. 191–203.

know whether or not ultra-theory's attack upon it will succeed, reason cannot dictate the choice between them, cannot determine that one demands our attention before the other. Faith and temperament must hold sway here, influencing whether we become Ungerian visionaries or Foucaultian sceptics. With caution in mind as to the ease of the shift from faith to infatuation, we will examine next the visionary programme. Since it takes a central place in the following chapter, it seems that faith and temperament have already spoken. Only at the end of that chapter will we know whether or not they have ushered us along a fruitful path.

7
Adjudication for Visionaries

> [T]he vision is yet for an appointed time, but at the end it shall speak, and not lie. The Old Testament, Habakkuk ii, 3.

Value talk—talk about moral, ethical, political and pragmatic values—can function on at least three related levels. First, value talk is appropriate at the level of the relevance of values of whatever kind to a particular activity, institution or social practice. For example, are members of particular professional groups *qua* members of those groups bound to act in accord with certain values? If the answer is affirmative then a second issue arises: which values? If values do indeed constrain the activity of participants in particular practices, it would be helpful to know exactly which values are in play and when. Here value talk could consist of an analysis of the respective importance of integrity and fairness or of efficiency and humanity in a particular profession. This second level of value talk is one of specification. Disagreement at this level might be expected about either specific entries on any list of values regarded as relevant to a particular activity, institution or practice or about the very list itself. In the former case, disagreement arises between either proponents of different values for inclusion upon a more or less agreed list or between those who disagree about the ranking of particular entries on the list. In the latter instance, the disagreement is between proponents of completely different lists.

A third level of value talk presents itself close on the heels of the second. It raises questions about the nature and basis of the values supposedly relevant to a specific activity, institution or practice. If, for example, the values of compassion and humanity are said to constrain participants in the practice 'commerce', then it is not unreasonable to request some account of the basis of those values' constraining power. Is it simply that our community and its merchants profess allegiance to those values? Or is it that all merchants and all communities profess belief in, and aspire to instantiate in conduct, those values? Alternatively, those values might demand the allegiance of merchants and others because it can be shown that rational beings must accept them and that this is true whether or not agents behave rationally. However unfashionable the term may currently be, this level of value talk will henceforth be referred to as foundational. This label is useful not merely in signifying that the issues raised here are ultimately epistemological, concerning the conditions under which moral knowledge and action are possible, but also because the position taken up at this level of value talk often conditions, perhaps occasionally completely determines, the positions taken up at the levels of relevance and specification.

This chapter examines these three levels of value talk as they arise within heretical accounts of adjudication. They are most economically defined as denying two claims that characterise orthodox accounts. One claim that orthodox accounts affirm and most heretical accounts deny, is that there is an important difference between 'easy cases', on the one hand, and 'hard cases', on the other. This denial does not commit heretics to the claim that adjudication is utterly unpredictable since the basis of their claim is justificatory. Heretics, remember, hold that easy and hard cases are qualitatively similar since decisions in each are neither rationally compelling nor authoritative. They deny neither that similar decisions may be made across time by judges nor that decisional outcomes cannot be foreseen. Yet they affirm that the bases of such decisions are found not in the unfolding of a distinctive, autonomous legal rationality but rather in the judges' implicit, shared prejudices and ideology. Another claim the orthodox affirm and heretics deny is that, in deciding cases, judges apply relatively determinate standards and invoke relatively determinate justificatory strategies to achieve closure of a choice open to them. Judges cannot do this, say many heretics, because of the truth of one claim, or a number of claims, about the indeterminacy of language and values. Such claims make *determinate* decision-making—that is, rationally compelling and politically legitimate decision-making—impossible. This claim can easily underpin heretics' denial of the hard case/easy case dichotomy.

What follows takes for granted that the two denials add up to a distinctive position and investigates heretics' account of the role of values within adjudication—an inquiry that raises issues of relevance and specification. Heretics' account of the nature and basis of the values that do and should inform adjudication is also examined and this, of course, raises issues of a foundational nature. The discussion establishes three important points. The first is that many heretics do indeed have a moral or political vision—complete or gestural—and take seriously the task of articulating, criticising and developing the values that do and should inform the law. This is significant for two reasons. First, it serves to dilute and deflect the hyperbolic, apocalyptic tone of some early reactions to the heresy. Heretics, remember, were said to have no place in the law school, were denied tenure and were generally demonised as overpaid revolutionaries.[1] They supposedly threatened

[1] A few of the many examples: C. Trillin, 'A Reporter at Large: Harvard Law' *New Yorker (Magazine)* 26 March 1984, 53–83 (on the tenure wars); P. Carrington, 'Of Law and the River' (1984) 34 *Journal of Legal Education* 222–228 (on the dangerously nihilistic nature of the heresy); and, on allegedly Jaguar-driving, wealthy heretics, B. Timmons, 'That's No Okie, That's My Torts Professor' *Wall Street Journal*, 3 April 1990, 20 and L. Menand, 'Radicalism for Yuppies' *The New Republic* 17 March 1986, 20–23.

the moral fibre of the law school, the law itself and the society and culture of which it is part. The basis of this threat was never explicitly articulated but one worry was often hinted at: heretics had no moral vision. As the discussion that follows shows, this worry and its cognate aspersions seem gratuitous if an indicator of moral seriousness—surely the antithesis of a dangerous nihilism—is a concern with articulating, criticising and developing the values that inform the law. There are few heretics who unambiguously eschew this task. Admittedly, some heretics are apparently extreme value sceptics, but even this doctrine has a respectable heritage within moral philosophy and has hardly, during the centuries since its inception, threatened the basis of either the law school or civilisation. Since many heretics gesture toward the moral and political vision they think the law should embody, it cannot be maintained that their critique of existing law and its constitutive values is entirely negative, that they have no answer to the question 'what would you put in its place?'[2] As the remainder of this chapter shows, nothing could be further from the truth.

Secondly, an appreciation of the moral and political vision of the heresy quells a more recent gripe about this body of thought. The gripe is rarely explicitly articulated, being more often delivered, by the ennui-laden, *sotto voce*. It holds not that heretics lack a moral and political vision but rather that their vision has failed.[3] Since the gripe is never fully articulated and argued through, we cannot be sure exactly when or why the vision failed. The discussion that follows serves to dispel the air of failure that nowadays wafts around heretical thought by replacing it with arguments that purport to show the strengths and weaknesses of heretics' moral and political vision. True, heretics face a number of difficulties, but few of them are so severe as to be insurmountable. As we will see, the most pervasive problem heretics face is that their accounts of the values that do and should inform the law are rarely fully developed.

The second point the discussion establishes is related to the first by way of amendment. Consideration of the accounts heretics offer of the role and nature of values within adjudication serves to dispel an impression probably encouraged by the statement of the first point, namely, that heretics embrace a single moral or political vision. This is a mistake. Rather, there are a number of such visions, although they are not all equally plausible or compelling. This leads directly to the final point the essay aims to establish. It is that heretics do not do particularly well when they undertake the task

[2] The question and its proponents are discussed by M. Fischl, 'The Question that Killed Critical Legal Studies' (1992) 17 *Law and Social Inquiry* 779–820, pp. 780–785.

[3] Two of the few examples of this gripe actually being articulated in print, though not by proponents and hence not developed in any way, are: C. Hussan, 'Expanding the Legal Vocabulary: The Challenge Posed by the Deconstruction and Defense of Law' (1986) 95 *Yale L. J.* 969–991, pp. 969–973 and N. Duxbury, *Patterns of American Jurisprudence* (Oxford, Clarendon 1995), p. 426 and fn. 24.

of articulating, criticising and developing the values that do and should inform the law. What follows aims to show where and how various heretical arguments come unstuck and hints at ways in which some arguments may be revived. Unlike many of the critical remarks directed at the heresy, this negative point is, as I hope the discussion shows, well founded: founded, that is, upon *arguments*. Hence, I hope to avoid the sheer lack of argument and plethora of unfounded assertions that have characterised many responses to the heresy. This should allow us to see more clearly the issues at stake in the dispute between orthodoxy and heresy and facilitate a genuine discussion.

Discussion of the first level of value talk—where questions are raised about the relevance of values to a particular practice or institution—can be gratifyingly brief. It is undoubtedly the case that heretics, like the orthodox, agree that values do indeed play a role within the existing practice and accounts of adjudication.[4] What is less clear is whether heretics also accept that values will play a role within post-orthodox, post-liberal adjudication (hereinafter I follow heretical bad practice by treating 'liberal' and 'orthodox' as synonyms). Furthermore, heretics' position on this issue is likely to be a function of their foundational account of the nature and basis of values. Thus, a sceptical account of the possibility of moral knowledge seems obviously in conflict with, and a rationalist account more supportive of, the claim that post-liberal adjudication must be informed by a particular set of values. Here one's foundational commitments determine the utility of value talk aimed at issues of specification. Accepting that this is generally the case, the emphasis of what follows is skewed towards the foundational level of heretical value talk, but not exclusively so. For, as will be seen, the issue of specification is an important concern of many heretics.

The chapter divides heretical positions on the nature and basis of values into those that are sceptical about values, those that are not, and those that are ambiguous. The first and third positions are dealt with in section I. The second position occupies section II. There are two possible value sceptical positions that heretics could take up but only the second is sustainable. The first—labelled extreme value scepticism—affirms: (i) that values are implicated within adjudication as it takes place in existing 'liberal' societies; (ii)

[4] It would be too tiresome and pedantic (even for me) to catalogue every heretical admission to this effect. Here are a few instances: R. Unger, *Knowledge and Politics* (New York, The Free Press 1975), pp. 88–100; *The Critical Legal Studies Movement* (Cambridge, Mass., Harvard U. P. 1986) pp. 17 and 88–89; and *What Should Legal Analysis Become?* (London, Verso 1996), p. 116. See also D. Kennedy, 'Form and Substance in Private Law Adjudication' (1976) 89 *Harvard L. R.* 1685–1778, pp. 1772–1773 (hereinafter referred to as '*FS*') and his 'Freedom and Constraint in Adjudication: A Critical Phenomenology' (1986) 36 *Journal of Legal Education* 518–562, pp. 533–535 (where he speaks the language of 'policy') and pp. 548–553; D. Cornell, *The Philosophy of the Limit* (London, Routledge, Chapman and Hall 1992), pp. 92, 94, 110, 148, 160 and 161.

that values would be similarly implicated within the process of adjudication as it would exist in the type of post-liberal society heretics aim to bring about; and (iii) that all value choices unavoidably suffer from rationality and legitimacy deficits. Obviously, the basis of this third claim must be some foundational position about the nature and basis of values. That is, extreme value sceptics must offer a plausible account of why value talk is best avoided, why it has no power over us—because, for example, such talk is ideological, self-interested, expressive only of a will to power and domination, or utterly lacking in rationality—if their position is to be taken seriously. One consequence of taking up extreme value scepticism is that its proponents run into exactly the same problems as those members of the orthodoxy who espouse strong value pluralism. For, if adjudication is in part a process of making and attempting to justify value choices, then extreme value scepticism and orthodox value pluralism struggle to show that adjudication is either a rationally compelling or politically legitimate activity. There is, however, a difference of degree here since orthodox value pluralists will face this problem less frequently than extreme value sceptics, the reason being that the former accept and the latter reject the hard/easy case dichotomy. What makes extreme value scepticism unsustainable as an account of adjudication is that it appears self-defeating: why would heretics want to affirm its three claims when so doing discredits not only the liberal practice and theory of adjudication but also the prospective practice of post-liberal adjudication? This particular question and the general contours of extreme value scepticism will be examined in section I (a).

The second value sceptical position that heretics could take up is elucidated in section I (b). When compared with extreme value scepticism, this position is rather limited (henceforth it is unimaginatively labelled 'moderate value scepticism'). It holds (i) that values are of course implicated in the existing practice and accounts of liberal adjudication and (ii) that some or all of those values are in some sense so problematic as to call into question both the legitimacy and rationality of present processes of adjudication. This position escapes the self-defeating consequence of extreme value scepticism because it leaves open and in fact encourages the possibility of developing an account of values and their role in adjudication free from legitimacy and rationality deficits. However, it does little to show what the basis of such values might be: moderate value sceptics are satisfied with 'trashing' liberal, orthodox values and occasionally recommending others to stand in their place. The dispute between moderate value sceptics and the orthodox therefore takes place within the domain of the second level of value talk. The dispute is about which values really are valuable and ought to impinge upon the practice of adjudication now and in the future. It is a dispute about the specific entries on a list of values or one between proponents of competing lists. The snag that besets moderate value sceptics is obvious: they must at some point begin the task of arguing that the values they embrace are better than those currently in play in adjudication. Such an account could highlight either or both the substantive content or the nature and basis of the values espoused. It must therefore move towards and take up a position within the third, foundational level of value talk. Unfortunately, moderate value sceptics are either unable or unwilling to take this extra step

Some heretics have adopted a particular body of thought in the hope that it serves as the vehicle of a moral vision that could support the heresy. The body of thought is deconstruction and it is argued, by some at least, that this approach brings with it an ethics, an account—albeit tentative—of what is good and bad in human life, of how we ought to react to and be treated by others. This position is considered in section I (c). It is not possible to itemise the constitutive claims of this position here for a reason that will be elaborated in that section, namely, that the position is not yet fully specified. This is one of the two reasons why this position must be regarded as a failure. An ethics of deconstruction has yet to be adequately and thoroughly formulated and the present debate on this issue, certainly in jurisprudential circles and only marginally less so in philosophical circles, is gestural. Therefore, the appropriate verdict upon the deconstructive strategy is a negative one. The second reason that undermines this position consists of a genuine doubt as to whether or not deconstructive thought and practice are compatible with any form of normative thought and practice. Some who assume the mantle of deconstruction within and beyond the legal academy have claimed there is an incompatibility. If this view is right, then the question of an ethics of deconstruction is pointless and so too is the question of the role of values within adjudication. This is not to say that proponents of this view must be unconcerned with the role that some—those as yet untouched by the 'truths' of deconstruction—think values play within adjudication. Far from it, since a continuing belief in the significance of values despite deconstruction's message obviously requires explanation and, as we will see, one particularly challenging explanation has been offered. That aside, as the debate now stands, the problems that ensnare deconstructive heretics in search of the normative substance of their practice and thought appear quite debilitating.

Section II analyses the position of a stout-hearted heretic who takes the step to the foundational level of value talk that moderate value sceptics eschew. His position is labelled, without pejoration, visionary. It is not a position that is sceptical about values although it accepts the first claim of moderate value scepticism, slightly amends the second and adds three other claims. Our visionary's first claim is, then, (i) that values are implicated within the existing practice and accounts of adjudication. The modification concerns that part of the second claim of moderate value scepticism which was initially formulated disjunctively, referring to either *some or all* of the values in play in the existing practice of adjudication. Our visionary can accept only the limited version of this claim, namely, (ii)* that *some* of the values implicated in the existing practice and accounts of liberal adjudication are in some sense problematic. The first of our visionary's additional three claims follows on from (ii)* and holds (iii) that some values within the existing practice of adjudication are indeed worthy of allegiance although presently marginalised or suppressed. This third claim brings with it an account of how those values might be reclaimed from the recesses of existing practice without a revolutionary change in that practice. The fourth claim goes slightly beyond the third. It asserts that (iv) there are, in addition to the commendable values immanent although not fully realised in our existing practice, other values that we must strive to uphold and realise in existing and future practice. The fifth claim will come as no surprise given the nature of the third and fourth claims since the obvious questions to ask of those claims are: why are those values worthy of allegiance? How is it that they generate good reasons for action? Hence claim (v) is foundational in the sense that it gives an account, the details of which will be examined below, of the normative basis and power of these values.

The visionary stance is less pessimistic about the nature of values than extreme value scepticism and more explicit in its account of them than moderate value scepticism. It offers a less problematic account of post-liberal, post-orthodox adjudication because it contains some hints as to the content, nature and basis of the values which will inform that practice. It also goes beyond the position of heretical proponents of deconstruction because it offers, first, a fairly fully worked out specification of the values it takes seriously and, second, an account of the basis of those values, of why they are worthy of realisation. Although our visionary's argument is not unproblematic, the problems it generates are qualitatively different from, and much more interesting than, those that ensnare the other heretical positions. That, at least, is the thrust of section II which concludes by suggesting that, problems notwithstanding, the visionary stance is a most promising strategy. It promises a coherent account of the nature and basis—as well as an elucidation of the specific kinds and role—of values within adjudication. It is a preamble to an overarching moral vision for the heretical programme, a vision the programme badly needs but which heretics have so far been loath to elucidate. Hence, the visionary stance has a presumptive claim to heretics' allegiance until such time as an ethics of deconstruction is fully developed and because neither value sceptical position is tenable. If a deconstructive ethics is untenable, and if the visionary stance is unproblematic, then that presumptive claim becomes conclusive.

I A SHORT HISTORY OF FAILURE

(a) Extreme value scepticism

The first two of the three claims that constitute extreme value scepticism serve only to situate that doctrine within legal scholarship At large, extreme value scepticism is marked by the third claim, namely, that value choices unavoidably suffer from rationality and legitimacy deficits. This is an interesting claim made all the more so by the fact that, within the history of moral philosophy, many diverse attempts have been made to substantiate it.[5] Almost all of these attempts have isolated either the nature of values themselves or that nature taken in conjunction with the limits of reason as the explanation of the problematic status of value choices. There has, however, been little agreement upon which particular properties of values—or which properties of reason—ensure that value choices lack legitimacy and rationality. Within the realm of heretical thought, however, two arguments to this end are encountered although the proponents of each are frequently ambiguous in their support. So, we will see that, while there are two versions of the first argument expressed in such a way as to suggest a commitment to extreme value scepticism, each version also appears, *in the same writers' hands*, to entail a commitment to moderate value scepticism. By contrast, instances of the second argument are relatively free from ambiguity.

The first argument to show that values unavoidably suffer from rationality and legitimacy deficits arises from one of the two versions of the fundamental contradiction. This argument is by now familiar. It is characteristic of Duncan Kennedy's early work and was subsequently taken to heart by a number of imitators.[6] One version holds that because the human condition is such that we are caught in a conflict between our need for the support of others, on the one hand, and our need for independence from others, on the other, then consistency in our moral, ethical, political or legal thought is impossible. Our values, in so far as they are premised upon this conflict, are *bound* to conflict. In a passage that had almost liturgical status for some heretics, Kennedy claimed that

> the goal of individual freedom is at the same time dependent on and incompatible with the communal coercive action that is necessary to achieve it. Others (family,

[5] For two related efforts—the first somewhat hasty, the second more considered—see A. J. Ayer, *Language, Truth and Logic* (Harmondsworth, Penguin 1971), pp. 110–116 and C. L. Stevenson, *Ethics and Language* (New Haven, Yale U. P. 1944).

[6] Kennedy's recent *A Critique of Adjudication* (Cambridge, Mass., Harvard U. P. 1997) tells us very little about values except (i) they are ideological or, at least, they seem to be constitutive elements of ideologies, and (ii) they are influenced by some or other version of the fundamental contradiction. It is very difficult to construct a coherent position from this different from both the extreme and moderate value scepticism apparent in the early work.

friends, bureaucrats, cultural figures, the state) are necessary if we are to become persons at all—they provide us the stuff of our selves and protect us in crucial ways against destruction. . . . But at the same time that it forms and protects us, the universe of others (family, friendship, bureaucracy, culture, the state) threatens us with annihilation and urges upon us forms of fusion that are quite plainly bad rather than good.[7]

This contradiction between self and other informs, because it is a precondition of, all our thought. Furthermore, not only do Kennedy and others accept that this meta-level conflict ensures micro-level value conflict, they also take it for granted that such micro-level conflict cannot be rationally resolved. In the face of the fundamental contradiction, reason is powerless. This is not, however, to say that the contradiction and the micro-level conflict it generates are always transparent to us; far from it, since processes of 'mediation' serve to hide it from us, to delude us into thinking that such conflicts can indeed be resolved rationally and legitimately.[8]

A second version of the fundamental contradiction—which, strictly speaking, need not contradict the first—holds that we are simultaneously committed to very abstract congeries or systems of values that are incompatible, conflict between them being irresolvable: 'we are divided, among ourselves and within ours[e]lves, between *irreconcilable* visions of humanity and society, and between radically different aspirations for our common future'.[9] The competing systems of values that inform these visions are usually described as 'individualist' and 'altruist', sometimes as 'substantive' and 'formal' and, rarely, as 'objective' and 'subjective'.[10] In the former guise the content of the two systems of values are described thus by Kennedy:

individualism is the making of a sharp distinction between one's interests and those of others, combined with the belief that a preference in conduct for one's own interests is legitimate . . . The form of conduct associated with individualism is self-reliance. This means an insistence on defining and achieving objectives without the help of others . . . It means . . . a firm conviction that I am entitled to enjoy the benefits of my efforts without an obligation to share or sacrifice them to the interests of others . . . The essence of altruism is the belief that one ought *not* to indulge a sharp preference for one's own interest over those of others. Altruism enjoins us to make sacrifices, to share, and to be merciful.[11]

[7] 'The Structure of Blackstone's *Commentaries*' (1979) 28 *Buffalo L. R.* 205–382, pp. 211–212. Henceforth referred to as '*BC*'.

[8] *BC*, pp. 214–216, 256–272 and 379–382.

[9] Kennedy, 'Form and Substance in Private Law Adjudication', *supra*, note 4, p. 1685 (emphasis supplied). Henceforth referred to as '*FS*'.

[10] The first formulation belongs, of course, to Kennedy's *FS*. The second and third appear in C. Dalton, 'An Essay in the Deconstruction of Contract Doctrine' (1985) 94 *Yale L. J.* 997–1114, pp. 999–1010 and 1066–1094; G. Frug, 'The Ideology of Bureaucracy in American Law' (1984) 97 *Harvard L. R.* 1276–1388, pp. 1279–1296.

[11] *FS*, pp. 1713–1717.

Again, it is claimed that these competing sets of values illustrate the parameters within which all our thought operates; all our thought is therefore conditioned by them. It cannot be a surprise, then, to be told that, *inter alia*, the legal 'problem of form' (ought we to regulate by means of rigorously defined rules or more flexible standards?), the choice of liability rule in tort law (one based on foreseeability of damage or upon a natural consequences test?) and the tension between freedom-promoting and freedom-denying rules in contract law are functions of the conflict between altruism and individualism.[12]

The argument from one or the other version of the fundamental contradiction qualifies as an instance of *extreme* value scepticism on two grounds. First, a number (although not all) of the renditions of the argument hold that the fundamental contradiction is universal. It defines the human condition *simpliciter* and not simply the condition of that segment of humanity living through western liberal capitalism. Jack Balkin puts this well:

> I do not believe that our moral and legal consciousness is dialectically structured because it is Liberal consciousness, so that if we could free ourselves from Liberal institutions our moral and legal debates would no longer display a crystalline structure. Our legal institutions and our system of moral values are Liberal, but the contradictions of our thought are not Liberal contradictions, but are only manifest in our Liberalism.[13]

When combined with the claim that the contradiction is either a cause or an example of value conflict, this ensures that value conflict too is universal. Secondly, many proponents of the fundamental contradiction argument suggest that value conflict generated by the contradiction cannot be rationally or legitimately resolved. Hence our situation is not one in which we are involved in an as yet unfinished quest for a metric by which conflicts between values can be solved. Rather, our condition is such that value conflicts can never be solved because no metric exists, although this clearly does not deny that such conflicts can be mediated, postponed or disguised.[14] These two reasons guarantee the truth of the third and crucial claim of extreme value scepticism, namely, that value choices suffer from rationality and legitimacy deficits.

[12] The form problem is, of course, the fulcrum of *FS*. For a discussion of liability rules in tort see A. Hutchinson, 'Of Kings and Dirty Rascals: The Struggle for Democracy' (1984) 9 *Queen's L. J.* 273–292, pp. 280–292; and, for some brief observations on contract see R. Gordon, '"Of Law and the River", and of Nihilism and Academic Freedom' (1985) 35 *Journal of Legal Education* 1–16, p. 2.

[13] 'The Crystalline Structure of Legal Thought' (1986) 39 *Rutgers L. R.* 1–110, p. 76. For some of Kennedy's statements that the fundamental contradiction is universal see: *BC*, pp. 210, 212, 213 and 221; *FS*, pp. 1684, 1722, 1766, 1767 and 1778.

[14] '[T]here is no metasystem that would, if only we could find it, key us into one mode or the other as circumstances required': *FS*, p. 1775.

The second argument used to support the claim that value choices unavoidably suffer from rationality and legitimacy deficits has a good deal in common with a traditional non-cognitivist position in moral philosophy.[15] That is to say, the argument appears committed to the view that the justification of particular value positions and choices between them is not a rational, although it may be an emotive or psychological, matter. That being so, and assuming a strong link between rationality and legitimacy, value choices must lack legitimacy.[16] Hence this argument is clearly an instance of extreme value scepticism. However, the argument does not have a great many heretical proponents and it is sometimes encountered only in discussions of other heretical and orthodox positions. For example, Alan Hutchinson and Patrick Monahan ascribe to 'advocacy scholarship'—an heretical alternative to orthodox theory and practice—the 'view that all social arrangements are arbitrary and contingent, [and] that *the best a theorist can do is make a personal commitment* to a particular set of values and then to defend them'.[17] Presumably, this is the best the theorist can do because the values to which she 'commits' herself cannot be rationally recommended to her, cannot be chosen on the basis of reason: 'commitments as such cannot be justified, and . . . a justification of anything must presuppose a previous commitment'.[18] Now, although Hutchinson and Monahan do not endorse advocacy scholarship—'CLSer's should want nothing to do with [it]'[19]—their own position is in one respect not far removed from it. Speaking for themselves, they hold that choosing between values and commitments in the course of disputes in life and in law is all of a piece: 'every doctrinal dispute is reducible to the contradictory claims of communal security and individual freedom. Any particular resolution of that dispute is simply an *arbitrary* choice'.[20] As a view about the rationality of value choice,

[15] Many of the standard non-cognitivist positions—although that label covers a multitude of sins—are outlined in W. D. Hudson, *Modern Moral Philosophy* (London, Macmillan, 2nd ed., 1988), chs 1–4.

[16] I examined the relationship between rationality and political legitimacy in ch. 4.

[17] 'Law, Politics and Critical Legal Scholars: The Unfolding Drama of American Legal Thought' (1984) 36 *Stanford L. R.* 199–245, p. 238 (emphasis supplied). The unsubstantiated claim that value choices are non-rational matters of commitment is a familiar refrain within heretical writings. Two examples are: *FS*, p. 1775 and J. Singer, 'The Player and the Cards: Nihilism and Legal Theory' (1984) 94 *Yale L. J.* 1–70, pp. 58 and 66.

[18] R. Trigg, *Reason and Commitment* (Cambridge, C. U. P. 1973), p. 93.

[19] 'Law, Politics and Critical Legal Scholars etc.', *supra*, note 17, p. 238.

[20] *Ibid*., p. 211 (emphasis supplied). For more of the same see: Hutchinson, *supra*, note 12, p. 280 and his *Dwelling on the Threshold: Critical Essays in Modern Legal Thought* (Toronto, Carswell 1988), p. 217. In the latter Hutchinson's authorial voice is heard in the judgment of the mythical Lefft, J. Hutchinson has recently renounced the 'debilitating nihilism' in some of these essays, although it seems that he means to refer to his then extreme scepticism about rule application and not his then—and continuing—value scepticism: 'A Postmodern's Hart: Taking Rules Sceptically' (1995) 58 *Modern L. R.* 788–819, p. 798. That Hutchinson's extreme value scepticism remains intact is clear from *Waiting for Coraf: A Critique of Law and Rights* (Toronto, University of Toronto Press 1995), pp. 86–87.

this is as much a matter of commitment as—and therefore indistinguishable from—the position allegedly taken by advocacy scholarship.

A related sceptical refrain is heard in David Kairys's comments about values. He observes that 'policy analysis and balancing of conflicting policies . . . do not require particular results and *inevitably impose certain subjective values*'.[21] Having said this, Kairys must believe that some values are subjective, but the remark need not be taken as endorsing a universal claim, namely, that *all* values in *all* conceivable societies are subjective and therefore suffer from legitimacy and rationality deficits. Of course, the 'therefore' in this proposition trades upon the richly ambiguous word 'subjective'. That ambiguity will not be completely resolved here, save to say that in the context of moral discourse, and in at least some senses, the word 'subjective' surely indicates a lack of rational power and legitimacy. Were this not the case it is difficult to envisage what power the subjectivity accusation could have. Now, if Kairys's comments are taken as indicators of the universal claim, then he is committed to extreme value scepticism. And that position, remember, is one in which value choices lack legitimacy and rationality. For if they do not, what power can the claims made by Kairys and Hutchinson and Monahan—claims that value choices impose *subjective* values, that they are *arbitrary* matters of personal commitment—possibly have?

It is now clear that heretics who are extreme value sceptics offer a pessimistic account of adjudication as practised now and in the future. For in so far as it is a process entailing value choices, adjudication must—because of the truth of extreme value scepticism—lack rationality and legitimacy. Extreme value scepticism appears to be a self-defeating position for heretics if by affirming it they hope to illustrate the ills of the present and the advantages of a different future. Since on this account the very idea of adjudication is objectionable, its existence now and in the future bespeaks a society seriously flawed and impoverished. What could heretics who are extreme value sceptics possibly see as the advantages—intellectual, emotional and political—of maintaining that adjudication now is, and will in the future continue to be, a process unavoidably lacking rationality and legitimacy? Two possibilities arise from the heretical literature. The first I label the 'edification' and the second the 'better future' strategy. They will be examined in turn. Each strategy generates particular problems of its own but both are beset by a general snag. Thus the conclusion is that neither strategy is particularly plausible.

The edification strategy holds that the truth of extreme value scepticism allows us to appreciate the limits of our reason and abilities, enforcing the point that we can avoid neither conflict nor irrationality in our decision-

[21] 'Law and Politics' (1984) 52 *George Washington L. R.* 243–262, p. 246 (emphasis supplied).

making. Of course, 'we can, as a matter of fact, decide if we have to . . . [but] [t]he only kind of imagery that conveys the process by which we act and act and act in one direction, but then reach the sticking point, is that of existentialist philosophy. We make commitments, and pursue them. The moment of abandonment is no more rational than that of beginning, and equally a moment of terror'.[22] This is a feature of our, the human condition; to deny it is to misunderstand something important about ourselves. Moreover, some heretics think that this is just the kind of misunderstanding to which the orthodox are prone. The orthodox supposedly think that decision-making in general and adjudication in particular are completely determinate processes, this view being caricatured 'as the belief that important questions about life can be answered by a formula, a mechanical decision procedure'.[23] An edifying philosophy, of which the edification strategy is but a part, aims to avert the danger 'that some given vocabulary, some way in which people might come to think of themselves' will lead them to think that all the important questions and choices that arise in life can be determinately and relatively easily answered. The edification strategy has 'sense only as a protest against attempts to close off the conversation'.[24] For some heretics the orthodox are guilty of just this closing of the conversation, of believing in a determinate method of making and justifying choices.

But it is not quite true that the orthodox think the conversation can be closed or believe that completely rational and legitimate adjudicative choices can be made. For, while the orthodox would accept that easy cases can be decided in this way, many of them seem committed to the view that decisions in some hard cases suffer from both legitimacy and rationality deficits. Thus the edification strategy serves only to mark out the difference between heretics and orthodox on the issue of the possibility and number of easy cases. While edifying philosophy constitutes 'an attempt to shake the rug out from under existing normal or abnormal systems of thought [supposedly manifest in the orthodoxy]'[25], the identification of this difference over easy cases surely falls far short of that ambitious aim. This slight misrepresentation of the orthodoxy is not, however, the most acute problem faced by proponents of the edification strategy. Far more problematic is the obvious incompatibility between this strategy, on the one hand, and any positive reconstructive programme, on the other. That is to say, the edification strategy, being premised upon extreme value scepticism, cannot be affirmed in conjunction with recipes for social, political and emotional change and development. At least, this is the case where such reconstructive programmes rest upon and seek to invoke particular values. This problem

[22] *FS*, p. 1775. [23] Singer, *supra*, note 17, p. 61.
[24] R. Rorty, *Philosophy and the Mirror of Nature* (Oxford, Basil Blackwell 1979), p. 377.
[25] Singer, *supra*, note 17, p. 57.

besets the better future strategy also and will be examined in a little more depth below. Suffice for the present to note that, puzzlingly, some proponents of the edification strategy do indeed link it with rather vague but nevertheless positive, reconstructive programmes.[26]

The better future strategy holds that the truth of extreme value scepticism and the pessimistic account of adjudication it generates shows that there are other and better means of resolving our disputes. Kennedy partially endorses one such possibility. He observes that '[t]he state, and with it the judge, are destined to disappear as people come to feel their brotherhood . . . Arbitrators are an improvement; mediators even better. But we attain the goal only when we surmount our alienation from one another and share ends to such an extent that contingency provides occasions for ingenuity but never for dispute'.[27] Thus, when combined with extreme value scepticism, the better future strategy need not be self-defeating since that better future will be one in which adjudication plays no role in our lives. Adjudication as we have so far understood it is best avoided. Of the alternatives—and thinking beyond Kennedy's vision of expanded altruism—proponents of the better future strategy often endorse a thorough-going programme of empowered, participatory democracy. The details of such a programme are rarely thoroughly worked out, but in some hands it is undoubtedly intended as an alternative to law and adjudication: '[a]n idiom of popular power could be developed, along with an accessible thesaurus of public empowerment to replace the elite lexicon of the law . . . [T]o achieve this state of affairs we must enhance and extend [but] . . . also quieten certain voices. For instance, lawyers will have to adopt a more humble tone and speak *sotto voce*, if at all'.[28]

In what the details of such a programme might consist and how, exactly, it presents an alternative to adjudication, are intriguing questions that, unfortunately, cannot be taken up here. The key question for present purposes arises thus. It is not a misrepresentation to interpret the programme of empowered democracy as a recipe for social, political and economic change; but, if it is such, how can it be recommended to us by extreme value sceptics? Unless they argue for the better future in value free or non-moral terms the danger they face is, of course, that of either falling victim to, or

[26] Singer, *supra*, note 17, pp. 66–70 and *FS*, p. 1771. This is especially odd in Singer's case since his exemplary edifying philosopher is Richard Rorty who insists that edifying philosophy is purely reactive, never constructive: see *supra*, note 24, pp. 366–368, 369, 377 and 378. For more on Singer's peculiar reading of Rorty, see J. Stick, 'Can Nihilism be Pragmatic?' (1986) 100 *Harvard L. R.* 332–401, pp. 341–345 and 366–367.

[27] *FS*, p. 1771. The endorsement is partial because Kennedy is describing the altruist vision, a vision—on the universalist reading of the argument from the fundamental contradiction, at least—in constant conflict with the individualist vision.

[28] Hutchinson, *Dwelling on the Threshold*, *supra*, note 20, p. 22. For a further instalment of Hutchinson's project see *Waiting for Coraf*, *supra*, note 20, chs. 1–3 and 7.

implicitly renouncing, their own value scepticism.[29] Moreover, it is unlikely, for two reasons, that extreme value sceptics could offer non-moral, value-free arguments in favour of their better future. First, it is just very difficult indeed to imagine what a non-moral, value-free argument in favour of, for example, empowered democracy, might look like. Suppose one were able to show that empowered democracy would make citizens happier and the community more efficient. Could it plausibly be maintained that the criteria of 'happiness' and 'efficiency' were either non-moral or value free? Many powerful arguments have been offered to show that the answer to this question must be in the negative.[30] Secondly, many heretics who take up the better future strategy would accept Hutchinson's claim that '[i]n a world where history cannot be side-stepped or bracketed, any claims to offer an *objective analysis or value-free judgment of any social practice* immediately become suspect'.[31] Obviously, they cannot accept this and persist in attempting to make non-moral, value-free arguments. Alternatively, they could make a moral or value-laden argument in favour of the specified better future but doing this would contradict their value scepticism. The conjunction of extreme value scepticism and the better future strategy is therefore unsustainable.

The snag that besets both edification and better future strategies can now be exposed. It informed the most serious specific problem both strategies faced, namely, their inability to combine extreme value scepticism with any positive, reconstructive programme. The underlying snag here is not, of course, solely that of developing a non-moral, non-evaluative programme of social, political and emotional change which could give agents reasons for action, but the source of that problem: extreme value scepticism itself. Accepting this foundational doctrine makes the development and recommendation of a reconstructive programme acutely problematic. Moreover, the doctrine is dubious for two independent and powerful reasons. First, in most heretical hands the arguments to support it are weak. They are not really arguments at all but assertions. It is asserted, as is plain from the statements cited above, either that it is just the case that we are caught in one or other version of the fundamental contradiction or that it is simply the

[29] The danger is vividly exemplified in Hutchinson, *Waiting for Coraf*, *supra*, note 20. Note his affirmation of Canadian Chief Justice Brian Dickson's remark that value choices 'must, by their very nature be arbitrary' (p. 87) and his affirmation of a conception of democracy, community and the good life (pp. 189, 206–207 and 225). Are the latter not values?

[30] Two good introductions to the vast literature about the alleged normative basis of conceptions of efficiency are: A. Buchanan, *Ethics, Efficiency and the Market* (Oxford, Clarendon 1985), pp. 4–13; J. Coleman, *Markets, Morals and the Law* (Cambridge, C. U. P. 1988), chs. 3 and 4; for similarly useful introductions to the problematic notion of happiness see J. S. Mill, *Utilitarianism, On Liberty and Considerations on Representative Government* (London, Dent Dutton 1972), pp. 5–11; J. J. C. Smart and B. Williams, *Utilitarianism: For and Against* (Cambridge, C. U. P. 1973), pp. 12–27.

[31] *Dwelling on the Threshold*, *supra*, note 20, p. 33 (emphasis supplied).

truth that value judgments are a matter of arbitrary, subjective commitment. But it is surely not unreasonable to want to hear the arguments that support these claims. Secondly, the argument some heretics do offer does not establish their case. It can be called 'the argument from moral experience' since it holds that, when faced with value choices, we are vividly aware of the indeterminacy of the arguments pro and con and that in this context rationally compelling arguments are rare indeed. The fact that our experience is like this supposedly warrants the inference that the subject matter in question—values and value choices—necessarily lacks rationality and legitimacy. This is surely the point of the value choice parables offered by Kennedy and Singer.[32]

Yet the argument from moral experience fails in three ways. First, it seems to be the case that moral experience and our experience of value choice in general is not univocal. This much is clear from the fact that many who deny extreme value scepticism and affirm some rationalist or realist account of the nature and basis of moral values could also point to moral experience to support their account. While it may be the case that our moral experience is sometimes like the sceptical picture—indeterminate and apparently devoid of rationality—it also seems to be the case that it is sometimes like the rationalist or realist picture, in which clear and determinate answers are available.[33] Secondly, our *experience* of moral or value choice does not necessarily tell us anything about the rationality or otherwise of those domains since our experience could be affected by variables beyond them. We might feel that value choices are indeterminate and non-rational but that could be because, for example, we are in the grip of certain false beliefs about the nature of values. We could experience moral choice the way Kennedy and Singer say we do and yet it could still be the case that a determinate, systematic, rationally compelling and true moral theory is available to us. The truth of the former does not, without more, impugn the truth of the latter.

Finally, it is difficult to see how the argument from moral experience could be used to support either argument from the fundamental contradiction. It is clear that either argument from the fundamental contradiction can entail the argument from moral experience. Since the fact that *all* our thought and values rest upon either the contradiction between self and others or that between individualism and altruism, and those contradictions are rationally irresolvable, then it follows that at least some of our value choices will take the form which the argument from moral experience says they do. What is equally clear is that the argument from moral experience

[32] *FS*, p. 1775; Singer, *supra*, note 17, p. 66.

[33] On the unreliable nature of appeals to moral experience/language, see J. Mackie, *Ethics* (Harmondsworth, Penguin Books 1977), ch. 1 and S. Blackburn, *Spreading the Word* (Oxford, Clarendon 1984), ch. 6.

does not entail the truth of either argument from the fundamental contradiction. This is because many reasons other than the truth of one or other of the fundamental contradictions could support the argument from moral experience. Until it is established that the argument from moral experience can only be a consequence of the truth of the fundamental contradictions, affirmation of the former cannot entail the latter. This means that heretics must turn to other arguments if they wish to establish the truth of the fundamental contradictions and hence the truth of extreme value scepticism. Arguing for—rather than simply affirming—the fundamental contradictions would probably require something like a transcendental argument. Even then, it is certain neither that this kind of argument would work nor that heretics would want to use it if it did.[34]

Extreme value sceptics, then, face a number of acute problems. Their pessimistic account of adjudication now and in the future is either self-defeating or must lead them, via the edification and better future strategies, to question their commitment to extreme value scepticism. Since they offer no plausible argument in favour of extreme value scepticism, renouncing that commitment is a viable option. We need now determine whether or not the heretical position we have labelled moderate value scepticism is any more plausible than the extreme variety.

(b) Moderate value scepticism

Moderate value scepticism, remember, holds that values are implicated in the current practice of adjudication; that some or all of those values are in some sense problematic; and that it is possible to offer a non-problematic account of values, some of which already do and others of which can, inform the existing and future practice of adjudication. It must also be noted that heretics are led to moderate value scepticism by two distinct paths. One path has already been hinted at in the discussion of extreme value scepticism. It is the path of those heretics whose accounts of one or other version of the argument from the fundamental contradiction are such that they seem committed both to the view that the contradiction is universal and that it is not. On the basis of the statements of the latter kind, these heretics qualify as moderate rather than extreme value sceptics. For moderate value sceptics the fundamental contradiction is not universal. It can be transcended: it is a partial truth in the sense that it holds only of current liberal

[34] This kind of argument seems out of sympathy with the 'anti-foundationalist' spirit of some heretical thought (see, for example, Singer, *supra*, note 17). A useful introduction to transcendental arguments, a classic example of which is Kant's transcendental deduction of the categories (I. Kant, *Critique of Pure Reason* (London, Macmillan 1929), pp. 120–175), is C. Taylor, 'The Validity of Transcendental Arguments' (1978–79) *Proceedings of the Aristotelian Society* 151–165.

capitalist societies.[35] Therefore, the fact that values and value choices lack rationality and legitimacy as a result of the truth of the fundamental contradiction will not necessarily hold true when the contradiction is overcome. In this latter situation it is perfectly coherent for heretics to maintain that values and value choices are completely rational and legitimate; they can hold, furthermore, that in a future society free from the fundamental contradiction, a value-laden practice of adjudication will be maximally rational and legitimate.

The second path by which some heretics arrive at moderate value scepticism avoids any version of the fundamental contradiction. Rather, this path involves arguing that the values informing some area of the law are unsatisfactory and should either (i) be replaced altogether with a different list of underpinning values or (ii) at least supplemented by other values. Mark Tushnet's proposal that the American constitution be interpreted so as to require socialism is a flippant example of the former, while Karl Klare's reconstruction of American labour law is an exemplary and serious instance of the latter.[36] Klare says that 'liberal collective bargaining law is . . . a form of political domination . . . articulat[ing] an ideology that aims to legitimate and justify unnecessary and destructive domination in the work place', but is also keen to stress the advantages this body of law has secured for workers. He holds, for instance, that 'collective bargaining law has endorsed and to some extent has actually engendered the democratic participation of employees in workplace governance'.[37] His objection to the existing practice of collective bargaining adjudication is that values such as those of democratic participation are incompletely realised and others are never even acknowledged. Hence:

Our political vision [and, *ex hypothesi*, the vision underpinning labour law] must encompass new notions of the meaning of work, indeed, that work should have meaning, that it should be a mode of self-expression and development . . . ; new conceptions of how to reconcile the industrial process with personal life and physical

[35] Some of Kennedy's remarks suggest this much: *BC*, pp. 211, 213, 215, 217 and 221; *FS*, pp. 1712, 1725, 1731, 1737–1738 and 1776. See also, Frug, *supra*, note 10, p. 1291 (the contradiction can be transcended, but contrast p. 1377); M. Tushnet, 'Legal Scholarship: Its Causes and Cure' (1981) 90 *Yale L. J.* 1205–1223, p. 1223; Dalton, *supra*, note 10, p. 1095. For M. Kelman, the contradiction is a matter of aesthetics and so, presumably, can be transcended: *A Guide to Critical Legal Studies* (Cambridge, Mass., Harvard U. P. 1987), pp. 54–63.

[36] M. Tushnet, 'Dia-Tribe' (1980) 78 *Michigan L. R.* 694–710, p. 697. Klare's programme for American labour law is contained in a number of articles, a few of the most notable being: 'Judicial Deradicalization of the Wagner Act and the Origins of Modern Legal Consciousness' (1978) 62 *Minnesota L. R.* 265–339; 'Labour Law as Ideology: Toward a New Historiography of Collective Bargaining Law' (1981) *Industrial Relations L. R.* 450–482; 'Critical Theory and Labour Relations Law' in D. Kairys (ed.), *The Politics of Law* (New York, Pantheon 1982) and 'Workplace Democracy and Market Reconstruction: An Agenda for Legal Reform' (1988) 38 *Catholic University L. R.* 1–68.

[37] 'Labour Law as Ideology', *supra*, note 36, pp. 452–453.

environment; a new set of values about the uses and allocation of social resources; and an end to racism, sexism and all forms of illegitimate hierarchy in the workplace.[38]

Once the process of either complete value substitution or mere value supplementation has been carried out, a value-laden practice of adjudication need create no difficulties. The process will be as rational and legitimate as any process of value choice. Since Klare and his fellow travellers are not extreme value sceptics, the inference must be that such processes are or can be both rational and legitimate.

Moderate value scepticism does not embrace a pessimistic account of adjudication and it therefore avoids the risk of being self-defeating. The problems it does face are nevertheless severe. There are two and they demonstrate that moderate value scepticism is incompletely developed at the level of specification and at the foundational level. The first problem is easily stated. In response to the question of which values should replace or supplement those that underpin existing areas of law and adjudication there is a cacophony of competing heretical voices. Each voice operates at the level of specification with the result that there is not only a series of disputes between particular heretics and members of the orthodoxy about the values that do and should inform a specific area of law, but equally many disputes between heretics about what values underpin which areas of law. Those heretics who are moderate value sceptics—heretics who can without fear of inconsistency espouse value scepticism in conjunction with some positive, reconstructive programme for law, politics and society—have argued that the law should be informed by and promote the values constitutive of, *inter alia*, civic republicanism, empowered democracy, fraternity and community.[39] What is required of the proponents of such a list is that the entries be fairly precisely delineated since there is no guarantee that our pre-reflective understanding ensures consistency between them. But this task has yet to be undertaken. Moderate value scepticism therefore lacks a sufficiently detailed account of both the content and contours of its constitutive values and is *prima facie* internally unstable.

Furthermore, moderate value scepticism is incomplete in another sense. Not only is the content of its constitutive values left vague, their foundation is also oblique. No plausible arguments are offered to explain the power of these values, to show why they should be regarded as worthy of allegiance and why they generate reasons for action. Rather, the values are simply asserted, it being assumed that they are worth pursuing, that they have some rational power over us. This lacuna is evident in Klare's work.

[38] 'Critical Theory and Labour Relations Law', *supra*, note 36, p. 81.

[39] For a thorough and reliable overview of the various programmes and values invoked by heretics see R. Bauman, 'The Communitarian Vision of Critical Legal Studies' (1988) 33 *McGill L. R.* 295–356, pp. 311–336.

As is obvious from one of the passages cited above, he is not shy of outlining the moral and political vision he thinks should underlie labour law. However, he is more than reticent about specifying the power of that vision, telling us nothing about why it 'must' be upheld and pursued. We know what the programme looks like but are left in the dark as to why it is worthy of our support, as to why it gives us good reasons for action. This is an acute problem if we think it important to have reasons for action.

(c) The ethics of deconstruction

Two questions structure the discussion in this section: does deconstruction call into question the very possibility of value talk? Or does it hold that philosophy and practice are unavoidably moral, political or ethical? Heretics writing under the influence of deconstruction have offered two diametrically opposed answers to these questions which, somewhat surprisingly, purportedly derive from Derridean deconstruction. Clearly, that body of thought encourages a variety of interpretations and its apparent malleability has not been greatly reduced by Jacques Derrida's own intervention in the debate about the relationship between justice and deconstruction.[40] No position is taken here upon the 'authenticity' of the jurisprudential versions of deconstruction examined. The debate about what a genuine deconstructive philosophy looks like and who, if anyone (other than Derrida), actually comes close to encapsulating it, is neither particularly fertile nor relevant for present purposes.[41] Rather, these writers' self-descriptions—their claims to be doing deconstruction—are accepted without question since our sole concern is to determine what lessons, if any, heretical deconstruction provides about the role and nature of values within adjudication.

Before turning to those matters a point about terminology must be noted. Deconstructive heretics' responses to the two questions roughly track the contours of a debate between philosophers and literary critics.[42] Further, for many participants the debate is focused upon just one aspect of value-

[40] 'Force of Law: The "Mystical Foundation of Authority"' in D. Cornell, M. Rosenfeld and D. Carlson (eds.), *Deconstruction and the Possibility of Justice* (London, Routledge, Chapman and Hall 1992), 3–67. For acute comment on Derrida's essay see D. LaCapra, 'Violence, Justice, and the Force of Law' (1990) 11 *Cardozo L. R.* 1065–1078.

[41] M. Kramer has hawkish views on this matter: see, for example, 'The Philosopher Judge: Some Friendly Criticisms of Richard Posner's Jurisprudence' (1996) 59 *Modern L. R.* 465–478, p. 471 and ch. 2 of his *Critical Legal Theory and the Challenge of Feminism* (Lanham, Rowman and Littlefield 1995).

[42] Instalments in the debate include, *inter alia*, J. Bernasconi, 'Deconstruction and the Possibility of Ethics' in J. Sallis (ed.), *Deconstruction and Philosophy* (Chicago, University of Chicago Press 1987) ch. 10, pp. 122–139; J. Hillis-Miller, *The Ethics of Reading* (New York, Columbia U. P. 1987); S. Critchley, *The Ethics of Deconstruction* (Oxford, Basil Blackwell 1992); J. Caputo, *Against Ethics* (Bloomington, Indiana U. P. 1993); R. Gashe, *Inventions of Difference* (Cambridge, Mass., Harvard U. P. 1994).

talk, namely, that area concerned with ethics and, even within this supposedly narrow domain, participants have defined the term somewhat differently from the way in which Anglo-American philosophers have defined it. Ethics is envisaged as not merely more inclusive than the domain of morality but as quite different from it; whereas the latter is concerned with the construction and content of a system of rules and obligations to which a good person must be responsive, the former is envisaged either as the primordial precondition of morality or as 'a way of being in the world that spans divergent value systems and allows us to criticize the repressive aspects of competing moral systems'.[43] Obviously, this has important implications for the nature and type of 'values' which deconstructive heretics think have a role within adjudication. We cannot therefore take it as an objection to these accounts that their value talk is somewhat different and removed from that of other heretics.

An affirmative answer to the first—and hence a negative answer to the second—question has been consistently espoused by Pierre Schlag. A positive answer to the second question has been offered by, *inter alios*, Drucilla Cornell and—albeit with a suspicion of inconsistency—Jack Balkin. Schlag's positive answer to the first question flows from an attack, inspired by deconstruction, upon what he calls normative legal thought. 'What should be done? How should we live? What should the law be? These are the momentous questions. These are the hard questions. These are the questions that animate virtually all of contemporary legal thought—from the most modest doctrinal reform proposals to the most ambitious utopian speculation'(*NPF*, p. 802).[44] This way of thinking, which characterises almost all orthodox and some heretical legal scholarship, is profoundly mistaken—'[n]ormative legal thought misunderstands its own situation' (*NN*, p. 187)—on three related grounds. First, it is blind to the politics of form. That is to say, it suffers from the illusion, generated by a view of language as a transparent and neutral medium, that linguistic and interpretative acts and choices have no effects in the world, do not foreclose options and do not constrain ways of thinking and doing. But, say Schlag and Derrida, they do. Such choices limit the horizon of opportunities available and this occurs not

[43] Cornell, *supra*, note 4, p. 13. The alternative view—which need not be incompatible with Cornell's since it, too, is derived from the work of E. Levinas and Derrida—is a simplistic rendering of Critchley, supra, note 42, ch. 1, especially pp. 1–9 and 31–44. For a standard Anglo-American view of the distinction see B. Williams, *Ethics and the Limits of Philosophy* (London, Fontana 1985), pp. 6–11.

[44] The essays by P. Schlag referred to in abbreviated form in text and notes are: 'Normativity and the Politics of Form' (1991) 139 *University of Pennsylvania L. R.*, 801–932 (*NPF*), also in P. Campos *et. al. Against the Law* (Durham, Duke U. P. 1998), 29–99; 'Normative and Nowhere to Go' (1990) 43 *Stanford L. R.* 167–191 (*NN*); '"*Le Hors de Texte, C'est Moi*": The Politics of Form and the Domestication of Deconstruction' (1990) 11 *Cardozo L. R.* 1631–1674 (*Texte*); and 'Values' (1994) 6 *Yale Journal of Law and the Humanities* 219–232 (hereinafter *V*).

just in those situations where interpretative choices are also performative acts—for example, where the judge's passing of sentence leads to the accused being imprisoned—but simply where we accept existing assumptions, patterns of thought and ways of meaning (*Texte*, pp. 1631–1647).[45] And, says Schlag, normative legal thought has a set of shared assumptions and patterns of thought despite the appearance of dissonance. The most important assumptions of normative legal thought include a commitment (i) to the generic rule of law values and (ii) to the attempt to reform existing legal practices and institutions so as better to adhere to or embody those values. Furthermore, normative legal thought, like any of the 'modern' enlightenment-forged humanities and human sciences, reinforces a particular and dubious conception of the human agent.

At this point the second mistake arises. It takes the form of a double bind. The first dimension is that the legal, social and cultural world normative legal thought knows is not the world 'out there'. A consequence of this is that the prescriptions normative legal thought generates for legal practice and institutions have little or no influence upon them. The second dimension is that normative legal thought's vision of the world—a world in which the generic rule of law values are manifest in the institutions and practices of the legal and administrative state—is appropriated by the state as a legitimation device. Hence normative legal thought

> becomes the mode of discourse by which bureaucratic institutions and practices represent themselves as subject to the rational ethical-moral control of autonomous agents (*when indeed they are not*), just as normative legal thought constructs us (you and me) to think and act as if we were at the center—in charge, so to speak—of our own normative legal thought (*when indeed we are not*). Normative legal thought can no longer be seen to govern, regulate or even describe human activity.
>
> In fact, as a further step in this degeneration/development, it now appears that it is very difficult to discern any significant difference between normative legal thought and the operation, performance, reproduction and proliferation of bureaucratic practices and institutions. The two collapse into each other. (*NN*, pp. 185–186; emphasis in original.)

The third mistake made by normative legal thought is also sketched in the previous statement: it misdescribes what we are. Normative legal thought has a conception of the human agent which holds that we are essentially autonomous, rational agents when in fact we are not: '[*t*]*raditional legal discourse rhetorically establishes the self of the legal thinker as a privileged individual subject—as the author of his own thoughts, the captain of his own ship*' (*Texte*, p. 1637; emphasis in original). The thrust of the 'twentieth-century knowledges' of sociology, economics and psychoanalysis is that we are much

[45] See also J. Derrida, *Writing and Difference* (London, Routledge and Kegan Paul 1978) ch. 10 and 'Signature Event Context' in his *Margins of Philosophy* (London, Harvester Wheatsheaf 1982).

more determined—much more the products of our environment and circumstances—than we care to admit (*Texte*, p. 1638). What we actually are, the task of generating an account of agents and identity in light of our twentieth century knowledges, is an important part of Schlag's work.[46]

Now, Schlag's bold argument raises many questions. His construct 'normative legal thought' and his account of its legitimating function cry out for analysis, as do his claims to have discovered a disjunction between the 'real' or 'true' pictures of the legal world and the person and the pictures of those phenomena within legal thought. Unfortunately, these pressing questions are beyond the scope of the present argument. Our task, remember, is to consider the role heretics think values do and should play within adjudication. This admittedly brief and overly simple sketch of Schlag's argument might lead one to suggest that his position on this issue would be unambiguous and straightforward. Schlag's scepticism about the values constitutive of normative legal thought suggests he would have little time for values at all, whether within existing and future schemes of adjudication or in life at large. On this view, Schlag's argument would, in so far as it embraced an account of the *value* of liberation from normative legal thought and the practices it (un)wittingly legitimates, run into the problems faced by extreme value scepticism. Moreover, this view generates an inconsistency in Schlag's argument since on at least three occasions he flirts with moral argument and judgment (*NN*, p. 174 and fn. 18 and 19)—practices apparently incompatible with extreme value scepticism. Were we to take these flirtations seriously and in conjunction with the recognition that, for all Schlag's sceptical fire and brimstone, his argument amounts to little more than a critique of some of the bad consequences that currently follow from normative thought and argument—*inter alia*, it 'leads us to equate the world established in value talk with our own' (*V*, p. 229)—then his value scepticism appears quite modest. This is reinforced by the fact that when operating on a broad canvas—the topic of 'human values in a postmodern world'—the only arguments Schlag makes against value talk that go beyond pointing to its present bad consequences highlight the ontological and historical questions that legal and philosophical practitioners of such talk often suppress (*V*, pp. 225–232). There is nothing particularly sceptical about arguments such as these: we would expect them to be made at some point by any self-conscious participant in the practice of evaluating human action, practices and institutions.

This leads to the thought that Schlag might well be a modest value sceptic. He seems to take up a characteristically modest position—that of articulating dissatisfaction with some features of present value talk while

46 The beginning of which seems to be 'Fish v. Zapp: The Case of the Relatively Autonomous Self' (1987) 76 *Georgetown L. J.* 37–58. Another instalment is 'The Problem of the Subject' (1991) 69 *Texas L. R.* 1627–1743.

not renouncing the practice altogether.[47] It would therefore not be too surprising to find Schlag offering another vision of value talk, another account of the values we should take seriously and some indication as to how they might be achieved. However, when regarded as a modest value sceptical position, Schlag's argument is even more problematic than those considered earlier. For Schlag gives no indication at all as to which values he thinks important. On the rare occasions when he does lapse into value talk, the values in question are always values of the other: the values of contemporary American law, of normative legal thought, of moral and legal philosophers. Since Schlag hardly spends any time engaged in value talk at the levels of specification and relevance, we cannot be surprised that he has equally little to say about foundational value matters (other than to assert that moral and legal philosophers often suppress or ignore ontological and historical questions). If Schlag is indeed a modest value sceptic, his scepticism is stunningly vague. It consists of some clear worries about existing value talk and normative legal thought without any indication as to which values we ought to take seriously and how those worries could be dissipated. It is no exaggeration to say that, considered as an instance of modest value scepticism, Schlag's position is much more problematic than those versions already encountered. By contrast, considered as an example of extreme value scepticism, Schlag's position at least achieves parity for it is just as problematic as the versions of that doctrine examined above.

Cornell's affirmative answer to the second question—by which she is committed to a negative answer to the first—is but part of her project. For she aims not only to show that deconstruction, which she renames the philosophy of the limit, 'is driven by an ethical desire to enact the ethical relation' (p. 62),[48] but also to illustrate 'the significance for legal interpretation of Derrida's . . . understanding of justice as an aporia that inevitably serves as the limit to any attempt to collapse justice into positive law' (p. 2). While Cornell's argument that deconstruction enacts the ethical relation—'by which I mean to indicate the aspiration to a non-violent relationship to the Other, and to Otherness more generally, that assumes responsibility to guard the Other against appropriation that would deny her difference and singularity' (p. 62)—is both challenging and important, it is not our central concern here. Far more important for present purposes are the implications Cornell hopes to derive from that argument, and from her related analyses of justice and the good, for the practice of adjudication. Before examining these implications in detail a little needs to be said about Balkin's affirmative answer to the second question.

[47] The arguments in this and the previous paragraph create trouble for M. Fischl's vigorously anti-normative reading of Schlag's work: see *supra*, note 2, pp. 800–807.

[48] Hereinafter, page numbers in brackets in the text refer to Cornell, *supra*, note 4.

Balkin argues that Derridean deconstruction is committed to a conception of justice. This will not be news to those familiar with Derrida's discussion of the relationship between deconstruction and justice, from which it is clear that Derrida thinks there is such a relationship, although his arguments to that end are neither particularly clear nor plausible. Balkin's argument does, however, have two remarkable features. First, he seeks to show that Derrida is committed, by virtue not only of his general arguments about the relationship between deconstruction and justice but also because of some of the claims made in his defence of Paul de Man, to a 'transcendental' conception of justice and other values. By 'transcendental' Balkin means a conception of justice that is 'indeterminate but is not reducible to any conventional notion of justice'; transcendental values 'are . . . indeterminate values or urges located in the human soul, which human beings articulate through positive morality and cultural conventions, and which nevertheless always escape this articulation'.[49] Such values neither indicate a single answer to our value choices—they 'are inchoate yearnings that we attempt to articulate through our cultural conventions'[50]—nor are they found solely in our laws and social conventions. Setting aside the problems this argument courts—the pre-eminent one being dissonance with many of the central claims of Derridean deconstruction—Balkin's resort to transcendental values is to some degree anticipated by Cornell. Her rethinking of deconstruction as the philosophy of the limit leads her to the view that it is a 'quasi-transcendental [form of] analysis' (p. ix). Within the adjudicative context it aims at

> destabilization of the relationship between the immanent and the transcendent . . . [which] is done in the name of justice but is not Justice. Justice 'is' the limit of the immanent norms of the legal system to the extent that these norms are identified as Justice. But for Derrida, this limit is not projected as a transcendental ideal. Rather, it is an unsurpassable aporia. Justice, in other words, operates, but it operates as aporia (p. 133).

Now, while Cornell is inclined, albeit hesitantly, to make the same startling move towards embracing a transcendental account of the values that deconstruction enacts as Balkin does, she differs from him in avoiding a rather difficult snag. This snag is the second remarkable feature of Balkin's answer to the second question and it provides a strong reason for hereinafter concentrating exclusively upon Cornell's argument.

The snag arises from the tension in Balkin's work between two claims. The first holds that deconstruction is an intellectual technique and as such has no necessary political, moral or ethical basis. As a technique it is neutral

[49] J. Balkin, 'Transcendental Deconstruction, Transcendent Justice' (1994) 92 *Michigan L. R.* 1131–1186, pp. 1138–39.

[50] *Ibid.*, p. 1141.

about such matters: it can be used to uphold or promote a particular ethical vision as well as to criticise and subvert that vision.[51] The second holds that 'when we try to make sense of Derrida's arguments about law and justice and read them charitably to avoid confusing and self-contradictory interpretations, we arrive at an important *variant* of deconstructive practice, which relies on the existence of human values that transcend any given culture'.[52] Now there need not be a contradiction here since Balkin's first claim may be applicable to most versions of deconstruction and the second relevant only to that variant concerned with law and justice. But this move is more difficult than Balkin might appreciate. It is tricky to argue that deconstruction—even just the Derridean version of it—is an easily segmented body of thought, parts of which have special 'application' to law while others are more appropriately 'applied' to different domains. (This image of deconstruction being 'applied' to areas of life and thought sits comfortably with Balkin's view that it is a technique or tool.) Rather, it is usually maintained that deconstruction remains the same whatever the areas—from aesthetics, literary criticism, the study of Hegel or the analysis of justice—in which it is utilised. Moreover, it can be plausibly argued that there is one core concept enacted in deconstruction that Balkin has missed, namely, the ethical relation. Hence, contrary to Balkin's view, it can be maintained that deconstruction has always been ethical and has never been just a neutral technique or tool.[53] Derrida's discussion of deconstruction and justice does not therefore signal a radical departure or a special variant of deconstruction but simply highlights what was always the case. In order for Balkin's argument to succeed he must look again at claims such as these and provide more in the way of argument than simply positing two types of deconstruction, one a normatively neutral 'technique', the other enmired in what he calls a 'normative chasm'.[54]

What, then, are the implications for adjudication that flow from Cornell's argument that deconstruction is ethical? It would be tempting to assume that, since deconstruction on Cornell's view enacts the ethical relation, then so too must legal doctrines and judicial decisions. There is an immediate problem with this. There is an obvious tension between the ethical relation and its insistence upon respect for the singularity and difference of the Other, on the one hand, and legal doctrines and decisions that almost always treat those subject to them as abstract yet equal rights-bearers, on the other.

[51] J. Balkin, pp. 1137–38 and 1176–1181. See also Balkin's 'Deconstructive Practice and Legal Theory' (1987) 96 *Yale L. J.* 743–786, p. 786 and 'Nested Oppositions' (1990) 99 *Yale L. J.* 1669–1705, p. 1671.

[52] 'Transcendental Deconstruction, Transcendent Justice', *supra*, note 49, p. 1138 (emphasis supplied).

[53] This is Cornell's view and it is not idiosyncratic: *supra*, note 4, p. 1. See also Bernasconi, *supra*, note 42, pp. 134–136.

[54] *Supra*, note 49, pp. 1176–1179.

Since the abstract legal person is all the law can see, the details and particularities of the person before the law are obliterated. Cornell is fully aware of this: 'law is inevitably unfaithful to the ethical relationship . . . [it] inevitably violates difference through the establishment of shared meaning and generalized standards' (p. 105). If law and adjudication violate the ethical substance of deconstruction, why bother with them?

The first part of Cornell's answer is taken from Emmanuel Levinas:

> He reminds us that we are inevitably fated to fall into law, understood now as a system of principles and not just as a positivist mechanism to distribute and redistribute violence and power. Why is this fall inescapable? I am never just alone with the Other. The entry of the third is inevitable, and with the entry of the third comes the need to make comparisons and to synchronize the competing demands of individuals within the space of a given legal system . . . Each Other has her claim, and her claim must be addressed. All claims, however, cannot be vindicated even if they must be heard. We need legal principles that guide us through the maze of competing legal interpretations, precisely because all claims cannot be vindicated (p. 105).

Surely this answer merely serves to subvert Cornell's argument that deconstruction, understood ethically, has implications for adjudication and law. Is not the reverse true? Does it not seem that the conjunction of adjudication, law and the presence of the third party have one very important implication for the philosophy of the limit, namely, that they clearly subvert its ethical aspiration? Cornell seeks to avoid this unwelcome conclusion by adding to the argument from Levinas a sketch of how law and adjudication can nevertheless serve to enact the ethical relation, albeit in a necessarily partial way.

The sketch begins with a distinction between two different but ultimately related senses of 'the good'. In a general sense the Good or, as Cornell also names it, the Law of Law, refers to acceptance of the ethical relation and hence respect for and responsibility towards the Other in all its detail and particularity. In this sense the Good is universal, 'an irremissable necessity for all subjects' (p. 92). While Cornell holds that the Good in this sense can never be completely realised—the call to the full realisation of the Good is the call 'to the commitment to the impossible' (p. 94)—it nevertheless structures our thought and action in the following way. 'The Law of Law or the Good, is precisely the echo of the Call of the other as a prescriptive command directed toward the future that *disrupts . . . the pretense of any system to have adequately represented the totality of what "is" Good*. The Law of Law "is" as rupture of the status quo' (p. 99; emphasis supplied). Furthermore, the Good in this sense must to some degree be realised within the good in the second sense. In the latter sense 'the good should be conceived as the universals within a given legal system conceptualized as an indeterminate *nomos*' (p. 92). Those universals can serve to make the *nomos* determinate only if they themselves have some determinate content and that can be derived from the Good; presumably, their content *must* be derived therefrom if law and adjudication are to have any legitimacy, although Cornell does not argue the point. Hence

'the projection of a horizon of the good within the *nomos* of any given legal system . . . is essential to the possibility of legal interpretation . . . [I]f all we do is interpret the *nomos* from within its own terms, without understanding its limit, we would not be faithful to the Good in . . . [the] strong sense . . . [W]e cannot escape the appeal to the Good as we interpret legal sentences' (pp. 93–94).

For Cornell, then, the Good enacts the ethical relation—the respect of Otherness and difference—and in so doing must also serve as a warning against assuming that the Good can ever be fully realised in our conventions and practices. It is to some degree immanent and to some degree transcendent. Furthermore, the Good must inform the good of the *nomos* in order to make determinate interpretation possible while also constantly serving to call into question the good of the *nomos*. For the *nomos* is, after all, a system of conventions and rules and cannot be assumed capable of completely enacting or capturing the Good. The Good therefore serves to inform the *nomos* while also disrupting it. Justice, in so far as it is distinct from the Good, serves a similar function, acting as a warning against the assumption that it can ever be achieved in an actually existing system of law and also operating as aporia in particular situations (pp. 131–135).

The way in which Cornell makes resort to law and adjudication palatable for the philosophy of the limit is to accept some degree of conflict while ensuring an even greater degree of dependence between the ethical relation or the Good, on the one hand, and the law or *nomos*, on the other. Whether or not this resolution of the tension is ultimately satisfactory is the second snag (call it the compatibility problem) that faces this account of the role of values within the present and future practice of adjudication. It will be examined, along with two other snags—the first being the vagueness problem and the third the redundancy problem—in the remainder of this section. Note that none of the three snags, unlike those that beset Schlag and extreme value sceptics, have their roots in any form of value scepticism. If there is anything we can be sure of, it is that Cornell is no value sceptic.

The vagueness problem consists of a worry about the utility of Cornell's conception of the Good when applied to judicial decision-making. Doubt sets in at the outset, when one considers any of the statements about the Good offered by Cornell and other deconstructionists. Simon Critchley's statement, while representative, is also particularly elegant: 'deconstruction [is] . . . an ethical demand which provides a compelling account of responsibility as an affirmation of alterity, of the otherness of the Other: "Yes, to the stranger" '.[55] How can this affirmation, or any injunction to respect the particularity and uniqueness of the Other, help one to decide particular cases, to make particular choices, to 'make comparisons and to synchronize the competing demands of individuals within the space of a given legal system' (p. 105)? One cannot be accused here of raising an unfair or inappropriate question because Cornell, as was made clear above, certainly thinks that the Good can inform the *nomos* and hence legal doctrine and judicial decision-making. The problem is surely the very vagueness of the Good. It is characterised in such a way as to make opaque its implications in any particular situation of choice.

An examination of the few instances in which Cornell seeks to criticise legal decisions and doctrines by reference to the Good does not alleviate the sense that the Good as characterised provides little or no guidance. For example, she discusses the famous Supreme Court abortion case of *Roe* v. *Wade* and some of its progeny (pp. 147–154). Cornell is critical of more recent cases that have apparently departed from *Roe*. In particular, she objects to the dissenting decision of Justice Sandra O'Connor in *Akron* v. *Akron Center for Reproductive Health*, accusing the Justice of 'an irresponsible act of judging[,] not by imaginatively recollecting her projection of the future, but by failing her responsibility to remember the actual conditions women would again face if the *Roe* framework was dismantled' (p. 152). Justice O'Connor ignored '[t]he call of women . . . for Justice' (*ibid.*) and in so doing, we are to infer, failed to respect the call of the Other. In Critchley's formulation, this was a case of 'No, to the Other'. This criticism raises the key question: who is the Other? Cornell's account of the ethical relation does nothing to answer that question as it arises in the abortion cases. For, as she recognises, in these cases 'the foetus can itself be recognized as the Other, with infinite right' (*ibid.*). It makes a great deal of difference whether the mother or the foetus is recognised as the Other—the implications of this decision could not be more serious. But the Good, the ethical relation, is silent as to how this choice is to be made. Further, if we suppose the choice does not have to be made since both foetus and mother are to be regarded as the Other, another problem arises: how are we to respect the Other in this situation? A decision either way seems to respect the Otherness of one as opposed to the Other. Is it impossible to respect the Otherness of each?

It might be objected here that we are expecting too much of this conception of the Good. We are expecting compelling, determinate answers when they are just not available. Moreover, it could be suggested that Cornell has counselled against such an unreasonable expectation in

[55] *Supra*, note 42, p. 189. Cornell's statements are very similar: *supra*, note 4, pp. 13, 82, 84–85 and 104–107.

claiming that 'law cannot be reduced to a set of technical rules, a self-sufficient mechanism that pulls us down the track through each new fact situation' (p. 102). The principles that underpin the law should be thought of 'as the light that comes from the lighthouse, . . . that guides us and prevents us going in the wrong direction . . . [but] which cannot determine the exact route we must take in any particular case' (p. 106). If it is added, further, that what is true of law is also true of a conception of the Good, then it seems that this is an argument to show that the worry about vagueness is misconceived. Yet this is a massive exaggeration. For the thrust of the worry about vagueness is not that Cornell's conception of the Good does not provide compelling, completely determinate guidance, but that in the cases in question it provides no guidance at all. The light from this particular lighthouse has gone out. Since we do not know who is the Other, or how to respect Otherness when faced with the competing claims of Others, our decisions must be made completely in the dark. Nor is this solely a consequence of the cases in question being concerned with abortion. It cannot be argued that this is just an exceptionally difficult area and it is thus unsurprising that Cornell's conception of the Good does not help us here. The argument is untenable because this conception of the Good operates no better in other, supposedly less difficult cases. For example, Cornell's discussion of *Bowers* v. *Hardwick* (pp. 159–167), a case involving the criminalisation of homosexuality, gives no indication that she can answer the question 'who is the Other?' any more plausibly in this, as opposed to the abortion, context.[56]

The compatibility snag arises in the shadow of the vagueness problem. The latter raises a worry about the almost complete lack of guidance Cornell's conception of the Good provides within the context of decision. The compatibility problem accepts this and raises the following question: is the vagueness of this conception of the Good a consequence of the fact that a deconstructive ethics is indeed incompatible with a systematic body of rules of recognition, adjudication and change (whatever their content)? The evidence to suggest incompatibility is overwhelming and well recognised by Cornell. She not only accepts, as was noted, that law 'inevitably violates difference' (p. 105), but also holds that Justice and the Good serve to disrupt systems of law (p. 99). However, it is not only law that is disrupted: the conception of the Good she offers stands distinct from 'morality' also, understood as the 'attempt to spell out how one *determines* a "right way to behave", behavioural norms which, once determined, can be translated into a system of rules' (p. 13). In the light of these statements, it is not unrea-

[56] In the context of *Bowers* the question would be: is the Other the homosexual man accused of a crime in this case or, for example, the Rev. Jerry Falwell and his new right 'moralists'?

sonable to conclude that the incompatibility here is strong enough to generate a contradiction and hence to support the claim that the ethics of deconstruction, on the one hand, and systems of critical and positive morality and law, on the other, are opposites. Whether we accept this strong view of the relationship or a weaker one that maintains only that there is a *prima facie* case of incompatibility, a great deal of weight falls upon Cornell's demonstration that the tension can be resolved. Is her argument a success?

The argument has two connected steps, neither of which is particularly plausible. The first seeks to show 'the inevitability and necessity of law' (p. 105), while the second shows how a legal system can be informed by legal principles that are in turn informed by Cornell's conception of the Good. The second step of this argument only makes sense if it has been established that law is indeed compatible with the ethical vision of the philosophy of the limit. The argument illustrating the necessity of law must therefore be intended to demonstrate such compatibility and it will henceforth be our prime concern. Furthermore, the second step raises, with its emphasis upon principles that operate like light from lighthouses, guiding but not determining a single correct path, questions which are the fulcrum of the vagueness problem and they need not be examined again. The weakness in the first step is that its constitutive claims fail to show that law and the ethical relation are compatible. The claims are: (i) 'law is inevitably unfaithful to the ethical relationship' (*ibid.*); (ii) the ethical relation is a product of the face to face, a matter of *my* responsibility towards *this* Other; and (iii) 'I am never just alone with the Other' (*ibid.*). That is to say, '[t]he third part[y?] interrupts the face to face' (*ibid.*) and makes law necessary for the reasons noted above. The surprise in Cornell's statement of these three claims is that she assumes they are compatible, that they add up to a consistent argument. As she states them, however, they plainly do not: their force, rather, is to demonstrate the incompatibility between the ethical relation and law. For it seems that Cornell has shown that the condition that makes law necessary—that I am never alone with the Other—also makes the realisation of the ethical relation impossible. Because I am never alone with the Other, because the third party is always here, I must 'make comparisons and synchronize competing demands' (*ibid.*). I must, that is, deny the ethical relation, since to make such comparisons and synchronisations I must 'violate[. . .] difference through the establishment of shared meaning and generalized standards'(*ibid.*), through law. Nor can this problem be avoided by following Levinas, as Critchley does, in reading the second claim as universal in the sense that it implies that every subject is responsible for every Other. Once this is done, it is clear that 'the ethical relation always takes place within a political context, within the public realm' but this still falls far short of showing that the ethical relation is compatible with law.[57] Moving the ethical relation from the face-to-face to faces-to-faces does not ensure compatibility with a body of general rules which compare and synchronise competing demands. Rather, the generality of these rules and their comparative, synchronising thrust apparently guarantees conflict with the ethical relation, understood as respect for difference and particularity.

The redundancy problem begins by highlighting one point of which we can be certain. For, regardless of the uncertainty as to what exactly Cornell's conception of the good and justice might entail for law and adjudication, it is clear that both serve as a warning against the assumption that existing conventions and legal systems are truly just and good. What is puzzling about this warning is neither the content of the claim nor even the way in which it may be supported. The puzzle is far simpler, much more elementary. It consists of wonderment that this claim needs be made, of doubt about being able to find anyone within contemporary legal and political philosophy—both orthodox and heretical—who would disagree with it. Nor does the claim have the merit of making explicit that which has been implicitly and unreflectively accepted, for it is hard to imagine a contemporary legal scholar unaware of questions about the moral and political legitimacy of some, perhaps even most, segments of her discipline. In a legal academy that is not unlike Schlag's picture of it—one in which normative questions are insistently asked (and rarely fruitfully answered)—the warning Cornell issues seems truly redundant. Certainly, it cannot serve to warn us against complacency, against accepting without question the justice of the law since our historical situation—our post-holocaust, post-civil rights, post-Vietnam time—is such as to make that virtually impossible, particularly for lawyers. In a time of heightened vigilance about the uses and abuses of formal political and less formal intellectual power, an exhortation to vigilance seems amusingly misplaced. Furthermore, if our present historical situation is rightly characterised as one in which separation between 'law and ethics, legality and morality, . . . validity and value, form and substance'[58] has taken hold, then the distinction Cornell warns us against eliding ought to be—as it is—a commonplace.

The problems that beset Cornell's account of the role of values in adjudication are obviously severe. They occupy that level of value talk earlier described as specification, raising questions about the values, or their specific content, in play in a particular domain. Until Cornell's conception of the Good can be shown actually to work for us, and that it is indeed compatible with law, her account of the role and nature of values in adjudication must be set aside. In light of this, and bearing in mind the snags

[57] See Critchley, *supra*, note 42, p. 225.

[58] C. Douzinas and R. Warrington, *Justice Miscarried* (London, Harvester Wheatsheaf 1994), p. 132.

ensnaring Balkin and Schlag, we can now examine whether or not a claim made in the introduction to this chapter is supportable. The claim was that Roberto Unger's project provided heretics with the best chance of developing a coherent ethical, political and moral vision. Although an apparently rash judgment, it has gained some plausibility from the arguments of this sub-section and the obituaries for extreme and moderate value scepticism issued at the end of sections I (a) and (b).

II THE VISION THING[59]

> When we're not 'merely' trashing, we switch to uselessly general Utopian theorizing. Mark Kelman, 'Trashing' (1984) 36 *Stanford L. R.*, p. 296.

> [W]e cannot be visionaries until we become realists. It is also true that to become realists we must make ourselves into visionaries. Roberto Unger, 'Legal Analysis as Institutional Imagination' (1996) 59 *M. L. R.*, p. 23.

If heretics thought themselves short of a vision, they would do well to consort with the works of Unger. He has provided a social ideal—a picture of a world better than that we know—a conception of the person truer to what we really are, and an institutional programme outlining the ways in which our existing practices and institutions such as law, democracy and the market, can be reformed so as to facilitate the social ideal and conception of the person. The contrast between Unger's grandiose scheme and some heretics' concern with the pettifogging business of trashing, marks an important temperamental and intellectual divide within the heresy, the basis of which need not be examined here. Nor need the whole of the Ungerian corpus be scrutinised in order to elucidate his account of the role, type and basis of values within adjudication. Rather, that account appears primarily within two texts—*The Critical Legal Studies Movement* and *What Should Legal Analysis Become?*[60]—although the social ideal and the conception of the person sketched in the former are more fully developed in two other works.[61] But there is an initial, pressing problem here. For, in attempting to discern, on the basis of these two works, Unger's view as to

[59] The phrase has been stolen from that acknowledged master of rhetoric and the *bon mot*, former President George Bush. M. Fischl, *supra*, note 2, uses the same phrase (p. 800) but is curiously loath to acknowledge the source of this brilliant *aperçu*.

[60] *Supra*, note 4. Referred to hereinafter in both text and notes as '*CLSM*' and '*WS*'. Some of the arguments of the latter appeared in Unger's 'Legal Analysis as Institutional Imagination' (1996) 59 *M. L. R.* 1–23.

[61] See *Passion: An Essay on Personality* (New York, The Free Press 1984), the introduction to which elucidates the conception of the person, and the three volumes of *Politics, A Work in Constructive Social Theory* (Cambridge, C. U. P. 1987), the main burden of which is to sketch the institutional programme required to make the social ideal a reality. For discussion of the latter see the symposium on *Politics* in (1987) 81 *Northwestern L. R.* 590–980.

the role and nature of values within adjudication, it becomes clear that they are incompatible. The discussion that follows will treat the works separately and highlight their differences. This reading is not an uncharitable one since it seems clear that any attempt to ensure complete consistency between these two works will fail. They show that Unger is caught between two potentially very different accounts of the substance and foundation of the values in play in adjudication. He is torn between an account that derives the values in play in adjudication from a conception of the self and an account of an ideal society, on the one hand, and an account that apparently derives those values solely from a commitment to democracy, on the other. Regardless of which view actually transpires to be 'really' Unger's, both, as we shall see, are problematic.

(a) The self and the social ideal

In *CLSM* Unger says adjudication has a tripartite structure. It consists of

> authoritative rules and precedents expressed today mainly by statutes and judicial decisions, organising principles and counterprinciples, and imaginative schemes of social life that assign distinct models of human association to different sectors of social practice . . . The interpretation of large bodies of rules and precedents must rely tacitly if not explicitly upon principles and counter-principles, and the understanding of principles and counter-principles must in turn presuppose conceptions of what the dealings among people can and should be like in each sphere of social life, even if these conceptions are said to be somehow embodied in the law rather than imported into it from outside (*CLSM*, p. 89).

This picture is one with which many of the orthodox would agree although their language would differ. The orthodox hold that the legal rules and precedents must be interpreted in light of their underpinning points, purposes or values—Ungerian 'principles' and 'counterprinciples'—which either add up to or flow from a coherent vision of the role of law in the political and social structure. Of course, there is little agreement about the constitutents of that vision, the principal contenders being either a combination of integrity and equality or liberty and utility.[62] What Unger takes to be the basis of his disagreement with the orthodox—although he never explicitly engages with their work, offering instead catty but amusing caricatures of it—and his main criticism of the contemporary practice of adjudication, is the prevailing espousal of both formalism and objectivism. By the former he refers to 'a commitment to, and therefore also a belief in the possibility of, a method of legal justification that contrasts with open-ended disputes about the basic terms of social life, disputes that people call ideo-

[62] These are crude characterisations of the respective positions of R. Dworkin, *Law's Empire* (London, Fontana 1986) and H. Hart, *The Concept of Law* (Oxford, Clarendon second edition 1994) and *Essays in Jurisprudence and Philosophy* (Oxford, Clarendon 1983), ch. 9.

logical, philosophical or visionary' (*CLSM*, p. 1). By the latter he has in mind the 'belief that the authoritative legal materials—the system of statutes, cases and accepted legal ideas—embody and sustain a defensible scheme of human association. They display, though always imperfectly, an intelligible moral order' (*CLSM*, p. 2).

Unger thinks both beliefs mistaken. Objectivism errs because '[t]he content of public and private law fails to present a single, unequivocal vision of democracy and the market. On the contrary, it contains in confused and undeveloped form the elements of different visions' (*CLSM*, pp. 7–8; *LA* p. 22). And formalism cannot be sustained except by either an untenable suppression of the multiple values and visions of human association that underpin existing legal rules and principles or by a misguided belief in objectivism. Once it is accepted that objectivism is false, recognised, that is, that there exist no 'types of social organisation with a built in [and necessary] legal structure' (*CLSM*, p. 6), it becomes difficult to maintain that the values and visions of human association said to underpin the law are in some sense necessary or compelling. Since such values and visions are eminently contestable—and contestable in just the same way and subject to just the same canons of argument that govern any ideological, philosophical or visionary dispute—formalism appears unsustainable. Unless, of course, formalists suppress the assumptions about values and the organisation of society that guide legal reasoning: '[c]oncealment of these assumptions is vital to the persuasive authority of the dominant legal ideas; seemingly uncontroversial technical conceptions commonly depend upon highly controversial, nontechnical premises' (*CLSM*, p. 88). Lest there be any doubt about what is involved in adjudication, on Unger's account, and about the consequences of rejecting objectivism, we need only note his sketch of post-objectivist legal doctrinal scholarship. This kind of scholarship he calls (interchangeably) 'deviationist' or 'expanded' doctrine. It is as much a prescription for the future practice of adjudication as a characterisation of a style of scholarship:

> The revised style of doctrine commits itself to integrate into standard doctrinal argument the explicit controversy over the right and feasible structure of society, over what the relations among people should be like in the different areas of social activity. In the rich North American countries of today, the imaginative vision of the ways in which people can have a life in common appeals to a particular ideal of democracy for the state and citizenship, to a picture of private community in the domain of the family and friendship, and to an amalgam of contract and impersonal technical hierarchy in the everyday realm of work and exchange. This social vision helps to make the entire body of law look intelligible and even justifiable. Above all it serves to resolve what would otherwise be incorrigible indeterminacy in the law. Just as the ambiguities of rules and precedents require recourse to imputed purposes or underlying policies and principles, so the ambiguities of these policies and

principles can be avoided only by an appeal to some background scheme of association of the kind just described. Yet the conflicting tendencies within the law constantly suggest alternative schemes of human association. The focused disputes of legal doctrine repeatedly threaten to escalate into struggles over the basic imaginative structure of social existence (*CLSM*, p. 17).[63]

It will be worthwhile to examine further this conception of doctrine as a means of specifying both the values Unger thinks should be implicated within adjudication and their basis.

Unger provides two examples of deviationist doctrine at work. They are drawn from the American law of equal protection and contract. His discussion of the former 'might be applied, with variations, to any Western liberal constitutional democracy' (*CLSM*, p. 50), while his examination of the latter could have drawn upon 'any common law or civilian jurisdiction in the West' (*CLSM*, p. 58). The account of equal protection consists of a critique of present doctrine and adjudication and the recommendation of an alternative guiding vision for future doctrine and adjudication. The faults of contemporary thought and practice consist in, *inter alia*, their commitment to 'a series of seemingly dogmatic assumptions and arbitrary distinctions' (*CLSM*, p. 52). Such assumptions and distinctions could only lose their dubious status were they supported by some defensible conception of the law's role in promoting and protecting a vision of society and the person in which equal protection rights are paramount. However, Unger holds that existing doctrine and practice have no such coherent, defensible vision and, therefore, no plausible account of law's role in implementing it. He supplies such a vision—consisting of 'the attempt to establish a form of social life that exhibits a more defensible conception of selfhood and association while maximising the corrigibility of social institutions' (*ibid.*)—on the basis of two beliefs. First, that it is normatively better than both the existing, fractured vision and any other alternative and, second, that this vision makes some sense of existing doctrine and practice and can also guide their future development.

Unger's discussion of contract law (which is far richer and complex than the account that follows) aims to establish two things. First, that existing contract law maintains an objectionable distinction between a realm in which self interest receives the imprimatur of law and the realm of communal or fraternal obligations 'in respect of . . . [which] each house is a domain into which the King's writ does not seek to run'.[64] His argument 'begin[s] by effacing the sharpness of the opposition between contract and community . . . [and] end[s] by suggesting a view of contract that can more

[63] Unger's account of legal scholarship in *WS* is more muted and less ambitious than this: see pp. 130–134.

[64] Per Atkin L. J. in *Balfour* v. *Balfour* [1919] 2 KB 571, p. 579.

readily accommodate both a broad range of different sorts of rights and obligations and a conception of community, as a heightened zone of mutual vulnerability' (*CLSM*, p. 86). Secondly, Unger attempts to show that were existing contract law to take seriously its commitment to doctrines designed to promote fairness and equality between contracting parties, it would 'invite[. . .] a transformation of the institutional basis of economic life' (*ibid.*). Unger holds that contract scholars and judges should engage in this enterprise. To kick-start it, his analysis of contract begins 'the search for the conditions under which a regime of contract can avoid becoming the disguise of a power order without constantly being overridden by [judicial] correction' (*ibid.*).

The values Unger claims are and should be tracked by these areas of law are not tidily listed and labelled. He is content to let them emerge gradually in the course of his exposition and critique of the law. It is nevertheless plain that, were we to label the values implicit in contract and equal protection on Unger's behalf, then we would have to speak the language of autonomy, equality, empowerment and participation. We should be concerned about the distribution of power in contractual relationships if we embrace a conception of autonomy which entails, *inter alia*, freedom from economic domination. Similarly, we should be worried about the potentially deleterious effects of regimes of legal regulation upon specific groups within our community if we accept that all citizens should be equally empowered to participate in the political, economic and cultural aspects of community life. That values such as these are in play here will not surprise a reader of Unger's institutional programme (pp. 25–40), from and by which deviationist doctrine is derived and inspired.

This specification of the values Unger thinks inform the best of contemporary doctrine and adjudication and which will, of course, inform future thought and practice, ought to worry us. Can we not raise against Unger an objection previously aimed at Klare, namely, that both the content of and relationships between the listed values are incompletely specified? And, that being so, the spectre of value conflict arises, a spectre that threatens to destabilise the normative vision said to inform the law. Can Unger avoid the objection? Although he does not formulate the objection and reply to it explicitly, he has to hand the bones of a rejoinder. It consists of the fact that Unger's value talk operates on two levels which we can designate, albeit rather clumsily, the micro- and macro-levels. Micro-level values, for Unger, are those immanent within existing thought, institutions and practices whereas macro-level values are derived from the social ideal and conception of the person.

This distinction is implicit within Unger's two instances of deviationist doctrine. His discussion of equal protection draws in a more direct way upon the macro-values embodied in the social ideal and the conception of the person than does his analysis of contract which, by contrast, is concerned with developing some of the micro-level values immanent within existing doctrine (see pp. 88–90). Although the two examples are stylistically different, this should not disguise the obvious interrelationship between macro- and micro-values. Some of the micro-level values immanent within our practices are but less abstract manifestations of the macro-level values constitutive of the social ideal and conception of the person. Furthermore, the macro-values determine those aspects of existing practices and institutions that are worthy of our support and respect. Nowhere is this interrelationship made more obvious by Unger than in his observation that 'internal development needs visionary thought . . . as a complement and corrective. When visionary thought works as theory rather than prophetic intuition, it characteristically takes the form of a systematic conception of society and personality . . . for which it claims normative authority' (*CLSM*, p. 91). This conception regulates the direction of internal development, the practice of thinking about 'the conflicts between the available ideals of social life in your own social world or legal tradition and their flawed actualizations in present society. You imagine the actualizations transformed, or you transform them in fact, if only by extending an ideal to some area of social life from which it had previously been excluded' (*CLSM*, p. 18). Regulation comes about in two ways. The social ideal and conception of the person select those practices, institutions or segments thereof most suitable for internal development *and* provide a check upon its direction. Hence the social ideal and conception of the person allow us to determine 'whether and why we should give weight to th[e] accident' (*CLSM*, p. 91) that some of our practices and institutions embody certain values.

Now, this 'interplay between practices and ideals' (*ibid.*), between social vision and conception of the person, on the one hand, and instances of legal doctrine or other practices, on the other, might enable Unger to avoid Klare's problem. For, although Unger does not neatly label the micro-level values he thinks should and do inform doctrine and adjudication, and although he does not elucidate the relationship between these values, the social ideal and conception of the person provide the means by which this could be done. Micro-level value conflict could be contained, and the relationship between such values determined, by reference to the macro-level values constitutive of the social ideal and conception of the person. Much weight is thus borne by these macro-level values since they undoubtedly constitute the dual foundation of Unger's institutional programme and his account of both deviationist doctrine and adjudication. But this simply raises an elementary question: what do the social ideal and conception of the person look like? We must be content to offer a brief but hopefully not overly misleading answer.

The social ideal insists upon the 'cumulative loosening of the fixed order of society' such that

> 'the life chances and life experiences of the individual should be increasingly freed from the tyranny of abstract social categories . . . The contrast between what a social world incorporates and what it excludes, between routine and revolution, should be broken down as much as possible; the active power to remake the [sic: and?] reimagine the structure of social life should enter into the character of everyday existence' (*CLSM*, p. 23).

Unger's guiding thought is that social structures are not beyond our control although we are often duped into thinking so. They are the product of human actions and since we create them we can also re-create them. They are, as he often remarks in *Politics*, 'plastic'. However, although social institutions and practices are malleable, they are also obviously constraining. Existing institutions, practices and structures limit the ways in which society can be organised and imagined, automatically ruling out alternatives (organising the economy according to principles X, Y and Z will usually make an alternative arrangement embodying A, B and C impossible). Hence, although ultimately plastic, social structures, practices and institutions manifest a high degree of resistance to change and tend towards rigidity and fossilisation. Unger's ideal body of structures, institutions and practices is one that manifests the lowest degree of resistance to challenge, change and development consistent with a necessary degree of stability. This openness to change is embodied in the institutional programme sketched in *CLSM* and described in detail in *Politics*. The

> guiding and unifying aim [of the programme is] . . . to remake all direct personal connections . . . by emancipating them from a background plan of social division and hierarchy . . . It wants the opportunities and experiences available to different categories of people to be more freely recombined. This facility of recombination matters both as a good in itself and as an occasion to improve the character of social life (*CLSM*, p. 26).

The conception of the person Unger invokes is hinted at in *CLSM* and thoroughly unpacked in *Passion*.[65] It consists of the recognition of 'the infinite quality of the personality' manifest in 'the power of the self eternally to transcend the limited imaginative and social worlds it constructs' (*ibid.*). In the introduction to *Passion* Unger develops the conception of the person as a response to two problems that determine the human condition. One is that of contextuality, the problem of defining 'our relation to the habitual settings of our actions . . . that we regularly take for granted' (*P*, pp. 3–4). Unger argues that the contexts in which our actions, thoughts and emotions

[65] *Supra*, note 61. Hereinafter referred to in both text and notes as *P* with accompanying page numbers.

make sense are neither completely avoidable—we cannot live meaningfully without them—nor are they completely immutable.[66] His conception of the person—excavated from the traditions of what he calls Christian-Romantic and Modernist thought about the self and elucidated by contrast with, *inter alia*, heroic and Confucian conceptions—is one in which the self, although incapable of complete independence from a background context, 'can always break through all contexts of practical or conceptual activity' (*P*, p. 8). Thus, for Unger, our identity is not completely defined by the particular family, community and social structures in which we are socialised since it is always possible for us to transcend their influence and change them. We are not on this view, which runs contrary to the arguments of some contemporary philosophical communitarians, just a list of our constitutive commitments and experiences and the contexts in which they were made available to us.[67] Rather, our essential nature is manifest in the capacity to move beyond, to call into question and to replace such commitments, experiences and contexts. This, then, is Unger's response to the problem of contextuality.

The 'other issue on which we must take a stand when we define a conception of identity concerns our relations to one another' (*P*, p. 4). This is the problem of solidarity, '[a] special paradox [that] marks our dealings with one another [because] [w]e present to one another both an unlimited need and an unlimited danger, and the very resources by which we attempt to satisfy the former aggravate the latter' (*P*, p. 20). Clearly there is more than a slight resonance between Unger's account of this problem and one version of Kennedy's fundamental contradiction. Unger deals with the problem of solidarity by reviving 'an ethics that sees love rather than altruism as its crowning ideal' (*P*, p. iix). His exploration of the emotions in *Passion* builds towards the conclusion that the only response to the problem of solidarity consistent with our context-transcending nature is to love the other: 'the significance of love lies . . . in the opportunity it presents for breaking out of the shell of character through the exposing of one's vulnerabilities, . . . the pushing of oneself into situations which shake up one's relations to others, and the putting at risk of what is most intimate and most important'.[68] Of all the passions, only love and the other 'higher virtues' of hope and faith reinforce our nature, our ability to transcend contexts. In

[66] S. Fish wrongly ascribes to Unger the view that humans are capable of completely transcending all contexts: *Doing What Comes Naturally* (Oxford, Clarendon 1989), pp. 427–430. The misrepresentation might be partially explained were this essay written prior to the publication of *P*.

[67] M. Sandel seems to take up this position in *Liberalism and the Limits of Justice* (Cambridge, C. U. P. 1982), chs. 1 and 4. For slightly different but related communitarian positions see: A. MacIntrye, *After Virtue* (London, Duckworth (second edition) 1985), ch. 15 and C. Taylor, *Sources of the Self* (Cambridge, C. U. P. 1989), part I.

[68] E. Weinrib, 'Enduring Passion' (1985) 94 *Yale L. J.* 1825–1841, p. 1835.

order to flourish, however, the higher virtues require not just appropriate individual character traits and modes of behaviour but also certain types of social structure and institutions. Unger puts it thus:

'[n]o social situation can preclude these epiphanies or determine the place and time of their happening. Cultures and collectivities differ, however, in their hospitality to these unruly occurrences, in their selection of the areas of social life that they recognize as appropriate to the assertion of faith, hope and love, and in their willingness to draw political inferences from these events . . . It is in the interstices of mutual vulnerability that the experiences of faith, hope and love have the best chance of taking hold. *An institutionalized condition of shared vulnerability* already represents, if only in a pale and distorted way, the net of actual involvements and potential reconciliations that is implied in the higher virtues' (*P*, p. 247; emphasis supplied).

Difficult it is to feign surprise at the obvious similarity between 'an institutionalised condition of shared vulnerability' and Unger's social ideal of a society in which we are freed from a constraining script limiting the types of behaviour, roles and institutions available to us. The social ideal, remember, amounts to the 'opening up of the practical and imaginative order of society to a principle of accelerated revision, to conflict and deliberation' (*P*, p. 266). And that ideal is but one side of the coin that has as its other side Unger's response to the problem of solidarity and his conception of the person. Lest there be any doubt about the relationship between social ideal and conception of the person, we need only note Unger's dictum that 'each [is] implied by the other'(*CLSM*, p. 91).[69]

This sketch of the social ideal and conception of the person shows how Unger *could* respond to the problem that ensnared Klare and other moderate value sceptics. The social ideal and conception of the person—Unger's macro-level values—*could* determine the relationships between and the content of the micro-level values manifest in our practices. Unger *could* thereby banish or at least contain value conflict; but we must be tentative here because it is not clear that Unger can successfully discharge this particular task. In fact, as we will soon see, a snag that can be called the contingency problem looms large, threatening to subvert the attempt to use macro-level values to inform the relationships between, and determine the content of, micro-level values. Moreover, even supposing Unger were to escape that problem, another lies in wait. Remember that, when considering Klare's moderate value scepticism, it was noted that he conspicuously refrained from providing any argument to show that the values he thought

[69] However, note that Unger equivocates about the relationship between the two. As well as statements that emphasise a strong link between them (one 'deploys' the other, one is the 'corresponding image' of the other (*CLSM*, pp. 26 and 27), both can be taken as 'a single, indivisible argument' (*P*, p. viii)), he also holds, somewhat surprisingly, that the one 'cannot [be] . . . deduce[d] from [the] . . . other', that there is merely 'an affinity' between them (*P*, p. 85).

should be in play in adjudication generated good reasons for action. Klare was content simply to assert those values, offering no account as to why they were worth pursuing, thereby culpably avoiding foundational level value talk. Does Unger face the same problem? On the basis of the exposition so far, he has provided no argument to show that macro- and micro-values are indeed worthy of support, that they generate good reasons for action. It also seems distinctly odd, given our sketch of them, to speak as we have so far done of Unger's conception of the person and social ideal as 'values'. Within the context of both philosophical and everyday moral thought, it is far more congenial to speak of 'justice', 'integrity' and the like as values. Notions as abstract as conceptions of the self do not seem accurately captured by such language Yet Unger's curious usage makes sense in light of the fact that, unlike moderate value sceptics, he does indeed provide a foundational argument specifically about the social ideal and conception of the person designed to show that they have normative power, that we ought to pursue them. The problem is that his argument is particularly implausible: let us label this, following Unger, the problem of normative ascription.

The contingency problem arises from the tension between the claim that macro-level values determine the institutional programme, the course of deviationist doctrine and the content of and relations between micro-level values, on the one hand, and the claim that the social world, institutions, cultural and intellectual practices are malleable and under-determined, on the other. As Unger notes in a discussion of different types of normative thought, '[t]he question . . . becomes whether you can fully acknowledge the contingency of social worlds . . . while nevertheless continuing to make normative claims'.[70] Since Unger constantly acknowledges the contingency of social worlds, and since the social ideal and conception of the person generate normative claims, it is puzzling that he regards the issue as posing a problem only for other normative thinkers and not himself. It is prima facie problematic to make normative claims—to prescribe, for example, which aspects of a social practice ought to be maintained and even enhanced by future action—while acknowledging that the social world in which the practice exists does not evolve according to any pre-existing laws, is somewhat fluid and can be constantly remade and reimagined. How can our values get purchase on such a liquid social world? Or, if that way of putting the question wrongly suggests that values stand outside the social world and its practices when they in fact only exist within it (*P*, *i*, p. 37), how do values operate within and influence the movements of this aqueous social world? Are they not bound to be—at best—rather like seaweed, rooted in the sea of the social world but nevertheless

[70] Unger, *Politics, A Work in Constructive Social Theory*, volume I, *supra*, note 61, p. 39 (hereinafter referred to in text and notes as *P* with accompanying volume and page numbers).

buffeted about by its currents, or—at worst—like flotsam, driven hither and thither with no influence at all?

Perhaps we have been beguiled by this watery metaphor. Unger uses another image to convey the nature of the social world that might keep the contingency problem at bay—he never tires of maintaining that society be envisaged as an 'artefact' (see *P*, *i*, ch. 1). To make an artefact assumes a guiding plan, a design which determines the nature and success of the construction. (When constructions do not go 'according to plan' they are invariably failures.) Since the social ideal and conception of the person supposedly inform the practice of deviationist doctrine and the institutional programme, it is not ridiculous to suggest that they constitute Unger's guiding plan. The analogy for the relationship between macro-values and the social world would then be that of the relationship between an architect's plan and the structure built according to it. Notice how tight a relationship this is. The plan determines almost every feature of the resulting structure including its proportions, its outward appearance and the materials used. It allows very little leeway for departures. Of course, not every detail will be determined such as, for example, the scheme of interior decoration and, no doubt, room will be left for amendment in light of changes in circumstances such as scarcity of particular materials. Nevertheless, it could not be said of implementing the architect's plan, as Unger says of the process of realising the social ideal and conception of the person, that '[a]t each crucial juncture in the advance toward more concrete levels of analysis, different conclusions might reasonably be drawn. At every point the foundations remain contestable and the implications loose'(*CLSM*, p. 56). If the macro-values have 'a directing force, although at every stage of the advance toward concreteness the transition to the next level remains loose and speculative' (*CLSM*, pp. 23–24), they are clearly dissimilar to the architect's plan. Moreover, these remarks of Unger's seem merely to repeat what he takes to be the truth of contingency but, in so doing, they undermine the directive force of the social ideal and conception of the person. If, at every stage in our attempts to instantiate those values the steps we take are underdetermined, our 'advance' is speculative and different paths could reasonably be taken, it becomes difficult to see just how the ideals 'direct' or 'regulate' the quest.

How can Unger respond to the contingency problem? He might accept, as seems clear, that the source of the problem is his desire to build into the process of bringing about the social ideal important features of the ideal. The ideal is, *inter alia*, a situation in which there is a far greater degree of contingency and malleability in society than we now experience: we are, remember, to be set free from background hierarchies and our roles and experiences are to be more freely recombined. And Unger's emphasis upon the loose and contingent connections between social ideal and conception of the person, on the one hand, and the practice of deviationist doctrine and the implementation of institutional programme, on the other, may just be an attempt to capture these features within our existing practice and political striving. But there is no reason why the process of achieving the ideal must be so marked by the features of the ideal, especially when incorporating those features seem to put at risk belief in our ability to bring about the ideal. Our existing practice and political striving must be galvanised by the social ideal and conception of the person. They are the goals we aim to attain, the banner under which Unger thinks we should march. We certainly cannot sustain attempts to bring them about while accepting that they could well, because of the truth of contingency, be unachievable. So, although we aim for an ideal that embodies heightened contingency, this need not mean that the achievement of the ideal is itself contingent or completely uncertain.

Another response Unger might make involves a couple of interpretative manoeuvres. The first would be to distinguish between a weak and strong sense of contingency in our thinking about society. The weak sense simply holds that society is an artefact, the product of our own hands. Societies are made by us—humankind—and we can therefore remake them. The weak sense aims to wean us away from what Unger would call an idolatrous and disempowering acceptance of any existing social order or segment thereof. What we make with our hands, minds and actions can also be remade. The strong sense of contingency incorporates the weak sense but adds to it the claim that we cannot be sure of anything in our attempts to remake social structures. This sense of contingency would seek to write large, for social life, the tired old cliché about expecting the unexpected. The second interpretative move involves arguing that when Unger speaks the language of contingency he has in mind only the weak sense. That sense does not seem to rob the macro-values of their directive or regulatory force whereas the strong sense does. In fact, the strong sense would seem to suggest the folly of attempting to bring about any ideals at all under conditions of radical uncertainty. By contrast, the weak sense, with its emphasis upon the fact that societies can be remade and reimagined, positively encourages the attempt to implement and achieve our ideals; if we are to *remake* and *reimagine*, we must surely do so according to some plan, some guiding vision.

Whether or not Unger would make these two interpretative manoeuvres is an open question. His texts do not obviously support one sense of contingency as opposed to the other,[71] except that a principle of interpretative

[71] Two representative statements illustrate the ambiguity: 'The intuitive core of the idea of contingency is the notion that *all* things or *some* things might be otherwise than they are' (*P*, *i*, p. 173, emphasis supplied); '. . . we lack a certain basis for discounting the possibility that a new approach to the assessment and remaking of ideals *might* change the character of nor-

charity would recommend the weak sense on the basis that it does less violence to the argument.[72] The damage done by the strong sense is severe: for instance, it is in obvious contradiction with what Unger must regard as stable features of the institutional programme such as the scheme of rights. If the social world is as contingent as the strong sense suggests, what hope is there of implementing a regime of Ungerian market or destabilisation rights, or of realising the rotating capital fund? Nor is it clear from his texts that Unger would embrace the first response to the contingency problem. The result of making that response is exactly the same as adopting the weak sense of contingency and there is certainly no incompatibility between them. Since there is no clear indication in the texts as to Unger's preferred response, it cannot therefore be said that he has a convincing solution to the contingency problem; however, it equally cannot be said that the contingency problem is fatal to his argument. Rather, it casts a shadow of doubt over Unger's project.

That shadow grows darker and is extended when the problem of normative ascription is introduced. Normative ascription is the label Unger gives to the argument by which he aims to show that the macro-values generate reasons for action, that they are to be pursued. The argument plays a particularly important role in *Passion* and *CLSM* since it is used therein to support, respectively, the conception of the person and the social ideal.[73] It consists of three moves. First, Unger invites us to look anew at what he takes to be the classical mode of arguing about values which is untroubled by the divide, vividly elucidated by David Hume, between fact and value.[74] This style of argument 'assume[s] rather than . . . demonstrate[s] the validity of ascribing normative force to conceptions of the self or to views of society with which those conceptions are bound up. It disregard[s] rather than . . . disprove[s] the distinction between normative and factual claims that constitutes the starting point of most modern moral and political philosophy' (*P*, pp. 39–40). In response to the thought that it is surely a mistake to attempt to neutralise Hume's argument by simply disregarding it, Unger

mative practice, and change us in the process . . . This element of pure givenness and *contingency* . . . suits a style of speculative thought that insists upon the empirical status of even its boldest claims' (*CLSM*, p. 97; emphasis supplied). Is Unger embracing the strong or weak sense of contingency here?

[72] Hutchinson and Monahan, *supra*, note 17, have no room for this principle in their discussion of Unger. They simply assume Unger is committed to the strong sense of contingency and are quite comfortable with the contradiction that follows from it: see pp. 233–236. For the same assumption see also their 'The Rights Stuff: Roberto Unger and Beyond' (1984) 62 *Texas L. R.* 1477–1539, pp. 1521–1522.

[73] *P*, pp. 39–47; *CLSM*, pp. 94–97. Versions of the argument also appear elsewhere: *P*, *i*, pp. 15–16 and 41–43; *P*, *ii*, pp. 350–368.

[74] D. Hume, *A Treatise of Human Nature* (Second edition, P. H. Nidditch (ed.), Oxford, Clarendon 1978), Book III, part I, p. 469. For a good treatment of the argument see the essays by A. MacIntyre, R. Atkinson, A. Flew, G. Hunter and W. Hudson in V. C. Chappell (ed.), *Hume: A Collection of Critical Essays* (London, Macmillan 1968).

holds that the commitment to the fact/value distinction is but part of 'an assumption of certain conceptual practices, especially natural science. This assumption is irrelevant to many other practices and incompatible with at least one other. The philosophical critics ask us . . . to abandon one practice—the classical style of normative argument—out of respect for the implicit ideas of another. Why should we?' (*P*, p. 41). Unger's second move, obviously, is to insist that the practice of ascribing normative force to quasi-factual or empirical conceptions of the person and society is indeed common in our culture. He says the practice is 'tenacious' (*P*, p. 3) but does not think this claim needs much support. Unger is content to point to the fact that this practice is common in religious conceptions of the world and to show that methods of moral argument other than the classical style either fall into indeterminacy when they succeed in eschewing any conception of the person, or remain determinate only by covertly assuming such a conception (*P*, p. 43; *CLSM*, pp. 95–96). The final move in the argument consists of Unger's attempt to show that denying the practice of normative ascription commits one to an extreme and unsustainable form of moral and epistemological scepticism (*P*, p. 46; *CLSM*, pp. 95–97).

The least problematic step in this argument is the second. It can easily be accepted that the urge to derive an 'ought' from an 'is' or values from facts is as strong now as it was in Hume's day. Yet it is difficult to know what to make of this. This urge could just as easily evidence some commendable truth about our condition and our world—as Unger seems to regard it—as an entirely objectionable truth illustrating both our blindness to logical consistency and unlimited capacity for self-deception. Further, this urge and associated practice can claim no special authority by virtue of the fact that they are common and have achieved longevity. For Unger to allow that it could would take him uncomfortably close to an idolatrous acceptance of a purely contingent and presumably plastic social practice. Many other practices, seemingly resting upon far more dangerous urges, have been with us just as long and are just as common. Torture, for example, is a common practice with a long and dismal history. It predates Damiens's terrible plight and includes the human rights abuses apparently institutionalised in many contemporary political regimes.[75] Presumably we would be loath to ignore Hume's lesson and simply ascribe normative force to this practice, one of the reasons for our hesitance being that the practice is itself normatively objectionable. And this raises the question of the basis of the normative judgment employed: by reference to what criteria have we concluded that that practice is objectionable? Moreover, a similar judgment

[75] Damiens' story is relayed by M. Foucault, *Discipline and Punish* (London, Penguin 1977), ch. 1. For equally dismal reading about the contemporary practice of torture, see any recent Amnesty International report or the now somewhat dated *Torture in the Eighties* (London, Amnesty International 1984).

surely lies behind Unger's preference for the practice of normative ascription. This practice of ascribing normative force to particular practices despite Hume's lesson is only worth engaging in if the practice in question is not normatively objectionable. How is that determined? The threat of an infinite regress looms if the normative status of a practice is determined by reference to other practices. The threat can be avoided if an attempt is made to conceive of some forms of moral argument as context- and practice-transcendent. The snag with this solution is that it is out of kilter with the contingent, non *a priori* tenor of most of Unger's work.

A proper understanding of the classical style of normative argument suggests it was indeed context- and practice-transcendent. Since it employed an epistemic and ontological category of intelligible essences 'in which each thing is conceived inchoately to be that which it ought to become . . . [and in which a] person's intelligible essence comprehended both brute actuality and normative ideal . . . [,] the ideal encompass[ing] the plenitude of what the person essentially was and what he therefore tended to by nature',[76] it ensured distance between the content of particular practices and what was morally good and virtuous. But this understanding of the classical style is not one Unger can accept. For, although the first step in his argument is to revive the classical style, he revives an emaciated version of it, cut adrift from the doctrine of intelligible essences.[77] This is especially problematic for Unger since only this doctrine allows the classical style to avoid Hume's argument.

At this point Unger might have us look again at part of the first and the third step in his argument. In conjunction these steps purport to rob Hume's argument of any power: to accept it is (i) to accept and privilege the practices of natural science understood in empiricist terms; and (ii) to commit oneself to an unsustainable moral and epistemological scepticism. To say that Unger's attempt to support these claims is incomplete is more than generous. The arguments, such as they are, seem to be obvious *non-sequiturs* (see *P*, pp. 41 and 46; *CLSM*, pp. 95–97). For example, many contemporary moral philosophers—realists and rationalists—rightly regard Hume's argument as compelling yet perfectly consistently offer arguments to establish the nature and basis of morality.[78] These philosophers are certainly neither moral nor epistemological sceptics. Further, although it seems plausible to locate Hume's argument within an intellectual and historical milieu in

[76] Weinrib, *supra*, note 68, p. 1827. The whole argument of this paragraph is derived from Weinrib's superb essay.

[77] The doctrine is rejected by Unger in *KP*, pp. 31 and 239. See Weinrib, *supra*, note 68, p. 1827, particularly fn. 5.

[78] For a rationalist attempt see A. Gewirth, *Reason and Morality* (Chicago, Univ. Chic. Press 1978) and his 'Can Any Final Ends be Rational?' (1991) 102 *Ethics* 66–95. Realists are well represented in a number of the essays in G. Sayre-McCord (ed.), *Moral Realism* (Ithaca, Cornell U. P. 1988) and by J. Dancy, *Moral Reasons* (Oxford, Basil Blackwell 1993).

which a particular conception of the nature of natural science was becoming dominant, this neither invalidates the argument nor commits one who accepts it to any particular account of the scientific enterprise. To think that Hume's argument is invalidated by an awareness of its context and background is to mistake the genesis of an argument for its validity.[79] To show that accepting the argument must commit one to a particular conception of the scientific enterprise would require a formidable degree of argumentation. Certainly, Unger has not yet come close to discharging the task.

(b) Democracy

The main burden of Unger's *WS* is to 'propose[.] a way to place legal analysis in the service of democratic experimentalism' (*WS*, p. 23). The latter is the label Unger adopts for the political programme and practice that flows from *Politics* and we need not examine it here. The main barrier to legal analysis becoming a tool of democratic experimentalism is the dominant conception of the nature and role of law, a conception Unger calls 'rationalising legal analysis'. The bulk of the book (*WS*, pp. 26–134) is a sustained attempt to show the ways in which rationalising legal analysis actually retards, but could also advance, democratic experimentalism and the democratic project of which it is but part. That project, as we would expect from Unger's previous work, 'is the effort to make a practical and moral success of society by reconciling the pursuit of two families of goods: the good of material progress, liberating us from drudgery and incapacity and giving arms and wings to our desires, and the good of emancipation, freeing us from the grinding schemes of social division and hierarchy' (*WS*, p. 6).

Neither the democratic project nor the whole of Unger's discussion of rationalising legal analysis will be examined here. Only a segment of the latter is of interest, namely, that part in which Unger answers the question '[h]ow should judges decide cases?' (*WS*, p. 113). The answer casts doubt over the argument of the previous section that, for Unger, the values in play in adjudication are derived from his social ideal and conception of the person. Why? The first step in Unger's account of how judges should decide cases is a point against rationalising legal analysis but its power is not confined solely to discrediting that doctrine. For, it apparently undermines *any* attempt to premise the practice of adjudication upon a particular set of

[79] The point is well made by K. Popper, *The Logic of Scientific Discovery* (London, Hutchinson 1961) p. 315. J. Boyle also rightly notes, as against Unger's first step, that some of Hume's arguments—contained, for example, in his accounts of causation and induction—are profoundly antithetical to the empiricist conception of science: 'Modernist Social Theory: Roberto Unger's *Passion*' (1985) 98 *Harvard L. R.* 1066–1083, p. 1076.

values, be they embodied in Unger's social ideal and conception of the person or in Dworkin's notions of integrity and equality. Such an attempt must fail because the truth about the current Anglo-American law-making process is that it yields, as laws, democratically engineered, *ad hoc* compromises between various factions and interest-groups within the polity. Hence, law lacks a property that both rationalising legal analysis and our previous account of Unger's thought need it to have since, when law is created in this way,

> [t]here is no developing [all-embracing] rational scheme that different fragments of law may be seen to exemplify. Rather than being a problem for democracy, the absence of such a latent scheme is, in a sense, a precondition for democratic vigor, for democracy expands by opening social life up to conscious experimentation. For the same reason, the devolution of law-completing and law-reconstructive responsibility to an insulated band of experts in rational deliberation makes no sense. Such an expertise properly belongs to the citizens (*WS*, p. 109).

Note that Unger's point is not that it is impossible to develop a scheme of values which the law can and should embody. Rather, it is that, in current conditions, any such scheme 'loses its purchase on reality' (*ibid.*).

The second step in Unger's account of how judges should decide cases flows directly from the first. He holds that judges should embrace this genealogy of law, accept as the basis of their practice the story about law that shows it to be, with the exception of the increasingly marginal body of common law doctrines (*WS*, p. 115), the embodiment of factional interests. Somewhat surprisingly, Unger holds that judges should decide cases through the process of 'purposive analogical reasoning' (*WS*, p. 114), but this is purposive analogical reasoning with a difference. Whereas almost any orthodox jurist could accept a role for this kind of reasoning, which seeks to draw analogies between cases by reference to the purposes and values that supposedly underlie the applicable propositions of law, few could accept the constraints Unger places on this process. There are two. First, this style of adjudication

> should acknowledge no drive towards systematic closure and abstraction: the conceptual ascent of purposive judgments toward prescriptive theory-like conceptions of whole fields of law and social life. Second, it should attempt to avoid any rigid contrast between the prospective and the retrospective genealogies of law: between law as it looks to those who struggle, in politics and public opinion, over its making and law as it looks after the fact to its professional and judicial interpreters. The purposes guiding the analogist must be *just as eclectic in character as those motivating the contestants in original law-making* (*WS*, p. 114; emphasis supplied).

Lest there were any doubt about Unger's position, note that:

> [w]hat matters is for the judge to form a view of these purposes that is continuous with the real world of discourse and conflict from which that fragment of law came.

Moreover, the view should recognise the contestable and factional quality of each of the interests, concerns and assumptions to which it appeals. *They count not because they are the best and the wisest but because they won*, and were settled, earlier down the road of law-making (*ibid.*; emphasis supplied).

These two steps locate adjudication firmly within the realm of democratic participation. Unger's position is therefore in stark contrast to all orthodox accounts of adjudication. But Unger's siting of adjudication within the realm of democracy is the very reason why he cannot hope to realise the social ideal and conception of the person through adjudication. His first step denies, albeit on contingent grounds, that there could be any correspondence between the social ideal and conception of the person, on the one hand, and the laws that issue from our current law-making process, on the other. His second step apparently guarantees dissonance between the social ideal and the conception of the person, on the one hand, and the practice of adjudication, on the other, by insisting that judges eschew the possibility of interpreting the law in light of a 'developing, rational scheme', or a 'prescriptive theory-like conception of a whole field of law'. As noted in the previous section, the social ideal and conception of the person seem admirably suited to the role of the law's developing rational scheme or prescriptive theory. However, as Unger makes abundantly clear, judges should ignore such things. They should apply the law in light of the interests—factional, *ad hoc*, temporary—registered through the democratic process and embodied in the law in question. Doing this manifests a 'general commitment to respect the capacity of parties and movements to win in politics, and to encode and enshrine their victories in law' (*WS*, p. 114).

Were we to derive Unger's account of the role and nature of values within adjudication solely from *WS* the conclusion would be that, if there is any value or values that should guide adjudication, then it is the value of democracy and the 'values' that emerge from the democratic process. So, in their decision-making, judges should defer to the values—whatever they might be—that won in the specific democratic contest that gave life to the law in question. This view generates two snags for Unger. The first is that the law cannot be consistent if the values that breathe life into it are the product of *ad hoc* compromises. This is an obvious consequence of the fact that those values are the product of a simple democratic process, that is, one which simply registers the vote of participants without any test for consistency and coherence. It may seem from *WS* that Unger would care little about this problem—after all, the tenor of his remarks is such to suggest that a patchwork of contradictory values underpinning the law is a fine testament to a vibrant democratic process. However, this attitude cannot be sustained if he is to avoid one of the failings that beset moderate value scepticism, namely, the inability to ensure that the values underpinning the law are consistent.

The second snag is altogether more pressing. If Unger's view is now that the only values in play in adjudication are those that emerge from the democratic process, then there is no guarantee that those values will be consistent with the values that animate Unger's wider project. While it is true that democracy is indeed one of those values, the values Unger invokes in other works—values that correlate around the social ideal and conception of the person and among which we must include 'participation', 'solidarity', 'equality'—will not automatically be embodied in the compromises that constitute the results of the law-making process. In fact, many of those values could quite easily be deliberately thwarted in existing schemes of democracy and law-making. It is rather startling, since the problem is so obvious and well known, that Unger is here at risk of being caught in a variant of the 'paradox of democracy'.[80] The paradox takes the form of a contradiction which can easily arise for a democrat, who we will regard henceforth as one committed to the principle that whatever the majority decide on an issue is right and should be done. If our democrat accepts this majoritarian principle she will not, without fear of contradiction, be able to accept any other non-democratic principle about right and wrong and about what should be done. For, any other such principle could lead her to affirm both X (do what the majority decide) and not-X (do whatever the non-democratic principle of right demands). Whether or not this actually is, strictly speaking, a contradiction need not worry us here since, even if it is not, there is nevertheless an obvious tension between the majoritarian principle and other, non-democratic principles. Unger apparently falls victim to this 'paradox' because, on the basis of works such as *Passion*, *CLSM* and *Politics*, he is committed to a set of values embodied in the social ideal and conception of the person. But, on the basis of *WS*, in particular his account therein of the way judges should decide cases, he seems unequivocally committed to the majoritarian principle. What else makes sense of his story of law-creation as one of *ad hoc* compromises between shifting factions?

Unger could avoid the paradox in two slightly different ways. Both promise to make his commitment to democracy consistent with the social ideal and conception of the person. The first path to consistency appears trite but will be considered nevertheless. It distinguishes between democracy as it actually exists and democracy in the future, particularly democracy as it will exist when some or all steps necessary to achieve the social ideal and conception of the person have been taken. In the latter context

[80] For a few of the many discussions see R. Wollheim, 'A Paradox in the Theory of Democracy' in P. Laslett and W. G. Runciman (eds.), *Philosophy*, *Politics and Society*, 2nd Series (Oxford, Basil Blackwell 1962); B. Barry, *Political Argument* (London, Routledge and Kegan Paul 1965), pp. 58–66 and 293–295; K. Graham, *The Battle of Democracy* (Brighton, Harvester Wheatsheaf 1986), ch. 5; and R. Harrison, *Democracy* (Routledge, London 1993), ch. 9.

it could well be the case that aspects of the political and economic structure are designed so as to ensure that whatever outcomes the democratic process yields, either through formal elections or the law-making process, are compatible with the social ideal and conception of the person. The social ideal and conception of the person could be to some degree institutionally enshrined by, for example, filtering the preferences that count in the democratic process. Many philosophers have been tempted by a similar strategy and have sought to distinguish between citizens' actual and real interests, or their external and internal preferences, or have constructed ideal situations of choice in which preferences or interests untainted by ideology or self-interest can be determined.[81] The unifying aim of such efforts is to bolster faith in democracy by ensuring that the preferences which generate democratic outcomes are neither utterly morally abhorrent nor destructive of democracy itself. Unger could leap upon this somewhat rickety bandwagon in an attempt to avoid the paradox. He could insist that his injunctions as to how judges should decide cases are intended for the future, for a time when our democratic processes will be fully compatible—because derived from—the social ideal and conception of the person. The difficulty with this solution—beyond its well-documented snags, such as the arrant instability of the distinctions drawn or the question-begging nature of the ideal situations of choice—is that nothing Unger says in *WS* supports this view. There is no indication that when he is describing adjudication his eyes are on the future rather than the present. And, in our present forms of democracy, Unger will certainly face the paradox.

The second path to consistency refuses the distinction which the first draws. It holds that whether Unger has in mind democracy now or in the future is irrelevant since, despite appearances, his commitment to the majoritarian principle is qualified. Nevertheless, accepting that our sketch of Unger's arguments about how judges should decide cases is accurate, on what grounds can we challenge appearances? Fortunately, Unger offers an important textual clue by way of one of the two constraints he places upon the process of democratic adjudication. He says the account of adjudication as we have so far sketched it is

> incomplete . . . [in the sense that] two large ideals bear upon its work and modify its course. The first is an ideal of concern with the litigants as real people, with their

[81] A few diverse examples are Wollheim and Barry, *supra*, note 80; W. Connolly, *The Terms of Political Discourse* (Oxford, Martin Robertson, 2nd ed. 1983), ch. 2; T. Benton, 'Realism, Power and Objective Interests' in K. Graham (ed.), *Contemporary Political Philosophy* (Cambridge, C. U. P. 1982); R. Dworkin, *Taking Rights Seriously* (London, Duckworth 1977), pp. 234–238 and 357–358; 'Is There a Right to Pornography?' (1981) 1 *Oxford Journal of Legal Studies* 177–212; and *Freedom's Law* (Oxford, Clarendon 1996), pp. 17–19.

vulnerabilities and expectations. The second is an ideal of commitment to make adjudication serve the larger goal of advancing the power of a free people to govern themselves (*WS*, p. 115).

The first ideal translates into the notion of equity as lawyers have traditionally understood it and does nothing to solve the paradox. The second ideal is, however, more pertinent. It apparently evinces an acceptance on Unger's behalf of constraints upon the majoritarian principle in the name of other values. Until this point Unger's account of how judges should decide cases has embodied the majoritarian principle: he maintains that judicial decision-making should track the democratic, factional compromises that generated the law in question. The paradox Unger faces is squaring his commitment to the majoritarian principle with his other values, values that might well not register in, or even be thwarted by, the democratic process. However, in accepting that judges should sometimes *not* track the democratic, factional compromises that yield laws—because the democratic process sometimes entrenches 'impediments to the enjoyment of rights' (*WS*, p. 118)—Unger surely qualifies his support for the majoritarian principle. He accepts that the principle, at least as it translates into the law-making process, can have objectionable consequences. It can be antidemocratic, in the sense that it can either entrench or fail to alleviate impediments to the enjoyment of 'rights composing the system of popular self government' (*ibid.*). Furthermore, it can surely be objectionable on other, non-democratic grounds when it entrenches or fails to alleviate impediments to the enjoyment of other rights. In these circumstances, judges should engage in either 'a bold remaking of the law' (*ibid.*) or in the 'structural but episodic intervention' (*ibid.*) he calls complex enforcement. And they should do this *regardless* of the democratic basis of the law in question.

This is the only qualification needed to avoid the paradox. For, if Unger's support of the majoritarian principle is filtered through other commitments and other values, then he can quite easily deny any tension between democracy and those other values. He can hold that the former must be made consistent with—perhaps because derived from—the latter. Further, were we to ask Unger why we should care about the fact that our existing political and economic processes entrench impediments to the enjoyment of rights, we could well guess the response. Would it not emphasise the importance of such rights to a particular kind of social structure and way of living? Would it not, in other words, found those rights upon the social ideal and conception of the person? And does not the justification for empowered democracy that Unger offered in *Politics* (*P*, *ii*, pp. 355–377), a justification closely connected to the social ideal and conception of the person, work equally well here, as a justification for action against impediments to the enjoyment of rights? If so, *WS* might, after all, be consistent with the rest of Unger's work.

(c) A failed vision?

In the work before *WS* Unger's main difficulties were the foundational level problems of contingency and normative ascription. Unger could acquit himself well at the level of specification since he has an obvious way—the distinction between micro- and macro-values—to avoid the difficulty that ensnares moderate value sceptics like Klare. However, because the contingency and normative ascription problems arise at the foundational level and beset Unger's account of which values generate reasons for action and why, it might be thought that they are particularly serious. So serious, in fact, as to call into question the claim that the visionary stance is the most promising account of the nature, basis and role of values in adjudication available to heretics. This assessment is too hasty.

First, it ignores the fact that both problems could be solved. That is, although Unger's own arguments on both points are weak, other arguments are available that do not have obviously unacceptable effects upon the main body of his work. Taking the problem of normative ascription first, it could be circumvented were Unger to argue for both social ideal and conception of the person in either moral realist or moral rationalist terms. That would involve, *inter alia*, showing the conception of the person to be a presupposition, and the social ideal a consequence, of his account of the moral values that bind us. It seems unlikely that the social ideal could function as the presupposition of such an account and makes little sense to regard the conception of the person as being a consequence of it—if we argue that certain values are binding upon 'us' we must know what 'we' look like at the outset. Adopting what Weinrib holds is the full-blown version of the classical style of normative argument is not an option for Unger lest he revoke his rejection of the notion of intelligible essences. By contrast, Unger could travel the moral realist or rationalist path with minimal disruption: he would only have to tone down his sceptical rhetoric about moral philosophy and give up on normative ascription.[82] One suspects that this would surely occur were Unger to acquaint himself more thoroughly with some contemporary work in the field. The contingency problem could also be fairly painlessly solved by Unger. The solution involves a simple acknowledgement of the ambiguity and a statement that he endorses the weak sense of contingency. The problem becomes debilitating only if Unger commits himself to the strong sense of contingency.

The second reason why it is hasty to take the problems of contingency

[82] Some examples of Unger's sceptical rhetoric are: *CLSM*, p. 56; *P*, pp. 43–44; and *P*, *i*, pp. 37–39.

and normative ascription as fatal to Unger's project is this. Those problems are small but important parts of an all-embracing programme of institutional, cultural and psychological development. The programme ranges from discussion of the details of particular segments of adjudication to sketches of the institutions and practices of a future society and includes an account of how interpersonal relations might be reconceived so as to track the higher virtues of love, hope and faith. To reject such an immense, ambitious programme because of the contingency and normative ascription problems is akin to scrapping a 1932 Rolls Royce Silver Shadow because of a faulty gear-box or destroying a Goya sketch because the charcoal is smudged. The problem is undoubtedly serious but should not be regarded, without a great deal of argument, as terminal.

The problem that *WS* presents is the paradox of democracy. There are ways in which Unger could avoid it without imperilling his other commitments. Again, this would not require much of him. A recasting of some of the language and a few of the arguments in his account of how judges should decide cases, so as to make clear that his commitment to democracy is filtered through, or qualified by, the values that constitute the social ideal and conception of the person, will suffice. However, taken in conjunction with the contingency and normative ascription problems, this point highlights the most unsatisfying aspect of Unger's work to date. For, how can it be that an enterprise so far developed, already rich in detail about our future institutions and modes of being, and crammed full with exhortations about the ways and means with which to change our existing practices, institutions and mentalities, is still vague about its guiding values and the way they interrelate? Until Unger explicitly tackles this issue we can only provisionally accept his programme; it can exert just a prima facie rather than compelling claim over us. However, despite its problems, we should resist the temptation to begin a requiem for Unger's programme, resist Menelaus's pessimistic verdict that '[v]anish'd are all the visionary joys'.[83] We should accept instead the judgment of Habakkuk: the vision is yet for an appointed time. Whether in the end it shall not lie remains to be established.

[83] A. Pope, *The Iliad and Odyssey of Homer* (London, Routledge 1890), Odyssey, IV, p. 341.

8
Conclusion

> Neither the defender of the status quo nor the proponent of radical change will find much comfort in these pages, which issue no clarion calls and recommend (if they recommend anything) only that we resist overheated and overdramatic characterizations of our situation. S. Fish, *There's no Such Thing as Free Speech* . . . (1994) p. viii.

Almost by definition, agnostics find it hard, as contemporary therapists might say, to 'commit'. It is clear by now that the temper of this book is, if anything, agnostic. Thus it is no surprise that Stanley Fish's uncharacteristically restrained but typically deflationary claim sums up our argument as accurately as his own. This position is not a conceit but a conclusion based upon evaluation of many of the most important orthodox and heretical arguments. As a result, the supposed battle between orthodoxy and heresy can now be seen in a clearer light and we can observe it in a somewhat detached way. Our overarching question—how different are orthodoxy and heresy?—received a deflationary answer, namely, 'not very'. The responses orthodox and heretical accounts of adjudication made to the problems of method, causality and values were charted and the conclusions reached will be reiterated in section I below. While the approach has been agnostic and detached, we have not been content simply to sit on fences or pursue an inane but comfortable *via media*. Hence not all of the conclusions reached were deflationary. Section II therefore defends those parts of the book that have a specific axe to grind and responds to what might be perceived as an omission.

I THE STORY SO FAR

The first part of the book established that orthodox accounts of adjudication begin by deploying the method of *Verstehen*. This is clearly the correct starting point, but the orthodox fail to come to grips with at least one difficult snag that method faces, namely, the plurality problem. There are other snags that allegedly ensnare the orthodox method, such as the incorrigibility problem and the ideology critique but these are either avoidable or highlight issues faced by any method. In addition, we examined whether, in taking up the method of *Verstehen*, the orthodoxy is thereby committed to methodological individualism. We concluded that it is not and that the orthodox method is best characterised by the label 'compatibilism'. The major failing of the orthodox was their inchoate implementation of this method. Compatibilism, remember, combines 'understanding' and 'explanation', insists that we must take seriously the meaning dimension of social action, practices and institutions, while accepting that such action, practices and institutions can be causally determined or influenced. Thus there is undoubtedly room in our efforts to make sense of the social world for both the hermeneutic interpretation of action and the pursuit and construction of a body of causal laws. Social life can be explained and understood by both an interpretative and a nomological net. When attention turned to values rather than method (although the two are, of course, unavoidably linked), it was established that strong value pluralism was a popular but not the only orthodox stance. If it arises within adjudication, strong value pluralism ensures that the determinacy condition cannot be satisfied and this puts one version of the law/politics distinction at risk. We also concluded that the legitimacy condition could not remedy the problems that arise from the collapse of the determinacy condition, at least not if the notions of legitimacy and authority are understood as some orthodox scholars understand them.

Part II began by considering the ways in which heretical legal scholars might loosen the grip of the orthodox method, might prise legal scholarship away from the method of *Verstehen* or the internal point of view. A number of arguments to this end were considered. It was established that only two might work: one version of the argument from the indeterminacy of language and a critical version of the ideology critique. The former did not, however, seem to pose a great problem for the orthodoxy since it invoked an account of meaning that the orthodox could easily—and probably do—accept. The critical version of the ideology critique seems powerful but, regrettably, the majority of heretics are attracted to non-critical versions of this critique. The problem with non-critical versions is that they are prone to redundancy, although we demonstrated this only in relation to one account. Our overall view of the other arguments intended to destabilise the orthodox method was that they were either so problematic or so ambitious as to never get off the ground. We then examined whether or not heretics might be tempted into the opposite sin of methodological individualism, namely, methodological holism. On balance, it seems that they are not, although some heretics are a little squeamish about explicitly articulating the method they employ in order to understand social life. Notwithstanding the confusion, we concluded that the heretical approach embodies compatibilism as does the orthodox approach. Finally, the heretical position on values was considered. While a majority of the orthodox are value pluralists, there is no such easily determinable heretical position. Heretics have taken a variety of positions on the nature of values and their role within adjudication, but we concluded that perhaps the most promising and certainly the most ambitious was that adopted by Roberto Unger. Although this position has some problems, they are not such as to make it unsustainable.

This sketch of the arguments of the book shows that there are some important similarities and differences between orthodoxy and heresy. That might not be considered the least bit newsworthy or interesting, but it is, for the following reason. Neither similarities nor differences arise where participants and observers of this debate might initially think. For example, the self-representations of the participants might lead one to believe that the orthodox think law a forum of reason, in which solutions to social problems and individual disputes are compelled by reasons eventually articulated by the work of many minds.[1] (The minds at work include those of judges, counsel, academic commentators and chroniclers of the law.) Those same self-representations often portray heretics as enemies of both reason and law, as non-believers who have nothing to put in their place. They smash the altars and churches, leaving us with no functional equivalents to do jobs that have to be done (disputes have to be resolved, don't they?). But it seems that the orthodox conception of the role of reason in law is far more modest than the stereotype suggests. We showed that the orthodox have a great deal of difficulty maintaining the determinacy condition and are unable to sustain what might be regarded as an important distinction between law and politics. The orthodox position therefore looks rather heretical, differing from it only in emphasis. Heretics are explicitly sceptical about either law's claim to be rational *simpliciter*, or law's claim to be a more rational process than, for example, collective local or national decision-making in an empowered democracy, for making social choices and resolving individual disputes. By contrast, the orthodox become sceptical about these matters only by default.

The hyperbole and publicity arising from the conflict between orthodoxy and heresy might also encourage the conclusion that these two approaches employ quite different methods to understand and explain law. Our analysis showed that they do not, despite the heretical tendency to deploy European 'fancy theory' and the orthodox taste for the supposedly mundane philosophers of the Anglo-American analytical tradition.[2] These two supposedly different traditions often bump up against the same issues although they tackle them in a different argot. Hence, questions of meaning, interpretation, causality, and values are live philosophical problems in both

[1] A view well expressed by the then Dean of Yale Law School, Professor A. Kronman, in 1994. He characterised 'the ethos of his institution [and the law at large?] . . . [as] ". . . faith in the power of reason" ': P. Schlag, *The Enchantment of Reason* (Durham, Duke U. P. 1998), p. 19.

[2] For some sources of fancy theory see D. Kennedy, 'Distributive and Paternalist Motives in Contract and Tort Law, With Special Reference to Compulsory Terms and Unequal Bargaining Power' (1982) 41 *Maryland L. R.* 563–658, p. 564, fn. 3.

traditions even though this can be obscured by the language of 'different traditions'. This is not to be insensitive to the different cultural conditions in which philosophical and political arguments are formulated and from which they derive some of their (illocutionary) meaning; but, equally, such sensitivity does not make the search for similarities impossible. And the similarity we discerned in both orthodox and heretical meditations on method was compatibilism. Despite the many protestations of difference by heretics, on the one hand, and somewhat shrill indignation of the orthodox, on the other, both are united in the belief that internal and external or reason-based and caused-based approaches are appropriate in the effort to understand social life. Orthodoxy and heresy are also similar in that both are, in deed if not in word, inchoate compatibilists: the former rarely go beyond the method of *Verstehen*, whereas the latter are inclined to be dismissive of the participants' point of view. The difference here is therefore one of tone or attitude; there is no great substantive dispute. Since the orthodox are inclined to take participants' views more seriously, they therefore take the task of rational reconstruction seriously (because participants do). Heretics are more sceptical of participants' views and thus uncomfortable with the enterprise of rational reconstruction. This is undoubtedly a divide arising from the degree of faith theorists have in the views of participants—the orthodox are believers and heretics non-believers—but the familiarity of the divide within the human sciences suggests that it surely cannot explain the controversy generated in our secular, de-mystified legal academy. Or perhaps it can, if the Benthamite task of secularisation and de-mystification of the law is still incomplete.[3]

Finally, note that the heretical critique of law, conceived in general terms, looks in some respects quite orthodox. While it must be conceded that some heretics apparently want rid of law altogether—think, for example, of Duncan Kennedy's hope that state and judge will disappear in a society of expanded altruism, or Allan Hutchinson's suggestion that a thesaurus of popular power and participation replace the elite lexicon of the law—many do not.[4] Rather, they criticise the law for impeding or ignoring some important values while exclusively and therefore harmfully promoting other values. Of the many examples of this argument in the heretical literature, perhaps the most notable are provided by William Simon and Karl Klare.[5]

[3] For a fine introduction see H. L. A. Hart, *Essays on Bentham* (Oxford, Clarendon 1982), ch. 1.

[4] See D. Kennedy, 'Form and Substance in Private Law Adjudication' (1976) 89 *Harvard L. R.* 1685–1778, p. 1771 and A. Hutchinson, *Dwelling on the Threshold: Critical Essays in Modern Legal Thought* (Toronto, Carswell 1988), p. 22.

[5] Both have written much on their respective proposals but the flavour can be gleaned from two early essays. They are: W. Simon, 'Visions of Practice in Legal Thought' (1984) 36 *Stanford L. R.* 469–507; K. Klare, 'Critical Theory and Labour Relations Law', ch. 4 of D. Kairys (ed.), *The Politics of Law* (New York, Pantheon 1982).

Simon's early work suggested that legal practice be reformulated to embody the notion of non-hierarchical community. Klare argued that American labour law inchoately embodies its supposed underpinning values, that it must realise these more completely and, in addition, incorporate an account of the value of work. Both proposals are in themselves very interesting but that is not our point. For, this heretical critique of areas of law for failing to track their underpinning values, or the demonstration that those values are incoherent, is also a central trope of orthodox doctrinal scholarship, along with the illustration that legal doctrines fail in their purpose or impact adversely upon non-legal life. So in this respect, at least, there is again no great difference between the two. Indeed, were two catalogues compiled listing the values that orthodox and heretical scholars thought particular areas of law should embody, it is unlikely that there would be much difference between them. Take contract law as an example. Both lists would undoubtedly include ideas like autonomy, freedom, fairness and good faith, although they would differ as to the relative importance of these and about the language appropriate to describe them (do they yield a vision of altruism or individualism, community or exchange?). But such differences are as likely to break out within the heresy and the orthodoxy as they are between orthodoxy and heresy, so the two positions cannot be distinguished on this dimension. Nor can we say that one group is clearly sceptical about the role of values in law and adjudication whereas the other is not.

The end product of our analysis of orthodoxy and heresy is a map. The map was constructed around one overarching question and three specific problems. This map is a better guide to the issues and arguments at stake between orthodoxy and heresy than anything heretics and orthodox have so far provided. Moreover, since it is a map constructed with regard to three problems that any effort to explain and understand almost any aspect of social life must address, it serves to position the dispute between orthodoxy and heresy within the wider currents of the human sciences. Of course, few heretical and orthodox legal scholars would affirm that their work is completely removed from the human sciences and thus free from the difficulties that must be addressed therein. We found that orthodox and heretics alike have either ignored or underestimated these problems and hence offered no or inadequate responses to them. We also found that it was not uncommon to misconstrue responses to these problems offered by social theorists and philosophers; indeed, misrepresentation often goes hand-in-hand with blindness as to the consequences of such responses. Yet what has been offered here is still a map, with all that this implies. It was constructed with a specific question and set of problems in mind; different questions and problems would almost certainly yield a different map. Besides the overarching question and the three problems, our map has been informed by another principle, namely, that of attempting to give scrupulous attention to the terrain itself. That is, to the arguments heretics and orthodox themselves use or are seemingly committed to; our map has thus been produced free from both hyperbole and hunches. Only then can we be clear about the contours of this alleged dispute.

II LOOSE ENDS

The relative paucity of specific clarion calls and recommendations in this book should not blind us to the fact that there are indeed some. In particular, it may be thought that the two areas where the book has prescriptions to offer are particularly problematic. There is, in addition, an objection that highlights what might be regarded as a particularly heinous omission in a book of this kind. These three points are examined in turn.

(a) Compatibilism: two additional difficulties

The book recommends compatibilism as a method for understanding and explaining social life in general and that specific part of it we know as adjudication. While efforts were made in chapters 3 and 6 to counter some objections to compatibilism, many others might be raised. Although they cannot all be considered here, some will be, namely, those that could conceivably hail from what Roberto Unger calls 'super-theorists'.[6] These social theorists and philosophers are compatibilists' fellow-travellers since, like them, they believe in the possibility and utility of systematic efforts to explain and understand social life. They are thus willing to take up the burdens—historical, philosophical, moral and epistemological—associated with that task. By contrast, objections to compatibilism that might be made by ultra-theorists—those enamoured of deconstruction—are ignored here. This is not because such objections are unworthy of attention but because, as should be plain from those sections of the book where efforts were made to engage with this body of thought, it is too demanding, raising issues that go beyond the already over-wide range of this work. Furthermore, since super-theorists are playing the same game as compatibilists, whereas ultra-theorists, contrary to Unger's view, appear not to be, the objections of the former would seem to be the more difficult and pertinent.

The first gripe about compatibilism concerns its ontological modesty. This complaint is most likely to be made by those super-theorists who maintain that methods for understanding and explaining the social world are determined by the constituents of that world. Hence, ontology determines

[6] *Social Theory: Its Situation and Its Task* (Cambridge, C. U. P. 1987), p. 165. This, remember, is the first of the three volumes that constitute Unger's *Politics*.

method. This claim partly constitutes a position within contemporary social and philosophical thought that is dubbed realism or, better, given the multiple associations and meanings attached to the former, critical realism.[7] Stated in this way, it seems that critical realism contradicts compatibilism since the latter apparently denies that ontology determines method. Most important for present purposes is the doubt expressed in chapter 3 as to whether the ontological claims made by proponents of different methods did indeed entail or support only those methods. Specifically, we rejected the claim that because action takes place within a rich context constituted by both structures and other actions, a method such as compatibilism, which seeks to integrate both reasons and causes, must be correct. Additionally, although less relevant here, chapter 6 rejected Unger's apparently ontological argument that the fluidity and contingency of the social world shows either the impossibility or improbability of a body of causal laws. Hence, there does indeed seem to be a conflict brewing between compatibilism and critical realism and that may be thought regrettable. For, beyond this putative dispute about the methodological implications of ontology, compatibilism and critical realism have much in common. Both, for example, seek to transcend the 'dispute' between methodological individualism and holism. In the effort to make sense of the social world both allocate a role to understanding and interpreting agents and their reasons, on the one hand, and to explaining and deducing the causal effects of structures, on the other. Moreover, critical realism is a well-developed and seemingly successful method within the social sciences.[8] Were compatibilism consistent with critical realism, it could only be strengthened by realism's success. The objection under consideration claims that they are inconsistent. Indeed, since ontology determines method, it holds that compatibilism's ontological modesty is a mistake.

We must look a little more carefully at the critical realist claim about ontology and method. What, exactly, does it maintain? A good formulation is offered by Margaret Archer. She holds that there is 'a necessary and a two-way linkage' between 'social ontology and explanatory methodology'.[9] She is clear that the linkage is not one of logical implication—things can exist that never enter into our social scientific explanations and some social facts are entirely neutral as to the method best employed to explain them. Rather, descriptions of the world and accounts of the constituents of the world set the parameters of our explanations in the following ways. First,

[7] A useful introduction to this programme is M. Archer *et al* (eds.), *Critical Realism: Essential Readings* (London, Routledge 1998). The most influential texts are those of R. Bhaskar, beginning with his *A Realist Theory of Science* (London, Verso 1997; first published 1975).

[8] See *Critical Realism*, *supra*, parts II and III and M. Archer, *Culture and Agency* (Cambridge, C. U. P. 1989).

[9] M. Archer, *Realist Social Theory: the Morphogenetic Approach* (Cambridge, C. U. P. 1995), p. 13.

Archer rightly concludes that ontology constrains explanation or method since the assertion that the world consists of only Xs, Ys and Zs conflicts with an attempt to explain that world by reference to Ps. If Xs, Ys and Zs are all that exists, it is surely inconsistent and mysterious to explain them by reference to what does not exist (Ps). Of course, were Xs, Ys and Zs derivable from a more fundamental category of Ps, then there would be no problem. But, if Ps are not part of the fabric of the world, how can they explain parts of it? Secondly, Archer holds: [i] that 'explanation cannot proceed without prior description, yet [ii] what something is defined as being through the concepts which describe it determines what exactly is to be explained, which [iii] necessarily circumscribes the explanatory project'.[10] The first claim here is surely true; one needs to have some idea what one is looking for in order to begin to explain it. The second is a little problematic, since it creates a misleading impression about description, namely, that we describe only in order to explain. That is surely not so. For example, many literary and poetic descriptions have no explanatory point at all, although they usually have an ontological referent (think of Romeo's reflections on Juliet's beauty). Beyond that, this claim seems only to reiterate Archer's point about ontology. If we take the world to be made up of only Xs, Ys and Zs, and we describe it so, it is bizarre to think that Ps (which are neither derivable from nor by-products of Xs, Ys and Zs) are in need of explanation. In this sense, our ontology and descriptions constrain our method and explanations; the third claim is therefore true. Note that affirming the world to be made up of Xs, Ys and Zs neither dictates a position as to the explanatory relationships between these elements (does X explain Y, or Y explain X? Does Z have any explanatory power at all?), nor requires the view that all these elements stand in need of explanation. How can affirming that the world is made up of Xs, Ys and Zs say anything about which element is the most important in explanatory terms? True, the affirmation sets the contours of the field in which any explanation operates—it describes the world, what we seek to explain and, of course, the concepts used in explanations must be part of that world. Yet the explanatory relationships between the constituents of that world and the explanatory power of particular constituents seem, prior to investigation, entirely open.

If this is all the critical realist position on ontology and method amounts to, then it creates no problem for compatibilism. Compatibilism denies that the ontological claim that both agents and structures exist entails compatibilism, since both methodological individualists and methodological holists can also make that ontological claim. Denying this entailment does not commit one to denying that ontology constrains method and explana-

[10] M. Archer, *Realist Social Theory*, p. 20.

tion in the ways noted in the previous paragraph. Indeed, compatibilism affirms a link between ontology and method in relation to language: since we are linguistically constituted beings, any effort to explain and understand social life must register this fact. Compatibilists are of course committed to making an ontological claim as a consequence of affirming their method, since they must hold that agents and structures exist. So, while they do not think a particular ontological claim entails their method, their method does indeed entail an ontological claim. In her treatment of the dispute between methodological individualists and methodological holists, Archer seemingly takes issue with this, maintaining that these methods are entailed by particular incompatible ontologies. Indeed, she sometimes characterises the dispute between methodological individualism and holism as being entirely ontological. If this is the only and best way in which to conceive it, then compatibilism's ontological modesty is again under threat.

It is unlikely, though, that this is the only or the best way to conceive the debate. Archer herself is aware of this when she accepts that it is the case 'that nobody disagrees that in social reality there are both individuals (X) and groups (Y)'.[11] This is a good characterisation of the position that many methodological individualists and holists take. And it is a position that they are perfectly entitled to take, without fear of contradiction. It makes perfect sense. Notice that their dispute thence cannot be adequately described as ontological, since the parties accept that both individuals and supra-individual facts or groups exist. Rather the dispute is surely about explanatory priority, about whether Xs can and must be explained in terms of Ys or vice versa. Nothing is gained from trying to cast this dispute in ontological terms, nor does there seem to be any necessity to do so. Yet Archer still makes the effort. After making the concession just noted, she nevertheless maintains that 'the crux of the matter . . . is not whether groups exist but what *constitutes* them. In other words, how should they properly be *described*?'[12] Why this ontological turn? Since Individualist and Holist agree that Xs and Ys exist, their dispute is surely not about how these things are best described, but about how they are best explained. There must be a description of X and Y that Individualist and Holist both accept, for if there is not, they cannot genuinely agree that X and Y exist. Disagreement about the constituents of X and Y is of course possible between those who accept that X and Y exist, just as we can agree about the existence of two kinds of cake yet argue about the ingredients. However, Archer is in danger of muddying the water here. For Individualist and Holist could accept that X is constituted by a, b and c, and that Y is constituted by d, e and f, yet still disagree as to how X and Y are best explained. Holist maintains that X is explained by reference to Y while Individualist holds just the opposite.

[11] M. Archer, *Realist Social Theory*, p. 18.

[12] *Ibid.*, (emphasis supplied).

Again, the attempt to convert the dispute into an ontological one looks unnecessary and unhelpful. This is not to deny that, as Archer rightly shows, some holists and individualists frame their dispute in ontological terms; it is to deny the necessity of so framing it, except in the situations already noted where ontology constrains method.

So, it seems that compatibilism's ontological modesty remains intact and that critical realism's ontological ambition is not as great as first imagined. The constraints ontology places on method need not and cannot be denied by compatibilists, although the critical realist's apparent tendency to reduce (or inflate?) every methodological dispute to an ontological disagreement must be resisted. We cannot, however, escape the maw of ontology just yet, for another objection might be raised against compatibilism's ontological modesty. This second gripe claims to discern a tension or contradiction between compatibilism's proclamations of ontological modesty, on the one hand, and the invocation in other parts of the book of the ontologically ambitious doctrine of moral realism. This doctrine will be examined in the following section. For now, simply note that a tension or contradiction only arises if there is no principled case for modesty in one context and ambition, or less modesty, in another. Moreover, a tension or contradiction could surely only be generated here were the compatibilist position one of ontological *abstinence* and not ontological *modesty*. Since the latter is the compatibilist position, some ontological claims are therefore permitted and have already been made. The fact that invoking moral realism entails another ontological claim is surely no cause for concern.

A third gripe about compatibilism is also ontologically motivated and altogether more intractable. It raises the question of the relation between agency and structure. The compatibilist view is that the relation is between separate but not completely independent properties that influence one another. In principle, then, the two must be distinguishable and relatively autonomous of one another, even though they cannot be envisaged as having a life without one another (just as we cannot conceive of *langue* without *parole*). While this view might accord with common sense and seems obvious, it has a powerful adversary within contemporary sociology in the form of Anthony Giddens's structuration theory.[13] We cannot do justice to the contours of this vastly ambitious body of work here and, thankfully, need not attempt to do so, since our focus is upon one specific claim. It is the claim that agency and structure are not and cannot be made distinct, that they blend or compact into one another. Thus there are not two discernible 'things' constitutive of the social landscape—agents and structures—but only one, namely, social practices. This claim is one of the

[13] See, *inter alia*, his *New Rules of Sociological Method* (London, Hutchinson 1976), chs. 2 and 3; *Central Problems in Social Theory* (London, Macmillan 1979), chs. 1, 2 and 3; and *The Constitution of Society* (Cambridge, Polity Press 1984), chs. 1 and 4.

most distinctive and challenging features of structuration theory and also the most difficult to refute. If it is correct, then compatibilism's insistence upon an agency/structure division must be wrong.

There is grave difficulty here, however. For it is unclear what would count as a demonstration of the truth or falsity of the agency/structure distinction. Structuration theory's claim that social practices are the fulcrum of social reality, and compatibilism's claim that such practices are separable into or side-effects of either agency or structure, appear ontological. How are such competing ontological claims to be evaluated? Even the most perceptive critics of structuration theory are occasionally tempted by the worthless argumentative gambit of bumping ontologies. John Thompson provides an example. He objects to structuration theory's claim that rules, resources and actions are the fulcrum of social reality and not structures on the ground that 'the study of rules (and resources) is not identical to, but rather distinct from and on a different level from, the analysis of social structure'.[14] Archer also avails herself of this gambit, affirming against Giddens's account of the agent that it 'generates an understratified notion, one which captures some salient features of the "actor" but cannot accommodate all the distinctive properties of either the "agent" or the "person"'.[15] The core of these comments is that things are really not the way Giddens thinks they are, that the social world is more stratified and complex than structuration theory's ontology would have us believe. The obvious question to raise here is this: how can we know? What is it that allows us to judge one such ontological claim (that the social world is made up of two distinctive types of thing, agents and structures) as better than another (that the social world is constituted by social practices which are reducible neither to agents nor structures)?

An appeal to ordinary experience or to what we called in chapters 1, 2 and 5 'practical theory' might help, but only if it speaks with one voice. It could well be the case that ordinary experience accommodates agents, structures and social practices, therefore providing no compelling support for either ontological claim. Another way in which claims such as these could be evaluated is by reference to their consistency with other important beliefs or theoretical positions and by virtue of their internal consistency and clarity. Giddens's work has been subject to a range of criticism on this last dimension. It has been argued that structuration theory's problems include *inter multos alia* an ambiguous account of rules, a mystifying notion of the 'virtual' existence of structures and an unacceptable account of the self. Only the most hasty would leap to the conclusion that this account of social reality is therefore entirely without merit and beyond

[14] 'The Theory of Structuration', ch. 3 of D. Held and J. Thompson (eds.), *Social Theory in Modern Societies: Anthony Giddens and his Critics* (Cambridge, C. U. P. 1989), p. 64.

[15] Archer, *supra*, note 9, p. 117.

hope. It is unlikely that the problems faced by structuration theory are such as to justify complete rejection nor is it true that other ontologically incompatible accounts of social reality are free from vice. Hence the intractability of this dispute.

Our conclusion is twofold: compatibilism is ontologically modest and this, to echo Fish again, is a good thing, too. Compatibilism brings with it ontological commitments such as those it shares with Archer's critical realism; it cannot therefore be regarded as espousing ontological abstinence. Those commitments are, however, nowhere near as strong as some compatibilists think (for example, the fabric of reality does not entail that compatibilism is the only appropriate method for understanding and explaining social life). This is what makes compatibilism's ontology 'modest'. There may be another, stronger reason to be ontologically modest. For, although the disagreement between compatibilism and structuration theory about agency and structure appears genuinely ontological, Willard Quine has suggested that such disputes are actually theoretical.[16] His thesis of ontological relativity seems to hold that ontologies do not and cannot determine theories and explanatory schemes. If anything, suggests Quine, theories and explanatory schemes determine ontologies. Whatever may be thought of this position, it at least has the virtue of turning attention to matters that may be easier to adjudicate than ontological disputes. A standard way in which to evaluate a theory or explanatory scheme is by virtue of its internal consistency. Many of the objections to structuration theory take this tack and it is very helpful. For it seems that the criteria of adequacy in this area are reasonably clear whereas the bumping of ontologies helps not a jot. Whereas the former allows some steps toward evaluation, the latter ends the process in something akin to the pantomime refrains of 'Oh yes there are (agents and structures)' and 'Oh no there aren't (there are just social practices)'. Until we know how to avoid such an *impasse*, ontological modesty is the only sensible response.

(b) The redundancy of realism and rationalism

The type of realism and rationalism we are interested in is moral realism and moral rationalism. Although they have been lumped together in an indiscriminate way in previous chapters, they must be distinguished here since they give rise to quite different sets of problems. For present purposes, moral realism holds that there are facts that make moral propositions either true or false and that these facts are either not completely, or not at all, determined by the wants, sentiments, desires or whims of agents. Moral rationalism, by contrast, maintains that some moral values or a par-

[16] See his *Ontological Relativity and Other Essays* (New York, Columbia U. P. 1969), ch. 2.

ticular fundamental moral principle can be shown by reason to be binding upon all purposive beings.[17] These formulations are undoubtedly crude and in proper meta-ethical discussion would require more by way of elucidation. For now, though, they serve to highlight two positions distinct from a family of non-cognitivist and emotivist meta-ethical doctrines.[18] These doctrines sometimes dismiss talk of moral truth as a mistake, or locate the truth of moral propositions in something other than the realm of facts, and also often minimise the role of reason in such matters. While realism and rationalism are similar because they deny these claims, it is clear from our crude definitions that they are not the same nor do they entail one another. So, for example, one can affirm rationalism and not affirm realism by resisting the claim that the moral principle established by reason in some sense corresponds to some fact of the matter.[19] Similarly, one can claim that moral propositions correspond without thereby being committed to the view that they are dialectically necessary truths established by reason.[20] Despite these obvious differences, both doctrines were invoked so as to rescue orthodoxy and heresy from some debilitating snags. More accurately, both doctrines were said to hold out *the promise* of solving two troublesome problems. For the orthodoxy, the difficulty moral realism and rationalism might circumvent is the plurality problem, itself a consequence of correctly adopting the internal point of view or the method of *Verstehen*. For the heresy, realism and rationalism promise to do better the job Unger assigns to normative ascription, since both doctrines accommodate rather than ignore the is/ought distinction. No argument was offered to show that only realism and rationalism could solve these problems nor is any such argument forthcoming.

Beyond these specific considerations, the salience of realism and rationalism derives from the assumption that they promise a greater degree of clarity and certainty in the effort to determine moral good and bad, right and wrong, than many other meta-ethical doctrines. How do they do this? First, by purporting to show exactly what it is that makes moral propositions right and wrong, better or worse and, second, by portraying that property, whatever it happens to be, in a particular way, namely, as independent

[17] See A. Gewirth, *Reason and Morality* (Chicago, University of Chicago Press 1978).

[18] This body of thought is not as homogenous as is sometimes thought: see C. Stevenson, *Ethics and Language* (New Haven, Yale U. P. 1945) and A. J. Ayer, *Language, Truth and Logic* (London, Penguin 1971), ch. 6. For a stimulating but somewhat jaundiced overview of emotivism and its consequences see A. MacIntyre, *After Virtue* (London, Duckworth 2nd. ed. 1985).

[19] Of course, Gewirth, *supra*, note 17, p. 175 claims that his rationally necessary fundamental moral principle—the principle of generic consistency—is true by virtue of its correspondence with the facts constitutive of the normative structure of action. Whether this would satisfy the realist conception of correspondence, and whether the normative structure of action is sufficiently 'factual', are open questions.

[20] See, for example, J. McDowell, 'Values and Secondary Qualities' in T. Honderich (ed.), *Morality and Objectivity* (London, Routledge and Kegan Paul 1985).

of shifting desires, sentiment, whim or emotion. On most realist views, it is the relationship between a moral proposition and some fact of the matter that determines the truth and falsity of that proposition. Whilst the fact of the matter is not conclusively affected by agents' desires, sentiments or whims, it is sometimes taken to trigger or resonate with some of their sensibilities. Contemporary rationalist views hold that the truth and power of moral propositions derive from their dialectical necessity and that, too, is independent of desires, sentiments or whims. Alan Gewirth's statement in favour of his version of moral rationalism has virtues that moral realism also hopes to display, namely, it establishes a fundamental moral principle and other subsequent moral propositions that are '*categorical* and *determinate*'.[21] Gewirth's principle of generic consistency 'is categorical in that it sets forth requirements for action that are normatively necessary, so that they cannot be rightly evaded by any prospective agent regardless of his variable inclinations, ideals or beliefs[; and it is] determinate in that it does not set forth, or allow, mutually opposed requirements for action'.[22]

This desire for determinacy and independence can indeed be seen as a reaction to what some have pejoratively dubbed 'the panic' about emotivism and non-cognitivism. These doctrines seemingly do not take our moral thought seriously and characterise it as massively inchoate and variable, dependent upon our apparently very different wants, desires and sentiments.[23] The supposedly pernicious consequences of emotivism and non-cognitivism have often been highlighted and equally often exaggerated. Realism and rationalism are indeed an antidote to these problems but it should not be assumed that all versions of emotivism and non-cognitivism display them. So, for example, although David Hume's account of morality rests upon agents' sentiments, it does not follow that morality is indeed subject to massive variations within a population or is hugely relativistic. Hume maintained that our sentiments are very stable and similar and therefore serve as a fairly determinate basis for moral judgments.[24] If this is true, then clearly Hume's non-cognitivist account of morality has an advantage that realism and rationalism also have, namely, providing morality with a stable base. They give quite different accounts, though, of why it is stable. Nevertheless, Hume's account of morality illustrates the mistake of assuming that the advantages of rationalism and realism cannot be shared by non-

[21] 'Replies to My Critics', in E. Regis Jnr. (ed.), *Gewirth's Ethical Rationalism* (Chicago, University of Chicago Press 1984), p. 192 (original emphasis).

[22] *Ibid.*

[23] The nature of the 'panic' is well captured by J. Waldron, 'The Irrelevance of Moral Objectivity', ch. 7 of R. P. George (ed.), *Natural Law Theory: Contemporary Essays* (Oxford, Clarendon 1992), pp. 167–171.

[24] D. Hume, *A Treatise of Human Nature* (Second edition, P. H. Nidditch (ed.), Oxford, Clarendon 1978; originally published 1739) Bk. III, part I, sc. II, pp. 474–476.

cognitivism and emotivism. Some versions of these doctrines can display some of rationalism's and realism's advantages, so our argument can only be put in limited terms. That is, it holds that realism and rationalism have advantages not had by many versions of non-cognitivism and emotivism and that no version of either of the latter has all the advantages of rationalism or realism.

It should now be clear that the general advantages of realism and rationalism recommend them as solutions to the plurality problem and as props for Unger's moral arguments. Realism and rationalism hold out the prospect of determinate answers to moral questions which are to some degree independent of individual sentiments and interests. They also purport to demonstrate how moral truth can be arrived at. They are therefore crucial aids to one faced with the supposed sea of different accounts of the moral value of some particular action, practice or institution. Of course, this does not show that the moral realist or rationalist will be able to show the moral value of any particular action, institution or practice since there is no guarantee that it has such value. Rather, it simply illustrates the nature and contours of the argument the realist or rationalist will make if it can be made. This kind of argument promises to solve the plurality problem by allowing the theorist to discriminate between better and worse accounts of the moral value of an action, practice or institution.

The specific problem Unger faced was how to offer arguments about the contours of moral value that neither invoked classical philosophical essentialism nor fell victim to the is/ought distinction. His attempt to solve the problem failed because, although he escaped essentialism, he did not solve the is/ought problem. He simply ignored it. Now, commending realism and rationalism as a better means—because neither essentialist nor insensitive to the is/ought distinction—of constructing the arguments about the contours of value Unger wants to make, is not to claim that they are the only meta-ethical doctrines that are in these respects better. Since almost all meta-ethical doctrines since Hume have been cognisant of the is/ought pitfall, it would be spurious indeed to commend realism and rationalism for being aware of it. Equally redundant would be a recommendation based upon rationalism's and realism's anti-essentialism, since yet again almost every meta-ethical position since Hume is similar in this respect. Realism and rationalism are not recommended for these spurious reasons, but for the reasons already articulated. In addition, there is much in these doctrines compatible with Unger's project, whereas there is little in other anti-essentialist doctrines sensitive to the is/ought distinction that is so compatible. Consider emotivism and non-cognitivism again. The claims some versions of these doctrines make about the basis of moral values, their relationship to our sentiments and desires and the plurality of these, suggest that Unger had them in mind when characterising the liberal's supposed commitment to the subjectivity of values.[25] That is a position Unger has always criticised and eschewed. Since they are indeed far distant from any belief in the subjectivity of values, and since they take seriously the is/ought divide, realism and rationalism therefore seem a better vehicle for Unger's task than the one he adopted and better, too, than many other meta-ethical doctrines.

Although realism and rationalism play only a limited role in our argument it might be maintained that even this is too much, since both doctrines are more trouble than they are worth. Some might argue that the doctrines are either redundant or are so minimally helpful as to be better avoided given the problems they generate. This redundancy objection takes a general form, in which it purports to discredit both realism and rationalism. The other infirmities to which these doctrines succumb are specific to one or the other, never or rarely affecting both. We will begin with the problems of realism and then examine the problems of rationalism.

Realism and rationalism can be regarded as redundant on the ground that meta-ethical doctrines of this kind make no difference to moral deliberation and action. So, whether an agent is a moral realist, rationalist, emotivist or whatever, makes no difference to the moral judgments they make: all will agree that, for example, in ordinary circumstances lying is morally wrong. Hence if the outcomes of moral deliberation are indeed independent of agents' meta-ethical views and can correspond despite meta-ethical disagreement, it seems pointless to waste labour in defending any particular meta-ethical position and entirely unforgivable to plunge methodological and other arguments into this quagmire. This objection is too hasty. First, it clearly does not, nor is it likely that any argument could, show the impossibility of meta-ethical positions determining the outcomes of moral deliberation, even though that may indeed be unlikely. Second, it ignores one obvious way in which meta-ethical doctrines can make a difference to actual moral practice and deliberation, although they are not guaranteed to do so. Realism and rationalism can make a difference not in relation to the outcomes arrived at, but rather in respect of the temper or tone of the practice of moral deliberation. It might be perceived as more serious, as less like a matter of 'mere' preference, or sentiment or whim. Realism and rationalism hold out the prospect of right moral answers and treat moral argumentation as in no way qualitatively different from other forms. On these views, reason plays an important role in the determination of moral outcomes and that process of reasoning can be every bit as precise and thorough as in other, supposedly 'harder' forms of deliberation. These considerations suggest a view of moral deliberation quite different from that engendered by emotivism and non-cognitivism.

[25] See *Knowledge and Politics* (New York, The Free Press 1975), chs. 2 and 3.

Of the many critics of moral realism, Simon Blackburn is perhaps the most acute. For this reason, we will focus upon his work, keeping in mind that if moral realism withstands his critical scrutiny, then it cannot be a completely worthless doctrine. Blackburn has offered at least three powerful arguments against this position. The first raises the issues of supervenience and entailment. Within philosophical discussions of moral realism, these ideas concern the relationship between moral propositions and naturalistic (non-moral) propositions. Blackburn takes moral realists to be committed to asserting a relationship between these two types of propositions such that moral propositions are supervenient upon naturalistic propositions but do not entail naturalistic propositions. Blackburn's account of the former relation holds that '[a] property M is supervenient upon properties $N_1 \ldots N_n$ if M is not identical with any of $N_1 \ldots N_n$ nor with any truth function of them, and it is logically impossible that a thing should become M, or cease to be M, or become more or less M than before, without changing in respect of some member of $N_1 \ldots N_n$'.[26] What he means by entailment in this context is that '[t]here is no moral proposition whose truth is entailed by any proposition ascribing naturalistic properties to its subject'.[27] The problem that besets moral realists is that their commitment to both supervenience and absence of entailment also seems to commit them to the following peculiarity. The moral realist 'has to say that the truth of a moral proposition consists in the existence of a state of affairs, which it reports; that the existence of this state of affairs is not entailed by the existence of other, naturalistic facts; yet that the continuation of these facts entails that the moral state of affairs continue as it is'.[28] Blackburn correctly notes that this is not actually an inconsistent position but it is nevertheless odd. For, one who takes it holds that naturalistic facts do not logically guarantee the existence of the state of affairs which a moral proposition reports, yet the continuation of those naturalistic facts does indeed guarantee the continued existence of the moral state of affairs.

A response to this argument is the affirmation of an identity between naturalistic and moral propositions, thus circumventing supervenience and affirming entailment between the two. Blackburn is uncomfortable with this response, as is clear from his adverse comments about the group of philosophers—so-called 'Cornell realists'—most often associated with it. His second argument against realism is not one about the impossibility of such an identity, but rather a family of related arguments about the implausibility or unhelpfulness of the position which affirms that identity. This, of course, is not a strong argument. Whatever weight it has can easily be reduced by noting the weaknesses of the anti-realist or, in Blackburn's case, quasi-realist alternative. The most troublesome aspect of Blackburn's quasi-

[26] S. Blackburn, *Essays in Quasi-Realism* (New York, O. U. P. 1993), p. 115.
[27] *Ibid*., p. 116. [28] *Ibid*., p. 118.

realism is his explanation of the relationship between moral and naturalistic propositions. This relationship is best understood, says Blackburn, as a matter of 'propositional reflection', yet it is not entirely clear that this is an obvious improvement upon the realist explanation.

Finally, Blackburn is one of many to aim a specific version of the redundancy objection at moral realism. The overall thrust of the argument is that thinking as a moral realist has no advantages. In particular, Blackburn makes efforts to show that the objectivist appearance of ordinary moral thought and language is just as easily captured by quasi-realism as by realism. This may well be right, but it is dubious for either realists or anti-realists to seek to make capital from ordinary moral thought if it is not univocal. That is, if ordinary moral thought and language contains both realist ('objectivist') and anti-realist aspects, the demonstration that one argument or another coheres with one aspect or another of ordinary thought and language is unhelpful. Indeed, a hunch about the multi-vocal nature of ordinary moral thought's meta-ethics has informed the arguments of this book. This is not to say that the substance of ordinary moral thought must be relativistic, that (*ceteris paribus*) what is morally wrong for agent Y is morally right for agent X. Rather, there is a great deal of substantive moral agreement in the face of meta-ethical disagreement or uncertainty. So, although X and Y agree that action p is morally wrong, they may well disagree as to what makes that claim true. None of this counts as an objection to Blackburn's argument. Casting doubt upon the assumption that ordinary moral thought and language are univocal neither strengthens nor weakens realism or anti-realism.

There is another variant of the redundancy objection aimed specifically at moral realism. Jeremy Waldron provides a clear example in his argument that moral realism cannot give a good account of moral motivation and action. Because it cannot do this, Waldron apparently thinks realism unworthy of serious attention.[29] But this version of the objection is recanted almost before it is fully articulated, since Waldron notes that there are at least two realist responses to it. The objection asserts that a feature of moral propositions is their capacity to generate action, to give agents good reasons to act. And, since realists hold that it is the existence or non-existence of facts in the world that makes moral propositions true or false, they must explain how it is that those facts motivate agents to act. While expressing some doubt about the capacity of facts to generate action, and heedless of the fact that were he given 50 pence change from the £5 tendered to pay for his 45 pence newspaper, he would undoubtedly act, Waldron notes that realists can say two things here. First, that moral facts are indeed 'mute' in regard to action, that something other than the existence of these facts is

[29] *Supra*, note 23.

required for agents to act upon them. Or, that they are not mute, that these moral facts simply have action-generating properties. The first response puts realism in no worse a position than other meta-ethical doctrines, since all must be charged with the task of providing an account of moral motivation and action. Nor is the second faced with exceptional problems, since it seems that some facts do indeed motivate actions. Since neither response is obviously crazy, it is somewhat premature to reject realism for having no account of moral motivation.

Objections to moral rationalism are just as plentiful as gripes about moral realism; hence our analysis of the former will be just as selective and truncated as the analysis of the latter. In this case, though, there is no particularly powerful critic whose work we can engage with so as to make the task more manageable. Although we examine only one version of moral rationalism—that developed by Gewirth—it has attracted a huge critical literature as well as a stalwart and exhaustive defence.[30] Our defence of moral rationalism will therefore consist of a statement of the weaknesses of a few of the more common objections to it. By far the most common objection is that directed at Gewirth's claim to have derived an 'ought' from an 'is'. If he claims to do this and fails, then our position is richly ironic, since the reason for commending rationalism and realism to Unger was their sensitivity to a distinction Gewirth seemingly ignores. Does Gewirth derive an 'ought' from an 'is'? And, more importantly, can he?

The objection to Gewirth on this score is misguided and it is difficult to see how he could have encouraged it.[31] The objection becomes salient only if insufficient regard is paid to the logical form of the argument. It gets off the ground only if the argument's starting point is the apparently factual claim that there are (potential) purposive agents (hereinafter 'PPAs') in the world. From this, Gewirth moves via a number of stages to the claim that PPAs must value their freedom and well-being, to the claim that PPAs must insist upon claim-rights to freedom and well-being, to the principle of generic consistency (hereinafter the PGC). The latter holds that agents must act in accordance with the generic rights of other PPAs as well as themselves.[32] Since the PGC is claimed by Gewirth to be a fundamental principle of morality and embodies an obvious 'ought', and since it is supposedly derived from an 'is' statement about PPAs, the argument does indeed seem to fall victim to Hume's fork. However, there are two reasons why this is not so.

[30] Gewirth's first book-length statement of his position is *Reason and Morality*, *supra*, note 17. One collection of responses is Regis (ed.), *supra*, note 21. A stout defence of Gewirth's argument is found in D. Beyleveld, *The Dialectical Necessity of Morality* (Chicago, University of Chicago Press 1991).

[31] See *Reason and Morality*, *supra*, note 17, p. 149.

[32] See *ibid.*, ch. 3 for thorough analysis.

First, for the is/ought problem to bite the argument must be assertoric and many have indeed taken it so; so understood, it clearly cannot derive ought from is. Assertoric arguments make claims based upon the properties of things and cannot deduce ought from is for these are incompatible properties of claims and propositions. Yet Gewirth's argument is dialectically necessary rather than assertoric, as he often notes. That is, it works in the manner of what I (and anyone else) must believe and do if I am a PPA. If I view myself thus, then there are certain things I must value, must regard as good for me and which I must assert claim-rights over. It is from this starting point that Gewirth proceeds to derive the PGC. But the argument is constructed from within the viewpoint of a PPA and shows what one must logically do and hold if one is a PPA. Because it is in this way dialectically necessary, the derivation of is from ought is not a problem. The argument does not purport to be about the nature of reality or propositions, but about the way I must view my agency qua PPA. Furthermore, the argument does not purport to establish the truth of the PGC but only to show that PPAs must, if they regard themselves as PPAs, act in accordance with it. This much might be accepted by Gewirth's critics but the objection could be pressed further. They might concede that Gewirth's argument is not explicitly assertoric but maintain that at some point it must depend upon an assertoric argument and that, when it does so, it falls victim to Hume's fork. It is very difficult to see how this could be demonstrated without ignoring the dialectical nature of the argument.[33]

The second reason why the argument does not fall victim to Hume's fork is that in one light it simply derives an ought from an ought. Gewirth often recognises this, so that when claiming to have made the derivation he says he does so only in a limited sense.[34] The part of the argument that involves the derivation of a moral claim (I must respect the claim-rights of others to freedom and well-being) from a prudential claim (I must have freedom and well-being) has been contested, but certainly not on the ground that it purports to move from fact to value or is to ought.[35] Rather, it is a move from prudential ought to moral ought. Indeed, Gewirth is quite content to accept the criticism that the arguments about the nature of agency (which PPAs themselves must make) are insufficiently factual or too normative to permit a derivation of is from ought. 'Hence, if being an agent, or engaging in action, is not something that can be stated as a "genuine, unadulterated

[33] See Beyleveld, *supra*, note 30, pp. 124–126.

[34] *Reason and Morality*, *supra*, note 17, pp. 102 and 149.

[35] On the move from prudential reasons to moral reasons see M. Kramer and N. Simmonds, 'Reason Without Reasons: A Critique of Alan Gewirth's Moral Philosophy' (1996) 34 *Southern Journal of Philosophy* 301–315; Alan Gewirth, '"Ought" and Reasons for Action' (1997) 35 *Southern Journal of Philosophy* 171–177; and Kramer and Simmonds, 'No Better Reasons: A Reply to Alan Gewirth' (1998) 36 *Southern Journal of Philosophy* 131–139.

statement of fact", this does not affect my general thesis'.[36] This is true, and Gewirth is surely right to direct attention to the central steps in his argument. After all, the claim to have bridged the is/ought divide in such a limited way is an unimportant aspect of an argument that purports to offer a dialectically necessary proof of the PGC.

Another objection to this version of moral rationalism also turns out to be something of a red herring. By contrast with the previous objection, this one is vague, masking a number of points. It is most likely motivated by the feeling, which often occurs after reading Gewirth, that morality surely cannot be or is not really like that. Subsequently, this feeling is often presented as a powerful and interesting thought in critical evaluation. The point revolves around the nature and contours of morality and some critics maintain that the logical nature of Gewirth's derivation of the PGC, and his demonstration of its rational necessity, are somehow untrue of moral experience. It has been maintained that the search for a fundamental moral principle is either objectionable *tout court* or destructive of the pluralistic aspects of ordinary moral thought. Whatever the specific point, the overarching claim is that morality is just not like that; it is neither a logical nor necessary business. Clearly there is not just one argument here, but many, linked only by an appeal to the nature of morality and ordinary moral experience.[37] Since that appeal establishes incompatible things in different writers' hands, its limited utility is evident, although this does not reduce the popularity of the argument. Even though the Janus-faced nature of this argument makes it difficult to assess, two things can be said about Gewirth's project that reduce its supposedly counter-intuitive nature. First, it is not intended to explicate or accommodate ordinary moral thought and practice but rather to ask how such thought and practice could be rationally justified. True, the question of rational justification is rarely asked by those who are immersed in the practice, but that does not make the question redundant. Similarly, it is no greater mistake to ask this question of our moral thought and practice than of any other practice. It is just false that such a question is irrelevant in relation to other practices and false that there is no effort to find a fundamental justificatory principle underlying those other practices.[38] Second, although the PGC is a single, fundamental moral principle, it does not have the effect of 'flattening out' moral experience, of turning us all into monists rather than pluralists. The PGC easily supports a diversity of moral argument and positions, as should be obvious once

[36] A. Gewirth, 'Replies to My Critics' in Regis (ed.), *supra*, note 21, pp. 223–224. Gewirth is quoting from p. 119 of W. D. Hudson's essay in the same volume.

[37] The essays by M. Singer, R. Bambrough, and K Nielson in Regis, *supra*, note 21, are examples of the overarching point being made in a number of different ways.

[38] A point well put by Gewirth in his reply to Bambrough in Regis, *supra,* note 21, pp. 195–196.

attention is given to the task of ensuring that PPAs' freedom and well-being is protected. Indeed, some have argued that Gewirth's emphasis upon both freedom and well-being creates a standard pluralistic snag, namely, that of reconciling the two.

One final point must be addressed before rationalism and realism are left behind. Even if rationalism and realism are defensible, and hence tying an account of law and adjudication to these doctrines is not a crass mistake, a problem remains. Having noted that rationalism and realism do not entail one another, that they can quite possibly pull in different directions, the following question arises: surely it is a mistake to base an account of method and adjudication upon such incompatible meta-ethical theories? This is just another way of maintaining that a choice must be made between the two, that one's wagon must be hitched to one or the other and not both. This is undoubtedly correct. Our task, though, has been a different one, namely, that of inclining legal theorists towards either or both of these positions as opposed to emotivism and non-cognitivism, which seem so natural and obvious to them. If MacIntyre is right and our culture is indeed dominated—he sometimes comes close to saying contaminated—by emotivism and non-cognitivism, then this should be no surprise.[39] We should expect rationalism, realism and MacIntyre's own virtue ethics to receive a frosty response, to be thought obviously wrong, not to say bizarre. Thus, although our concern has been simply to put moral rationalism and realism on the agenda of legal philosophy, this must not detract from the fact that at some point a choice must be made between them. This is neither the place nor time to make and justify such a choice.

(c) No theory of legal rationality

The previous chapters may well be criticised by proponents of what Pierre Schlag calls the 'Thumper' school of jurisprudence.[40] He does not have in mind a group of jurists more enamoured than most of a particularly brutal and pugilistic approach to legal philosophy, but those who are temperamentally at the other end of the spectrum. That is, those who, like Walt Disney's amiable rabbit in *Bambi*, think that if one cannot speak well of someone or thing, then one should not speak at all. Both Schlag and Mark Kelman suggest—perhaps not without tongue in cheek—that this attitude motivates the negative reaction of many American jurists to heretical legal thought.[41] Heretics spend all their time trashing and have nothing at all positive to say. Offering no alternative, having no vision, is regarded as a

[39] In MacIntyre's eyes, emotivism is in the main responsible for the 'grave cultural loss' or the 'disappearance' of a particular conception of morality: *After Virtue, supra*, note 18, p. 21.
[40] P. Schlag, 'Normative and Nowhere to Go' (1990) 43 *Stanford L. R.* 167–191, p. 175.
[41] Schlag, *ibid.*, M. Kelman, 'Trashing' (1984) 36 *Stanford L. R.* 293–348, p. 297.

particularly grievous omission. We have shown that this is not an accurate characterisation of much heretical thought. For now, imagine the objection being put against the arguments of this book. If some heretical thought is indeed relentlessly negative and critical, attacking the orthodoxy without an alternative in mind, then this judgment is surely true of the arguments herein, but more so. Those arguments not only criticise the orthodoxy in the absence of an alternative, but do exactly the same in relation to the heresy. The sin is therefore surely compounded: Thumper will be doubly appalled. A calming notice is necessary.

It consists of two points. First, there is a programme of sorts herein, as already noted. One positive dimension of the book is its commendation and defence of compatibilism. Second, there are some indications how normative argument might fruitfully proceed—that, after all, is one reason underlying our support for moral realism and rationalism. Hence, niceness (in the form of constructive recommendations) coexists with critique. These points might not suffice, though, because the book purports to be about adjudication yet it recommends and defends, albeit partially, a position about method in the human sciences and one or two within moral philosophy. What about law and adjudication? It was stated at the outset that we were to explore normative and methodological issues as they arose within accounts of adjudication and not to construct an account of our own. The project was dubbed a second-order enquiry, an enquiry about how to conduct a particular kind of enquiry, namely, the development of a 'theory', 'model', 'account', 'explanation' or 'understanding' of adjudication. But surely, Thumper might maintain, you can say a little more about the first-order fulcrum of this project, about the ways in which judges do and should reason when deciding hard cases?

We are indeed committed to developing such an account and not simply in order to have something constructive to say. The commitment arises by virtue of some arguments used against orthodoxy and heresy. For example, in the discussion of the problems the orthodoxy has with the determinacy condition, it was argued that incommensurability entails a rationality deficit. If, in deciding hard cases, judges must choose between incommensurables, then their choices are not compelled by reasons even though informed by Reason. This becomes a problem if the orthodox wish to distinguish legal from ideological, visionary or political disputes on the basis of their higher rationality quotient. For it seems that choices between incommensurables in hard cases are no more rational than the choices made in these other, non-legal contexts. Assume that this version of the law/politics distinction is worthwhile, although it burdens us with the task of speaking up for law as a means of solving individual disputes and making social choices, of showing that it is better than alternative methods, such as empowered democracy or social mediation. Espousing it entails that decisions in hard cases must be compelled by reasons, which might be regarded as an impossibly high standard for adjudication to achieve. Recall also that some heretical attacks upon orthodox accounts of adjudication were criticised for lumbering the orthodoxy with a deductive, almost algorithmic conception of the rationality of adjudication. Note, for example, Joseph Singer's claim that the orthodoxy regard judicial decision-making as a process in which 'theories or arguments . . . necessarily lead to certain results'.[42] This suggests something akin to a deductive, logically inexorable process in which the decision is compelled by the reasons supporting it. In such instances, we would expect judges to be 'driven' to decide a case in a particular way, even though they have no sympathy with and perhaps even regret the result.[43] While such sentiments sometimes surface in easy cases, it would be odd to find them in hard cases since these are regarded as lacking certainty, as lacking an obvious right answer, as cases in which the decision is not compelled by reasons.

The difficulty is this. The problem posed for the orthodox (judicial decisions must have a higher rationality quotient than merely being informed by Reason) appears inconsistent with the argument used against Singer (it is a mistake to ascribe to the orthodox belief in an axiomatic, deductive conception of legal rationality). Surely the conception of legal rationality Singer ascribes to the orthodox is exactly the same as that which we say the orthodox *must* (although they do not) espouse in order to maintain the law/politics distinction? Let us call this conception of legal rationality 'deductivism'. It maintains that judicial decisions should be compelled by reasons and not merely informed by Reason. The latter view we will dub, for want of a better label, 'reasonableness'. It requires that judicial decisions be based on reasons, but neither that those reasons undergo any process of critical assessment nor that they be shown to be the most powerful for the decision in question. Whether it is inconsistent to affirm that the orthodox must regard legal decisions as compelled by reasons, and affirm that this does not commit them to Singer's version of deductivism, depends primarily upon the possibility of a *via media* between deductivism and reasonableness. If there is no such middle way the difficulty could only be avoided by changing the terms of the initial debate. In particular, this problem in the account of legal rationality could be dissolved either by denying the existence of incommensurability and affirming that there are right answers in hard cases, or by rejecting this version of the law/politics distinction. Each possibility will be examined in turn.

Heretical scholarship provides little succour for those in search of the

[42] J. Singer, 'The Player and the Cards: Nihilism and Legal Theory' (1984) 94 *Yale L. J.* 1–70, p. 10.

[43] See the remarks of Lewis J. in the Tabard case discussed by N. MacCormick, *Legal Reasoning and Legal Theory* (Oxford, Clarendon, revised ed. 1993), ch. II, pp. 20–21.

middle way. This literature is founded upon the assumption that if adjudication is not compelled by reasons, then it lacks determinacy (by which is meant justificatory determinacy and not predictability). Heretics often infer from this that adjudication must also lack legitimacy. Things are not much better when orthodox scholarship is examined. Many orthodox scholars think the most that can be said about the process of hard case decision-making is that it is informed by Reason but certainly not compelled by reasons. They do not see a path between deductivism and reasonableness. Alternatively, some orthodox scholars develop accounts of the distinctive nature of legal rationality that hint at such a *via media* but which ultimately prove to be implausible. Consider three examples. Recall that Neil MacCormick's account of hard-case adjudication emphasises the significance of consequentialist arguments and arguments from coherence and consistency. These are the kinds of considerations judges use to determine the contours of the applicable proposition of law in a hard case or to establish whether there is indeed such a proposition. Recall also that consequentialist arguments are, for MacCormick, the most significant and powerful and that the considerations embodied in such arguments are plural and incommensurable.[44] The latter not only makes deductivism impossible but also clearly blocks the middle path. For, if consequentialist arguments are truly the most important in second-order justification, and they are truly incommensurable, then *ex hypothesi* the choice between such arguments cannot be compelled by reasons. Rather, choices between incommensurables are only informed by Reason.

Cass Sunstein's account of adjudication looks more promising for, with the claim that '[a]nalogical reasoning is the key to legal casuistry', he might be taken to have carved out a path between deductivism and reasonableness.[45] In so far as analogical reasoning is distinctive of legal reasoning, and if legal decisions produced by such reasoning have a higher rationality quotient than those simply informed by Reason, then Sunstein generates a distinction between legal argument, on the one hand, and ideological, visionary and political arguments, on the other. This distinction is further buttressed by the idea of incompletely theorised agreements. These, according to Sunstein, play a pervasive role in law and take a number of forms. They exist when there is 'agreement on a general principle alongside disagreement about particular cases'; that is, 'people who accept the principle need not agree on what it entails in particular cases'.[46] In addition, incompletely theorised agreements arise when 'people agree on a mid-level principle but disagree about both general theory and particular cases' and where there is agreement 'on particular outcomes, accompanied by agreement[.] on the

[44] *Ibid.*, chs. V and VI.

[45] *Legal Reasoning and Political Conflict* (New York, O. U. P. 1996), p. 32.

[46] *Ibid.*, p. 35.

narrow or low-level principles that account for them'.[47] However, the hope that Sunstein provides a plausible *via media* is dashed by the appearance of two problems.

The first is old and obvious and affects any account of analogical reasoning in law. Such a process of reasoning only works by way of assessing similarities and differences between the fact situations and the legal questions in particular cases. The kind of argument produced looks like this: because case 2 has features P, Q, Y and Z and raises legal question *, it should be decided in the same way as case 1, which has features S, P, Q, and R and raises legal questions * and **. Clearly, a lot of questions about factual and other similarities and differences—plaintiff in case 1 was not bald whereas plaintiff in case 2 was—have already been ruled out in this formulation, but certainly not by analogical reasoning. Holding that analogical reasoning is the fulcrum of legal reasoning therefore seems strikingly reductionist, since in order for that process to begin judges do and must employ arguments and a body of assumptions that make some pathways of analogy possible and plausible and others impossible and implausible. Hence, '[t]here is no way to compare the relative cogency of . . . two competing analogical options without resort to some values or principles that are extraneous to the process of analogical reasoning itself'.[48] Surely such values and principles are equally if not more important than analogical reasoning in law since they make that process work. And, when we examine how these values and principles are justified—by means of arguments from coherence, consequences and consistency, or by reference to arguments from the institutional morality of law—they are not obviously qualitatively different from visionary, ideological or political disputes.

To succeed Sunstein's *via media* must show not only that analogical reasoning is unique to law (which is, of course, highly unlikely), but also that it is a process in which outcomes are more than merely informed by Reason (although they need not be compelled by reasons). Since analogical arguments must be animated by arguments about the principles and values that inform some area of law, and since these arguments seem at most to be informed by Reason, this path looks unpromising. But this might be too hasty. For the second feature of Sunstein's account—incompletely theorised agreements—may solve this problem. This idea promises not only to bring an end to the seemingly endless analogy-mongering which competent lawyers can engage in, by preventing argument about the underpinning values and principles of some area of law breaking out into widespread nor-

[47] *Legal Reasoning and Political Conflict*, pp. 36 and 37 respectively.

[48] A. Hutchinson, 'The Reasoning Game: Some Pragmatic Suggestions' (1998) 61 *Modern L. R.* 263–280, p. 267. Lest this be regarded as a singularly heretical thought about analogy, see N. MacCormick, *supra*, note 43, ch. VII, pp. 185–194.

mative disputation.[49] It might also ensure that argument about such underpinning principles and values is more than merely informed by Reason. This is where we meet the second problem that ensnares Sunstein's theory of legal rationality: the idea of incompletely theorised agreements does not show that choices in hard cases are more than merely informed by Reason. Indeed, as Sunstein occasionally characterises them, it is doubtful that incompletely theorised agreements are even informed by Reason.

Maintaining that decisions in hard cases are compelled by reasons runs counter to the tenor of the idea of incompletely theorised agreements. If an incompletely theorised agreement is the basis of a decision, then it is possible that the judges converged on an outcome without having any reasons in common for it and without, on Sunstein's view, ever having tried to show that the reasons they had were the most powerful. The reason why the latter task must be eschewed, even though it is actually quite common in the cases, is that it risks generating disagreement about general principles, since appeal to such principles is the most obvious way for judges to show that the reasons for their decisions are compelling. So, the most Sunstein could say of decisions reached on the basis of incompletely theorised agreements is that they are informed by Reason. Hence, when he says that a 'modest judge joins an opinion that is incompletely theorised, he has to rely on a reason or principle, *justifying* one outcome rather than another',[50] he must be invoking the idea of justification in the weak sense. That is, the reason justifies the outcome only in the sense that it is forwarded as a reason for the outcome, but not as the only, or the best, or the most compelling reason. The judge therefore has reasons for his decision but they are not, or cannot be shown to be, compelling without the existence of incompletely theorised agreements being threatened. Yet we cannot even be sure that the decision reached must be informed by Reason, in the sense of tracking genuine but not compelling reasons, since Sunstein accepts that 'the incompletely theorised agreement may be nothing to celebrate. It may be wrong or unreliable. The fact that people converge may be a kind of coincidence or an accident'.[51] If the incompletely theorised agreement underpinning a decision in a hard case is wrong, and thus the decision itself is wrong, that presumably means that the reasons for it are specious. If that is so, it cannot be informed by Reason, even though it appears to be by those who made it. For many legal philosophers such decisions would be treated as exceptional, in the sense that their lack of rational power would *prima facie* affect their legitimacy and special steps would be taken to show why, if at all, they should be followed. Oddly, Sunstein seems to regard such decisions as entirely unexceptional, requiring no special attention.

[49] They operate as the foundation of analogies: *supra*, note 45, pp. 6 and 90–100.
[50] *Supra*, note 45, p. 51(emphasis supplied). [51] *Ibid.*

The second argument that might succeed in providing a middle way between deductivism and reasonableness is not really an argument. It is an idea, often thought suggestive by legal philosophers and equally often beguilingly unhelpful. The idea is that of 'weight'. It hints at a legal rationality in which decisions are more than informed by Reason, for the idea of 'weighing' seems by definition to involve sorting and assessment, to entail the critical evaluation of the reasons for and against decision or action. This idea is beguiling, though, because it often leads jurists to lapse into metaphor, to speak in a mysterious way. One instance was encountered in chapter 4 when Steven Burton's discussion of adjudication was examined. Burton undoubtedly thinks that the idea of weight and the notion of weighing reasons provide insight into adjudication and he may be right. Yet the general problem faced by any theory of legal rationality reliant upon this notion is that of generating a plausible account of the weighing process. Burton does not succeed in providing one because, although he speaks of judges 'weighing' and 'gauging' reasons, he identifies no single scale by which they do this. Were there many such scales in play then the job of identifying them would be important, since knowledge of the available scales would help in assessing and predicting the outcomes of cases. Again, Burton provides no such outline of possible scales.

If metaphorical talk is avoided and the notion of weighing reasons is to be helpful in this context, then assigning determinate weight is the key to understanding the process. This implies that the process of weighing be understood in mathematical terms as either summing the weight of all pre-established reasons on each side of a dispute or as establishing a rank ordering of reasons for and against. Burton dismisses both possibilities, the former on the ground that it is fanciful to imagine that the weight of reasons is accessible to judges prior to deciding a case, and the latter because there is no means of combining reason rankings.[52] These are hardly insuperable problems. Envisaging judges summing the weight of reasons in cases, their weight being known in advance, is certainly fanciful if one is already enamoured by Burton's account of the weighing process. Yet this alternative differs only slightly from Burton's own account. Proponents of the alternative must certainly agree with Burton that reasons for decision 'must be identified before any are assigned a weight'.[53] While accepting this, Burton rejects the next and seemingly small step the alternative account insists upon, namely, that in addition to being identified prior to decision, the weight of these reasons is also established in advance. For Burton, the weight of such reasons is only established by reference to the congeries of reasons in the particular case. The most likely grounds on which to suggest

[52] S. Burton, *Judging in Good Faith* (Cambridge, C. U. P. 1992), p. 59.
[53] *Ibid.*, p. 55.

that this alternative account is independently implausible—implausible for reasons other than a commitment to Burton's account—would highlight the fact that participants in the practice do not describe adjudication in this way. It is unlikely, though, that the language of weight and weighing is completely absent from the practice and much more likely that it is but incompletely formulated. That is to say, judges most likely do speak of weighing reasons but do not explicate exactly what is involved. Whether weighing is a matter of summing weight or the legal equivalent of constructing a Calder mobile is unlikely to be determined by the language of participants.[54] Recourse to the language of participants is also unlikely to show the absence of a method for systematically combining rankings in a systematic way and, since many ways of accomplishing this task have been developed in theories of rational choice, it is premature to dismiss the possibility altogether.

We, too, are in danger of being beguiled by the language of weighing. In the present context it is especially appealing since it promises to show that judicial decisions are more than merely informed by Reason. To thoroughly unpack the two versions of weighing noted here would demand the articulation of a general theory of legal practical reason and that will not be attempted. Rather, note only that this idea is suggestive yet in some forms also richly problematic. That might be enough for some to abandon it altogether. In the present context that means abandoning the search for a path between deductivism and reasonableness. Abandoning the search for a *via media* does not preclude the possibility of affirming either deductivism or reasonableness, although only the former supports the version of the law/politics distinction deployed here. Let us therefore examine two ways in which deductivism, and hence the law/politics distinction, could be supported. The first stems from Ronald Dworkin's denial that incommensurability plays a role in adjudication, which makes deductivism possible, and his argument that there are right answers in hard cases, which suggests that there is a stringent legal rationality in which decisions are more than merely informed by Reason.[55] His denial of incommensurability is difficult to assess, and for the same reason why affirmations of incommensurability are difficult to assess. Both claims are almost exclusively informed by appeals to moral experience. Since it is unlikely that moral experience is univocal on this matter, both claims have some support. The problem, though, is determining how to proceed from here. Neither those who affirm nor those who deny incommensurability provide much guidance. Even if Dworkin's

[54] *Ibid*., p. 58.

[55] The Dworkinian view of incommensurability is stated in P. Amselek and N. MacCormick (eds.), *Controversies About Law's Ontology* (Edinburgh, E. U. P. 1991), pp. 88–90. On right answers and objectivity see R. Dworkin, *A Matter of Principle* (New York, O. U. P. 1986), chs 5–7; *Law's Empire* (London, Fontana 1986), pp. 78–86 and ch. 7; and 'Objectivity and Truth: You'd Better Believe It' (1996) 25 *Philosophy and Public Affairs* 87–139.

denial is correct, and it is true that incommensurability plays no role in adjudication, it is uncertain that he provides much of a prop for deductivism. The fact that Dworkin's 'right-answer' talk conjures up the image of a legal rationality in which we can say for sure that answer X in case Y is correct and, by extension, compelled by reasons, may serve to mislead. This is because what Dworkin has in mind by the claim that there are right answers to interpretive and moral questions, both of which constitute the fulcrum of his account of adjudication, is simply that we think there are right answers. That is, saying 'that one interpretation of some text or social practice can be on balance better than others, that there can be a "right answer" to the question of which is best even when it is controversial what the right answer is', is just a matter of emphasis.[56] The language of right answers and of objectivity is but a means of distinguishing, for example, those propositions applicable to all (slavery is wrong) from those unique to a particular perspective or relative to taste (rum raisin ice cream is the best).

Dworkin provides no account of what makes right answers right, other than the account of law as integrity. The right answer in a hard case is that which fits both the brute facts of legal history and portrays the law in the best possible moral and political light. How this might be transformed into deductivism is oblique, for two reasons. The first begins with Dworkin's observation that '[n]o electronic magician could design from my arguments a computer program that would supply a verdict everyone would accept once the facts of the case and the text of all past statutes and judicial decisions were put at the computer's disposal'.[57] Knowing nothing about the strategies of computer programme design makes it unwise and hazardous to comment. Nevertheless, a prerequisite for such a programme might be the conversion of arguments into their logical form, most likely that of the open hypothetical, and that is surely also the starting point of deductivism.[58] If Dworkin is not persuaded that his account of legal rationality can be so converted, then it is unlikely to be a version of deductivism, despite the language of right answers.

Secondly, if arguments portraying some area of law in the best moral and political light must invoke other interpretive, higher order moral concepts such as justice, either arbitrariness or an infinite regress beckons.[59] A regress threatens because interpretive disputes about such higher order concepts are not constrained by appeal to the brute facts of some practice or other and it is therefore difficult to see how they could be resolved. If these interpretive disputes are exactly the same as those that rage around proposi-

[56] *Law's Empire*, *supra*, note 55, p. 80. [57] *Ibid.*, p. 412.

[58] On the task of conversion see N. MacCormick, *supra*, note 43, ch. II.

[59] The argument here belongs to N. Simmonds, 'Imperial Visions and Mundane Practices' (1987) 46 *Cambridge L. J.* 465–488, pp. 469–480.

tions of law, but without the requirement of fit, the question we are left with is: which interpretation of these higher order moral concepts portrays them in their best moral and political light? If we answer: that which invokes other interpretive moral concepts, then we are ensnared. By contrast, if the answer is: decide which interpretation of these higher order moral concepts is best by reference to notions of 'human nature or the theory of the self',[60] being neither moral-cum-political concepts nor interpretive concepts, then arbitrariness lurks. For, an argument is required but never provided, showing that these concepts are not moral-cum-political, when they have often been regarded as such, or demonstrating why they should lie beyond the bounds of Dworkin's general theory of interpretation. This is a theory, remember, that promises to be of general application, to subsume and elucidate the nature of interpretation in all fields in which it is found. It therefore seems odd to place disputes about human nature and the self beyond the interpretive pale.

For these reasons, law as integrity is an unlikely prop for deductivism. Our flirtation with moral realism and rationalism suggests another avenue for deductivism, although it too proves to be something of a dead end. Deductivism seems to work best in easy cases, one hallmark of which is absence of doubt about the applicable propositions of law. In hard cases there is doubt that can be remedied, it is sometimes suggested, by normative argument. Arguments of principle from the surrounding institutional morality and policy or consequentialist arguments are, of course, familiar examples. Now, if such arguments can draw upon a determinate moral rationality, then deductivism might be possible, since morality might fill the gaps or resolve the ambiguity in the relevant law. While the law may be in doubt, moral realism and rationalism would have us believe that the injunctions of morality are not.[61] These injunctions may inform hard case adjudication, making it an almost completely determinate process. Since we have already invoked realism and rationalism in other contexts, it might seem both perverse and inconsistent not to put the doctrines to work within an account of adjudication. Is it?

The question should be answered in the negative, albeit a qualified negative. The reason is the existence of doubt about the possibility of any substantive account of morality always being able to settle each and every hard legal question. In our hands rationalism and realism have been silent about the substance of morality, having been invoked simply as accounts of what it is that gives moral propositions their rational power or what makes them true or false. The basis of the doubt has nothing to do with these

[60] *Law's Empire*, *supra*, note 55, p. 425.

[61] M. Moore has propounded this type of view. See *inter alia* his 'Law as a Functional Kind', ch. 8 of R. George (ed.), *supra*, note 23, pp. 229–232 and 'Moral Reality' (1982) *Wisconsin Law Review* 1061–1156.

claims, though. For even if we imagine that realism and rationalism generate detailed, substantial accounts of what morality requires, it is still possible that morality so conceived does not generate an answer to a particular hard case. Analogously, it can be maintained that however thorough and meta-ethically respectable Unger's normative vision might be, however detailed his assessment of what the democratic compromises underlying the law entail, or what the social ideal and conception of the self demand, it is still not guaranteed to solve every hard case. The point is not just that we have no reason to expect any substantive moral theory to be more complete than any legal system, but also that hard legal choices might be underdetermined by moral theories. (This is quite different from the claim that legal choices can be over-determined by moral theory as when choice Y is a consequence of theories 1, 2 and 3.) It is easy to see how particular moral theories mandate results in hard cases dealing with, for example, the legality of marital rape (likely that this will be an instance of over-determination). Yet it is not at all clear that any moral theory gives unequivocal guidance as to when past consideration should be good consideration, or when the actions of third parties are so unforeseeable as to relieve a defendant of liability in tort or the criminal law. This is not to say such questions lack a moral dimension, since they are clearly other-regarding and concern matters of harm, responsibility and attribution. These questions fall within the domain of the moral as well as the legal. The point simply expresses doubt as to the existence of unambiguous, determinate moral guidance on such issues.

This view seemingly runs contrary to that burgeoning body of contemporary jurisprudential scholarship which seeks to explicate the moral foundations of many legal doctrines. Armed with the classics of ancient and modern moral philosophy, and some hybrids, these scholars show that some area of law embodies the principle of utility, the Kantian categorical imperative or Rawlsian principles of justice. The shadow of this doubt need not fall over this work unless it is carried out in the belief that moral philosophy can deal with all hard legal questions. And, of course, that is rarely entertained. This is true of some of the most thorough work of this genre, which employs Gewirth's moral rationalism not simply to justify the institution of (Anglo-American) contract law, but also to determine specific doctrinal choices within it. Roger Brownsword has argued that Gewirth's principle of generic consistency (the PGC) requires a good faith regime in English contract law, underpins the relaxation of the doctrine of privity and supports many aspects of product liability law.[62] In doing so, he has never

[62] '"Good Faith in Contracts" Revisited' (1996) 49 *Current Legal Problems* 111–157; D. Beyleveld and R. Brownsword, 'Impossibility, Irrationality, and Strict Product Liability' (1991) 20 *Anglo-American L. R.* 257–284; and, again with D. Beyleveld, 'Privity, Transitivity and Rationality' (1991) 54 *Modern L. R.* 48–71.

claimed that each and every hard case—contractual or otherwise—could be resolved by deploying the PGC. Such a claim would indeed be a hostage to fortune and the doubt expressed here shows why it should not be made. But this coolness about moral rationalism's ability to resolve all hard (legal) cases might be thought especially strange in light of the efforts made in the book to place this doctrine, along with moral realism, on the jurisprudential agenda. The coolness does not generate inconsistency, though, since endorsing the value of these doctrines in some contexts—they might solve the plurality problem and allow us to make moral arguments while taking the gap between is and ought seriously—does not entail regarding them as valuable in all contexts, nor is it plausible to regard such different contexts as relevantly similar. Furthermore, neither the doubt nor the coolness it implies provide an insuperable obstacle to realism and rationalism; doubts can be dissipated just as furrows can be removed from brows.

It is time to take stock. The question under discussion is: can one consistently contend that the orthodox must regard hard case decisions as more than simply informed by Reason, while also claiming that they are not Singerian deductivists? A perfectly valid affirmative answer insists upon a *via media* between deductivism and reasonableness, although few orthodox scholars and even fewer heretics explore this possibility. Moreover, the discussion showed how elusive a plausible version of this answer is; the work which we thought might provide a good answer did not, and the remaining possibility was disturbingly vague. This part of our search has not therefore borne much fruit, although there are a few seedlings which, with a good deal of work and cultivation, may generate a good crop. Two versions of a negative answer to this question were therefore examined, similar in that both canvassed the possibility that some of the orthodox might be deductivists. This would show that Singer was right after all, except for the fact that many of the orthodox have never described themselves as deductivists. An argument that they *should* so regard themselves is easily derived from the version of the law/politics distinction in play here. The conclusion reached was again disappointing, since it was thought unlikely that either of these negative answers would work.

A final possibility presents itself. Perhaps we have mistaken the source of the problem. It may not reside in the rationality (or lack of it) of adjudication, but in the law/politics distinction. It is that distinction which, after all, forced the search for an account of legal rationality such that judicial decisions are more than merely informed by Reason. It might therefore seem appropriate to take a different tack altogether and reject this version of the law/politics distinction. Few if any orthodox scholars have done this, although few if any explicitly address the distinction save in the most vague terms, highlighting specifically 'legal' features of one domain not had by the other, but which do not serve to generate an interesting and important distinction. In this context, one hears talk about the greater use of precedent in one domain as opposed to another, or the different conceptions of appropriate argument in the different forums, and so on. But none of these observations seem capable of generating a powerful case for law as a means of resolving disputes as opposed to, for example, democratic forums or methods of conciliation. Yet why attempt to make such a case? If the law/politics distinction as formulated here is rejected, there is no need to continue with this quest. Within contemporary jurisprudence the most elegant and challenging version of this argument belongs to Unger. An interesting question, which will only be raised here, is: how much of this argument can the orthodox accept?

Unger locates adjudication firmly within the realm of democratic participation. His account of adjudication therefore contrasts vividly with orthodox accounts. These accounts are antidemocratic if and when they regard judges as privileged interpreters and developers of the democratic scheme embodied in statute law. On this view, law is but the incompletely formulated outcome of the bargains and compromises reached in the political process which judges are left to develop by means of reasoned elaboration, arguments of principle and policy or some such regime. The judges' position is privileged because they work insulated from the democratic fray and methods of accountability therein. But the arrogation of this power by judges, or the explicit granting of it as a gift from the political community, is objectionable for Unger. For him, 'the devolution of law-completing and law-reconstructive responsibility to an insulated band of experts makes no sense. Such an expertise properly belongs to the citizens'.[63] The standard arguments in favour of insulating adjudication from politics (the latter being, as he constantly reminds us, the primary source of most of our law) are dismissed by Unger as clogs upon the democratic project. His view is that judges should apply the law in light of the interests registered through the democratic process and embodied in the law in question. Judges should 'recognise the contestable and factional quality of the interests, concerns and assumptions to which [they] . . . appeal . . . [Such interests] . . . count not because they are the best and wisest but because they won, and were settled, earlier down the road of lawmaking'.[64] This style of adjudication manifests 'a more general commitment to respect the capacities of parties and movements to win in politics, and to encode and enshrine their victories in law'.[65] Where the law in question is judge-made, judges are to behave as if it were the product of politics:

[63] *What Should Legal Analysis Become?* (London, Verso 1996), p. 109. Unger notes, in one of his more pungent sentences, that 'only a democracy in the grip of an antidemocratic superstition will entrust to a cadre of juristic mystagogues the task of elaborating these agreements': *ibid.*, p. 110.

[64] *Ibid.*, p. 114.

[65] *Ibid.*

a common law after democracy and within democracy must mean something different, and develop in a different way, from a common law outside and before democracy. To be tolerable within democracy a common law cannot represent the cumulative discovery and refinement of a natural and stable world of custom by a group of legal wise men. Nor can it be the basic system of private law categories defining the necessary legal forms of free economies and societies. It exists on sufferance as a body of historical compromises that the people choose occasionally to revise . . . We strengthen its continuing vitality and authority by bringing to its case-by-case development the assumptions and analogies in the political making, and the judicial construction, of statutory law.[66]

It seems obvious from this that if any single value guides adjudication at all, it is the value of democracy. In so far as this translates into the belief that whatever values or results emanate from the democratic process are in themselves valuable, then, as was noted in the previous chapter, Unger faces the paradox of democracy. Whether or not he can avoid the problem is not our concern. Rather, our interest lies with the explicit and challenging renunciation of the law/politics divide. Certainly, this account of adjudication and legal rationality is one in which an argument that adjudication is more or less rational than other forms of decision making is inappropriate. Although nothing like the law/politics distinction as we have understood it exists in Unger's work, there is a distinction of sorts, but it is unlikely to commit him to any view as to the greater rationality or legitimacy of adjudication. The distinction arises from the fact that Unger sees the judiciary performing slightly different tasks from those of the legislature, but these are merely different points on a spectrum. Adjudication and legislation are both part of the democratic project but the former, for Unger, can sometimes do work that the latter cannot. In particular, the institution of adjudication might be better than most at dissolving some impediments to popular self-government and at closing gaps that might arise between custom and equity. In general terms, though, Unger has neither room for, nor need of a law/politics distinction.

The orthodox are likely to be ambivalent about this bold strategy. It may seem distasteful because it makes law far less significant than the orthodox are wont to believe, and to take away law's role as protector, as a force against the tyranny of the majority. (The orthodox must not forget, though, that the Ungerian world is one in which there is room for individual rights.) Yet the appeal of this argument is obvious, since it conclusively rejects the exceptionally problematic quest for a special or unique legal rationality, thus giving up the idea that law is a particularly special or important means of resolving disputes. The conclusion of this section therefore echoes the overall deflationary argument of the book. The orthodox must either develop an account of legal rationality showing that decisions are more than

[66] *Ibid.*, p. 115.

merely informed by Reason, or they should do as heretics have always done, and give up on the law/politics distinction. This can be restated so as to avoid privileging the orthodoxy. Heretics have shown time and again what many orthodox scholars must now accept, namely, that law is no more rational nor legitimate a process for resolving individual disputes and social conflicts than many other actual or imaginable methods. Since the argument of the book is that orthodoxy and heresy are nowhere near as different as they are often assumed to be, this is music to my ears. Whether the supposed disputants will find the tune so appealing remains to be seen.

Index

'advocacy scholarship' 305, 306
agency/agents 249, 252, 255, 262
  autonomous 254
  created by structures 265
  rules that 'govern' or 'determine' 265
  task of generating an account of 317
  understanding and interpreting 357
agnosticism 277, 284–93
  methodological 251, 288, 289, 292
  theoretical 251
agreements:
  incompletely theorised 375, 377
  moral, substantive 368
Akron case 323
Alexy, Robert 6
Althusser, Louis 234, 235, 236, 238
Altman, Andrew 204–5, 212, 213, 214–15
altruism 12, 161, 202, 203, 204, 205, 258
  expanded 308
  individualism and 303, 304, 310
anthropology 251, 252–3, 260, 266
Apel, Karl-Otto 119
aporia 318, 319
arbitrariness 11, 75, 207, 306, 310, 330, 380, 381
  choice 158–9, 305
  representation 286
Archer, Margaret 357–8, 359, 360, 362
arguments 11, 31–2, 37, 82, 132, 250
  consequentialist 5, 6, 50, 109, 149, 150, 375
  foundational 336
  ideological 190–1, 375
  metaphysical 194, 202, 205, 208
  methodological 29, 35, 279, 366
  moral 86, 309, 365, 366, 371, 383
  normative 194, 278, 279, 340, 341, 373
  ontological 127, 128, 194, 357
association 278, 328, 329, 330
Austin, J. L. 66–7, 82
authority 141, 151, 167, 169, 224, 385
  justification of 166, 168, 178
  persuasive 182, 329
  Raz's account 178
  see also legitimacy
autonomy 10, 219–20, 331
  relative 238

Balkin, Jack 113–14, 190, 304, 315, 318, 320, 327
behaviour 17, 19, 56, 58, 69, 70
  external accounts of 57
  meaning and 21
  publicly available 25
  rule-governed 62, 231
  social 99, 170, 245
behaviourism 96
  epistemological 290, 291
beliefs 14, 36, 58, 61, 69, 71, 88, 129, 245, 285
  coherence of 286
  consequences of 135, 225, 239
  corrigibility of some 240
  ideological 223, 224, 225, 226, 227, 228
  obfuscatory 223, 225, 239, 247
  see also values
Bell, John 49, 52
Bentham, Jeremy 150
Blackburn, Simon 367–8
Borges, Jorge Luis 208
Bourdieu, Pierre 256
Bowers v. Hardwick 324
Brownsword, Roger 382
bureaucracy 218, 223, 258, 316
Burton, Steven 2, 154–62 *passim*, 164, 378–9

Caldwell case (1981) 97–100, 102
causal laws 95–6, 114, 280, 281
  general 282
  impossibility or improbability of 357
  quest to explain all aspects of social life by reference to 277
  Unger's problems 283
causality 20, 32, 35, 36, 56, 95, 126, 130
  analysis of 68, 110
  meaning and 96, 108
  plausible accounts of 241
certainty 3, 46
choices 4, 5, 6, 46, 108, 148, 154
  adjudication without 197
  arbitrary 158–9, 305
  compelled by reason 140, 153, 155, 177
  custom narrows 198
  determinate method of making and justifying 307
  doctrinal 204, 205, 257, 382
  easy case 140, 192
  hard case 140, 154, 160, 192, 196, 382
  illegitimate 142
  indeterminacy of 142
  interpretative 13, 315–16
  justifiable 2, 3, 10, 138, 142, 143
  justification of 290–1
  legitimate 182, 202, 307
  linguistic 315–16

choices (*Cont.*):
  moral 310
  rational 223, 307, 379
  rationally defensible 202
  value 153, 299, 302, 304, 305, 310, 312, 313, 319
citizenship 161, 329
class 245
  consciousness 105
  conflict 235
  interests 235, 237, 239
'clingfilm' problem 53, 54, 55
closure 274, 275, 296
Cohen, Gerry 244, 245, 247
coherence 3, 5, 16, 46, 95, 111, 131
  arguments from 196, 375, 376
  attempt to distinguish 193
  commitment to 190, 192
  indeterminacy and 216
  possibility of 132
collective action 102, 171
Collingwood, R. G. 38–9, 113
commensurability 87
common law 2, 101, 131, 132, 136–7, 343
  after democracy 385
compatibilism 38, 96–7, 117, 118–34, 251, 265, 267–84
  additional difficulties 356–62
  commendation and defence of 373
  Dworkin's 105, 107, 108, 110, 112, 115, 117
  inchoate 113
  MacCormick's 104, 107, 108, 112, 117
  Raz's 105, 106, 107, 108, 112
  structuralism and 266–7
  see also incompatibilism; methodological compatibilism
compromises 237, 384
  ad hoc 344, 345
  democratic 347, 382
  factional 347
  historical 385
conflict 96, 145, 150, 190, 231, 237, 302, 322
  meta-level 303
  micro-level 203
  role 262, 263
  see also value conflict
consciousness 214
  discursive 261
  false 13, 190, 209, 230, 235, 261
  'genetic account' of the production of 254
  practical 261
consequences 27, 63, 109–10, 131, 150, 206, 252, 277, 290
  arguments of/from 196, 376
consequentialism 3, 5, 6, 46, 62, 149, 150, 243
consistency 3, 4, 5, 46, 95, 131, 136, 144, 328
  arguments of/from 196, 375, 376
context 66, 93, 96, 98, 103, 122, 151, 177, 181, 208, 357, 367, 391
  institutional and imaginative 280
  nature of action and 123
contingency 256, 335, 336, 337, 349
  foundational level problems 348
  heightened 338
  strong sense of 338, 348
  weak sense of 338, 339, 348
contradiction 16, 19, 107, 159, 212, 233, 238, 360
  doctrinal 258
  indeterminacy and 201–6
coordination 165, 169, 170, 171, 172, 174
Cornell, Drucilla 7, 315, 318, 319, 320–6, 367
correspondence theory 241, 268, 289, 290, 291–2
corrigibility 126, 227, 240, 330
Cotterrell, Roger 107–8
Critchley, Simon 322, 323, 325
critical accounts of ideology 225–6, 227, 230, 232–6 *passim*, 239, 245
  criticism of 242
'critical legal feminism' 137
Critical Legal Studies Movement 258, 327
'critical race theory' 137
culture 9, 84, 88, 109, 198
  agent as a product of 254
  determination or mediation through 261

Dalton, Clare 7
Davidson, Donald 68, 120, 129, 213–14
decisions 2, 3, 4, 14, 40, 97, 105, 187–8, 328
  hard case 36, 95, 149, 157, 231, 236, 307, 374, 375, 377
  ideological 263, 269, 272–3, 274, 290
  indeterminate 163, 171–6, 177, 180, 181, 198, 236, 290
  justification for/justifiability of 7, 131, 141, 198
  legitimate 136, 141, 170, 171, 181, 236, 296
  more than merely informed by reason 379, 383, 385–6
  rationality deficit 154, 194
  reasons for 99, 101–2, 111, 155–6, 160, 168, 193
deconstruction 7, 9, 137, 243, 300
  claims of 242
  ethics of 10, 300, 301, 314–27
  heretical proponents of 301
deduction 274
  see also D-N method
deductivism 374, 375, 378, 379, 383

deliberation 335
moral 366
practical 263
democracy 327, 342–8
commitment to 328, 349
common law after 385
empowered 309, 313, 347, 373
value of 385
democratic experimentalism 342
denial 128, 262, 264, 296
Derrida, Jacques 7, 242, 272, 284, 314, 315, 319, 320
description 60, 61, 68, 86, 87, 232, 292, 357–8
descriptive accuracy 49, 50, 51–2
descriptive theory 75, 78, 79, 82, 83, 88
desires 149, 362, 365–6
ethical 318
determinacy 143, 195–200 *passim*, 210, 275
denial of 205
desire for 364
justifactory 375
law lacks 15
determinacy condition 136, 137, 182
characterisation of 142
denying 140
fulfilment of 141
value pluralism and 145–63
determination 254, 261
determinism 96n., 129
deviationist doctrine 329, 330, 331, 332, 337, 338
Diplock, W. J. K., Lord 100, 101
directives 164–6, 167, 168, 173, 174, 176
good reason to follow 170
mistaken 172, 177, 178, 179–80, 181
ultra vires 179
disputes 4, 28, 37, 132, 138, 172, 305
coordination 174
doctrinal 160
ideological 160, 328–9, 376
interpretative 73, 380
normative 376–7
ontological 360, 362
philosophical 96n., 160, 328–9
political 373, 376
unregulated 151–2
visionary 160, 328–9, 373, 376
division:
agency/structure 361
social 333, 342
D-N method 19, 20, 22, 23, 25, 26, 133, 279, 280, 281–2, 283
commitment to 117
Drayton, Michael 182
Dummett, Michael 213
Durkheim, Emile 243
Dworkin, Ronald 1, 2, 51, 79, 136, 164, 167, 203
incommensurability 379–80
internal point of view 113
plurality problem 77, 86, 114
'protestant' theory of interpretation 114, 115, 116, 152
'right answers thesis' 152–3, 154
value pluralism 149, 153
WORKS:
Law's Empire 4, 5, 6, 46, 60, 61, 62, 71, 73, 105, 107, 110, 112, 115, 152
A Matter of Principle 152, 153
Taking Rights Seriously 5, 6, 50, 152

EAL (Economic Analysis of Literature) literature 30–1
'easy' cases 4, 5, 15, 36, 182
choices made in 140, 192
eclecticism 29, 251, 267–84
economics 93, 105, 127, 220, 316
neoclassical 30–1
Edmund-Davies, Lord (Herbert Edmund Davies) 99, 100, 101
emotivism 25, 26, 32, 365, 366, 372
empiricism 33, 34, 52, 54, 96, 109, 341
empowerment 331
epistemology 31, 35, 53, 84, 122, 143, 200, 219, 236, 240
empiricist 33, 155
ideology critique and 227–8, 229
rationalist 34
equality 10, 26, 222, 328, 331, 345
ethics 88, 93
deconstruction 10, 300, 301, 314–27
explicit 78, 85, 86
virtue 372
Evine, Simon 129

face-to-face 325, 326
facts 26, 33, 34, 50, 54–5, 59, 124, 241
access to 58, 240
brute 53, 60, 61, 73, 200, 380
empirical 200, 281
epistemologically dubious account of 84
moral 368–9
naturalistic 367
nature of 51, 58, 60, 87, 88
qualitative distinction between theories and 53
societal 18, 22
faith 293, 335, 346, 349
bad 232
good 3, 258
see also 'good faith thesis'
fallibility argument 172, 177–82
Feinman, Jay 228, 240

fetishism 235, 245
Finnis, John 80–7 *passim*
  Natural Law and Natural Rights 72n., 75–6, 77–9, 83
Fish, Stanley 205–6, 210, 211, 216, 219, 351, 361
'fit' criticism 3, 48, 51–63, 72
  reformulated 60, 63, 69, 79, 80, 87
formalism 328, 329
Foucault, Michel 249, 284, 286, 287, 288, 289, 293, 340n.
Frank, Jerome 270–1nn., 273
free will 96n.
freedom 289, 370
Freud, Sigmund 259–60, 263, 264
Friedman, Lawrence 108–9
Frug, Gerald 189
fundamental contradiction 12, 203, 205, 334
  argument from 304, 310

Gabel, Peter 228, 240, 247, 261
gauging 156, 157
Gewirth, Alan 364, 369, 370, 371, 372, 382
Gibson, Peter, Lord Justice 101
Giddens, Anthony 119, 261, 360, 362
'good faith thesis' 155, 165
Gordon, Robert 228
Gramsci, Antonio 234, 237
Greenawalt, Kent 50
Grice, Paul 64–5

Habermas, Jürgen 105, 119, 164
'hard' cases 4–6 *passim*, 15, 73, 138, 182, 205, 382
  choices made in 140, 154, 160, 192, 196, 373
  compelling justificatory reasons impossible in 158
  difference between easy cases and 296
  right answers to 150, 152–3, 380
harm 241, 242, 263, 382
Hart, Herbert 30, 80
Hegel, G. W. F. 115, 320
hegemony 234, 237
Heller, Thomas 248, 253, 254, 255, 261, 284
heresy:
  constructing 187–248
  orthodoxy and 1–17, 136–45
hermeneutics 81–2, 113, 118, 125
  depth 123
Hicks, Sir John 31
hierarchy 116, 187, 228, 342
  background 337
  social 7
holism 18, 21, 22, 114–18, 291, 357–9 *passim*
Hollis, Martin 32, 97, 98–9, 101, 131
Holmes, Oliver Wendell 155
Hood, Thomas 187, 188
Horwitz, Morton 108–9
'How' question 18, 21, 22, 26, 27, 33
Hume, David 88, 129, 149, 150, 240, 243, 287, 339, 341, 342, 369, 370
  metaphysical account of identity 222
  non-cognitivist account of morality 364–5
Hutchinson, Alan 305, 306, 309

ideology 59, 69–70, 110, 113, 115, 190, 195, 275
  decisions based on 263, 269, 272–3, 274, 290
  heretics and 227–33
  non-critical accounts 225–7 *passim*, 232, 233, 234–9, 247
  unconsciousness and 262
  see also critical accounts of ideology; ideology critique
ideology critique 14, 29, 70
  indeterminacy and 190–1, 206, 209, 215, 224–48
illegitimacy condition 136, 141, 144, 226
illocutionary acts 66–7, 120
illusion 133, 230
  constitutive of class societies 245
immanent critique 212, 215, 216
incommensurability 32, 83, 86–7, 88, 146, 147–8, 152, 288
  coordination problems and 176–7
  decisions resting upon 176
  reason and 154, 155, 173, 174
incomparability claim 145, 146, 147, 150–1, 152, 181
incompatibilism 106, 107, 116, 131
incorrigibility 25, 56, 101, 120, 133, 256
  problem of 51, 59, 60, 62, 63–70
indeterminacy 136–42, 275, 310, 340
  all-embracing, proof of 271
  charitable interpretation of 143
  contradiction and 201–6
  death of 188–217
  empirical 194–201, 216
  language 13, 14, 15, 143, 206–17
  method and 189–94
  value 11, 13, 14, 15, 139, 143
individualism 12, 93, 201, 258
  altruism and 202–5 *passim*, 303, 304, 310
  see also methodological individualism
individuals 359
  'bracketing' 253
  sovereign 93–134
induction, *see* D-N method
institutional schemata 121, 123–4, 132, 265
  causal power of 126
institutions 24, 36, 55, 56, 59, 61, 121, 209
  constraining and contingent nature of 215

determination of self by 254
effort to explain and understand 266
plasticity and contingency of 278
reasons agents have for accepting 58
structures and 73, 120, 123
see also social structures
intention 63, 97, 120, 277
meaning and 64–9, 94, 101, 207, 208
interest groups 13–14, 161, 226, 230, 238, 343
interests 115, 117, 164, 226, 365
actual and real 346
ad hoc 344
articulating an account of 241
class 235, 237, 239
competing 230
factional 344
group 234, 235, 237, 239
temporary 344
internal point of view 60, 76, 78, 89, 94, 105, 110
acceptance of rules 71
central case of 77, 81
Dworkin and 113
incorrigible 67
'internal perspective' 113–14
MacCormick and 72–3, 113
methodological sense of 87, 88
plurality of 74
Raz and 62, 113
tension between external and 96
undifferentiated 80
interpretation 5–6, 13, 53, 96, 97, 101, 139, 287
constructive 62, 73, 74, 75
interpretative charity 87, 338–9
interpretativism 96, 125
intuitionism 147
is/ought distinction 365, 366, 370, 371

jurisprudence 22, 28, 45, 54, 56–7, 72, 108
compatibilism and 118
contemporary 384
grounding in critical perspective 190
orthodox, radical nature of 135
'Thumper' school of 372
justice 76, 165, 326, 336, 380
as aporia 318
deconstruction and 314, 319, 320
indeterminate 319
law and 262, 320

Kairys, David 183, 306
Kaldor, Nicholas, Lord 31
Kant, Immanuel 243, 382
Kelman, Mark 7, 11, 12, 137, 139, 204, 232, 233, 327, 372
response to 'how' question 246–7
response to 'why' question 247
Kennedy, Duncan 137, 257–9, 284, 291, 302–3, 308, 310
binary oppositions 251
compatibilism 133–4, 277, 282
denial 264
eclecticism 251
explanatory priority 286, 290
fundamental contradiction 334
ideology 275
indeterminacy 199, 200–2, 203, 204
modern/postmodern project 9
WORK:
Critique of Adjudication 194–5, 229–30, 231, 232, 236, 237, 238, 262–3, 267–76 *passim*, 283
kinship 252, 261, 264
Lévi-Strauss's accounts 256–7, 259–60
oppositions underpinning 255
other societies' systems of 253
Klare, Karl 312, 313–14, 331, 332, 335, 336, 348
knowledge 33, 34, 55, 148, 181, 200, 227, 285

language 22, 80, 81, 139, 202, 359
abstract 126
identity created in 254
indeterminacy of 13, 14, 15, 143, 206–17, 296
knowledge obtained through 55, 235
learning 213–14, 266
Saussurian account of 254
structuralist accounts of 265
transparent and neutral medium 315
langue 255, 360
law 69, 71, 97, 100, 132, 151, 158
adjudication and 321, 322
alternative to 308
as integrity 211, 212
changes in 111–12
contract 12, 101, 203, 228, 304, 330–1, 382
duty to uphold 155, 157
equal protection 330
ethical relation compatible with 326
ideology and 115, 230
indeterminacy in 142, 195–6
'internal' and 'external' accounts 107, 108–9, 190
justice and 262, 320
Law of 321
liberal collective bargaining 312
obligation to obey 164, 165, 166, 167, 171, 179
positive reconstructive programme for 313

law (*Cont.*):
prospective and retrospective genealogies of 343
public 258, 329
statute 384, 385
threat to 296–7
see also causal laws; law/politics distinction
law/politics distinction 14, 160–2, 236–7, 374, 383–6 *passim*
affirmed 230–1
endangered 154
espousal of appropriate version 238
problematised 227
worthwhile version 373
legitimacy 82, 83, 117, 224, 322, 377, 385
deficits 299, 302, 305, 307
value choices lack 305, 312
legitimacy condition 136, 140
characterisation of 142
fulfilment of 141
value pluralism and 163–82
Lenin, V. I 234
Levinas, Emmanuel 321, 325
Levin, Joel 2, 154, 158–9, 160–1, 162
Lévi-Strauss, Claude 251–2, 252–3, 255–7, 259–61, 262, 264, 266, 285
liberalism 139, 230, 236, 238, 274, 289, 365–6
contradictions of thought manifest in 304
Locke, John 243
logic 23, 26, 33, 37, 38
bureaucratic 223
internal 194, 271
standard 126, 199
logical positivism 199
Louch, A. R. 126
love 334, 335, 349
Lyotard, Jean-François 284

MacCormick, Neil 1, 2, 50–1, 136, 166, 375
compatibilism 104, 107, 108, 112, 117
conventionalism 167
incomparability claim 150–1
internal point of view 80, 113
plurality problem 114
value pluralism 149, 153
Verstehen 103
WORKS:
H. L. A. Hart 28n., 73, 81–2
Legal Reasoning and Legal Theory 4, 5, 60, 61–2, 71, 73, 81, 88, 104, 109, 149–50
On Legal Decisions and Their Consequences 6, 46
MacIntyre, A. 25, 135, 372
Mackie, John 34, 152
Maclean case 157
Man, Paul de 45, 319
Mannheim, Karl 235, 236
market 327, 329
Marx, Karl 229, 243, 244, 245, 247
Marxism 234, 235, 245, 281
neo- 268
Mauss, Marcel 256
meaning 18, 31, 118, 123, 131
behaviour and 21
causality and 95, 96, 108
covert 97, 101
illocutionary 66–7, 120
indeterminacy of 212
intention and 64–9, 94, 101, 207, 208
language and 139, 207, 208
non-natural 65
overt 97, 98
social action and 20, 34, 112
word 11, 139, 208, 213, 287
mediation 237, 281, 303
group interests 239
social 373
through culture 261
Meirs, David 49
Melden, A. I. 129
meta-ethical theories 149, 365, 372
meta-narratives 9
collapse of 283, 289
delegitimation of 286
illegitimacy 285
suspicion of 283, 284
metaphysics 35, 36, 93, 199, 200, 202, 205, 211, 229
methodological compatibilism 97, 117, 118, 119, 256, 277
archetypal 292
arguments which recommend 123
methodological individualism 94, 115–16
hallmark of 18
holism and 357, 359
incorrigibility thesis and 63
strong 104, 114, 117
weak 117, 118
method(ology) 17–22, 31, 34, 36, 57–8, 103, 112, 113, 283
causal 281
critique of 267
deductive-nomological 96
empiricist 53
Finnis's 75–6
indeterminacy and 189–94
internal point of view and 72–3
interpretative 125, 130, 281
non-empiricist 54
ontology and 356–7, 359, 360

scientific 27, 28, 56, 125, 130, 284, 288, 291, 292, 373
see also D-N; holism; methodological compatibilism; methodological individualism; *Verstehen*
Meyerson, Denise 203
Mill, James 243
Mill, John Stuart 243
mind 82, 199
dichotomy of body and 229
unconscious 259
misrepresentation 237, 262, 270, 292, 307, 308
models 52–3
consensus 49
interstitial legislator 49
rights 49
unconscious 260, 266
see also D-N method
modernism 9–10
modified conventionalism 166, 167, 170, 171, 172, 177
Monahan, Patrick 305, 306
monists 145, 146, 371
moral philosophy 164, 314, 373, 382
descriptive sciences and 80
extreme value scepticism and 297, 302
non-cognitive position 305
moral rationalism 26, 32, 348, 362–6 *passim*, 372, 381
ability to resolve hard cases 383
Gewirth's 382
objections to 369, 371
support for 373
moral realism 26, 32, 149, 362–7 *passim*, 372, 381, 383
gripes about 360, 369
support for 373
moral values 32, 60, 77, 86, 145, 151
morality 71, 83, 84, 85, 88, 93, 152, 371
critical and positive 325
Good stands distinct from 324
Hume's non-cognitivist account of 364–5
institutional 376, 381
legality and 326
primordial precondition 315
political 6, 73, 74
positive 319
motivation 368, 369
myth 223–4, 226, 229, 252, 261, 264

Nietzsche, Friedrich 221, 286, 287
nihilism 195, 297
nomos 321, 322, 323
non-cognitivism 32, 305, 365, 366, 372
panic about 364
'normal justification thesis' 168–76, 178, 180, 181
restatement of 179
normative ascription 336, 340, 341, 348, 349
normative vision 331
norms 61, 103, 166, 254
identified as Justice 319
morally binding 71

Oakeshott, Michael 234
objectivism 328, 329, 368, 380
obligations 164, 165, 166, 167, 179, 331
blanket 171
communal or fraternal 330
construction and content of a system of 315
general 171
perspicuous 211
O'Connor, Justice Sandra 323
ontology 33, 34, 35, 122, 127
abstinence 360
claims 240, 279–80
constrains method 358, 360
modesty 360, 362
social 64, 68, 69, 214, 215, 357
structuration theory's 361
orthodoxy:
constructing 60–2
criticising 48–60
heresy and 1–17, 136–45
otherness 10, 318, 321, 323, 324, 325
and difference 322

'paradox of democracy' 345, 347, 349, 385
Pareto, Vilfredo 31
parole 255, 360
participation/participants 10, 55, 61, 69, 70, 75, 77, 99, 331, 345
democratic 312–13, 344
interpretation of practice 109, 115
language of 379
see also points of view
Paterson, Alan 50
Peller, G. 11, 145, 200, 206–16, 229, 232, 233, 242, 243, 286
person(s) 335, 337–8, 344, 345, 346
see also self
PGC (principle of generic consistency) 369, 370, 371, 371–2, 383
philosophy 27, 31, 32, 39, 97, 187, 217, 218, 289, 372
'analytical' 30
deconstructive 276
edifying 307
ethical 314
existentialist 307

philosophy (*Cont.*):
  language 30, 82, 143, 215
  of the limit 321, 322
  orthodox doctrinal scholarship and 189
  political 80, 93, 151, 164, 220, 314, 326, 339
  postmodern 242
  social 164
pluralism 135–84, 372
plurality problem 51, 59–60, 62, 69, 70–89
  MacCormick and Dworkin's embrace of 114
  plausible solution to 93–4
points of view 59, 77, 112, 126, 157, 256
  external 96, 105, 267, 269, 271, 272
  internal 267, 269, 270, 271
  see also internal point of view
policy 6, 50, 138, 150, 269
politics 6, 66, 78, 79, 198, 217
  capacity of parties and movements to win in 344
  positive reconstructive programme for 313
  role in adjudication 238
  see also law/politics distinction
positivism 1, 96, 131, 151
  logical 199
post-structuralism 242
Postema, Gerald 115
postmodernism 9, 243
power:
  critical 212, 216, 226, 233
  explanatory 260, 275
  rational 306, 377, 381
  social structures 214
  will to 286, 287, 288, 289
PPAs (potential purposive agents) 369, 370, 372
'practical theory' 361
practice(s) 49, 50, 52, 57–8, 59, 70, 109
  acceptance of 73, 74, 77, 78, 80, 81, 84, 85
  determination of self by 254
  effort to explain and understand 266
  plasticity and contingency of 278
  representational 206–11, 215, 216, 232
  value of 64, 67, 72, 75
  volitional commitment to 81, 82
  see also social practice(s)
pragmatism 290, 291, 292
precedent 6, 101, 139, 328
  ambiguities of 329–30
  greater use of 384
predictability 3, 46, 100, 138, 141, 198, 215
  lack of 142
  surrogates for 192, 193
principle(s) 5, 26, 50, 140, 147, 149, 154, 321
  altruistic 205
  arguments of 381, 384
  justifactory, fundamental 371
  majoritarian 345, 346, 347
  moral 364, 371
  narrow or low-level 376
  non-democratic 345
  normative 254
  organising 328
  underpinning 376, 377
priority 147, 286, 290, 291
privileging 246
psychoanalysis 255, 269, 316
psychology 220, 262, 275

Quine, Willard 54, 212, 213, 281, 362

rankings 378, 379
rational reconstruction 3, 113, 189, 190, 192, 202, 205
  impossibility of 208, 216, 224
'rationalising legal analysis' 342, 343
rationality 159–60, 210, 216, 224
  determinate 160
  no theory of 372–86
  substantive 89, 99
rationality deficit 153, 154, 158, 194, 299, 302, 305, 307
  incommensurability entails 373
Rawls, John 382
Raz, Joseph 1, 2, 51, 136, 166
  compatibilism 105, 106, 107, 108, 112
  detached statements 81
  Ealing directives 178, 179, 180
  incomparability claim 147
  internal point of view 80, 113
  modified conventionalism 166, 167
  normal justification thesis 168
  value pluralism 149, 153
  Verstehen 103
  WORKS:
  The Authority of Law 151
  Ethics in the Public Domain 46, 62, 71, 106
  The Morality of Freedom 148, 151, 152, 167, 168, 171–3 *passim*, 176–8 *passim*
  Practical Reason and Norms 151
realism 270, 341, 382
  critical 357, 360, 362
  redundancy of 362–72
  see also moral realism
reason 9, 22, 28, 29, 31, 154, 160, 375
  choices compelled by 140, 153, 155–6, 177
  compelling 377
  decisions more than merely informed by 379, 383, 385–6

determinacy condition and 155, 157
incommensurabilty and 176
indeterminate 148, 173
reasonableness 375, 378, 379, 383
reasoning 13, 14, 48, 49, 60, 62, 169–70
analogical 376
assumptions that guide 329
reconstruction 96, 123–4
see also rational reconstruction
redundancy 128, 322, 326
conceptual 235
objection 366, 368
'reflective equilibrium' 78
regulation 331, 332
reification 229, 233, 235
Kelman's notion of 246
unavoidable 247
relativism 159
relativity 285, 286
representation 243, 285, 290
accuracy in 291, 292
arbitrariness of 286
crisis of 283, 284, 286, 289
impossible 276, 284
Re Selectmove case (1995) 97, 101
Ricoeur, Paul 119
'right answers thesis' 150, 152–3, 154–5
rights 49, 73, 164, 331, 339
abuses 340
equal 320
equal protection 330
impediments to the enjoyment of 347–8
innate 244
Roe v. Wade 323
roles 24, 31, 35, 99, 113, 144, 158–9
assigned to author and agent 250
judicial 262
legitimizing 228
limiting types of 335
procrustean and reductive 261
socially created character of 229
Rorty, Richard 289, 290, 291, 294
Rudden, Bernard 50
rule of law 219, 226, 231
generic values 3, 28, 95, 144, 316
rules 7, 17, 18, 61, 103, 215, 324
acceptance of 58, 71, 73, 80, 81, 84, 85
ambiguities of 329–30
application of 143–4, 153, 231
constitutive 24, 27, 254
constraining and contingent nature of 215
'governing' or 'determining' agents 265
grammatical 66, 254, 261
individualists prefer 204, 205
liability 203, 204, 205
volitional commitment to 81, 82
Sartre, Jean-Paul 248
Saussure, F. de 254
scepticism 13, 286, 293
external 288, 289
internal 286, 288, 289
moral and epistemological 340, 341
see also value scepticism
schemata 158
see also institutional schemata
Schlag, Pierre 7, 242, 243, 245, 252, 253–4, 315, 327
conception of the self 217, 218–24
modest value scepticism 317–18, 322
normative legal thought 316
redundancy problem 326
'Thumper' school of jurisprudence 372
Schutz, Alfred 79, 127
sciences 19, 22, 24–6 *passim*, 53, 93, 95–6, 284, 316, 341, 342
causal explanation in 107
compelling method for 96–7
competing philosophies 51
descriptive 80
general problems within 239
method(ology) in 27, 28, 56, 125, 130, 268, 288, 292, 373
philosophy of 27, 31, 97
self 188
autonomous 253, 254
conception of 217, 218–24, 336, 382
disappearance of 190, 191, 217–24
genealogy of 266
genetic account of 254
and others 201, 202, 203, 241, 303
social ideal and 328–42
structuralist account of 254
theory of 381
thought about 334
self-consciousness 255, 270
reinterpretation of 261
semantic theory 64–5
semiotics 255, 269
separation thesis 94
Shiner, Roger 82–3
Simpson, A. W. B. 131–2, 273
Singer, Joseph 7, 11, 159–60, 195–9, 202, 284, 310, 374, 383
Skinner, Quentin 66, 67, 119, 120
social action 17–23 *passim*, 25, 27–8, 31, 47, 78, 122
attempts to explain 95
causality and 29, 36, 106, 110–11, 116, 277
description of 76
'facts' of 58, 59
inescapable features of 32
knowledge of 55, 57, 80, 83, 88
meaning and value dimensions 34

social action (*Cont.*):
  method and 124
  purposive 24, 55, 56, 58, 70
  rule-governed 70
  theory and 125
  Verstehen and 55–6, 58, 59
social change 250, 278, 280
social ideal 327, 342, 343, 344, 346, 348, 382
  self and 328–42
  values that correlate around 345
social practice(s) 55, 61, 62, 71, 119, 291, 328, 360, 362
  aspects which ought to be maintained 336
  constraining and contingent nature of 215
  contingent, legitimating 229
  interpretation of 380
  purely contingent and presumably plastic 340
social reality 63, 69, 70, 87, 107, 359
  agents systematically misguided about 225, 227, 239
  constrained and distorted awareness 262
  falsely represented 223
  fundamental constituents 119
  illusions part of 245
  immutable and natural 229
  no objective structure to 214
  perceiving the true nature of 245
  true picture 242
social structures 120, 121, 123, 124, 126, 265, 333
  constraining power of 214
  determination of self by 254
  linguistic 255
  plasticity and contingency of 278
social theory 242, 268–9, 279
  antinecessitarian 277
  deep structure 281, 282
  scientistic 277
sociology 10, 93, 215, 220, 222, 360
  structuralist thought in 252
  Weberian 268–9
Socrates 161
solidarity 10, 345
  problem of 334, 335
Solkin, David 187, 188
Soper, Philip 164, 165, 166
standards 11, 61, 103, 139, 151, 204
  behavioural 222
  preference for 205
  relatively determined 46, 138, 196
Stick, John 198
structuralism 29, 242, 251–67, 283, 292
structuration theory 361
structures 269
  agent created by 265
  all-pervasive power of 266
  causal effects 357
  existence of 358, 359
  inter-subjective 255
  manipulating and creating 249
  'virtual' existence of 361
  see also social structures
subjectivity 11, 12, 13, 139, 265, 366
Sunstein, Cass 2, 375, 377
suppression 262–3, 264, 301

tension 238, 304, 320, 360
  affirming ideology critique 243
  democracy and other values 347
  natural science and social understanding 277
Thompson, John 127, 361
  Critical Hermeneutics 119–21, 123
tort 203, 204, 258, 382
totemism 255, 257, 259–60
truth 11, 26, 32, 94, 114, 116, 117, 203, 242
  a priori 202
  analysis of 68
  correspondence theory of 241, 289, 290, 291–2
  methods for determining 199
  misplaced suspicion about the notion of 276
  ontological 128
  philosophical accounts of 268, 287
  theory of 240, 241, 268
Tushnet, Mark 312

übermensch 221
'ultra-theory' 214, 215, 292, 293, 356
unconscious:
  brooding presence of 257
  invoking 260–1, 262
  Lévi-Strauss's invocation of 260
  roles of 252, 256
  two meanings of 258
unconsciousness 259, 262, 264
Unger, Roberto 7, 10–12 *passim*, 137, 160, 284, 293, 356, 369, 385
  causal laws 357
  compatibilism 133, 251, 267
  discomfort with method 283
  law/politics distinction 384
  moral arguments 365
  normative vision 382
  subjectivity of values 139, 366
  WORKS:
  The Critical Legal Studies Movement 327, 328, 329–33, 335, 337, 339, 340, 341, 345
  Passion 327 n., 333, 334, 339, 345
  Politics 277–82 *passim*, 292, 333–7 *passim*,

340–2 *passim*, 345, 347
What Should Legal Analysis Become? 188, 327, 342–4, 346–7, 347
'universalisation project' 230
Urmson, J. O. 147
utilitarians 145, 146
utility 328
utterances 63–4, 65, 213, 252
context of 272
illocutionary 66, 120
ironic 66

value conflict 71, 140, 146–7, 148, 149, 153, 335
micro-level 303, 332
value pluralism 135, 136
and determinacy condition 145–63
and legitimacy condition 163–82
orthodox 299
value scepticism:
extreme 297–9 *passim*, 302–11, 317, 318, 322, 327
moderate 301, 311–14, 327, 335, 336, 344, 348
value talk 295–349
values 10, 12, 33, 34, 46, 58, 264, 385
adjudication and 143–5
altruistic 12
conflicting 71, 140, 146, 147, 148, 149, 153
constitutive 47, 144
generic rule of law 3, 28, 95, 144
immanent 331, 332
incommensurate 152, 153, 163, 176
indeterminacy of 11, 13, 14, 15, 139, 143, 319
individualistic 12, 22
macro-level 331, 335, 336, 337, 339
micro-level 331, 332, 335, 348
multiple 329
political 86, 145, 173
problem of 24–7, 32
subjectivity of 11, 12, 13, 139, 306, 366
transcendental 319
see also moral values; *also under headings above prefixed* 'value'
Verstehen approach 20–3 *passim*, 26, 28, 84, 87, 88, 118
commitment to 62, 114, 115, 116
displaced 200–1
improved account of nature of 35
loosening the hold of 190
necessity of 56–7
orthodox invocation of 104, 108, 115
social action and 55–6, 58, 59
strategies designed to weaken 29
varieties 34
viewpoints, *see* points of view
virtues 334–5, 349, 364
visionaries 32, 295–349

Waldron, Jeremy 368
Weaver, Max 49, 52
Weber, Max 27, 105, 116, 243, 268–9
Wednesbury directives 178, 180–1
weighing process 156, 157, 167, 168, 377, 379
Weinrib, Ernest 348
well-being 370, 372
will 149, 170
to power 286, 287, 288, 289, 299
Williams v. Roffey case (1990) 101
Winch, Peter 105–6, 116, 126
Wright, Georg von 119